Langenscheidt

Universal French Dictionary

French – English
English – French

edited by the
Langenscheidt editorial staff

Langenscheidt

New York · Berlin · Munich · Vienna · Zurich

Compiled by LEXUS with: / Réalisé par LEXUS:

Sandrine François · Jane Goldie
Claire Guerreau · Julie Le Boulanger
Peter Terrell

1. 2. 3. 4. 5.   12 11 10 09 08

© 2008 Langenscheidt KG, Berlin and Munich
Printed in Germany

Contents / Table des matières

Abbreviations / Abréviations

and	&	et
see	→	voir
registered trademark	®	marque déposée
adjective	*adj*	adjectif
adverb	*adv*	adverbe
agriculture	AGR	agriculture
anatomy	ANAT	anatomie
architecture	ARCH	architecture
astronomy	ASTR	astronomie
astrology	ASTROL	astrologie
attributive	*atr*	devant le nom
motoring	AUTO	automobiles
aviation	AVIAT	aviation
biology	BIOL	biologie
botany	BOT	botanique
British English	*Br*	anglais britannique
chemistry	CHIM	chimie
commerce, business	COMM	commerce
computers, IT term	COMPUT	informatique
conjunction	*conj*	conjonction
cooking	CUIS	cuisine
economics	ÉCON	économie
education	EDU	éducation
education	ÉDU	éducation
electricity	ÉL	électricité
electricity	ELEC	électricité
especially	*esp*	surtout
euphemism	*euph*	euphémisme
familiar, colloquial	F	familier
feminine	*f*	féminin
figurative	*fig*	figuré

finance	FIN	finance
formal	*fml*	langage formel
feminine plural	*fpl*	féminin pluriel
geography	GEOG	géographie
geography	GÉOGR	géographie
geology	GÉOL	géologie
geometry	GÉOM	géométrie
grammar	GRAM	grammaire
historical	HIST	historique
IT term	INFORM	informatique
interjection	*int*	interjection
invariable	*inv*	invariable
law	JUR	juridique
law	LAW	juridique
linguistics	LING	linguistique
literary	*litt*	littéraire
masculine	*m*	masculin
nautical	MAR	marine
mathematics	MATH	mathématiques
medicine	MED	médecine
medicine	MÉD	médecine
masculine and feminine	*m/f*	masculin et féminin
military	MIL	militaire
motoring	MOT	automobiles
masculine plural	*mpl*	masculin pluriel
music	MUS	musique
noun	*n*	nom
nautical	NAUT	marine
plural noun	*npl*	nom pluriel
singular noun	*nsg*	nom singulier
oneself	o.s.	se, soi
popular, slang	P	populaire
pejorative	*pej*	péjoratif

pejorative	*péj*	péjoratif
pharmacy	PHARM	pharmacie
photography	PHOT	photographie
physics	PHYS	physique
plural	*pl*	pluriel
politics	POL	politique
preposition	*prep*	préposition
preposition	*prép*	préposition
pronoun	*pron*	pronom
psychology	PSYCH	psychologie
something	*qch*	quelque chose
someone	*qn*	quelqu'un
radio	RAD	radio
railroad	RAIL	chemin de fer
religion	REL	religion
singular	*sg*	singulier
someone	s.o.	quelqu'un
sports	SP	sport
something	*sth*	quelque chose
subjunctive	*subj*	subjonctif
noun	*subst*	substantif
theater	THEA	théâtre
theater	THÉÂT	théâtre
technology	TECH	technique
telecommunications	TÉL	télécommunications
telecommunications	TELEC	télécommunications
typography, typesetting	TYP	typographie
television	TV	télévision
vulgar	V	vulgaire
auxiliary verb	*v/aux*	verbe auxiliaire
intransitive verb	*v/i*	verbe intransitif
transitive verb	*v/t*	verbe transitif
zoology	ZO	zoologie

La Prononciation / Pronunciation

Les consonnes / Consonants

[b]	*bag*	*bouche*
[d]	*dear*	*dans*
[f]	*fall*	*foule*
[g]	*give*	*gai*
[h]	*hole*	et *hop*
[j]	*yes*	ra*dio*
[k]	*come*	*qui*
[l]	*land*	*la*
[m]	*mean*	*mon*
[n]	*night*	*nuit*
[p]	*pot*	*pot*
[r]	*right* (*la langue vers le haut*)	*reine*
[s]	*sun*	*sauf*
[t]	*take*	*table*
[v]	*vain*	*vain*
[w]	*wait*	*oui*
[z]	*rose*	*rose*
[ŋ]	*bring*	*feeling*
[ʃ]	*she*	*chat*
[ʧ]	*chair*	*cha-cha-cha*
[dʒ]	*join*	*adjuger*
[ʒ]	*leisure*	*juge*
[θ]	*think*	langue entres les dents
[ð]	*the*	langue derrière les dents du haut

Les voyelles anglaises / English vowels

[ɑ:]	f*a*r	*â*me
[æ]	m*a*n	s*a*lle
[e]	g*e*t	s*e*c
[ə]	utt*er*	l*e*
[ɜ:]	abs*ur*d	b*eu*rre
[ɪ]	st*i*ck	*i* très court
[i:]	n*ee*d	s*i*
[ɒ]	*i*n-l*a*ws	ph*a*se
[ɔ:]	m*o*re	ess*o*r
[ʌ]	m*o*ther	entre *à* et *eux*
[ʊ]	b*oo*k	b*ou*quin (*très court*)
[u:]	h*oo*t	s*ou*s

Les diphtongues anglaises / English diphthongs

[aɪ]	t*i*me	*aïe*
[aʊ]	cl*ou*d	*ciao*
[eɪ]	n*a*me	*nez suivi d'un y court*
[ɔɪ]	p*oi*nt	*cow-boy*
[oʊ]	s*o*	*eau*

['] indique que la syllabe suivante est accentuée: *ability* [ə'bɪlətɪ]

Some French words starting with h have ' before the h. This ' is not part of the French word. It shows i) that a preceding vowel does not become an apostrophe and ii) that no elision takes place. (This is called an aspirated h).

'hanche	la hanche, les hanches [no z sound between *les* and *hanches*]
habit	l'habit, les habits [a z sound between *les* and *habits*]

A

à *lieu* in; *direction* to; **au bout de la rue** at/to the end of the street; **~ 2 heures d'ici** 2 hours from here; **~ cinq heures** at five o'clock; **~ Noël** at Christmas; **~ demain** until tomorrow; **c'est ~ moi** it's mine, it belongs to me; **aux cheveux blonds** with blonde hair; **~ pied** on foot; **~ dix euros** at ou for ten euros

abaissement *m* lowering; (*humiliation*) abasement; **abaisser** lower; *fig* (*humilier*) humble; **s'~** drop; *fig* demean o.s.

abandonner abandon; *pouvoir* give up; SP withdraw from; **s'~** (*se confier*) open up; **s'~ à** give way to

abasourdi amazed

abat-jour *m* (lamp)shade

abattre *arbre* fell; AVIAT shoot down; *animal* slaughter; *péj* (*tuer*) kill; *fig* (*épuiser*) exhaust; (*décourager*) dishearten; **s'~** collapse

abbaye *f* abbey

abcès *m* abscess

abdomen *m* abdomen

abeille *f* bee

aberrant F absurd

abêtir make stupid

abîmer spoil, ruin; **s'~** be ruined; *d'aliments* spoil

aboiement *m* barking

abolir abolish; **abolition** *f* abolition

abominable appalling

abondance *f* abundance

abonné, ~e *m/f* subscriber; **abonnement** *m* subscription; *de transport, de spectacles* season ticket; **abonner: s'~ à** subscribe to

abord *m*: **d'~** first; **au premier ~** at first sight; **~s** surroundings; **aborder 1** *v/t* (*prendre d'assaut*) board; (*heurter*) collide with; *fig: question* tackle; *personne* approach **2** *v/i* land (**à** at)

aboutir *d'un projet* succeed; **~ à** end at; *fig* lead to; **aboutissement** *m* (*résultat*) result

aboyer bark

abréger abridge

abréviation *f* abbreviation

abri *m* shelter; **être sans ~** be homeless

abricot *m* apricot; **abricotier** *m* apricot (tree)

abriter (*loger*) take in, shelter; **~ de** (*protéger*) shelter from; **s'~** take shelter

abrupt abrupt; *pente* steep

abruti stupid; **~ qn** be bad for s.o.'s brain; (*surmener*) exhaust s.o.

absence *f* absence; *absent* absent; *air* absent-minded; **absenter: s'~** leave, go away

absolu absolute; **absolument** absolutely

absorber absorb; *nourriture* eat; *boisson* drink; **s'~ dans** be absorbed in

abstenir: s'~ POL abstain; **s'~ de faire qc** refrain from doing sth; **abstention** *f* POL abstention

abstrait abstract

absurdité *f* absurdity; **~(s)** nonsense

abus *m* abuse; **~ de confiance** breach of trust; *abuser* overstep the mark; **~ de qc** misuse ou abuse sth; **s'~** be mistaken; *abusif, -ive* excessive; *emploi d'un mot incorrect*

académie *f* academy

acajou *m* mahogany

accabler: être accablé de be weighed down by; **~ qn de qc** heap sth on s.o.

accalmie *f aussi fig* lull

accaparer ÉCON, *fig* monopolize

accéder: ~ à reach, get to; INFORM access; *à l'indépendance, au pouvoir* gain; *d'un chemin* lead to

accélérateur *m* AUTO gas pedal, *Br* accelerator; **accélérer** *aussi* AUTO accelerate

accent *m* accent; (*intonation*) stress; **mettre l'~ sur qc** *fig* put the emphasis on sth; **accentuer** *syllabe* stress, accentuate

acceptable acceptable; **accepter** accept; (*reconnaître*) agree; **~ de faire** agree to do

accès *m aussi* INFORM access; MÉD fit

accessoire 1 *adj* incidental **2** *m* detail; **~s** accessories; THÉÂT props

accident *m* accident; *événement fortuit* mishap; *par* **~** by accident, accidentally; **accidentel, ~le** accidental

acclamation *f* acclamation; **~s** cheers, cheering; *acclamer* cheer

acclimater: s'~ become acclimatized

accolade *f* embrace; *signe* brace, *Br* curly bracket

accommodation *f* adaptation; **accommoder** adapt; CUIS prepare; **s'~ à** adapt to; **s'~ de** make do with

accompagnateur, -trice *m/f* guide; MUS accompanist; **accompagner** accompany

accomplir accomplish; *souhait* realize

accord *m* agreement; MUS chord; **d'~** OK, alright; *être* **~** agree; *tomber* **d'~** come to an agreement; **accordé:**

(bien) ~ in tune

accordéon accordion

accorder *crédit* grant; GRAM make agree; MUS tune; **s'~** get on; GRAM agree; **s'~ qc** allow o.s. sth

accouchement *m* birth; **accoucher** give birth (*de* to)

accouder: **s'~** lean (one's elbows); **accoudoir** *m* armrest

accoupler connect; **s'~** BIOL mate

accourir come running

accoutumance *f* MÉD dependence; **accoutumer**: ~ *qn à qc* get s.o. used to sth; **s'~ à qc** get used to sth

accrocher *manteau* hang up; AUTO collide with; **s'~ à** hang on to; *fig* cling to

accroître increase; **s'~** grow

accroupir: **s'~** crouch, squat

accueil *m* reception, welcome; **accueillir** greet, welcome

accumulation *f* accumulation; **accumuler** accumulate; **s'~** accumulate

accusation *f* accusation; JUR prosecution; *plainte* charge; **accusé**, **~e** *m/f* **1** JUR: *l'~* the accused **2** COMM: *accusé m de réception* acknowledgement (of receipt); **accuser** (*incriminer*) accuse (*de* of); (*faire ressortir*) emphasize

acerbe caustic

acéré sharp

acharnement *m* grim determination; **acharner**: **s'~ à faire qc** be bent on doing sth; **s'~ sur** ou **contre qn** pick on s.o.

achat *m* purchase; *faire des ~s* go shopping

acheter buy

achever finish; **s'~** finish

acide 1 *adj* sour; CHIM acidic **2** *m* CHIM acid

acier *m* steel

acné *f* acne

à-coup *m* jerk; *par ~s* in fits and starts

acoustique acoustic

acquéreur *m* purchaser; **acquérir** acquire; *droit* win

acquiescer: ~ *à* agree to

acquis acquired; *résultats* achieved

acquisition *f* acquisition

acquitter *facture* pay; JUR acquit; **s'~ de** carry out; *dette* pay

âcre acrid; *goût*, *fig* bitter; **âcreté** *f* bitterness

acrobate *m/f* acrobat; **acrobatie** *f* acrobatics *pl*

acte *m* (*action*) action, deed; (*document officiel*) act; THÉÂT act; *~ de mariage* marriage certificate

acteur, **-trice** *m/f* actor; actress

actif, **-ive 1** *adj* active **2** *m* COMM assets *pl*

action *f* action; COMM share; *~s* stock, shares *pl*; **actionnaire** *m/f* shareholder

actionner operate; *alarme etc*

activate
activer (accélérer) speed up
activité f activity
actualiser update
actualité f current events pl; **~s** TV news sg
actuel, ~le current, present; (d'actualité) topical; **actuellement** currently, at present
adaptation f adaptation; **adapter** adapt; **s'~ à** adapt to
addition f addition; au restaurant check, Br bill; **additionner** add
adéquat suitable; montant adequate
adhérent, ~e m/f member; **adhérer** stick, adhere (**à** to)
adhésif, -ive 1 adj sticky, adhesive 2 m adhesive
adieu m goodbye; **faire ses ~x** say one's goodbyes (**à qn** to s.o.)
adjectif m GRAM adjective
adjoint, ~e m/f & adj assistant, deputy
admettre (autoriser) allow; (accueillir) admit, allow in; (reconnaître) admit
administrateur, -trice m/f administrator; **administratif**, -ive administrative; **administration** f administration; (direction) management, running
admirateur, -trice 1 adj admiring 2 m/f admirer; **admiration** f admiration; **admirer** admire

admissible candidat eligible; **ce n'est pas ~** that's unacceptable
admission f admission
adolescence f adolescence; **adolescent**, ~e m/f adolescent, teenager
adopter adopt; **adoption** f adoption
adorable adorable; **adorer** REL worship; fig (aimer) adore
adosser; **s'~ contre** ou **à** lean against ou on
adoucir soften; **s'~ du temps** become milder
adrénaline f adrenalin
adresse f address; (habileté) skill; **~ électronique** email address
adresser lettre address (**à** to); remarque direct (**à** at); **~ la parole à** address, speak to; **s'~ à qn** apply to s.o.; (être destiné à) be aimed at s.o.
adroit skillful, Br skilful
adulte 1 adj adult; plante mature 2 m/f adult, grown-up
adultère 1 adj adulterous 2 m adultery
adverbe m GRAM adverb
adversaire m/f opponent, adversary
adversité f adversity
aération f ventilation; **aérer** ventilate; literie, pièce air
aérien, ~ne air atr; vue aerial
aérobic f aerobics
aérodynamique aerodynamic

aéronautique aeronautical
aéroport *m* airport
aérosol *m* aerosol
affable affable
affaiblir weaken; **s'~** weaken
affaire *f* (*question*) matter, business; (*entreprise*) business; *marché* deal; (*bonne occasion*) bargain; JUR case; (*scandale*) affair, business; **~s biens personnels** things, belongings; **les ~s étrangères** foreign affairs; **affairer: s'~** busy o.s.
affaisser **s'~** *du terrain* subside; *d'une personne* collapse
affamé hungry (*de* for)
affectation *f* *d'une chose* allocation; *d'un employé* assignment; MIL posting; (*pose*) affectation; **affecter** (*destiner*) allocate; *employé* assign; MIL post; (*émouvoir*) affect
affectif, **-ive** emotional
affection *f* affection; MÉD complaint
affectueux, **-euse** affectionate
affermir strengthen
affichage *m* billposting; INFORM display; **affiche** *f* poster; **afficher** *affiche* stick up; *attitude*, INFORM display
affilier: s'~ à club join; **être affilié à** be a member of
affiner refine
affinité *f* affinity
affirmatif, **-ive** affirmative;

personne assertive; **affirmation** *f* statement; **affirmer** (*prétendre*) maintain; *autorité* assert
affligeant distressing, painful; **affliger** distress
affluence *f*: **heures** *fpl* **d'~** rush hour *sg*; **affluent** *m* tributary; **affluer** come together
affolement *m* panic; **affoler** (*bouleverser*) madden, drive to distraction; *d'une foule*, *d'un cheval* panic; **s'~** panic
affranchir free; *lettre* meter, *Br* frank
affreux, **-euse** horrible; *peur*, *mal de tête* terrible
affront *m* insult, affront; **affronter** confront, face; SP meet; **s'~** confront ou face each other; SP meet
afin: **~ de faire** in order to do, so as to do; **~ que** (+ *subj*) so that
africain, **~e** African; **Africain**, **~e** *m/f* African; **Afrique** *f*: **l'~** Africa
agaçant annoying; **agacement** *m* annoyance; **agacer** annoy; (*taquiner*) tease
âge *m* age; **Moyen-Âge** Middle Ages *pl*; **personnes** *fpl* **du troisième ~** senior citizens; **quel ~ a-t-il?** how old is he?, what age is he?; **âgé** elderly; **~ de deux ans** aged two, two years old
agence *f* agency; *d'une banque* branch; **~ immobilière**

realtor's, *Br* estate agent's; ~ **matrimoniale** marriage bureau

agenda *m* diary; ~ **électronique** (personal) organizer

agenouiller: s'~ kneel (down)

agent *m* agent; ~ **de change** stockbroker; ~ **immobilier** realtor, *Br* real estate agent; ~ **de police** police officer

agglomération *f* built-up area; *concentration de villes* conurbation

aggraver make worse; **s'~** worsen

agile agile; **agilité** *f* agility

agios *mpl* ÉCON bank charges

agir act; ~ **sur qn** affect s.o.; **il s'agit de** it's about

agitation *f* hustle and bustle; POL unrest; (*nervosité*) agitation; **agiter** *bouteille* shake; *mouchoir, main* wave; (*préoccuper, énerver*) upset; **s'~** *d'un enfant* fidget; (*s'énerver*) get upset

agneau *m* lamb

agonie *f* death throes *pl*

agrafer *vêtements* fasten; *papier* staple; **agrafeuse** *f* stapler

agrandir enlarge; **agrandissement** *m* enlargement; *d'une ville* expansion

agréable pleasant (*à* to)

agrément *m* approval, consent; *les ~s* (*attraits*) the delights

agresser attack; **agresseur** *m* attacker; *pays* aggressor;

agressif, -ive aggressive; **agression** *f* attack; PSYCH stress

agriculteur *m* farmer; **agriculture** *f* agriculture, farming

agrumes *mpl* citrus fruit

ahuri astounded; **ahurissant** astounding

aide 1 *f* help, assistance; **à l'~ de qc** with the help of sth; **avec l'~ de qn** with s.o.'s help **2** *m/f* (*assistant*) assistant; **aider 1** *v/t* help; **s'~ de qc** use sth **2** *v/i* help; ~ **à qc** contribute to sth

aïeul, ~e *m/f* ancestor; **aïeux** ancestors

aigle *m* eagle

aigre sour; *vent* bitter; *critique* sharp; *voix* shrill

aigu, ~ë sharp; *son* high-pitched; *conflit* bitter; *intelligence* keen; MÉD, GÉOM, GRAM acute

aiguille *f* needle; *d'une montre* hand; *tour* spire

aiguiser sharpen; *fig: appétit* whet

ail *m* garlic

aile *f* wing; AUTO fender, *Br* wing

ailier *m* SP wing, winger

ailleurs somewhere else, elsewhere; **d'~** besides; **par ~** moreover

aimable pleasant

aimant *m* magnet

aimer like; *parent, enfant, mari etc* love; ~ **mieux** prefer

aine f groin

aîné, ~e 1 adj elder; *de trois ou plus* eldest; **2** adj eldest; **il est mon ~ de deux ans** he is two years older than me

ainsi this way, thus fml; **~ que** and, as well as

air m air; *aspect* look; MUS tune; *se donner des ~s* give o.s. airs; **airbag** m airbag

aire f area; **~ de jeu** playground

aisance f ease; *(richesse)* wealth

aise f ease; **être à l'~** be comfortable; **être mal à l'~** be uncomfortable; **prendre ses ~s** make o.s. at home

aisselle f armpit

ajourner postpone *(de* for); JUR adjourn

ajouter add; **s'~ à** be added to

ajuster adjust; *vêtement* alter; *(viser)* aim at; *(joindre)* fit *(à* to)

alarme f alarm; **donner l'~** raise the alarm; **~ antivol** burglar alarm; **alarmer** alarm; **s'~ de** be alarmed by

album m album

alcool m alcohol; **alcoolique** adj & m/f alcoholic; **alcoolisme** alcoholism; **alco(o)-test** m Breathalyzer®, Br Breathalyser®

aléatoire uncertain; INFORM, MATH random

alentour: ~s mpl surroundings pl; **aux ~s de** in the vi-

cinity of; *(autour de)* about

alerte 1 adj alert **2** f alarm; **~ à la bombe** bomb scare; **alerter** alert

algèbre f algebra

Algérie f: **l'~** Algeria; **algérien, ~ne** Algerian; **Algérien, ~ne** m/f Algerian

algue f BOT seaweed

aligner TECH align *(sur* with); *(mettre une ligne)* line up; **s'~** line up; **s'~ sur qc** align o.s. with sth

aliment m foodstuff; **~s** food; **alimentation** f food; *en eau, en électricité* supply; **~ de base** staple diet; **alimenter** feed; *en eau, en électricité* supply *(en* with); *conversation* keep going

alinéa m paragraph

allaiter breast-feed

allécher tempt

allée f *(avenue)* path; **~s et venues** comings and goings

allégé yaourt low-fat; *confiture* low-sugar; **alléger** lighten; *impôt, tension* reduce

allègre cheerful

Allemagne f: **l'~** Germany; **allemand, ~e 1** adj German **2** m langue German; **Allemand, ~e** m/f German

aller 1 v/i go; **~ en voiture** go by car; **~ chercher** go for, fetch; **comment allez-vous?** how are you?; **je vais bien** I'm fine; **ça va?** is that OK?; *(comment te portes-tu?)* how are you?; **ça va**

bien merci fine, thanks; **~ bien avec** go well with; **on y va!** F let's go!; **allez!** go on!; **allons! allons donc!** come now!; **s'en ~** leave; *d'une tâche* disappear; **cette couleur te va bien** that color really suits you **2** *v/aux*: **je vais partir demain** I'm going to leave tomorrow **3** *m*: **~ et retour** round trip, *Br* return trip; **billet ~ et retour** round-trip ticket, *Br* return ticket; **~ simple** one-way ticket, *Br* single; **match** *m* **~** away game

allergie *f* allergy; **allergique** allergic (**à** to)

alliance *f* POL alliance; (*mariage*) marriage; (*anneau*) wedding ring; **allié,** **~e 1** *adj* allied; *famille* related by marriage **2** *m/f* ally; *famille* relative by marriage

allô hello

allocation *f* allowance; **~ chômage** workers' compensation, *Br* unemployment benefit

allonger lengthen, make longer; *jambes* stretch out; **s'~** get longer; (*s'étendre*) lie down

allumage *m* AUTO ignition; **allumer 1** *v/t* light; *chauffage, télévision etc* turn on **2** *v/i* turn the lights on; **allumette** *f* match

allure *f* (*démarche*) walk; (*vi-*

tesse) speed; (*air*) appearance; **avoir de l'~** have style

allusion *f* allusion

alors then; (*par conséquence*) so; **~ que** *temps* when; *opposition* while

alouette *f* lark

alourdir make heavy

Alpes *fpl*: **les ~** the Alps

alphabet *m* alphabet

alpinisme *m* mountaineering; **alpiniste** *m/f* mountaineer

altercation *f* argument

altérer *denrées* spoil; *couleur* fade; *vérité* distort; *texte* alter

alternance *f* alternation; *de cultures* rotation; **alternatif** *f* alternative; **alterner** alternate

altitude *f* altitude

alto *m* alto; **à cordes** viola

altruisme *m* altruism

aluminium *m* aluminum, *Br* aluminium

amabilité *f* kindness

amadouer softsoap

amaigri thinner; **amaigrir**: **~ qn** cause s.o. to lose weight; **s'~** lose weight, get thinner

amalgame *m* mixture, amalgamation

amande *f* almond

amant *m* lover

amarrer MAR moor

amas *m* pile; **amasser** amass

amateur *m* lover; *non professionnel* amateur; **en ~** as a hobby

ambassade f embassy; **ambassadeur**, **-drice** m/f ambassador

ambiance f (atmosphère) atmosphere

ambigu, **~ë** ambiguous; **ambiguïté** f ambiguity

ambitieux, **-euse 1** adj ambitious **2** m/f ambitious person; **ambition** f ambition

ambivalence f ambivalence

ambulance f ambulance; **ambulancier** m paramedic, Br ambulance man

ambulant traveling, Br travelling

âme f soul; **état** m d'**~** state of mind; **~ charitable** do-gooder

amélioration f improvement; **améliorer** improve; **s'~** improve, get better

aménager appartement arrange, lay out; terrain develop; vieille maison convert

amende f fine

amender improve; projet de loi amend

amener bring; (causer) cause; **s'~** turn up

amer, **-ère** bitter

américain, **~e 1** adj American **2** m LING American English; **Américain**, **~e** m/f American; **américaniser** Americanize

amérindien, **~ne** Native American; **Amérindien**, **~ne** m/f Native American

Amérique f: l'**~** America; l'**~**

centrale Central America; l'**~ latine** Latin America; l'**~ du Nord** North America; l'**~ du Sud** South America

amertume f bitterness

ameublement m (meubles) furniture

ameuter rouse

ami, **~e 1** m/f friend; (amant) boyfriend; (maîtresse) girlfriend; **devenir ~ avec qn** make friends with s.o. **2** adj friendly; **amiable**: **à l'~** amicably; JUR out of court; **arrangement** amicable, friendly; JUR out-of-court

amical, **~e 1** adj friendly **2** f association

amincir 1 v/t make thinner; d'une robe make look thinner **2** v/i get thinner

amiral m admiral

amitié f friendship; **~s** best wishes

amnésie f amnesia

amnistie f amnesty

amoindrir diminish, lessen; **s'~** diminish

amollir soften

amonceler pile up

amont: **en ~** upstream (**de** from)

amoral amoral

amorcer begin; INFORM boot up

amorphe sans énergie listless

amortir choc cushion; bruit muffle; douleur dull; dettes pay off; **amortisseur** m AUTO shock absorber

amour *m* love; **~s** love life; **faire l'~** make love; **amoureux, -euse** *regard* loving; *vie love atr*; *personne* in love (**de** with); **tomber ~** fall in love; **amour-propre** *m* pride

amphithéâtre *m* amphitheater, *Br* amphitheatre; *d'université* lecture hall

ample *vêtements* loose; *sujet* broad; *ressources* ample; **ampleur** *f d'un désastre etc* scale

amplification *f* TECH amplification; *fig* growth; **amplifier** TECH amplify; *fig: problème* magnify; *idée* expand

ampoule *f sur la peau* blister; *de médicament* ampoule; *lampe* bulb

amputer amputate; *fig* cut

amusant funny, amusing

amuse-gueule *m* appetizer

amuser amuse; **s'~** have a good time, enjoy o.s.; **s'~ à faire qc** have fun doing sth, enjoy doing sth; **faire qch pour s'~** do sth for fun

amygdale *f* ANAT tonsil; **amygdalite** *f* tonsillitis

an *m* year; **le jour** *ou* **le premier de l'~** New Year's Day; **elle a 15 ~s** she's 15 (years old)

analogie *f* analogy; **analogique** INFORM analog; **analogue** analogous (**à** with)

analphabète illiterate; **analphabétisme** *m* illiteracy

analyse *f* analysis; *de sang* test; **analyser** analyze; *Br* analyse; *sang* test; **analytique** analytical

ananas *m* BOT pineapple

anarchie *f* anarchy; **anarchiste** *m* anarchist

anatomie *f* anatomy

ancêtres *mpl* ancestors

anchois *m* anchovy

ancien, ~ne old; *de l'Antiquité* ancient; **anciennement** formerly

ancre *f* anchor

Andorre *f*: **l'~** Andorra

âne *m* donkey; *fig* ass

anéantir annihilate

anecdote *f* anecdote

anémie *f* MÉD anemia, *Br* anaemia

anesthésie *f* MÉD anesthesia, *Br* anaesthesia

ange *m* angel

angine *f* MÉD throat infection; **~ de poitrine** angina

anglais, ~e 1 *adj* English **2** *m langue* English; **Anglais, ~e** *m/f* Englishman; English-woman; **les ~** the English

angle *m* angle; *(coin)* corner; **~ mort** blind spot

Angleterre *f*: **l'~** England

anglophone English-speaking

angoisse *f* anguish; **angoisser** distress

anguille *f* eel

anguleux, -euse angular

animal *m* animal; **~ domestique** pet **2** *adj* animal *atr*

animateur, -trice *m/f d'une*

émission host, presenter; *d'une discussion* moderator; *d'activités culturelles, d'une entreprise* leader; *de dessin animé* animator; **animation** *f* (*vivacité*) liveliness; *de mouvements* hustle and bustle; *de dessin animé* animation; **animé** *rue, quartier* busy; *conversation* lively, animated; **animer** *fête* liven up; (*stimuler*) animate; *discussion, émission* host; **s'~** come to life; *d'une personne, discussion* become animated

animosité *f* animosity

anneau *m* ring

année *f* year; **les ~s 90** the 90s; **bonne ~!** happy New Year!

annexe *f d'un bâtiment* annex; *d'un document* appendix; *d'une lettre* enclosure

anniversaire *m* birthday; *d'un événement* anniversary

annonce *f* announcement; *dans journal* ad (*vertisement*); (*présage*) sign; **petites~s** classified ads; **annoncer** announce; **s'~ bien/mal** be off to a good/bad start

annotation *f* annotation

annuaire *m*: **~ du téléphone** phone book

annuel, ~le annual, yearly

annulaire *m* ring finger

annulation *f* cancellation; *d'un mariage* annulment; **annuler** cancel; *mariage an*-

nul

anodin harmless; *personne* insignificant; *blessure* slight

anomalie *f* anomaly

anonyme anonymous; **société** *f* **~** incorporated *ou* Br limited company

anorak *m* anorak

anorexie *f* anorexia; **anorexique** anorexic

anormal abnormal

anse *f d'un panier etc* handle; GÉOGR cove

antagonisme *m* antagonism

antarctique 1 *adj* Antarctic **2** *m* **l'Antarctique** Antarctica, the Antarctic

antécédents *mpl* history

antenne *f* ZO antenna, feeler; TV, *d'une radio* antenna, Br aerial

antérieur (*de devant*) front; (*d'avant*) previous, earlier; **~ à** prior to, before

anthropologie *f* anthropology

antibiotique *m* antibiotic

antibrouillard *m* fog lamp

anticipation *f* anticipation; **payer par ~** pay in advance; **d'~** *roman* science-fiction

anticiper anticipate; **~ un paiement** pay in advance

anticonstitutionnel, ~le unconstitutional

antidater backdate

antidérapant *m* AUTO non-skid tire *ou* Br tyre

antidote *m* MÉD antidote

antigel *m* antifreeze

antipathie f antipathy

antipelliculaire: *shampoing* m ~ dandruff shampoo

antiquaire m antique dealer; **antique** ancient; *meuble antique*; *péj* antiquated; **antiquités** fpl antiques

antisémite 1 *adj* anti-Semitic **2** *m/f* anti-Semite

antiseptique m & *adj* antiseptic

antisocial antisocial

antiterroriste anti-terrorist

antivol m anti-theft device

anxiété f anxiety; **anxieux, -euse** anxious

août m August

apaiser *personne* calm down; *douleur* soothe; *soif, faim* satisfy

apathie f apathy

apercevoir see; **s'~ de qc** notice sth

apéritif m aperitif

à-peu-près m approximation

apitoyer: ~ **qn** move s.o. to pity; **s'~ sur qn** feel sorry for s.o.

aplanir flatten, level; *fig*: *différend* smooth over

aplatir flatten; **s'~** (*s'écraser*) be flattened; **s'~ devant** kowtow to

aplomb m self-confidence; (*audace*) nerve; **d'~** vertical, plumb; **je ne suis pas d'~** *fig* I don't feel a hundred percent

apostrophe f (*interpellation*) rude remark; *signe* apostro-phe

apparaître appear; **faire ~** bring to light

appareil m device; AVIAT plane; **qui est à l'~?** TÉL who's speaking?; ~ **ménager** household appliance; ~ **photo** camera

apparemment apparently

apparence f appearance; **en** ~ on the face of things; **sauver les ~s** save face; **apparent** visible; (*illusoire*) apparent

apparenté related (**à** to)

apparition f appearance

appartement m apartment, *Br* flat

appartenir belong (**à** to); **il m'appartient pas d'en décider** it's not up to me to decide

appauvrir impoverish; **s'~** become impoverished; **appauvrissement** m impoverishment

appel m call; MIL (*recrutement*) draft, *Br* call-up; JUR appeal; ÉDU roll-call; **faire** ~ **à qc** (*nécessiter*) require; **faire** ~ **à qn** appeal to s.o.; **appeler** call; (*nécessiter*) call for; **en** ~ **à qn** approach s.o.; **comment t'appelles-tu?** what's your name?, what are you called?

appendice m appendix; **appendicite** f MÉD appendicitis

appétissant appetizing; **appétit** m appetite; **bon ~!** enjoy (your meal)!

applaudir applaud, clap; **applaudissements** *mpl* applause, clapping

applicateur *m* applicator; **application** *f* application; **appliquer** apply; **s'~** *d'une personne* work hard; **~ Y sur X** smear X with Y

apport *m* contribution; **apporter** bring

appréciation *f* estimate; (*jugement*) opinion; COMM appreciation; **apprécier** estimate; *personne, musique, la bonne cuisine* appreciate

appréhender: ~ qc be apprehensive about sth; **~ qn** JUR arrest s.o.; **appréhension** *f* apprehension

apprendre learn; *nouvelle aussi* hear (*par qn* from s.o.); **~ qc à qn** (*enseigner*) teach s.o. sth; (*raconter*) tell s.o. sth

apprenti, ~e *m/f* apprentice; *fig* beginner; **apprentissage** *m* learning; *d'un métier* apprenticeship

apprivoiser tame

approbateur, -trice approving; **approbation** *f* approval

approcher 1 *v/t* bring closer (*de* to) **2** *v/i* approach; **s'~ de** approach

approfondir deepen; (*étudier*) go into in detail

approprié appropriate, suitable (*à* for); **approprier: s'~ qc** appropriate sth

approuver *loi* approve; *personne, manières* approve of

approvisionnement *m* supply (*en* of)

approximatif, -ive approximate; **approximation** *f* approximation

appui *m* support; *d'une fenêtre* sill; **prendre ~** lean on; **appuyer 1** *v/t* lean on; (*tenir debout*) support; *fig* candidat, idée support, back **2** *v/i*: **~ sur** bouton press, push; *fig* stress; **s'~** lean on; *fig* rely on

après 1 *prép* after; **d'~ les journaux** going by what the papers say **2** *adv* afterward **3** *conj*: **~ que** after

après-demain the day after tomorrow

après-midi *m ou f* afternoon

apr. J.-C. (= **après Jésus-Christ**) AD (= anno Domini)

aptitude *f* aptitude

aquarelle *f* watercolor, *Br* watercolour

aquarium *m* aquarium

arabe 1 *adj* Arab **2** *m langue* Arabic; **Arabe** *m/f* Arab; **Arabie** f: **l'~ Saoudite** Saudi (Arabia)

araignée *f* spider

arbitrage *m* arbitration

arbitre *m* referee; **libre ~** free will; **arbitrer** arbitrate

arbre *m* tree; TECH shaft

arbuste *m* shrub

arc *m* ARCH arch; GÉOM arc

arc-en-ciel m rainbow

arche f arch; *Bible* Ark

archéologie f archeology, Br archaeology; **archéologique** archeological, Br archaeological; **archéologue** m/f archeologist, Br archaeologist

archet m archer; MUS bow

archevêque m archbishop

architecte m/f architect; **architecture** f architecture

arctique 1 adj Arctic **2** m l'Arctique the Arctic

ardent soleil blazing; désir burning; défenseur fervent; **ardeur** f fig ardor, Br ardour

ardoise f slate

ardu arduous

arène f arena; ~s arena

arête f d'un poisson bone; d'une montagne ridge

argent m silver; (monnaie) money; ~ **liquide** ou **comptant** cash

argot m slang

argument m argument; **argumenter** argue

aride arid, dry

aristocrate m/f aristocrat; **aristocratie** f aristocracy

armateur m shipowner

arme f weapon (aussi fig); ~ à **feu** firearm; **armée** f army; ~ **de l'air** airforce; **armement** m arming; ~s armaments; **armer** arm (**de** with); fig equip (**de** with)

armistice m armistice

armoire f cupboard; pour les vêtements closet, Br wardrobe

arnaque f F rip-off F; **arnaquer** F rip off F

aromate m herb; (épice) spice; (parfum) arôme m flavor, Br flavour; (odeur) aroma

arracher pull out; pommes de terre pull up; ~ **qc à qn** snatch sth from s.o.; **s'~ à** ou **de qc** free o.s. from sth; **s'~ qc** fight over sth

arrangement m arrangement; **arranger** arrange; objet fix; différend settle; cela **m'arrange** that suits me; **s'~ avec qn** pour faire qch come to an arrangement with s.o. about sth; **s'~ pour** faire qch manage to do sth

arrestation f arrest; **en état d'~** under arrest

arrêt m (interruption) stopping; d'autobus stop; JUR judgment; **sans** ~ constantly; **arrêter 1** v/i stop **2** v/t stop; moteur turn off; voleur arrest; jour, date set; ~ **de faire qch** stop doing sth; **s'~** stop

arrière 1 adv back; **en** ~ backward; regarder back; (à une certaine distance) behind; **en** ~ **de** behind **2** adj inv rear **3** m AUTO, SP back; **à l'**~ in back, at the back

arrière-goût m aftertaste; **arrière-grand-mère** f great-grandmother; **arrière-grand-père** m great-grandfather; **arrière-pensée** f ul-

terior motive; **arrière-petit--fils** m great-grandson
arrivée f arrival; SP finish line; **arriver** arrive; *d'un événement* happen; **~ à faire qch** manage to do sth; **~ à qn** happen to s.o.; **j'arrive!** (I'm) coming!
arrogance f arrogance; **arrogant** arrogant
arrondir *vers le haut* round up; *vers le bas* round down; **arrondissement** m *d'une ville* district
arroser water; **~ qch** fig have a drink to celebrate sth; **arrosoir** m watering can
art m art; **avoir l'~ de faire qch** have a knack for doing sth
artère f ANAT artery; *(route)* main road
arthrite f arthritis
artichaut m artichoke
article m article, item; JUR article, clause; *de presse*, GRAM article; **~s de luxe** luxury goods
articulation f ANAT joint; *d'un son* articulation; **articuler** *son* articulate
artificiel, **~le** artificial
artisan m craftsman; **artisanal** hand-made; *fromage*, *pain etc* traditional
artiste 1 m/f artist; *comédien*, *chanteur* performer **2** adj artistic
as m ace
ascenseur m elevator, Br lift

ascension f ascent; fig *(progrès)* rise; **l'Ascension** REL Ascension
asiatique Asian; **Asiatique** m/f Asian; **Asie** f: **l'~** Asia
asile m shelter; POL asylum; **~ de vieillards** old people's home; **demandeur** m **d'~** asylum seeker
aspect m *(vue)* look; *(point de vue)* angle, point of view; *d'un problème* aspect; *(air)* appearance; **à l'~ de** at the sight of
asperge f BOT stalk of asparagus; **~s** asparagus
asperger sprinkle; **~ qn de qch** spray s.o. with sth
asphyxier asphyxiate
aspirateur m vacuum (cleaner); **aspirer** *de l'air* breathe in, inhale; *liquide* suck up; **~ à (faire) qch** aspire to (doing) sth
aspirine f aspirin
assagir: **s'~** settle down
assaillir *vedette* mob; **être assailli de** be assailed by; *de coups de téléphone* be bombarded by
assainir *(nettoyer)* clean up; *eau* purify
assaisonnement m seasoning
assassin m murderer; *d'un président* assassin; **assassinat** m assassination; **assassiner** murder; *un président* assassinate
assemblée f gathering; *(réu-*

nion) meeting; **~ générale**
annual general meeting; **assembler** assemble; **s'~** assemble, gather

asseoir: s'~ sit down

assez enough; *(plutôt)* quite;
~ d'argent enough money; **~
grand** big enough

assidu *élève* hard-working

assiette *f* plate; **ne pas être
dans son ~** *fig* be under
the weather

assigner assign

assimiler *(comparer)* compare; *connaissances, étran-
gers* assimilate

assis: être ~ be sitting; **assise**
f fig basis

assistance *f (public)* audience; *(aide)* assistance; assistant, **~e** *m/f* assistant;
~e sociale social worker;
assister 1 *v/i:* **~ à qc** attend
sth, be (present) at sth **2** *v/t:*
~ qn assist s.o

association *f* association; associé, **~e** *m/f* partner; associer associate **(à** with); **s'~**
join forces; COMM go into
partnership; **s'~ à** *douleur*
share in

assoiffé thirsty

assombrir: s'~ darken

assommant F deadly boring;
assommer stun; F bore to
death

Assomption *f* REL Assumption

assorti matching; **~ de** ac-
companied by; **assortiment**

m assortment

assoupir send to sleep; *fig:
douleur, sens* dull; **s'~** doze
off; *fig* die down

assourdir deafen; *bruit* muffle

assumer take on, assume

assurance *f* assurance; *(contrat)* insurance

assuré, ~e 1 *(sûr)* confident **2**
m/f insured party; **~ment** assuré-
ment certainly; **assurer** succès ensure; **par une assurance** insure; **s'~** take out insurance; **s'~ de qc** *(vérifier)*
make sure of sth, check sth

asthme *m* asthma

astiquer *meuble* polish; *casserole* scour

astre *m* star

astrologie astrology

astronaute *m/f* astronaut

astronomie *f* astronomy; astronomique astronomical
(aussi fig)

astuce *f (ingéniosité)* astute-
ness; *(truc)* trick; **astucieux,
-euse** astute

atelier *m* workshop; *d'un artiste* studio

athée *m/f* atheist; **athéisme**
m atheism

athlète *m/f* athlete; **athlétisme** *m* athletics *sg*

Atlantique *m:* **l'~** the Atlantic

atlas *m* atlas

atmosphère *f* atmosphere

atome *m* atom

atout *m fig* asset

atroce dreadful, atrocious;

atrocité *f* atrocity

attachant captivating

attaché-case *m* executive briefcase

attacher 1 *v/t* attach, fasten; *animal* tie up; *prisonnier* secure; *chaussures* do up **2** *v/i* CUIS (*coller*) stick; **s'~ à** become attached to

attaquant, ~e *m/f* SP striker; **attaque** *f* attack; **~ à la bombe** bomb attack; **attaquer** attack; *travail, sujet* tackle; **s'~ à** attack; *problème* tackle

attarder: s'~ linger

atteindre reach; *d'un projectile* strike, hit; *d'une maladie* affect

atteinte *f* fig attack; **porter ~ à qc** undermine sth; **hors d'~** out of reach

attendant: en ~ in the meantime; **en ~ qu'il arrive** (*subj*) while waiting for him to arrive; **attendre** wait; **~ qn** wait for s.o.; **s'~ à qc** expect sth; **~ un enfant** be expecting a baby

attendrir *fig: personne* move; *cœur* soften; **s'~** be moved (**sur** by); **attendrissement** *m* tenderness

attentat *m* attack; **~ à la bombe** bombing, bomb attack; **~ à la pudeur** indecent assault

attente *f* wait; (*espoir*) expectation

attentif, -ive attentive (**à** to); **attention** *f* attention; (**fais**) **~!** look out!, (be) careful!;

faire ~ à qc pay attention to sth

atténuer reduce; *propos, termes* tone down

atterrir AVIAT land; **~ en catastrophe** crash-land

attestation *f* certificate; **attester** certify; (*prouver*) confirm

attirance *f* attraction; **attirer** attract; **s'~ des critiques** come in for criticism

attitude *f* attitude; *d'un corps* pose

attraction *f* attraction

attrait *m* attraction

attraper catch; (*duper*) take in

attrayant attractive

attribuer attribute; *prix* award; *part, rôle* allot; *valeur* attach; **s'~** take; **attribution** *f* allocation; *d'un prix* award; **~s** (*compétence*) competence

attrister sadden

attroupement *m* crowd; **attrouper: s'~** gather

aube *f* dawn; **à l'~** at dawn

auberge *f* inn; **~ de jeunesse** youth hostel

aubergine *f* BOT eggplant, *Br* aubergine

aucun, ~e 1 *adj avec négatif* no, not …any; *avec positif, interrogatif* any **2** *pron avec négatif* none; **~ des deux** neither of the two; *avec positif, interrogatif* anyone, anybody

audace f daring, audacity; péj
audacity; **audacieux, -euse**
(courageux) daring, auda-
cious; (insolent) insolent
au-delà beyond; ~ **de** above; ~
au-dessous: ~ (**de**) below; ~
au-dessus: ~ (**de**) above; ~
au-devant: **aller** ~ **de** meet;
désirs anticipate
audible audible
audience f d'un tribunal
hearing
audiovisuel, .le audiovisual
auditeur, -trice m/f listener;
FIN auditor; (**audition** f audition; (ouïe) hearing; **de témoins** examination
augmentation f increase; de
salaire raise, Br rise; **augmenter** 1 v/t increase; salarié give a raise ou Br rise
to 2 v/i increase, rise
aujourd'hui today
auparavant beforehand;
deux mois ~ two months
earlier
auprès: ~ **de** beside, near
auquel → **lequel**
auriculaire m little finger
aurore f dawn
ausculter MÉD sound
aussi 1 adv too, also; **il est** ~
grand que moi he's as tall as
me 2 conj therefore
aussitôt immediately; ~ **que**
as soon as
austère austere
Australie f: **l'~** Australia; **australien, ~ne** Australian;
Australien, ~ne m/f Austral-

ian
autant (tant) as much (que
as); avec pluriel as many
(que as); comparatif: ~ **de**
... **que** ... as much ... as
...; avec pluriel as many ...
as ...; (pour) ~ **que je sache**
(subj) as far as I know; **en**
faire ~ do the same
auteur m/f author; d'un crime
perpetrator
authenticité f authenticity;
authentique authentic
autiste autistic
auto f car, automobile
autobiographie f autobiography
autocollant 1 adj adhesive 2
m sticker
autodéfense f self-defense,
Br self-defence
autodidacte self-taught
auto-école f driving school
autographe m autograph
automatique adj & m automatic; **automatiquement**
automatically; **automatiser**
automate
automne m fall, Br autumn
automobile f car, automobile; **automobiliste** m/f
driver
autonomie f independence;
POL autonomy
autoradio m car radio
autorisation f authorization,
permission; **autoriser** authorize, allow; **autoritaire**
authoritarian; **autorité** f authority

autoroute *f* highway, *Br* motorway

auto-stop *m*: **faire de l'~** hitchhike

autour: **~ (de)** around

autre 1 *adj* other/une **~** ... another ...; **nous ~s Américains** we Americans; **rien d'~** nothing else; **~ part** somewhere else; **d'~ part** on the other hand 2 *pron*: **un/une ~** another (one); **l'~** the other (one); **les ~s** the others; (*autrui*) other people; **l'un l'~**, **les uns les ~** each other, one another

autrefois in the past

autrement (*différemment*) differently; (*sinon*) otherwise

Autriche *f*: **l'~** Austria; **autrichien, ~ne** Austrian; **Autrichien, ~ne** *m/f* Austrian

autrui other people *pl*, others *pl*

auxquelles, auxquels → **lequel**

av. (= **avenue**) Ave (= avenue)

aval 1 *adv*: **en ~** downstream (**de**) from) 2 *m* FIN guarantee

avalanche *f* avalanche

avaler swallow

avance *f* advance; *d'une course* lead; **d'~** in advance; **en ~** ahead of time; **avancement** *m* progress; (*promotion*) promotion; **avancer** 1 *v/t chaise, date* bring forward; *main* put out; *argent*

advance; *thèse* put forward 2 *v/i* make progress; MIL advance; *d'une montre* be fast; **s'~ vers** come up to

avant 1 *prép* before; **~ tout** above all; **~ de faire qch** before doing sth 2 *adv temps* before; *espace* in front of; **en ~** forward 3 *conj*: **~ que** (+ *subj*) before 4 *adj*: **roue** *f* **~** front wheel; **5 m** front; *d'un navire* bow; SP forward

avantage *m* advantage; **~s sociaux** fringe benefits; **avantager** suit; (*favoriser*) favor, *Br* favour

avant-dernier, -ère last but one

avant-hier the day before yesterday

avant-première *f* preview

avant-propos *m* foreword

avant-veille *f*: **l'~** two days before

avare 1 *adj* miserly 2 *m* miser; **avarice** *f* miserliness

avarié *nourriture* bad

avec with

avenir *m* future; **à l'~** in future; **d'~** promising

Avent *m* Advent

aventure *f* adventure; (*liaison*) affair; **aventurer**: **s'~** venture (**dans** into)

avenue *f* avenue

avérer: **s'~** (+ *adj*) prove

averse *f* shower

aversion *f* aversion (**pour** *ou* **contre** to); **prendre qn en ~** take a dislike to s.o.

avertir inform (*de* of); (*mettre en garde*) warn (*de* of); **avertissement** *m* warning; **avertisseur** *m* AUTO horn

aveu *m* confession

aveuglant blinding; **aveugle 1** *adj* blind **2** *m/f* blind man; blind woman; **aveugler** blind

aviateur, -trice *m/f* pilot; **aviation** *f* aviation, flying

avide greedy, avid (*de* for); **avidité** *f* greed

avilissant degrading

avion *m* (air)plane, *Br* (aero-) plane; **aller en ~** fly, go by plane; **par ~** (by) airmail

aviron *m* oar; SP rowing

avis *m* opinion; (*information*) notice; **à mon ~** in my opinion; **changer d'~** change one's mind; **sauf ~ contraire** unless otherwise stated

aviser: **~ qn de qc** advise *ou* inform s.o. of sth; **s'~ de qc** notice sth; **s'~ de faire qch** take it into one's head to do sth

av. J.-C. (= *avant Jésus-Christ*) BC (= before Christ)

avocat, ~e 1 *m/f* lawyer; (*défenseur*) advocate **2** *m* BOT avocado

avoir 1 *v/t* (*posséder*) have, have got; (*obtenir*) get; **j'ai froid/chaud** I am cold/hot; **~ 20 ans** be 20; **il y a** there is; **avec pluriel** there are; **qu'est-ce qu'il y a?** what's the matter?; **il y a un an** a year ago **2** *v/aux* have; **j'ai déjà parlé** I have *ou* I've already spoken; **je lui ai parlé hier** I spoke to him yesterday **3** *m* COMM credit; (*possessions*) possessions *pl*

avoisiner: **~ qc** border on sth

avortement *m* miscarriage; **provoqué** abortion; **avorter 1** *v/t* **femme** terminate the pregnancy of; **se faire~** have an abortion **2** *v/i* miscarry; *fig* fail

avouer: **~ (avoir fait qc)** confess (to having done sth)

avril *m* April

axe *m* axle; GÉOM axis; *fig* basis

B

babiller babble

bâbord *m* MAR: **à ~** to port

bac[1] *m* **bateau** ferry; **récipient** container

bac[2] *m* F, **baccalauréat** *m* exam that is a prerequisite for university entrance

bâche *f* tarpaulin

bâcler F botch F

badaud *m* onlooker

badiner joke

baffe *f* F slap

bafouiller 1 *v/t* stammer **2** *v/i* F talk nonsense

bagages *mpl* baggage, luggage; *fig* (*connaissances*) knowledge; *faire ses ~* pack

bagarre *f* fight; **bagarrer** F: *se ~* fight

bagnole *f* F car

bague *f* ring; *~ de fiançailles* engagement ring

baguette *f* stick; MUS baton; *pain* French stick; *~s pour manger* chopsticks

baie[1] *f* BOT berry

baie[2] *f* (*golfe*) bay; *Baie d'Hudson* Hudson Bay

baigner *enfant* bathe, *Br* bath; *se ~* go for a swim; **baignoire** *f* (bath) tub

bail *m* lease

bâiller yawn; *d'un trou* gape; *d'une porte* be ajar

bain *m* bath; *salle f de ~s* bathroom; *être dans le ~ fig* (*au courant*) be up to speed; *~ de bouche* mouthwash; **bain-marie** *m* CUIS double boiler

baiser 1 *m* kiss **2** *v/t* kiss; V screw V

baisse *f* fall; *être en ~* be falling; **baisser 1** *v/t* lower; *radio, chauffage* turn down **2** *v/i de forces* fail; *de lumière* fade; *d'une température, d'un prix* drop, fall; *de vue* deteriorate; *se ~* bend down

bal *m* dance; *formel* ball

balade *f* walk, stroll; **balader** walk; *se ~* go for a walk *ou* stroll

baladeur *m* Walkman®

balai *m* broom; *donner un coup de ~ à qch* give sth a sweep

balance *f* scales *pl*; COMM balance; ASTROL *Balance* Libra; **balancer** *jambes* swing; F (*lancer*) chuck F; F (*jeter*) chuck out F; *se ~* swing; **balançoire** *f* swing

balayer sweep; *fig: gouvernement* sweep from power; *soucis* sweep away

balbutier stammer

balcon *m* balcony

baleine *f* whale

ballade *f* ballad

balle *f* ball; *d'un fusil* bullet; *de marchandises* bale

ballet *m* ballet

ballon *m* ball; *pour enfants,* AVIAT balloon

ballotter 1 *v/t* buffet **2** *v/i* bounce up and down

balnéaire: *station f ~* seaside resort

balourd clumsy

balte Baltic; **Baltique**: *la (mer) ~* the Baltic (Sea)

balustrade *f* balustrade

bambou *m* bamboo

banal (*mpl -als*) banal; **banalité** *f* banality

banane *f* banana; **bananier** *m* banana tree

banc *m* bench, seat; *~ de sable* sandbank

bancaire bank *atr*

bancal (*mpl -als*) *table* wobbly

bandage *m* MÉD bandage

bande f de terrain, de tissu strip; MÉD bandage; (rayure) stripe; (groupe) group; péj gang, band; **bander** MÉD bandage; **~ les yeux à qn** blindfold s.o.

bandit m bandit; (escroc) crook

banlieue f suburbs pl; **de ~** suburban

bannière f banner

bannir banish

banque f bank; **~ du sang** blood bank

banquet m banquet

banquette f seat

banquier m banker

baptême m baptism; **baptiser** baptize

bar m bar; meuble cocktail cabinet

baraque f shack

barbant F boring

barbare 1 adj barbaric **2** m/f barbarian

barbe f beard; **à papa** cotton candy, Br candy floss

barbecue m barbecue

barber F bore rigid F

barbu bearded

barder F: **ça va ~** there's going to be trouble

baromètre m barometer

barque f MAR boat

barrage m dam; (barrière) barrier

barre f bar; MAR helm; (trait) line; **~ des témoins** JUR witness stand

barreau m bar; d'échelle rung

barrer (obstruer) block, bar; mot cross out; **se ~** F leave

barrette f barrette, Br hairslide

barrière f barrier; (clôture) fence; **~s douanières** customs barriers

bar-tabac m bar-cum-tobacco store

bas, ~se 1 adj low; GÉOGR lower; instrument bass; voix deep **2** adv low; parler in a low voice, quietly; **en ~** downstairs; **là~** there **3** m bottom; (vêtement) stocking; **au ~ de** at the bottom of

basané weatherbeaten; naturellement swarthy

bas-côté m d'une route shoulder

basculer topple over

base f base; d'un édifice foundation; fig: d'une science basis; **de ~** basic; **à ~ de lait** milk-based

base de données database

base-ball m baseball

baser base (**sur** on); **se ~ sur** draw on; d'une idée be based on

basilic m BOT basil

basket(-ball) m basketball; baskets fpl sneakers, Br trainers

basque 1 adj Basque **2** m langue Basque; **Basque** m/f Basque

basse-cour f farmyard; animaux poultry

bassine f bowl

bélier

bataille f battle; **livrer ~** give battle; **batailler** fig battle

bâtard m bastard; **chien** mongrel

bateau m boat; **faire du ~** go sailing; **mener qn en ~** fig put s.o. on, Br have s.o. on

bâti 1 adj built on; **bien ~** well-built **2** m frame

bâtiment m building; **secteur** construction industry; MAR ship

bâtir build

bâton m stick; **parler à ~s rompus** make small talk; **~ de rouge** lipstick; **~ de ski** ski pole ou stick

battant 1 adj pluie driving **2** m d'une porte leaf; personne fighter

batte f de base-ball bat

battement m de cœur beat; de temps interval

batterie f ÉL battery; MUS drums pl; dans un orchestre percussion; **batteur** m CUIS whisk; électrique mixer; MUS drummer; en base-ball batter; **battre 1** v/t beat; **cartes** shuffle **2** v/i beat; d'un volet bang; **se ~** fight

bavard, ~e 1 adj talkative **2** m/f chatterbox; **bavarder** chatter; (divulguer un secret) talk

baver drool, slobber; **bavure** f fig blunder, blooper F; **sans ~** impeccable

Bd (= **boulevard**) Blvd (= Boulevard)

B.D. f (= **bande dessinée**) comic strip

béant gaping

béat péj: sourire silly

beau, bel, belle (mpl beaux) beautiful, lovely; homme handsome; **il fait beau (temps)** it's lovely weather; **il a beau dire ...** it's no good him saying ...

beaucoup adv: **~ de** lots of, a lot of; **~ de gens** lots ou a lot of people, many people; **je n'ai pas ~ d'argent** I don't have a lot of ou much money; **~ trop cher** much too expensive

beau-fils m son-in-law; d'un remariage stepson; **beau-frère** m brother-in-law; **beau-père** m father-in-law; d'un remariage stepfather

beauté f beauty

beaux-arts mpl: **les ~** fine art

beaux-parents mpl parents-in-law

bébé m baby

bec m d'un oiseau beak; d'un récipient spout; MUS mouthpiece; F mouth

bedaine f (beer) belly

bégayer stutter, stammer

béguin m fig F: **avoir le ~ pour** have a crush on

beige beige

beignet m CUIS fritter

belge Belgian; **Belge** m/f Belgian; **Belgique: la ~** Belgium

bélier m ZO ram; ASTROL **Bé-**

lier Aries
belle → *beau*
belle-famille *f* in-laws *pl*
belle-fille *f* daughter-in-law; *d'un remariage* stepdaughter; **belle-mère** *f* mother--in-law; *d'un remariage* stepmother; **belle-sœur** *f* sister-in-law
belliqueux, -euse warlike
bémol *m* MUS flat
bénédiction *f* blessing
bénéfice *m* benefit; COMM profit; **bénéficier: ~ de** benefit from; **bénéfique** beneficial
Bénélux: **le ~** the Benelux countries *pl*
bénévolat voluntary work; **bénévole 1** *adj travail* voluntary **2** *m/f* volunteer
bénin, -igne *tumeur* benign; *accident* minor
bénir bless; **bénit** consecrated; *eau f ~e* holy water
béquille *f* crutch; *d'une moto* stand
berceau *m* cradle; **bercer** rock; *se ~ d'illusions* delude o.s.
béret *m* beret
berger *m* shepherd; *chien* German shepherd, *Br aussi* Alsatian
berline *f* AUTO sedan, *Br* saloon
bermuda(s) *m (pl)* Bermuda shorts *pl*
berner fool
besogne *f* job, task

besoin *m* need; **avoir ~ de (faire) qch** need (to do) sth; **au ~** if need be
bestial bestial
bétail *m (sans pl)* livestock
bête 1 *adj* stupid **2** *f animal*; *(insecte)* insect; **chercher la petite ~** nitpick; **bêtement** stupidly; **bêtise** *f* stupidity; **dire des ~s** talk nonsense; **une ~** a stupid thing to do/say
béton *m* concrete
betterave *f* beet, *Br* beetroot
beugler *de bœuf* low; F *d'une personne* shout
beurre *m* butter; **~ de cacahuètes** peanut butter
bévue *f* blunder
biais 1 *adv*: **en ~** diagonally; **de ~** *regarder* sideways **2** *m fig (aspect)* angle; **par le ~ de** through
biberon *m* (baby's) bottle
Bible *f* bible
bibliothèque *f* library; *meuble* bookcase
bic® *m* ballpoint (pen)
bicentenaire *m* bicentennial, *Br* bicentenary
biceps *m* biceps
biche *f* ZO doe
bicyclette *f* bicycle; **aller en** *ou* **à ~** cycle
bidon 1 *m*: **~ à essence** gas *ou Br* petrol can
bidonville *m* shanty town
bidule *m* F gizmo F
bien 1 *m* good; *(possession)* possession; **le ~** ce qui est

juste good; *faire le ~* do good; *faire du ~ à qn* do s.o. good; *~s (possessions)* property; *(produits)* goods **2** *adj* good; *(beau, belle)* good-looking; *être ~* feel well; *(à l'aise)* be comfortable; *ce sera très ~ comme ça* that will do very nicely; *se sentir ~* feel well; *avoir l'air ~* look good; *des gens ~* respectable people **3** *adv* well; *(très)* very; *~ des fois* lots of times; *eh ~* well; *oui, je veux ~* yes please **4** *conj ~ que* (+ *subj*) although

bien-être *m* welfare; *sensation agréable* well-being
bienfait *m* benefit
bien-fondé *m* legitimacy
bienheureux, -euse happy; REL blessed
bienséance *f* propriety
bientôt soon; *à ~!* see you (soon)!
bienveillance *f* benevolence
bienvenu, ~e 1 *adj* welcome **2** *m/f* *être le/la ~(e)* be welcome **3** *f* *souhaiter la ~e à* welcome
bière *f* beer; *~ blanche* wheat beer; *~ brune* dark beer, *Br* bitter; *~ pression* draft (beer), *Br* draught (beer)
bifteck *m* steak
bifurquer *v/i ~ (vers)* fork (off onto); *fig* branch out (into)
bigame 1 *adj* bigamous **2** *m/f* bigamist; **bigamie** *f* bigamy
bijou *m* jewel; *~x* jewelry, *Br*

jewellery; **bijouterie** *f* jewelry store, *Br* jeweller's; **bijoutier, -ère** *m/f* jeweler, *Br* jeweller
bikini *m* bikini
bilan *m* balance sheet; *fig (résultat)* outcome; *faire le ~ de* take stock of
bilingue bilingual
billard *m* billiards *sg*; *table* billiard table; *~ américain* pool
bille *f* marble; *billard (billiard)* ball; *stylo m (à) ~* ball-point (pen)
billet *m* ticket; *(petite lettre)* note; *~ (de banque)* bill, *Br* (bank)note; **billeterie** *f* ticket office; *automatique* ticket machine; FIN ATM, *Br aussi* cash dispenser
biochimie *f* biochemistry
biodégradable biodegradable
biodiversité *f* biodiversity
biographie *f* biography
biologie *f* biology; **biologique** biological; *aliments* organic
biotechnologie *f* biotechnology
bis 1 *adj*: *24 ~* 24A **2** *m* encore
biscornu *fig* weird
biscotte *f* rusk
biscuit *m* cookie, *Br* biscuit
bise *f*: *faire la ~ à* kiss
bisexuel, ~le bisexual
bisou *m* F kiss
bissextile: *année f ~* leap year

bistro(t) m bistro
bit m INFORM bit
bitume m asphalt
bizarre strange, bizarre
blafard wan
blague f joke; **sans ~!** no kidding!; **blaguer** joke
blaireau m badger; **pour se raser** shaving brush
blâme m blame; (sanction) reprimand
blanc, blanche 1 adj white; page blank; **nuit f blanche** sleepless night **2** m white; textile (household) linen; par opposé aux couleurs whites pl; dans un texte blank **3** m/f **Blanc, Blanche**, white, White
blancheur f whiteness; **blanchir** f v/t whiten; mur whitewash; linge launder, wash; du soleil bleach; fig: innocenter clear **2** v/i go white
blasé blasé
blasphème m blasphemy; **blasphémer** blaspheme
blé m wheat, Br corn
blêmir turn pale
blesser hurt (aussi fig); dans un accident injure; à la guerre wound; **se ~** injure ou hurt o.s.; **blessure** f d'accident injury; d'arme wound
bleu 1 adj blue; viande very rare **2** m blue; fromage blue cheese; sur la peau bruise; fig (novice) rookie F
blindage m armor, Br armour; **blinder** armor, Br ar-

mour; fig F harden
bloc m block; POL bloc; de papier pad; **faire ~** join forces
bloc-notes m notepad
blocus m blockade
blond, blonde 1 adj blonde; tabac Virginian; sable golden **2** m/f blonde **3** f bière beer, Br aussi lager
bloquer block; mécanisme jam; roues lock; compte freeze
blouson m jacket, blouson
bluff m bluff; **bluffer** bluffer
bobard m F tall tale ou Br story
bocal m (glass) jar
bock m: **un ~** a (glass of) beer
bœuf m steer; viande beef
bohémien, ~ne m/f gipsy
boire drink; (absorber) soak up
bois m matière, forêt wood; **en ~** wooden
boisson f drink; **~s alcoolisées** alcohol
boîte f box; en tôle can, Br aussi tin; F (entreprise) company; **~ (de nuit)** nightclub; **en ~** canned, Br aussi tinned; **~ à gants** glove compartment; **~ aux lettres** mailbox, Br letterbox
boiter limp; fig: de raisonnement be shaky; **boiteux, -euse** table etc wobbly; fig: raisonnement shaky; **être ~ d'une personne** have a limp
boîtier m case, housing
bol m bowl

bombardement *m* bombing; *avec obus* bombardment; **bombarder** bomb; *avec obus, questions* bombard; **bombe** *f* bomb; *(atomiseur)* spray; *~ à retardement* time bomb; **bombé** bulging

bon, ~ne 1 *adj* good; *route, moment* right; *de ~ foi personne* sincere; *être ~ en qch* be good at sth; *à quoi ~?* what's the use?; *witticism*; *~ anniversaire!* happy birthday!; *~ voyage!* have a good trip!, bon voyage!; *~ne chance!* good luck!; *~ne année!* Happy New Year!; *~ne nuit!* good night!; *ah ~* really **2** *adv*: *sentir ~* smell good; *tenir ~* not give in; *trouver ~ de faire qch* think it right to do sth **3** *m* COMM voucher; *avoir du ~* have its good points; *~ d'achat* gift voucher; *~ du Trésor* Treasury bond

bonbon *m* candy, *Br* sweet; *~s* candy, *Br* sweets

bond *m* leap; *d'une balle* bounce

bondé packed

bondir jump, leap *(de* with)

bonheur *m* happiness; *(chance)* luck; *par ~* luckily; *au petit ~* at random

bonhomme *m* F *(type)* guy F

boniment *m* battage spiel F, sales talk; F *(mensonge)* fairy story

bonjour *m* hello

bonne *f* maid

bonnet *m* hat; *gros ~ fig* F big shot F; *~ de douche* shower cap

bonsoir *m* hello, good evening

bonté *f* goodness

bonus *m* no-claims bonus

bord *m* edge; *(rive)* bank; *d'une route* side; *d'un verre* brim; *au ~ de la mer* at the seaside; *être au ~ des larmes* be on the verge of tears; *monter à ~* go on board

bordel *m* F brothel; *(désordre)* mess F

bordélique F chaotic

border *m* edge *(de* with); *(être le long de)* border; *enfant* tuck in

bordure *f* border, edging; *en ~ de forêt, ville* on the edge of

borne *f* boundary marker; ÉL terminal; *~s fig* limits; *dépasser les ~s* go too far; **borné** narrow-minded; **borner**: *se ~ à (faire)* restrict o.s. to (doing)

bosse *f* *(enflure)* lump; *d'un bossu, d'un chameau* hump; *du sol* bump

bosser F work hard

bossu, ~e *m/f* hunchback

botanique 1 *adj* botanical **2** *f* botany

botte *f chaussure* boot

bouc *m* goat; *~ émissaire fig* scapegoat

bouche f mouth; *de métro en-trance*; ~ *d'aération* (air) vent; ~ *d'incendie* (fire) hydrant

bouché blocked; *temps* over-cast

bouche-à-bouche m MÉD mouth-to-mouth resuscita-tion

bouchée f mouthful

boucher[1] v/t block; *trou* fill (in); *se* ~ *d'un évier* get blocked; *se* ~ *le nez* hold one's nose

boucher[2], -ère m/f butcher (*aussi fig*)

boucherie f *magasin* butch-er's; *fig* slaughter

bouchon m top; *de liège* cork; *fig*: trafic hold-up

boucle f loop; *de ceinture* buckle; *de cheveux* curl; ~ *d'oreille* earring; **bouclé** *cheveux* curly; **boucler** *cein-ture* fasten; *porte* lock; MIL surround; *en prison* lock away

bouddhisme m Buddhism; **bouddhiste** m Buddhist

bouder 1 v/i sulk **2** v/t: *qn/qc* give s.o./sth the cold shoulder

boudin m: ~ (*noir*) blood sau-sage, *Br* black pudding

boue f mud

bouée f MAR buoy

bouffée f *de fumée, vent* puff; *de parfum* whiff

bouffer F eat

bouffi bloated

bouger move; *de prix* change

bougie f candle; AUTO spark plug

bouillie f baby food

bouillir boil; *fig* be boiling (with rage); *faire* ~ boil; **bouilloire** f kettle

bouillon m (*bulle*) bubble; CUIS stock; **bouillonner** bub-ble; *fig*: *d'idées* seethe

bouillotte f hot water bottle

boulanger, -ère m/f baker; **boulangerie** f bakery

boule f ball; *jeu* m *de* ~s bowls *sg*

bouleau m BOT birch (tree)

boulevard m boulevard

bouleversement m upheav-al; **bouleverser** (*mettre en désordre*) turn upside down; *traditions* overturn; *émo-tionnellement* shatter

boulimie f bulimia

boulot m F work

bouquet m bouquet

bouquin m F book; **bouqui-ner** read

bourde f blunder, blooper F

bourdon m ZO bumblebee; **bourdonner** *d'insectes* buzz; *de moteur* hum; *d'oreilles* ring

bourgeois, ~e **1** adj middle-class **2** m/f member of the middle classes

bourgeoisie f middle classes *pl*

bourgeon m BOT bud

bourrasque f gust

bourratif, -ive stodgy

bourré crammed (*de* with); F

(*ivre*) drunk, sozzled F

bourrer *coussin* stuff; *pipe* fill; *se ~ de qc* F stuff o.s. with sth

bourru surly

bourse f *d'études* grant; (*porte-monnaie*) coin purse, Br purse; *Bourse (des valeurs)* Stock Exchange

boursouf(f)lé swollen

bousculer (*heurter*) jostle; (*presser*) rush; *fig*: *traditions* overturn

bousiller F *travail* screw up F; (*détruire*) wreck

boussole f compass

bout m end; (*morceau*) piece; *au ~ de* at the end of; *d'un ~ à l'autre* right the way through; *être à ~* be at an end; *venir à ~ de* overcome

bouteille f bottle; *de butane* cylinder

boutique f store, Br shop; *de mode* boutique

bouton m button; *de porte* handle; ANAT spot, zit F; BOT bud; **bouton-d'or** m BOT buttercup; **boutonner** button; BOT bud; **boutonneux**, *-euse* spotty

bovin 1 *adj* cattle *atr* **2** *mpl* ~*s* cattle *pl*

bowling m bowling, Br ten-pin bowling; *lieu* bowling alley

boxe f boxing; **boxer** box; **boxeur** m boxer

boycott m boycott; **boycotter** boycott

B.P. (= *boîte postale*) PO Box (= Post Office Box)

bracelet m bracelet

braconnier m poacher

braguette f fly

brailler bawl

braiser CUIS braise

brancard m (*civière*) stretcher

branche f branch; *de céleri* stick

brancher connect up (*sur* to; *à une prise* plug in; **branché** F (*informé*) clued up; (*en vogue*) trendy

brandir brandish

braquer 1 *v/t*: *~ sur* aim *ou* point at **2** *v/i* AUTO turn the wheel; *se ~ contre* *fig* turn against

bras m arm; *avoir le ~ long* *fig* have influence

brasse f stroke

brasser *bière* brew; **brasserie** f *usine* brewery; *établissement* restaurant

brave 1 *adj* brave; (*before the noun*) good **2** m: *un ~* a brave man; **braver** (*défier*) defy; **bravoure** f bravery

break m AUTO station wagon, Br estate (car)

brebis f ewe

bredouiller mumble

bref, *-ève* **1** *adj* brief, short **2** *adv* briefly, in short

Brésil: *le ~* Brazil; **brésilien**; *~ne* Brazilian; **Brésilien**, *~ne* m/f Brazilian

Bretagne: *la ~* Britany

bretelle f *de lingerie* strap;

d'autoroute ramp, *Br* slip
road; ~*s de pantalon* suspenders, *Br* braces

brevet *m* diploma; *pour invention* patent; **breveter**
patent

bric-à-brac *m inv* bric-a-brac

bricolage *m* do-it-yourself,
DIY; **bricole** *f* little thing;
bricoler do odd jobs

brièvement briefly; **brièveté**
f briefness, brevity

brigade *f* MIL brigade; *de police* squad; *d'ouvriers* gang

brillamment brilliantly; **brillant** shiny; *couleur* bright;
fig brilliant; **briller** shine
(*aussi fig*); **faire ~ meuble**
polish

brin *m d'herbe* blade; *de corde* strand

brindille *f* twig

brioche *f* CUIS brioche; F
(*ventre*) paunch

brique *f* brick

briquet *m* lighter

brise *f* breeze

brisé broken

briser **1** *v/t* break; *vie,
bonheur* destroy; (*fatiguer*)
wear out **2** *v/i de la mer*
break; **se ~ de verre etc**
break; *des espoirs* be shattered

britannique British; **Britannique** *m/f* Briton, Britisher,
Brit F; **les ~s** the British

broc *m* pitcher

brocante *f magasin* second-hand store

broche *f* CUIS spit; *bijou*
brooch

brochet *m* pike

brochette *f* CUIS skewer; *plat*
shish kebab

brochure *f* brochure

brocolis *mpl* broccoli *sg*

broncher *sans ~* without
batting an eyelid

bronches *fpl* ANAT bronchial
tubes

bronchite *f* MÉD bronchitis

bronze *m* bronze

bronzé tanned; **bronzer** **1** *v/t
peau* tan **2** *v/i* get a tan; **se ~**
sunbathe

brosse *f* brush; *coiffure* crew-cut; **~ à dents/cheveux**
toothbrush/hairbrush; **brosser** brush; **se ~ les dents**
brush one's teeth

brouhaha *m* hubbub

brouillard *m* fog; *il y a du ~*
it's foggy

brouille *f* quarrel; **brouiller**
œufs scramble; *cartes* shuffle; *papiers* muddle; *radio*
jam; *involontairement* cause
interference to; *amis* cause
to fall out; **se ~** *du ciel* cloud
over; *de vitres* mist up;
d'idées get muddled; *d'amis*
fall out

brouillon *m* draft; *papier m ~*
scratch paper, *Br* scrap paper

broussailles *fpl* undergrowth

broyer grind; **~ du noir** *fig* be
down

bru f daughter-in-law

brugnon m BOT nectarine

bruine f drizzle

bruit m sound; *qui dérange* noise; (*rumeur*) rumor, Br rumour; *faire du ~* make a noise; *fig* cause a sensation

brûlant burning (*aussi fig*); (*chaud*) burning hot; *liquide* scalding; **brûlé** burnt; **brûler 1** v/t burn; *d'eau bouillante* scald; *électricité* use; *~ un feu rouge* go through a red light **2** v/i burn; *se ~* burn o.s.; *d'eau bouillante* scald o.s.; **brûleur** m burner; **brûlure** f sensation burning; *lésion* burn; *~s d'estomac* heartburn

brume f mist

brun, ~e 1 adj brown; *cheveux, peau* dark **2** m/f dark-haired man/woman; *une ~e* a brunette **3** m couleur brown

brushing® m blow-dry

brusque abrupt, brusque; (*soudain*) abrupt, sudden; **brusquement** abruptly, suddenly; **brusquer** rush

brut, ~e 1 adj raw; *poids, revenu* gross; *pétrole* crude; *sucre* unrefined; *champagne* very dry **2** m crude (petroleum) **3** f brute brutal; **brutalement** brutally; **brutaliser** ill-treat; **brutalité** f brutality

Bruxelles Brussels

bruyant noisy

buanderie f laundry room

bûcher¹ m woodpile; (*échafaud*) stake

bûcher² v/i work hard; ÉDU F hit the books, Br swot

budget m budget

buée f steam, condensation

buffet m buffet; *meuble* sideboard

buisson m shrub, bush

bulbe f BOT bulb

bulgare 1 adj Bulgarian **2** m langue Bulgarian; **Bulgare** m/f Bulgarian; **Bulgarie**: *la ~* Bulgaria

bulle f bubble

bulletin m (*formulaire*) form; (*rapport*) bulletin; *à l'école* report card; *~ (de vote)* ballot (paper); *~ de salaire* paystub, Br payslip

bureau m office; *meuble* desk; *~ de change* exchange office, Br bureau de change; *~ de poste* post office; *~ de tabac* tobacco store, Br tobacconist's

bureaucratie f bureaucracy; **bureautique** f office automation

bus m bus

buste m bust

but m (*cible*) target; (*objectif*) aim, goal; *d'un voyage* purpose; SP goal; *sans ~* aimlessly; **buteur** m goalscorer

buté stubborn

buter: *~ contre qch* bump into sth; *~ sur un problème* hit a problem; *se ~* fig dig one's heels in

butin m booty; *de voleurs* haul

butte f (*colline*) hillock; **être**

en ~ à be exposed to

buvable drinkable; **buvette** f bar; **buveur, -euse** m/f drinker

C

c' → ce

ça that; **~ va?** how are things?; (*d'accord?*) ok?; **~ y est** that's it; **c'est ~!** that's right

cabale f (*intrigue*) plot

cabane f (*baraque*) hut

cabaret m (*boîte*) night club

cabine f cabin; *d'un camion* cab; **~ téléphonique** phone booth

cabinet m *petite pièce* small room; *d'avocat* office; *de médecin* office, Br surgery; (*clientèle*) practice; POL Cabinet

câble m cable

cabosser dent

cabrer: **se ~** *d'un animal* rear

cabriolet m AUTO convertible

cacah(o)uète f BOT peanut

cacao m cocoa; BOT cocoa bean

cache-cache m: **jouer à ~** play hide-and-seek; **cache-nez** m scarf; **cacher** hide; **se ~ de** hide from

cachet m seal; *fig* (*caractère*) style; PHARM tablet; (*rétribution*) fee; **~ de la poste** postmark

cachette f hiding place; **en ~**

secretly

cachotterie f: **faire des ~s** be secretive; **cachottier, -ère** secretive

cactus m cactus

cadavre m (dead) body, corpse; *d'un animal* carcass

caddie® m cart, Br trolley

cadeau m present, gift; **faire un ~ à** qn give s.o. a present

cadenas m padlock

cadence f tempo rhythm; *de travail* rate

cadet, ~te m/f younger; *de plus de deux* youngest; **il est mon ~ de trois ans** he's three years younger than me

cadran m dial; **~ solaire** sundial

cadre m frame; *fig* framework; *d'une entreprise* executive; (*environnement*) surroundings *pl*

cafard m ZO cockroach; **avoir le ~** F be feeling down

café m coffee; *établissement* café; **~ crème** coffee with milk, Br white coffee

cafétéria f cafeteria

cafetière f coffee pot; **~ électrique** coffee maker

cage f cage

cagibi m F box room

cagneux, -euse knock-kneed

cagoule f hood; (*passe-montagne*) balaclava

cahier m notebook; ÉDU exercise book

cahoter jolt

cahoteux, -euse bumpy

caille f quail

cailler *du lait* curdle; *du sang* clot

caillou m pebble, stone

caisse f chest; *pour le transport* crate; *de champagne, vin* case; (*argent*) cash; (*guichet*) cashdesk; *dans un supermarché* checkout; **caissier, -ère** m/f cashier

cajoler (*câliner*) cuddle

calamité f disaster, calamity

calcium m calcium

calcul 1 m calculation

calcul 2 m MÉD stone; **~ rénal** kidney stone

calculatrice f: **~ (de poche)** (pocket) calculator; **calculer** calculate; **calculette** f pocket calculator

calé F: **être ~ en qch** be good at sth

caleçon m *d'homme* boxer shorts pl; *de femme* leggings pl

calembour m pun

calendrier m calendar; *emploi du temps* schedule, Br timetable

caler *moteur* stall; TECH wedge

califourchon: à ~ astride

câlin 1 adj affectionate 2 m (*caresse*) cuddle

calmant 1 adj soothing; *contre douleur* painkilling 2 m tranquilizer, Br tranquillizer; *contre douleur* painkiller

calme 1 adj calm; *Bourse, vie* quiet 2 m calmness; MAR calm; (*silence*) peace and quiet; **calmement** calmly; **calmer** *personne* calm down; *douleur* relieve; **se ~** calm down

calomnie f slander; *écrite* libel; **calomnier** insult; *par écrit* libel

calorie f calorie

calquer trace

calvitie f baldness

camarade m/f friend; POL comrade

cambriolage m break-in, burglary; **cambrioler** burglarize, Br burgle

cambrioleur, -euse m/f house-breaker, burglar

camelote f F junk

caméra f camera

caméscope m camcorder

camion m truck, Br aussi lorry

camionnette f van

camomille f BOT camomile

camoufler camouflage; *fig: intention* hide; *faute* cover up

camp m camp (*aussi* MIL, POL); **ficher le ~** F get lost F

campagne f country, countryside; MIL, *fig* campaign; **à la ~** in the country

camper camp; **se ~ devant** plant o.s. in front of; **campeur, -euse** *m/f* camper

camping *m* (**terrain de**) campground, campsite; **faire du ~** go camping

Canada le ~ Canada; **canadien, ~ne** Canadian; **Canadien, ~ne** *m/f* Canadian

canal *m* channel; (*tuyau*) pipe; (*bras d'eau*) canal

canalisation *f* (*tuyauterie*) pipes *pl*, piping; **canaliser** *fig* channel

canapé *m* sofa; GASTR canapé

canapé-lit *m* sofa-bed

canard *m* duck; F newspaper

canari *m* canary

cancans *mpl* gossip

cancer *m* MÉD cancer; ASTROL *Cancer* Cancer

candeur *f* ingenuousness

candidat, ~e *m/f* candidate; **candidature** *f* candidacy; **à un poste** application; **candide** ingenuous

cane *f* (female) duck; **caneton** *m* duckling

canette *f* (*bouteille*) bottle

caniche *m* poodle

canicule *f* heatwave

canif *m* pocket knife

canin dog *atr*, canine

canine *f* canine

canne *f* cane, stick; **~ à pêche** fishing rod

cannelle *f* cinnamon

canoë *m* canoe; *activité* canoeing

canon *m* MIL gun; HIST cannon; *de fusil* barrel

canot *m* small boat; **~ pneumatique** rubber dinghy; **~ de sauvetage** lifeboat

cantine *f* canteen

canular *m* hoax

caoutchouc *m* rubber; (*bande élastique*) rubber band

cap *m* GÉOGR cape; AVIAT, NAUT course

capable capable (**de faire** of doing)

capacité *f* (*compétence*) ability; (*contenance*) capacity

cape *f* cape

capitaine *m* captain

capital 1 *adj* essential **2** *m* capital; **capitaux** capital **3** *f* *ville* capital (city); *lettre* capital (letter)

capitalisme *m* capitalism

capituler capitulate

capot *m* AUTO hood, Br bonnet

capote *f* *vêtement* greatcoat; AUTO top, Br hood; **~ (anglaise)** F condom

caprice *m* whim; **capricieux, -euse** capricious

Capricorne *m* ASTROL Capricorn

capter *regard* catch; RAD, TV pick up

capteur *m*: **~ solaire** solar panel

captif, -ive *m/f & adj* captive; **captivant** *personne* captivating; *lecture* gripping;

captiver *fig* captivate; **captivité** *f* captivity

capture *f* capture; *(proie)* catch; **capturer** capture

capuche *f* hood

car¹ *m* bus, *Br aussi* coach

car² *conj* for

carabine *f* rifle

carabiné F: *un ... carabiné* one hell of a ... F

caractère *m* character; *avoir bon ~* be good-natured; **caractériel** *troubles* emotional; *personne* emotionally disturbed

caractériser be characteristic of; **caractéristique** *f & adj* characteristic

carambolage *m* AUTO pile-up

caramel *m* caramel

caravane *f* AUTO trailer, *Br* caravan

carboniser burn

carburant *m* fuel

carburateur *m* TECH carburet(t)or

cardiaque MÉD **1** *adj* cardiac, heart *atr* **2** *m/f* heart patient

cardinal: *les quatre points mpl cardinaux* the four points of the compass

cardiologue *m/f* cardiologist, heart specialist

carême *m* REL Lent

carence *f* *(incompétence)* inadequacy; *(manque)* deficiency

caresse *f* caress; **caresser** caress; *idée* play with; *espoir* cherish

cargaison *f* cargo; *fig* load

caricature caricature

carie *f* MÉD: *une ~* a cavity

carié *dent* bad

caritatif, *~ive* charitable

carnage *m* carnage

carnassier, *-ère* carnivorous

carnaval *m* carnival

carnet *m* notebook; *de tickets, timbres* book

carnivore 1 *adj* carnivorous **2** *m* carnivore

carotte *f* carrot; *poil de ~* ginger

carpe *f* ZO carp

carpette *f* rug

carré 1 *adj* square; *fig: réponse* straightforward **2** *m* square

carreau *m* *de fenêtre* pane; *cartes* diamonds; *à ~x* checked

carrefour *m* crossroads *sg* *(aussi fig)*

carrelage *m* *(carreaux)* tiles *pl*

carrément bluntly, straight out

carrière *f* quarry; *profession* career; *militaire m de ~* professional soldier

carrosserie *f* AUTO bodywork

carrure *f* build

cartable *m* schoolbag; *à bretelles* satchel

carte *f* card; *dans un restaurant* menu; GÉOGR map; NAUT, *du ciel* chart; *~ bancaire* debit card, banker's card; *~ de crédit* credit card;

~ d'embarquement boarding pass; **~ d'identité** identity card; **~ postale** postcard; **~ téléphonique** phonecard

carton m cardboard; *boîte* cardboard box; **~ jaune/rouge** *en football* yellow/red card

cartouche f cartridge; *de cigarettes* carton

cas m case; **en aucun ~** under no circumstances; **dans ce ~-là** in that case; **en tout ~** in any case; **en ~ de** in the event of

casanier, -ère m/f stay-at-home

cascade f waterfall

case f (*hutte*) hut; (*compartiment*) compartment; *dans formulaire* box; *dans mots-croisés, échiquier* square

caser put; (*loger*) put up; **se ~** (*se marier*) settle down

caserne f barracks; **~ de pompiers** fire station

casier m *courrier* pigeonholes pl; *bouteilles, livres* rack; **~ judiciaire** criminal record

casino m casino

casque m helmet; *de radio* headphones pl; **casquette** f cap

cassable breakable

casse-cou m inv daredevil; **casse-croûte** m snack; **casse-noisettes** m nutcrackers pl; **casse-pieds** m/f inv F pain in the neck F

casser 1 v/t break; *noix* crack; JUR quash; **les pieds à qn** F (*embêter*) get on s.o.'s nerves F; **se ~** break 2 v/i break

casserole f (*sauce*)pan

casse-tête m fig: *problème* headache

cassette f cassette; **~ vidéo** video

cassis m BOT blackcurrant; (*crème f de*) **~** blackcurrant liqueur

castrer castrate

cataclysme m disaster

catalogue m catalog, Br catalogue; **cataloguer** catalog, Br catalogue; F *péj* label

catalytique AUTO: **pot** m **~** catalytic converter

cataracte f waterfall; MÉD cataract

catastrophe f disaster, catastrophe; **en ~** in a rush; **catastrophique** disastrous, catastrophic

catch m wrestling

catéchisme m catechism

catégorie f category; **catégorique** categorical

cathédrale f cathedral

catholique 1 adj (Roman) Catholic 2 m/f Roman Catholic

cauchemar m nightmare (*aussi fig*)

cause f cause; JUR case; **à ~ de** because of; **être en ~** d'honnêteté be in question

causer 1 v/t (*provoquer*) cause 2 v/i (*s'entretenir*) chat

(*avec qn* with s.o. about);
causette *f* chat; *faire la ~*
have a chat

caustique CHIM, *fig* caustic

caution *f* security; *pour logement* deposit; JUR bail; *fig*
(*appui*) backing; **cautionner**
stand surety for; JUR bail; *fig*
(*se porter garant de*) vouch
for; (*appuyer*) back

cavaler F: *~ après qn* chase
after s.o.

cavalier, -ère 1 *m/f pour cheval* rider; *pour bal* partner 2
m aux échecs knight 3 *adj*
offhand, cavalier

cave *f* cellar; *~ (à vin)* wine
cellar

caverne *f* cave

caviar *m* caviar

cavité *f* cavity

CD *m* (= *compact disc*) CD;
CD-Rom *m* CD-Rom

ce *m* (*cet m, cette f, ces pl*)
1 *adj* this, *pl* these; *~ livre-ci*
this book; *~ livre-là* that
book; *ces jours-ci* these
days 2 *pron c'est pourquoi*
that is *ou* that's why; *c'est
triste* it's sad; *ce ~ sont mes
enfants* these are my children; *c'est un acteur* he is
ou he's an actor; *c'est que
tu as grandi!* how you've
grown!; *ce que tu fais* what
you're doing; *ce qui me
plaît* what I like; *ce qu'il
est gentil!* isn't he nice!;
sur ~ with that

ceci this

cécité *f* blindness

céder 1 *v/t* give up; *cédez le
passage* AUTO yield, *Br* give
way 2 *v/i* give in (*à* to); (*se
casser*) give way

cédille *f* cedilla

cèdre *m* BOT cedar

ceinture *f* belt; ANAT waist; *~
de sécurité* seatbelt

cela that; *à ~ près* apart from
that

célèbre famous

célébrer celebrate

célébrité *f* fame; *personne* celebrity

céleri *m* BOT: *~ (en branche)*
celery; *~(-rave)* celeriac

célibat *m* single life; *d'un prêtre* celibacy; **célibataire** 1
adj single, unmarried 2 *m*
bachelor 3 *f* single woman

celle, celles → *celui*

cellophane *f* cellophane

cellule *f* cell

cellulose *f* cellulose

Celsius Celsius

celui *m* (*celle f, ceux mpl,
celles fpl*) the one, *pl* those;
~ qui ... *personne* he who ...;
chose the one which; *celle
de Claude* Claude's; *celui-
ci* this one; *celui-là* that one

cendre *f* ash; *~s de cigarette*
cigarette ash; **cendrier** *m*
ashtray

cène *f* REL: *la ~* (Holy) Communion; *la Cène peinture*
the Last Supper

censé: *il est ~ être malade*
he's supposed to be sick

censure f censorship; *organe* board of censors; **censurer** censor

cent 1 *adj* hundred **2** m a hundred, one hundred; *monnaie* cent; *pour* ~ per cent; *centaine* f: *une* ~ *de* a hundred or so; *des* ~s *de* hundreds of; **centenaire 1** *adj* hundred-year-old **2** m *fête* centennial, *Br* centenary; **centième** hundredth; **centilitre** m centiliter, *Br* centilitre; **centimètre** m centimeter, *Br* centimetre; *ruban* tape measure

central, ~e **1** *adj* central **2** m TÉL telephone exchange **3** f power station; **centraliser** centralize

centre m center, *Br* centre; ~ *d'accueil* temporary accommodations *pl*; **centrer** center, *Br* centre

centre-ville m downtown area, *Br* town centre

cep m vine stock

cèpe m BOT cèpe, boletus

cependant yet, however

cercle m circle; ~ *vicieux* vicious circle

cercueil m casket, *Br* coffin

céréales *fpl* (breakfast) cereal

cérébral cerebral

cérémonie f ceremony; *sans* ~ *repas etc* informal; *se présenter etc* informally; *mettre à la porte* unceremoniously

cerf m deer

cerf-volant m kite

cerise f cherry; **cerisier** m cherry (-tree)

cerne m: *avoir des* ~s have bags under one's eyes; **cerner** (*encercler*) surround; *fig: problème* define

certain **1** *adj* certain; *être* ~ *de qc* be certain of sth; *d'un* ~ *âge* middle-aged **2** *pron:* **certains**, -aines some (people)

certainement certainly; (*sûrement*) probably

certes certainly

certificat m certificate; ~ *de mariage* marriage certificate; **certifier** guarantee; ~ *qc à qn* assure s.o. of sth

certitude f certainty

cerveau m brain

cervelle f brains *pl*; *se brûler la* ~ *fig* blow one's brains out

ces → **ce**

cesser stop; ~ *de faire qch* stop doing sth; **cessez-le--feu** m ceasefire

cession f disposal

c'est-à-dire that is, that is to say

cet, cette → **ce**

ceux → **celui**

chacun, ~e each (one); *c'est--pour soi* it's every man for himself

chagrin m grief; *faire du* ~ *à* upset

chahut m F racket, din; **chahuter** heckle

chaîne f chain; *radio*, TV

channel; **~s** AUTO snow chains; **~ hi-fi** hi-fi

chair f flesh; **avoir la ~ de poule** have goosebumps

chaise f chair; **~ longue** (*transatlantique*) deck chair

chalet m chalet

chaleur f heat; *plus modérée* warmth (*aussi fig*); **chaleureusement** warmly

chamailler F: **se ~** bicker

chambre F (bed)room; JUR, POL chamber; **~ à air** *de pneu* inner tube; **~ à coucher** bedroom; **~ à un lit** single (room); **~ à deux lits** twin-bedded room; **~ d'amis** spare room

chambré *vin* at room temperature

chameau m camel

champ m field (*aussi fig*); **~ de courses** racecourse

champagne m champagne

champêtre country *atr*

champignon m fungus; *nourriture* mushroom

champion, ~ne m/f champion; **championnat** m championship

chance f luck; (*occasion*) chance; **bonne ~!** good luck!; **avoir de la ~** be lucky; **c'est une ~ que** (+ *subj*) it's lucky that

chanceler stagger; *d'un gouvernement* totter

chanceux, -euse lucky

chandail m sweater

change m exchange; **taux m**

de ~ exchange rate; **donner le ~ à qn** deceive s.o.; **changeant** changeable; **changement** m change; **~ de vitesse** AUTO gear shift; **changer** 1 v/t change (**en** into); (*échanger*) exchange (**contre** for) 2 v/i change; **~ d'avis** change one's mind; **se ~** change

chanson f song

chant m song; *action de chanter* singing; *d'église* hymn

chantage m blackmail

chanter sing; *d'un coq* crow; **faire ~ qn** blackmail s.o.

chanteur, -euse m/f singer

chantier m REL shipyard

chaos m chaos; **chaotique** chaotic

chaparder F pinch F

chapeau m hat; **chapeauter** *fig* head up

chapelet m REL rosary

chapelle f chapel

chapelure f CUIS breadcrumbs pl

chapitre m chapter; *division de budget* heading; *fig* subject

chaque each

charbon m coal; **~ de bois** charcoal

charcuterie f CUIS cold cuts pl, Br cold meat; *magasin* pork butcher's; **charcutier** m pork butcher

charge f load; *fig* burden; ÉL, JUR, MIL charge; (*responsa-*

bilité) responsibility; **avoir des enfants à ~** have dependent children; **~s** charges; (*impôts*) costs; **~s fiscales** taxation

chargement *m* loading; *ce qui est chargé* load; **charger 1** *v/t navire,* arme load; *batterie,* JUR charge; (*exagérer*) exaggerate; **~ qn de qc** put s.o. in charge of sth; **se ~ de** look after **2** *v/i* charge

chariot *m pour bagages, achats* cart, *Br* trolley; (*charrette*) cart

charisme *m* charisma

charitable charitable; **charité** *f* charity; **faire la ~ à qn** give s.o. money

charmant charming, delightful; **charme** *m* charm; **charmer** charm

charnière *f* hinge

charnu fleshy

charognard *m* scavenger

charpente *f* framework; **charpentier** *m* carpenter

charte *f* charter

charter *m* charter

chasse¹ *f*: **~ d'eau** flush

chasser *gibier* hunt; (*expulser*) drive away; *employé* dismiss; **chasseur** *m* hunter; AVIAT fighter; *dans un hôtel* bellhop, *Br* bellboy

châssis *m* frame; AUTO chassis

chaste chaste

chat¹ *m* cat

chat² *m* INFORM chatroom; *conversation* (online) chat

châtaigne *f* chestnut; **châtaignier** *m* chestnut (tree); **châtain** *inv* chestnut

château *m* castle; **~ fort** (fortified) castle; **~ d'eau** water tower

châtier punish; **châtiment** *m* punishment

chaton *m* kitten

chatouiller tickle

chatte *f* cat

chatter INFORM chat (online)

chaud 1 *adj* hot; *plus modéré* warm; **il fait ~** it's hot/warm **2** *m* *plus modéré* warmth; **j'ai ~** I'm hot/warm; **chaudière** *f* boiler

chauffage *m* heating; **~ central** central heating

chauffard *m* F roadhog

chauffer 1 *v/t* heat (up), warm (up); *maison* heat; **se ~** warm o.s.; *d'un sportif* warm up **2** *v/i* warm *ou* heat up; *d'un moteur* overheat

chauffeur *m* driver; *privé aussi* chauffeur; **~ de taxi** taxi *ou* cab driver

chaussée *f* pavement, *Br* roadway

chausser *bottes* put on; **se ~** put one's shoes on; **chaussette** *f* sock; **chausson** *m* slipper; **chaussure** *f* shoe; **~s de marche** hiking boots;

~s de ski ski boots

chauve bald; **chauve-souris** *f* bat

chauvinisme *m* chauvinism

chef *m* (*meneur*), POL leader; (*patron*) boss; *d'une entreprise* head; *d'une tribu* chief; CUIS chef; **au premier ~** first and foremost; *de propre* **mon ~** on my own initiative

chef-d'œuvre *m* masterpiece

chemin *m* way; (*route*) road; (*allée*) path; **~ de fer** railroad, *Br* railway

cheminée *f* chimney; (*âtre*) fireplace; (*encadrement*) mantelpiece; *de bateau* funnel

cheminot *m* rail worker

chemise *f* shirt; (*dossier*) folder; **~ de nuit de femme** nightdress; **chemisier** *m* blouse

chêne *m* BOT oak (tree)

chenil *m* kennels *pl*

chenille *f* ZO caterpillar

chèque *m* COMM check, *Br* cheque; **~ de voyage** traveler's check, *Br* traveller's cheque; **chéquier** *m* checkbook, *Br* chequebook

cher, -ère 1 *adj* dear (**à qn** to s.o.); *coûteux* dear, expensive **2** *adv*: **payer qch ~** pay a high price for sth **3** *m/f* **mon cher, ma chère** my dear

chercher look for; **~ à faire qch** try to do sth; **aller ~** fetch, go for; **venir ~** collect,

come for; **envoyer ~** send for

chéri darling

chétif, -ive puny

cheval *m* horse; AUTO horsepower; **aller à ~** ride; **être à ~ sur qch** straddle sth; **chevalier** *m* HIST knight; **chevalière** *f* signet ring

chevelu *personne* long-haired; **chevelure** *f* hair

chevet *m* bedhead; **table** *f* **de ~** nightstand, *Br aussi* bedside table

cheveu *m* hair; **~x** hair; **aux ~x courts** short-haired

cheville *f* ANAT ankle; TECH peg

chèvre *f* goat

chevreau *m* kid

chevreuil *m* deer; CUIS venison

chez: **~ lui** at his place; *direction* to his place; **~ Marcel** at Marcel's; **quand nous sommes ~ nous** when we are at home; **rentrer ~ soi** go home; **aller ~ le coiffeur** go to the hairdresser *ou Br* hairdresser's; **~ Molière** in Molière

chez-soi *m* home

chiant F boring

chic 1 *m* style **2** *adj* chic; (*sympathique*) decent

chicaner quibble (**sur** over)

chicorée *f* BOT chicory

chien *m* dog; **temps de ~** *fig* F filthy weather; **~ d'aveugle** seeing-eye dog, *Br* guide dog; **chienne** f dog; **le chien et la ~** the dog and the bitch

chier V shit; **ça me fait ~** P it pisses me off P

chiffon m rag; **~ (à poussière)** duster; **chiffonner** crumple; fig F bother

chiffre m number; (code) cipher

Chili: le ~ Chili; **chilien, ~ne** 1 adj Chilean; **Chilien, ~ne** m/f Chilean

chimie f chemistry

chimiothérapie f chemotherapy

chimique chemical

Chine: la ~ China; **chinois, ~e** 1 adj Chinese 2 m langue Chinese; **Chinois, ~e** m/f Chinese

chiot m pup

chips mpl chips, Br crisps

chirurgie f surgery; **~ esthétique** plastic surgery; **chirurgien, ~ne** m/f surgeon; **~ dentiste** dental surgeon

choc m shock; **d'opinions, intérêts** clash

chocolat m chocolate

chœur m choir **en ~** in chorus

choisir choose; **~ de faire** decide to do; **choix** m choice; (assortiment) range; **de (premier) ~** choice

cholestérol m cholesterol

chômage m unemployment; **être au ~** be unemployed; **~ partiel** short time; **chômeur, -euse** m/f unemployed person; **les ~s** the unemployed pl

chope f beer mug

choquant shocking; **choquer: ~ qc** knock sth; **~ qn** shock s.o.

chorale f choir

chose f thing; **autre ~** something else; **c'est ~ faite** it's done

chou m BOT cabbage; **~x de Bruxelles** Brussels sprouts

chouette 1 f owl 2 adj F great

chou-fleur m cauliflower

chrétien, ~ne adj & m/f Christian

christianisme m Christianity

chrome m chrome

chronique 1 adj chronic 2 f d'un journal column; reportage report; **chroniqueur** m pour un journal columnist

chronologique chronological

chronométrer time

chuchoter whisper

chut: ~! hush

chute f fall; **~ des cheveux** hair loss

ci: à cette heure~ at this time; **comme ~ comme ça** F so-so; **par~ par-là** here and there

cible f target; **cibler** target

ciboulette f BOT chives pl

cicatrice f scar (aussi fig); **cicatriser (se) ~** heal

ci-contre opposite; **ci-dessous** below; **ci-dessus** above

cidre m cider

ciel *m* sky; REL heaven

cigale *f* cicada

cigare *m* cigar

cigarette *f* cigarette

ci-inclus enclosed; **ci-joint** enclosed, attached

cil *m* eyelash

ciment *m* cement

cimetière *m* cemetery

ciné *m* F movie theater, *Br* cinema; **cinéma** *m* movie theater, *Br* cinema; *art* cinema, movies *pl*

cinglé F mad, crazy

cinq five; *le ~ mai* May fifth, *Br* the fifth of May; **cinquantaine** *f* about fifty; *elle approche la ~* she's getting on for fifty; **cinquante** fifty; **cinquantième** fiftieth **cinquième** fifth

cintre *m* arch; *pour vêtements* coathanger

cirage *m* *pour parquet* wax, polish; *pour chaussures* polish

circonférence *f* circumference

circonspect circumspect

circonstance *f* circumstance

circuit *m* circuit; *de voyage* tour; SP track

circulaire *adj* & *f* circular

circulation *f* circulation; *voitures* traffic; *voitures circulate; *faire ~ nouvelles* spread

cire *f* wax; **cirer** polish; *parquet aussi* wax

cirque *m* circus

cirrhose *f*: *~ du foie* cirrhosis

of the liver

ciseaux *mpl* scissors *pl*

citadin, ~e 1 *adj* town atr, city atr **2** *m/f* town-dweller, city-dweller

citation *f* quotation; JUR summons *sg*

cité *f* city; *~ universitaire* fraternity house, *Br* hall of residence

citoyen, ~ne *m/f* citizen; **citoyenneté** *f* citizenship

citron *m* lemon; *~ vert* lime; **citronnier** *m* lemon (tree)

civière *f* stretcher

civil 1 *adj* civil; *non militaire* civilian; *état m ~* marital status **2** *m* civilian; *en ~* in civilian clothes; *policier* in plain clothes; **civilisation** *f* civilization

civique civic

civisme *m* public-spiritedness

clair 1 *adj* clear; *couleur* light; *chambre* bright **2** *adv* *voir* clearly; *dire, parler* plainly **3** *m*: *~ de lune* moonlight

clairière *f* clearing

clairvoyant perceptive

clandestin secret, clandestine; *passager m ~* stowaway

claque *f* slap; **claquer 1** *v/t argent* slam; *argent* F blow; *~ des doigts* snap one's fingers **2** *v/i* *d'un fouet* crack; *des dents* chatter; *d'un volet* slam

clarifier clarify

clarinette f clarinet

clarté f (*lumière*) brightness; (*transparence*) clarity

classe f class; *il a de la ~* he's got class; *~ économique* economy class

classement m position, place; BOT, ZO classification; *de lettres* filing; **classer** classify; *actes, dossiers* file; *une affaire* consider a matter closed

classique 1 adj classical; (*traditionnel*) classic **2** m in littérature classical author; MUS classical music; *film, livre* classic

clause f clause; *~ pénale* penalty clause

clavicule f collarbone

clavier m keyboard

clé f key; TECH wrench; *~ de fa* MUS bass clef; *fermer à ~* lock; *sous ~* under lock and key

clef → **clé**

clément merciful

clergé m clergy

clic m bruit, INFORM click

client, ~e m/f (*acheteur*) customer; *d'un médecin* patient; *d'un avocat* client; **clientèle** f customers pl, clientèle; *d'un médecin* patients pl; *d'un avocat* clients pl

cligner: *~ (des yeux)* blink; *~ de l'œil à qn* wink at s.o.

clignotant m turn signal, Br indicator; **clignoter** d'une lumière flicker

climat m climate (*aussi fig*)

climatisation f air conditioning; **climatisé** air conditioned

clin m: *~ d'œil* wink; *en un ~ d'œil* in a flash

clinique 1 adj clinical **2** f clinic

cliquer INFORM click (*sur* on)

clochard, ~e m/f hobo, Br tramp

cloche f bell f; F (*idiot*) nitwit F; **clocher 1** m steeple F; **clocher 2** v/i F: *ça cloche* something's not right

cloison f partition

cloîtrer fig: *se ~* shut o.s. away

clonage m cloning; **clone** m clone; **cloner** clone

clope m ou f F cigarette, Br F fag; (*mégot*) cigarette end

cloque f blister

clôture f *d'un débat* closure; *d'un compte* closing; (*barrière*) fence

clou m nail; fig main attraction; MÉD boil; **clouer** nail; *être cloué au lit* be confined to bed

clown m clown

club m club; *~ de gym* gym

coaguler *du lait* curdle; *du sang* coagulate

cobaye m ZO, fig guinea pig

coca m F Coke®

coccinelle f ladybug, Br ladybird; F AUTO Volkswagen® beetle

cocher *sur une liste* check, Br

aussi tick off

cochon 1 *m* ZO, *fig* pig **2** *adj* **cochon**, **~ne** F dirty; **cochonnerie** *f* F: **des ~s** filth; *nourriture* junk food

coco *m*: **noix** *f* **de ~** coconut

cocotte *f* CUIS casserole; F darling; *péj* tart; **~ minute** pressure cooker

code *m* code; **~ confidentiel** PIN number; **~ pénal** penal code; **se mettre en ~** switch to low beams; **~ postal** zip-code, *Br* postcode

cœur *m* heart; **de bon ~** glad-ly; **par ~** by heart; **j'ai mal au ~** I feel nauseous

coffre *m* **meuble** chest; FIN safe; AUTO trunk, *Br* boot; **coffre-fort** *m* safe

cogérer co-manage

cognac *m* brandy, cognac

cogner *d'un moteur* knock; **~ à** *ou* **contre qc** bang against sth; **se ~ à** *ou* **contre qc** bump into sth

cohabiter cohabit

cohérent *théorie* consistent, coherent

cohue *f* crowd, rabble

coiffer: **~ qn** do s.o.'s hair; **se ~** do one's hair; **coiffeur** *m* hairdresser, hair stylist; **coiffeuse** *f* hairdresser, hair stylist; *meuble* dressing table; **coiffure** *f* **de cheveux** hair-style

coin *m* corner; *cale* wedge

coincer squeeze; *porte, tiroir* jam; **coincé dans un em-**

bouteillage stuck in a traffic jam

coïncidence *f* coincidence

col *m* collar; *d'une bouteille, d'un pull* neck; GÉOGR col; **~ blanc/bleu** white-collar/blue-collar worker

colère *f* anger; **se mettre en ~** get angry

colique *f* colic; *(diarrhée)* di-arrhea, *Br* diarrhoea

colis *m* parcel, package

collaborateur, **-trice** *m/f* collaborator (*aussi* POL *péj*); **collaboration** *f* collabora-tion, cooperation; POL *péj* collaboration; **collaborer** collaborate, cooperate (**avec** with; **à** on); POL *péj* collaborate

collant 1 *adj* sticky; *vêtement* close-fitting; F *personne* clingy **2** *m* pantyhose *pl*, *Br* tights *pl*

colle *f* glue; *fig* P question tough question; *(retenue)* detention

collecte *f* collection; **collec-tif**, **-ive** collective; **voyage** *m* **~** group tour

collection *f* collection; **col-lectionner** collect; **collec-tionneur**, **-euse** *m/f* collec-tor

collège *m* **école** junior high, *Br* secondary school; **collé-gien**, **~ne** *m/f* junior high student, *Br* secondary school pupil

collègue *m/f* colleague, co-worker

coller 1 v/t stick, glue **2** v/i stick (**à** to); **se ~ contre mur** press o.s against; *personne* cling to

collier m *bijou* necklace; *de chien* collar

colline f hill

collision f collision; **entrer en ~ avec** collide with

colocataire m/f roommate, Br flatmate

colombe f dove (*aussi fig*)

Colombie: la ~ Colombia; **colombien, ~ne** Colombian; **Colombien, ~ne** m/f Colombian

colonie f colony; **~ de vacances** summer camp

colonne f column

colorant 1 adj shampoing color atr, Br colour atr **2** m dye; *dans la nourriture* coloring, Br colouring; **colorer** color, Br colour

coma m coma

combat m fight; MIL *aussi* battle; **mettre hors de ~** put out of action; **combattant 1** adj fighting **2** m combatant; **combattre** fight

combien 1 adv *quantité* how much; *avec pl* how many **2** m: **tous les ~** how often; **on est le ~ aujourd'hui?** what date is it today?

combinaison f combination; (*astuce*) scheme; *de mécanicien* coveralls pl, Br boiler suit; *lingerie* (full-length) slip; **~ de plongée** wet suit

combiner combine; *voyage, projet* plan

comble 1 m fig: *sommet* height; **~s** pl attic; **de fond en ~** from top to bottom **2** adj full (to capacity); **combler** *trou* fill in; *déficit* make good; *personne* overwhelm; **~ qn de qch** shower s.o. with sth

combustible 1 adj combustible **2** m fuel

comédie f comedy; **~ musicale** musical; **comédien, ~ne** m/f actor; *qui joue le genre comique* comic actor

comestible 1 adj edible **2** mpl **~s** food

comique 1 adj THÉÂT comic; (*drôle*) funny, comical **2** m comedian; *acteur* comic (actor); *genre* comedy

comité m committee

commande f COMM order; TECH control; INFORM command; **commander 1** v/t COMM order; (*ordonner*) command, order; MIL be in command of; TECH control **2** v/i (*diriger*) be in charge; COMM order

comme 1 adv like; **noir ~ la nuit** as black as night; **~ ci ~ ça** F so-so; **~ vous voulez** as you like; **~ si** as if; **il travaillait ~ ...** he was working as a ...; **moi, ~ les autres, je ...** like the others, I ... **2** conj as

commencement *m* beginning, start; **commencer** begin, start; **~ qc par qc** start sth with sth; **~ par faire qc** start by doing sth

comment how; **~?** (*qu'avez--vous dit?*) pardon me?, *Br* sorry?; **~!** *surpris* what!

commentaire *m* comment; RAD, TV commentary; **commenter** comment on; RAD, TV commentate on

commerçant, **~e 1** *adj*: **rue f ~e** shopping street **2** *m/f* merchant, trader

commerce *m* trade, commerce; (*magasin*) store, *Br* shop; *fig* (*rapports*) dealings *pl*; **commercial** commercial; **commercialiser** market

commettre commit; *erreur* make

commis *m*: **~ voyageur** commercial traveler *ou Br* traveller

commissaire *m* commission member; *de l'UE* Commissioner; SP steward; **commissariat** *m* commissionership; **~ (de police)** police station

commission *f* commission; (*message*) message

commode 1 *adj* handy; *arrangement* convenient; **pas ~ personne** awkward **2** *f* chest of drawers; **commodité** *f* convenience

commotion *f* MÉD: **~ cérébrale** stroke

commun 1 *adj* common; *œu-*

vre joint; **mettre en ~ argent** pool **2** *m*: **hors du ~** out of the ordinary

communal (*de la commune*) local

communauté *f* community; *de hippies* commune

communication *f* communication; (*message*) message; **~ téléphonique** telephone call

communion *f* REL Communion

communiquer 1 *v/t* communicate; *maladie* pass on, give (**à qn** to s.o.) **2** *v/i* communicate

communisme *m* communism; **communiste** *m/f* & *adj* Communist

commutateur *m* switch

compact compact

compagne *f* companion; *dans couple* wife

compagnie *f* company; **~ aérienne** airline

compagnon *m* companion; *dans couple* husband; *employé* journeyman

comparaison *f* comparison; **par ~ à** compared with; **comparer** compare (**à** to, **avec** with)

compartiment *m* compartment; *de train* car, *Br* compartment

compas *m* compass

compassion *f* compassion

compatible compatible

compatir: **~ à** sympathize

with

compatriote *m/f* compatriot
compenser compensate for
compétence *f (connaissances)* ability, competence;
JUR jurisdiction; **compétent** competent, skillful, *Br* skilful; JUR competent
compétitif, -ive competitive; **compétition** *f* competition
compiler compile
complaire: se ~ dans/à faire delight in/in doing
complet, -ète 1 *adj* complete; *hôtel, description, jeu de cartes* full; *pain* whole wheat, *Br* wholemeal **2** *m* suit; **complètement** completely; **se ~** complement each other
complexe *adj & m* complex
complication *f* complication
complice *m/f* JUR: **être ~ de** be an accessory to **2** *m/f* accomplice
compliment *m* compliment; **mes ~s** congratulations
compliqué complicated; **compliquer** complicate; **se ~** become complicated
comporter *(comprendre)* comprise; *(impliquer)* involve; **se ~** behave (o.s)
composer 1 *v/t (former)* make up; MUS compose; *livre, poème* write; *numéro* dial **2** *v/i* transiger come to terms *(avec* with); **se ~ de** consist of
compositeur, -trice *m/f* com-

poser
composter *billet* punch
compote *f:* **~ de pommes** stewed apples
compréhension *f* understanding
comprendre understand; *(inclure)* include; *(comporter)* comprise
compresse *f* MÉD compress
comprimé *m* tablet
compris *(inclus)* included; **y ~** including
compromettre compromise
comptabilité *f* accountancy; *(comptes)* accounts *pl*; **comptable** *m/f* accountant
comptant: au ~ cash
compte *m* account; *(calcul)* calculation; **~s** accounts; **en fin de ~** when all's said and done; **se rendre ~ de** realize; **tenir ~ de qc** take sth into account; **~ courant** checking account, *Br* current account; **~ rendu** report; *de réunion* minutes *pl*; **compter 1** *v/t* count; *(prévoir)* allow; *(inclure)* include; **~ faire** plan on doing **2** *v/i* count; **~ sur** rely on; **à ~ de** starting (from); **compteur** *m* meter
comptoir *m d'un café* bar; *d'un magasin* counter
con, ~ne P **1** *adj* damn stupid F **2** *m/f* damn idiot F
concentration *f* concentration; **concentrer** concentrate; **se ~** concentrate

(**sur** on)

concept *m* concept

conception *f* (*idée*) concept; (*planification*) design; BIOL conception

concernant concerning, about; **concerner** concern

concert *m* MUS concert; **de ~ avec** together with

concession *f* concession; AUTO dealership

concevable conceivable; **concevoir** (*comprendre*) understand, conceive; (*inventer*) design; BIOL, *plan, idée* conceive

concierge *m/f* superintendent, *Br* caretaker; *d'école* janitor, *Br aussi* caretaker; *d'un hôtel* concierge

concis concise

concitoyen, **~ne** *m/f* fellow citizen

conclure conclude; **~ de** conclude from; **conclusion** *f* conclusion

concombre *m* cucumber

concours *m* competition; (*assistance*) help

concret, **-ète** concrete

concurrence *f* competition; **faire ~ à** compete with; **concurrent**, **~e 1** *adj* rival **2** *m/f* competitor

condamnation *f* sentence; *action* sentencing; *fig* condemnation

condamner JUR sentence; *malade* give up; (*réprouver*) condemn; *porte* block up

condescendance *f péj* condescension

condition *f* condition; **~ préalable** prerequisite; **à (la) ~ que** (+ *subj*) on condition that; **conditionner** (*emballer*) package; PSYCH condition

condoléances *fpl* condolences

conducteur, **-trice 1** *m/f* driver **2** *m* PHYS conductor

conduire **1** *v/t* take; (*mener*) lead; *voiture* drive; EL conduct; **se ~** behave **2** *v/i* AUTO drive; (*mener*) lead

conduit *m d'eau, de gaz* pipe; **~ d'aération** ventilation shaft

conduite *f* (*comportement*) behavior, *Br* behaviour; *direction* management; *d'eau, de gaz* pipe; AUTO driving

cône *m* cone

confection *f* making; *industrie* clothing industry

conférence *f* conference; (*exposé*) lecture; **être en ~** be in a meeting

confesser confess; **~ qn** REL hear s.o.'s confession; **se ~** REL go to confession; **confession** *f* confession; (*croyance*) faith

confiance *f* confidence; **faire à** trust; **confiant** confident; (*crédule*) trusting

confidence *f* confidence; **faire une ~ à** confide in; **confident**, **~e** *m/f* confidant; **con-**

fidentiel, **~le** confidential

confier: **~ qc à qn** (*laisser*) entrust s.o. (with sth); **se ~ à** confide in

confirmation *f* confirmation (*aussi* REL); **confirmer** confirm (*aussi* REL)

confiserie *f* confectionery; *magasin* confectioner's; **~s** candy, *Br* sweets

confisquer confiscate (**à** from)

confiture *f* jelly, *Br* jam

conflit *m* conflict; **d'idées** clash

confondre confuse; (*déconcerter*) take aback; **se ~** (*se mêler*) merge

conforme: **~ à** in accordance with; **conformiste** *m/f* conformist

confort *m* comfort; **confortable** comfortable; *somme* sizeable

confronter confront; (*comparer*) compare

confusion *f* confusion; (*embarras*) embarrassment

congé *m* vacation, *Br* holiday; MIL leave; *avis de départ* notice; **prendre ~ de** take one's leave of; **~ de maladie** sick leave

congélateur *m* freezer; **congelé** *aliment* frozen; **congeler** freeze

congénital congenital

congestion *f* MÉD congestion; **~ cérébrale** stroke; **congestionné** *visage* flushed

congrès *m* convention, conference; **Congrès** *aux États-Unis* Congress

conique conical

conjecture *f* conjecture

conjoint, **~e 1** *adj* joint **2** *m/f* spouse

conjonctivite *f* MÉD conjunctivitis

conjugaison *f* GRAM conjugation

conjugal conjugal; *vie* married

conjuguer *efforts* combine; GRAM conjugate

connaissance *f* knowledge; (*conscience*) consciousness; *personne connue* acquaintance; **~s** *d'un sujet* knowledge; **connaisseur** *m* connoisseur; **connaître** know; (*rencontrer*) meet; **s'y ~ en** be an expert on

connecter TECH connect; **se ~** INFORM log on

connerie *f* V: **une ~** a damn stupid thing to do/say

connexion *f* connection; **hors ~** INFORM off-line

connu well-known

conquérir conquer

conquête *f* conquest

consacrer REL consecrate; (*dédier*) dedicate; *temps, argent* spend; **se ~ à** dedicate *ou* devote o.s. to

conscience *f* moral conscience; *physique*, PSYCH consciousness; **prendre ~**

contact

de become aware of

consécutif, -ive consecutive; *~ à* resulting from

conseil *m* advice; (*conseiller*) adviser; (*assemblée*) council; *un ~* a piece of advice; *~ d'administration* board of directors

conseiller *personne* advise; *~ qc à qn* recommend sth to s.o.

consentir 1 *v/i* consent, agree (*à* to) **2** *v/t prêt, délai* agree

conséquence *f* consequence; *en ~* consequently

conservation *f* preservation; *des aliments* preserving

conserve *f* preserve; *en boîte* canned food, *Br aussi* tinned food; **conserver** keep; *aliments* preserve

considérable considerable; **considération** *f* consideration; **considérer** consider

consigne *f orders pl*; *d'une gare* baggage checkroom, *Br* left luggage office; *pour bouteilles* deposit; ÉDU detention

consistance *f* consistency; **consistant** *liquide, potage* thick; *mets* substantial; **consister**: *~ en/dans* consist of; *~ à faire* consist in doing

consolation *f* consolation

console *f* console; *jouer à la ~* play computer games

consoler consolet; *se ~ de* get over

consolider consolidate

consommateur, -trice *m/f* consumer; *dans un café* customer; **consommation** *f* consumption; *dans un café* drink; **consommer 1** *v/t* consume, use **2** *v/i dans un café* drink

consonne *f* consonant

conspiration *f* conspiracy; **conspirer** conspire

constamment constantly

constance *f* (*persévérance*) perseverance; *en amour* constancy

constant constant; *ami* staunch; *efforts* persistent

constater observe

consternation *f* consternation; **consterner** fill with consternation, dismay

constipation *f* MÉD constipation

constituer constitute; *comité, société* form; *rente* settle (*à* on); *se ~ fortune* build up

constitution *f* (*composition*) composition; ANAT, POL constitution; *d'un comité, d'une société* formation

construction *f* construction, building; **construire** construct, build; *théorie, roman* construct

consul *m* consul; **consulat** *m* consulate

consultation *f* consultation; **consulter 1** *v/t* consult **2** *v/i* be available for consultation

contact *m* contact; *se mettre*

en ~ avec contact; *mettre/*
couper le ~ AUTO switch
the engine on/off

contagieux, -euse contagious; *rire* infectious

contaminer contaminate;
MÉD *personne* infect

conte *m* story, tale

contempler contemplate

contemporain *m & adj* contemporary

contenir contain; *foule* control; *larmes* hold back; *peine*
suppress; *se ~* contain o.s.

content pleased, content (*de*
with)

contenu *m* content

contestation *f* discussion;
(opposition) protest; **contester** challenge

contexte *m* context

continent *m* continent

contingent *m (part)* quota

continu continous; ÉL *courant* direct; **continuer 1** *v/t*
continue; *rue, ligne* extend
2 *v/i* continue, go on; *de route* extend; *~ à ou de faire*
continue to do, go on doing;
continuité *f* continuity;
d'une tradition continuation

contorsion *f* contorsion

contour *m* contour; *d'une fenêtre, d'un visage* outline; *~s*
(courbes) twists and turns

contourner get around

contraceptif, -ive contraceptive; **contraception** *f* contraception

contracter *dette* incur; *mala-*

die aussi contract; *obligation, engagement* enter into;
assurance take out; *habitude*
acquire

contradiction *f* contradiction

contraindre: *~ qn à faire qc*
force s.o. to do sth; **contrainte** *f* constraint; *sans ~*
freely, without restraint

contraire 1 *adj sens* opposite;
principes conflicting; *vent*
contrary **2** *m*: *le ~ de* the opposite *ou* contrary of; *au ~*
on the contrary

contrarier *personne* annoy;
projet thwart

contraster contrast

contrat *m* contract

contravention *f* infringement; *(procès-verbal)* ticket

contre 1 *prép* against; *(en
échange)* (in exchange) for;
tout ~ qch right next to
sth; *par ~* on the contrary;
*quelque chose ~ la
diarrhée* something for diarrhea **2** *m*: *le pour et le ~* the
pros and the cons *pl*

contrebande *f* smuggling;
marchandises contraband;
contrebandier *m* smuggler

contrebasse *f* double bass

contrecœur: *à ~* reluctantly

contrecoup *m* after-effect

contredire contradict

contrée *f* country

contrefaire counterfeit; *signature* forge; *personne, gestes* imitate; *voix* disguise

contre-nature unnatural

contrepartie f compensation; **en ~** in return

contre-plaqué m plywood

contrer counter

contresens m misinterpretation; **prendre une route à ~** go down a road the wrong way

contretemps m hitch

contribuable m taxpayer; **contribuer** contribute (**à** to); **~ à faire** help to do

contrôle m (vérification) check; (domination) control; (maîtrise de soi) self-control; **~ douanier** customs inspection; **~ radar** radar speed check; **contrôler** identité, billets etc check; (maîtriser, dominer) control; **se ~** control o.s.

controversé controversial

contusion f MÉD bruise

convaincre (persuader) convince; **~ qn de faire qch** persuade s.o. to do sth

convalescent, ~e m/f convalescent

convenable suitable; (correct) personne respectable; salaire adequate; **convenance** f: **les ~s** the proprieties

convenir: **~ à qn** suit s.o.; **~à qc** be suitable for sth; **~ de qc** (décider) agree on sth; **~ que** (reconnaître que) admit that; **comme convenu** as agreed

convention f convention

converger converge

conversation f conversation; **~ téléphonique** telephone conversation, phonecall

conversion f conversion

convertir convert

conviction f conviction

convive m/f guest; **convivialité** f conviviality, friendliness; INFORM user-friendliness

convocation f d'une assemblée convening; JUR summons sg

convoi m convoy

convoquer assemblée convene; JUR summons; candidat notify; employé, écolier call in

convoyer MIL escort

convulsion f convulsion

coopération f cooperation; **coopérer** cooperate (**à** in)

coordination f coordination

coordonnées fpl MATH coordinates pl; de personne contact details

copain m F pal

copie f copy; ÉDU paper; **copier** copy (sur qn from s.o.)

copieux, -euse copious

copine f F pal

copropriétaire m/f co-owner, part owner

coq m rooster

coquelicot m BOT poppy

coquetier m eggcup

coquetterie f flirtatiousness; (élégance) stylishness

coquillage m shell; **des ~s**

shellfish

coquille f shell; erreur misprint, typo

coquin, ~e 1 adj enfant naughty 2 m/f rascal

corbeau m ZO crow

corbeille f basket; au théâtre circle

corbillard m hearse

corde f rope; MUS, de tennis string

cordialité f cordiality

cordon m cord; ~ littoral offshore sand bar

cordonnier m shoe repairer

Corée f: la ~ Korea; coréen, ~ne 1 adj Korean 2 m langue Korean; **Coréen**, ~ne m/f Korean

corne f horn

cornée f cornea

corneille f crow

corner m en football corner

cornet m sachet (paper) cone; MUS cornet

cornichon m gherkin

corporation f body; HIST guild

corporel, ~le hygiène personal; châtiment corporal; art body atr

corps m body; mort aussi corpse; MIL corps; **prendre** ~ take shape

corpulence f stoutness, corpulence

correct correct; tenue suitable; F (convenable) acceptable, ok F

correcteur m: ~ orthographique spellchecker

correction f qualité correctness; (modification) correction; (punition) beating

correspondance f correspondence; de train ete connection; **correspondre** correspond; de salles communicate; ~ à réalité correspond with; preuves tally with; idées fit in with

corridor m corridor

corriger correct; épreuve proof-read; (battre) beat

corrompre corrupt; (soudoyer) bribe

corrosion f corrosion

corruption f corruption; (pot-de-vin) bribery

corsage m blouse

corse Corsican; **Corse 1** m/f Corsican 2 f la Corse Corsica

corsé vin full-bodied; sauce spicy; café strong; facture stiff; problème tough

cortège m cortège; (défilé) procession

cortisone f cortisone

corvée f chore; MIL fatigue

cosmétique m & adj cosmetic

cosmopolite m & adj cosmopolitan

costaud F sturdy

costume m costume; pour homme suit

cote f en Bourse quotation; d'un document identification code

côte f ANAT rib; (*pente*) slope; *à la mer* coast; *viande* chop; *~ à ~* side by side

côté m side; *à ~* (*près*) nearby; *à ~ de* next to; *de ~* aside; *de l'autre ~ de* on the other side of; *du ~ de* in the direction of; *sur le ~* on one's/its side; *mettre de ~* put aside

côtelette f CUIS cutlet

cotisation f contribution; *à une organisation* subscription

coton m coton

côtoyer rub shoulders with; *qc* border sth

cottage m cottage

cou m neck

couchant 1 m west **2** adj: *soleil* m *~* setting sun

couche f layer; *de peinture aussi* coat; *de bébé* diaper, Br nappy

coucher 1 v/t (*mettre au lit*) put to bed; (*héberger*) put up; (*étendre*) put *ou* lay down **2** v/i sleep; *se ~* go to bed; (*s'étendre*) lie down; *du soleil* set, go down **3** m: *~ du soleil* sunset

coucou m cuckoo; (*pendule*) cuckoo clock

coude m ANAT elbow; *d'une route* turn

coudre sew; *bouton* sew on; *plaie* sew up

couette f comforter, Br quilt

couler 1 v/i flow, run; *d'eau de bain* run; *d'un bateau* sink **2** v/t *liquide* pour; (*mouler*)

cast; *bateau* sink

couleur f color, Br colour

coulisse f: *~s* THÉÂT wings; *dans les ~s* fig behind the scenes

couloir m passage, corridor; *d'un bus, avion* aisle

coup m blow; *dans jeu* move; *boire un ~* F have a drink; *du ~* and so; *après ~* after the event; *tout d'un ~, tout à ~* suddenly, all at once; *coup de couteau* stab; *coup de foudre: ce fut le ~* it was love at first sight; *coup de main: donner un ~ à qn* give s.o. a hand; *coup d'œil: au premier ~* at first glance; *coup de pied* kick; *coup de poing* punch; *donner un ~ à qn* punch; *coup de téléphone* (phone) call; *coup de soleil: avoir un ~* have sun stroke

coupable 1 adj guilty **2** m/f culprit, guilty party

coupe¹ f de cheveux, d'une robe cut

coupe² f (*verre*) glass; SP cup; *de fruits, glace* dish

coupe-ongles m inv nail clippers pl

couper 1 v/t cut; *morceau, eau* cut off; *robe, chemise* cut out; *vin* dilute; *animal* castrate **2** v/t: *se ~* cut o.s.; (*se trahir*) give o.s. away

couple m couple

coupon m de tissu remnant; COMM coupon; (*ticket*) ticket

coupure f cut; *de journal* cutting; *(billet de banque)* bill, Br note; **~ de courant** power outage, Br power cut

cour f court; ARCH courtyard; *Cour internationale de justice* International Court of Justice

courage m courage, bravery; **courageux, -euse** brave, courageous

couramment fluently

courant 1 *adj* current; *eau* running; *langage* everyday **2** *m* current *(aussi* ÉL*);* **~ d'air** draught, Br draft; **être au ~ de qch** know about sth

courbature f stiffness; **avoir des ~s** be stiff

courbe 1 *adj* curved **2** f curve; **courber** bend; **se ~** *(se baisser)* stoop, bend down

coureur m runner; *péj* skirt-chaser

courge f BOT squash, Br marrow

courgette f BOT zucchini, Br courgette

courir 1 *v/i* run *(aussi d'eau);* *d'un bruit* go around **2** *v/t* *risque, danger* run; **~ les magasins** go around the stores

couronne f crown; *de fleurs* wreath; **couronnement** m coronation

courrier m mail, Br aussi post; *(messager)* courier; **~ électronique** electronic mail, e-mail

courroie f belt

cours m course; ÉCON price; *de devises* rate; *(leçon)* lesson; **à l'université** class, Br aussi lecture; **donner libre ~ à** give free rein to; **en ~ de route** on the way

course f **à pied** running; SP race; *en taxi* ride; *(commission)* errand; **~s** *(achats)* shopping; **faire des ~s** go shopping

court¹ m *(aussi* **~ de tennis**) (tennis) court

court² *adj* short; **à ~ de** short of

court-circuit m ÉL short circuit

courtier m broker

courtisane f courtesan

courtoisie f courtesy

cousin, ~e m/f cousin

coussin m cushion

coût m cost; **coûter 1** *v/t* cost; **combien ça coûte?** how much is it?, how much does it cost? **2** *v/i* cost; **~ cher** be expensive

couteau m knife

coûteux, -euse expensive, costly

coutume f custom; **avoir ~ de faire** be in the habit of doing

couture f sewing; *d'un vêtement, bas etc* seam

couvée clutch; *fig* brood

couvent m convent

couver 1 *v/t* hatch; *personne* pamper **2** *v/i* *d'un feu* smolder, Br smoulder; *d'une révolution* be brewing

couvercle m cover

couvert 1 adj ciel overcast; ~ **de** covered with ou in 2 m à table place setting; ~**s** flatware, Br cutlery; **mettre le** ~ set the table; **couverture** f cover; sur un lit blanket

couvrir cover (**de** with ou in); ~ **qn** fig (protéger) cover (up) for s.o.; **se** ~ (s'habiller) cover o.s. up; du ciel cloud over

covoiturage m carpooling; **faire du** ~ carpool

crabe m crab

cracher spit

crachin m drizzle

craie f chalk

craindre fear, be frightened of; ~ **de faire** be afraid of doing; ~ **que (ne)** (+ subj) be afraid that

crainte f fear; **de** ~ **de** for fear of

craintif, -ive timid

cramoisi crimson

crampe f MÉD cramp

crampon m crampon

cran m notch; **il a du** ~ F he's got guts F

crâne m skull

crâner F (pavaner) show off

crapaud m zo toad

crapule f villain

craquelé cracked

craquement m crackle; **craquer** crack; d'un parquet creak; de feuilles crackle; d'une couture split; d'une personne (s'effondrer) crack

crasse 1 adj ignorance crass 2 f dirt

cravate f necktie, Br tie

crayon m pencil; ~ **à bille** ballpoint pen; ~ **de couleur** crayon

créance f COMM debt; **créancier, -ère** m/f creditor

création f creation; de mode, design design; **créativité** f creativity

créature f creature

crèche f day nursery; de Noël crèche, Br crib

crédibilité f credibility; **crédit** m credit; (prêt) loan; (influence) influence; **acheter à** ~ buy on credit; **faire** ~ **à qn** give s.o. credit

créditeur, -trice 1 m/f creditor 2 adj solde credit atr; **être** ~ be in credit

crédule credulous

créer create; institution set up; COMM produit design

crématorium m crematorium

crème 1 f cream; ~ **anglaise** custard; ~ **dépilatoire** hair remover; ~ **solaire** suntan cream 2 m coffee with milk, Br white coffee 3 adj inv cream

créneau m AUTO space; COMM niche

crêpe f CUIS pancake

crépiter crackle

crépu frizzy

crépuscule m twilight

crétin, ~e *m/f* idiot, cretin

creuser hollow out; *trou* dig; *fig* look into

creux, -euse 1 *adj* hollow; **assiette** *f* **creuse** soup plate 2 *adv*: **sonner** ~ ring hollow 3 *m* hollow

crevaison *f* flat, *Br* puncture

crevant F (*épuisant*) exhausting; (*drôle*) hilarious

crevasse crack; **se** ~ crack

crever 1 *v/t ballon* burst; *pneu* puncture 2 *v/i* burst; F (*mourir*) kick the bucket F; F AUTO have a flat *ou Br* puncture

crevette *f* shrimp

cri *m* shout, cry; **c'est le dernier** ~ *fig* it's all the rage

cribler sieve; **criblé de** *fig* riddled with

cric *m* jack

crier 1 *v/i* shout; ~ **au scandale** protest 2 *v/t* shout

crime *m* crime; (*assassinat*) murder; **criminel**, ~le 1 *adj* criminal 2 *m/f* criminal; (*assassin*) murderer

crinière *f* mane

criquet *m* ZO cricket

crise *f* crisis; MÉD attack; ~ **cardiaque** heart attack

crisper *muscles* tense; *visage* contort; *fig* F irritate; **se** ~ tense up

crisser squeak

cristal *m* crystal

critère *m* criterion

critique 1 *adj* critical 2 *m* critic 3 *f* criticism; *d'un film etc* review; **critiquer** criticize;

(*analyser*) look at critically

croc *m* (*dent*) fang; *de boucherie* hook

crochet *m* hook; *ouvrage* crochet; *d'une route* sharp turn; ~**s en typographie** square brackets

crochu *nez* hooked

crocodile *m* crocodile

croire 1 *v/t* believe; (*penser*) think; ~ **qc de qn** believe sth about s.o. 2 *v/i*: ~ **à qc** believe in sth; ~ **en Dieu** believe in God 3: **il se croit intelligent** he thinks he's intelligent

croisade *f* crusade

croisement *m* crossing (*aussi* BIOL); *animal* cross; **croiser** 1 *v/t* cross (*aussi* BIOL); ~ **qn dans la rue** pass s.o. in the street 2 *v/i* MAR cruise; **se** ~ *de routes* cross; *de personnes* meet

croisière *f* MAR cruise

croissance *f* growth

croissant *m de lune* crescent; CUIS croissant

croître grow

croix *f* cross; **mettre une** ~ **sur qc** *fig* give sth up

croquer 1 *v/t* crunch; (*dessiner*) sketch 2 *v/i* be crunchy

croquis *m* sketch

crotte *f* droppings *pl*

crouler collapse (*aussi fig*)

croupir stagnate (*aussi fig*)

croustillant crusty

croûte *f de pain* crust; *de fromage* rind; MÉD scab

croûton *m* crouton
croyance *f* belief; **croyant,**
~e *m/f* REL believer
cru 1 *adj* raw; *lumière, verité*
harsh; *paroles* blunt **2** *m* (*do-maine*) vineyard; *de vin* wine
cruauté *f* cruelty
cruche *f* pitcher
crucial crucial
crucifier crucify; **crucifix** *m*
crucifix
crudité *f* crudeness; *de paro-les* bluntness; *de lumière*
harshness; *de couleur gar-ishness;* **~s** CUIS raw vegeta-bles
cruel, ~le cruel
crustacés *mpl* shellfish *pl*
Cuba *f* Cuba; **cubain, ~e** Cu-ban; **Cubain, ~e** *m/f* Cuban
cube MATH **1** *m* cube **2** *adj* cu-bic; **cubisme** *m* ART cubism
cueillir pick
cuiller, cuillère *f* spoon; **cuil-lerée** *f* spoonful
cuir *m* leather; **~ chevelu**
scalp
cuirasse *f* armor, *Br* armour
cuire cook; *au four* bake; *rôti*
roast
cuisine *f* cooking; *pièce*
kitchen; **la ~ italienne** Ital-ian cooking *ou* cuisine; **cui-siner** cook; **cuisinière** *f*
cook; (*fourneau*) stove
cuisse *f* ANAT thigh; CUIS *de*
poulet leg
cuisson *f* cooking; *du pain*
baking; *d'un rôti* roasting
cuit cooked, done; *rôti, pain*

done
cuivre *m* copper; **~ jaune**
brass; **~s** brasses
cul *m* V ass P, *Br* arse P
cul-de-sac *m* blind alley; *fig*
dead end
culminer *fig* peak
culotte *f* short pants *pl, Br*
short trousers *pl; de femme*
panties *pl*
culpabilité *f* guilt, culpability
culte *m* worship; (*religion*) re-ligion; (*service*) church ser-vice; *fig* cult
cultivateur, -trice *m/f* farm-er; **cultiver** cultivate (*aussi*
fig); *légumes, tabac* grow;
se ~ improve one's mind
culture *f* culture; AGR cultiva-tion; *de légumes, fruits etc*
growing
culturel, ~le cultural
cumuler: ~ des fonctions
have more than one position
cupidité *f* greed, cupidity
cure *f* MÉD course of treat-ment; **~ de repos** rest cure
curé *m* curate
cure-dent *m* tooth pick
curiosité *f* curiosity; *objet ra-re* curio
curry *m* curry
curseur *m* INFORM cursor
cuvée *f de vin* vatful; *vin*
wine, vintage; **cuver 1** *v/i*
mature **2** *v/t:* **~ son vin** *fig*
sleep it off
cuvette *f* (*bac*) basin; *de cabi-net* bowl
CV *m* (= *curriculum vitae*) ré-

sumé, *Br* CV (= curriculum vitae)
cybercafé *m* Internet café
cycle *m* cycle; **cyclisme** *m* cycling; **cycliste** *m/f* cyclist
cyclone *m* cyclone

cygne *m* swan
cylindre *m* cylinder
cynique 1 *adj* cynical **2** *m/f* cynic
cystite *f* MÉD cystitis

D

dactylo *f* typing; *personne* typist
daigner: ~ *faire qch* deign to do sth
daim *m* ZO deer; *peau suede*
dalle *f* flagstone
daltonien, ~ne colorblind, *Br* colourblind
dame *f* lady; *aux échecs, cartes* queen; *jeu m de* ~s checkers *sg*, *Br* draughts *sg*
damner damn
Danemark: *le* ~ Denmark
danger *m* danger; *courir un* ~ be in danger
dangereux, -euse dangerous
danois, ~ **1** *adj* Danish **2** *m langue* Danish; **Danois**, ~e *m/f* Dane
dans in; *boire* ~ *un verre* drink from a glass
danse *f* dance; *action* dancing; ~ *folklorique* folk dance; **danser** dance; **danseur, -euse** *m/f* dancer
dard *m* *d'une abeille* sting
date *f* date; *de longue* ~ *amitié* long-standing; ~ *limite* deadline; ~ *limite de conservation* use-by date; da-

ter **1** *v/t* date **2** *v/i* ~ *de* date from; *à* ~ *de ce jour* from today
datte *f* date
davantage more
de 1 *prép origine* from; *possession* of; *il vient* ~ *Paris* he comes from Paris *la maison* ~ *mon père* my father's house; *un film* ~ *Godard* a movie by Godard; ~ *jour* by day; *trembler* ~ *peur* shake with fear; *cesser* ~ *travailler* stop working **2** *partitif*: *du pain* (some) bread; *des petits pains* (some) rolls; *je n'ai pas d'argent* I don't have any money, I have no money; *est-ce qu'il y a des disquettes?* are there any diskettes?
dé *m jeu* dice; ~ (*à coudre*) thimble
dealer *m* dealer
déambuler stroll
débâcle *f de troupes* rout; *d'une entreprise* collapse
déballer unpack
débandade *f* stampede
débarbouiller: ~ *un enfant*

wash a child's face

débardeur *m vêtement* tank top

débarquement *m de marchandises* unloading, disembarkation; *de passagers* landing, disembarkation; **débarquer 1** *v/t marchandises* unload; *passagers* land, disembark **2** *v/i* land, disembark; **~ chez qn** *fig* F turn up at s.o.'s place

débarrasser *table etc* clear; **~ qn de qc** take sth off s.o.; **se ~ de** get rid of

débat *m* debate; *(polémique)* argument

débattre: **~ qc** discuss *ou* debate sth; **se ~** struggle

débauche *f* debauchery; **débaucher** *(licencier)* lay off; F lead astray

débile 1 *adj* weak; F idiotic **2** *m*: **~ mental** mental defective

débit *m (vente)* sale; *d'un stock* turnover; *d'une usine* output; *(élocution)* delivery; FIN debit; **débiter** *marchandises* sell (retail); *péj: fadaises* talk; *texte étudié* deliver, *péj* recite; *d'une pompe* deliver; *d'une usine, de produits* output; *bois, viande* cut up; FIN debit *(de* with); **débiteur, -trice** *1 m/f* debtor **2** *adj compte* overdrawn; *solde de* débit

déblayer *endroit* clear; *débris* clear (away)

débloquer 1 *v/t* TECH release;

prix, compte unfreeze; *fonds* release **2** *v/i* F be crazy; **se ~ d'une situation** get sorted out

déboguer debug

déboires *mpl* disappointments

déboisement *m* deforestation

déboîter 1 *v/t* MÉD dislocate **2** *v/i* AUTO pull out; **se ~ l'épaule** dislocate one's shoulder

débonnaire kindly

débordé snowed under (*de* with); **~ par les événements** overwhelmed by events; **déborder** *d'une rivière* overflow its banks; *du lait, de l'eau* overflow

débouché *m d'une vallée* entrance; COMM outlet; **~s** *d'une profession* prospects; **déboucher 1** *v/t tuyau* unblock; *bouteille* uncork **2** *v/i*: **~ de** emerge from; **~ sur** lead to (*aussi fig*)

débourser *(dépenser)* spend

debout standing; *objet* upright, on end; *être* **~** stand; *(levé)* be up, be out of bed; **se mettre ~** stand up, get up

déboutonner unbutton

débraillé untidy

débrancher ÉL unplug

débrayer AUTO declutch; *fig* down tools

débris *mpl* debris *sg*; *fig* remains

débrouillard resourceful; **débrouiller** disentangle; *fig: affaire* clear up; **se ~** cope

début *m* beginning, start; **~s** THÉÂT, POL debut; **débutant**, **~e** *m/f* beginner

décacheter *lettre* open

décadent decadent

décaféiné: café *m* ~ decaffeinated coffee, decaff F

décalage *m dans l'espace* moving; (*différence*) difference; *fig* gap; **décaler** *rendez-vous* change the time of; *dans l'espace* move

décamper F clear out

décaper *surface* clean; *meuble vernis* strip

décapiter decapitate

décapotable *f* (**voiture** *f*) **~** convertible

décapsuleur *m* bottle opener

décarcasser: se ~ F bust a gut F

décéder die

déceler (*découvrir*) detect; (*montrer*) point to

décembre *m* December

décemment decently; (*raisonnablement*) reasonably

décennie *f* decade

décent decent,

décentralisation *f* decentralization

déception *f* disappointment

décerner *prix* award

décès *m* death

décevoir disappoint

déchaîner *fig* provoke; **se ~**

d'une tempête break; *d'une personne* fly into a rage

décharge *f* JUR acquittal; *dans fusillade* discharge; **~ électrique** electric shock; **décharger** unload; *arme* fire; *accusé* acquit; *colère* vent (**contre** on); **~ qn de qch** relieve s.o. of sth

décharné skeletal

déchausser: se ~ take one's shoes off

déchéance *f* decline; JUR forfeiture

déchets *mpl* waste

déchiffrer decipher

déchiqueté *côte* jagged; **déchiqueter** *corps, papier* tear to pieces

déchirant heart-breaking; **déchirer** *tissu* tear; *papier* tear up; *fig: silence* pierce; **se ~** *d'une robe* tear; **se ~ un muscle** tear a muscle

décidé (*résolu*) determined (**à faire qc** to do sth); **décidément** really; **décider 1** *v/t* decide on; *question* settle; decide; **~ qn à faire qc** convince s.o. to do sth; **~ de faire qch** decide to do sth **2** *v/i* decide; **se ~** make one's mind up, decide (**à faire qch** to do sth)

décimal decimal

décimer decimate

décimètre: double ~ ruler

décisif, -ive decisive; **décision** *f* decision; (*fermeté*) determination

déclaration *f* declaration, statement; *d'une naissance* registration; *de vol, perte* report; **déclarer** declare; *naissance* register; *se ~* declare o.s.; *en amour* declare one's love; *d'un feu, d'une épidémie* break out

déclencher trigger; *se ~* be triggered

déclic *m bruit* click

déclin *m* decline

décliner 1 *v/i du soleil* go down; *du jour, des forces, du prestige* wane; *de la santé* decline **2** *v/t offre* decline

décoder decode; **décodeur** *m* decoder

décoiffer *cheveux* ruffle

décollage *m* AVIAT take-off; **décoller 1** *v/t* peel off **2** *v/i* AVIAT take off; *se ~* peel off

décolleté 1 *adj robe* low-cut **2** *m* neckline

décolorer *tissu, cheveux* bleach; *se ~* fade

décombres *mpl* rubble

décommander cancel; *se ~* cancel

décomposer *produit* break down (**en** into); CHIM decompose; *se ~ d'un cadavre* decompose; *d'un visage* become contorted

décompresser F unwind, chill out F

décompte *m* deduction; *d'une facture* breakdown

déconcentrer: *~ qn* make it

hard for s.o. to concentrate

déconcertant disconcerting

déconfit disheartened

déconfiture *f* collapse

décongeler *aliment* thaw out

décongestionner *route* decongest; *nez* clear

déconnecter unplug, disconnect; *se ~* INFORM log off, log out

déconner P *actions* fool around; *paroles* talk crap P

déconseiller advise against

décontenancer disconcert

décontracter relax; *se ~* relax

décor *m* decor; *fig (cadre)* setting; *~s de théâtre* sets, scenery; **décorateur, -trice** *m/f* decorator; THÉÂT set designer; **décorer** decorate (**de** with)

découler: *~ de* arise from

découper cut up; *photo* cut out (**dans** from); *se ~ sur* fig stand out against

décourager discourage (**de faire qc** from doing sth); *se ~* lose heart, become discouraged

découvert, ~e 1 *adj tête, épaules* bare, uncovered; *à ~* FIN overdrawn **2** *m* overdraft **3** *f* discovery; **découvrir** uncover; *(trouver)* discover; *ses intentions* reveal; *(comprendre)* find (**que** that); *se ~ d'une personne* take off a couple of layers; *(enlever son chapeau)* take

off one's hat; *du ciel* clear
décret *m* decree
décrire describe; ~ *une orbite autour de* orbit
décrocher *tableau* take down; *fig* F *prix, bonne situation* land F; *le téléphone* pick up the receiver; *pour ne pas être dérangé* take the phone off the hook
décroître decrease, decline
déçu disappointed
décupler increase tenfold
dédaigner 1 *v/t* scorn; *personne* treat with scorn **2** *v/i*: ~ *de faire qch* disdain to do sth; **dédaigneux, -euse** disdainful; **dédain** *m* disdain
dedans inside
dédicace *f* dedication; **dédier** dedicate
dédommager compensate (*de* for)
dédouanement *m* customs clearance; **dédouaner**: ~ *qch* clear sth through customs; ~ *qn fig* clear s.o.
dédoublement *m*: ~ *de personnalité* split personality; **dédoubler** split in two; *se* ~ split
dédramatiser play down, downplay
déduction *f* deduction; **déduire** COMM deduct; (*conclure*) deduce (*de* from)
déesse *f* goddess
défaillance *f* weakness; *fig* shortcoming; *technique* fail-

ure; **défaillir** weaken; (*se trouver mal*) feel faint
défaire undo; (*démonter*) take down, dismantle; *valise* unpack; *se* ~ come undone; *se* ~ *de qn/qc* get rid of s.o./ sth; **défait** *visage* drawn; *chemise, valise* undone; *armée, personne* defeated; **défaite** *f* defeat; **défaitisme** *m* defeatism
défaut *m* (*imperfection*) defect; *morale* shortcoming, failing; (*manque*) lack; JUR default; *faire* ~ be lacking; *par* ~ INFORM default *atr*
défavorable unfavorable, *Br* unfavourable; **défavorisé** disadvantaged; *les milieux* ~**s** the underprivileged classes
défectueux, -euse defective
défendre defend; *à qn de faire qc* forbid s.o. to do sth
défense *f* defense, *Br* defence *f*; *d'un éléphant* tusk; ~ *de fumer* no smoking; **défenseur** *m* defender; *d'une cause* supporter; JUR defense attorney, *Br* counsel for the defence; **défensif, -ive** *adj & f* defensive
déférent deferential; **déférer**: ~ *qn à la justice* prosecute s.o.
défi *m* challenge; (*bravade*) defiance
défiance *f* distrust, mistrust
déficience *f* deficiency; ~ *immunitaire* immune deficien-

cy

déficit m deficit; **déficitaire** *balance* showing a deficit; *compte* in debit

défier (*provoquer*) challenge; (*braver*) defy; **~ qn de faire qch** dare s.o. to do sth

défigurer disfigure; *fig: réalité* misrepresent

défilé m parade; GÉOGR pass; **~ de mode** fashion show; **défiler** parade, march

défini definite; **bien ~** well defined; **définir** define; **définitif, -ive** definitive; **en définitive** in the end; **définition** definition; **définitivement** definitely; (*pour de bon*) for good

déflagration f explosion

défoncer *voiture* smash up, total; *porte* break down; *terrain* break up

déformer deform; *chaussures* stretch (out of shape); *visage, fait* distort; *idée* misrepresent; **se ~ de chaussures** lose their shape

défouler: se ~ give vent to one's feelings

défroisser *vêtement* crumple

défunt, ~e 1 *adj* late **2** *m/f: le ~* the deceased

dégagement m *d'une route* clearing; *de chaleur* release; **dégager** (*délivrer*) free; *route* clear; *odeur, chaleur* give off; **se ~** free o.s.; *d'une route, du ciel* clear

dégât m damage; **~s** damage

---

dégel m thaw (*aussi* POL)

dégeler 1 *v/t frigidaire* defrost; *crédits* unfreeze **2** *v/i d'un lac* thaw

dégénérer degenerate (**en** into)

dégivrer defrost; TECH de-ice

déglutir swallow

dégonfler let the air out of, deflate; **se ~** deflate; *fig* F lose one's nerve

dégourdi resourceful; **dégourdir** *membres* loosen up; **se ~ les jambes** stretch one's legs

dégoût m disgust; **dégoûtant** disgusting; **dégoûter** disgust; **~ qn de qc** put s.o. off sth; **se ~ de qc** take a dislike to sth

dégrader MIL demote; *édifice* damage; (*avilir*) degrade; **se ~** deteriorate; *d'un édifice* fall into disrepair

degré m degree; (*échelon*) level

dégressif, -ive *tarif* tapering

dégringoler fall

dégriser sober up

déguerpir clear off

dégueulasse P disgusting; **dégueuler** F vomit

déguisement m disguise; *pour bal masqué etc* costume; **déguiser** disguise; *enfant* dress up (**en** as); **se ~** disguise o.s.; *pour bal masqué etc* dress up

dégustation f tasting; **déguster** taste

dehors 1 *adv* outside **2** *prép*: **en ~ de** outside **3** *m* exterior

déjà already; *c'est qui déjà?* F who's he again?

déjeuner 1 *v/i midi* (have) lunch; *matin* (have) breakfast **2** *m* lunch; *petit ~* breakfast

déjouer thwart

DEL *f* (= *diode électroluminescente*) LED (= light-emitting diode)

délabré dilapidated

délacer loosen, unlace

délai *m* (*temps imparti*) time allowed; (*date limite*) deadline; (*prolongation*) extension; *sans ~* without delay

délaisser (*abandonner*) leave; (*négliger*) neglect

délassement *m* relaxation; **délasser** relax; *se ~* relax

délateur, -trice *m/f* informer; **délation** *f* denunciation

délayer dilute, water down; *fig*: *discours* pad out

délecter: *se ~ de* take delight in

délégué, ~e *m/f* delegate; **déléguer** delegate

délibération *f* deliberation; (*décision*) resolution; **délibéré** deliberate; **délibérer** deliberate

délicat delicate; *problème* tricky; (*plein de tact*) tactful; **délicatesse** *f* delicacy; (*tact*) tact; **délicatement** delicately

délicieux, -euse delicious

délier loosen, untie; *~ la langue à qn* loosen s.o.'s tongue

délimiter define

délinquance *f* crime, delinquency

délire *m* delirium; *enthousiasme* frenzy; *foule en ~* ecstatic crowd; **délirer** be delirious; F *être fou ~* be stark raving mad

délit *m* offense, *Br* offence; *commettre un ~ de fuite* leave the scene of an accident

délivrance *f* release; (*soulagement*) relief; (*livraison*) delivery; *certificat* issue

délivrer release; (*livrer*) deliver; *certificat* issue

délocaliser relocate

déloyal disloyal; *concurrence f ~e* unfair competition

deltaplane *m* hang-glider; *faire du ~* go hang-gliding

déluge *m* flood

demain tomorrow; *à ~!* see you tomorrow!

demande *f* (*requête*) request; *écrite* application; ÉCON demand; *sur ou à la ~ de* at the request of; **demandé** popular, in demand; **demander** ask for; *somme d'argent* ask; (*nécessiter*) call for; *~ qch à qn* ask s.o. for sth; (*vouloir savoir*) ask s.o. sth; *~ à qn de faire qc* ask s.o. to do sth; *se ~ si* wonder if

démanger: *le dos me démange* my back itches; *ça me démange depuis longtemps* I've been itching to do it for ages

démanteler dismantle

démaquillant *m* cleanser; *lait m* ~ cleansing milk; **démaquiller**: *se* ~ take off one's make-up

démarcation *f* demarcation

démarchage *m* selling

démarche *f* step (*aussi fig*); *faire des* ~*s* take steps

démarquer: *se* ~ stand out (*de* from)

démarrage *m* start; **démarrer** start (up)

démasquer unmask

démêlé *m* argument; *avoir des* ~*s avec la justice* have problems with the law; **démêler** disentangle; *fig* clear up

déménager move; **déménageurs** *mpl* movers, removal men

démence *f* dementia; **dément** demented; *c'est* ~ *fig* F it's unbelievable

démener: *se* ~ struggle; (*s'efforcer*) make an effort

démenti *m* denial

démentir (*nier*) deny; (*infirmer*) belie

démerder: *se* ~ F manage, sort things out

démesuré enormous; *orgueil* excessive

démettre *poignet* dislocate;

se ~ *de ses fonctions* resign one's office

demeure *f* residence; **demeurer** (*habiter*) live; (*rester*) stay, remain; **demeuré** retarded

demi 1 *adj* half; *une heure et* ~*e* an hour and a half; *il est quatre heures et* ~*e* it's four thirty, it's half past four **2** *adv* half; *à* ~ half **3** *m* half; *bière* half a pint; *en football, rugby* halfback

demi-cercle *m* semi-circle

demi-finale *f* semi-final

demi-frère *m* half-brother

demi-heure *f* half-hour

démilitariser demilitarize

demi-litre *m* half liter *ou* Br litre

demi-mot: *il nous l'a dit à* ~ he hinted at it to us

demi-pension *f* American plan, Br half board

demi-pression *f* half-pint of draft *ou* Br draught beer

demi-sel *m* slightly salted butter

demi-sœur *f* half-sister

démission *f* resignation; *fig* renunciation; **démissionner 1** *v/i* resign; *fig* give up **2** *v/t* sack

demi-tarif *m* half price

demi-tour *m* AUTO U-turn; *faire* ~ *fig* turn back

démocrate democrat; **démocratie** *f* democracy

démodé old-fashioned

démographique demographic; **poussée** f ~ population growth

demoiselle f (*jeune fille*) young lady; ~ **d'honneur** bridesmaid

démolir demolish (*aussi fig*); **démolition** f demolition

démon m demon

démonstration f demonstration

démonter dismantle; *fig* disconcert

démontrer demonstrate, prove; (*faire ressortir*) show

démoraliser demoralize

démordre: **il n'en démordra pas** he won't change his mind

démotiver demotivate

démuni penniless

dénaturer distort

dénicher find

dénier deny

dénigrer denigrate

dénivellation f difference in height

dénombrer count

dénomination f name

dénoncer denounce; *à la police* report; *contrat* terminate; **se ~ à la police** give o.s. up to the police; **dénonciateur, -trice** m/f informer; **dénonciation** f denunciation

dénoter indicate, denote

dénouement m ending; **dénouer** loosen; **se ~** *fig d'une scène* end; *d'un mystère* be cleared up

denrée f: **~s** (*alimentaires*) foodstuffs

dense dense; **densité** f density; *du brouillard, d'une forêt* denseness

dent f tooth; **j'ai mal aux ~s** I've got toothache; **avoir une ~ contre qn** have a grudge against s.o.; **dentaire** dental

dentelle f lace

dentier m false teeth pl; **dentifrice** m toothpaste; **dentiste** m/f dentist

dénuder strip

dénué: **~ de qc** devoid of sth; **~ de tout** deprived of everything; **dénuement** m destitution

déodorant m deodorant

dépannage m AUTO *etc* repairs pl; (*remorquage*) recovery; **dépanner** repair; (*remorquer*) recover; **~ qn** *fig* F help s.o. out; **dépanneur** m repairman; *pour voitures* mechanic; **dépanneuse** f wrecker, *Br* tow truck

départ m departure; SP, *fig* start; **au ~** at first

départager decide between

départemental departmental; **route ~e** secondary road

dépassé out of date, old-fashioned; **dépasser** *personne* pass; AUTO pass, *Br* overtake; *but etc* overshoot; *fig* exceed; **se ~** surpass o.s.

dépaysement m disorienta-

dépression

tion; *changement agréable* change of scene

dépêcher dispatch; **se ~ de faire qch** hurry to do sth; **dépêche-toi!** hurry up!

dépendance f dependence; **~s bâtiments** outbuildings; **entraîner une (forte)** ~ be (highly) addictive; **dépendre:** ~ **de** depend on; *moralement* be dependent on

dépens mpl: **aux ~ de** at the expense of

dépense f expenditure; *d'essence, d'électricité* consumption, use; **dépenser** spend; *son énergie, ses forces* use up; *essence* consume, use; **se ~** exert o.s., be physically active; **dépensier, -ère 1** *adj* extravagant **2** *m/f* spendthrift

dépérir waste away; *fig d'une entreprise* go downhill

dépeuplement m depopulation

dépilatoire: crème f ~ hair remover, depilatory cream

dépistage m *d'un criminel* tracking down; MÉD screening

dépit m spite; **en ~ de** in spite of

dépité crestfallen

déplacé out of place; *(inconvenant)* uncalled for; POL displaced; **déplacer** move; *personnel* transfer; *problème* shift the focus of; **se ~** move; *(voyager)* travel

déplaire: ~ **à qn** *(fâcher)* offend s.o.; **cela lui déplaît de faire ...** he dislikes doing ...

déplaisant unpleasant

dépliant m leaflet; **déplier** unfold

déploiement m MIL deployment; *de forces, courage* display

déplorable deplorable

déporter POL deport; **se ~** *d'un véhicule* swing

déposer 1 *v/t* put down; *armes* lay down; *passager* drop; *roi* depose; *argent, boue* deposit; *projet de loi* table; *ordures* dump; *plainte* lodge **2** *v/i d'un liquide* settle; JUR testify; **se ~ de la boue** settle; **dépôt** m deposit; *chez le notaire* lodging; *d'un projet de loi* tabling; *des ordures* dumping; *(entrepôt)* depot

dépouiller *animal* skin; *(voler)* rob *(de* of); *(examiner)* go through; **le scrutin ou les votes** count the votes

dépourvu ~ de devoid of; **prendre qn au ~** take s.o. by surprise

dépoussiérer dust; *fig* modernize

dépraver deprave

déprécier *chose* decrease the value of; *personne* belittle; **se ~** depreciate, lose value; *d'une personne* belittle o.s.

dépression f depression; **fai-**

re une ~ be depressed

déprime f depression; **déprimer** depress

dépuceler deflower

depuis 1 prép since; espace from; **j'attends ~ une heure** I have been waiting for an hour; **~ quand permettent-ils que ...?** since when do they allow ...? **2** adv since **3** conj: **~ que** since

député m POL MP, Member of Parliament; **~ européen** m Euro MP

déraciner uproot; (extirper) root out, eradicate

dérailler go off the rails; fig F: d'un mécanisme go on the blink; (déraisonner) talk nonsense; **dérailleur** m d'un vélo derailleur

déraisonnable unreasonable

dérangement m disturbance; **déranger** disturb

déraper AUTO skid

déréglé vie wild

déréglementer deregulate

dérégler mécanisme upset

dérision f derision; **tourner en ~** deride

dérisoire derisory, laughable

dérivatif m diversion; **dériver 1** v/t MATH derive; cours d'eau divert **2** v/i MAR, AVIAT drift; **~ de** d'un mot be derived from

dermatologue m/f dermatologist

dernier, -ère last; (le plus récent) mode, roman etc latest;

extrême utmost; **ce ~** the latter; **dernièrement** recently, lately

dérobée: à la ~ furtively; **dérober** steal; **~ qch à qn** rob s.o. of sth, steal sth from s.o.; **se ~ à** discussion shy away from; obligations shirk

déroger JUR: **~ à** make an exception to, depart from

déroulement m unfolding; **le ~ du projet** the running of the project; **dérouler** unroll; bobine, câble unwind; **se ~** take place; d'une cérémonie go (off)

dérouter (déconcerter) disconcert

derrière 1 adv behind **2** prép behind **3** m back; ANAT bottom; **de ~** patte etc back atr

dès from, since; **~ lors** from then on; (par conséquent) consequently; **~ lundi** as of Monday; **~ que** as soon as

désabuser disillusion

désaccord m disagreement

désaffecté disused; église deconsecrated

désagréable unpleasant, disagreeable

désappointement m disappointment

désapprobateur, -trice disapproving

désapprouver disapprove of

désarmement m MIL disarmament; **désarmer** disarm (aussi fig)

désarroi m disarray

désastre *m* disaster

désavantage *m* disadvantage; **désavantager** put at a disadvantage

désaveu *m* disowning; *d'un propos* retraction; **désavouer** disown; *propos* retract

descendance *f* descendants *pl*; **descendant**, **~e** *m/f* descendant

descendre 1 *v/i* go/come down; *d'un bus* get off; *d'une voiture* get out; *de température, prix* go down; *d'un chemin* drop; AVIAT descend; **~ chez qn** stay with s.o.; **~ de qn** be descended from s.o. **2** *v/t* (*porter vers le bas*) bring down; (*emporter*) take down; *passager* drop off; F (*abattre*) shoot down; *vallée, rivière* descend; **~ les escaliers** come/go downstairs; **descente** *f* descent; (*pente*) slope; *en parachute* jump; **~ de lit** bedside rug

description *f* description

désemparé at a loss

déséquilibré PSYCH unbalanced

désert 1 *adj* deserted; *une île* **~e** a desert island **2** *m* desert; **déserter** desert; **déserteur** *m* MIL deserter

désertification *f* desertification

désertion *f* desertion

désespérant depressing

désespérer 1 *v/t* drive to despair **2** *v/i* despair

désespoir *m* despair; *en ~ de cause* in desperation

déshabillé *m* negligee; **déshabiller** undress; **se ~** get undressed

déshériter disinherit

déshonorer disgrace, bring dishonor *ou Br* dishonour on

déshydraté *aliments* dessicated; *personne* dehydrated; **déshydrater**: **se ~** become dehydrated

design *m*: **~ d'intérieurs** interior design

désigner (*montrer*) point to, point out; (*appeler*) call; (*nommer*) appoint (*pour* to), designate

désillusion *f* disillusionment

désinfectant *m* disinfectant

désintéressé disinterested, impartial; (*altruiste*) selfless; **désintéresser**: **se ~ de** lose interest in

désintoxication *f*: *faire une cure de ~* go into detox

désinvolture *f* casualness

désir *m* desire; (*souhait*) wish

désirer want; *sexuellement* desire; **~ faire qch** want to do sth; **désireux**, **-euse** eager (*de faire* to do)

désister POL: **se ~** withdraw, stand down

désobéir disobey; **~ à** disobey; **désobéissant** disobedient

désobligeant disagreeable

désodorisant m deodorant

désolé upset (*de* about, over); *je suis* ~ I am so sorry

désopilant hilarious

désordre m untidiness; *en* ~ untidy

désorganisé disorganized

désormais now; *à partir de maintenant* from now on

désosser remove the bones from

despote m despot; **despotique** despotic

dessécher dry out; *de fruits* dry

dessein m intention; *à* ~ intentionally; *dans le* ~ *de faire qc* with the intention of doing sth

desserrer loosen

dessert m dessert

desservir *des transport publics* serve; (*s'arrêter à*) stop at; *table* clear; ~ *qn* do s.o. a disservice

dessin m drawing; (*motif*) design; **dessiner** draw

dessoûler F sober up

dessous 1 *adv* underneath; *en* ~ underneath 2 m underside; *ci-* ~ below; *les voisins du* ~ the downstairs neighbors

dessous-de-plat m inv table mat

dessus 1 *adv* on top; *sens* ~ **dessous** upside down; *en* ~ on top; *par* ~ over; *ci-* ~ above 2 m top; *les voisins*

du ~ the upstairs neighbors; *avoir le* ~ *fig* have the upper hand; **dessus-de-lit** m inv bedspread

déstabilisant unnerving; **déstabiliser** destabilize

destin m destiny, fate

destinataire m addressee

destination f destination; **destinée** f destiny; **destiner** mean, intend (*à* for)

destituer dismiss; MIL discharge

destructeur, -trice destructive; **destruction** f destruction

désuet, -ète obsolete; *mode* out of date

détachable detachable; **détacher** detach; *ceinture* undo; *chien* release; *employé* second; (*nettoyer*) clean; *se* ~ *sur* stand out against

détail m detail; COMM retail trade; *vendre au* ~ sell retail; *prix m de* ~ retail price; *en* ~ detailed

détaillant m retailer

détartrage m descaling

détecteur m sensor

détective m detective

déteindre fade; ~ *sur* come off on; *fig* rub off on

détendre slacken; *se* ~ *d'une corde* slacken; *fig* relax

détenir hold; JUR detain, hold

détente f *d'une arme* trigger; *fig* relaxation; POL détente

détention f holding; JUR detention

détenu, **~e** *m/f* inmate

détergent *m* detergent

détériorer damage; **se~** deteriorate

déterminant decisive; **déterminer** establish, determine

déterrer dig up

détester detest, hate

détonation *f* detonation

détour *m* detour; *d'un chemin, fleuve* bend; **sans ~** *fig:* dire qch straight out

détourné *fig* indirect; **détourner** *trafic* divert; *avion* hijack; *tête, yeux* turn away; *de l'argent* embezzle; **se ~** turn away

détresse *f* distress

détriment *m*: **au ~ de** to the detriment of

détritus *m* garbage, *Br* rubbish

détroit *m* strait

détromper put right

détruire destroy; *(tuer)* kill

dette *f* debt

deuil *m* mourning; *il y a eu un ~ dans sa famille* there's been a bereavement in his family

deux 1 *adj* two; *les ~* both; *nous ~* the two of us, both of us; *en ~* in two, in half; *~ à ou par ~* in twos, two by two; *~ fois* twice **2** *m* two; **deuxième** second; *étage* third, *Br* second; **deux-pièces** *m inv bikini* two-piece swimsuit; *appartement* two-room apartment; **deux--points** *m inv* colon

dévaliser *banque* rob, raid; *maison* burglarize, *Br* burgle; *personne* rob; *fig: frigo* raid

dévalorisant demeaning; **dévalorisation** *f* drop in value; *fig* belittlement; **dévaloriser** devalue; *fig* belittle

dévaluation *f* devaluation; **dévaluer** devalue

devancer be ahead of; *désir, objection* anticipate

devant 1 *adv* in front; *droit ~* straight ahead **2** *prép* in front of; *passer ~ l'église* go past the church; *~ Dieu* before God **3** *m* front

devanture *f* shop window

dévaster devastate

développement *m* development; **développer** develop; **se ~** develop

devenir become; *il devient vieux* he's getting old; *que va-t-il ~?* what's going to become of him?

dévergondé *sexuellement* promiscuous

déverser *ordures* dump; *passagers* disgorge

dévêtir undress

déviation *f* *d'une route* detour; *(écart)* deviation

dévier 1 *v/t* divert, reroute **2** *v/i* deviate (*de* from)

deviner guess

devis *m* estimate

dévisager stare at

devise *f* FIN currency; *(moto,*

règle de vie) motto; **~s étran-**
gères foreign currency
dévisser unscrew
dévoiler unveil; *secret* reveal,
disclose
devoir 1 *v/t de l'argent* owe **2**
v/aux: *il doit le faire* he has
to do it, he must do it; *il au-*
rait dû me le dire he should
have told me; *tu devrais*
l'acheter you should buy
it; *ça doit être cuit* it should
be done **3** *m* duty; *pour*
l'école homework
dévorer devour
dévouement *m* devotion; **dé-**
vouer: *se ~ pour* dedicate
one's life to
dextérité *f* dexterity, skill
diabète *m* diabetes *sg*
diable *m* devil; **diabolique** di-
abolical
diagnostic *m* MÉD diagnosis;
diagnostiquer MÉD diagnose
diagonal, ~e **1** *adj* diagonal **2**
f diagonal (line); *en ~e* diagonally
diagramme *m* diagram
dialogue *m* dialog, *Br* dialogue
diamant *m* diamond
diamètre *m* diameter
diapositive *f* slide
diarrhée *f* diarrhea, *Br* diarr-
rhoea
dictateur *m* dictator; **dictatu-**
re *f* dictatorship
dictée *f* dictation
dictionnaire *m* dictionary

diesel *m* diesel
diète *f* diet
Dieu *m* God; *~ merci!* thank
God!
diffamer slander
différence *f* difference; **diffé-**
rencier differentiate
différend *m* dispute
difficile difficult; (*exigeant*)
hard to please; **difficulté** *f*
difficulty
difformité *f* deformity
diffusion *f* spread; RAD, TV
broadcast; *de chaleur etc* diffusion
digérer digest
digestion *f* digestion
digital digital; *empreinte f ~e*
fingerprint
digne (*plein de dignité*) dignified; *~ de* worthy of; **dignité**
f dignity; (*charge*) office
digue *f* dyke
dilapider squander
dilater expand; *pupille* dilate
dilemme *m* dilemma
diluer dilute
dimanche *m* Sunday
dimension *f* dimension; (*tail-*
le) size; *d'une faute* magnitude
diminuer 1 *v/t nombre, prix*
reduce; *joie, forces* diminish; *mérites* detract from;
souffrances lessen, decrease
2 *v/i* decrease
diminutif *m* diminutive; **di-**
minution *f* decrease, decline; *d'un nombre, prix* reduction

dinde *f* turkey; dindon *m* turkey

dîner **1** *v/i* dine **2** *m* dinner

dingue F crazy, nuts F

diplomate *m* diplomat; diplomatie *f* diplomacy

diplôme *m* diploma; *universitaire* degree; diplômé diploma holder; *de l'université* graduate

dire say; *(informer, révéler, ordonner)* tell; **~ à qn de faire qch** tell s.o. to do sth; **à vrai ~** to tell the truth; **cela va sans ~** that goes without saying

direct direct; **en ~** *émission* live; directement directly; directeur, -trice **1** *adj comité* management **2** *m/f* manager; *plus haut dans la hiérarchie* director; ÉDU principal, *Br* head teacher; direction *f* *(sens)* direction; *(gestion, directeurs)* management; AUTO steering; **~ assistée** power steering; directive *f* instruction; *de l'UE* directive

dirigeant *m* leader; diriger manage, run; *pays* lead; *orchestre* conduct; *voiture* steer; *arme, critique* aim **(contre** at); *regard, yeux* turn **(vers** to); *personne* direct; **se ~ vers** head for

discerner make out; **~ le bon du mauvais** tell good from bad

discipline *f* discipline

disc-jockey *m* disc jockey,

DJ

discontinu *ligne* broken; *effort* intermittent

discorde *f* discord

discothèque *f* *(boîte)* discotheque, disco; *collection* record library

discours *m* speech

discréditer discredit

discret, -ète *(qui n'attire pas l'attention)* unobtrusive; *couleur* quiet; *robe* simple; *(qui garde le secret)* discreet; discrétion *f* discretion

discrimination *f* discrimination

disculper clear, exonerate; **se ~** clear o.s.

discussion *f* discussion; *(altercation)* argument; discuter discuss; *(contester)* question

disjoncter **1** *v/t* ÉL break **2** *v/i* F be crazy; disjoncteur *m* circuit breaker

disparaître disappear; *(mourir)* die; *d'une espèce* die out; **faire ~** get rid of

disparition *f* disappearance; *(mort)* death; **espèce en voie de ~** endangered species

dispenser: **~ qn de (faire) qc** excuse s.o. from (doing) sth

disperser disperse; **se ~** *(faire trop de choses)* spread o.s. too thin

disponibilité *f* availability; disponible available

disposer *(arranger)* arrange;

~ de qn/qc have s.o./sth at one's disposal; **se ~ à faire qc** get ready to do sth

dispositif *m* device

disposition *f* (*arrangement*) arrangement; *d'une loi* provision; (*humeur*) mood; (*tendance*) tendency; **être à la ~ de qn** be at s.o.'s disposal; **avoir des ~s pour qch** have an aptitude for sth

disputer match play; **~ qc à qn** compete with s.o for sth.; **se ~** quarrel, fight

disqualifier disqualify

disque *m* disk; SP discus; **~ compact** compact disc; **disquette** *f* diskette, disk; **~ de sauvegarde** backup disk

dissertation *f* ÉDU essay

dissimuler conceal, hide (*à* from)

dissiper dispel; *brouillard* disperse; *fortune* squander; **se ~ du brouillard** clear

dissoudre dissolve

dissuader: **~ qn de faire qc** dissuade s.o. from doing sth, persuade s.o. not to do sth; **dissuasion** *f* dissuasion

distance *f* distance; **prendre ses ~s avec qn** distance o.s. from s.o.; **distancer** outdistance

distiller distill; **distillerie** *f* distillery

distinct distinct; **~ de** different from; **distinctif, -ive** distinctive; **distinguer** (*percevoir*) make out; (*différen-*

cier) distinguish (*de* from); **se ~** (*être différent*) stand · out (*de* from)

distraction *f* (*passe-temps*) amusement; (*inattention*) distraction

distraire *du travail, des soucis* distract (*de* from); (*divertir*) amuse, entertain; **se ~** amuse o.s.; **distrait** absent-minded

distribuer distribute; *courrier* deliver; **distributeur** *m* distributor; **~ automatique** vending machine

dit (*surnommé*) referred to as; (*fixé*) appointed

divaguer talk nonsense

divan *m* couch

diverger diverge; *d'opinions* differ

divers (*différent*) different, varied; *au pl* (*plusieurs*) various

diversifier diversify

diversion *f* diversion

diversité *f* diversity

divertir amuse, entertain; **divertissement** *m* amusement, entertainment

divin divine; **divinité** *f* divinity

diviser divide; **se ~** be divided (*en* into); **division** *f* division

divorce *m* divorce; **demander le ~** ask for a divorce; **divorcé, ~e** *m/f* divorcee; **divorcer** get a divorce (*d'avec* from)

dix ten; **dix-huit** eighteen; **dixième** tenth; **dix-neuf** nineteen; **dix-sept** seventeen; **dizaine** *f:* **une ~ de** about ten, ten or so

D.J. *m/f* (= **disc-jockey**) DJ, deejay (= disc jockey)

docile docile

docteur *m* doctor; **doctorat** *m* doctorate, PhD

doctrine *f* doctrine

document *m* document; **documentation** *f* documentation; **documenter**: **se ~** collect information

dodu chubby

dogmatique dogmatic

doigt *m* finger; **~ de pied** toe; **croiser les ~s** keep one's fingers crossed

dollar *m* dollar

domaine *m* estate; *fig* domain

dôme *m* dome

domestique 1 *adj* domestic **2** *m* servant

domicile *m* place of residence; **domicilié: ~ à** resident at

domination *f* domination; **dominer 1** *v/t* dominate **2** *v/i* (*prédominer*) be predominant; **se ~** control o.s.

dommage *m:* (**quel**) **~!** what a pity!; **c'est ~ que** (+ *subj*) it's a pity (that); **~s et intérêts** JUR damages

dompter *animal* tame; *rebelle* subdue; **dompteur** *m* trainer

DOM-TOM *mpl* (= **départe-**ments et territoires d'outre-mer) overseas departments and territories of France

don *m* donation; (*cadeau, aptitude*) gift; **~ du ciel** godsend; **donation** *f* donation

donc *conclusion* so; **écoutez ~!** do listen!; **comment ~?** how (so)?; **allons ~!** come on!

données *fpl* data *sg* (*aussi* INFORM), information; **donner 1** *v/t* give **2** *v/i:* **~ sur la mer** look onto the sea

dont whose; **le film ~ elle parlait** the movie she was talking about; **la manière ~ elle me regardait** the way (in which) she was looking at me

doré *bijou* gilded; *couleur* golden

dorénavant from now on

dorer gild

dormeur, -euse *m/f* sleeper; **dormir** sleep

dortoir *m* dormitory

dos *m* back; **~ d'âne** *m* speed bump; *pont* hump-backed bridge

dose *f* MÉD dose; PHARM proportion; **doser** measure out

dossier *m* d'une chaise back *f*; de documents file, dossier; **~ médical** medical record(s)

douane *f* customs *pl*; **douanier, -ère 1** *adj* customs *atr* **2** *m/f* customs officer

double 1 *adj* double **2** *m*

deuxième exemplaire duplicate; *au tennis* doubles (match); **le ~** double, twice as much; **doubler 1** *v/t* double; AUTO pass, *Br* overtake; *film* dub; *vêtement* line 2 *v/i* double; **doublure** *f d'un vêtement* lining

doucement gently; *(bas)* softly; *(lentement)* slowly; **douceur** *f d'une personne* gentleness; **~s** *(jouissance)* pleasures; *(sucreries)* sweet things

douche *f* shower; **prendre une ~** shower, take a shower

doué gifted; **~ de qc** endowed with sth

douleur *f* pain

douloureux, -euse painful

doute *m* doubt; **sans ~** without doubt; **sans aucun ~** undoubtedly; **douter:** **~ de qn/qch** doubt s.o./sth; **se ~ de qc** suspect sth; **se ~ que** suspect that; **douteux, -euse** doubtful

doux, douce sweet; *temps* mild; *personne* gentle; *au toucher* soft

douzaine *f* dozen; **douze** twelve; **douzième** twelfth

dragée *f* sugared almond

draguer *rivière* dredge; F *femmes* try to pick up; **dragueur** *m* F ladies' man

dramatique dramatic; **dramatiser** dramatize; **drame** *m* drama

drap *m de lit* sheet

drapeau *m* flag

drap-housse *m* fitted sheet

dresser put up; *contrat* draw up; *animal* train; **~ contre qn** set s.o. against s.o.; **se ~** straighten up; *d'une tour* rise up; *d'un obstacle* arise

drogue *f* drug; **~ douce** soft drug; **~ récréative** recreational drug; **drogué, -e** *m/f* drug addict; **droguer** drug; **se ~** take drugs; MÉD *(traiter)* give medication to; **se ~** take drugs; MÉD *péj* pop pills; **droguerie** *f* hardware store

droit 1 *adj côté* right; *ligne* straight; *(debout)* erect; *(honnête)* upright **2** *adv tout ~* straight ahead **3** *m* right; *(taxe)* fee; JUR law; **être en ~ de faire qch** be entitled to do sth; **~s d'auteur** royalties

droite *f* right; *côté* right-hand side; **à ~** on the right(-hand side)

drôle funny; **une ~ d'idée** a funny idea

dubitatif, -ive doubtful

duc *m* duke

duchesse *f* duchess

duel *m* duel

dûment duly

dune *f* (sand) dune

Dunkerque Dunkirk

duper dupe

duplex *m* duplex

duquel → lequel

dur 1 *adj* hard; *climat* harsh;

viande tough **2** *adv travailler, frapper* hard

durable durable, lasting; *croissance, utilisation de matières premières* sustainable

durant during; *des années ~* for years

durcír 1 *v/t* harden **2** *v/i: se ~* harden

durée *f* duration; *~ de vie* life; *d'une personne* life expectancy

durement harshly; *être frappé ~ par* be hard hit by

durer last

duvet *m* down; (*sac de couchage*) sleeping bag

DVD *m* DVD (= digitally versatile disk)

dynamique 1 *adj* dynamic **2** *f* dynamics

dynamo *f* dynamo

dyslexique dyslexic

E

eau *f* water; *tomber à l'~* fall in the water; *fig* fall through; *~ courante* running water; *~ gazeuse* carbonated water, *Br* fizzy water; *~ de Javel* bleach

eau-de-vie *f* brandy

ébahi dumbfounded

ébaucher *tableau, roman* rough out; *texte* draft; *~ un sourire* smile faintly

ébéniste *f* cabinetmaker

éblouir dazzle (*aussi fig*)

éboueur *m* garbageman, *Br* dustman

éboulement *m* landslide

ébouriffé tousled; **ébouriffer** *cheveux* ruffle

ébranler shake; *s'~* move off

ébriété *f* inebriation

ébruiter *nouvelle* spread

ébullition *f* boiling point; *être en ~* be boiling

écaille *f* de coquillage, tortue shell; *de poisson* scale; *de peinture, plâtre* flake; *matière* tortoiseshell; **écailler** *poisson* scale; *huître* open; *s'~ de peinture* flake (off); *de vernis à ongles* chip

écart *m* (*intervalle*) gap; (*différence*) difference; *moral* indiscretion; *à l'~* at a distance (*de* from)

écarter *jambes* spread; *fig: idée* reject; *danger* avert; *s'~ de* (*s'éloigner*) stray from

écervelé scatterbrained

échafaudage *m* scaffolding

échancré low-cut

échange *m* exchange; *~s extérieurs* foreign trade; *en ~* in exchange (*de* for); **échanger** exchange (*contre* for); **échangeur** *m* interchange

échantillon *m* COMM sample

échappement *m* AUTO exhaust; *tuyau m d'~* tail pipe;

échapper *d'une personne* ~ **à qn** escape from s.o.; ~ **à qc** escape sth; *l'*~ **belle** have a narrow escape; **s'**~ escape

écharde *f* splinter

écharpe *f* scarf; *de maire* sash; **en** ~ MÉD in a sling

échauffer heat; **s'**~ SP warm up; ~ **les esprits** get people excited

échéance *f d'un contrat* expiration date, *Br* expiry date; *de police* maturity

échec *m* failure; **essuyer un** ~ meet with failure

échecs *mpl* chess; **jouer aux** ~ play chess

échelle *f* ladder; *d'une carte, des salaires* scale; **à l'**~ **mondiale** on a global scale

échelonner space out; *paiements* spread, stagger (**sur un an** over a year)

échevelé disheveled, *Br* dishevelled

échiner F: **s'**~ **à faire qch** go to great lengths to do sth

échiquier *m* chessboard

écho *m* echo

échotier, -ère *m/f* gossip columnist

échouer fail; (**s'**)~ *d'un bateau* run aground

éclabousser spatter

éclair *m* flash of lightning; CUIS eclair; **comme un** ~ in a flash; **éclairage** *m* lighting

éclaircie *f* clear spell; **éclaircir** lighten; *fig: mystère* clear up; **s'**~ *du ciel* clear

éclairer light; ~ **qn** light the way for s.o.; *fig* enlighten s.o.

éclat *m de verre* splinter; *de métal* gleam; *des yeux* sparkle; *de couleurs, fleurs* vividness; ~ **de rire** peal of laughter; **un** ~ **d'obus** a piece of shrapnel; **éclatant** dazzling; *couleur* vivid; *rire* loud; **éclater** *d'une bombe* blow up, explode; *d'un ballon, pneu* burst; *d'un coup de feu* ring out; *d'une guerre, d'un incendie* break out; *fig: d'un groupe, parti* break up; ~ **en sanglots** burst into tears

éclipser eclipse (*aussi fig*); **s'**~ F vanish, disappear

éclore *d'un oiseau* hatch out; *de fleurs* open

écluse *f* lock

écœurement *m* disgust; (*découragement*) discouragement; **écœurer** disgust, sicken; (*décourager*) dishearten; ~ **qn** *d'un aliment* make s.o. feel nauseous

école *f* school; ~ **maternelle** nursery school; ~ **primaire** elementary school, *Br* primary school ~ **publique** state school; **écolier** *m* schoolboy; **écolière** *f* schoolgirl

écologie *f* ecology; **écologique** ecological

économe economical, thrifty

économie *f* economy; *science*

economics *sg*; **~ souterraine** black economy; **~s** savings; **économiser** save; **~ sur qc** save on sth; **économiseur** *m* **d'écran** INFORM screen saver

écorce *f d'un arbre* bark; *d'un fruit* rind

écorcher *animal skin*; (*égratigner*) scrape; *fig: nom, mot* murder

écossais, ~e Scottish; **Écossais, ~e** *m/f* Scot; **Écosse** *f*: **l'~** Scotland

écoulement *m* flow; COMM sale; **écouler** COMM sell; **s'~** flow; *du temps* pass; COMM sell

écourter shorten; *vacances* cut short

écoute *f*: **être à l'~** be always listening out; **aux heures de grande ~** RAD at peak listening times; TV at peak viewing times; **écouter 1** *v/t* listen to **2** *v/i* listen; **écouteur** *m* TÉL receiver; **~s** RAD headphones

écran *m* screen; **porter à l'~** TV adapt for television; **~ tactile** touch screen; **~ total** sunblock

écrasant overwhelming; **écraser** crush; *cigarette* stub out; (*renverser*) run over; **s'~ au sol** *d'un avion* crash

écrémé: **lait** *m* **~** skimmed milk

écrevisse *f* crayfish

écrier: **s'~** cry out

écrire write; **comment est-ce que ça s'écrit?** how do you spell it?; **écrit** *m* document; **l'~ examen** the written exam; **par ~** in writing; **écriteau** *m* notice; **écriture** *f* writing; COMM entry; **les (Saintes) Écritures** Holy Scripture

écrivain *m* writer

écrou *m* nut

écrouler: **s'~** collapse

écru *couleur* natural

écueil *m* reef; *fig* pitfall

éculé *chaussure* worn-out; *fig* hackneyed

écume *f* foam

écureuil *m* squirrel

écurie *f* stable

édenté toothless

édifice *m* building; **édifier** erect; *fig* build up

éditer *livre* publish; *texte* edit; **éditeur, -trice** *m/f* publisher; (*commentateur*) editor; **édition** *f* publishing; *action de commenter* editing; (*tirage*) edition; **maison** *f* **d'~** publishing house; **éditorial** *m* editorial

édredon *m* eiderdown

éducatif, -ive educational; **education** *f* education; (*culture*) upbringing

éduquer educate; (*élever*) bring up

effacer erase; **s'~** *d'une inscription* wear away; *d'une personne* fade into the background

effarement *m* fear; **effarer**

frighten

effectif, -ive 1 adj effective **2** m manpower, personnel; **effectivement** true enough

effectuer carry out

efféminé péj effeminate

effervescent effervescent; fig: foule excited

effet m effect; COMM bill; **en ~** sure enough; **faire de l'~** have an effect; **~s** (personal) effects

efficace remède effective; personne efficient; **efficacité** f effectiveness; **d'une personne** efficiency

effleurer brush against; (aborder) touch on

effondrement m collapse; **effondrer: s'~** collapse

efforcer: s'~ de faire qch try very hard to do sth

effort m effort; **faire un ~** make an effort, try a bit harder

effraction f JUR breaking and entering

effrayant frightening; **effrayer** frighten; **s'~** be frightened (**de qch**)

effroi m fear

effronterie f impertinence, effrontery

effroyable terrible, dreadful

égal 1 adj equal; surface even; vitesse steady; **ça lui est ~** it's all the same to him **2** m equal; **sans ~** unequaled; Br unequalled; **également** (pareillement) equally; (aus-

si) as well, too; **égaler** equal; **égaliser 1** v/t haies, cheveux even up; sol level **2** v/i SP tie the game, Br equalize; **égalité** f equality; en tennis deuce; **être à ~** be level; en tennis be at deuce

égard m: **à cet ~** in that respect; **à l'~ de qn** to(ward) s.o.; **par ~ pour** out of consideration for; **~s** respect

égarer personne lead astray; chose lose; **s'~** get lost; du sujet stray from the point

égayer cheer up

église f church

égocentrique egocentric

égoïsme m selfishness, egoism; **égoïste 1** adj selfish **2** m/f egoist

égorger: ~ qn cut s.o.'s throat

égout m sewer

égoutter drain

égratignure f scratch

Égypte f: **l'~** Egypt; **égyptien, ~ne** Egyptian; **Égyptien, ~ne** m/f Egyptian

éjecter eject; F personne kick out

élaborer projet draw up

élan m momentum; SP run-up; **de tendresse** upsurge; de générosité fit; (vivacité) enthusiasm

élancer v/i: **ma jambe m'élance** I've got shooting pains in my leg; **s'~** dash; SP take a run-up

élargir widen, broaden; vêtement let out; débat widen

élastique 1 *adj* elastic **2** *m* elastic; *de bureau* rubber band

électeur, -trice *m/f* voter; **élection** *f* election; **électorat** *m* droit franchise; *personnes* electorate

électricien, ~ne *m/f* electrician; **électricité** *f* electricity; **~ statique** static (electricity); **électrique** electric; **électriser** electrify

électrocuter electrocute

électroménager: appareils *mpl* **~s** household appliances

électronique 1 *adj* electronic; **livre ~** e-book, electronic book **2** *f* electronics

élégance *f* elegance; **élégant** elegant

élément *m* element; (*composante*) component; *d'un puzzle* piece; **~s** (*rudiments*) rudiments; **élémentaire** elementary

éléphant *m* elephant

élevage *m* breeding; **~ (du bétail)** cattle farming

élève *m/f* pupil

élevé high; *esprit* noble; *style* elevated; **bien/mal ~** well/badly brought up; **élever** raise; *prix, température* raise, increase; *statue* put up, erect; *enfants* bring up, raise; *animaux* breed; **s'~** rise; *d'une tour* rise up; *d'un cri* go up; **s'~ contre** rise up against; **s'~ à** amount

to; **éleveur, -euse** *m/f* breeder

élimination *f* elimination; *des déchets* disposal; **éliminatoire** *f* qualifying round; **éliminer** eliminate; *difficultés* get rid of

élire elect

elle *f* she; *après prép* her; *chose* it

elle-même herself; *chose* itself

elles *fpl* they; *après prép* them

elles-mêmes themselves

éloigné remote

éloigner move away; *soupçon* remove; **s'~** move away (**de** from); **s'~ de qn** distance o.s. from s.o.

éloquence *f* eloquence; **éloquent** eloquent

élu 1 *adj*: **le président ~** the President elect **2** *m/f* POL (elected) representative

élucider *mystère* clear up; *question* clarify

émacié emaciated

e-mail *m* e-mail

émanciper emancipate; **s'~** become emancipated

emballage *m* packaging; **emballer** *package; fig* F thrill; **s'~** *d'un moteur* race; *fig* F get excited; **emballé sous vide** vacuum packed

embargo *m* embargo

embarquer 1 *v/t* load **2** *v/i ou* **s'~** embark; **s'~ dans** F get involved in

embarras 92

embarras *m* difficulty; (*gêne*) embarrassment; *être dans l'~* be in an embarrassing position; *sans argent* be short of money; **embarrassant** embarrassing; (*encombrant*) cumbersome; **embarrasser** embarrass; (*encombrer*) *escaliers* clutter up

embaucher take on, hire

embellir 1 *v/t* make more attractive; *fig* embellish **2** *v/i* become more attractive

embêtant F annoying; **embêter** F (*ennuyer*) bore; (*contrarier*) annoy; *s'~* be bored

emblème *m* emblem

emboîter insert; *le pas à qn* fall into step with s.o. (*aussi fig*); *s'~* fit together

embolie *f* embolism

embonpoint *m* stoutness

embouchure *f* GÉOGR mouth; MUS mouthpiece

embouteillage *m* traffic jam

emboutir crash into

embranchement *m* branch; (*carrefour*) intersection, *Br* junction

embrasser kiss; *période, thème* take in, embrace; *métier* take up; *~ du regard* take in at a glance

embrayage *m* AUTO clutch; *action* letting in the clutch

embrouiller muddle; *s'~* get muddled

embryon *m* embryo

éméché F tipsy

émeraude *f & adj* emerald

émerger emerge

émerveiller amaze; *s'~* be amazed (*de* by)

émetteur *m* RAD, TV transmitter

émettre *radiations etc* give off, emit; RAD, TV broadcast, transmit; *opinion* voice; *action, nouveau billet* issue; *emprunt* float

émeute *f* riot

émietter crumble

émigration *f* emigration; **émigré, ~e** *m/f* emigré; **émigrer** emigrate

émincer cut into thin slices

éminent eminent

émission *f* emission; RAD, TV program, *Br* programme; COMM, FIN issue

emmagasiner store

emmêler *fils* tangle; *fig* muddle

emménager: *~ dans* move into

emmener take

emmerder F: *~ qn* get on s.o.'s nerves; *s'~* be bored rigid

emmitoufler wrap up; *s'~* wrap up

émotion *f* emotion; F (*frayeur*) fright

émouvant moving; **émouvoir** (*toucher*) move; *s'~* be moved

emparer: *s'~ de* seize; *clés, héritage* grab; *des doutes, de la peur* overcome

empâter: *s'~* thicken

empêchement m: *j'ai eu un ~* something has come up; **empêcher** prevent; ~ *qn de faire qc* prevent ou stop s.o. doing sth; *(il) n'empêche que* nevertheless

empereur m emperor

empiéter: ~ *sur* encroach on

empiffrer F: *s'~* stuff o.s.

empiler pile (up)

empire m empire; *fig (maîtrise)* control

empirer get worse, deteriorate

emplacement m site

emplette f purchase; *faire des ~s* go shopping

emplir fill; *s'~* fill *(de* with)

emploi m *(utilisation)* use; ÉCON employment; ~ *du temps* schedule, *Br* timetable; *chercher un ~* be looking for work ou for a job

employé, ~e m/f employee; **employer** use; *personnel* employ; *s'~ à faire qc* strive to do sth; **employeur, -euse** m/f employer

empocher pocket

empoigner grab, seize

empoisonner poison

emporter take; *prisonnier* take away; *(entraîner, arracher)* carry away; *du courant* sweep away; *d'une maladie* carry off; *l'~ sur qn/qc* get the better of s.o./sth; *s'~* fly into a rage

empreinte f impression; *fig* stamp; ~ *génétique* genetic fingerprint

empresser: *s'~ de faire qc* rush to do sth; *s'~ auprès de qn* be attentive to s.o.

emprise f hold

emprisonnement m imprisonment; **emprisonner** imprison

emprunt m loan; **emprunter** borrow *(à* from); *chemin, escalier* take

ému moved, touched

en¹ *prép* in; *direction* to; *agir ~ ami* act as a friend; ~ *voiture* by car; ~ *or* of gold; *en même temps* while, when; *mode* by

en² *pron*: *qu'~ pensez-vous?* what do you think about it?; *il y ~ a deux* there are two (of them); *j'~ ai* I have some; *j'~ ai cinq* I have five; *je n'~ ai pas* I don't have any; *il ~ est mort* he died of it

encadrer *tableau* frame; *encadré de deux gendarmes* fig flanked by gendarmes

encaisser COMM take; *chèque* cash; *fig* take

en-cas m CUIS snack

encastrer build in

enceinte¹ *adj* pregnant

enceinte² f enclosure; ~ *(acoustique)* speaker

encens m incense

encercler encircle

enchaîner chain up; *fig: pensées, faits* link (up)

enchanté enchanted; ~! how do you do?; **enchanter** *(ra-*

vir) delight; (*ensorceler*) enchant

enchère *f* bid; *vente f aux ~s* auction

enchevêtrer tangle; *fig*: *situation confuse*; *s'~ de fils* get tangled up; *d'une situation* get muddled

enclin: *être ~ à faire qch* be inclined to do sth

encoche *f* notch

encolure *f* neck; *tour de cou* neck (size)

encombrant cumbersome; *être ~ d'une personne* be in the way; **encombrer** *maison* clutter up; *rue, passage* block; *s'~ de* load o.s. down with

encore *de nouveau* again; (*toujours*) still; *pas ~* not yet; *~ une bière?* another beer?; *~ plus rapide* even faster

encourageant encouraging; **encourager** encourage; *projet, entreprise* foster

encrasser dirty; *s'~* get dirty

encre *f* ink

encyclopédie *f* encyclopedia

endetter: *s'~* get into debt

endeuillé bereaved

endive *f* chicory

endolori painful

endommager damage

endormi asleep; *fig* sleepy; **endormir** send to sleep; *douleur* dull; *s'~* fall asleep

endosser *vêtement* put on; *responsabilité* shoulder; *chè-*

que endorse

endroit *m* (*lieu*) place; *d'une étoffe* right side

enduire *de* cover with; **enduit** *m de peinture* coat

endurance *f* endurance

endurcir harden

endurer endure

énergie *f* energy; **énergique** energetic; *protestation* strenuous

énervant irritating; **énerver**: *~ qn* (*agacer*) get on s.o.'s nerves; (*agiter*) make s.o. edgy; *s'~* get excited

enfance *f* childhood

enfant *m ou f* child

enfer *m* hell (*aussi fig*)

enfermer shut *ou* lock up; *champ* enclose; *s'~* shut o.s. up

enfiler *aiguille* thread; *perles* string; *vêtement* slip on; *rue* turn into

enfin (*finalement*) at last; (*en dernier lieu*) lastly, last; (*bref*) in a word

enflammer set light to; *allumette* strike; MÉD inflame; *fig*: *imagination* fire; *s'~* catch; MÉD become inflamed; *fig*: *de l'imagination* take flight

enfler swell; **enflure** *f* swelling

enfoncer 1 *v/t clou, pieu* drive in; *couteau* thrust, plunge (*dans* into); *porte* break down **2** *v/i dans sable etc* sink (*dans* into); *s'~* sink

enfreindre infringe

enfuir: *s'~* run away

engagement *m* (*obligation*) commitment; *personnel* recruitment; THÉÂT booking; (*mise en gage*) pawning

engager (*lier*) commit (*à* to); *personnel* hire; TECH (*faire entrer*) insert; *discussion* begin; (*entraîner*) involve (*dans* in); THÉÂT book; (*mettre en gage*) pawn; *s'~* (*se lier*) commit o.s. (*à faire qc* to doing sth); (*commencer*) begin; MIL enlist

engelure *f* chillblain

engendrer *fig* engender

engin *m* machine; MIL missile; F *péj* thing

englober include

engloutir (*dévorer*) devour, wolf down; *fig* engulf

engouffrer devour, wolf down; *s'~ dans* de l'eau pour in; *fig*: *dans un bâtiment* rush into; *dans une foule* be swallowed up by

engourdir numb; *s'~* go numb

engraisser fatten

engrenage *m* gear

engueuler F bawl out; *s'~* have an argument

énigme *f* enigma; (*devinette*) riddle

enivrer intoxicate; *fig* exhilarate

enjamber step across; *d'un pont* span

enjeu *m* stake

enjoliveur *m* AUTO wheel trim, hub cap

enjoué cheerful, good humored, *Br* good-humoured

enlèvement *m* (*rapt*) abduction, kidnap; **enlever** take away, remove; *vêtement* take off, remove; (*kidnapper*) abduct, kidnap; *~ qc à qn* take sth away from s.o.

enneigé *route* blocked by snow; *sommet* snow-capped

ennemi, *~e* **1** *m/f* enemy **2** *adj* enemy *atr*

ennui *m* boredom; *~s* problems; **ennuyer** (*contrarier*, *agacer*) annoy; (*lasser*) bore; *s'~* be bored; **ennuyeux**, *-euse* (*contrariant*) annoying; (*lassant*) boring

énoncé *m* statement; *d'une question* wording; **énoncer** state; *~ des vérités* state the obvious

énorme enormous; **énormément** enormously; *~ de* F an enormous amount of

énormité *f* enormity

enquête *f* inquiry; *policière aussi* investigation; (*sondage d'opinion*) survey; **enquêter**: *~ sur* investigate

enraciné deep-rooted

enregistrement *m* registration; *de disques* recording; AVIAT check-in; **enregistrer** register; *disques* record; *bagages* check in

enrhumer: *s'~* catch (a) cold

enrichir enrich; *s'~* get richer

enrouer : *s'~* get hoarse

enrouler *tapis* roll up; *~ autour de qch* wind sth around sth

enseignant, *~e* m/f teacher

enseignement m education; *d'un sujet* teaching; **enseigner** teach (*qc à qn* s.o. sth)

ensemble 1 *adv* (*simultanément*) together **2** m (*totalité*) whole; (*groupe*) group, set; MUS, *vêtement* ensemble; MATH set; *dans l'~* on the whole

ensevelir bury

ensoleillé sunny

ensommeillé sleepy

ensuite then; (*plus tard*) after

entacher smear

entaille f cut; (*encoche*) notch; **entailler** notch; *s'~ la main* cut one's hand

entamer start; *économies* make

entasser *choses* pile up; *personnes* cram

entendre hear; (*comprendre*) understand; (*vouloir dire*) mean; *~ faire qc* intend to do sth; *~ dire que* hear that; *s'~* (*avec qn*) get on (with s.o.); (*se mettre d'accord*) come to an agreement (with s.o.); *entendu regard* knowing; *bien ~* of course; **entente** f agreement

enterrement m burial; *cérémonie* funeral; **enterrer** bury

en-tête m heading; INFORM

header; COMM letterhead; *d'un journal* headline

entêtement m stubbornness; **entêter**: *s'~* persist (*dans* in; *à faire qc* in doing sth)

enthousiasme m enthusiasm; **enthousiasmer**: *s'~ pour* be enthusiastic about

enticher: *s'~ de personne* become infatuated with; *activité* develop a craze for

entier, *-ère* whole, entire; (*intégral*) intact; *confiance*, *satisfaction* full

entonnoir m funnel

entorse f MÉD sprain

entortiller (*envelopper*) wrap

entourage m entourage; (*bordure*) surround; **entourer**: *~ de* surround with; *s'~ de* surround o.s. with

entraide f mutual assistance; **entraider**: *s'~* help each other

entrailles fpl intestines

entrain m liveliness; **entraînement** m SP training; TECH drive; **entraîner** (*charrier, emporter*) sweep along; SP train; *fig* result in; *frais* entail; *personne* drag; TECH drive; *s'~* train

entrave f hindrance; **entraver** hinder

entre between; *le meilleur d'~ nous* the best of us; *~ autres* among other things

entrebâiller half open

entrechoquer: *s'~* knock against one another

entrecôte f rib steak

entrée f entrance, way in; *accès au théâtre, cinéma* admission; *(billet)* ticket; *(vestibule)* entry(way); CUIS starter; INFORM *touche* enter (key); *de données* input; ~ **interdite** no admittance

entrejambe m crotch

entrelacer interlace

entremets m CUIS dessert

entremise f: **par l'~ de** through (the good offices of)

entreposer store; **entrepôt** m warehouse

entreprenant enterprising; **entreprendre** undertake; **entrepreneur, -euse** m/f entrepreneur; **entreprise** f enterprise; *(firme)* company, business

entrer 1 v/i enter/go in, enter; ~ **dans** come/go into, enter; *voiture* get into; *pays* enter; *catégorie* fall into; *l'armée, le parti etc* join **2** v/t bring in; INFORM input, enter

entre-temps in the meantime

entretenir *maison, machine etc* maintain; *famille* keep, support; *amitié* keep up; **s'~ de qc** talk to each other about sth

entretien m maintenance, upkeep; *(conversation)* conversation

entrevoir glimpse; *fig* foresee

entrevue f interview

entrouvrir half open

énumérer list, enumerate

envahir invade; *d'un sentiment* overwhelm; **envahissant** *personne* intrusive; *sentiments* overwhelming

enveloppe f *d'une lettre* envelope; **envelopper** wrap; **enveloppé de** *brume, mystère* enveloped in

envenimer poison *(aussi fig)*

envergure f *d'un oiseau, avion* wingspan; *fig* scope; *d'une personne* caliber, Br calibre

envers 1 *prép* toward, Br towards **2** m *d'une feuille* reverse; *d'une étoffe:* wrong side; **à l'~** pull inside out; *(en désordre)* upside down

envie f *(convoitise)* envy; *(désir)* desire *(de* for); **avoir ~ de** *(faire)* **qc** want (to do) sth; **envier** envy; ~ **qc à qn** envy s.o. sth

environ 1 *adv* about **2** *mpl:* ~**s** surrounding area; **dans les** ~**s** in the vicinity

environnement m environment

envisager *(considérer)* think about; *(imaginer)* envisage

envoi m shipment; *d'un fax* sending

envoler: **s'~** fly away; *d'un avion* take off; *fig: du temps* fly

envoyé m envoy; *d'un journal* correspondent; **envoyer** send; *gifle* give

éolienne f wind turbine
épais, **~se** thick; *foule* dense; **épaisseur** f thickness; **épaissir** thicken
épancher: **s'~** pour out one's heart (**auprès de** to)
épanouir: **s'~** blossom
épargne f saving; **~s** (*économies*) savings; **épargner 1** *v/t* save; *personne* spare; **~ qc à qn** spare s.o. sth **2** *v/i* save
éparpiller scatter
épars sparse
épatant F great, terrific; **épater** astonish
épaule f shoulder
épave f wreck (*aussi fig*)
épée f sword
épeler spell
éperdu *besoin* desperate; **~ de** beside o.s. with
épi m ear
épice f spice; **épicer** spice; **épicerie** f grocery store, *Br* grocer's; **épicier**, **-ère** *m/f* grocer
épidémie f epidemic
épier spy on; *occasion* watch for
épilepsie f epilepsy; **crise d'~** epileptic fit
épiler remove the hair from
épinards *mpl* spinach
épine f *d'une rose* thorn; *d'un hérisson* spine, prickle; **épineux**, **-euse** *problème* thorny
épingle f pin; **~ de sûreté** safety pin; **tiré à quatre ~s**

fig well turned-out
Épiphanie f Epiphany
épisode m episode
éploré tearful
éplucher peel; *fig* scrutinize; **épluchures** *fpl* peelings
éponge f sponge; **éponger** sponge down; *flaque* sponge up; *déficit* mop up
époque f age, epoch; **meubles** *mpl* **d'~** period *ou* antique furniture
époumoner: **s'~** F shout o.s. hoarse
épouse f wife; **épouser** marry; *principe etc* espouse
épousseter dust
époustouflant F breathtaking
épouvantable dreadful
épouvantail m scarecrow
épouvanter horrify; *fig* terrify
époux m husband; **les ~** the married couple
éprendre: **s'~ de** fall in love with
épreuve f trial; *SP* event; *imprimerie* proof; *photographie* print; **à toute ~** confiance *etc* never-failing; **à l'~ du feu** fireproof
éprouver test, try out; (*ressentir*) experience
épuisé exhausted; *livre* out of print; **épuiser** exhaust; **~ les ressources** be a drain on resources; **s'~** tire o.s. out (**à faire qch** doing sth); *d'une source* dry up

épurer purify

équateur *m* equator

équilibre *m* balance, equilibrium; **équilibrer** balance

équipage *m* crew

équipe *f* team; *d'ouvriers* gang; **~ de nuit** night shift; **~ de secours** rescue party; **équipement** *m* equipment; **équiper** equip (*de* with)

équitable just, equitable

équitation *f* riding

équivalent 1 *adj* equivalent (*à* to) **2** *m* equivalent

équivoque 1 *adj* equivocal, ambiguous **2** *f* ambiguity; (*malentendu*) misunderstanding

érable *m* BOT maple

érafler scratch; **éraflure** *f* scratch

ère *f* era

érection *f* erection

éreinter exhaust; **s'~** exhaust o.s. (*à faire qch* doing sth)

ériger erect; **s'~ en** set o.s. up as

érosion *f* erosion

érotisme *m* eroticism

errer roam; *des pensées* stray

erreur *f* mistake, error; **~ de calcul** miscalculation

érudit erudite; **érudition** *f* erudition

éruption *f* eruption; MÉD rash

escabeau *m* (*tabouret*) stool; (*marchepied*) stepladder

escalade *f* climbing; **~ de violence etc** escalation in; **escalader** climb

escalator *m* escalator

escale *f* stopover; **faire ~ à** MAR call at; AVIAT stop over in

escalier *m* stairs *pl*, staircase; **dans l'~** on the stairs; **~ de secours** fire escape

escalope *f* escalope

escamoter (*dérober*) make disappear; *antenne* retract; *fig: difficulté* get around

escapade *f: faire une ~** get away from it all

escargot *m* snail

escarpement *m* slope

esclaffer: s'~ guffaw, laugh out loud

esclavage *m* slavery; **esclave** *m/f* slave

escompte *m* discount; **escompter** discount; *fig* expect

escorter escort

escrime *f* fencing; **escrimer: s'~** fight, struggle (*à* to)

escroc *m* crook

espace *m* space; **espacer** space out; **s'~** become more and more infrequent

Espagne *f* Spain; **espagnol, ~e 1** *adj* Spanish **2** *m langue* Spanish; **Espagnol, ~e** *m/f* Spaniard

espèce *f* kind, sort (*de* of); BIOL species; **~ d'abruti!** *péj* idiot!; **en ~s** COMM cash

espérer 1 *v/t* hope for; **~ que** hope that; **~ faire qc** hope to do sth **2** *v/i* hope; **~ en** trust in

espiègle mischievous

espion, ~e *m/f* spy; **espionnage** *m* espionage, spying; **espionner** spy on

espoir *m* hope

esprit *m* spirit; (*intellect*) mind; (*humour*) wit

esquisse *f* sketch; *fig: d'un roman* outline; **esquisser** sketch; *fig: projet* outline

esquiver dodge; **s'~** slip away

essai *m* (*test*) test, trial; (*tentative*) attempt, try; *en rugby* try; *en littérature* essay; **à l'~** on trial

essaim *m* swarm

essayage *m*: **cabine** *f* d'**~** changing cubicle; **essayer** try; (*mettre à l'épreuve, évaluer*) test; *vêtement* try on; **de faire qc** try to do sth; **s'~ à qc** try one's hand at sth

essence *f* essence; *carburant* gas, *Br* petrol; BOT species

essentiel, ~le **1** *adj* essential **2** *m*: **l'~** the main thing; *de sa vie* the main part

essieu *m* axle

essor *m fig* expansion

essorer wring out; *d'une machine à laver* spin

essoufflé out of breath

essuie-glace *m* (windshield) wiper, *Br* (windscreen) wiper; **essuie-mains** *m* handtowel; **essuyer** wipe; *fig* suffer

est **1** *m* east **à l'~ de** (to the) east of **2** *adj* east, eastern

est-ce que: **~ c'est vrai?** is it true?; **est-ce qu'ils se por-**

tent bien? are they well?

esthéticienne *f* beautician

esthétique esthetic, *Br* aesthetic

estimatif, -ive estimated; **devis** *m* **~** estimate; **estimation** *f* estimation; *des coûts* estimate

estime *f* esteem; **estimer** *valeur* estimate; (*respecter*) have esteem for; (*croire*) feel, think; **s'~ heureux** consider o.s. lucky

estival summer *atr*

estomac *m* stomach

Estonie *f* Estonia

estrade *f* podium

estropier cripple

estuaire *m* estuary

et and; **~ ... ~ ...** both ... and

étable *f* cowshed

établi *m* workbench

établir *entreprise* establish, set up; *, contact, ordre* establish; *salaires, prix* set, fix; *facture, liste* draw up; *record* set; *culpabilité* establish, prove; *raisonnement, réputation* base (*sur* on); **s'~** (*s'installer*) settle; **établissement** *m* establishment; *de salaires, prix* setting; *d'une facture, liste* drawing up; *d'un record* setting; *d'une loi, d'un impôt* introduction

étage *m* floor, story, *Br* storey; *d'une fusée* stage

étagère *f meuble* bookcase,

shelves *pl*; *planche* shelf

étain *m* pewter

étalage *m* display; **faire ~ de** *qch* show sth off; **étaler** *carte* spread out; *peinture, paiements* spread (**sur** over); *vacances* stagger; *marchandises* display; *fig* (*exhiber*) show off; **s'~ de** *peinture* spread; *de paiements* be spread out (**sur** over); (*se vautrer*) sprawl; *par terre* fall flat

étanche watertight; **étancher** make watertight

étang *m* pond

étape *f lieu* stopover, stopping place; *d'un parcours* stage, leg; *fig* stage

état *m* state; (*liste*) statement, list; **en tout ~ de cause** in any case, anyway; **hors d'~** out of order

États-Unis *mpl*: **les ~** the United States

été *m* summer

éteindre *incendie, cigarette* put out; *électricité, radio, chauffage* turn off; **s'~ de** *feu, lumière* go out; *de télé etc* go off; *euph* (*mourir*) pass away

étendre *malade, enfant* lay (down); *beurre, enduit* spread; *peinture* apply; *bras* stretch out; *linge* hang up; *vin* dilute; *sauce* thin; *influence* extend; **s'~** extend, stretch (**jusqu'à** as far as, to); *d'une personne* lie

down; *d'un incendie, d'une maladie* spread; *d'un tissu* stretch; **étendue** *f* extent; *d'eau* expanse; *de connaissances, d'une catastrophe* extent

éternel, ~le eternal; **éternité** *f* eternity

éternuer sneeze

éthique 1 *adj* ethical **2** *f* ethics

étinceler sparkle; **étincelle** *f* spark

étiqueter label (*aussi fig*)

étiquette *f* label; (*protocole*) etiquette

étirer: **s'~** stretch

étoffe *f* material; **étoffer** *fig* flesh out

étoile *f* star (*aussi fig*); **~ filante** falling star, *Br* shooting star; **~ de mer** starfish

étonnement *m* astonishment, surprise; **étonner** astonish, surprise; **s'~ de** be astonished *ou* surprised at; **s'~ que** (+ *subj*) be suprised that

étouffant stifling, suffocating; **étouffée** *CUIS*: **à l'~** braised; **étouffer** suffocate; *avec un oreiller* smother, suffocate; *fig*: *bruit* quash; *révolte* put down, suppress; *cri* smother; *scandale* hush up

étourderie *f* foolishness; *action* foolish thing to do

étourdi foolish, thoughtless; **étourdir** daze; **~ qn** *d'alcool, de succès* go to s.o.'s head;

étourdissement *m* (*vertige*) dizziness, giddiness

étrange strange

étranger, **-ère 1** *adj* strange; *de l'étranger* foreign **2** *m/f* stranger; *de l'étranger* foreigner **3** *m*: *à l'~* abroad; *investissement* foreign, outward

étrangler strangle; *fig*: *critique, liberté* stifle

être 1 *v/i* be; *nous sommes lundi* it's Monday; *nous avons été éliminé* we were eliminated; *~ à qn appartenir à* belong to s.o. **2** *v/aux* have; *elle n'est pas encore arrivée* she hasn't arrived yet; *elle est arrivée hier* she arrived yesterday **3** *m* being; *personne* person

étreindre grasp; *ami* embrace, hug; *de sentiments* grip; **étreinte** *f* hug, embrace; *de la main* grip

étrenner use for the first time

étrennes *fpl* New Year's gift

étroit narrow; *tricot* tight, small; *amitié* close; *être ~ d'esprit* be narrow-minded

étroitesse *f* narrowness

étude *f* study; *salle à l'école* study room; *de notaire* office; *activité* practice; *faire des ~s* study; *~ de marché* market research; **étudiant**, *~e m/f* student; **étudier** study

étui *m* case

étuvée *CUIS*: *à l'~* braised

euphorique euphoric

euro *m* euro

Europe *f*: *l'~* Europe; **européen**, *~ne* European; **Européen**, *~ne m/f* European

eux *mpl* they; *après prép* them

eux-mêmes *mpl* themselves

évacuation *f* evacuation

évacuer evacuate; *s'~* escape

évadé *m* escaped prisoner, escapee; *s'évader* *s'~* escape

évaluer (*estimer*) evaluate; *tableau, meuble* value; *coût, nombre* estimate

évanouir: *s'~* faint; *fig* vanish, disappear

évaporer: *s'~* evaporate

évasif, **-ive** evasive; **évasion** *f* escape

éveil *m* awakening; *en ~* alert; **éveiller** wake up; *fig* arouse; *s'~* wake up; *fig* be aroused

événement *m* event

éventail *m* fan; *fig*: *de marchandises* range

éventé *boisson* flat; **éventer** fan; *fig*: *secret* reveal

éventualité *f* eventuality, possibility; **éventuel**, *~le* possible

évêque *m* bishop

évertuer: *s'~ à faire qc* try one's hardest to do sth

évident obvious

évier *m* sink

éviter avoid; *~ qc à qn* spare s.o. sth; *~ de faire qc* avoid doing sth

évoluer develop, evolve; **évolution** *f* development; *BIOL* evolution

évoquer *esprits* conjure up; **~ un problème** bring up a problem

exact *nombre, poids* exact, precise; *reportage* accurate; *calcul, date, solution* right, correct; *personne* punctual; **exactitude** *f* accuracy; *(ponctualité)* punctuality

ex æquo: *être* ~ tie, draw

exagération *f* exaggeration; **exagérer** exaggerate

exalter excite; *(vanter)* exalt

examen *m* exam; MÉD examination; **passer un** ~ take an exam; **être reçu à un** ~ pass an exam; **examiner** examine

exaspérer exasperate

excédent *m* excess; *budgétaire, de trésorerie* surplus; **~ de bagages** excess baggage; **excéder** exceed; *(énerver)* irritate

excellence *f* excellence; **Ex-cellence** Excellency; **excellent** excellent; **exceller** *(dans* en; *en* in, at; **à faire qch** at doing sth)

excepté 1 *adj:* **la Chine ~e** except for China **2** *prép* except; **~ que** except for the fact that; **~ si** unless, except if; **excepter** exclude, except; **exception** *f* exception; **à l'~ de** with the exception of; **exceptionnel, ~le** exceptional

excès *m* excess; **à l'~** to excess, excessively; **~ de vitesse** speeding; **excessif, -ive**

excessive

excitation *f* excitement; *(provocation)* incitement (**à** to); *sexuelle* arousal; **exciter** excite; *(provoquer)* incite (**à** to); *sexuellement* arouse; *appétit* whet; *imagination* stir

exclamation *f* exclamation; **exclamer: s'~** exclaim

exclure exclude

exclusion *f* expulsion; **à l'~ de** to the exclusion of; *(à l'exception de)* with the exception of

exclusivité *f* COMM exclusivity, sole rights *pl*; **en ~** exclusively

excursion *f* trip, excursion

excuse *f* excuse; **~s** apology; **excuser** excuse; **s'~** apologize (**de** for); **excusez-moi** excuse me

exécuter *ordre, projet* carry out; MUS perform; *loi, jugement* enforce; *condamné* execute; **exécution** *f* *d'un ordre, projet* carrying out; MUS performance; *d'une loi, un jugement* enforcement; *d'un condamné* execution

exemplaire 1 *adj* exemplary **2** *m* copy; *(échantillon)* sample; **en deux ~s** in duplicate

exemple *m* example; **par ~** for example; **donner l'~** set a good example

exempt exempt (**de** from); *souci* free (**de** from); **exempter** exempt (**de** from);

exemption f exemption

exercer corps exercise; influence exert, use; pouvoir use; profession practice, Br practise; mémoire train; MIL drill; **s'~** (s'entraîner) practice, Br practise; **exercice** m exercise (aussi ÉDU); d'une profession practice; COMM fiscal year, Br financial year; MIL drill

exhiber exhibit; document produce; **s'~** make an exhibition of o.s.; **exhibitionniste** m exhibitionist

exigeant demanding; **exigence** f demand; **exiger** demand

exigu, **~ë** tiny

exil m exile; **exilé**, **~e** m/f exile; **exiler** exile; **s'~** go into exile

existence f existence; **exister** exist

exonérer exempt

exorbitant exorbitant

exotique exotic

expansion f expansion

expatrier argent move abroad ou out of the country; **s'~** settle abroad

expédier send; COMM ship, send; travail do quickly

expéditeur, **-trice** m/f sender; COMM shipper, sender; **expédition** f sending; COMM shipment; (voyage) expedition

expérience f experience; scientifique experiment

expérimenté experienced;

expérimenter (tester) test

expert, **~e** adj & m/f expert; **expertise** f (estimation) valuation; JUR expert testimony

expier expiate

expiration f d'un délai expiration, Br expiry; de souffle exhalation; **expirer** d'un contrat, délai expire; (respirer) exhale; (mourir) die, expire fml

explication f explanation; **expliquer** explain; **s'~** explain o.s.; **s'~ avec qn** talk things over with s.o.

exploit m sportif, médical feat; amoureux exploit

exploitant, **~e** m/f agricole farmer

exploitation f d'une ferme, ligne aérienne running; du sol farming; de richesses naturelles péj: des ouvriers exploitation; (entreprise) operation

exploiter ferme, ligne aérienne run; sol farm; richesses naturelles exploit (aussi péj)

explorateur, **-trice** m/f explorer; **explorer** explore

exploser explode (aussi fig); **~ de rire** F crack up F; **explosif**, **-ive** adj & m explosive; **explosion** f explosion (aussi fig)

exportateur, **-trice** **1** adj exporting **2** m exporter; **exportation** f export; **exporter** export

exposé *m* account, report; ÉDU presentation; **exposer** *art, marchandise* exhibit, show; *problème, programme* explain; *à l'air, à la chaleur* expose (*aussi* PHOT); **exposition** *f d'art, de marchandise* exhibition; *d'un problème* explanation; *au soleil* exposure (*aussi* PHOT)

exprès¹ *adv* (*intentionnellement*) deliberately, on purpose; (*spécialement*) expressly

exprès², **-esse 1** *adj* express **2** *adj inv* **lettre** *f* **exprès** express letter

express 1 *adj inv* express **2** *m* train express; *café* espresso

expressément expressly

expression *f* expression

exprimer express; **s'~** express o.s.

expulser expel; *d'un pays* deport; **expulsion** *f* expulsion; *d'un pays* deportation

exquis exquisite

extase *f* ecstasy

extension *f des bras, jambes* stretching; (*prolongement*) extension; *d'une épidémie* spread; INFORM expansion

exténuer exhaust

extérieur 1 *adj* external; *mur aussi* outside **2** *m* (*partie externe*) outside, exterior; **à l'~ de** outside; **extérioriser** express, let out; **s'~** *d'un senti-* ment find expression; *d'une personne* express one's emotions

exterminer exterminate

externaliser COM outsource

externe external

extincteur *m* extinguisher

extinction *f* extinction (*aussi fig*)

extirper *mauvaise herbe* pull up; MÉD remove; *fig renseignement* drag out

extorquer extort

extorsion *f* extortion

extraction *f* extraction

extrader extradite

extraire extract

extrait *m* extract

extraordinaire extraordinary

extraterrestre *m/f* extraterrestrial, alien

extravagance *f* extravagance; *d'une personne, d'une idée* eccentricity

extraverti extrovert

extrême 1 *adj* extreme **2** *m* extreme; **à l'~** to extremes

Extrême-Orient *m:* **l'~** the Far East

extrémiste *m/f* POL extremist; **extrémité** *f d'une rue* (very) end; *d'un doigt* tip; (*situation désespérée*) extremity; **~s** ANAT extremities

exubérant exuberant

exulter exult

eye-liner *m* eyeliner

F

fable *f* fable

fabricant, **-e** *m/f* manufacturer, maker; **fabrication** *f* making; *industrielle* manufacture; **fabriquer** make; *industriellement aussi* manufacture; *histoire* fabricate

fabuleux, **-euse** fabulous

fac *f* (= **faculté**) uni, university

façade *f* façade

face *f* face; *d'une pièce* head; **en ~** (**de**) opposite; **faire ~ à** face up to; **face-à-face** *m inv* face-to-face (debate)

fâché annoyed; **fâcher** annoy; **se ~** get annoyed; **se ~ avec qn** fall out with s.o.; **fâcheux**, **-euse** annoying; (*déplorable*) unfortunate

facile easy; *personne* easy-going; **facilement** easily; **facilité** *f* easiness; *à faire qc* ease; **~s de paiement** easy terms; **faciliter** make easier, facilitate

façon *f* (*manière*) way, method; **de ~ (à ce) que** (+subj) so that; **de toute ~** anyway, anyhow; **de cette ~** (in) that way; **à la ~ de** like, in the style of

facteur *m* mailman, *Br* postman; MATH, *fig* factor

factrice *f* mailwoman, *Br* postwoman

facture *f* bill; COMM invoice; **facturer** invoice

facultatif, **-ive** optional

faculté *f* faculty

fade insipid

faible **1** *adj* weak; *bruit, lumière, espoir* faint; *avantage* slight **2** *m pour personne* soft spot; *pour chocolat etc* weakness; **faiblesse** *f* weakness; **faiblir** weaken

faille *f* GÉOL fault; *dans théorie* flaw

faillible fallible; **faillir**: **il a failli gagner** he almost won

faim *f* hunger; **avoir ~** be hungry; **mourir de ~** starve (*aussi fig*)

fainéant, **~e** **1** *adj* idle, lazy **2** *m/f* idler

faire **1** *v/t* do; *robe, meuble, repas, liste* make; **~ de la natation/du ski** swim/ski, go swimming/skiing; **cinq plus cinq font dix** five and five are *ou* make ten; **ça ne fait rien** it doesn't matter; **~ rire qn** make s.o. laugh; **~ peindre la salle de bain** have the bathroom painted **2** *v/i*: **~ vite** hurry up, be quick **3** *impersonnel*: **il fait chaud/froid** it's warm/cold **4**: **ça ne se fait pas** it's not done; **se ~ rare** become rarer; **se ~ à qc** get used to sth; **je ne m'en fais pas** I'm not worrried

faisable feasible

faisan *m* pheasant

faisceau *m* bundle; **de lumière** beam

fait[1] *m* fact; *(action)* act; *(événement)* development; **au ~** by the way; **de ce ~** consequently; **en ~** in fact; **tout à ~** absolutely; **un ~ divers** a brief news item

fait[2] *adj*: **être ~ pour qn/qch** be made for s.o./sth.; **c'est bien ~ pour lui** serves him right!

falaise *f* cliff

falloir: **il faut un visa** you need a visa, you must have a visa; **il faut l'avertir** we have to warn him; **il me faut sortir, il faut que je sorte** *(subj)* I have to go out, I must go out; **s'il le faut** if necessary; **il aurait fallu prendre le train** we should have taken the train; **comme il faut** respectable; **il ne faut pas que je sorte** *(subj)* I mustn't go out

falsifier *argent* forge; *document* falsify; *vérité* misrepresent

famélique starving

fameux, -euse *(célèbre)* famous; *(excellent)* wonderful

familiariser familiarize; **familiarité** *f* familiarity; **familier, -ère** familiar

famille *f* family

famine *f* famine

fanatique 1 *adj* fanatical **2** *m/f* fanatic; **fanatisme** *m* fanaticism

faner: **se ~** fade

fanfare *f* *(orchestre)* brass band; *(musique)* fanfare; **fanfaron, ~ne 1** *adj* boastful **2** *m* boaster

fantaisie *f* imagination; *(caprice)* whim

fantasme *m* fantasy; **fantasmer** fantasize

fantasque strange, weird

fantastique 1 *adj* fantastic; *(imaginaire)* imaginary **2** *m*: **le ~** fantasy

fantôme *m* ghost

farce *f* *au théâtre* farce; *(tour)* joke; CUIS stuffing; **farceur, -euse** *m/f* joker; **farcir** CUIS stuff; *fig* cram

fard *m* make-up; **~ à paupières** eye shadow

fardeau *m* burden *(aussi fig)*

farder: **se ~** make up

farine *f* flour; **~ de maïs** corn starch, *Br* cornflour

farouche *(timide)* shy; *volonté, haine* fierce

fascination *f* fascination; **fasciner** fascinate

faste *m* pomp

fast-food *m* fast food restaurant

fastidieux, -euse tedious

fastueux, -euse lavish

fatal fatal; *(inévitable)* inevitable; **fatalisme** *m* fatalism;

fataliste 1 *adj* fatalistic **2** *m/f*
fatalist; **fatalité** *f* fate

fatigant tiring; (*agaçant*) tiresome; **fatigue** *f* tiredness; **fatiguer** tire; (*importuner*) annoy; **se ~** get tired

faubourg *m* (working-class) suburb

fauché F broke F; **faucher** *fig* mow down; F (*voler*) pinch F

faufiler: se ~ dans une pièce slip into a room

faune *f* wildlife, fauna

faussaire *m* forger; **fausser** *calcul*, *vérité* distort; *clef* bend

faute *f* mistake; (*responsabilité*) fault; **par sa ~** because of him; **~ de** for lack of; **sans ~** without fail

fauteuil *m* armchair; **~ roulant** wheelchair

fauve 1 *adj* tawny **2** *m félin* big cat

faux, fausse 1 *adj* false; *incorrect aussi* wrong; *bijoux* imitation, fake; **fausse couche** *f* miscarriage; **~ témoignage** perjury **2** *adv*: **chanter ~** sing out of tune **3** *m copie* forgery, fake

faux-filet *m CUIS* sirloin

faux-monnayeur *m* counterfeiter, forger

faux-semblant *m* pretense, *Br* pretence

faveur *f* favor, *Br* favour; **de ~** *traitement* preferential; *prix* special; **en ~ de** in favor of

favorable favorable, *Br* favourable; **favori, ~te** *m/f & adj* favorite, *Br* favourite; **favoriser** favor, *Br* favour; **faciliter**, *avantager* promote; **favoritisme** *m* favoritism, *Br* favouritism

fax *m* fax; **faxer** fax

féconder fertilize; **fécondité** *f* fertility

fécule *f* starch

fédéral federal; **fédération** *f* federation

fée *f* fairy

feeling *m* feeling; **avoir un bon ~ pour qc** have a good feeling about sth

feindre: ~ l'étonnement pretend to be astonished, feign astonishment; **~ de faire qch** pretend to do sth; **feinte** *f* feint

fêler: se ~ crack

félicitations *fpl* congratulations; **féliciter** congratulate (**de** on)

fêlure *f* crack

femelle *f & adj* female

féminin 1 *adj* feminine; *sexe* female; *problèmes*, *magazines*, *mode* women's **2** *m* GRAM feminine; **féministe** *m/f & adj* feminist; **féminité** *f* femininity

femme *f* woman; (*épouse*) wife; **~ battue** battered wife; **~ au foyer** homemaker, *Br* housewife

fendre split; (*fissurer*) crack; *cœur* break; **se ~** split; (*se fissurer*) crack

fenêtre f window
fenouil m BOT fennel
fente f crack; *d'une boîte à lettres, jupe* slit; *pour pièces de monnaie* slot
fer m iron; **à cheval** horseshoe; **à repasser** iron
férié: *jour* m ~ (public) holiday
ferme[1] adj firm; *terre* f ~ dry land, terra firma **2** adv *travailler* hard; *s'ennuyer* ~ be bored stiff
ferme[2] f farm
fermé closed, shut; *robinet* off; *club* exclusive
fermenter ferment
fermer 1 v/t close, shut; *eau, gaz, robinet* turn off; *manteau* fasten; **ferme-la!** shut up! **2** v/i close, shut; *d'un manteau* fasten; *se* ~ close, shut
fermeté f firmness
fermeture f closing; *définitive* closure; *mécanisme* fastener; ~ **éclair** zipper, Br zip (fastener)
fermier 1 adj *œufs, poulet* free-range **2** m farmer
féroce fierce, ferocious; **férocité** f fierceness, ferocity
ferré, ~e: *voie* f ~e (railroad *ou* Br railway) track
ferroviaire railroad atr, Br railway atr
fertile fertile; ~ **en** full of; **fertilité** f fertility
fervent fervent
fesse f buttock; ~**s** butt, Br

bottom; **fessée** f spanking
festin m feast
festival m festival
festivités fpl festivities
fêtard m F reveler, Br reveller; **fête** f festival; *(soirée)* party; *publique* holiday; REL feast (day), festival; *jour d'un saint* name day; **les** ~**s** (*de fin d'année*) the holidays, Christmas and New Year; **faire la** ~ party; ~ **foraine** fun fair; **Fête des mères** Mother's Day; **Fête nationale** Bastille Day; **fêter** celebrate; *(accueillir)* fête
feu m fire; AUTO, MAR light; *de circulation* (traffic) light, Br (traffic) lights pl; *d'une cuisinière* burner; *fig (enthousiasme)* passion; **coup** m **de** ~ shot; **prendre** ~ catch fire; **vous avez du** ~? got a light?; ~ **arrière** AUTO taillight
feuillage m foliage; **feuille** f leaf; *de papier* sheet; ~ **d'impôt** tax return; ~ **de paie** payslip; **feuilleter** *livre etc* leaf through
feuilleton m serial; TV soap opera
feutre m felt; *stylo* felt-tipped pen; *chapeau* fedora
février m February
fiable reliable
fiançailles fpl engagement; **fiancé**, ~e m/f fiancé; **fiancer**: *se* ~ **avec** get engaged to

fibre f fiber, Br fibre; **avoir la ~ paternelle** fig be a born father; **la ~ patriotique** patriotic feelings

ficeler tie up; **ficelle** f string; pain thin French stick

fiche f pour classement index card; formulaire form; ÉL plug

ficher F (faire) do; (donner) give; (mettre) stick; **fiche-moi la paix!** leave me alone!; **je m'en fiche** I don't give a damn

fichier m INFORM file; **~ joint** attachment

fichu F (inutilisable) kaput F; (sale) filthy; **être mal ~ santé** be feeling rotten

fictif, -ive fictitious; **fiction** f fiction

fidèle 1 adj faithful **2** m/f REL, fig: **les fidèles** the faithful pl; **fidélité** f faithfulness

fier[1]: **se ~ à** trust

fier[2], **-ère** adj proud (de of); **fierté** f pride

fièvre f fever; **avoir de la ~** have a fever; **fiévreux, -euse** feverish

figer congeal; **se ~** fig: d'un sourire become fixed

figue f fig; **figuier** m fig tree

figurant, ~e m/f de théâtre walk-on; de cinéma extra; **figure** f figure; (visage) face; **figuré** figurative; **figurer** figure; **se ~ qc** imagine sth

fil m thread; de métal, ÉL, TÉL wire; **coup** m **de ~** TÉL (phone) call

filature f spinning; usine mill; **prendre qn en ~** fig tail s.o.

file f line; d'une route lane; **~ (d'attente)** line, Br queue

filer 1 v/t spin; F (donner) give; (épier) tail F **2** v/i F (partir vite) race off; **du temps** fly past

filet m d'eau trickle; de pêche, tennis net; CUIS fillet

filial, ~e 1 adj filial **2** f COMM subsidiary

fille f girl; parenté daughter; **vieille ~** old maid; **fillette** f little girl

filleul m godson; **filleule** f goddaughter

film m movie, Br aussi film; **couche** film; **~ policier** detective movie ou Br aussi film; **filmer** film

fils m son; **~ à papa** (spoilt) rich kid

filtre m filter; **filtrer 1** v/t filter; fig screen **2** v/i filter through; fig leak

fin[1] f end; **à la ~** in the end; **mettre ~ à qc** put an end to sth; **sans~** endless; parler endlessly

fin[2] **1** adj fine; (mince) thin; taille, cheville slender; esprit refined; (rusé, malin) sharp **2** adv fine(ly)

final, ~e 1 adj final **2** m: **~e** MUS finale **3** f SP final; **finale 1** m MUS finale **2** f SP final; **finaliser** finalize; **finaliste** m/f finalist

finance f finance; **financer** fund, finance; **financier, -ère 1** adj financial **2** m financier

finesse f (délicatesse) fineness

fini 1 adj finished **2** m finish; **finir** v/t finish **2** v/i finish; ~ **de faire qc** finish doing sth; ~ **par faire qc** finish up doing sth

finlandais, ~e 1 adj Finnish **2** m langue Finnish; **Finlandais, ~e** m/f Finn; **Finlande** f: **la ~** Finland

firme f firm

fisc m tax authorities pl

fissure f crack

fixe 1 adj fixed; adresse, personnel permanent **2** m basic salary; **fixer** fasten; (déterminer) fix, set; PHOT fix; (regarder) stare at; **se ~** (s'établir) settle down

flageolet m flageolet bean

flagrant flagrant; **en ~ délit** red-handed

flair m sense of smell; fig intuition; **flairer** smell (aussi fig)

flambant: ~ **neuf** brand new; **flamber 1** v/i blaze **2** v/t CUIS flambé

flamme f flame; fig fervor, Br fervour

flan m flan

flancher quail

flâner stroll

flanquer flank; F (jeter) fling; coup give

flaque f puddle

flasque flabby

flatter flatter; **se ~ de qc** congratulate o.s. on sth; **flatterie** f flattery; **flatteur, -euse 1** adj flattering **2** m/f flatterer

flèche f arrow; d'un clocher spire; **monter en ~** de prix skyrocket

fléchir 1 v/t bend; (faire céder) sway **2** v/i d'une poutre bend; fig (céder) give in; (faiblir) weaken; d'un prix, de ventes fall

flegmatique phlegmatic

flemme f F laziness; **j'ai la ~ de le faire** I can't be bothered

flétrir: **se ~** wither

fleur f flower; d'un arbre blossom; **fleurir** flower, bloom; fig flourish; **fleuriste** m/f florist

fleuve m river

flexibilité f flexibility; **flexible** flexible

flic m F cop fn

flinguer F gun down

flipper 1 m pinball machine; jeu pinball **2** v/i F freak out F

flirter flirt

flocon m flake; ~ **de neige** snowflake

Floride f Florida

florissant fig flourishing

flot m flood (aussi fig); **~s** waves; **remettre à ~** refloat (aussi fig)

flottant floating; vêtements baggy

flotte f fleet; F (eau) water; F (pluie) rain; **flotter** d'un bateau float; d'un drapeau flutter; d'un sourire, air hover; fig waver

flou blurred, fuzzy; robe loose-fitting

fluctuation f fluctuation; **fluctuer** COMM fluctuate

fluide 1 adj fluid; circulation moving freely **2** m PHYS fluid; **fluidité** f fluidity

fluorescent fluorescent

flûte f MUS, verre flute; pain thin French stick

fluvial river atr

flux m MAR flow

fœtus m fetus, Br foetus

foi f faith; **être de bonne/mauvaise ~** be sincere/insincere

foie m liver; **une crise de ~** a stomach upset

foire f fair

fois f time; **une ~** once; **deux ~** twice; **trois ~** three times; **il était une ~ ...** once upon a time there was ...; **quatre ~ six** four times six; **à la ~** at the same time

foisonner be abundant

folie f madness; **faire des ~s achats** go on a spending spree

folk m folk (music)

folklore folklore

follement madly

fomenter foment

foncé couleur dark; **foncer** de couleurs darken; AUTO speed along; **~ sur** rush at

foncier, -ère COMM land

foncièrement fundamentally

fonction f function; (poste) office; **faire ~ de** act as; **en ~ de** according to; **prendre ses ~s** take up office

fonctionnaire m/f public servant

fonctionnement m functioning; **fonctionner** work; du système function

fond m bottom; d'une salle, armoire back; d'une peinture background; (contenu) content; d'un problème heart; d'un pantalon seat; **à ~** thoroughly; **au ~, dans le ~** basically

fondamental fundamental

fondateur, -trice m/f founder; **fondation** f foundation; **fondé 1** adj well-founded **2** m: **~ de pouvoir** authorized representative; **fondement** m fig basis; **sans ~** groundless; **fonder** found; **~ qch sur** base sth on; **se ~ sur** d'une personne base o.s. on; d'une idée be based on

fondre 1 v/t neige melt; dans l'eau dissolve; métal melt down **2** v/i de la neige melt; dans l'eau dissolve; **~ sur** pounce on

fonds m 1 sg fund; d'une bibliothèque collection; **~ de commerce** business **2** pl (argent) funds

fondu melted

fondue f CUIS fondue; **~ bour-guignonne** beef fondue

fontaine f fountain; (*source*) spring

fonte f métal cast iron; **~ des neiges** spring thaw

football m soccer; Br aussi football; **~ américain** football, Br American football; **footballeur, -euse** m/f soccer player, Br aussi footballer

footing m jogging; **faire du ~** jog, go jogging

force f strength; (*violence*) force; **à ~ de travailler** by working; **de ~** by force; **~s armées** armed forces

forcené, **~e** m/f maniac

forcer force; **se ~** force o.s.

forestier, -ère 1 adj forest atr 2 m ranger, Br forest warden

forêt f forest

forfait m COMM package; (*prix*) all-in price; **déclarer ~** withdraw

formaliser: **se ~ de** take offense ou Br offence at; **formalité** f formality

format m format; **formater** format

formation f formation; (*éducation*) training; **~ continue** continuing education

forme f form; **en ~ de** in the shape of; **être en ~** be in form, be in good shape; **formel, ~le** formal; (*explicite*) categorical; **formellement** adv: **~ interdit** strictly for-

bidden; former form; (*instruire*) train; **se ~** form

formidable enormous; F great F

formulaire m form

formulation f wording

formule f formula; **formuler** formulate; vœux, jugement express

fort 1 adj strong; (*gros*) stout; coup, pluie heavy; somme big; **être ~ en qch** be good at sth 2 adv parler loudly; pousser, frapper hard; (*très*) extremely; (*beaucoup*) a lot 3 m strong point; MIL fort; **fortement** pousser hard; (*beaucoup*) greatly

fortifier strengthen

fortuit chance

fortune f luck; **de ~** makeshift

fosse f pit; (*tombe*) grave; **fossé** m ditch; fig gulf; **fossette** f dimple

fossile m & adj fossil

fou, folle 1 adj mad; (*incroyable*) incredible; **être ~ de qn/qc** be mad ou crazy about s.o./sth; **~ de joie** etc beside o.s. with 2 m/f madman; madwoman

foudre f lightning; **coup** m **de ~** fig love at first sight

foudroyer strike down; **~ qn du regard** give s.o. a withering look

fouet m whip; CUIS whisk

fougueux, -euse fiery

fouiller 1 v/i dig; (*chercher*) search 2 v/t de police search;

en archéologie excavate
fouiner nose around
foulard m scarf
foule f crowd; **une ~ de**
masses of
fouler trample; sol set foot
on; **se ~ la cheville** twist
one's ankle; **foulure** f sprain
four m oven; TECH kiln; fig F
(insuccès) flop F
fourchette f fork; (éventail)
bracket; **fourchu** forked;
cheveux mpl **~s** split ends
fourgon m baggage car, Br
luggage van; camion van;
fourgonnette f small van
fourmi f ant
fourmillements mpl pins and
needles; **fourmiller** swarm
(**de** with)
fournaise f fig oven; **fourneau** m furnace; CUIS stove
fourni: **bien ~** well stocked
fournir supply (**de**, **en** with);
occasion provide; effort
make; **~ qc à qn** provide
s.o. with sth; **fournisseur**
m supplier; **~ d'accès (Internet)** Internet service provider, ISP; **fourniture** f supply;
~s scolaires school stationery and books
fourré[1] m thicket
fourré[2] adj CUIS filled; vêtement lined
fourrer stick, shove; (remplir)
fill; **se ~ dans** get into
fourrière f pound
fourrure f fur
fourvoyer: **se ~** go astray

foutre F do; (mettre) stick;
coup give; **se ~ de qn** make
fun of s.o.; indifférence not
give a damn about s.o.; **je
m'en fous!** I don't give a
damn!
foyer m fireplace; d'une famille home; de jeunes club;
(pension) hostel; d'un théâtre foyer; d'un incendie seat;
d'une infection source
fracas m crash; **fracasser**
shatter
fractionner divide (up) (**en**
into)
fracture f MÉD m fracture;
fracturer coffre break open;
jambe fracture
fragile fragile; santé frail;
cœur weak; **fragiliser** weak-
en; **fragilité** f fragility
fragment m fragment
fraîcheur f freshness; (froideur) coolness (aussi fig);
fraîchir du vent freshen; du
temps get cooler
frais[1], **fraîche 1** adj fresh;
(froid) cool; peinture wet;
nouvelles recent; **servir ~**
serve chilled; **il fait ~** it's cool
2 adv freshly, newly **3** m:
prendre le ~ get a breath
of fresh air
frais[2] mpl expenses pl; COMM
costs pl; **faire des ~** incur
costs; **à mes ~** at my (own)
expense; **~ bancaires** bank
charges; **~ généraux** over-
head, Br overheads
fraise f strawberry

framboise f raspberry

franc¹, **franche** adj frank; regard open; COMM free

franc² m franc

français, **~e 1** adj French **2** m langue French; **Français**, **~e** m/f Frenchman; Frenchwoman; **les ~** the French pl; **France** f: **la ~** France

franchir cross; obstacle negotiate

franchise f caractère frankness; (exemption) exemption; COMM franchise; d'une assurance deductible, Br excess

franco adv: **~ (de port)** carriage free; **y aller ~** fig F go right ahead

francophone 1 adj French-speaking **2** m/f French speaker

franc-parler m outspokenness

frange f bangs pl, Br fringe

frappant striking; **frappe** f INFORM keying; **faute** f **de ~** typo, typing error; **frapper 1** v/t hit, strike; (impressionner) strike **2** v/i (agir) strike; **à la porte** knock (**à** at); **~ dans ses mains** clap (one's hands)

fraternel, **~le** brotherly, fraternal; **fraternité** f brotherhood

fraude f fraud; ÉDU cheating; **passer en ~** smuggle; **frauduleux**, **-euse** fraudulent

frayer: **se ~** chemin clear

frayeur f fright

fredonner hum

frein m brake; **sans ~** fig unbridled; **~ à main** parking brake, Br hand brake; **freiner 1** v/i brake **2** v/t fig curb, check

frêle frail

frelon m hornet

frémir shake; de feuilles quiver; de l'eau simmer; **frémissement** m shiver; de feuilles quivering

frénésie f frenzy; **avec ~** frenetically

fréquemment frequently; **fréquence** f frequency; **quelle est la ~ des bus?** how often do the buses go?; **fréquent** frequent; situation common

fréquentation f d'un théâtre etc attendance; **tes ~s** (amis) the company you keep; **fréquenter** endroit go to regularly, frequent; personne see; groupe go around with

frère m brother

fret m freight

frétiller wriggle

friable crumbly

friand: **être ~ de qc** be fond of sth; **friandises** fpl sweet things

fric m F money, dosh F

friche f AGR: **en ~** (lying) fallow

friction f friction; de la tête scalp massage; **frictionner** massage

frigidaire *m* refrigerator
frigide frigid
frigo *m* F icebox, fridge; **fri-
gorifier** refrigerate
frileux, **-euse**: **être ~** feel the
cold
frimer show off; **frimeur**, **-eu-
se** show-off
fringues *fpl* F clothes, gear F
frire 1 *v/i* fry **2** *v/t*: **faire ~** fry
frisé curly; **friser** *cheveux*
curl; *fig*: *le ridicule* verge on
frissonner shiver
frit fried; **(pommes) frites** *fpl*
(French) fries, Br *aussi*
chips; **friteuse** *f* deep fryer;
friture *f poissons* Br white-
bait, *small fried fish*; *huile*
oil; *à la radio*, TÉL interference
frivole frivolous; **frivolité** *f*
frivolity
froid 1 *adj* cold (*aussi fig*); **j'ai
~** I'm cold; **prendre ~** catch
(a) cold **2** *m* cold; **humour** *m*
à ~ dry humor; **froidement**
fig coldly; *(calmement)*
coolly; *tuer* in cold blood;
froideur *f* coldness
froissement *m bruit* rustle;
froisser crumple; *fig* offend; **se ~** crumple; *fig* take
offense *ou* Br offence
fromage *m* cheese; **~ blanc**
fromage frais; **~ à tartiner**
cheese spread
froncer gather; **~ les sourcils**
frown
front *m* front; ANAT forehead;
de ~ from the front; *fig*

head-on; **marcher de ~** walk
side by side
frontière *f* frontier, border
frotter 1 *v/t* rub **2** *v/t* rub (**de**
with); *meuble* polish; *sol*
scrub; *allumette* strike
frousse *f* F fear; **avoir la ~** be
scared
fructifier BOT bear fruit; *d'un
placement* yield a profit
fructueux, **-euse** fruitful
fruit *m* fruit; **~s** fruit; **~s de
mer** seafood
frustrant frustrating; **frustration** *f* frustration
fugitif, **-ive 1** *adj* runaway; *fig*
fleeting **2** *m/f* fugitive
fugue *f d'un enfant* escapade;
MUS fugue; **faire une ~** run
away
fuir **1** *v/i* flee; *du temps* fly;
d'un tuyau leak; *d'un robinet*
drip; *d'un liquide* leak out **2**
v/t shun; *question* avoid; **fuite** *f* flight (**devant** from);
d'un tuyau etc leak; **prendre
la ~** take flight
fulgurant dazzling; *vitesse*
lightning
fumé smoked; *verre* tinted
fumée *f* smoke; **fumer**
smoke; **fumeur**, **-euse** *m/f*
smoker
funèbre funeral *atr*; *(lugubre)*
gloomy
funérailles *fpl* funeral
funeste fatal
fur: **au ~ et à mesure** as I/you
etc go along; **au ~ et à mesure que** as

fureter ferret around

fureur *f* fury; **faire ~** be all the rage

furie (*colère*) fury; *femme* shrew; **furieux, -euse** furious (*contre qn* with s.o.; **de qch** with *ou* at sth)

furtif, -ive furtive, stealthy

fuseau *m*: **~ horaire** time zone

fusée *f* rocket

fusible *m* ÉL fuse

fusil *m* rifle; **~ de chasse** shotgun; **fusiller** execute by firing squad

fusion *f* COMM merger; PHYS fusion; **fusionner** COMM merge

futé cunning, clever

futile futile; *personne* frivolous

futur *m & adj* future

fuyant *menton* receding; *regard* evasive

G

gabarit *m* size; TECH template

gâcher *fig* spoil; *travail* bungle; *temps, argent* waste

gâchis *m* (*désordre*) mess; (*gaspillage*) waste

gadget *m* gadget

gaffe *f* F blooper F, blunder; **faire ~ à** F be careful of

gaffer F make a gaffe *ou* blooper F

gage *fig* forfeit; (*preuve*) token; **tueur à ~s** hitman; **mettre en ~** pawn

gagnant, ~e 1 *adj* winning **2** *m/f* winner

gagne-pain *m* livelihood

gagner win; *salaire, amitié etc* earn; *place, temps* gain; *endroit* reach; *de peur etc* overcome; **~ sa vie** earn one's living

gai cheerful; *un peu ivre* tipsy; **gaieté** *f* cheerfulness

gain *m* gain; (*avantage*) benefit; **~s** profits; *d'un employé* earnings

gaine *f* sheath

galant galant; **homme ~** gentleman

galaxie *f* galaxy

galère *f*: **il est dans la ~** *fig* F he's in a mess; **galérer** F sweat

galerie *f* gallery; AUTO roofrack; **~ d'art** art gallery; **~ marchande** mall

galet *m* pebble

Galles *fpl*: **le pays** *m* **de ~** Wales; **gallois, ~e 1** *adj* Welsh **2** *m langue* Welsh; **Gallois, ~e** *m/f* Welshman; Welsh woman

galop *m* gallop; **galoper** gallop

galopin *m* urchin

galvaniser galvanize

gambader gambol, leap

gamin, ~e 1 *m/f* kid **2** *adj*

childlike

gamme f MUS scale; fig range; **bas de ~** downscale, Br downmarket

gang m gang

gangster m gangster

gant m glove; **~ de toilette** washcloth, Br facecloth

garage m garage; **garagiste** m auto mechanic; propriétaire garage owner

garant, ~e m/f guarantor; **garantie** f guarantee; **garantir** guarantee

garce F F bitch

garçon m boy; (serveur) waiter; **~ d'honneur** best man; **~ manqué** tomboy; **garçonnière** f bachelor apartment ou Br flat

garde[1] f care (de of); MIL guard; **prendre ~** be careful; **être de ~** be on duty; **mettre qn en ~** put s.o. on their guard; **~ à vue** police custody

garde[2] m guard; **~ forestier** (forest) ranger

garde-boue m AUTO fender, Br wing

garde-fou m railing

garde-malade m/f nurse

garder objet keep; vêtement keep on; (surveiller) guard; malade, enfant look after; **se ~ de faire qch** be careful not to do sth

garderie f daycare center, Br daycare centre

gardien, ~ne m/f de prison guard, Br warder; d'un musée attendant; d'immeuble, d'école janitor; fig guardian; **~ (de but)** goalkeeper **~ de la paix** police officer

gare[1] f station; **~ routière** bus station

gare[2]: **~ à toi!** watch out!); ça va mal se passer you'll be for it!

garer park; **se ~** park; pour laisser passer move aside

gargariser: se ~ gargle

gargouiller gurgle; de l'estomac rumble

garnement m rascal

garnir (fournir) fit (de with); (orner) trim (de with); **garniture** f légumes vegetables pl

gars m F guy F

gasoil m gas oil, Br diesel

gaspillage m waste; **gaspiller** waste; **gaspilleur, -euse 1** adj wasteful **2** m/f waster

gastroentérite f gastroenteritis

gastronome m/f gourmet; **gastronomie** f gastronomy

gâteau m cake; **~ sec** cookie, Br biscuit

gâter spoil; **se ~** d'un aliment spoil; du temps deteriorate

gauche 1 adj left; manières gauche **2** f left; **à ~** on the left (de of); **gaucher, -ère 1** adj left-handed **2** m/f left-hander

gaufre f waffle; **gaufrette** f wafer

gaver *oie* force-feed; **~ qn de qch** *fig* stuff s.o. full of sth

gaz *m* gas; **mettre les ~** step on the gas; **~ à effet de serre** greenhouse gas

gaze *f* gauze

gazeux, -euse *boisson* carbonated, *Br* fizzy

gazinière *f* gas cooker

gazole *m* gas oil, *Br* diesel

gazon *m* grass

gazouiller twitter

géant, ~e 1 *adj* gigantic, giant *atr* **2** *m/f* giant

geindre groan

gel *m* frost; *fig*: *des prix* freeze; *cosmétique* gel

gélatine *f* gelatine

gelée *f* frost; CUIS aspic; *confiture* jelly, *Br* jam; **geler 1** *v/t* freeze **2** *v/i il d'une personne* freeze; **il gèle** there's a frost

Gémeaux *mpl* ASTROL Gemini

gémir groan; **gémissement** *m* groan

gênant (*embarrassant*) embarrassing

gencive *f* gum

gendarme *m* policeman; **gendarmerie** *f* police force; *lieu* police station

gendre *m* son-in-law

gêne *f* (*embarras*) embarrassment; (*dérangement*) inconvenience; *physique* difficulty; **sans ~** shameless; **gêner** bother; (*embarrasser*) embarrass; (*encombrer*) be in the way

général, ~e 1 *adj* general; **en ~** generally **2** *m* MIL general **3** *f* THÉÂT dress rehearsal; **généraliser** generalize; **se ~** spread; **généraliste** *m* MÉD generalist; **généralités** *fpl* generalities

générateur *m* generator; **générer** generate

généreux, -euse generous; **générosité** *f* generosity

génétique genetic; **génétiquement** genetically; **~ modifié** genetically modified, GM

génétiquement genetically; **~ modifié** genetically modified, GM

Genève Geneva

génial of genius; (*formidable*) terrific; **génie** *m* genius; TECH engineering; **avoir du ~** be a genius; **~ civil** civil engineering

genou *m* knee; **à ~x** on one's knees

genre *m* kind, sort; GRAM gender; **bon chic, bon ~** preppie *atr*

gens *mpl* people *pl*

gentil, ~le nice; *enfant* good; **gentillesse** *f* (*amabilité*) kindness

géographie *f* geography

géologie *f* geology; **géologue** *m/f* geologist

géomètre *m/f* geometrician; **géométrie** *f* geometry

gérance *f* management; **gé-**

rant, **~e** *m/f* manager

gerbe *f de blé* sheaf

gercé *lèvres* chapped

gérer manage

gériatrie *f* geriatrics

germain: cousin *m* ~, cousine *f* ~e (first) cousin

germe *m* germ (*aussi fig*); **germer** germinate

gestation *f* gestation

geste *m* gesture; **gesticuler** gesticulate

gestion *f* management; **gestionnaire** *m/f* manager

ghetto *m* ghetto

gibier *m* game

giboulée *f* wintry shower

gicler spurt

gifle *f* slap (in the face); **gifler** slap (in the face)

gigantesque gigantic

gigaoctet *m* gigabyte

gigot *m d'agneau* leg

gigoter F fidget

gilet *m* vest, *Br* waistcoat; (*chandail*) cardigan; **~ de sauvetage** lifejacket

gin *m* gin; **~ tonic** gin and tonic

gingembre *m* BOT ginger

girafe *f* giraffe

giratoire: sens *m* ~ traffic circle, *Br* roundabout

gisement *m* GÉOL deposit; **~ pétrolifère** *ou* **de pétrole** oilfield

gitan, ~e *m/f* gypsy

gîte *m* holiday home

givre *m* frost; **givré** covered with frost; *avec du sucre*

frosted; F (*fou*) crazy

glace *f* ice; (*miroir*) mirror; AUTO window; (*crème glacée*) ice cream; *d'un gâteau* frosting, *Br* icing; *d'une tarte* glaze; **glacer** freeze; (*intimider*) petrify; *gâteau* frost, *Br* ice; *tarte* glaze; **se ~** freeze; *du sang* run cold; **glacial** icy (*aussi fig*); **glacière** *f* cool bag; *fig* icebox; **glaçon** *m* icicle; *artificiel* icecube

glaise *f* (*aussi* **terre *f ~***) clay

gland *m* acorn

glande *f* gland

glander F hang around F

glaner *fig* glean

glapir shriek

glauque *eau* murky; *couleur* blue-green

glissade *f* slide; *accidentelle* slip; **glissant** slippery; **glissement** *m* **~ de terrain** landslide; **glisser 1** *v/t* slip (*dans* into) **2** *v/i* slide; *sur l'eau* glide (*sur* over); (*déraper*) slip; *être glissant* be slippery; **se ~ dans** slip into

global *prix, somme* total, overall; **globalisation** *f* globalization; **globe** *m* globe; **~ oculaire** eyeball

gloire *f* glory; **glorieux, -euse** glorious; **glorifier** glorify

glousser cluck; *rire* giggle

gluant sticky

glycine *f* wisteria

gnangnan F *film, livre* sloppy F

goal *m* goalkeeper

gobelet *m* tumbler; *en carton, plastique* cup

gober gobble; F *mensonge* swallow

godet *m* récipient pot; *de vêtements* flare

gogo F: **à** ~ galore

goinfrer: **se** ~ *péj* stuff o.s.

golf *m* SP golf; *terrain* golf course

golfe *m* GÉOGR gulf

gomme *f* gum; *pour effacer* eraser; **gommer** (*effacer*) erase

gond *m* hinge; *sortir de ses* ~**s** fly off the handle

gondole *f* gondola

gonflable inflatable; **gonfler 1** *v/i* swell **2** *v/t* blow up; (*exagérer*) exaggerate

gonzesse *f* F *péj* chick F

gorge *f* throat; (*poitrine*): *(poitrine)* bosom; GÉOGR gorge; *avoir mal à la* ~ have a sore throat; **gorgée** *f* mouthful; **gorger**: **se** ~ gorge o.s. (*de* with)

gosier *m* throat

gosse *m/f* F kid F

goudron *m* tar

gouffre *m* abyss; *fig* depths *pl*

goujat *m* boor

goulot *m* neck; *boire au* ~ drink from the bottle

goulu greedy

gourd numb (with the cold)

gourde *f* récipient water bottle; *fig* F moron F

gourer F: **se** ~ goof F, *Br* boob F

gourmand, ~**e1** *adj* greedy **2** *m/f* gourmand; **gourmandi-** se *f* greediness; ~**s** *mets* delicacies; **gourmet** *m* gourmet

gourmette *f* chain

gourou *m* guru

gousse *f* pod; ~ **d'ail** clove of garlic

goût *m* taste; *de bon* ~ tasteful, in good taste; *de mauvais* ~ tasteless, in bad taste; *avoir du* ~ have taste; **goûter 1** *v/t* taste; *fig* enjoy **2** *v/i prendre un goûter* have an afternoon snack **3** *m* afternoon snack

goutte *f* drop; *de pluie* raindrop; **goutte-à-goutte** *m* MÉD drip; **goutter** drip; **gouttière** *f* gutter

gouvernement *m* government; **gouverner** *pays* govern; *passions* master, control; MAR steer; **gouverneur** *m* governor

grâce *f* grace; (*bienveillance*) favor, *Br* favour; JUR pardon; *faire* ~ **à qn de qc** spare s.o. sth; ~ **à** thanks to; **gracier** reprieve; **gracieux, -euse** graceful; **à titre** ~ se free

grade *m* rank; **gradé** *m* MIL noncommissioned officer

gradins *mpl* SP bleachers, *Br* terraces

graduellement gradually

graduer (*augmenter*) gradually increase; *instrument* graduate

graffitis *mpl* graffiti *sg ou pl*

grain *m* grain; MAR squall; ~ **de**

beauté mole, beauty spot; **~ de raisin** grape

graine *f* seed

graissage *m* lubrication, greasing; **graisse** *f* fat; TECH grease; **graisser** grease, lubricate; (*salir*) get grease on; **graisseux, -euse** greasy

grammaire *f* grammar; **grammatical** grammatical

gramme *m* gram

grand 1 *adj* big; (*haut*) tall; (*adulte*) grown-up; (*long*) long; (*important, glorieux*) great; **il est ~ temps** it's high time; **~e surface** *f* supermarket; **les ~es vacances** *fpl* the summer vacation, *Br* the summer holidays; **~ ensemble** new development, *Br* (housing) estate **2** *adv* **ouvrir** wide **3** *m* giant, great man

grand-chose: **pas ~** not much

Grande-Bretagne: **la ~** Great Britain

grandeur *f* (*taille*) size; **~ nature** lifesize

grandiose magnificent

grandir 1 *v/i* grow **2** *v/t*: **~ qn** make s.o. look taller; *de l'expérience* strengthen s.o.

grand-mère *f* grandmother

grand-père *m* grandfather

grands-parents *mpl* grandparents *pl*

granit(e) *m* granite

granuleux, -euse granular

graphique 1 *adj* graphic **2** *m*

chart; MATH graph; INFORM graphic

grappe *f* cluster; **~ de raisin** bunch of grapes

grappin *m*: **mettre le ~ sur qn** get one's hands on s.o.

gras, ~se 1 *adj* fatty, fat; *personne* fat; *cheveux, peau* greasy; **faire la ~se matinée** sleep late **2** *m* CUIS fat

gratification *f* (*prime*) bonus; PSYCH gratification; **gratifier**: **~ qn de qc** present s.o. with sth

gratiné CUIS with a sprinkling of cheese; *fig* F *addition* colossal

gratitude *f* gratitude

gratte-ciel *m* skyscraper; **gratter** scrape; (*griffer, piquer*) scratch; (*enlever*) scrape off; *mot* scratch out; **se ~** scratch; **grattoir** *m* scraper

gratuit free; *fig* gratuitous

gravats *mpl* rubble

grave serious; *son* deep; **ce n'est pas ~** it's not a problem

graver engrave; *disque* cut

gravier *m* gravel

gravillon *m* grit; **~s** gravel, *Br* loose chippings *pl*

gravir climb

gravité *f* seriousness; PHYS gravity

gravure *f* ART engraving; (*reproduction*) print

gré *m*: **bon ~, mal ~** like it or not; **contre mon ~** against

my will; **de bon ~** willingly;
de son plein ~ of one's own
free will

grec, **~que 1** adj Greek **2** m
langue Greek; **Grec**, **~que**
m/f Greek; **Grèce**: **la ~**
Greece

greffe graft; **~ du cœur** MÉD
heart transplant; **greffer**
graft; cœur, poumon transplant

greffier m clerk of the court
grêle[1] adj jambes skinny;
voix shrill

grêle[2] f hail; **grêler**: **il grêle**
it's hailing; **grêlon** m hail-
stone

greloter shiver
grenade f BOT pomegranate;
MIL grenade

grenadine f grenadine,
pomegranate syrup

grenier m attic
grenouille f frog
grès m sandstone; poterie
stoneware

grésiller sizzle; RAD crackle
grève[1] f strike; **être en ~**, **faire ~** be on strike; **se mettre
en ~** go on strike; **~ de la
faim** hunger strike

grève[2] f (plage) shore
gréviste m/f striker
gribouillage m scribble;
(dessin) doodle; **gribouiller**
scribble; (dessiner) doodle

grief m grievance
grièvement blessé seriously
griffe f claw; COMM label; fig
(empreinte) stamp; **griffer**

scratch

griffonner scribble
grignoter 1 v/t nibble on; économies nibble away at **2** v/i
nibble

grill m broiler, Br grill; **grilla-
de** f broil, Br grill

grillage m wire mesh; (clôture) fence

grille f d'une fenêtre grille;
(clôture) railings pl; d'un
four rack; (tableau) grid;
grille-pain m inv toaster;
griller 1 v/t viande broil,
Br grill; pain toast; café,
marrons roast **2** v/i d'une
ampoule burn out; **~ un
feu rouge** go through a red
light

grillon m cricket
grimace f grimace; **faire des
~s** pull faces

grimper climb
grincement m de porte
squeaking; **grincer** d'une
porte squeak; **~ des dents**
grind one's teeth

grincheux, **-euse** grouchy
grippe f MÉD flu; **prendre qn
en ~** take a dislike to s.o.;
grippé MÉD: **être ~** have flu

gris gray, Br grey; temps, vie
dull; (ivre) tipsy

grisant exhilarating
grisâtre grayish, Br greyish
griser: **~ qn** go to s.o.'s head;
se laisser ~ par get carried
away by

grisonner go gray ou Br grey
grognement m (plainte)

grumbling; *d'un cochon etc* grunt; **grogner** (*se plaindre*) grumble; *d'un cochon* grunt; **grognon**, **ne**: *être* ~ be grumpy

grommeler mutter

gronder 1 *v/i* growl; *du tonnerre* rumble; *d'une révolte* brew **2** *v/t* scold

gros, **~se 1** *adj* big; (*corpulent*) fat; *lèvres* thick; *rhume*, *souliers* heavy; *chaussettes* thick; *plaisanterie* coarse; *vin* rough; ~ *mots mpl* bad language **2** *adv*: *gagner* ~ win a lot; *en* ~ (*globalement*) on the whole; COMM wholesale **3** *m personne* fat man; COMM wholesale trade

groseille *f* BOT currant; ~ *à maquereau* gooseberry

grossesse *f* pregnancy

grosseur *f* (*corpulence*) fatness; (*volume*) size; (*tumeur*) growth

grossier, **-ère** (*rudimentaire*) crude; (*indélicat*) coarse; (*impoli*) rude; *erreur* big

grossir 1 *v/t au microscope* magnify; *nombre*, *rivière* swell; (*exagérer*) exaggerate; ~ *qn d'une robe etc* make s.o. look fatter **2** *v/i d'une personne* put on weight

grotesque grotesque

grotte *f* cave

grouiller: ~ *de* be swarming with; *se* ~ F get a move on

groupe *m* group; ~ *sanguin* blood group; **grouper**

group; *se* ~ *autour de qn* gather around s.o.

grue *f* ZO, TECH crane

grumeleux, **-euse** lumpy

gué *m* ford

guenilles *fpl* rags

guêpe *f* wasp

guère: *ne* ... ~ hardly

guéridon *m* round table

guérir 1 *v/t* cure (*de* of) **2** *v/i* heal; *d'un malade* get better; **guérison** *f* (*rétablissement*) recovery

guerre *f* war; *en* ~ at war; *faire la* ~ be at war (*à* with); ~ *civile* civil war; ~ *des gangs* gang warfare; **guerrier**, **-ère 1** *adj* warlike **2** *m* warrior

guet *m*: *faire le* ~ keep watch; **guet-apens** *m* ambush; **guetter** keep an eye open for; (*épier*) watch

gueule *f* F mouth; (*visage*) face; *ta* ~! F shut it! F; ~ *de bois* hangover; **gueuler** F yell

gueuleton *m* F enormous meal

guichet *m de banque*, *poste* wicket, F window; *de théâtre* box office; ~ *automatique* ATM, *Br aussi* cash dispenser

guide 1 *m* guide **2** *f* girl scout, *Br* guide **3**: ~*s fpl* guiding reins; **guider** guide

guidon *m de vélo* handlebars *pl*

guillemets *mpl* quote marks

guindé stiff

guirlande f garland; **~s de Noël** tinsel

guise f: **agir à sa ~** do as one likes; **en ~ de** as, by way of

guitare f guitar; **guitariste** m/f guitarist

guttural guttural

Guyane: la ~ Guyana

gym f gym; **gymnase** m SP gym; **gymnaste** m/f gymnast; **gymnastique** f gymnastics SG; *corrective, matinale* exercises pl

gynécologue m/f MÉD gynecologist, Br gynaecologist

gyrophare m flashing light

H

habile skillful, Br skilful; **habileté** f skill; **habilité** JUR authorized

habillé (*élégant*) dressy; **habiller** dress; **s'~** get dressed, dress; **élégamment** get dressed up

habit m: **~s** clothes

habitable inhabitable; **habitant, ~e** m/f inhabitant; **habitation** f *living*; (*domicile*) residence; **habiter 1** v/t live in **2** v/i live

habitude f habit, custom; **d'~** usually; **par ~** out of habit; **habitué, ~e** m/f regular; **habituel, ~le** usual; **habituer: ~ qn à qch** get s.o. used to sth; **s'~ à** get used to

'hache f ax, Br axe; **'hacher** chop; **viande** f **hachée** ground beef, Br mince

'hachisch m hashish

'hachoir m *appareil* meat grinder, Br mincer; *couteau* cleaver; *planche* chopping board

haddock m smoked haddock

'haie f hedge; SP hurdle; *pour chevaux* fence, jump; **une ~ de policiers** fig a line of police

'haillons mpl rags

'haine f hatred; **'haineux, -euse** full of hatred

'haïr hate

'hâle m (sun)tan

haleine f breath; **hors d'~** out of breath

'haleter pant

'hall m *d'hôtel, immeuble* foyer; *de gare* concourse

'halle f market

halloween m Halloween

hallucination f hallucination

halogène m: (**lampe** f) **~** halogen light

'halte f stop; **faire ~** halt, make a stop

haltère m dumbbell; **faire des ~s** do weightlifting

haltérophilie f weightlifting

'hamac m hammock

'hameau m hamlet

hameçon m hook

'hamster m hamster

'hanche f hip

'handicap m handicap; 'handicapé, ~e 1 adj disabled, handicapped 2 m/f disabled ou handicapped person

'hangar m shed; AVIAT hangar

'hanter haunt

'hantise f fear, dread

'happer catch; fig: de train, bus hit

'haras m stud farm

'harassant travail exhausting

'harceler harass

'hard m hardcore; MUS hard rock

'hardi bold

'hareng m herring

'hargne f bad temper; 'hargneux, -euse venomous; chien vicious

'haricot m BOT bean; c'est la fin des ~s F that's the end

harmonie f harmony; harmoniser match (up); MUS harmonize; s'~ de couleurs go together; s'~ avec go with

'harpe f MUS harp

'harpon m harpoon

'hasard m chance; au ~ at random; par ~ by chance; 'hasarder hazard; se ~ à faire qc venture to do sth

'hâte f hurry, haste; en ~ in haste; avoir ~ de faire qc be eager to do sth; 'hâter hasten; se ~ hurry

'hausse f increase, rise; 'hausser increase; ~ les épaules shrug (one's shoulders)

'haut 1 adj high; immeuble tall, high; cri, voix loud; fonctionnaire high-level 2 adv high; de ~ from above; de ~ en bas from top to bottom; regarder qn up and down; en ~ above; en ~ de at the top of 3 m top; du ~ de from the top of; des ~ et des bas ups and downs

'hautain haughty

'hauteur f height; fig haughtiness; être à la ~ de qc be up to sth

hebdomadaire m & adj weekly

hébergement m accommodation, Br accommodations pl, Br accommodation; héberger: ~ qn put s.o. up; fig take s.o. in

hébreu m: l'~ Hebrew

hectare m hectare (approx 2.5 acres)

'hein F eh?; c'est joli, ~? it's pretty, isn't it?

'hélas alas

'héler hail

hélice f MAR, AVIAT propeller; escalier m en ~ spiral staircase

hélicoptère m helicopter

hémisphère m hemisphere

hémorragie f hemorrhage, Br haemorrhage

'hennir neigh

hépatite f hepatitis

herbe f grass; CUIS herb; mauvaise ~ weed; fines ~s herbs

héréditaire hereditary; hérédité f heredity

homard

hérésie *f* heresy; **hérétique 1** *adj* heretical **2** *m/f* heretic

'**hérissé** ruffled

'**hérisson** *m* hedgehog

héritage *m* inheritance; **hériter 1** *v/t* inherit **2** *v/i*: **~ de qc** inherit sth; **~ de qn** receive an inheritance from s.o.; **héritier, -ère** *m/f* heir

'**hernie** *f* MÉD hernia; **~ discale** slipped disc

héroïne[1] *f drogue* heroin

héroïne[2] *f* heroine

héroïque heroic

héroïsme *m* heroism

'**héron** *m* heron

'**héros** *m* hero

herpès *m* herpes

hésitation *f* hesitation; **hésiter** hesitate

hétérogène heterogeneous

hétérosexuel, ~le heterosexual

heure *f* hour; **arriver à l'~** arrive on time; **de bonne ~** early; **à tout à l'~!** see you soon!; **quelle ~ est-il?** what time is it?; **il est six ~s** it's six (o'clock); **~ locale** local time; **~s d'ouverture** opening hours

heureusement luckily, fortunately; **heureux, -euse** happy; *(chanceux)* fortunate

'**heurt** *m de deux véhicules* collision; *fig (friction)* clash; '**heurter** collide with; *fig* offend; **se ~** collide *(à* with); *fig (s'affronter)* clash *(sur* over)

hiberner hibernate

'**hibou** *m* owl

'**hideux, -euse** hideous

hier yesterday

'**hiérarchie** *f* hierarchy

high-tech *inv* high tech, hi--tech

hilare grinning

hippique SP equestrian; **concours** *m* **~** horse show; **hippodrome** *m* race course

hirondelle *f* swallow

hirsute hairy

hispanique Hispanic

'**hisser** *drapeau, voile* hoist; *(monter)* lift, raise; **se ~** pull o.s. up

histoire *f* history; *(récit, conte)* story; **faire des ~s** make a fuss

historique 1 *adj* historic **2** *m* chronicle

hiver *m* winter

H.L.M. *m ou f* (= **habitation à loyer modéré**) low cost housing

'**hocher**: **~ la tête** *approbation* nod (one's head); *désapprobation* shake one's head

'**hockey** *m* **sur gazon** field hockey, *Br* hockey; **sur glace** hockey, *Br* ice hockey

'**holding** *m* holding company

'**hold-up** *m* holdup

'**hollandais, ~e 1** *adj* Dutch **2** *m langue* Dutch; **Hollandais, ~e** *m/f* Dutchman; Dutchwoman; '**Hollande: la ~** Holland

'**homard** *m* lobster

homéopathie *f* homeopathy
homicide *m* homicide; ~ **involontaire** manslaughter; ~ **volontaire** murder
hommage *m* homage; **rendre ~ à** pay homage to
homme *m* man; ~ **d'affaires** businessman; ~ **d'État** statesman
homologue *m* counterpart, opposite number; **homologuer** *record* ratify; *tarif* authorize
homophobe homophobic
homosexuel, ~le *m/f & adj* homosexual
'Hongrie *f*: **la ~** Hungary; **'hongrois, ~e 1** *adj* Hungarian **2** *m langue* Hungarian; **Hongrois, ~e** *m/f* Hungarian
honnête honest; *(convenable)* decent; *(passable)* reasonable; **honnêteté** honesty
honneur *m* honor, *Br* honour; **en l'~ de** in honor of; **faire ~ à qc** honor sth; **honorable** honorable, *Br* honourable; **honoraire 1** *adj* honorary **2 ~s** *mpl* fees; **honorer** honor, *Br* honour; **honorifique** honorific
'honte *f* shame; **avoir ~ de** be ashamed of; **'honteux, -euse** *(déshonorant)* shameful; *(déconfit)* ashamed
'hooligan *m* hooligan
hôpital *m* hospital; **à l'~** in the hospital, *Br* in hospital
'hoquet *m* hiccup; **avoir le ~**
have (the) hiccups
horaire 1 *adj* hourly **2** *m emploi du temps* timetable, schedule; *des avions, trains etc* schedule, *Br* timetable
horizon *m* horizon
horizontal horizontal
horloge *f* clock
'hormis but
hormonal hormonal; **hormone** *f* hormone
horodateur *m dans parking* pay and display machine
horoscope *m* horoscope
horreur *f* horror; *(monstruosité)* monstrosity; **avoir ~ de qc** detest sth; *(quelle)* ~! how awful!
horrible horrible
horrifiant horrifying
'hors: ~ **de** *(à l'extérieur de)* outside; ~ **de danger** out of danger; ~ **sujet** beside the point; **être ~ de soi** be beside o.s.
'hors-bord *m* outboard
'hors-d'œuvre *m* CUIS appetizer, starter
'hors-jeu offside
horticulture *f* horticulture
hospice *m* REL hospice; *(asile)* home
hospitalier, -ère hospitable; MÉD hospital *atr*
hospitaliser hospitalize
hospitalité *f* hospitality
hostile hostile; **hostilité** *f* hostility
'hot-dog *m* hot dog
hôte *m* host; *(invité)* guest

hôtel *m* hotel; **~ de ville** town hall

hôtellerie *f*: **l'~** the hotel business

hôtesse *f* hostess; **~ de l'air** air hostess

'houblon *m* BOT hop

'houille *f* coal

'houle *f* MAR swell; **'houleux, -euse** *fig* stormy

'housse *f* protective cover

'houx *m* BOT holly

'hublot *m* NAUT porthole; AVIAT window

'huer boo, jeer

huile *f* oil; **~ solaire** suntan oil; **huiler** oil

'huis *m*: **à ~ clos** behind closed doors; JUR in camera; **huissier** *m* JUR bailiff

'huit eight; **~ jours** a week; **demain en ~** a week tomorrow; **'huitaine** *f*: **une ~ de** about eight, eight or so; **une ~ (de jours)** a week; **'huitième** eighth

huître *f* oyster

humain human; *traitement* humane; **humaniser** humanize; **humanitaire** humanitarian; **humanité** *f* humanity

humble humble

humecter moisten

'humer breathe in

humeur *f* mood; (*tempérament*) temperament; **être de bonne/mauvaise ~** be in a good/bad mood

humide damp; (*chaud et ~*) humid; **humidifier** moisten; *atmosphère* humidify; **humidité** *f* dampness; humidity

humiliation *f* humiliation; **humiliant** humiliating; **humilier** humiliate

humour *m* humor, *Br* humour; **avoir de l'~** have a (good) sense of humor

'huppé exclusive

'hurlement *m d'un loup* howl; *d'une personne* scream; **'hurler** *d'un loup* howl; *d'une personne* scream; **~ de rire** roar with laughter

hydratant *cosmétique* moisturizing

hydraulique hydraulic

hydroélectrique hydroelectric

hydrogène *m* CHIM hydrogen

hydroglisseur *m* jetfoil

hygiène *f* hygiene; **avoir une bonne ~ de vie** have a healthy lifestyle; **hygiénique** hygienic; **papier ~** toilet paper; **serviette ~** sanitary napkin, *Br* sanitary towel

hymne *m* hymn; **~ national** national anthem

hyperactif, -ive hyperactive

hypersensible hypersensitive

hypertension *f* MÉD high blood pressure

hypertexte: **lien** *m* **~** hypertext link

hypnotiser hypnotize

hypocrisie *f* hypocrisy; **hy-**

pocrite 1 *adj* hypocritical **2**
m/f hypocrite
hypothèque *f* COMM mortgage

hypothèse *f* hypothesis; **hy-**
pothétique hypothetical
hystérie *f* hysteria; **hystéri-**
que hysterical

I

ici here; **jusqu'~** to here; (*jus-*
qu'à maintenant) so far; **par**
~ this way; (*dans le coin*)
around about here; **d'~ là**
by then, by that time
icône *f* icon
idéal *m & adj* ideal; **idéaliser**
idealize; **idéalisme** *m* ideal-
ism; **idéaliste 1** *adj* idealist
2 *m/f* idealist
idée *f* idea; (*opinion*) view;
avoir dans l'~ de faire qch
be thinking of doing sth; **tu**
te fais des ~s (*tu te trompes*)
you're imagining things; **~**
fixe obsession
identifier identify (**avec, à**
with); **s'~ avec** *ou* **à** identify
with
identique identical (**à** to)
identité *f* identity; **pièce** *f* **d'~**
identity, ID
idéologie *f* ideology
idiomatique idiomatic
idiot, ~e 1 *adj* idiotic **2** *m/f* idiot; **idiotie** *f* idiocy; **dire des**
~s talk nonsense
idole *f* idol
idylle *f* romance
ignare *péj* **1** *adj* ignorant **2** *m/f*
ignoramus
ignoble vile

ignorance *f* ignorance; **igno-**
rant ignorant; **ignorer** not
know; *personne, talent* ignore
il he; *chose* it; *impersonnel* it;
~ va pleuvoir it is *ou* it's going to rain
île *f* island; **les ~s britan-**
niques the British Isles
illégal illegal
illégitime *enfant* illegitimate
illettré illiterate
illicite illicit
illimité unlimited
illisible illegible; *mauvaise*
littérature unreadable
illogique illogical
illuminer light up, illuminate;
par projecteur floodlight
illusion *f* illusion; **se faire**
des ~s delude o.s.; **illusoire**
illusory
illustration *f* illustration; **il-**
lustrer illustrate; **s'~** distinguish o.s. (**par** by)
îlot *m* (small) island; *de mai-*
sons block
ils *mpl* they
image *f* picture; *dans un mi-*
roir reflection, image; (*res-*
semblance) image
imaginaire imaginary; **ima-**

gination *f* imagination; **ima-giner** imagine; (*inventer*) devise; **s'~ que** imagine that

imbattable unbeatable

imbécile 1 *adj* idiotic **2** *m/f* idiot, imbecile

imbiber soak (*de* with)

imbu: ~ **de** *fig* full of

imitation *f* imitation; THÉÂT impersonation; **imiter** imitate; THÉÂT impersonate

immaculé immaculate

immangeable inedible

immatriculation *f* registration; **plaque f d'~** AUTO license plate, *Br* number plate; **immatriculer** register

immature immature

immédiat 1 *adj* immediate **2** *m*: **dans l'~** for the moment; **immédiatement** immediately

immense immense

immerger immerse; **s'~ d'un** *sous-marin* submerge

immeuble *m* building

immigrant, **~e** *m/f* immigrant; **immigration** *f* immigration; **immigrer** immigrate

imminent imminent

immiscer: **s'~ dans qc** interfere in sth

immobile immobile

immobilier, **-ère 1** *adj*: **biens** *mpl* **~s** real estate **2** *m* property

immobiliser immobilize; *train*, *circulation* bring to a standstill; *capital* tie up; **s'~**

(*s'arrêter*) come to a standstill

immonde foul

immoral immoral; **immoralité** *f* immorality

immortaliser immortalize; **immortalité** *f* immortality; **immortel**, **~le** immortal

immuniser: **im-munisé contre** *fig* immune to; **immunité** *f* JUR, MÉD immunity

impact *m* impact

impair 1 *adj* odd **2** *m* blunder

impardonnable unforgiveable

imparfait imperfect

impartial impartial

impasse *f* dead end; *fig* deadlock, impasse

impassible impassive

impatience *f* impatience; **impatient** impatient; **impatienter**: **s'~** get impatient

impayé unpaid

impeccable impeccable

impénétrable impenetrable

impératif, **-ive 1** *adj* imperative **2** *m* (*exigence*) requirement; GRAM imperative

impératrice *f* empress

imperceptible imperceptible

imperfection *f* imperfection

impérieux, **-euse** *personne* imperious; *besoin* urgent

impérissable immortal; *souvenir* unforgettable

imperméable waterproof; **imperméable 1** *adj tissu* waterproof **2** *m* raincoat

impersonnel, **~le** impersonal
impertinence *f* impertinence; **impertinent** impertinent
imperturbable imperturbable
impétueux, **-euse** impetuous
impitoyable pitiless
implacable implacable
implanter *fig* introduce; *usine* set up; **s'~** become established; *d'une industrie* set up
implicite implicit
impliquer *personne* implicate; (*entraîner*) mean, involve; (*supposer*) imply
implorer *aide* beg for; **~ qn de faire qch** implore *ou* beg s.o. to do sth
impoli rude, impolite
impopulaire unpopular
importance *f* importance; *d'une ville* size; *d'une somme, catastrophe* magnitude; **important 1** *adj* important; *ville, somme* large, sizeable **2** *m*: **l'~, c'est que ...** the important thing is that ...
importateur, **-trice 1** *adj* importing **2** *m* importer; **importation** *f* import; **importer 1** *v/t* import; *mode, musique* introduce **2** *v/i* matter, be important (*à* to); **n'importe quand** any time; **n'importe quoi!** nonsense!
importun troublesome; **importuner** bother
imposable taxable

imposant imposing; **imposer** impose; *marchandise* tax; **s'~** (*être nécessaire*) be essential; (*se faire admettre*) gain recognition
impossible 1 *adj* impossible **2** *m*: **faire l'~ pour faire qch** do one's utmost to do sth
imposteur *m* imposter
impôt *m* tax; **déclaration** *f* **d'~s** tax return
impotent crippled
impraticable *projet* impractical; *rue* impassable
imprécis vague, imprecise
imprégner impregnate (**de** with); **imprégné de** *fig* full of
impression *f* impression; *imprimerie* printing; **impressionnant** impressive; (*troublant*) upsetting; **impressionner** impress; (*troubler*) upset; **impressionniste** *m/f* & *adj* impressionist
imprévisible unpredictable
imprévu 1 *adj* unexpected **2** *m*: **sauf ~** all being well
imprimante *f* INFORM printer; **~ laser** laser printer; **~ à jet d'encre** ink-jet (printer); **imprimé** *m* (*formulaire*) form; *tissu* print; **poste ~s** printed matter; **imprimer** print; INFORM print out; *édition* publish
improbable unlikely, improbable
improductif, **-ive** unproduc-

tive

impropre *mot, outil* inappropriate; **~ à la consommation** unfit for human consumption

improviste: à l'~ unexpectedly

imprudence *f* imprudence; **imprudent** imprudent

impudence *f* impudence; **impudent** impudent

impudique shameless

impuissance *f* powerlessness; MÉD impotence; **impuissant** powerless; MÉD impotent

impulsif, -ive impulsive; **impulsion** *f* impulse; **à l'économie** boost

impuni unpunished

impur *eau* dirty, polluted; *(impudique)* impure

imputer attribute (**à** to); FIN charge (**sur** to)

inabordable *prix* unaffordable

inacceptable unacceptable

inaccessible inaccessible; *personne* unapproachable; *objectif* unattainable

inachevé unfinished

inactif, -ive idle; *population* non-working; *remède, méthode* ineffective; *marché* slack

inadéquat inadequate; *méthode* unsuitable

inadmissible unacceptable

inadvertance *f*: **par ~** inadvertently

inanimé inanimate; *(mort)* lifeless; *(inconscient)* unconscious

inaperçu: passer ~ pass unnoticed

inapproprié inappropriate

inapte: ~ à unsuited to; MÉD, MIL unfit for

inattendu unexpected

inattention *f* inattentiveness; **erreur d'~** careless mistake

inaudible inaudible

inaugurer inaugurate

inavouable shameful

incapable incapable (**de faire** of doing)

incapacité *f* *(inaptitude)* incompetence; **de faire qch** inability

incarcérer imprison

incassable unbreakable

incendiaire incendiary; *discours* inflammatory; **incendie** *m* fire; **~ criminel** arson; **incendier** set fire to

incertain uncertain; *temps* unsettled; *(hésitant)* indecisive; **incertitude** *f* uncertainty

incessamment any minute now

inchangé unchanged

incident *m* incident; **~ de parcours** mishap

incinérer incinerate; *cadavre* cremate

incisif, -ive incisive; **incision** *f* incision

inciter encourage (**à faire qch** to do sth); *péj* egg on, incite

inclinable tilting; **inclinaison** f slope

inclination f fig inclination (**pour** for); **~ de tête** (salut) nod; **incliner** tilt; **s'~** bend; *pour saluer* bow; **s'~ devant qc** (céder) yield to sth; **s'~ devant qn** aussi fig bow to s.o.

inclure include; *dans une lettre* enclose; **ci-inclus** enclosed; **jusqu'au 30 juin ~** to 30th June inclusive

incohérence f de comportement inconsistency; de discours incoherence

incolore colorless, Br colourless

incomber: **il vous incombe de le lui dire** it is your duty to tell him

incommoder bother

incomparable incomparable

incompatibilité f incompatibility; **incompatible** incompatible

incompétence f incompetence; **incompétent** incompetent

incomplet, -ète incomplete

incompréhensible incomprehensible; **incompréhension** f lack of understanding

incompris misunderstood (**de** by)

inconcevable inconceivable

inconditionnel, ~le 1 adj unconditional **2** m/f fan, fanatic

inconfortable uncomfortable

inconnu, ~e 1 adj (ignoré) unknown; (étranger) strange **2** m/f stranger

inconscient unconscious; (irréfléchi) irresponsible

inconsidéré rash, thoughtless

inconsistant inconsistent; fig: raisonnement flimsy

inconsolable inconsolable

incontestable indisputable; **incontesté** outright

incontournable: **être ~** be a must

inconvénient m disadvantage m; **si vous n'y voyez aucun ~** if you have no objection

incorporer incorporate (**à** with, into); MIL draft

incorrect wrong, incorrect; tenue, langage improper

incorrigible incorrigible

incrédule (sceptique) incredulous; **incrédulité** f incredulity

incriminer personne blame; JUR accuse; paroles, actions condemn

incroyable incredible, unbelievable

inculpé, ~e m/f: **l'~** the accused, the defendant; **inculper** JUR charge, indict (**de, pour** with)

inculquer: **~ qc à qn** instill ou Br instil sth into s.o.

inculte terre waste atr, uncultivated; (ignorant) uneducated

incurable incurable

incursion f MIL raid, incursion; fig: *dans la politique etc* venture (***dans*** into)

Inde f: *l'~* India

indécent indecent; *(incorrect)* inappropriate, improper

indécis undecided; *personne, caractère* indecisive

indéfini indefinite; *(imprécis)* undefined

indéfinissable indefinable

indélicat *personne, action* tactless

indemne unhurt; **indemniser** compensate (***de*** for); **indemnité** f *(dédommagement)* compensation; *(allocation)* allowance

indéniable undeniable

indépendance f independence; **indépendant** independent (***de*** of); *travailleur* freelance; **indépendantiste** (pro-)independence *atr*

indescriptible indescribable

indésirable undesirable

indéterminé unspecified

index m index; *doigt* index finger

indicateur, -trice m *(espion)* informer; TECH gauge, indicator

indicatif m TÉL code

indication f indication; *(information)* piece of information; *~s* instructions

indice m *(signe)* sign, indica-

tion; JUR clue

indien, ~ne Indian; *d'Amérique aussi* native American; **Indien** m/f Indian; *d'Amérique aussi* native American

indifférence f indifference; **indifférent** indifferent

indigène *adj & m/f* native

indigeste indigestible; **indigestion** f MÉD indigestion

indignation f indignation

indigne unworthy; *parents* unfit

indigner make indignant; *s'~ de qc/contre qn* be indignant about sth/with s.o.

indiqué appropriate; *ce n'est pas ~* it's not advisable; **indiquer** indicate, show; *d'une pendule* show; *(recommander)* recommend

indirect indirect

indiscipline f indiscipline; **indiscipliné** undisciplined; *cheveux* unmanageable

indiscret, -ète indiscreet; **indiscrétion** indiscretion

indispensable indispensable

indistinct indistinct

individu m individual; **individualisme** m individualism; **individuel, ~le** individual; *secrétaire* private, personal; *liberté* personal; *chambre* single; *maison* detached

indivisible indivisible

indolent lazy, indolent

indolore painless

indomptable fig indomitable

indu: *à une heure ~e* at some

ungodly hour
indubitable indisputable
induire: ~ *qn en erreur* mislead s.o.
indulgence *f* indulgence; *d'un juge* leniency; **indulgent** indulgent; *juge lenient*
industrialisé industrialized; **industrialiser** industrialize; **industrie** *f* industry; **industriel**, **~le 1** *adj* industrial **2** *m* industrialist
inébranlable solid (as a rock)
inédit (*pas édité*) unpublished; (*nouveau*) original, unique
inégal unequal; *surface* uneven; *rythme* irregular; **inégalité** *f* inequality; *d'une surface* unevenness
inepte inept; **ineptie** *f* ineptitude; **~s** nonsense
inépuisable inexhaustible
inerte *corps* lifeless, inert; PHYS inert; **inertie** *f* inertia
inespéré unexpected, unhoped-for
inestimable *tableau* priceless; *aide* invaluable
inévitable inevitable; *accident* unavoidable
inexact inaccurate
inexcusable inexcusable, unforgivable
inexistant non-existent
inexplicable inexplicable
inexprimable inexpressible
infaillible infallible
infantile *mortalité* infant *atr*; *péj* infantile; *maladie* children's

infarctus *m* MÉD: ~ *du myocarde* coronary (thrombosis)
infatigable tireless, indefatigable
infect disgusting; *temps* foul; **infecter** infect; *air*, *eau* pollute; **s'~** become infected; **infectieux**, **-euse** infectious; **infection** *f* MÉD infection
inférieur, **~e 1** *adj* lower; *qualité* inferior **2** *m/f* inferior; **infériorité** *f* inferiority
infernal infernal
infidèle unfaithful; REL pagan *atr*; **infidélité** *f* infidelity
infiltrer: **s'~ dans** get into; *fig* infiltrate
infime tiny, infinitesimal
infini 1 *adj* infinite **2** *m* infinity
infirme 1 *adj* disabled **2** *m/f* disabled person; **infirmerie** *f* infirmary; ÉDU sickbay; **infirmier**, **-ère** *m/f* nurse; **infirmité** *f* disability
inflammation *f* MÉD inflammation
inflation *f* inflation
inflexible inflexible
infliger *peine* inflict (**à** on); *défaite* impose
influence *f* influence; **influencer** influence; **influent** influential
influer: ~ *sur* affect
info *f* F RAD, TV news item; **les ~s** the news *sg*
informaticien, **~ne** *m/f* com-

puter scientist

information f information; JUR inquiry; **une ~** a piece of information; **les ~s** RAD, TV the news sg; **traitement** m **de l'~** data processing

informatique 1 adj computer atr **2** f information technology, IT; **informatiser** computerize

informe shapeless

informer inform; **s'~** find out (**de qc auprès de qn** about sth from s.o.)

infraction f infringement (**à** of)

infranchissable impossible to cross; obstacle insurmountable

infrarouge infrared

infrastructure f infrastructure

infroissable crease-resistant

infructueux, -euse unsuccessful

infusion f herb tea

ingénierie f engineering; **ingénieur** m engineer

ingéniosité f ingeniousness

ingrat, ~e ungrateful; tâche thankless; **ingratitude** f ingratitude

ingrédient m ingredient

ingurgiter gulp down

inhabitable uninhabitable; **inhabité** uninhabited

inhalateur m MÉD inhaler; **inhaler** inhale

inhérent inherent (**à** in)

inhibé inhibited; **inhibition** f PSYCH inhibition

inhospitalier, -ère inhospitable

inhumain inhuman

ininflammable non-flammable

ininterrompu uninterrupted; pluie, musique non-stop

initial, ~e 1 adj initial **2** f initial (letter)

initiation f initiation; **~ à** fig introduction to

inimitié f enmity

initiative f initiative

initié, ~e m/f insider; **initier** initiate (**à** in); fig introduce (**à** to)

injecté: ~ (**de sang**) bloodshot; **injecter** inject; **injection** f injection

injoignable unreachable, uncontactable

injure f insult; **~s** abuse; **injurier** insult, abuse

injuste unfair, unjust; **injustice** f injustice; d'une décision aussi unfairness

inlassable tireless

inné innate

innocence f innocence; **innocent** innocent; **innocenter** clear

innombrable countless; auditoire, foule vast

innovant innovative; **innovation** f innovation

inoccupé personne idle; maison unoccupied

inodore odorless, Br odourless

inoffensif, -ive harmless; *humour* inoffensive

inondation *f* flood; **inonder** flood; ~ *de fig* inundate with

inopiné unexpected

inopportun ill-timed

inorganique inorganic

inoubliable unforgettable

inouï unheard-of

inoxydable stainless

inquiet, -ète anxious, worried (*de* about); **inquiéter** worry; **s'~** worry (*de* about); **inquiétude** *f* anxiety

insaisissable elusive; *différence* imperceptible

insatiable insatiable

insatisfaisant unsatisfactory; **insatisfait** unsatisfied; *mécontent* dissatisfied

inscription *f* inscription; (*immatriculation*) registration; **inscrire** (*noter*) write down, note; *dans registre* enter; *examen* register; (*graver*) inscribe; **s'~** put one's name down; *à l'université* register; *à un cours* enroll, *Br* enrol (*à* for)

insecte *m* insect; **insecticide** *m* insecticide

insécurité *f* insecurity; POL security problem

insensé mad, insane

insensibiliser numb; **insensible** ANAT numb; *personne* insensitive (*à* to)

insérer insert; *annonce* put; **insertion** *f* insertion

insigne *m* (*emblème*) insig-

nia; (*badge*) badge

insignifiant insignificant

insinuer insinuate; **s'~ dans** worm one's way into

insipide insipid

insistance *f* insistence; **insistant** insistent; **insister** insist; F (*persévérer*) persevere; ~ *pour faire qch* insist on doing sth; ~ *sur qc* (*souligner*) stress sth

insolation *f* sunstroke

insolence *f* insolence; **insolent** insolent

insolite unusual

insoluble insolvent

insomnie *f* insomnia

insonoriser soundproof

insouciant carefree

insoumis rebellious

insoutenable (*insupportable*) unbearable; *argument* untenable

inspecter inspect; **inspecteur, -trice** *m/f* inspector; **inspection** *f* inspection

inspiration *f fig* inspiration; **inspirer** 1 *v/i* breathe in, inhale 2 *v/t* inspire; **s'~ de** be inspired by

installation *f* installation; ~ **électrique** wiring; ~**s** facilities; **installer** install; *appartement*: fit out; (*loger, placer*) put; **s'~** (*s'établir*) settle down; *à la campagne etc* settle; *d'un médecin, dentiste* set up

instant *m* instant, moment; *à l'~* just this minute; *dans un*

~ in a minute; **pour l'** for the moment; **instantané 1** *adj* immediate; *café* instant; *mort* instantaneous **2** *m* PHOT snap(shot)

instaurer establish

instinct *m* instinct; **instinctif, -ive** instinctive

instituer introduce; **institut** *m* institute; ~ **de beauté** beauty salon; **instituteur, -trice** *m/f* (primary) school teacher; **institution** *f* institution

instructeur *m* MIL instructor; **instructif, -ive** instructive; **instruction** *f* (*enseignement, culture*) education; MIL training; JUR preliminary investigation; INFORM instruction; ~**s** instructions; **instruire** ÉDU educate, teach; MIL train; JUR investigate; **instruit** (well-)educated

instrument *m* instrument

insu: à l'~ de unbeknownst to

insubordination *f* insubordination

insuffisance *f* deficiency; ~ **respiratoire** respiratory problem; **insuffisant** *quantité* insufficient; *qualité* inadequate

insulaire 1 *adj* island *atr* **2** *m/f* islander

insuline *f* insulin

insulte *f* insult; **insulter** insult

insupportable unbearable

insurger: s'~ contre rise up against

insurrection *f* insurrection

intact intact

intégral full, complete; *texte* unabridged

intégration *f* (*assimilation*) integration

intègre of integrity

intégrer (*assimiler*) integrate; (*incorporer*) incorporate; **intégriste** *m/f* & *adj* fundamentalist

intégrité *f* (*honnêteté*) integrity

intellectuel, **~le** *m/f* & *adj* intellectual

intelligence *f* intelligence; **intelligent** intelligent

intempéries *fpl* bad weather

intempestif, -ive untimely

intenable *situation*, *froid* unbearable

intense intense; **intensif, -ive** intensive; **intensification** *f* intensification; *d'un conflit* escalation; **intensifier** intensify; **s'~** intensify; *d'un conflit* escalate; **intensité** *f* intensity

intenter: ~ **un procès contre** start proceedings against

intention *f* intention; **avoir l'~ de faire qch** intend to do sth; **à l'~ de** for; **intentionné: bien** ~ well-meaning; **mal** ~ ill-intentioned; **intentionnel, ~le** intentional

interactif, -ive interactive

intercéder: ~ **pour qn** intercede for s.o.

intercepter intercept; *soleil* shut out

interchangeable interchangeable

interdiction *f* ban; **interdire** ban; ~ **à qn de faire qc** forbid s.o. to do sth; **interdit** forbidden; *(très étonné)* taken aback

intéressant interesting; *(avide)* selfish; *prix* good; *situation* well-paid; **intéressé** interested; *(concerné)* concerned; **intéresser** interest; *(concerner)* concern; **s'~ à** be interested in; **intérêt** *m* interest; *(égoïsme)* self-interest; **~s** COMM interest

interface *f* interface

intérieur 1 *adj poche* inside; *porte, vie* inner; *politique, vol* domestic; *mer* inland **2** *m* inside; *d'une auto etc* interior; **à l'~ (de)** inside

intérim *m* interim; *travail* temporary work; **intérimaire 1** *adj travail* temporary **2** *m/f* temp

interlocuteur, -trice *m/f*: **mon/son ~** the person I/she was talking to

intermédiaire 1 *adj* intermediate **2** *m/f* intermediary; COMM middleman

interminable interminable

intermittence *f*: **par ~** intermittently

international, **~e** *m/f & adj* international

interne 1 *adj* internal; *oreille*

inner; *d'une société* in-house **2** *m/f* *élève* boarder; *médecin* intern, *Br* houseman; **~** terner intern

Internet *m* Internet; **sur ~** on the Internet

interpeller call out to; *de la police*, POL question

interphone *m* intercom; *d'un immeuble* entry phone

interposer: **s'~** *(intervenir)* intervene

interprète *m/f* interpreter; *(porte-parole)* spokesperson; **interpréter** interpret; *rôle*, MUS play

interrogation *f* question; *d'un suspect* questioning, interrogation; **interrogatoire** *m par police* questioning; *par juge* cross-examination; **interroger** question; *de la police* question, interrogate; *d'un juge* cross-examine

interrompre interrupt; **s'~** break off

interrupteur *m* switch; **interruption** *f* interruption; **sans ~** without stopping

intersection *f* intersection

intervalle *m* space, gap; *de temps* interval

intervenir intervene; *d'une rencontre* take place; **intervention** *f* intervention; MÉD operation; *(discours)* speech

interview *f* interview; **interviewer** interview

intestin 1 *adj* internal **2** *m* intestin

intime 1 adj intimate; *ami* close; *pièce* cozy, Br cosy; *vie private* **2** m/f close friend
intimider intimidate
intimité f intimacy; *vie privée* privacy
intituler call; *s'~* be called
intolérable intolerable; **intolérance** f intolerance; **intolérant** intolerant
intoxication f poisoning; *~ alimentaire* food poisoning; **intoxiquer** poison; *fig* brainwash
intransigeant intransigent
intrépide intrepid
intrigue f plot; *~s* scheming, plotting; **intriguer 1** v/i scheme, plot **2** v/t intrigue
introduction f introduction; **introduire** introduce; *visiteur* show in; *(engager)* insert; *s'~ dans* gain entry to
introuvable impossible to find
introverti, *~e* m/f introvert
intrus, *~e* m/f intruder
intuitif, *-ive* intuitive; **intuition** f intuition; *(pressentiment)* premonition
inusable hard-wearing
inutile *qui ne sert pas* useless; *(superflu)* pointless, unnecessary; **inutilisable** unuseable
invalide 1 adj *(infirme)* disabled **2** m/f disabled person; **invalider** JUR, POL invalidate; **invalidité** f disability
invariable invariable

invasion f invasion
invendable unsellable
inventaire m inventory; COMM *opération* stocktaking
inventer invent; *histoire* make up; **inventeur**, *-trice* m/f inventor; **invention** f invention
inverse 1 adj MATH inverse; *sens* opposite; *dans l'ordre ~* in reverse order **2** m opposite, reverse; **inverser** invert; *rôles* reverse
investigation f investigation
investir FIN invest; *(cerner)* surround; **investissement** m FIN investment
invétéré inveterate
investisseur, *-euse* m investor
invincible invincible; *obstacle* insuperable
invisible invisible
invitation f invitation; **invité**, *~e* m/f guest; **inviter** invite; *~ qn à faire qch* urge s.o. to do sth
invivable unbearable
involontaire unintentional; *témoin* unwilling; *mouvement* involuntary
invoquer *Dieu* call on, invoke; *aide* call on; *texte*, *loi* refer to; *solution* put forward
invraisemblable unlikely, improbable
Iran m: *l'~* Iran; **iranien**, *~ne* Iranian; **Iranien**, *~ne* m/f Iranian

Iraq *m*: *l'~* Iraq; **iraquien, ~ne** Iraqi; **Iraquien, ~ne** *m/f* Iraqi

irascible irascible

irlandais, ~e 1 *adj* Irish **2** *m* *langue* Irish (Gaelic); **Irlandais, ~e** *m/f* Irishman; Irishwoman; **Irlande** *f*: *l'~* Ireland

ironie *f* irony; **ironiser** be ironic

irraisonné irrational

irrationnel, ~le irrational

irréalisable *projet* impracticable; *rêve* unrealizable

irréaliste unrealistic

irréconciliable irreconcilable

irrécupérable beyond repair; *personne* beyond redemption; *données* irretrievable

irréductible indomitable; *ennemi* implacable

irréel, ~le unreal

irréfléchi thoughtless, reckless

irréfutable irrefutable

irrégulier, -ère irregular; *surface, terrain* uneven; *étudiant, sportif* erratic

irrémédiable *maladie* incurable; *erreur* irreparable

irremplaçable irreplaceable

irréparable *faute, perte* irreparable; *vélo* beyond repair

irréprochable irreproachable

irrésistible irresistible

irrésolu *personne* indecisive; *problème* unresolved

irrespirable unbreathable

irresponsable irresponsible

irrigation *f* AGR irrigation

irritable irritable; **irritation** *f* irritation; **irriter** irritate; **s'~** get irritated

islam, Islam *m* REL Islam; **islamique** Islamic; **islamiste** Islamic fundamentalist

islandais, ~e 1 *adj* Icelandic **2** *m langue* Islandic; **Islandais, ~e** *m/f* Icelander; **Islande** *f*: *l'~* Iceland

isolation *f* insulation; *contre le bruit* soundproofing; **isolé** isolated; TECH insulated; **isolement** *m* isolation; **isoler** isolate; *prisonnier* place in solitary confinement; ÉL insulate

Israël *m* Israel; **israélien, ~ne** Israeli; **Israélien, ~ne** *m/f* Israeli

issu: *être ~ de parenté* come from; *résultat* stem from

issue *f* way out (*aussi fig*), exit; (*fin*) outcome; *à l'~ de* at the end of

Italie *f*: *l'~* Italy; **italien, ~ne 1** *adj* Italian **2** *m langue* Italian; **Italien, ~ne** *m/f* Italian

itinéraire *m* itinerary

IVG *f* (= **interruption volontaire de grossesse**) termination, abortion

ivoire *m* ivory

ivre drunk; *~ de joie, colère* wild with; **ivresse** *f* drunkenness; **ivrogne** *m/f* drunk

J

jacasser chatter

jacinthe f BOT hyacinth

jade m jade

jaillir shoot out (*de* from)

jalousie f jealousy; (*store*) Venetian blind; **jaloux, -ouse** jealous

jamais ◇ *positif* ever; **à ~** for ever, for good; ◇ *négatif* never; **ne ... ~** never; **je ne lui ai ~ parlé** I've never spoken to him

jambe f leg

jambon m ham

jante f rim

janvier m January

Japon m: **le ~** Japan; **japonais, ~e 1** adj Japanese **2** m langue Japanese; **Japonais, ~e** m/f Japanese

jappement m yap

jaquette f d'un livre dust jacket

jardin m garden; **~ botanique** botanical gardens pl; **~ public** park; **jardinage** m gardening; **jardiner** garden; **jardinier** m gardener; **jardinière** f à fleurs window box; femme gardener

jargon m jargon; péj (charabia) gibberish

jarret m back of the knee; CUIS shin

jaser gossip

jatte f bowl

jauge f gauge; **jauger** gauge

jaunâtre yellowish; **jaune 1** adj yellow **2** m: **~ d'œuf** egg yolk; **jaunir** go yellow; **jaunisse** f MÉD jaundice

jazz m jazz; **jazzman** m jazz musician

je I

jean m jeans pl; **veste m en ~** denim jacket

jeep f jeep

Jésus-Christ Jesus (Christ)

jet m (*lancer*) throw; (*jaillissement*) jet; de sang spurt; **~ d'eau** fountain

jetable disposable

jetée f MAR jetty

jeter throw; (*se défaire de*) throw away; **~ un coup d'œil à qch** glance at sth

jeton m token; de jeu chip

jeu m play (*aussi* TECH); activité, en tennis game; (*série, ensemble*) set; de cartes deck, Br pack; MUS playing; THÉÂT acting; **~ ~** gambling; **être en ~** be at stake; **~ de mots** play on words

jeudi m Thursday

jeun: à ~ on an empty stomach

jeune 1 adj young; **~s mariés** newly-weds **2** m/f: **un ~** a young man; **les ~s** young people pl, the young pl

jeûne m fast; **jeûner** fast

jeunesse f youth; *caractère jeune* youthfulness

J.O. *mpl* (= ***Jeux Olympiques***) Olympic Games

joaillerie f *magasin* jewelry store, Br jeweller's; *articles* jewelry, Br jewellery; **joaillier, -ère** m/f jeweler, Br jeweller

jogging m jogging; (*survêtement*) sweats pl, Br tracksuit; **faire du ~** go jogging

joie f joy; **débordant de ~** jubilant

joindre join; *efforts* combine; *à un courrier* enclose (**à** with); *personne* contact, get in touch with; *mains* clasp; **se ~ à qn pour faire qch** join s.o. in doing sth

joint m joint; *d'étanchéité* seal, gasket; *de robinet* washer

joli pretty

joncher strew (**de** with)

jonction f junction

jongler juggle; **jongleur** m juggler

joue f cheek

jouer 1 v/t play; *argent, réputation* gamble; THÉÂT *pièce* perform; *film* show; **la comédie** put on an act 2 v/i play; *d'un acteur* act; *parier* gamble; **~ au football** play football; **~ d'un instrument** play an instrument; **~ sur cheval etc** put money on

jouet m toy

joueur, -euse m/f player; *de*

jeux d'argent gambler; **être beau/mauvais ~** be a good/bad loser

jouir have an orgasm, come; **~ de qc** enjoy sth; (*posséder*) have sth; **jouissance** f enjoyment; JUR possession

jour m day; (*lumière*) daylight; (*ouverture*) opening; **au grand ~** in broad daylight; **de nos ~s** these days; **du ~ au lendemain** overnight; **être à ~** be up to date; **se faire ~** *de problèmes* come to light; **deux ans ~ pour ~** two years to the day; **il fait ~** it's (getting) light; **au petit ~** at first light

journal m (news)paper; *intime* diary; TV, *à la radio* news sg; **journalisme** m journalism; **journaliste** m/f journalist

journée f day

jovial jovial

joyeux, -euse joyful; **~ Noël!** Merry Christmas!

jubilation f jubilation; **jubiler** be jubilant; *péj* gloat

jucher perch

judiciaire legal

judicieux, -euse sensible, judicious

judo m judo

juge m judge; **~ d'instruction** examining magistrate; **~ de touche** SP linesman; **jugement** m judge(ment); *en matière criminelle* sentence; **porter un ~ sur** pass judge(e)-

ment on; **juger 1** *v/t* JUR try; (*évaluer*) judge; ~ *qc/qn in-térèssant* consider sth/s.o. interesting; ~ *que* think that; ~ *de qn/qc* judge s.o./sth **2** *v/i* judge
juif, -ive *adj* Jewish; **Juif, -ive** *m/f* Jew
juillet *m* July
juin *m* June
jumeau, jumelle *m/f* & *adj* twin; **jumeler** *villes* twin; **jumelles** *fpl* binoculars
jument *f* mare
jungle *f* jungle
jupe *f* skirt
juré *m* JUR juror; **jurer** swear (*de qch* to sth)
juridiction *f* jurisdiction
juridique legal
juron *m* curse
jury *m* JUR jury; *d'un concours* panel, judges *pl*; ÉDU board of examiners
jus *m* juice

jusque 1 *prép*: *jusqu'à lieu* as far as, up to; *temps* until; *jusqu'où vous allez?* how far are you going? **2** *adv* even, including **3** *conj*: *jusqu'à ce qu'il s'endorme* (*subj*) until he falls asleep
juste 1 *adj* fair, just; *salaire, récompense* fair; (*précis*) right, correct; *vêtement* tight **2** *adv* just; *viser, tirer* accurately; *chanter* ~ sing in tune; **justesse** *f* accuracy; *de* ~ only just; **justice** *f* fairness, justice; JUR justice; *la* ~ the law; *faire* ~ *à qn* do s.o. justice
justification *f* justification; **justifier** justify; ~ *de qc* prove sth
juteux, -euse juicy
juvénile youthful; *délinquance* ~ juvenile delinquency
juxtaposer juxtapose

K

kaki khaki
kamikaze *m/f* suicide bomber
kangourou *m* kangaroo
kébab *m* kabob, *Br* kebab
kermesse *f* fair
kérosène *m* kerosene
ketchup *m* ketchup
kg (= *kilogramme*) kg (= kilogram)
kidnapping *m* kidnapping; **kidnapper** kidnap

kilo(gramme) *m* kilo(gram); **kilométrage** *m* mileage; **kilomètre** *m* kilometer, *Br* kilometre; **kilo-octet** *m* kilobyte, k
kinésithérapeute *m/f* physiotherapist
kiosque *m* pavilion; COMM kiosk; ~ *à journaux* newsstand
kit *m*: *en* ~ kit

klaxon *m* AUTO horn; **klaxonner** sound one's horn, hoot
km (= *kilomètre*) km (= kilometer)

knock-out *m* knockout
K-O *m* (= *knock-out*) KO
Ko *m* (= *kilo-octet m*) k (= kil-
obyte)

L

la[1] → **le**
la[2] *pron personnel* her; *chose*
it
là here; *dans un autre lieu
qu'ici* there; *causal* hence;
par ~ that way; *là-bas* (over)
there
laboratoire *m* laboratory, lab
laborieux, -euse laborious;
personne hardworking
labourer plow, *Br* plough
labyrinthe *m* labyrinth, maze
lac *m* lake
lacer tie
lacérer lacerate
lacet *m de chaussures* lace; *de
la route* sharp turn
lâche 1 *adj* loose; *personne*
cowardly **2** *m* coward
lâcher 1 *v/t* let go of; (*laisser
tomber*) drop; (*libérer*) release; *ceinture* loosen; *juron,
vérité* let out; SP leave behind **2** *v/i de freins* fail;
d'une corde break
lâcheté *f* cowardice
lacrymogène *gaz* tear *atr*;
grenade tear-gas *atr*
lacune *f* gap
là-dedans inside; **là-des-
sous** underneath; *derrière*
behind it; **là-dessus** on it,

on top; *à ce moment* at that
instant; *sur ce point* about it;
là-haut up there
laid ugly; **laideur** *f* ugliness;
(*bassesse*) meanness
lainage *m étoffe* woolen *ou
Br* woollen fabric; *vêtement*
woolen, *Br* woollen; **laine** *f*
wool; **laineux, -euse** fleecy
laïque 1 *adj* REL secular; (*sans
confession*) State *atr* **2** *m/f*
lay person
laisse *f* leash
laisser leave; (*permettre*) let;
se ~ aller let o.s. go
laisser-aller *m* casualness
laissez-passer *m* pass
lait *m* milk; **laitage** *m* dairy
product; **laitier, -ère** dairy
atr
laiton *m* brass
laitue *f* BOT lettuce
lambin, ~e *m/f* F slowpoke F,
Br slowcoach F
lambris *m* paneling, *Br* panelling
lame *f blade*; (*plaque*) strip;
(*vague*) wave
lamentable deplorable; **la-
menter: se ~** complain
lampadaire *m* floor lamp;
dans la rue street light

lampe f lamp; **~ de poche** flashlight, Br torch

lancé established; **lancement** m launch; **lancer** throw; avec force hurl; injure shout, hurl (à at); cri give; fusée, COMM launch; INFORM programme run; moteur start; **se ~ sur** marché enter; piste de danse step out onto; **se ~ dans** des activités take up; des explications launch into; des discussions get involved in

langage m language

langouste f spiny lobster

langue f tongue; LING language; **mauvaise ~** gossip; **~ maternelle** mother tongue

languette f d'une chaussure tongue

languir languish; d'une conversation flag

lanière f strap

laper lap up

lapider stone

lapin m rabbit

laps m: **~ de temps** period of time

laque f lacquer

larcin m petty theft

lard m bacon

lardon m lardon, diced bacon

large 1 adj wide; épaules, hanches broad; mesure, rôle large; (généreux) generous **2** adv: voir; **au ~** open sea; **prendre le ~** fig take off; largesse f generosity; largeur f width; **~ d'es-** prit broad-mindedness

larme f tear; **une ~ de** a drop of; larmoyer des yeux water; (se plaindre) complain

laryngite f laryngitis

las, ~se weary

laser m laser

lasser weary, tire; **se ~ de** tire ou weary of

latent latent

latéral lateral, side atr

latitude f latitude

latte f lath; de plancher board

lauréat, ~e m/f prizewinner

laurier m laurel; **feuille f de ~** CUIS bayleaf

lavabo m (wash)basin; **~s** toilets

lavage m washing

lavande f lavender

laver wash; tâche wash away; laverie f: **~ automatique** laundromat, Br laundrette; lavette f dishcloth; fig péj spineless individual

lave-vaisselle m dishwasher

laxatif, -ive adj & m laxative

laxisme m laxness

le complément d'objet direct him; chose it; oui, je ~ sais yes, I know

le, f **la**, pl **les** article défini the; **le garçon/les garçons** the boy/the boys; **je me suis cassé la jambe** I broke my leg; **j'aime le vin** I like wine; **les dinosaures avaient ...** dinosaurs had ...; **le premier mai** May first, Br the first of May; **ouvert le samedi**

open (on) Saturdays; *10 euros les 5* 10 euros for 5; *tu connais la France?* do you know France; *le printemps est là* spring is here; *je ne parle pas l'italien* I don't speak Italian

leader *m* POL leader

lécher lick

leçon *f* lesson

lecteur, **-trice 1** *m/f* reader; *à l'université* foreign language assistant **2** *m* INFORM drive; ~ *de CDs* CD player; **lecture** *f* reading

ledit, ladite the said

légal legal; **légaliser** *signature* authenticate; *(rendre légal)* legalize; **légalité** *f* legality

légende *f* legend; *sous image* caption; *d'une carte* key

léger, -ère light; *erreur, retard* slight; *mœurs* loose; *(frivole, irréfléchi)* thoughtless; *à la légère* lightly; **légèrement** lightly; *(un peu)* slightly; **légèreté** *f* lightness; *(frivolité, irréflexion)* thoughtlessness

légion *f* legion; ~ *étrangère* Foreign Legion; **légionnaire** *m* legionnaire

législation *f* legislation

légitime legitimate

legs *m* legacy

léguer bequeath

légume *m* vegetable

lendemain *m*: *le* ~ the next *ou* following day; *le* ~ *de son*

élection the day after he was elected

lent slow; **lentement** slowly; **lenteur** *f* slowness

lentille *f* TECH lens; *légume sec* lentil

léopard *m* leopard

lequel, laquelle *(pl lesquels, lesquelles)* interrogatif which (one); *relatif, avec personne* who; *avec chose* which

les¹ → **le**

les² *pron* personnel them

lesbien, -ne *adj & f* lesbian

léser injure; *intérêts* damage; *droits* infringe

lésiner skimp *(sur* on)

lésion *f* MÉD lesion

lessive *f* *produit* laundry detergent, *Br* washing powder; *liquide* detergent; *linge* laundry; *faire la* ~ do the laundry

leste agile; *propos* crude

léthargie *f* lethargy

lettre *f* letter; *à la* ~, *au pied de la* ~ literally; *en toutes* ~s in full; *fig* in black and white; ~s literature; *études* arts; **lettré** well-read

leucémie *f* MÉD leukemia, *Br* leukaemia

leur 1 *adj possessif* their **2** *pron personnel*: *le/la* ~, *les* ~s theirs **3** *complément d'objet indirect* (to) them

leurrer *fig* deceive

levé: **être**- be up; **levée** *f* lifting; *d'une séance* adjournment; *du courrier* collec-

tion; *aux cartes* trick; **lever 1**
v/t raise, lift; *poids, interdiction* lift; *impôts* collect **2** *v/i*
de la pâte rise; **se** ~ get up;
du soleil rise; *du jour* break
3 *m*: ~ *du jour* daybreak; ~
du soleil sunrise

levier *m* lever; ~ **de vitesse**
gear shift, *surtout Br* gear lever

lèvre *f* lip

levure *f* yeast; ~ **chimique**
baking powder

lézard *m* lizard

lézarde *f* crack

liaison *f* connection; *amou-
reuse* affair; *de train* link;
LING liaison

liant sociable

libellule *f* dragonfly

libéral liberal; **profession** *f*
~**e** profession; **libéralisme**
m liberalism

libérateur, -trice 1 *adj* liberat-
ing **2** *m/f* liberator; **libération** *f* liberation; *d'un prisonnier* release; ~ **conditionnelle** parole; **libérer** liberate; *prisonnier* release,
free (*de* from); *gaz, d'un engagement* release

liberté *f* freedom, liberty;
mettre en ~ free, release

librairie *f* bookstore, *Br*
bookshop

libre free (*de faire* to do); **libre-service** *m* self-service;
magasin self-service shop

Libye *f* Libya; **libien**, ~**ne** Libyan; **Libyen**, ~**ne** *m/f* Libyan

licence *f* license, *Br* licence;
diplôme degree

licenciement *m* layoff; (*renvoi*) dismissal; **licencier** lay
off; (*renvoyer*) dismiss

lié: **être** ~ **par** be bound by;
être très ~ **avec qn** be very
close to s.o.

lien *m* tie, bond; (*rapport*)
connection; **avoir un** ~ **de
parenté** be related

lier tie (up); *d'un contrat* be
binding on; CUIS thicken;
pensées, personnes connect;
~ **amitié avec qn** make
friends with s.o.

lierre *m* BOT ivy

lieu *m* place; ~**x** premises; JUR
scene; **au** ~ **de (faire)** *qch* instead of (doing) sth; **avoir** ~
take place; **donner** ~ **à** give
rise to; **en premier** ~ in the
first place; **s'il y a** ~ if necessary

lièvre *m* hare

ligne *f* line; *d'autobus* number; **garder la** ~ keep one's
figure; **entrer en** ~ **de compte** be taken into consideration; **pêcher à la** ~ go angling; **en** ~ INFORM on line;
achats en ~ on-line shopping

liguer: **se** ~ join forces (*pour*
to do)

lilas *m* & *adj inv* lilac

limace *f* slug

lime *f* file; ~ **à ongles** nail file;
limer file

limitation *f* limitation; ~ **de**

vitesse speed limit; **limite** *f* limit; (*frontière*) boundary; **à la ~** if absolutely necessary; **date** *f* ~ deadline; **vitesse** *f* ~ speed limit; **limiter** limit (**à** to)

limoger POL dismiss

limonade *f* lemonade

limousine *f* limousine

lin *m* BOT flax; *toile* linen

linéaire linear

linge *m* linen; (*lessive*) washing

lingerie *f* lingerie

linguiste *m/f* linguist

lion *m* lion; ASTROL **Lion** Leo; **lionne** *f* lioness

liposuccion *f* liposuction

liqueur *f* liqueur

liquidation *f* liquidation; *vente au rabais* sale

liquide 1 *adj* liquid; *argent* *m* ~ cash **2** *m* liquid; ~ **de freins** brake fluid; **liquider** liquidate; *stock* sell off; *problème* dispose of

lire read

lis *m* BOT lily

lisible legible

lisse smooth; **lisser** smooth

liste *f* list; ~ **d'attente** waiting list; ~ **de commissions** shopping list; **lister** list; **listing** *m* printout

lit *m* bed; **aller au** ~ go to bed; ~ **de camp** cot, Br camp bed; **literie** *f* bedding

litige *m* dispute

litre *m* liter, Br litre

littéraire literary; **littérature** *f* literature

littoral 1 *adj* coastal **2** *m* coastline

livraison *f* delivery

livre[1] *m* book; ~ **de poche** paperback

livre[2] *f* *poids, monnaie* pound

livrer *marchandises* deliver; *prisonnier* hand over; *secret* divulge; **se** ~ (*se confier*) open up; (*se soumettre*) give o.s. up; **se** ~ **à** (*se confier*) confide in; *activité* indulge in; *l'abattement* give way to

livret *m* booklet; *d'opéra* libretto

livreur *m* delivery man; ~ **de journaux** paper boy

lobby *m* lobby

lobe *m*: ~ **de l'oreille** earlobe

local 1 *adj* local **2** *m* (*salle*) premises *pl*; **locaux** premises; **localisation** *f* location; *de software etc* localization; **localiser** locate; (*limiter*) localize; *de software* localize

locataire *m/f* tenant; **location** *f* par propriétaire renting out; *par locataire* renting; (*loyer*) rent; *au théâtre* reservation

logement *m* accommodations, Br accommodation, *pl* (*appartement*) apartment, Br aussi flat; **loger 1** *v/t* accommodate **2** *v/i* live; **logeur** *m* landlord; **logeuse** *f* landlady

logiciel *m* INFORM software

logique 1 *adj* logical **2** *f* logic

loi f law

loin far (*de* from); *dans le passé* long ago; *dans l'avenir* a long way off; *au ~* in the distance

lointain 1 adj distant **2** m distance

loisir m leisure; *~s* leisure activities

Londres London

long, longue 1 adj long; *à ~ terme* in the long term; *à la longue* in time; *être ~ (à faire qch)* take a long time (doing sth) **2** adv: *en dire ~* speak volumes **3** m: *de deux mètres de ~* two meters long; *le ~ de* along

longer follow

longitude f longitude

longtemps a long time

longuement for a long time; *parler* at length

longueur f length; *sur la même ~ d'onde* on the same wavelength

loquace talkative

loque f rag

loquet m latch

lorgner eye; *héritage, poste* have one's eye on

lors: *dès ~* from then on; *~ de* during

lorsque when

lot m (*destin*) fate; *à la loterie* prize; (*portion*) share; COMM batch

loterie f lottery

loti: *bien/mal ~* well/badly off

lotion f lotion

lotissement m (*parcelle*) plot; *terrain loti* housing development

louable praiseworthy; **louange** f praise

louche¹ adj sleazy

louche² f ladle

loucher squint

louer¹ rent

louer² (*vanter*) praise (*de, pour* for)

loup m wolf

loupe f magnifying glass

louper F *travail* botch; *bus, miss*

lourd heavy; *plaisanterie* clumsy; *temps* oppressive; **lourdaud, ~e 1** adj clumsy **2** m/f oaf; **lourdement** heavily

loyal honest; *adversaire* fair-minded; *ami* loyal

loyer m rent

lubie f whim

lubrifiant m lubricant; **lubrifier** lubricate

lucarne f skylight

lucide lucid; (*conscient*) conscious; **lucidité** f lucidity

lucratif, -ive lucrative

lueur f faint light; *une ~ d'espoir* a glimmer of hope

luge f toboggan; *faire de la ~* go tobogganing

lugubre gloomy, lugubrious

lui *complément d'objet indirect, masculin* (to) him; *féminin* (to) her; *chose, animal* (to) it; *après prép, masculin* him; *animal* it

lui-même himself; *de chose* itself
luire glint, glisten
lumière *f* light; **à la ~ de** in the light of
lumineux, -euse luminous; *ciel, couleur* bright; *affiche* illuminated; *idée* brilliant
lunaire lunar
lunatique lunatic
lundi *m* Monday
lune *f* moon; **~ de miel** honeymoon
lunette *f*: **~s** glasses; **~s de soleil** sunglasses; **~s de ski** ski goggles
lustre *m* (*lampe*) chandelier; *fig* luster, *Br* lustre; **lustrer** polish

lutte *f* fight, struggle; *SP* wrestling; **lutter** fight, struggle; *SP* wrestle
luxe *m* luxury; **de ~** luxury *atr*
Luxembourg: **le ~** Luxemburg; **luxembourgeois, ~e** of/from Luxemburg, Luxemburg *atr*; **Luxembourgeois, ~e** *m/f* Luxemburger
luxer: **se ~ l'épaule** dislocate one's shoulder
luxueux, -euse luxurious
luxuriant luxuriant
lycée *m* senior high, *Br* grammar school; **lycéen, ~ne** *m/f* student (at a lycée)
lyophilisé freeze-dried
lyrique lyric; *qui a du lyrisme* lyrical; **artiste ~** opera singer

M

M. (= *monsieur*) Mr
ma → **mon**
macabre macabre
macédoine *f*: **~ de légumes** mixed vegetables *pl*; **~ de fruits** fruit salad
macérer *CUIS*: **faire ~** marinate
mâcher chew
machin *m* F thing
machinal mechanical
machine *f* machine; *NAUT* engine; *fig* machinery; **~ à laver** washing machine; **~ à sous** slot machine
machisme *m* machismo; **macho 1** *adj* male chauvinist **2**

m macho type
mâchoire *f* jaw; **mâchonner** chew (on); (*marmonner*) mutter
maçon *m* bricklayer; *avec des pierres* mason; **maçonnerie** *f* masonry
maculer spatter
madame *f*: **Madame Durand** Mrs Durand; **mesdames et messieurs** ladies and gentlemen
mademoiselle *f*: **Mademoiselle Durand** Miss Durand
madone *f* Madonna
magasin *m* (*boutique*) store, *surtout Br* shop; (*dépôt*)

store room; **grand ~** department store; **magasinier** *m* storeman

magazine *m* magazine

mage *m*: **les Rois ~s** the Three Wise Men, the Magi

magicien, ~ne *m/f* magician; **magie** *f* magic; **magique** magic, magical

magistral *ton* magisterial; *fig* masterly; **cours** *m* ~ lecture

magistrat *m* JUR magistrate

magnanime magnanimous

magner: se ~ F move it F

magnétique magnetic

magnétophone *m* tape recorder

magnétoscope *m* video (recorder)

magnifique magnificent

magouille *f* F scheming; **~s électorales** election shenanigans F

mai *m* May

maigre thin; *résultat, salaire* meager, *Br* meagre; **maigrir** get thin, lose weight

mailing *m* mailshot

maille *f* stitch

maillet *m* mallet

maillot *m* SP shirt, jersey; *de coureur* vest; **~ (de bain)** swimsuit

main *f* hand; **fait à la ~** handmade; **prendre qc en ~** take sth in hand; **perdre la ~** *fig* lose one's touch; **sous la ~** to hand, within reach

main-d'œuvre *f inv* manpower, labor, *Br* labour

maint *fml* many; **à ~es reprises** time and again

maintenance *f* maintenance

maintenant now; **~ que** now that

maintenir keep; *tradition* uphold; *(tenir fermement)* hold; *d'une poutre* hold up; *(soutenir)* maintain; **se ~** *d'un prix* hold steady; *d'une tradition, de la paix* last; **se ~ au pouvoir** stay in power; **maintien** *m* maintenance; **~ de la paix** peace keeping

maire *m* mayor; **mairie** *f* town hall

mais 1 *conj* but **2** *adv*: **~ bien sûr!** of course!; **~ non!** no!

maïs *m* BOT corn, *Br aussi* maize; *en boîte* sweet corn

maison *f* house; *(chez-soi)* home; COMM company; **à la ~** at home; **pâté ~** homemade pâté; **~ de campagne** country house

maître *m* master; *(professeur)* school teacher; *(peintre, écrivain)* maestro; **~ chanteur** blackmailer; **~ d'hôtel** maitre d', *Br* head waiter; **~ nageur** swimming instructor

maîtresse 1 *f* mistress *(aussi amante)*; *(professeur)* schoolteacher **2** *adj*: **idée ~** main idea

maîtrise *f* mastery; *diplôme* MA, master's (degree); **~ de soi** self-control; **maîtri-**

ser master; *cheval* gain control of; *incendie* bring under control

majestueux, -euse majestic

majeur 1 *adj* major; *être* ~ JUR be of age 2 *m* middle finger; **majorité** *f* majority

majuscule *f & adj:* (*lettre* *f*) ~ capital (letter)

mal 1 *m* evil; (*maladie*) illness; (*difficulté*) difficulty; **faire** ~ hurt; **avoir** ~ **aux dents** have toothache; **se donner du** ~ go to a lot of trouble; **faire du** ~ **à qn** hurt s.o.; ~ **de mer** seasickness **2** *adv* badly; **pas** ~ not bad; **se sentir** ~ feel ill **3** *adj:* **faire/dire qc de** ~ do/say sth bad

malade ill, sick; **tomber** ~ fall ill; ~ **mental** mentally ill; **maladie** *f* illness

maladresse *f* clumsiness; **maladroit** clumsy

malaise *m* discomfort; POL malaise; **faire un** ~ faint

malavisé ill-advised

malchance *f* bad luck

mâle *m & adj* male

malédiction *f* curse

malencontreux, -euse unfortunate

malentendant hard of hearing

malfaiteur *m* malefactor

malgré in spite of

malheur *m* misfortune; (*malchance*) bad luck; **par** ~ unfortunately; **malheureusement** unfortunately;

malheureux, -euse unfortunate; (*triste*) unhappy; (*insignifiant*) silly little

malhonnête dishonest; **malhonnêteté** *f* dishonesty

malice *f* malice; (*espièglerie*) mischief; **malicieux, -euse** malicious; (*coquin*) mischievous

malin, -igne (*rusé*) crafty, cunning; (*méchant*) malicious; MÉD malignant

malle *f* trunk; **mallette** *f* little bag

malodorant foul-smelling

malpoli impolite

malpropre dirty

malsain unhealthy

malt *m* malt

Malte *f* Malta; **maltais, ~e** Maltese; **Maltais, ~e** *m/f* Maltese

maltraiter mistreat, maltreat

malveillant malevolent

malvoyant, ~e 1 *adj* visually impaired **2** *m/f* visually impaired person

maman *f* Mom, *Br* Mum

mamelle *f de vache* udder; *de chienne* teat

mamie *f* F granny

mammifère *m* mammal

manager *m* manager

manche[1] *m d'outils* handle; *d'un violon* neck

manche[2] *f* sleeve; SP round; **la Manche** the English Channel

manchette *f* cuff; *d'un journal* headline

mandarine *f* mandarin (orange)

mandat *m* POL term of office, mandate; *(procuration)* proxy; *de la poste* postal order; *~ d'arrêt* arrest warrant; **mandataire** *m/f à une réunion* proxy

manège *m* riding school; *(carrousel)* carousel, *Br* roundabout; *fig* game

mangeable edible, eatable

mangeoire *f manger*

manger eat; *argent, temps* eat up; *mots* swallow

maniable *voiture* easy to handle

maniaque fussy; **manie** *f* mania

manier handle

manière *f* way, manner; *~s* manners; *affectées* airs and graces; *à la ~* de in the style of; *de cette ~* (in) that way; *de toute ~* anyway; *d'une ~ générale* generally speaking; *de ~ à faire qch* so as to do sth; **maniéré** affected

manifestant, -e *m/f* demonstrator; **manifestation** *f de joie etc* expression; POL demonstration; *culturelle, sportive* event

manifeste 1 *adj* obvious **2** *m* POL manifesto; **manifester 1** *v/t* show; *se ~ de maladie, problèmes* manifest itself/themselves **2** *v/i* demonstrate

manipulateur, -trice manipu-

lative; **manipulation** *f d'un appareil* handling; *d'une personne* manipulation; *~ génétique* genetic engineering; **manipuler** handle; *personne* manipulate

mannequin *m dans magasin* dummy; *personne* model

manœuvre 1 *f* maneuver, *Br* manoeuvre; *d'un outil, une machine etc* operation **2** *m* unskilled laborer *ou Br* labourer; **manœuvrer** maneuver, *Br* manoeuvre

manoir *m* manor (house)

manque *m* lack; *par ~ de* for lack of; **manqué** unsuccessful; *rendez-vous* missed; **manquer 1** *v/i (être absent)* be missing; *(faire défaut)* be lacking; *(échouer)* fail; *tu me manques* I miss you; *~ à promesse* fail to keep; *devoir fail in* **2** *v/t (être absent à)* miss; *examen* fail; *elle a manqué (de) se faire écraser* she was almost run over **3** *impersonnel* **il manque de preuves** there's a lack of evidence

manteau *m* coat; *de neige* blanket; *~ de cheminée* mantelpiece

manucure *f* manicure

manuel, -le *adj & m* manual; *~ d'utilisation* instruction manual

manufacturé: *produits mpl ~s* manufactured goods

manuscrit 1 *adj* handwritten

2 *m* manuscript

maquereau *m* zo mackerel; F (*souteneur*) pimp

maquette *f* model

maquillage *m* make-up; **maquiller** make up; *crime, vérité* conceal; **se ~** put one's make-up on

marais *m* swamp

marathon *m* marathon

marbre *m* marble

marc *m*: **~ de café** coffee grounds *pl*

marchand, ~e 1 *adj valeur* market *atr*; *rue* shopping *atr*; **marine merchant** *atr* **2** *m/f* merchant, storekeeper, *Br* shopkeeper; **marchander** haggle, bargain; **marchandise** *f*: **~s** merchandise; **train m de ~** freight train

marche *f* walking; *d'escalier* step; MUS, MIL march; *des événements* course; (*démarche*) walk; **~ arrière** AUTO reverse; **mettre en ~** start (up)

marché *m* market; (*accord*) deal; (**à**) **bon ~** cheap; **par-dessus le ~** into the bargain; **~ boursier** stock market; **le Marché Commun** POL the Common Market; **~ noir** black market

marcher walk; MIL march; *d'une machine* run, work; F (*réussir*) work; *d'un bus, train* run; **faire ~ qn** pull s.o.'s leg

mardi *m* Tuesday; **Mardi gras**

Mardi Gras, *Br* Shrove Tuesday

mare *f* pond; **~ de sang** pool of blood

marécage *m* swamp; **marécageux, -euse** swampy

marée *f* tide; **~ basse/haute** low/high tide; **~ noire** oil slick

margarine *f* margarine

marge *f* margin; **en ~ de** on the fringes of

marguerite *f* daisy

mari *m* husband

mariage *m fête* wedding; *état* marriage

marié 1 *adj* married **2** *m* (bride)groom; **mariée** *f* bride; **marier** marry; **se ~** get married; **se ~ avec** marry, get married to

marijuana *f* marijuana

marin 1 *adj air* sea *atr*; *animaux* marine **2** *m* sailor

marine *f* MIL navy; (*bleu*) **~** navy (blue)

marionnette *f* puppet; *avec des ficelles aussi* marionnette

marmelade *f* marmalade

marmite *f* (large) pot

marmonner mutter

maroquinerie *f* leather goods shop; *articles* leather goods *pl*

marquant remarkable

marque *f* mark; COMM brand; *de voiture* make; (*signe*) trademark; **~ déposée** registered trademark; **de ~**

COMM branded; *fig: personne* distinguished; **marquer** mark; (*noter*) write down; *personnalité* leave its mark on; *d'un baromètre etc* show; (*accentuer*) *taille* emphasize; **~ un but** score (a goal); **marqueur** *m* marker pen

marraine *f* godmother

marrant F funny

marre: **j'en ai ~** I've had enough

marrer: **se ~** have a good laugh

marron 1 *m* chestnut **2** *adj inv* brown; **marronnier** *m* chestnut tree

mars *m* March

marteau *m* hammer; **~ piqueur** pneumatic drill; **marteler** hammer

martyr, **~e**[1] *m/f* martyr; **martyre**[2] *m* martyrdom; **martyriser** abuse; *petit frère, camarade de classe* bully

masculin male; GRAM masculine

masque *m* mask; **masquer** mask

massacre *m* massacre; **massacrer** massacre

massage *m* massage

masse *f* masse; ÉL ground,; **en ~** in large numbers, en masse; *manifestation* massive; **une ~ de choses à faire** masses *pl* (of things) to do

massif, **-ive 1** *adj* massif; *or, chêne* solid **2** *m* massif; **~**

de fleurs flowerbed

massue *f* club

mastiquer *nourriture* chew

mat[1] MATT; *son* dull

mat[2] *inv aux échecs* checkmated

mât *m* mast

match *m* game, *Br aussi* match; **~ nul** tied game, *Br* draw

matelas *m* mattress; **~ pneumatique** air bed

matelot *m* sailor

matérialiser: **se ~** materialize; **matériau** *m* material; **matériel**, **~le 1** *adj* material **2** *m de camping*, SP equipment; INFORM hardware

maternel, **~le 1** *adj* maternal; **langue** *f* **~le** mother tongue **2** *f* nursery school; **maternité** *f* motherhood; *établissement* maternity hospital; (*enfantement*) pregnancy

mathématicien, **~ne** *m/f* mathematician; **mathématique 1** *adj* mathematical **2** *fpl*: **~s** mathematics

matière *f* material; PHYS, PHIL matter; (*sujet*) subject; **entrée en ~** introduction; **en ~ de** when it comes to; **~ première** raw material

matin *m* morning; **le ~** in the morning; **tous les lundis ~s** every Monday morning; **matinal** morning *atr*; **être ~** be an early riser; **matinée** *f* morning; (*spectacle*) matinée; **faire la grasse ~** sleep late

matou *m* tom cat

matricule *m* number

matrimonial matrimonial

maturité *f* maturity

maudire curse; **maudit** F damn F

mauvais 1 *adj* bad; (*erroné*) wrong **2** *adv* bad; **il fait ~** the weather is bad

mauve mauve

maximum *adj & m* maximum; **au ~** at most, at the maximum

mayonnaise *f* mayonnaise, mayo F

me me; *complément d'objet indirect* (to) me; **je ~ suis coupé** I've cut myself; **je ~ lève à …** I get up at …

mec *m* F guy F

mécanicien *m* mechanic; **mécanique 1** *adj* mechanical **2** *f* mechanics; **mécanisme** *m* mechanism

méchanceté *f* nastiness; *action, parole* nasty thing to do/say; **méchant**, *~e* **1** *adj* nasty; *enfant* naughty **2** *m* F: **les gentils et les ~s** the goodies and the baddies

mèche *f de bougie* wick; *d'explosif* fuse; *de perceuse* bit; *de cheveux* strand

méconnaissable unrecognizable

mécontent unhappy, displeased (**de** with); **mécontenter** displease

médaille *f* medal; **médaillon**

m medallion

médecin *m* doctor

médecine *f* medicine; **les ~s douces** alternative medicines

média *m* media *pl*

médiateur, **-trice** *m/f* mediator

médiatique media *atr*

médical medical

médicament *m* medicine, drug

médiéval medieval, *Br* mediaeval

médiocre mediocre; **~ en** ÉDU poor at

médire: **~ de qn** run s.o. down

méditation *f* meditation; **méditer 1** *v/t* think about, reflect on **2** *v/i* meditate (**sur** on)

Méditerranée: **la ~** the Mediterranean; **méditerranéen**, **~ne** Mediterranean; **Méditerranéen**, **~ne** *m/f* Mediterranean *atr*

méduse *f* ZO jellyfish

meeting *m* meeting

méfait *m* JUR misdemeanor, *Br* misdemeanour; **~s de la drogue** harmful effects

méfiance *f* mistrust, suspicion; **méfiant** suspicious; **méfier**: **se ~ de** mistrust, be suspicious of; (*se tenir en garde*) be wary of

mégaoctet *m* INFORM megabyte

mégarde *f*: **par ~** inadvertently

mention

mégot m cigarette butt
meilleur 1 adj better; **le ~ ...** the best ... **2** m: **le ~** the best
mél m email
mélancolie f gloom, melancholy
mélange m mixture; de thés blend; action mixing; de thés blending; **mélanger** mix; thés blend; (brouiller) jumble up, mix up
mêlée f fray, melee; en rugby scrum; **mêler** mix; (réunir) combine; (brouiller) jumble up, mix up; ~ **qn à qc** fig involve s.o. in sth; **se ~ à qc** get involved with sth; **se ~ de qc** interfere in sth
mélodie f tune, melody; **mélodieux, -euse** tuneful, melodious; voix melodious
mélodramatique melodramatic; **mélodrame** m melodrama
melon m BOT melon
membre m ANAT limb; fig member
même 1 adj: le/la ~, les ~s the same; **la bonté** ~ kindness itself **2** pron: le/la ~ the same one; **les** ~**s** the same ones; **cela revient au** ~ it comes to the same thing **3** adv even; ~ **pas** not even; **faire le** ~ do the same; **de** ~! likewise!; **être à ~ de faire** be able to do; **tout de** ~ all the same; **quand** ~ all the same; **moi de** ~ me too
mémoire 1 f memory; **à la** ~

de in memory of **2** m (exposé) report; (dissertation) thesis; ~**s** memoirs; **mémorable** memorable; **mémoriser** memorize
menace f threat; **menacer** threaten (de with; **de faire** to do)
ménage m (famille) household; (couple) (married) couple; **faire le** ~ clean house, Br do the housework; **ménagement** m consideration; **ménager**[1] v/t treat with consideration; temps, argent use sparingly; (arranger) arrange; **ménager**[2], **-ère 1** adj household atr **2** f home-maker, housewife
mendiant, ~e m/f beggar; **mendier 1** v/i beg **2** v/t beg for
mener 1 v/t lead; (amener, transporter) take **2** v/i: ~ **à d'un chemin** lead to; **ne ~ à rien des efforts** come to nothing; **meneur** m leader; péj ringleader
mensonge m lie; **mensonger, -ère** false
mensualité f somme à payer monthly payment; **mensuel, ~le** monthly
mental mental; **calcul** m ~ mental arithmetic; **mentalité** f mentality
menteur, -euse m/f liar
menthe f BOT mint
mention f mention; à un examen grade, Br aussi mark;

mentionner mention

mentir lie (**à** to)

menton *m* chin

menu **1** *adj* slight; *morceaux* small **2** *adv* finely, fine **3** *m* menu (*aussi* INFORM); (*repas*) set meal; **par le ~** in minute detail

menuisier *m* carpenter

méprendre: **se ~** be mistaken (**sur** about)

mépris *m* (*indifférence*) disdain; (*dégoût*) scorn; **méprisable** despicable; **méprisant** scornful; **mépriser** *argent, ennemi* despise; *conseil, danger* scorn

mer *f* sea; **en ~** at sea; **la Mer du Nord** the North Sea

mercenaire *m* mercenary

mercerie *f* *magasin* notions store, *Br* haberdashery; *articles* notions, *Br* haberdashery *pl*

merci **1** *int* thanks, thank you (**de, pour** for); **~ bien** thanks a lot, thank you very much **2** *f* mercy

mercredi *m* Wednesday

merde *f* P shit P; **merder** P screw up P

mère *f* mother

méridional southern

mérite *m* merit; **mériter** deserve; **~ le détour** be worth a visit

merle *m* blackbird

merveille *f* wonder, marvel; **à ~** wonderfully well; **merveilleux, -euse** wonderful

mes → **mon**

mésaventure *f* mishap

mesquin mean

message *m* message; **messager, -ère** *m/f* messenger, courier; **messagerie** *f* parcels service; **électronique** electronic mail; **~ vocale** voicemail

messe *f* REL mass

mesure *f* measurement; *disposition* measure, step; MUS (*rythme*) time; **à ~ que** as; **être en ~ de faire qch** be in a position to do sth; **outre ~** excessive; **sur ~** *fig* tailor-made; **mesurer** measure; *risque, importance* gauge; *paroles* weigh; **se ~ avec qn** pit o.s. against s.o.

métal *m* metal; **métallique** metallic

métamorphoser: **se ~** metamorphose

météo *f* weather forecast

météore *m* meteor

météorologie *f* meteorology; *service* weather office

méthode *f* method

méticuleux, -euse meticulous

métier *m* profession; *manuel* trade; (*expérience*) experience; *machine* loom

métrage *m* *d'un film* footage; **court ~** short

mètre *m* meter, *Br* metre; (*règle*) tape measure

métrique metric

métro *m* subway, *Br* under-

ground; **à Paris** metro
métropole *f* metropolis; *de colonie* mother country
mettre put; *vêtements, lunettes, chauffage* put on; *réveil* set; *argent dans entreprise* put in; *~ deux heures à faire qc* take two hours to do sth; *se ~ à faire* start to do
meuble *m* piece of furniture; *~s* furniture; **meubler** furnish
meurtre *m* murder; **meurtrier, -ère 1** *adj* deadly **2** *m/f* murderer
meurtrir bruise; **meurtrissure** *f* bruise
meute *f* pack; *fig* mob
mexicain, ~e *adj* Mexican; **Mexicain, ~e** *m/f* Mexican; **Mexique:** *le ~* Mexico
mi-... half; *à mi-chemin* halfway; *(à la) mi-janvier* mid-January
mi-bas *mpl* knee-highs, pop socks
miche *f* large round loaf
micro *m* mike; INFORM computer, PC; *d'espionnage* bug
microbe *m* microbe
microfilm *m* microfilm
micro-ondes *m* microwave
microphone *m* microphone
microscope *m* microscope
midi *m* noon, twelve o'clock; *(sud)* south; *le Midi* the South of France
mie *f de pain* crumb
miel *m* honey
mien: *le mien, la mienne, les*

miens, les miennes mine
miette *f* crumb
mieux 1 *adv comparatif de bien* better; *superlatif de bien* best; *le ~* best; *de ~ en ~* better and better; *tant ~* so much the better; *vous feriez ~ de ...* you would ou you'd do best to ... **2** *m: (progrès)* progress; *j'ai fait de mon ~* I did my best; *le ~, c'est de ...* the best thing is to ...
mièvre insipid
mignon, ~ne *(charmant)* cute; *(gentil)* nice
migraine *f* migraine
migration *f* migration; **migrer** migrate
mijoter CUIS simmer; *fig* hatch
milieu *m (centre)* middle; *biologique, social* environment; *au ~ de* in the middle of; *le ~* the underworld
militaire 1 *adj* military **2** *m* soldier; *les ~s* the military *sg ou pl*
militant active
militer: *~ dans* be an active member of; *~ pour/contre* *fig* militate for/against
mille 1 (a) thousand **2** *m measure* mile; *~ marin* nautical mile
millénaire 1 *adj* thousand-year old **2** *m* millennium
milliard *m* billion; **milliardaire** *f* billionaire
millième thousandth

millier *m* thousand

milligramme *m* milligram

millimètre millimeter, *Br* millimetre

million *m* million; **millionnaire** *m/f* millionaire

minable mean, shabby; *un salaire ~* a pittance

mince thin; *personne* slim; *espoir* slight; *somme, profit* small; *argument* flimsy

mine[1] *f* appearance, look; *avoir bonne/mauvaise ~* look/not look well

mine[2] *f* mine (*aussi* MIL); *de crayon* lead; *miner* undermine; MIL mine

minéral *adj & m* mineral

minéralogique AUTO: **plaque** *f ~* license plate, *Br* number plate

mineur[1] *adj* JUR, MUS minor

mineur[2] *m* (*ouvrier*) miner

miniature *f* miniature

minimal minimum; **minime** minimal; *salaire* tiny; **minimiser** minimize; **minimum** *adj & m* minimum; *au ~* at the very least; *un ~ de* the least little bit of

ministère *m* department; (*gouvernement*) government; REL ministry; **ministre** *m* minister; *~ des Affaires étrangères* Secretary of State, *Br* Foreign Secretary; *~ de l'Intérieur* Secretary of the Interior, *Br* Home Secretary

minitel *m* small home terminal connected to a number of data banks

minorité *f* JUR, POL minority

minuit *m* midnight

minuscule **1** *adj* tiny, minuscule; *lettre* small, lower case **2** *f* small *ou* lower-case letter

minute *f* minute

minuterie *f* time switch

minutie *f* meticulousness; **minutieux, -euse** meticulous

miracle *m* miracle; **miraculeux, -euse** miraculous

mirage *m* mirage; *fig* illusion

miroir *m* mirror

miroiter sparkle

mise *f au jeu* stake; *de ~* acceptable; *~ en bouteilles* bottling; *~ en marche ou route* start-up; **miser** stake (*sur* on)

misérable wretched; **misère** *f* destitution; (*chose pénible*) misfortune

miséricordieux, -euse merciful

misogyne *m* misogynist

missile *m* MIL missile

mission *f* mission; (*tâche*) task

mite *f* ZO (*clothes*) moth

mi-temps 1 *f* SP half-time **2** *m* part-time job; *à ~ travail* part-time

mitigé moderate; *sentiments* mixed

mi-voix: *à ~* under one's breath

mixer, mixeur *m* CUIS blender; **mixte** mixed; **mixture** *f*

MM (= *Messieurs*) Messrs.
Mme (= *Madame*) Mrs
Mo *m* (= *mégaoctet*) Mb (= megabyte)
mobile 1 *adj* mobile; (*amovible*) movable; *feuilles* loose; *ombres* moving **2** *m* motive; ART mobile
mobilier, -ère 1 *adj* JUR movable, personal **2** *m* furniture
mobilisation *f* mobilization; **mobilité** *f* mobility
mobylette® *f* moped
moche F ugly; (*méprisable*) mean
mode¹ *m* method; ~ *d'emploi* instructions (for use); ~ *de vie* life-style
mode² *f* fashion; *être à la* ~ be fashionable, be in fashion
modèle *m* model; *tricot* pattern; **modeler** model
modem *m* INFORM modem
modération *f* moderation; **modéré** moderate; **modérer** moderate; *se* ~ control o.s.
moderne modern; **modernisation** *f* modernization; **moderniser** modernize
modeste modest; **modestie** *f* modesty
modification *f* modification; **modifier** modify
modique modest
module *m* TECH module; **moduler** modulate
moelle *f* marrow; ~ *épinière* spinal cord; **moelleux, -euse** *lit* soft; *chocolat, vin* smooth

mœurs *fpl* morals; (*coutumes*) customs
moi me; *avec* ~ with me
moi-même myself
moindre lesser; *prix* lower; *quantité* smaller; *le/la* ~ the least
moine *m* monk
moineau *m* sparrow
moins 1 *adv* less; *au ou du* ~ at least; *à* ~ *que ... ne* (+ *subj*) unless; *de* ~ *en* ~ less and less; *20 euros de* ~ 20 euros less **2** *m*: *le* ~ the least **3** *prép* MATH minus; *dix heures* ~ *cinq* it's five of ten , *Br* it's five to ten; *il fait* ~ *deux* it's 2 below zero
mois *m* month
moisi 1 *adj* moldy, *Br* mouldy **2** *m* BOT mold, *Br* mould; **moisir** go moldy *ou Br* mouldy; **moisissure** *f* BOT mold, *Br* mould
moisson *f* harvest; **moissonner** harvest
moite damp, moist
moitié *f* half; *à* ~ *vide/endormi* half-empty/-asleep; ~ ~ fifty-fifty
molaire *f* molar
molécule *f* molecule
molester rough up
molette *f* *de réglage* knob
mollesse *f* softness; *d'une personne, d'actions* lethargy
mollet¹, -te *adj* soft; *œuf* soft-boiled
mollet² *m* calf

péj vile concoction

môme m/f F kid F

moment m moment; **d'un ~ à l'autre** at any moment; **par ~s** at times, sometimes; **pour le ~** for the moment

momentané temporary; **momentanément** for a short while

mon m, **ma** f, **mes** pl my

monarchie f monarchy; **monarque** m monarch

monastère m monastery

monceau m mound

mondain vie society atr

mondanités fpl social niceties

monde m world; **gens** people pl; **tout le ~** everybody, everyone; **mettre au ~** bring into the world

mondial world atr, global; **mondialisation** f globalization

monétaire monetary; marché money atr

moniteur, -trice 1 m/f instructor **2** m INFORM monitor

monnaie f money; (pièces) change; (unité monétaire) currency

monologue m monolog, Br monologue

monopole m monopoly; **monopoliser** monopolize

monospace m people carrier, MPV

monotone monotonous; **monotonie** f monotony

monsieur m (pl messieurs) dans lettre Dear Sir; **Mon-**sieur Durand Mr Durand; **bonjour ~** good morning

monstre 1 m monster **2** adj colossal

mont m mountain

montage m TECH assembly; d'un film editing; d'une photographie montage; ÉL connecting

montagnard, ~e 1 adj mountain atr **2** m/f mountain dweller; **montagne** f mountain; **à la ~** in the mountains; **~s russes** roller coaster; **montagneux, -euse** mountainous

montant 1 adj robe high-necked; mouvement upward **2** m somme amount

montée f sur montagne ascent; (pente) slope; de prix, de température rise; **monter 1** v/t climb, go/come up; valise take/bring up; machine assemble; tente put up; THÉAT put on; film edit; entreprise set up; cheval ride **2** v/i come/go upstairs; d'avion, de route climb; des prix rise, go up; de baromètre, fleuve rise; **~ dans** avion, train get on; voiture get in(to) **3**: **se ~ à** de frais amount to

montre f (wrist)watch

montrer show; **~ qn/qc du doigt** point at s.o./sth

monture f (cheval) mount; de lunettes frame; d'un diamant setting

moucher

monument *m* monument;
  monumental monumental
moquer: se ~ de (*railler*)
  make fun of; (*dédaigner*)
  not care about; (*tromper*)
  fool; (*moquerie*) mockery
moquette *f* wall-to-wall carpet
moqueur, -euse 1 *adj* mock-
  ing **2** *m/f* mocker
moral, ~e 1 *adj* moral; *souf-*
  france, santé spiritual **2** *m*
  morale *f* morality, morals
  pl; *d'une histoire* moral
morbide morbid
morceau *m* piece; *d'un livre*
  passage
morceler divide up
mordant biting; **mordre** bite;
  d'un acide eat into
morfondre: se ~ mope; (*s'en-*
  nuyer) be bored
morgue *f lieu* mortuary,
  morgue
moribond dying
morne gloomy
morose morose
mors *m* bit
morsure *f* bite
mort[1] *f* death
mort[2], **~e 1** *adj* dead; *eau*
  stagnant; *yeux* lifeless;
  membre numb; *ivre* ~ dead
  drunk; *être ~ de rire* F die
  laughing **2** *m/f* dead man;
  dead woman; **les ~s** the
  dead *pl*
mortalité *f* mortality; **taux** *m*
  de ~ death rate, mortality;
  mortel, ~le mortal; *blessure*,

dose, *maladie* fatal; *péché*
  deadly
morue *f* cod
morveux, -euse *m/f* F squirt F
mosaïque *f* mosaic
Moscou Moscow
mosquée *f* mosque
mot *m* word; (*court message*)
  note; **bon ~** witticism; **~ clé**
  key word; **~ de passe** password; **gros ~** rude word,
  swearword; **~ à ~** word for
  word
motard *m* motorcyclist, biker; *de la gendarmerie* motorcycle policeman
moteur, -trice 1 *m* engine,
  motor; *fig: personne* driving
  force (**de** behind) **2** *adj arbre*
  drive; *force* driving
motif *m* motive, reason; (*for-*
  me) pattern; MUS theme, motif; *en peinture* motif
motion *f* POL motion
motivation *f* motivation; **mo-**
  tiver motivate; (*expliquer*)
  be the reason for, prompt;
  (*justifier par des motifs*) give
  a reason for
moto *f* motorbike, motorcycle; **faire de la ~** ride one's
  motorbike; **motocycliste**
  m/f motorcyclist
motoriser mechanize; **je suis**
  motorisé F I have a car
mou, molle soft; *caractère, ré-*
  sistance weak
mouche *f* fly
moucher: se ~ blow one's
  nose

moucheron *m* gnat

mouchoir *m* handkerchief

moudre grind

moue *f* pout; *faire la ~* pout

mouette *f* seagull

moufle *f* mitten

mouillé wet; **mouiller 1** *v/t* wet; (*humecter*) dampen; *liquide* water down **2** *v/i* MAR anchor

moule 1 *m* mold, *Br* mould; CUIS tin **2** *f* ZO mussel

mouler mold, *Br* mould

moulin *m* mill; **~ (à vent)** windmill; **~ à café** coffee grinder

mourir die (**de** of); **~ de froid** freeze to death

mousse *f* foam; BOT moss; CUIS mousse; **mousser** lather; **mousseux, -euse 1** *adj* foamy **2** *m* sparkling wine

moustache *f* mustache, *Br* moustache

moustique *m* mosquito

moutarde *f* mustard

mouton *m* sheep; *viande* mutton; *fourrure* sheepskin

mouvement *m* movement; *trafic* traffic; **en ~** moving; **mouvementé** eventful; *débat* lively

mouvoir: **se ~** move

moyen, ~ne 1 *adj* average; *classe* middle; **Moyen Âge** *m* Middle Ages *pl*; **Moyen--Orient** *m* Middle East **2** *m* (*façon, méthode*) means *sg*; **~s** (*argent*) means *pl*; *intellectuelles* faculties; **au ~ de,**

par le ~ de by means of **3** *f* average; *statistique* mean; **en ~ne** on average; **moyenâgeux, -euse** medieval

moyennant for

Mt (= **Mont**) Mt (= Mount)

muer *d'oiseau* molt, *Br* moult; *de voix* break

muet, ~te dumb; *fig* silent

mufle *m* muzzle; *fig* F boor

mugir moo; *du vent* moan

muguet *m* BOT lily of the valley

mule *f* mule

multicolore multicolored, *Br* multicoloured

multimédia *m & adj* multimedia

multinational, ~e 1 *adj* multinational **2** *f*: **multinationale** multinational

multiplication *f* multiplication; *la ~ de* (*augmentation*) the increase in the number of; **multiplier** multiply; **se ~** *d'une espèce* multiply

multitude *f*: **une ~ de** a host of; *la ~ péj* the masses *pl*

multiusages versatile

municipal town *atr*; *conseil* municipal; **municipalité** *f* (*commune*) municipality; *conseil* town council

munir: **~ de** fit with; *personne* provide with; **se ~ de qc** *d'un parapluie, de son passeport* take sth

mur *m* wall

mûr ripe

muraille *f* wall

mûre f BOT mulberry; *des ronces* blackberry

murer *enclos* wall in; *porte* wall up

mûrier m mulberry (tree)

mûrir ripen

murmure m murmur; **murmurer** murmur; *(médire)* talk

muscle m muscle; **musclé** muscular; **musculation** f body-building

museau m muzzle

musée m museum

museler muzzle *(aussi fig)*; **muselière** f muzzle

musical musical; **musicien, ~ne 1** *adj* musical **2** m/f musician; **musique** f music; ~ **de fond** piped music

must m must

musulman, ~e m/f & *adj* Muslim

mutation f change; BIOL mutation; *de fonctionnaire* transfer

mutiler mutilate

mutuel, ~le mutual

myope shortsighted

myrtille f bilberry

mystère m mystery; **mystérieux, -euse** mysterious

mystifier fool, take in

mystique 1 *adj* mystical **2** m/f mystic **3** f mystique

mythe m myth; **mythologie** f mythology

mythomane m/f pathological liar

N

nabot m *péj* midget

nacre f mother-of-pearl

nage f swimming; *style* stroke; *être en* ~ *fig* be dripping with sweat

nageoire f fin

nager 1 v/i swim **2** v/t: ~ *la* **brasse** do the breaststroke

naïf, naïve naive

nain, ~e m/f & *adj* dwarf

naissance f birth *(aussi fig)*; **naître** be born *(aussi fig)*; *faire* ~ *sentiment* give rise to

naïveté f naivety

nana f F chick F, girl

nantir provide *(de* with)

nappe f tablecloth; *de gaz, pétrole* layer

narcotique m & *adj* narcotic

narguer taunt

narine f nostril

narquois taunting

narrateur, -trice m/f narrator; **narration** f narration

nasal nasal

natal *pays etc* of one's birth, native; **natalité** f: *(taux m de)* ~ birth rate

natation f swimming

natif, -ive native

nation f nation; **national, ~e 1** *adj* national **2** *mpl:* **natio-**

naux nationals **3** f highway;
nationaliser nationalize;
nationaliste 1 adj nationalist; péj nationalistic **2** m/f
nationalist; **nationalité** f nationality

natte f (tapis) mat; de cheveux braid, plait

naturalisation f naturaliza-
tion

nature 1 adj yaourt plain; thé,
café without milk or sugar;
personne natural **2** f nature;
~ morte ART still life; naturel, ~le **1** adj natural **2** m (caractère) nature; (spontanéi-
té) naturalness; **naturellement** naturally

naufrage m shipwreck; **faire
~** be shipwrecked

nausée f nausea; **j'ai la ~** I'm
nauseous, Br I feel sick;
nauséeux, -euse nauseous

nautique nautical; ski water
atr

nautisme m water sports and
sailing

naval naval; construction ship
atr

navet m rutabaga, Br swede;
fig turkey F, Br flop

navette f shuttle; **faire la ~**
shuttle

navigable navigable; **navigation** f sailing; (pilotage) navigation; **~ aérienne** air travel; **~ spatiale** space travel;
naviguer d'un navire, marin
sail; d'un avion fly; (conduire), INFORM navigate; **~ sur**

Internet surf the Net

navire m ship

navrant upsetting; navré: **je
suis ~** I'm so sorry

ne: je ~ comprends pas I
don't understand, I do not
understand; **ne ... guère**
hardly; **ne ... jamais** never;
ne ... personne nobody; **ne
... plus** no longer; not any
more; **ne ... que** only; **ne
... rien** nothing, not anything; → aussi **guère, jamais**
etc

né born; **~e Lepic** nee Lepic

néanmoins nevertheless

néant m nothingness

nécessaire 1 adj necessary **2**
m necessary; **le strict ~** the
bare minimum; **~ de toilette**
toiletries pl; **nécessité** f necessity; **nécessiter** require,
necessitate

néerlandais, ~e 1 adj Dutch
2 m langue Dutch; **Néerlandais, ~e** m/f Dutchman;
Dutchwoman

néfaste harmful

négatif, -ive adj & m negative; **négation** f negation;
GRAM negative

négligé 1 adj travail careless;
tenue untidy; épouse, enfant
neglected **2** f negligee; **négligence** f negligence, care-
lessness; d'une épouse, d'un
enfant neglect; (nonchalan-
ce) casualness; **négligent**
careless, negligent; parent
negligent; geste casual; né-

gliger neglect; *occasion* miss; *avis* disregard; **~ de faire** fail to do

négoce *m* trade; **négociant** *m* merchant; **négociateur, -trice** *m/f* negotiator; **négociation** *f* negotiation; **négocier** negotiate

neige *f* snow; **neiger** snow

néon *m* neon

nerf *m* nerve; *(vigueur)* energy; **être à bout de ~s** be at the end of one's tether

nerveux, -euse nervous; *(vigoureux)* full of energy; AUTO responsive; **nervosité** *f* nervousness

n'est-ce pas: *il fait beau, ~?* it's a fine day, isn't it?; *tu la connais, ~?* you know her, don't you?

net, ~te 1 *adj (propre)* clean; *(clair)* clear; *différence* distinct; COMM net **2** *adv (aussi* **nettement)** *tué* outright; *refuser* flatly; *parler* plainly; **netteté** *f* cleanliness; *(clarté)* clarity

nettoyage *m* cleaning; **~ ethnique** ethnic cleansing; **~ à sec** dry cleaning; **nettoyer** clean; F *(ruiner)* clean out F; **~ à sec** dryclean

neuf¹ nine

neuf², neuve *adj* new; **refaire à ~** *maison etc* renovate; *moteur* recondition

neutraliser neutralize; **neutralité** *f* neutrality; **neutre** neutral

neuvième ninth

neveu *m* nephew

névralgie *f* MÉD neuralgia

névrosé, ~e *m/f* neurotic

nez *m* nose

ni neither, nor; *je n'ai ~ intérêt ~ désir* I have neither interest nor inclination; **sans sucre ~ lait** without sugar or milk, with neither sugar nor milk; **~ moi non plus** neither *ou* nor do I, me neither

niais stupid; **niaiserie** *f* stupidity

niche *f dans un mur* niche; *d'un chien* kennel; **nicher** nest; *fig* F live

nicotine *f* nicotine

nid *m* nest; **~ de poule** *fig* pothole

nièce *f* niece

nier: **~ (avoir fait)** deny (doing)

nigaud 1 *adj* silly **2** *m* idiot, fool

niveau *m* level; ÉDU standard; *outil* spirit level; **~ de vie** standard of living; **niveler** *terrain* level; *fig: différences* even out

noble noble; **noblesse** *f* nobility

noce *f* wedding; **faire la ~** F paint the town red

nocif, -ive harmful, noxious

nocturne 1 *adj* night *atr*; ZO nocturnal **2** *f:* **un match joué en ~** an evening match

Noël *m* Christmas; **joyeux ~!**

Merry Christmas!; **le père ~** Santa Claus, *Br aussi* Father Christmas

nœud *m* knot (*aussi* NAUT); *fig: d'un problème* nub; **~ papillon** bow tie

noir 1 *adj* black; (*sombre*) dark; **il fait ~** it's dark **2** *m* black; (*obscurité*) dark; **travail** *m* **au ~** moonlighting

Noir *m* black man

noircir blacken

Noire *f* black woman

noisetier *m* hazel; **noisette** *f* & *adj inv* hazelnut

noix *f* walnut

nom *m* name; GRAM noun; **au ~ de qn** *in ou Br* on behalf of s.o.; **~ de famille** surname, family name; **~ de jeune fille** maiden name

nombre *m* number; **sans ~** countless; **nombreux, -euse** numerous, many; **famille large**

nombril *m* navel

nomination *f* appointment; **à un prix** nomination

nommer name, call; **à une fonction** appoint; **se ~** be called

non no; **j'espère que ~** I hope not; **moi ~ plus** me neither; **c'est normal, ~?** that's normal, isn't it?

non-alcoolisé non-alcoholic

nonchalant nonchalant, casual

nonobstant notwithstanding

non-polluant environ-

mentally friendly, non-polluting

nord 1 *m* north; **au ~ de** (to the) north of **2** *adj* north; *hemisphère* northern

nord-américain, ~e North-American; **Nord-Américain, ~e** *m/f* North-American

nord-est *m* north-east

nord-ouest *m* north-west

normal, ~e 1 *adj* normal **2** *f*: **inférieur/supérieur à la ~e** above/below average; **normalement** normally; **normalisation** *f* normalization; TECH standardization; **normalité** *f* normality

norme *f* norm; TECH standard

Norvège: la ~ Norway; **norvégien, ~e 1** *adj* Norwegian **2** *m langue* Norwegian; **Norvégien, ~e** *m/f* Norwegian

nos → notre

nostalgie *f* nostalgia; **avoir la ~ de son pays** be homesick

notaire *m* notary

notamment particularly

note *f* note; *à l'école* grade, *Br* mark; (*facture*) check, *Br* bill; **~ de frais** expense account; **~ de service** memo; **noter** (*écrire*) write down; (*remarquer*) note

notice *f* note; (*mode d'emploi*) instructions *pl*

notifier *v/t*: **~ qch à qn** notify s.o. of sth

notion *f* (*idée*) notion, concept; **~s** basics *pl*

nôtre, *pl* **nos** our

nôtre: *le/la* **~**, *les* **~s** ours

nouer tie; *relations* establish

nougat *m* nougat

nouilles *fpl* noodles

nounou *f* F nanny

nounours *m* teddy bear

nourrice *f* child minder

nourrir feed; *fig*: *espoir* nurture

nourrisson *m* infant

nourriture *f* food

nous *sujet* we; *complément d'objet direct* us; *complément d'objet indirect* (to) us; **~ ~ sommes levés tôt** we got up early; **~ ~ aimons** we love each other

nouveau, **nouvelle** (*m* **nouvel** *before a vowel or silent* h; *mpl* **nouveaux**) **1** *adj* new; *de ou* **à ~** again; **Nouvel An** *m* New Year('s) **2** *m/f* new person

nouveau-né 1 *adj* newborn **2** *m* newborn baby

nouveauté *f* novelty

nouvelle *f* (*récit*) short story; *une* **~** *dans les médias* a piece of news; **nouvelles** *fpl* news *sg*; **Nouvelle Zélande** *f* New Zealand

novembre *m* November

novice 1 *m/f* novice **2** *adj* inexperienced

noyade *f* drowning

noyau *m* pit, *Br* stone; PHYS nucleus; *fig* (small) group

noyer[1] *v/t* drown; AUTO flood;

se **~** drown; *se suicider* drown o.s.

noyer[2] *m arbre, bois* walnut

nu 1 *adj* naked; *arbre, bras, tête etc* bare **2** *m* ART nude

nuage *m* cloud; **nuageux, -euse** cloudy

nuance *f* shade; *fig* slight difference; (*subtilité*) subtlety; **nuancé** subtle; **nuancer** qualify

nucléaire 1 *adj* nuclear **2** *m*: *le* **~** nuclear power

nudiste *m/f & adj* nudist; **nudité** *f* nudity

nuée *f d'insectes* cloud; *de journalistes* horde

nuire: **~ à** hurt, harm

nuit *f* night; *il fait* **~** it's dark

nul, **~le 1** *adj* no; (*non valable*) invalid; (*sans valeur*) hopeless; (*inexistant*) nonexistent; **~le part** nowhere **2** *pron* no-one; **nullement** not in the least; **nullité** *f* JUR invalidity; *fig* hopelessness; *personne* loser

numérique numerical; INFORM digital

numéro *m* number; **~ vert** toll-free number, *Br* Freefone number; **numéroter 1** *v/t* number **2** *v/i* TÉL dial

nuque *f* nape of the neck

nurse *f* nanny

nutritif, -ive nutritional; *aliment* nutritious; **nutrition** *f* nutrition

nylon *m* nylon

obéir obey; **~ à** obey; **obéissance** *f* obedience; **obéissant** obedient

obèse obese; **obésité** *f* obesity

objecter: **~ qch pour ne pas faire qch** give sth as a reason; **~ que** object that; **objectif**, **-ive 1** *adj* objective **2** *m* objective; PHOT lens; **objection** *f* objection; **objectivité** *f* objectivity

objet *m* object; **de réflexions**, **d'une lettre** subject

obligation *f* obligation; COMM bond; **obligatoire** compulsory, obligatory

obligeant obliging; **obliger** oblige; **(forcer)** force; **être obligé de faire qc** be obliged to do sth

oblique oblique

oblitérer *timbre* cancel

obscène obscene

obscur obscure; *nuit, rue* dark; **obscurcir** darken; **s'~** grow dark; **obscurité** *f* obscurity; *de la nuit, d'une rue* darkness

obséder obsess

obsèques *fpl* funeral

observateur, **-trice** *m/f* observer; **observation** *f* observation; *d'une règle* observance; **observatoire** *m* observatory; **observer** ob-

serve; *changement* notice; **faire ~ qc à qn** point sth out to s.o.

obsession *f* obsession

obstacle *m* obstacle; SP hurdle; *pour cheval* jump; **faire ~ à qc** stand in the way of sth

obstination *f* obstinacy; **obstiné** obstinate; **obstiner**: **s'~ à faire qc** persist in doing sth

obstruction *f* obstruction; *dans tuyau* blockage; **obstruer** obstruct, block

obtenir get, obtain

obturer seal; *dent* fill

obtus MATH, *fig* obtuse

obus *m* MIL shell

occasion *f* opportunity; *marché* bargain; **d'~** second-hand; **à l'~** when the opportunity arises; **occasionner** cause

Occident *m*: **l'~** the West; **occidental**, **~e** western; **Occidental**, **~e** *m/f* Westerner

occulte occult

occupant 1 *adj* occupying **2** *m* occupant; **occupation** *f* occupation; **occupé** busy; *pays, appartement* occupied; *chaise* TÉL busy; **occuper** occupy; *personnel* employ; **s'~ de politique** *etc* take an interest in; *malade, organisation* look after

occurrence *f*: **en l'~** as it hap-

ondée

pens

océan m ocean

octet m INFORM byte

octobre m October

oculaire eye atr

oculiste m/f eye specialist

odeur f smell; **~ corporelle** BO

odieux, -euse hateful, odious

odorant scented

odorat m sense of smell

œil m (pl **yeux**) eye; **à vue d'~** visibly

œillet m BOT carnation

œuf m egg; **~s brouillés** scrambled eggs; **~ à la coque** soft-boiled egg; **~ sur le plat** fried egg

œuvre 1 f work; **~ d'art** work of art; **mettre en ~** (employer) use; (exécuter) carry out **2** m ART, littérature works pl

offense f (insulte) insult; (péché) sin; **offenser** offend; **s'~ de** take offense ou Br offence at

office m office; REL service; **d'~** automatically; **faire ~ de** act as

officiel, ~le official

officier m officer

officieux, -euse semi-official

officinal plante medicinal

offre f offer; **~ d'emploi** job offer; **offrir** offer; cadeau give; **s'~ qc** treat o.s. to sth

offusquer offend

oie f goose

oignon m onion; BOT bulb

oiseau m bird; **à vol d'~** as the crow flies

oiseux, -euse idle

oisif, -ive idle; **oisiveté** f idleness

olive f olive; **olivier** m olive (tree)

olympique Olympic

ombrage m shade; **ombragé** shady; **ombrageux, -euse** cheval skittish; personne touchy; **ombre** f shade; (silhouette) shadow; fig (anonymat) obscurity; **de regret** hint

ombrelle f sunshade

omelette f omelet, Br omelette

omettre leave out, omit; **~ de faire** fail ou omit to do; **omission** f omission

omnibus m: (**train** m) **~** slow train

on (après que, et, où, qui, si souvent **l'on**) (nous) we; (tu, vous, indéterminé) you; (quelqu'un) someone; (eux, les gens) they, people; autorités they; **~ m'a dit que...** I was told that ...; **~ ne sait jamais** you never know, one never knows fml

oncle m uncle

onction f REL unction; **onctueux, -euse** smooth; fig smarmy F, unctuous

onde f wave; **sur les ~s** RAD on the air; **grandes ~s** long wave

ondée f downpour

on-dit *m* rumor, *Br* rumour
ondoyer *du blés* sway
ondulation *f de terrain* undulation; *de coiffure* wave; **onduler** *d'ondes* undulate; *de cheveux* be wavy
onéreux, -euse expensive
ongle *m* nail; *zo* claw
onguent *m* cream, salve
onze eleven; **le ~** the eleventh; **onzième** eleventh
opaque opaque
opéra *m* opera; *bâtiment* opera house
opérable MÉD operable; **opérateur, -trice** *m/f* operator; *en cinéma* cameraman; FIN trader; **opération** *f* operation; *action* working; FIN transaction; **opérer 1** *v/t* MÉD operate on; *(produire)* make; *(exécuter)* implement **2** *v/i* MÉD operate; *(avoir effet)* work; *(procéder)* proceed; **se faire ~** have an operation
opiner: **~ de la tête** nod in agreement
opiniâtre stubborn; **opiniâtreté** *f* stubbornness
opinion *f* opinion
opium *m* opium
opportun *ou* opportune; *moment* right; **opportuniste** *m/f* opportunist; **opportunité** *f* timeliness; *(occasion)* opportunity
opposant, ~e 1 *adj* opposing **2** *m/f* opponent; **les ~s** the opposition; **opposé 1** *adj*

pôles opposite; *opinions* conflicting; **être ~ à qc** be opposed to sth **2** *m* opposite; **à l'~ de qn** unlike s.o.; **opposer** bring into conflict; *argument* put forward; **s'~ à qn/à qc** oppose s.o./sth; **opposition** *f* opposition; *(contraste)* contrast
oppresser oppress, weigh down; **oppression** *f* oppression
opprimer oppress
opter: **~ pour** opt for
opticien, ~ne *m/f* optician
optimisme *m* optimism; **optimiste 1** *adj* optimistic **2** *m/f* optimist
option *f* option
optique 1 *adj nerf* optic; *verre* optical **2** *f science* optics; *fig* viewpoint
opulent wealthy; *poitrine* ample
or[1] *m* gold
or[2] *conj* now
orage *m* storm; **orageux, -euse** stormy
oraison *f* REL prayer
oral *adj* & *m* oral
orange *f* & *adj inv* orange; **oranger** *m* orange tree
orateur, -trice *m/f* orator
orbital orbital
orbite *f* ANAT eyesocket; ASTR orbit *(aussi fig)*
orchestre *m* orchestra; *de théâtre* orchestra, *Br* stalls *pl*
orchidée *f* orchid
ordinaire 1 *adj* ordinary **2** *m*

essence regular; **d'~** ordinarily

ordinateur *m* computer

ordonnance *f* arrangement, layout; (*ordre*) order (*aussi* JUR); MÉD prescription; ordonné tidy; **ordonner** organize; (*commander*) order; MÉD prescribe

ordre *m* order; **~ du jour** agenda; **de premier ~** first-rate; **mettre en ~** tidy

ordures *fpl* (*détritus*) garbage, *Br* rubbish; *fig* filth

oreille *f* ear; *d'un bol* handle; **dur d'~** hard of hearing

oreiller *m* pillow

oreillons *mpl* MÉD mumps *sg*

orfèvre *m* goldsmith

organe *m* organ; (*voix, porte-parole*) voice; *d'un mécanisme* part

organisation *f* organization; **organiser** organize; **s'~** *d'une personne* get organized; **organiseur** *m* INFORM personal organizer

organisme *m* organism; ANAT system; (*organisation*) organization, body

orgue *m* organ

orgueil *m* pride; **orgueilleux, -euse** proud

Orient *m*: **l'~** the East; *Asie* the East, the Orient; **oriental, ~e** east, eastern; *d'Asie* eastern, Oriental; **Oriental, ~e** *m/f* Oriental

orientation *f* direction; *d'une maison* exposure; **orienter**

orient, *Br* orientate; (*diriger*) direct; **s'~** get one's bearings; **s'~ vers** *fig* go in for

orifice *m* opening

originaire original; **être ~ de** come from; **original 1** *adj* original; *péj* eccentric **2** *m ouvrage* original; *personne* eccentric; **origine** *f* origin; **à l'~** originally; **originel, ~le** original

orme *m* BOT elm

ornement *m* ornament; **ornementer** ornament

orner decorate (**de** with)

orphelin, ~e *m/f* orphan; **orphelinat** *m* orphanage

orteil *m* toe

orthographe *f* spelling

ortie *f* BOT nettle

os *m* bone

osciller PHYS oscillate; *d'un pendule* swing; **~ entre** *fig* waver between

osé daring; **oser: ~ faire** dare to do

osier *m* BOT osier; **en ~** wicker

ossements *mpl* bones; **osseux, -euse** ANAT bone *atr*; *visage, mains* bony

ostensible evident

otage *m* hostage

ôter remove; MATH take away

ou or; **~ bien** or (else); **~ ... ~ ...** either ... or

où where; **d'~ vient-il?** where does he come from?; **d'~ l'on peut déduire que ...** from which it can be deduced that

...; **le jour ~** ... the day when
...

ouate f absorbent cotton, Br cotton wool; **ouater pad**, quilt

oubli m forgetting; (omission) oversight; **tomber dans l'~** sink into oblivion; **oublier** forget; **~ de faire** forget to do

ouest 1 m west; **à l'~ de** (to the) west of **2** adj west, western

oui yes

ouï-dire: par ~ by hearsay

ouïe f hearing; **~s** zo gills

ouragan m hurricane

ourler hem; **ourlet** m hem

ours m bear; **ourse** f she-bear; **la Grande Ourse** ASTR the Great Bear

oursin m zo sea urchin

outil m tool; **outillage** m tools pl

outrage m insult; **outrager** insult

outrance f excessively; **à ~** excessively

outre 1 prép in addition to **2** adv: **en ~** besides; **passer ~** ignore

outré: être ~ de ou **par** be outraged by

outre-Atlantique on the other side of the Atlantic

outre-Manche on the other side of the Channel

outre-mer: d'~ overseas atr

ouvert open; **ouverture** f opening; MUS overture

ouvrable working; **jour** m **~** workday; **ouvrage** m work; **ouvragé** ornate

ouvre-boîtes m can opener, Br aussi tin opener; **ouvre-bouteilles** m bottle opener

ouvrier, -ère 1 adj working-class **2** m/f worker

ouvrir 1 v/t open; radio, gaz turn on **2** v/i d'un magasin open; **s'~** open; fig open up

ovale m & adj oval

ovni m (= **objet volant non identifié**) UFO (= unidentified flying object)

oxygène m oxygen

P

pacifier pacify; **pacifique 1** adj personne peace-loving; coexistence peaceful **2** m **le Pacifique** the Pacific; **pacifiste** m/f & adj pacifist

pacte m pact; **pactiser: ~ avec** come to terms with

pagaie f paddle

pagaïe, pagaille f F mess

page f page; **~ d'accueil** INFORM home page

paie, paye f pay; **paiement** m payment

païen, ~ne m/f & adj pagan

paillasson m doormat

paille f straw

pain *m* bread; **~ au chocolat** chocolate croissant; **~ complet** whole wheat *ou Br* wholemeal bread; **~ d'épice** gingerbread; **petit ~** roll

pair **1** *adj nombre* even **2** *m*: **hors ~** unrivaled; *Br* unrivalled; **fille** *f* **au ~** au pair

paire *f*: **une ~ de** a pair of

paisible peaceful; *personne* quiet

paître graze

paix *f* peace; *(calme)* peace and quiet

Pakistan: **le ~** Pakistan; pakistanais, **~e** Pakistani; Pakistanais, **~e** *m/f* Pakistani

palais *m* **1** palace; **~ de justice** law courts *pl* **2** ANAT palate

pale *f* blade

pâle pale; *fig*: *style* colorless, *Br* colourless; *imitation* pale

Palestine: **la ~** Palestine; palestinien, **~ne** Palestinian; Palestinien, **~ne** *m/f* Palestinian

palette *f de peinture* palette

pâleur *f* paleness, pallor

palier *m d'un escalier* landing; TECH bearing; *(phase)* stage

pâlir go pale; *de couleurs* fade

palissade *f* fence

pallier alleviate; *manque* make up for

palme *f* BOT palm; *de natation* flipper; **palmier** *m* BOT palm tree

pâlot, **~te** pale

palper feel; MÉD palpate

palpitant *fig* exciting, thrilling; **palpitations** *fpl* palpitations; **palpiter** *du cœur* pound

pamplemousse *m* grapefruit

pan *m de vêtement* tail; *de mur* section

panache *m* plume; **avoir du ~** have panache; **panaché** *m* shandy-gaff, *Br* shandy

pancarte *f* sign; *de manifestation* placard

pané breaded

panier *m* basket

panique *f* panic; **paniquer** panic

panne *f* breakdown; **~ en panne** have a breakdown; **tomber en ~ sèche** run out of gas *ou Br* petrol; **~ d'électricité** power outage, *Br* power failure

panneau *m* board; TECH panel; **~ de signalisation** roadsign

panorama *m* panorama

pansement *m* dressing; **panser** *blessure* dress; *cheval* groom

pantalon *m* pants *pl*, *Br* trousers *pl*; **un ~** a pair of pants

pantelant panting

pantois *inv*: **rester ~** be speechless

pantoufle *f* slipper

paon *m* peacock

papa *m* dad

papal REL papal; **pape** *m* REL pope

paperasse f (souvent au pl ~s) péj papers pl

papeterie f magasin stationery store, Br stationer's

papi, papy m F grandpa

papier m paper; ~ (d')**aluminium** kitchen foil; ~ **hygiénique** toilet tissue; ~s **d'identité** identification, ID

papillon m butterfly; TECH wing nut; F (contravention) (parking) ticket

paquebot m liner

pâquerette f BOT daisy

Pâques msg ou fpl Easter; **joyeuses** ~! happy Easter

paquet m packet; de sucre, café bag; de la poste parcel

par lieu through; passif, moyen by; ~ **terre** on the ground; ~ **beau temps** in fine weather; ~ **curiosité** out of curiosity; ~ **hasard** by chance; ~ **diviser** ~ **quatre** divide by four; ~ **an** a year; **finir** ~ **faire** finish by doing

parabolique: antenne f ~ satellite dish

paracétamol m paracetamol

parachute m parachute; **parachutiste** m/f parachutist; MIL para(trooper)

parade f parade; en escrime parry; à un argument counter

paradis m paradise

paradoxe m paradox

parages mpl: ; **dans les** ~ around; **dans les** ~ **de** in the vicinity of

paragraphe m paragraph

paraître appear; d'un livre come out, be published; **il paraît que** it seems that, it would appear that; **laisser** ~ show

parallèle 1 adj parallel (**à** to) **2** f MATH parallel (line) **3** m GÉOGR parallel (aussi fig)

paralyser paralyse; **paralysie** f paralysis

paramètre m parameter

paranoïaque m/f & adj paranoid

parapharmacie f (non-dispensing) pharmacy; **produits** toiletries pl

paraplégique m/f & adj paraplegic

parapluie m umbrella

parasite 1 adj parasitic **2** m parasite; ~s radio interference

parasol m parasol; de plage beach umbrella

paratonnerre m lightning rod, Br lightning conductor

paravent m windbreak

parc m park; pour enfant playpen

parcelle f de terrain parcel

parce que because

par-ci adv: , **par-là** espace here and there; temps now and then

parcimonie f: **avec** ~ parcimoniously

parcourir région travel through; distance cover; texte read quickly

parcours *m* route; *course d'automobiles* circuit

par-derrière from behind

par-dessous underneath

pardessus *m* overcoat

par-dessus over

par-devant from the front

pardon *m* forgiveness; *~!* sorry!; *~?* excuse me?; *pardonner: ~ qc à qn* forgive s.o. sth

pare-brise *m* windshield, *Br* windscreen

pare-chocs *m* bumper

pareil, *~le* **1** *adj* similar (*à* to); (*tel*) such; *c'est toujours ~* it's always the same **2** *adv*: *habillés ~* similarly dressed, dressed the same way

parent, *~e* **1** *adj* related **2** *m/f* relative; *~s* (*mère et père*) parents; *parenté* *f* relationship

parenthèse *f* parenthesis, *Br* (round) bracket; *entre ~s fig* by the way

parer *attaque* ward off; *en escrime* parry

paresse *f* laziness; *paresseux, -euse* lazy

parfait 1 *adj* perfect; *avant le substantif* complete **2** *m* GRAM perfect (tense)

parfois sometimes

parfum *m* perfume; *d'une glace* flavor, *Br* flavour

pari *m* bet; **parier** bet

parisien, *~ne* Parisian, of/ from Paris; *Parisien*, *~ne* *m/f* Parisian

parité *f* ÉCON parity

parking *m* parking lot, *Br* car park; *édifice* parking garage, *Br* car park

parlant *comparaison* striking; *preuves* decisive

Parlement *m* Parliament; **parlementaire 1** *adj* Parliamentary **2** *m/f* Parliamentarian

parler 1 *v/i* speak, talk; *sans ~ de* not to mention **2** *v/t*: *~ affaires* talk business; *~ anglais* speak English

parmi among

parodie *f* parody

paroi *f* partition

paroisse *f* REL parish

parole *f* word; *faculté* speech; *donner la ~ à qn* give s.o. the floor

parquer *bétail* pen; *réfugiés* dump

parquet *m* (*parquet*) floor; JUR public prosecutor's office

parrain *m* godfather; *dans un club* sponsor

parsemer sprinkle (*de* with)

part *f* share; (*fraction*) part; *faire ~ de qc à qn* inform s.o. of sth; *de la ~ de qn* in *ou Br* on behalf of s.o.; *d'une ~ ... d'autre* on the one hand ... on the other hand; *autre ~* elsewhere; *nulle ~* nowhere; *quelque ~* somewhere; *à ~ traiter etc* separately; *à ~ cela* apart from that

partage *m* division; **partager**

share; (*couper, diviser*) divide (up)

partenaire *m/f* partner

parterre *m de fleurs* bed; *au théâtre* rear orchestra, *Br* rear stalls *pl*

parti¹ *m* side; POL party; **prendre ~ pour** side with; **tirer ~ de qc** turn sth to good use; **~ pris** preconceived idea

parti² *adj* F: **être ~** (*ivre*) be tight

partial biassed

participant, ~e *m/f* participant; **participer: ~ à** participate in, take part in; *bénéfices* share; *frais* contribute to; *douleur, succès* share in

particularité *f* special feature; **particulier, ~ère 1** *adj* particular, special; *privé* private; **~ à** peculiar to **2** *m* (*privé*) individual; **particulièrement** particularly

partie *f; d'un jeu* game; JUR party; *lutte* struggle; **en ~** partly; **faire ~ de qch** be part of sth

partiel, ~le partial

partir leave (**à, pour** for); SP start; *de la saleté* come out; **~ de qc** (*provenir de*) come from sth; **à ~ de** (*starting*) from

partisan, ~e *m/f* supporter; MIL *m* partisan

partition *f* MUS score; POL partition

partout everywhere

parure *f* finery; *de bijoux* set

parvenir arrive; **faire ~ à qn** forward sth to s.o.; **~ à faire** manage to do

parvenu, ~e *m/f* upstart

pas¹ *m* step, pace; **faux ~** stumble; *fig* blunder, faux pas

pas² *adv* not; **ne ... ~** not; **il ne pleut ~** it's not raining; **il n'a ~ plu** it didn't rain

passable acceptable

passage *m* passage; *fig* (*changement*) changeover; **~ à niveau** grade crossing, *Br* level crossing; **de ~** passing

passager, ~ère 1 *adj* passing **2** *m/f* passenger

passant, ~e *m/f* passerby

passe *f* SP pass

passé 1 *adj* past **2** *prép*: **~ dix heures** after ten o'clock **3** *m* past; **composé** GRAM perfect

passe-partout *m* skeleton key

passe-passe *m*: **tour** *m* **de ~** conjuring trick

passeport *m* passport

passer 1 *v/i* pass, go past; *d'un film* show; **~ chez qn** drop by at s.o.'s place; **~ de mode** go out of fashion; **~ en seconde** AUTO shift into second; **~ pour qc** pass as sth; **faire ~** *personne* let past; *plat, journal* pass; **laisser ~** *personne* let past; *lumière* let in; *chance* let slip **2** *v/t* *frontière* cross; *(omettre)* miss (out); *temps* spend; *examen* take; *vêtement* slip on; *film* show; *contrat* enter into; **~ qc à qn** pass s.o. sth, pass sth to s.o. **3**: **se ~** *(se produire)* happen; **se ~ de qc** do without sth

passerelle *f* footbridge; MAR gangway; AVIAT steps *pl*

passe-temps *m* hobby, pastime

passif, -ive 1 *adj* passive **2** *m* GRAM passive; COMM liabilities *pl*

passion *f* passion; *passionnant* exciting; **passionné, ~e 1** *adj* passionate **2** *m/f* enthusiast; **passionner** excite; **se ~ pour** have a passion for

passivité *f* passiveness, passivity

passoire *f* sieve

pastel *m* pastel

pastèque *f* BOT watermelon

pasteur *m* REL pastor

pasteuriser pasteurize

pastille *f* pastille

patate *f* F potato, spud F

patauger flounder

pâte *f* paste; CUIS: *à pain* dough; *à tarte* pastry; **~s** pasta *sg*

pâté *m* paté; **~ de maisons** block of houses

patère *f* coat peg

paternaliste paternalistic

paternel, ~le paternal

pâteux, ~euse doughy; *bouche* dry

pathétique touching; F *(mauvais)* pathetic

pathologique pathological

patience *f* patience; **patient, ~e** *m/f* & *adj* patient; **patienter** wait

patin *m*: **faire du ~** go skating; **~ à roulettes** roller skate; **patinage** *m* skating; **patiner** skate; AUTO skid; *de roues* spin; **patineur, -euse** *m/f* skater; **patinoire** *f* skating rink

pâtisserie *f* cake shop; *gâteaux* cakes; **pâtissier, -ère** *m/f* pastrycook

patois *m* dialect

patrie *f* homeland

patrimoine *m* heritage

patriote 1 *adj* patriotic **2** *m/f* patriot

patron *m* boss; *(propriétaire)* owner; *d'une auberge* landlord; REL patron saint; *de couture* pattern

patronne *f* boss; *(propriétaire)* owner; *d'une auberge* landlady; REL patron saint

patronner sponsor

patrouille *f* patrol

patte *f* paw; *d'un oiseau* foot; *d'un insecte* leg; F hand, paw *péj*

paume *f* palm

paumer F lose

paupière *f* eyelid

pause *f* *(silence)* pause; *(interruption)* break; **~ café** coffee break

pauvre 1 *adj* poor **2** *m/f* poor

person; **les ~s** the poor *pl*;
pauvreté *f* poverty

pavé *m* paving; (*chaussée*)
pavement, *Br* road surface;
pierres rondes cobbles *pl*;
un ~ a paving stone; **rond**
a cobblestone; **paver** pave

pavillon *m* (*maisonnette*)
small house; MAR flag

pavot *m* BOT poppy

payable payable

payant *spectateur* paying;
parking which charges; *fig*
profitable

payer 1 *v/t* pay; **~ qc dix euros** pay ten euros for sth **2**
v/i pay **3**: **se ~ qc** treat o.s.
to sth

pays *m* country; **mal** *m* **du ~**
homesickness

paysage *m* landscape

paysan, ~ne 1 *m/f* small farmer; HIST peasant **2** *adj mœurs*
country *atr*

Pays-Bas *mpl*: **les ~** the
Netherlands

PC *m* (= ***personal computer***)
PC

PDG *m* (= ***président-direc-
teur général***) President,
CEO (= Chief Executive
Officer)

péage *m* d'une autoroute toll-
booth; ***autoroute à ~*** turnpike, toll road

peau *f* skin; *cuir* leather

pêche[1] *f* BOT peach

pêche[2] *f* fishing; *poissons*
catch

péché *m* sin; **pécher** sin

pêcher[1] *m* BOT peach tree

pêcher[2] **1** *v/t* fish for; (*attraper*) catch **2** *v/i* fish; **~ à la ligne** go angling

pêcheur, -eresse *m/f* sinner

pêcheur *m* fisherman; **~ à la
ligne** angler

pédagogie *f* education,
teaching; **pédagogique** educational; *méthode* teaching

pédale *f* pedal; **pédaler à vélo**
pedal

pédéraste *m* homosexual

pédestre: **sentier** *m* **~** footpath; **randonnée** *f* **~** hike

pédiatre *m/f* MÉD pediatrician

pédicure *m/f* podiatrist, *Br*
chiropodist

pègre *f* underworld

peigne *m* comb; **peigner**
comb; **se ~** comb one's hair

peignoir *m* robe, *Br* dressing
gown

peindre paint; (*décrire*) depict

peine *f* (*punition*) punishment; (*effort*) trouble; (*difficulté*) difficulty; (*chagrin*)
sorrow; **ce n'est pas la ~**
there's no point, it's not
worth it; **valoir la ~ de faire
qc** be worth doing sth; **à ~**
scarcely, hardly

peiner 1 *v/t* upset **2** *v/i* labor,
Br labour

peintre *m* painter

peinture *f* paint; *action, tableau* painting; *description*
depiction

péjoratif, -ive pejorative
pelage *m* coat
peler peel
pèlerin *m* pilgrim
pelle *f* spade
pellicule *f* film; **~s** dandruff
pelote *f* de fil ball
peloter F grope, feel up
peloton *m* ball; MIL platoon; SP pack; **pelotonner** wind into a ball; **se ~ contre qn** snuggle up to s.o.
pelouse *f* lawn
peluche *f* jouet soft toy; **ours** *m* **en ~** teddy bear
pelure *f* de fruit peel
pénaliser penalize; **pénalité** *f* penalty
penchant *m* (*inclination*) liking, penchant
pencher **1** *v/t* pot tilt; **penché** *écriture* sloping; **~ la tête en avant** bend *ou* lean forward **2** *v/i* lean; *d'un plateau* tilt; *d'un bateau* list; **se ~ sur un problème** *fig* examine a problem
pendant[1] **1** *prép* during; *avec chiffre* for **2** *conj*: **~ que** while
pendant[2] *adj* oreilles pendulous; (*en instance*) pending
penderie *f* armoire, *Br* wardrobe
pendre hang; **se ~** hang o.s.
pendule **1** *m* pendulum **2** *f* (*horloge*) clock
pénétrer **1** *v/t* penetrate; *pensées, personne* fathom out **2** *v/i*: **~ dans** penetrate; *mai-*

son, *bureaux* get in
pénible *travail, vie* hard; *nouvelle* painful; *caractère* difficult
pénicilline *f* penicillin
péninsule *f* peninsula
pénis *m* penis
pénitence *f* REL penitence; (*punition*) punishment; **pénitencier** *m* penitentiary, *Br* prison
pénombre *f* semi-darkness
pense-bête *m* reminder
pensée *f* thought; BOT pansy; **penser** think; **~ à** (*réfléchir à*) think about; **faire ~ à qn à faire qch** remind s.o. to do sth; **~ faire qch** (*avoir l'intention*) be thinking of doing sth; **penseur** *m* thinker; **pensif, -ive** thoughtful
pension *f* (*allocation*) allowance; *logement* rooming house, *Br* boarding house; *école* boarding school; **~ complète** American plan, *Br* full board; **pensionnaire** *m/f* *d'un hôtel* guest; *écolier* boarder; **pensionnat** *m* boarding school
pente *f* slope; **en ~** sloping
Pentecôte: **la ~** Pentecost
pénurie *f* shortage
pépin *m* de fruit seed
perçant *regard, froid* piercing
percée *f* breakthrough
percepteur *m* tax collector
perception *f* perception; *des impôts* collection; *bureau* tax office

percer 1 v/t make a hole in; *porte* make; (*transpercer*) pierce **2** v/i *du soleil* break through; **perceuse** f drill

percevoir perceive; *impôts* collect

perche f zo perch; *en bois, métal* pole

percher (**se**) ~ *d'un oiseau* perch; F live; **perchoir** m perch

percolateur m percolator

percussion f MUS percussion

percuter crash into

perdant, ~e 1 adj losing **2** m/f loser

perdre 1 v/t lose; *occasion* miss; *son temps* waste; *se* ~ *disparaître* disappear; *d'une personne* get lost **2** v/i: ~ **au change** lose out

perdrix f partridge

père m father (*aussi* REL)

perfection f perfection; **perfectionnement** m perfecting; **perfectionner** perfect; **se** ~ **en anglais** improve one's English

perfide treacherous

perforer perforate; *cuir* punch

performance f performance; **performant** high-performance

péril m peril; **périlleux, -euse** perilous

périmé out of date

périmètre m MATH perimeter

période f period; **en** ~ **de** in times of; **périodique 1** adj

périodique 2 m periodical

périphérie f *d'une ville* outskirts pl; **périphérique** m beltway, Br ringroad

périr perish; **périssable** *nourriture* perishable

péritel: prise f ~ scart

perle f pearl; (*boule percée*) bead; fig: *personne* gem; *de sang* drop; **perler: la sueur perlait sur son front** he had beads of sweat on his forehead

permanence f permanence; **être de** ~ be on duty; **en** ~ constantly; permanent; ~ **1** adj permanent **2** f *coiffure* perm

perméable permeable

permettre allow, permit; ~ **à qn de faire qch** allow s.o. to do sth; **se** ~ **qc** allow o.s. sth

permis m permit; **passer son** ~ sit one's driving test; ~ **de conduire** driver's license, Br driving licence; ~ **de séjour** residence permit

permission f permission; MIL leave

perpendiculaire perpendicular (**à** to)

perpétrer JUR perpetrate

perpétuel, ~le perpetual; **perpétuer** perpetuate; **perpétuité** f: **à** ~ in perpetuity; JUR *condamné* to life imprisonment

perplexe perplexed, puzzled

perron m steps pl

185 **peu**

perroquet *m* parrot
perruque *f* wig
persécuter persecute
persévérance *f* perseverance; persévérer persevere (**dans** in)
persienne *f* shutter
persil *m* BOT parsley
persistance *f* persistence; persister persist (**à faire** in doing); **~ dans sa décision** stick to one's decision
personnage *m* character; (*dignitaire*) important person
personnalité *f* personality
personne¹ *f* person; **deux ~s** two people; **par ~** per person, each; **les ~s âgées** the old *pl*, old people *pl*
personne² *pron* no-one, nobody; **il n'y avait ~** no-one there; **il n'y avait pas ~** there wasn't anyone there; **je ne vois jamais ~** I never see anyone; **qui que ce soit** anyone, anybody
personnel, ~le **1** *adj* personal; *conversation, courrier* private **2** *m* personnel *pl*, staff *pl*
perspective *f* perspective; *fig: pour l'avenir* prospect
perspicace shrewd; perspicacité *f* shrewdness
persuader persuade (**de faire** to do); **se ~** convince o.s.
perte *f* loss; *fig* (*destruction*) ruin; **à ~ de vue** as far as the eye can see; **une ~ de temps** a waste of time

pertinent relevant
perturbateur, -trice disruptive; perturber *personne* upset; *trafic* disrupt
pervers perverse; pervertir pervert
pesant heavy; pesanteur *f* PHYS gravity
pèse-personne *f* scales *pl*
peser weigh; *fig* weigh up; *mots* weigh
pessimisme *m* pessimism; pessimiste **1** *adj* pessimistic **2** *m/f* pessimist
pétale *f* petal
pétard *m* firecracker; F (*bruit*) racket F
péter F fart F
pétillant sparkling; pétiller *du feu* crackle; *d'une boisson, d'yeux* sparkle
petit, ~e **1** *adj* small, little; **~ à ~** gradually, little by little; **~ ami** *m* boyfriend; **~e amie** *f* girlfriend **2** *m/f* child; **une chatte et ses ~s** a cat and her young; **attendre des ~s** be pregnant
petite-fille *f* granddaughter
petit-fils *m* grandson
pétition *f* petition
pétrifier turn to stone; *fig* petrify
pétrin *m* fig F mess
pétrir knead
pétrole *m* oil, petroleum; **~ brut** crude (oil); pétrolier, -ère **1** *adj* oil *atr* **2** *m* tanker
peu **1** *adv*: **~ gentil** not very nice; **~ après** a little after;

j'ai ~ dormi I didn't sleep much; **~ de pain** not much bread; **~ de choses à faire** not many things to do; **~ de gens** few people; **dans ~ de temps** in a little while; **un ~** a little, a bit; **un tout petit ~** just a very little, just a little bit; **un ~ de chocolat** a little chocolate, a bit of chocolate; **un ~ plus long** a bit *ou* little longer; **de ~ rater le bus** etc only just; **à ~ ~ près** little by little; **à ~ près** (*plus ou moins*) more or less; (*presque*) almost

peuple *m* people; **peupler** *région* populate; *maison* live in

peuplier *m* poplar

peur *f* fear (**de** of); **avoir ~** be frightened, be afraid (**de** of); **faire ~ à** frighten s.o.; **de ~ que** (+*subj*) in case; **peureux**, **-euse** fearful, timid

peut-être perhaps, maybe

phare *m* MAR lighthouse; AVIAT beacon; AUTO headlight; **se mettre en (pleins) ~s** switch to full beam

pharmacie *f* pharmacy, *Br aussi* chemist's; *science* pharmacy; **médicaments** pharmaceuticals *pl*; **pharmacien**, **~ne** *m/f* pharmacist

phénomène *m* phenomenon

philosophe *m* philosopher; **philosophie** *f* philosophy; **philosophique** philosophical

phobie *f* phobia

photo *f* photo; *l'art* photography; **prendre qn en ~** take a photo of s.o.

photocopie *f* photocopy; **photocopier** photocopy; **photocopieur** *m*, **photocopieuse** *f* photocopier

photographe *m/f* photographer; **photographie** *f* photograph; *l'art* photography; **photographier** photograph

phrase *f* GRAM sentence; MUS phrase; **sans ~s** straight out

physicien, **~ne** *m/f* physicist

physique 1 *adj* physical **2** *m* physique **3** *f* physics

piailler *d'un oiseau* chirp; F *d'un enfant* scream

pianiste *m/f* pianist; **piano** *m* piano; **~ à queue** grand piano

pic *m* pick; *d'une montagne* peak; **à ~** *tomber* steeply

pichet *m* pitcher, *Br* jug

pickpocket *m* pickpocket

pick-up *m* pick-up (truck)

pie *f* ZO magpie

pièce *f* piece; *de machine* part; (*chambre*) room; (*document*) document; *de monnaie* coin; *de théâtre* play; **cinq euros (la) ~** five euros each; **mettre en ~s** smash to smithereens; **~ jointe** enclosure

pied *m* foot; *d'un meuble* leg; *d'un champignon* stalk; **à ~** on foot; **~s nus** barefoot; **au ~ de** at the foot of; **mettre**

sur ~ set up
piège *m* trap; **piégé: voiture** *f*
~**e** car bomb; **piéger** trap;
voiture booby-trap
piercing *m* body piercing
pierre *f* stone; ~ **tombale**
gravestone; **pierreux, -euse**
sol stony
piétiner 1 *v/t* trample; *fig*
trample underfoot **2** *v/i fig*
(*ne pas avancer*) mark time
piéton, ~e 1 *m/f* pedestrian **2**
adj: **zone** *f* ~**ne** pedestria-
nized zone, *Br* pedestrian
precinct
pieu *m* stake; F pit F
pieuvre *f* octopus
pieux, -euse *adj* pious
pigeon *m* pigeon
piger F understand, get F
pigment *m* pigment
pile¹ *f* (*tas*) pile; ÉL battery;
monnaie tails
pile² *adv*: **s'arrêter** ~ stop
dead; **à deux heures** ~ at
two o'clock on the dot
piler *ail* crush; *amandes* grind
pilier *m* pillar (*aussi fig*)
pillage *m* pillage, plunder;
piller pillage
pilote 1 *m* pilot; AUTO driver **2**
adj: **usine** *f* ~ pilot plant; **pi-**
loter pilot; AUTO drive
pilule *f* pill
piment *m* pimento; *fig* spice
pimenter spice up
pin *m* BOT pine
pinard *m* F wine
pince *f* pliers *pl*; *d'un crabe*
pincer; ~ **à épiler** tweezers

pl; ~ **à linge** clothespin, *Br*
clothespeg
pinceau *m* brush
pincer pinch; MUS pluck
ping-pong *m* ping-pong
pinson *m* chaffinch
pintade *f* guinea fowl
pioche *f* pickax, *Br* pickaxe;
piocher dig
pioncer F sleep, *Br* kip F
pipe *f* pipe
pipi *m* F pee F
pique *m aux cartes* spades
pique-nique *m* picnic
piquer *d'une abeille, des or-*
ties sting; *d'un moustique,*
serpent bite; *d'épine* prick;
fig: *curiosité* excite; *fig* F
(*voler*) pinch F; **se** ~ prick
o.s.; *se faire une piqûre* inject
o.s.
piquet *m* stake; ~ **de tente**
tent peg; ~ **de grève** picket
line
piquette *f* cheap wine
piqûre *f d'abeille* sting; *de*
moustique bite; MÉD injection
pirate *m* pirate; ~ **informati-**
que hacker; ~ **de l'air** hijacker; **pirater** pirate
pire worse; **le/la** ~ the worst
piscine *f* (swimming) pool; ~
couverte/en plein air in-
door/outdoor pool
pisser F pee F, piss F
piste *f* track; AVIAT runway; *ski*
alpin piste; *ski de fond* trail;
~ **cyclable** cycle path
pistolet *m* pistol

piston m piston; **pistonner** F pull strings for

pitié f pity; **avoir ~ de qn** take pity on s.o.

pitoyable pitiful

pittoresque picturesque

pivot m pivot

pizza f pizza

PJ (= **pièce(s) jointe(s)**) enclosure(s)

placard m (*armoire*) cabinet, *Br* cupboard; (*affiche*) poster; **placarder** *avis* stick up

place f de ville square; (*lieu*) place; (*siège*) seat; (*espace libre*) room, space; (*emploi*) position; **sur ~** on the spot; **à la ~ de** instead of; **~ de place ce avec** change places with

placement m (*emploi*) placement; FIN investment; **agence f de ~** employment agency; **placer** put, place; (*procurer emploi à*) find a job for; *argent* invest; *dans une famille etc* find a place for; **se ~** take one's place

plafond m ceiling

plage f beach; *lieu* seaside resort

plagiat m plagiarism

plaider 1 v/i JUR plead **2** v/t: **~ la cause de qn** defend s.o.; *fig* plead s.o.'s cause

plaidoyer m JUR speech for the defense *ou Br* defence; *fig* plea

plaie f cut; *fig* wound

plaignant, ~e m/f JUR plaintiff

plaindre pity; **se ~** complain

(*de* about; *à* to)

plaine f plain

plainte f complaint; (*lamentation*) moan

plaire: **s'il vous plaît, s'il te plaît** please; **Paris me plaît** I like Paris; **ça me plairait d'aller …** I would like to go …; **se ~ de personnes** be attracted to each other

plaisance f: **port m de ~** marina

plaisanter joke; **plaisanterie** f joke

plaisir m pleasure; **par ~, pour le ~** for pleasure; **faire ~ à** please

plan 1 *adj* flat, level **2** m (*surface*) surface; (*projet, relevé*) plan; **premier ~** foreground; **sur ce ~** in that respect; **sur le ~ économique** in economic terms

planche f plank; **~ à voile** sailboard

plancher m floor

planer hover; *fig* live in another world

planète f planet

planeur m glider

planifier plan

planning m: **~ familial** family planning

planquer F hide; **se ~** hide

plant m AGR seedling; (*plantation*) plantation

plante[1] f plant

plante[2] f: **~ du pied** sole of the foot

planter plant; *jardin* plant up;

poteau hammer in; *tente* put up

plaque *f* plate; (*inscription*) plaque; ~ **électrique** hotplate; ~ **tournante** turntable; *fig* hub

plaquer *argent, or* plate; *meuble* veneer; *fig* pin (**contre** to, against); F (*abandonner*) dump F; *au rugby* tackle

plastique *adj* & *m* plastic

plat 1 *adj* flat; *eau* still **2** *m* dish

plateau *m* tray; *de théâtre* stage; TV, *d'un film* set; GÉOGR plateau; ~ **de fromages** cheeseboard

plate-bande *f* flower bed

plate-forme *f* platform; ~ **de lancement** launch pad

platine 1 *m* CHIM platinum **2** *f*: ~ **laser** *ou* **CD** CD player

platitude *f* dullness; (*lieu commun*) platitude

plâtre *m* plaster; **plâtrer** plaster

plausible plausible

plein 1 *adj* full (**de** of); **en ~ air** in the open (air); **en ~ Paris** in the middle of Paris; **en ~ jour** in broad daylight **2** *adv*: ~ **de** F lots of, a whole bunch of F **3** *m*: **faire le ~** AUTO fill up

pleurer 1 *v/i* cry; ~ **sur** complain about **2** *v/t* (*regretter*) mourn

pleurnicher F snivel

pleuvoir rain; **il pleut** it's raining

pli *m* fold; *d'une jupe* pleat; *d'un pantalon* crease; (*enveloppe*) envelope; (*lettre*) letter; **plier 1** *v/t* (*rabattre*) fold; (*courber, ployer*) bend **2** *v/i* bend; *fig* (*céder*) give in; **se ~ à** (*se soumettre*) submit to

plomb *m* lead; **sans ~** *essence* unleaded

plombage *m* filling

plomberie *f* plumbing; **plombier** *m* plumber

plongée *f* diving; **plonger 1** *v/i* dive **2** *v/t* plunge; **se ~ dans** bury o.s. in; **plongeur, -euse** *m/f* diver

pluie *f* rain; *fig* shower

plumage *m* plumage; **plume** *f* feather; **plumer** pluck; *fig* fleece

plupart: **la ~ d'entre nous** most of us; **pour la ~** mostly; **la ~ du temps** most of the time

pluriel, ~le *adj* & *m* plural

plus 1 *adv* more (**que, de** than); ~ **grand** bigger; ~ **efficace** more efficient; **le ~ grand** the biggest; **le ~ efficace** the most efficient; ~ **il vieillit ~ il dort** the older he gets the more he sleeps; **le ~** the most; **tu en veux ~?** do you want some more?; **20 euros de ~** = 20 euros more; **nous n'avons ~ d'argent** we have no more money, we don't have any more money; **elle n'y habite ~**

she doesn't live there any more, she no longer lives there; **je ne le reverrai ~ jamais** I won't see him ever again; **moi non ~** me neither **2** *prép* MATH plus

plusieurs several

plutôt rather

pluvieux, -euse rainy

pneu *m* tire, *Br* tyre

pneumonie *f* pneumonia

poche *f* pocket; zo pouch; **livre** *m* **de ~** paperback; **argent de ~** pocket money

pocher œufs poach

pochette *f pour photos etc* folder; *d'un disque, CD* sleeve; *(sac)* bag

poêle 1 *m* stove **2** *f* frypan, *Br* frying pan

poème *m* poem

poésie *f* poetry; *(poème)* poem

poète *m* poet; **poétique** poetic; *atmosphère* romantic

poids *m* weight; *fig (charge, fardeau)* burden; *(importance)* weight; **perdre/prendre du ~** lose/gain weight

poignard *m* dagger; **poignarder** stab

poignée *f petit nombre* handful; *d'une valise etc* handle; **~ de main** handshake

poignet *m* wrist

poil *m* hair; **à ~** naked; **poilu** hairy

poinçonner argent hallmark; *billet* punch

poing *m* fist; **coup** *m* **de ~** punch

point¹ *m* point; *de couture* stitch; **deux ~s** colon; **être sur le ~ de faire** be on the point of doing; **à ~** viande medium; **à ce ~** so much; **~ du jour** dawn; **~ de vue** point of view

point² *adv litt:* **il ne le fera ~** he will not do it

pointe *f* point; *d'asperge* tip; **en ~** pointed; **de ~** technologie leading-edge; *secteur* high-tech; **une ~ de** a touch of

pointer 1 *v/t sur liste* check, *Br* tick off **2** *v/i d'un employé* clock in

pointillé *m:* **les ~s** the dotted line

pointilleux, -euse fussy

pointu pointed; *voix* high-pitched

pointure *f* (shoe) size

point-virgule *m* GRAM semi-colon

poire *f* pear

poireau *m* BOT leek

poirier *m* BOT pear (tree)

pois *m* BOT pea; **petits ~** garden peas

poison 1 *m* poison **2** *m/f fig* F nuisance, pest

poisson *m* fish; **Poissons** *mpl* ASTROL Pisces

poissonnerie *f* fish shop, *Br* fishmonger's

poitrine *f* chest; *(seins)* bosom

poivre *m* pepper; **poivrer**

pepper
poivron *m* bell pepper, *Br* pepper
polaire polar; **pôle** *m* pole; *fig* center, *Br* centre, focus; **~ Nord** North Pole; **~ Sud** South Pole
poli (*courtois*) polite; *métal, caillou* polished
police *f* police; **~ d'assurance** insurance policy
policier, -ère 1 *adj* police *atr; film, roman* detective *atr* **2** *m* police officer
polir polish
politesse *f* politeness
politicien, ~ne *m/f* politician
politique 1 *adj* political; **homme ~** *m* politician **2** *f d'un parti etc* policy; (*affaires publiques*) politics *sg*
pollen *m* pollen
polluer pollute; **pollution** *f* pollution; **~ atmosphérique** air pollution
Pologne: la ~ Poland; **polonais, ~e 1** *adj* Polish **2** *m langue* Polish; **Polonais, ~e** *m/f* Pole
poltron, ~ne *m/f* coward
polyclinique *f* (general) hospital
polycopié *m* (photocopied) handout
polystyrène *m* polystyrene
polyvalence *f* versatility; **polyvalent** multipurpose; *personne* versatile
pommade *f* MÉD ointment
pomme *f* apple; **~ de terre** po-

tato
pommette *f* ANAT cheekbone
pommier *m* BOT apple tree
pompe[1] *f faste* pomp; **~s funèbres** funeral director
pompe[2] *f* TECH pump; **à essence** gas pump, *Br* petrol pump; **pomper** pump; *fig* (*épuiser*) knock out
pompeux, -euse pompous
pompier *m* firefighter; **~s** fire department, *Br* fire brigade
pomponner F: **se ~** get dolled up F
poncer sand
ponctualité *f* punctuality; **ponctuel, ~le** *personne* punctual; *fig: action* one-off
ponctuer punctuate
pondération *f d'une personne* level-headedness; *de forces* balance; ÉCON weighting; **pondéré** *personne* level--headed; *forces* balanced; ÉCON weighted
pondre *œufs* lay; *fig* F come up with; *roman* churn out
poney *m* pony
pont *m* bridge; MAR deck; **faire le ~** make a long weekend of it
pontage *m*: **~ coronarien** (heart) bypass
pop *f* MUS pop
populaire popular; **populariser** popularize; **popularité** *f* popularity
population *f* population
porc *m* hog, pig; *fig* pig; *viande de* pork

porcelaine f porcelain

porcherie f hog ou pig farm

pore m pore; **poreux, -euse** porous

pornographique pornographic

port[1] m port; **~ de pêche** fishing port

port[2] m d'armes carrying; courrier postage

portable 1 adj portable **2** m ordinateur laptop; téléphone cellphone, cell, Br mobile

portail m ARCH portal; d'un parc gate

portant mur load-bearing; **à bout ~** at point-blank range; **bien ~** well; **mal ~** not well

portatif, -ive portable

porte f door; d'une ville gate; **mettre qn à la ~** show s.o. the door

porte-bagages m AUTO roof rack; filet luggage rack; **porte-bonheur** m lucky charm; **porte-clés** m keyring; **porte-documents** m briefcase

portée f zo litter; d'une arme range; (importance) significance; **être à la ~ de qn** fig be accessible to s.o.

portefeuille m portfolio (aussi POL, FIN); (porte-monnaie) billfold, Br wallet

portemanteau m coat rack; sur pied coatstand

porte-monnaie m coin purse, Br purse

porte-parole m spokesperson

porter 1 v/t carry; un vêtement, des lunettes etc wear; (apporter) take; bring; yeux, attention turn (**sur** to); toast drink; fruits, nom bear; **~ plainte** make a complaint **2** v/i d'une voix carry; **~ sur** (appuyer sur) rest on; (concerner) be about **3**: **il se porte bien/mal** he's well/not well; **se ~ candidat** be a candidate, run

porteur m d'un message bearer

portier m doorman

portière f de train, voiture door

portion f portion

portrait m portrait

portugais, ~e 1 adj Portuguese **2** m langue Portuguese; **Portugais, ~e** m/f Portuguese; **Portugal: le ~** Portugal

pose f d'un radiateur installation; de moquette fitting; de papier peint, rideaux hanging; (attitude) pose; **posé** poised, composed; **poser 1** v/t (mettre) put (down); compteur, radiateur install, Br instal; moquette fit; papier peint, rideaux hang; problème pose; question ask; **se ~ en** set o.s. up as **2** v/i pose

positif, -ive positive

position f position

possédé possessed (**de** by); **posséder** own, possess;

pourboire

possesseur *m* owner; **possession** *f* possession, ownership

possibilité *f* possibility; **possible 1** *adj* possible; **le plus souvent ~** as often as possible; **autant que ~** as far as possible **2** *m*: **faire tout son ~** do everything one can

poste¹ *f* mail, *Br aussi* post; (**bureau** *m* **de**) **~** post office; **mettre à la ~** mail, *Br aussi* post

poste² *m* post; (*profession*) position; RAD, TV set; TÉL extension; **~ de secours** first-aid post; **~ de travail** INFORM work station

poster *soldat* post; *lettre* mail, *Br aussi* post

postérieur 1 *adj dans l'espace* back *atr*, rear *atr*; *dans le temps* later; **~ à qch** after sth **2** *m* F posterior F

postérité *f* posterity

posthume posthumous

postier, -ère *m/f* post office employee

postillonner splutter

postuler apply for

posture *f* position, posture; *fig* position

pot *m* pot; **~ à eau** water jug; **prendre un ~** F have a drink; **avoir du ~** F be lucky

potable fit to drink; **eau ~** drinking water

potage *m* soup; **potager, -ère**: **jardin** *m* **~** kitchen garden

pot-au-feu *m* boiled beef dinner

pot-de-vin *m* F kickback F, bribe

poteau *m* post; **~ indicateur** signpost

poterie *f* pottery; *objet* piece of pottery

potion *f* potion

potiron *m* BOT pumpkin

pou *m* louse

poubelle *f* trash can, *Br* dustbin

pouce *m* thumb

poudre *f* powder; **chocolat** *m* **en ~** chocolate powder; **poudrier** *m* powder compact

pouffer: **~ de rire** burst out laughing

poulailler *m* henhouse; *au théâtre* gallery, *Br* gods *pl*

poulain *m* ZO foal

poule *f* hen; **poulet** *m* chicken

poulpe *m* octopus

pouls *m* pulse

poumon *m* lung

poupée *f* doll (*aussi fig*)

poupon *m* little baby

pour 1 *prép* for; **~ 20 euros de courses** 20 euros' worth of shopping; **je l'ai dit ~ te prévenir** I said that to warn you **2** *conj*: **~ que** (+ *subj*) so that; **il parle trop vite ~ que je le comprenne** he speaks too fast for me to understand **3** *m*: **le ~ et le contre** the pros and the cons *pl*

pourboire *m* tip

pourcentage *m* percentage

pourparlers *mpl* talks

pourpre purple

pourquoi why

pourri rotten (*aussi fig*);
pourrir 1 *v/i* rot; *fig: d'une situation* deteriorate **2** *v/t* rot; *fig* (*corrompre*) corrupt; (*gâter*) spoil; **pourriture** *f* rot (*aussi fig*)

poursuite *f* chase, pursuit; *fig* pursuit; **~s** JUR proceedings;
poursuivre pursue, chase; *fig: bonheur* pursue; *de pensées* haunt; JUR sue; *malfaiteur* prosecute; (*continuer*) carry on with

pourtant yet

pourvoir 1 *v/t emploi* fill; **~ de** *voiture, maison* equip with **2** *v/i:* **~ à besoins** provide for; **se ~ de** provide o.s.

pourvu: **~ que** (+ *subj*) provided that; *exprimant désir* hopefully

pousse *f* AGR shoot; **poussée** *f* thrust; MÉD outbreak; *de fièvre* rise; *fig: de racisme etc* upsurge; **pousser 1** *v/t* push; *du vent* drive; *cri, soupir* give; *fig: recherches* pursue; **se ~** *d'une foule* push forward; *pour faire de la place* move over **2** *v/i* push; *de cheveux, plantes* grow; **poussette** *f pour enfants* stroller, *Br* pushchair

poussière *f* dust; *particule* speck of dust

poussin *m* chick

poutre *f* beam

pouvoir 1 *v/aux* be able to, can; *je ne peux pas aider* I can't ou cannot help; *je ne pouvais pas accepter* I couldn't accept, I wasn't able to accept; *il se peut que* (+ *subj*) it's possible that; *tu aurais pu me prévenir!* you could have ou might have warned me! **2** *m* power; *procuration* power of attorney; *les* **~s publics** the authorities

prairie *f* meadow; *plaine* prairie

praline *f* praline

praticable *projet* feasible; *route* passable

pratique 1 *adj* practical **2** *f* practice; *expérience* practical experience; **pratiquement** (*presque*) practically; *dans la pratique* in practice; **pratiquer** practice, *Br* practise; *sports* play; *technique* use; TECH *trou, passage* make

pré *m* meadow

préado *m/f* pre-teen

préalable 1 *adj* (*antérieur*) prior; (*préliminaire*) preliminary **2** *m* condition; *au* **~** beforehand

préavis *m* notice

précaire precarious

précaution *f* caution; *mesure* precaution; *par* **~** as a precaution

précédent 1 *adj* previous **2** *m*

precedent; **précéder** precede

prêcher preach

précieux, -euse precious

précipice *m* precipice

précipitamment hastily, in a rush; **précipitation** *f* haste; **~s** *temps* precipitation; **précipiter** (*faire tomber*) plunge (**dans** into); (*pousser*) hurl; (*brusquer*) precipitate; *pas* hasten; **se ~** (*se jeter*) throw o.s.; (*se dépécher*) rush

précis 1 *adj* precise **2** *m* précis, summary; **préciser** specify; **~ que** (*souligner*) make it clear that; **précision** *f* accuracy; *d'un geste* preciseness; *pour plus de* **~s** for further details

précoce early; *enfant* precocious; **précocité** *f* earliness; *d'un enfant* precociousness

préconçu preconceived

précurseur 1 *m* precursor **2** *adj*: *signe* *m* **~** warning sign

prédateur, -trice 1 *adj* predatory **2** *m/f* predator

prédécesseur *m* predecessor

prédestiner predestine (**à qc** for sth; **à faire** to do)

prédiction *f* prediction

prédilection *f* predilection; **de ~** favorite, *Br* favourite

prédire predict

prédominer predominate

préfabriqué prefabricated

préface *f* preface

préférable preferable (**à** to);

préféré favorite, *Br* favourite; **préférence** *f* preference; **de ~** preferably; **préférer** prefer (**à** to); **~ faire qc** prefer to do sth; *je préfère que tu viennes* (*subj*) **demain** I would *ou* I'd prefer you to come tomorrow, I'd rather you came tomorrow

préfet *m* prefect; **~ de police** chief of police

préfixe *m* prefix

préjudice *m* harm; **porter ~ à** harm

préjugé *m* prejudice

prélever *échantillon* take; *montant* deduct (**sur** from)

préliminaire preliminary

préluder *fig*: **~ à** be the prelude to

prématuré premature

préméditer premeditate

premier, -ère 1 *adj* first; *rang* front; *objectif, cause* primary; *nombre* prime; **au ~ étage** on the second floor, *Br* on the first floor; *Premier ministre* Prime Minister; *le* **~ août** August first, *Br* the first of August **2** *m/f*: *partir le* **~** leave first **3** *m* second floor, *Br* first floor; *en* **~** first **4** *f* THÉÂT first night; AUTO first (gear); *en train* first (class)

prémisse *f* premise

prémonition *f* premonition; **prémonitoire** *rêve* prophetic

prendre 1 *v/t* take; (*enlever*) take away; *froid* catch; *poids* put on; **~ qch à qn** take sth (away) from s.o. **2** *v/i* (*durcir*) set; *de mode* catch on; *d'un feu* take hold; **à droite** turn right **3**: **se ~** (*se laisser attraper*) get caught; **se ~ d'amitié pour qn** take a liking to s.o.

prénom *m* first name; **deuxième** *f* middle name

préoccuper preoccupy; (*inquiéter*) worry; **se ~ de** worry about

préparatifs *mpl* preparations; **préparation** *f* preparation; **préparer** prepare; (*organiser*) arrange; **~ qn à qch** prepare s.o. for sth; **~ un examen** prepare for an exam; **se ~** get ready; *de dispute, d'orage* be brewing

prépondérant predominant

préposé *m* (*facteur*) mailman, *Br* postman; *au vestiaire* attendant; *des douanes* official; **préposée** *f* (*factrice*) mailwoman, *Br* postwoman

préretraite *f* early retirement

près 1 *adv* close, near; **de ~** closely **2** *prép*: **de ~ qch** near sth, close to sth; **~ de 500** nearly 500

présage *m* omen

presbyte farsighted, *Br* longsighted

prescription *f* rule; MÉD prescription; **prescrire** stipulate; MÉD prescribe

présence *f* presence; **en ~ de** in the presence of; **présent 1** *adj* present **2** *m* present (*aussi* GRAM); **les ~s** those present; **à ~** at present; **à ~ que** now that; **jusqu'à ~** till now

présentateur, **-trice** *m/f* TV presenter; **~ météo** weatherman; **présentation** *f* presentation; **présenter** present; *chaise* offer; *personne* introduce; *pour un concours* put forward; *billet* show, present; *condoléances, félicitations* offer; *difficultés, dangers* involve; **se ~** introduce o.s.; *pour un poste, un emploi* apply; *aux élections* run; *de difficultés* come up

préservatif *m* condom

préserver protect (**de** from); *bois, patrimoine* preserve

présidence *f* chairmanship; POL presidency; **président**, **-e** *m/f d'une réunion* chair; POL president; **présidentiel**, **-le** presidential; **présider** *réunion* chair

présomption *f* presumption; **présomptueux**, **-euse** presumptuous

presque almost, nearly

presqu'île *f* peninsula

pressant *besoin* pressing, urgent; *personne* insistent

presse *f* press; **mise *f* sous ~** going to press

pressé *lettre, requête* urgent; *citron* fresh; **je suis ~** I'm in a hurry

prime

pressentiment *m* foreboding, presentiment; **pressentir**: ~ *qch* have a premonition that sth is going to happen; ~ *qn pour un poste* approach s.o., sound s.o. out

presser 1 *v/t bouton* push, press; *fruit* squeeze; (*harceler*) press; *pas* quicken; *affaire* speed up; (*étreindre*) press, squeeze; **se** ~ **contre** press (o.s.) against **2** *v/i* be urgent; **se** ~ hurry up

pressing *m magasin* dry cleaner

pression *f* pressure; *bouton* snap fastener, *Br aussi* press-stud fastener; (*bière f*) ~ draft beer, *Br* draught beer; **faire** ~ **sur** pressure, put pressure on

prestance *f* presence

prestation *f* (*allocation*) allowance; ~*s familiales* child benefit

prestige *m* prestige

présumer 1 *v/t*: ~ *que* presume *ou* assume that **2** *v/i*: ~ *de* overrate

prêt[1] *adj* ready (*à* for; *à faire* to do)

prêt[2] *m* loan; ~ *immobilier* mortgage

prêt-à-porter *m* ready-to-wear clothes *pl*

prétendre 1 *v/t* maintain; ~ *faire qch* claim to do sth **2** *v/i*: ~ *à* lay claim to sth; **prétendu** so-called

prétentieux, **-euse** pretentious

prêter 1 *v/t* lend **2** *v/i*: ~ *à* give rise to; **se** ~ *à d'une chose* lend itself to; *d'une personne* be a party to

prétexte *m* pretext; **sous** ~ **de faire** on the pretext of doing

prêtre *m* priest; **prêtresse** *f* woman priest

preuve *f* proof, evidence; MATH proof; **faire** ~ **de courage** show courage

prévenance *f* consideration

prévenir (*avertir*) warn (*de* of); (*informer*) inform (*de* of); *besoin, question* anticipate; *crise, maladie* avert

préventif, **-ive** preventive; **prévention** *f* prevention; ~ *routière* road safety

prévision *f* forecast; ~*s météorologiques* weather forecast

prévoir (*pressentir*) foresee; (*planifier*) plan; **comme prévu** as expected; **prévoyance** *f* foresight; **prévoyant** farsighted

prier 1 *v/i* REL pray **2** *v/t* (*supplier*) beg; REL pray to; ~ *qn de faire qc* ask s.o. to do sth; *je vous en prie* don't mention it

prière *f* REL prayer; (*demande*) entreaty; **faire sa** ~ say one's prayers

primaire primary; *péj* narrow-minded

prime[1]: *de* ~ *abord* at first sight

prime² *f d'assurance* premium; *de fin d'année* bonus; *(cadeau)* free gift

primer 1 *v/i* take precedence **2** *v/t* take precedence over

primeur *f*: **avoir la ~ de** *nouvelle* be the first to hear *objet* have first use of; **~s** early fruit and vegetables

primitif, -ive primitive; *couleur, sens* original

primordial essential

prince *m* prince; **princesse** princess

principal, ~e 1 *adj* main, principal **2** *m*: **le ~** the main thing **3** *m/f* principal, *Br* head teacher

principe *m* principle; **par ~** on principle; **en ~** in principle

printemps *m* spring

priorité *f* priority (**sur** over); *sur la route* right of way

pris place taken; *personne* busy

prise *f* hold; *d'un pion, une ville etc* capture, taking; *de poissons* catch; ÉL outlet, *Br* socket; *d'un film* take; **être aux ~s avec** be struggling with; **~ de conscience** awareness; **~ de courant** outlet, *Br* socket

prison *f* prison; **prisonnier, -ère** *m/f* prisoner

privation *f* deprivation

privatisation *f* privatization; **privatiser** privatize

privé 1 *adj* private **2** *m*: **en ~** in private; **priver**: **~ qn de** deprive s.o. of; **se ~ de** go without

privilège *m* privilege; **privilégier** favor, *Br* favour

prix *m* price; *(valeur)* value; *(récompense)* prize; **à tout ~** at all costs; **hors de ~** prohibitive; **au ~ de** at the cost of; **~ fort** full price; **~ de revient** cost price

probabilité *f* probability; **probable** probable

probant convincing

problème *m* problem

procédé *m (méthode)* method; TECH process; **~s** *(comportement)* behavior, *Br* behaviour

procéder proceed; **~ à qc** carry out sth

procès *m* JUR trial

processus *m* process

procès-verbal *m* minutes *pl*; *(contravention)* ticket

prochain, ~e 1 *adj* next **2** *m/f*: **son ~** one's neighbor *ou Br* neighbour

proche 1 *adj* close (**de** to), near; *ami* close; *événement* recent; **~ de** *fig* close to **2** *mpl*: **~s** family and friends

proclamer *roi, république* proclaim; *résultats, innocence* declare

procréer procreate

procuration *f* proxy, power of attorney; **procurer** get, procure *fml*

prodigieux, -euse enormous,

tremendous

prodigue extravagant; **prodiguer** lavish

producteur, -trice 1 *adj* producing **2** *m/f* producer; **productif, -ive** productive; **production** *f* production; **produire** *se* ~ happen; **produit** *m* product; *d'un investissement* yield; ~ **d'entretien** cleaning product; ~ **fini** end product

profane 1 *adj rel, musique* secular **2** *m/f fig* lay person; **profaner** desecrate, profane

proférer *menaces* utter

professeur *m* teacher; *d'université* professor

profession *f* profession; **professionnel, ~le** *m/f & adj* professional

profil *m* profile

profit *m* COMM profit; *(avantage)* benefit; **profitable** beneficial; COMM profitable; **profiter:** ~ **de qc** take advantage of sth; ~ **à qn** be to s.o.'s advantage

profond deep; *personne, pensées* deep, profound; *influence* profound; **profondément** deeply, profoundly; **profondeur** *f* depth

programme *m* program, *Br* programme; INFORM program; ~ **télé** TV program; **programmer** TV schedule; INFORM program; **programmeur, -euse** *m/f* programmer

progrès *m* progress; *d'un incendie, d'une épidémie* spread; **progresser** progress; *d'une incendie, d'une épidémie* spread; **progressif, -ive** progressive; **progression** *f* progress

prohiber ban, prohibit; **prohibition** *f* ban; **la Prohibition** HIST Prohibition

proie *f* prey *(aussi fig)*; **en** ~ **à** prey to

projecteur *m* (*spot*) spotlight; *au cinéma* projector

projection *f* projection

projet *m* project; *personnel* plan; *(ébauche)* draft; ~ **de loi** bill; **projeter** *(jeter)* throw; *film* screen; *travail, voyage* plan

proliférer proliferate

prologue *m* prologue

prolongation *f* extension; ~**s** SP overtime; *Br* extra time; **prolonger** prolong; *mur, route* extend; *se* ~ continue

promenade *f* walk; *en voiture* drive; **promener** take for a walk; *se* ~ go for a walk; *en voiture* go for a drive; **promeneur, -euse** *m/f* stroller, walker

promesse *f* promise; **prometteur, -euse** promising; **promettre** promise (*qc à qn* s.o. sth, sth to s.o., *de faire* to do); *se* ~ **de faire qc** make up one's mind to do sth

promiscuité *f* overcrowding;

sexuelle promiscuity

promontoire *m* promontory

promoteur, -trice 1 *m/f* (*instigateur*) instigator **2** *m*: ~ **immobilier** property developer; **promotion** *f* promotion; *sociale* advancement; ÉDU class, *Br* year; **en** ~ on special offer; **promouvoir** promote

prompt swift

pronom *m* GRAM pronoun

prononcé *fig* marked, pronounced; *accent, traits* strong; **prononcer** (*dire*) say, utter; (*articuler*) pronounce; *discours* give; JUR *sentence* pass, pronounce; **se** ~ **d'un mot** be pronounced; (*se déterminer*) express an opinion; **se** ~ **pour/ contre qch** come out in favor *ou Br* favour of /against sth; **prononciation** *f* pronunciation; JUR passing

propager *idée, nouvelle* spread; BIOL propagate; **se** ~ spread; BIOL reproduce

propension *f* propensity (**à** for)

propice favorable, *Br* favourable; *moment* right

proportion *f* proportion; **toutes ~s gardées** on balance; **proportionnel, ~le** proportional (**à** to)

propos 1 *mpl* (*paroles*) words **2** *m* (*intention*) intention; **à** ~ at the right moment; **mal à** ~, **hors de** ~ at the wrong moment; **à** ~! by the way; **à** ~ **de** (*au sujet de*) about

proposer suggest, propose; (*offrir*) offer; **se** ~ **de faire** propose doing; **se** ~ offer one's services; **proposition** *f* (*suggestion*) proposal, suggestion; (*offre*) offer; GRAM clause

propre 1 *adj* own; (*net*) clean; (*approprié*) suitable; **à** (*particulier à*) characteristic of **2** *m*: **mettre au** ~ make a clean copy of; **propreté** *f* cleanliness

propriétaire *m/f* owner; *qui loue* landlord; *femme* landlady; **propriété** *f* ownership; (*caractéristique*) property

propulser propel; **propulsion** *f* propulsion

proscrire (*interdire*) ban; (*bannir*) banish

prospectus *m* brochure; FIN prospectus

prospère prosperous; **prospérer** prosper; **prospérité** *f* prosperity

prosterner: **se** ~ prostrate o.s.

prostituée *f* prostitute; **prostitution** *f* prostitution

protecteur, -trice 1 *adj* protective; *péj*: *ton* patronizing **2** *m* protector; (*mécène*) sponsor, patron; **protection** *f* protection; **protéger** protect (**contre, de** from); *arts, artistes* be a patron of

protéine *f* protein

pull(-over)

protestant, ~e REL m/f & adj
Protestant
protestation f (plainte) protest; (déclaration) protestation; **protester** protest
prothèse f prosthesis
protocole m protocol
prototype m prototype
prouesse f prowess
prouver prove
provenance f origin; **en ~ de avion**, train from
provenir: ~ **de** come from
proverbe m proverb
providence f providence
province f province
proviseur m principal, Br head (teacher)
provision f supply; ~**s** (vivres) provisions; (achats) shopping; d'un chèque funds pl; **chèque** m **sans ~** bad check ou Br cheque
provisoire provisional
provocant, **provocateur**, -trice provocative; **provocation** f provocation; **provoquer** provoke; accident cause
proximité f proximity; **à ~ de** near, in the vicinity of
prude prudish
prudence f caution, prudence; **prudent** cautious, prudent; conducteur careful
prune f BOT plum
pruneau m prune
prunier m plum (tree)
PS m (= Parti socialiste) Socialist Party; (= Post Scriptum) PS (= postscript)
psaume m psalm

pseudonyme m pseudonym
psychanalyser psychoanalyze; **psychanalyste** m/f psychoanalyst
psychiatre m/f psychiatrist
psychologie f psychology; **psychologique** psychological; **psychologue** m/f psychologist
psychopathe m/f psychopath
puant stinking; fig arrogant; **puanteur** f stink
pub f: **une ~** an ad; **faire de la ~** do some advertising
public, **publique 1** adj public **2** m public; d'un spectacle audience
publication f publication
publicitaire advertising atr; **publicité** f publicity; COMM advertising; (affiche) ad
publier publish
publipostage m mailshot
puce f ZO flea; INFORM chip
pudeur f modesty; **pudique** modest; discret discreet
puer 1 v/i stink; ~ **des pieds** have smelly feet **2** v/t stink of
puéril childish
puis then
puiser draw (**dans** from)
puisque since
puissance f power; d'une armée strength; **puissant** powerful; musculature, médicament strong
puits m well; d'une mine shaft; ~ **de pétrole** oil well
pull(-over) m sweater, Br

aussi pullover
pullover swarm
pulsation f beat, beating
pulsion f drive; **~s** fpl **de mort** death wish
pulvériser solide pulverize (aussi fig); liquide spray
punaise f ZO bug; (clou) thumbtack, Br drawing pin
punir punish; **punition** f punishment
pupille 1 m/f JUR ward 2 f ANAT pupil
pur pure; whisky straight
purée f puree; **~** (**de pommes de terre**) mashed potatoes pl
pureté f purity

purge f purge; **purger** TECH bleed; POL purge; JUR peine serve
purification f purification; **purifier** purify
pur-sang m thoroughbred
pus m pus
pute f F slut
puzzle m jigsaw (puzzle)
P.-V. m (= procès-verbal) ticket
pyjama m pajamas pl, Br pyjamas pl
pyramide f pyramid
Pyrénées fpl Pyrenees
pyromane m pyromaniac; JUR arsonist

Q

quadragénaire m/f & adj forty-year old
quadrillé papier squared; **quadriller** fig: région put under surveillance
quadruple quadruple
quai m d'un port quay; d'une gare platform
qualification f qualification; (appellation) name; **qualifier** qualify; **~ qn d'idiot** describe s.o. as an idiot; **se ~** SP qualify
qualité f quality; **de ~** quality atr; **en ~ d'ambassadeur** as ambassador, in his capacity as ambassador
quand when; **~ je serai de retour** when I'm back

quant à as for
quantifier quantify
quantité f quantity; **une ~ de grand nombre** a great many; **abondance** a great deal of
quarantaine f MÉD quarantine; **une ~ de** about forty, forty or so; **avoir la ~** be in one's forties; **quarante** forty
quart m quarter; de vin quarter liter, Br quarter litre; **~ d'heure** quarter of an hour; **~ de finale** quarter-final
quartier m (quart) quarter; d'orange segment; d'une ville area; **~ général** MIL headquarters pl
quasiment virtually
quatorze fourteen

quatre four; **quatre-vingt(s)** eighty; **quatre-vingt-dix** ninety; **quatrième** fourth

quatuor *m* MUS quartet

que 1 *pron relatif personne* who, that; *chose, animal* which, that; **les étudiants ~ j'ai rencontrés** the students (who *ou* that) I met **2** *pron interrogatif* what; **qu'y a-t-il?** what's the matter?; **qu'est-ce que c'est?** what's that? **3** *adv dans exclamations:* **~ c'est beau!** it's so beautiful!; **~ de fleurs!** what a lot of flowers! **4** *conj* that; **je croyais ~ ...** I thought (that) ...; **plus grand ~ moi** bigger than me; **aussi petit ~ cela** as small as that; **ne ... ~** only

quel, ~le what, which; **~le femme!** what a woman!

quelconque (*médiocre*) mediocre; **un travail ~** some sort of job

quelque some; **~s** some, a few; **~ ... que** (+ *subj*) whatever, whichever

quelque chose something; *avec interrogatif, conditionnel aussi* anything

quelquefois sometimes

quelques-uns, quelques-unes a few, some

quelqu'un someone, somebody; *avec interrogatif, conditionnel aussi* anyone, anybody

querelle *f* quarrel; **quereller:**

se ~ quarrel; **querelleur, -euse** quarrelsome

question *f* question; **questionnaire** *m* questionnaire; **questionner** question (**sur** about)

quête *f* search; (*collecte*) collection

queue *f* *d'un animal* tail; *d'un fruit* stalk; *d'une casserole* handle; *d'un train* rear; *d'une classe* bottom; *d'une file* line, *Br* queue; **faire la ~** stand in line, *Br* queue (up); **à la ~, en ~** at the rear

qui *interrogatif* who; *relatif, personne* who, that; *relatif, chose, animal* which, that

quiconque whoever; (*n'importe qui*) anyone, anybody

quincaillerie *f* hardware; *magasin* hardware store

quinquagénaire *m/f* & *adj* fifty-year old

quintal *m* hundred kilos *pl*

quinte *f*: **~ (de toux)** coughing fit

quinzaine *f* *de jours* two weeks *pl*, *Br aussi* fortnight; **une ~ de personnes** about fifteen people *pl*; **quinze** fifteen; **~ jours** two weeks, *Br aussi* fortnight

quitte: être ~ envers qn be quits with s.o.

quitter leave; *vêtement* take off; **se ~** part; **ne quittez pas** TÉL hold the line please

quoi what; **après ~, il ...** after which he ...; **à ~ bon?** what's the point?; **il n'y a pas de ~!** don't mention it; **~ que** (+ *subj*) whatever

quoique (+ *subj*) although, though

quotidien, ~ne *adj* daily; **de tous les jours** everyday **2** *m* daily

R

rabâcher keep on repeating

rabais *m* discount, reduction; **rabaisser** *prix* reduce; *mérites* belittle

rabattre 1 *v/t siège* pull down; *couvercle* shut; *col* turn down **2** *v/i fig*: **se ~ sur** fall back on; *d'une voiture* pull back into

râblé stocky

rabot *m* plane

rabougri stunted

rabrouer snub

racaille *f* rabble

raccommoder mend; *chaussettes* darn

raccompagner: **je vais vous ~ chez vous** *à pied* I'll take you home

raccord *m* join; *d'un film* splice; **raccorder** join

raccourci *m* shortcut; **en ~** briefly; **raccourcir 1** *v/t* shorten **2** *v/i* get shorter

raccrocher *v/t* put back up; **~ le téléphone** hang up; **se ~ à** *v/t* TÉL hang up; se ~ à **2** *v/i* TÉL hang up; **se ~ à** cling to

race *f* race; (*ascendance*) descent; ZO breed

rachat *m* d'un *otage* ransoming; *d'une société* buyout; **racheter** buy back; *otage*

ransom; *fig*: *faute* make up for; **se ~** make amends

racine *f* root

racisme *m* racism; **raciste** *m/f & adj* racist

racler scrape; **se ~ la gorge** clear one's throat

raconter tell

radar *m* radar

radeau *m* raft

radiateur *m* radiator

radiation *f* radiation; *d'une liste* deletion

radical *adj & m* radical

radier strike out

radieux, -euse radiant; *temps* glorious

radin F mean, tight

radio *f* radio; (*radiographie*) X-ray

radioactif, -ive radioactive

radiocassette *f* radio cassette player

radiographie *f procédé* radiography; *photo* X-ray

radioréveil radio alarm

radis *m* BOT radish

radoter ramble

radoucir make milder; **se ~ du temps** get milder

rafale *f de vent* gust; MIL burst

raffermir *chair* firm up; *auto-*

ramification

rité re-assert

raffinage *m* refining; **raffiné** refined; **raffiner** refine; **raffinerie** *f* refinery

raffoler: ~ **de** adore

rafraîchir 1 *v/t* cool down; *mémoire* refresh **2** *v/i du vin* chill; **se** ~ *de la température* get cooler; *d'une personne* have a drink (in order to cool down); **rafraîchissant** refreshing (*aussi fig*); **rafraîchissement** *m de la température* cooling; ~**s** (*boissons*) refreshments

rage *f* rage; MÉD rabies *sg*; **rageur, -euse** furious

ragoût *m* CUIS stew

raide *personne*, *membres* stiff; *pente* steep; *cheveux* straight; (*ivre*, *drogué*) stoned; **raideur** *f* stiffness; *d'une pente* steepness; **raidir**: **se** ~ *de membres* stiffen up

raie *f* (*rayure*) stripe; *des cheveux* part, *Br* parting; ZO skate

rail *m* rail; ~ **de sécurité** crash barrier

railler mock; **raillerie** *f* mockery

raisin *m* grape; ~ **sec** raisin

raison *f* reason; **avoir** ~ be right; **avoir** ~ **de** get the better of; **à** ~ **de** at a rate of; **à plus forte** ~ all the more so; **en** ~ **de** (*à cause de*) because of; ~ **sociale** company name; **raisonnable** reasona-

ble; **raisonnement** *m* reasoning; **raisonner 1** *v/i* reason **2** *v/t*: ~ **qn** make s.o. see reason

rajeunir 1 *v/t thème* modernize; ~ **qn** make s.o. look (years) younger **2** *v/i* look younger

rajouter add

rajuster adjust; *coiffure* put straight

ralenti *m* AUTO idle; *dans un film* slow motion; **au** ~ *fig* at a snail's pace; **ralentir** slow down; **ralentissement** *m* slowing down; **ralentisseur** *m de circulation* speed-bump

râler moan; F beef F; **râleur, -euse** F **1** *adj* grumbling **2** *m/f* grumbler

rallier rally; (*s'unir à*) join; **se** ~ **à** rally to

rallonger 1 *v/t* lengthen **2** *v/i* get longer

rallumer télé, *lumière* switch on again; *fig* revive

ramassage *m* collection; *de fruits* picking; **ramasser** collect; *ce qui est par terre* pick up; *fruits* pick; F *coup* get

rame *f* oar; *de métro* train

rameau *m* branch

ramener take back; (*rapporter*) bring back; *l'ordre* restore; **se** ~ **à** (*se réduire à*) come down to

ramer row; **rameur, -euse** *m/f* rower

ramification *f* ramification

ramollir soften; *se ~* soften; *fig* go soft

rampant crawling; BOT creeping; *fig*: *inflation* rampant

rampe *f* ramp; *d'escalier* bannisters *pl*; *au théâtre* footlights *pl*

ramper crawl; BOT creep

rance rancid

rancœur *f* resentment (**contre** toward)

rançon *f* ransom; **la ~ de** *fig* the price of

rancune *f* resentment; **rancunier, -ère** resentful

randonnée *f* walk; *en montagne* hill walk; **randonneur** *m* walker; *en montagne* hillwalker

rang *m* row; (*niveau*) rank; **être au premier ~** be in the forefront

rangée *f* row

ranger put away; *chambre* tidy up; *voiture* park; (*classer*) arrange; *se ~* (*s'écarter*) move aside; AUTO pull over; *fig* (*assagir*) settle down; *se ~ à une opinion* come around to a point of view

ranimer *personne* bring around; *fig*: *force* revive

rap *m* MUS rap

rapace 1 *adj* *animal* predatory; *personne* greedy **2** *m* bird of prey

rapatrier repatriate

râpe *f* *grater*; TECH rasp; **râper** CUIS grate; *bois* file; **râpé** CUIS grated; *manteau* threadbare

rapide 1 *adj* fast, rapid; *coup d'œil*, *décision* quick **2** *m* *dans l'eau* rapid; *train* fast train; **rapidité** *f* speed, rapidity

rapiécer patch

rappel *m* reminder; *d'un ambassadeur*, *produit* recall; THÉÂT curtain call; MÉD booster; **rappeler** call back; *ambassadeur* recall; *~ qc/qn à qn* remind s.o. of sth/s.o.; *se ~ qc* remember sth

rapport *m* *écrit*, *oral* report; (*lien*) connection; (*proportion*) proportion; COMM return; MIL briefing; **~s (sexuels)** sexual relations; **par ~ à** compared with; **être en ~ avec** be in touch with; **rapporter** return, bring/take back; *d'un chien* fetch; COMM bring in; (*relater*) report; *se ~ à* be connected with; **rapporteur** *m* reporter; *enfant* sneak

rapprochement *m* *fig* reconciliation; POL rapprochement; *analogie* connection; **rapprocher** bring closer (**de** to); *établir un lien* connect; *se ~* come closer

rapt *m* abduction

raquette *f* racket

rare rare; *marchandises* scarce; (*peu dense*) sparse; **se raréfier** *se ~* become rare; *de l'air* become rarefied; **rarement** rarely; **rareté** *f* rarity

ras short; **rempli à ~ bord** full to the brim; **faire table ~e** make a clean sweep

raser shave; *barbe* shave off; (*démolir*) raze to the ground; *murs* hug; F (*ennuyer*) bore

rasoir *m* razor; **~ électrique** electric shaver

rassasier satisfy

rassembler collect, assemble; **se ~** gather

rasseoir replace; **se ~** sit down again

rassis stale; *fig* sedate

rassurer reassure; **rassurez-vous** don't be concerned

rat *m* rat

ratatiner: se ~ shrivel up

rate *f* ANAT spleen

raté, ~e 1 *adj* unsuccessful; *occasion* missed **2** *m/f personne* failure

râteau *m* rake

rater 1 *v/t* miss; *examen* fail **2** *v/i d'une arme* misfire; *d'un projet* fail

ration *f* ration; *fig* (fair) share

rationaliser rationalize; **rationnel, ~le** rational; **rationner** ration

ratisser rake; (*fouiller*) search

rattacher *chien* tie up again; *cheveux* put up again; *lacets* do up again; *conduites d'eau* connect; *idées* connect; **se ~ à** be linked to

rattraper recapture; *objet qui tombe* catch; (*rejoindre*) catch up (with); *retard* make up; *imprudence* make up for; **se ~** make up for it; (*se raccrocher*) get caught

rature *f* deletion

rauque hoarse

ravages *mpl* devastation; **les ~ du temps** the ravages of time; **ravager** devastate

ravaler swallow; *façade* clean up

rave *f*: **céleri ~** celeriac

rave *f* rave

ravi delighted (**de** with; **de faire** to do)

ravir (*enchanter*) delight

raviser: se ~ change one's mind

ravissant delightful

ravisseur, -euse *m/f* abductor

ravitaillement *m* supplying; **en carburant** refueling, *Br* refuelling; **ravitailler** supply; **en carburant** refuel

raviver revive

rayé striped; *papier* lined; *verre, carrosserie* scratched; **rayer** scratch; *mot* score *ou* scratch out

rayon *m* ray; MATH radius; *d'une roue* spoke; (*étagère*) shelf; *de magasin* department; **~ laser** laser beam; **rayonner de chaleur** radiate; *d'un visage* shine; **~ de** *fig* radiate

rayure *f* stripe; *sur un meuble, du verre* scratch

raz *m*: **~ de marée** tidal wave

réacteur *m* reactor; AVIAT jet engine; **réaction** *f* reaction; **avion** *m* **à ~** jet (aircraft); **réactionnaire** *m/f* & *adj* reactionary

réagir react (**à** to; **contre** against)

réalisable feasible; **réalisateur, -trice** *m/f* director; **réalisation** *f* *d'un projet* execution, realization; *création, œuvre* creation; *d'un film* direction; **réaliser** *projet* carry out; *rêve* fulfill, *Br* fulfil; *vente* make; *film* direct; *bien, capital* realize; (*se rendre compte*) realize; **se ~** *d'un rêve* come true; *d'un projet* be carried out

réalisme *m* realism; **réaliste 1** *adj* realistic **2** *m/f* realist; **réalité** *f* reality

réanimer resuscitate

rébarbatif, -ive off-putting, daunting

rebelle 1 *adj* rebellious **2** *m/f* rebel; **rebeller: se ~** rebel; **rébellion** *f* rebellion

rebondir bounce; (*faire un ricochet*) rebound; **faire ~ qch** *fig* get sth going again; **rebondissement** *m fig* unexpected development

rebord *m* edge; *d'une fenêtre* sill

rebours *m*: **compte** *m* **à ~** countdown

rebrousser: ~ chemin retrace one's footsteps

rebut *m* dregs *pl*; **mettre au ~**

get rid of

rebuter (*décourager*) dishearten; (*choquer*) offend

récapituler recap

récemment recently

recenser *population* take a census of

récent recent

récépissé *m* receipt

récepteur *m* receiver

réception *f* reception; *d'une lettre, de marchandises* receipt; **réceptionniste** *m/f* receptionist, desk clerk

récession *f* ÉCON recession

recette *f* COMM takings *pl*; CUIS, *fig* recipe

recevoir receive; **être reçu à un examen** pass an exam

rechange *m*: **de ~** spare *atr*

rechargeable pile rechargeable; **recharger** *camion, arme* reload; *accumulateur* recharge; *briquet* refill

réchaud *m* stove

réchauffement *m* warming; **~ de la planète** global warming; **réchauffer** warm up

recherche *f* search (**de** for); *scientifique* research; **~ de la police** search; **rechercher** look for, search for; (*prendre*) fetch

rechute *f* MÉD relapse

récif *m* reef

récipient *m* container

réciproque reciprocal

récit *m* account; (*histoire*) story; **réciter** recite

réclamation *f* claim; (*protes-*

tation) complaint
réclame f advertisement
réclamer secours, aumône
ask for; son õ claim; (nécessiter) call for
réclusion f imprisonment
récolte f harvesting; de produits harvest, crop; fig crop;
récolter harvest
recommander recommend;
lettre register
recommencer start again
récompense f reward; récompenser reward (**de** for)
réconcilier reconcile
reconduire: ~ **qn** chez lui
take s.o. home; à la porte
see s.o. out
réconforter console, comfort
reconnaissance f recognition; d'une faute acknowl-
edg(e)ment; (gratitude) gratitude; MIL reconnaissance;
reconnaissant grateful (**de**
for); **reconnaître** recognize;
faute acknowledge; **se** ~ de
deux personnes recognize
each other; **se** ~ **à** be recognizable by; **reconnu** known
reconstituer reconstitute;
ville, maison restore; événement reconstruct
reconstruire rebuild
reconvertir: **se** ~ retrain
recopier notes copy out
record m record; **recordman**
m record holder; **recordwoman** f record holder
recourbé bent
recours m recourse, resort;

avoir ~ **à** resort to
recouvrer recover; santé regain
recouvrir recover; enfant
cover up again; (couvrir entièrement) cover (**de** with);
(cacher, embrasser) cover
récréation f relaxation; ÉDU
recess; Br recreation
récriminations fpl recrimi-
nations
recrudescence f new outbreak
recrue f recruit; **recruter** recruit
rectangle m rectangle; **rectangulaire** rectangular
rectifier rectify; (ajuster) adjust; (corriger) correct
recto m d'une feuille front
reçu m receipt
recueil m collection; **recueillir** collect; personne take in;
se ~ meditate
recul m d'un fusil recoil;
d'une armée retreat; de la
production drop; fig detachment; **reculer 1** v/t push
back; décision postpone **2**
v/i back away, recoil; MIL retreat; d'une voiture back, reverse; ~ **devant** fig back
away from; **reculons**: **à** ~
backward, Br backwards
récupérer 1 v/t recover, retrieve; ses forces regain;
vieux matériel salvage;
temps make up **2** v/i recover
recyclable recyclable; **recyclage** m du personnel re-

training; TECH recycling; recycler retrain; TECH recycle

rédacteur, -trice *m/f* editor;
(*auteur*) writer; **~ en chef**
editor-in-chief; **rédaction** *f*
editing; (*rédacteurs*) editorial team

redescendre 1 *v/i* come/go
down again; **~ d'une voiture**
get out of a car again **2** *v/t*
bring/take down again;
montagne come down again

redevable: être ~ de qc à qn
owe s.o. sth; **redevance** *f*
d'un auteur royalty; TV licence fee

rédiger write

redire repeat, say again; (*rapporter*) repeat; **trouver à ~ à**
find fault with

redoubler 1 *v/t* double **2** *v/i*
ÉDU repeat a class; *d'une
tempête* intensify; **~ d'efforts** redouble one's efforts

redoutable formidable; *hiver*
harsh; **redouter** dread (*de
faire* doing)

redresser *ce qui est courbe*
straighten; *ce qui est tombé*
set upright; **se ~ d'un pays**
recover

réduction *f* reduction; MÉD
setting; **réduire** reduce; *personnel* cut back; **se ~ à**
amount to; **réduit 1** *adj* reduced; *possibilités* limited
2 *m* small room

rééducation *f* MÉD rehabilita-
tion

réel, ~le real

refaire do again; *examen* re-
take; *erreur* repeat; **remettre
en état: maison** do up

réfectoire *m* refectory

référence *f* reference; **~s** (*recommandation*) reference

référendum *m* referendum

référer: en ~ à consult; **se ~ à**
refer to

réfléchir 1 *v/t* reflect **2** *v/i*
think (**à, sur** about)

reflet *m de lumière* glint; *dans
miroir* reflection (*aussi fig*)

réflexe *m* reflex

réflexion *f* reflection; (*remarque*) remark

réforme *m* reform; **la Réforme**
REL the Reformation; **réformer** reform; MIL discharge

refouler push back; PSYCH repress

refrain *m* refrain, chorus

réfréner control

réfrigérateur *m* refrigerator

refroidir cool down; *fig* cool;
se ~ du temps get colder;
MÉD catch a chill; **refroidis-
sement** *m* cooling; MÉD chill

refuge *m* refuge, shelter;
pour piétons traffic island;
en montagne (mountain)
hut; **réfugié, ~e** *m/f* refugee;
réfugier: se ~ take shelter

refus *m* refusal; **refuser** refuse; **~ de** ou **se ~ à faire** refuse to do

réfuter refute

regagner win back, regain;
endroit get back to

régal *m* treat; **régaler** regale

(**de** with)

regard *m* look; **regardant** *avec argent* careful with one's money; *ne pas être* ~ *sur* not be too worried about; **regarder 1** *v/t* look at; *télé* watch; *(concerner)* regard, concern; ~ **qn faire qch** watch s.o. doing sth **2** *v/i* look; *se* ~ look at o.s.; *de plusieurs personnes* look at each other

régate *f* regatta

régime *m* POL government, régime; MÉD diet; *fiscal* system

région *f* region; ~ **sinistrée** disaster area; **régional** regional

régir govern

régisseur *m* THÉÂT stage manager; *dans le film* assistant director

réglage *m* adjustment

règle *f* rule; *instrument* ruler; **en ~ générale** as a rule; **~s** *(menstruation)* period

réglé *organisé* settled; *vie* well-ordered; *papier* ruled

règlement *m* settlement; *(règles)* regulations *pl*; **réglementaire** in accordance with the rules; *tenue* regulation *atr*; **réglementer** control, regulate

régler *affaire* settle; TECH adjust; COMM pay, settle; *épicier etc* pay, settle up with

règne *m* reign; **régner** reign

régression *f* regression

regret *m* regret (**de** about); **à ~** with regret, reluctantly; **être au ~ de faire** regret to do; **regrettable** regrettable; **regretter** regret; *personne absente* miss; **~ d'avoir fait qc** regret doing sth, regret having done sth; **je ne regrette rien** I have no regrets; **je regrette mais …** I'm sorry (but) …

régulariser put in order; *situation* regularize; TECH regulate; **régularité** *f* regularity; *d'élections* legality; **régulier, -ère** regular; *allure, progrès* steady; *écriture* even; *(réglementaire)* lawful; *(correct)* honest; **régulièrement** regularly

réhabiliter rehabilitate; *quartier* renovate, redevelop

rehausser raise; *fig (accentuer)* emphasize

rein *m* ANAT kidney; **~s** lower back

reine *f* queen

réitérer reiterate

rejaillir spurt

rejeter reject; *(relancer)* throw back; *(vomir)* bring up; *responsabilité, faute* lay (**sur** on)

rejoindre *personne* join, meet; *(rattraper)* catch up with; MIL rejoin; *autoroute* get back onto; **se ~** meet

réjouir make happy, delight; **se ~ de** be delighted about; **réjouissance** *f* rejoicing

relâche *f:* **sans ~** without a break, nonstop

relâcher *corde, emprise* loosen; *prisonnier* release; **se ~** *d'un élève, de la discipline* become slack

relais *m* SP, ÉL relay; **prendre le ~ de** take over from

relancer *balle* throw back; *moteur* restart; *fig: économie* kickstart; *personne* contact again

relater relate

relatif, -ive relative; **~ à** relating to; **relation** *f* relationship; (*connaissance*) acquaintance; **être en ~ avec qn** be in touch with s.o.; **~s** relations; (*connaissances*) contacts; **relativement** relatively; **~ à** compared with; (*en ce qui concerne*) relating to; **relativiser** look at in context

relaxer: se ~ relax

relayer take over from; TV, *radio* relay; **se ~** take turns

reléguer relegate

relève *f* relief; **prendre la ~** take over

relevé 1 *adj manche* turned up; *style* elevated; CUIS spicy **2** *m de compteur* reading; **~ de compte** bank statement; **relever 1** *v/t* raise; (*remettre debout*) pick up; *col, chauffage* turn up; *manches* roll up; *siège* put up; *économie* improve; (*ramasser*) collect; *défi* take up; *faute* find;

adresse, date copy; (*relayer*) take over from; **se ~** get up; *fig* recover **2** *v/i:* **~ de** (*dépendre de*) be answerable to; (*ressortir de*) be the responsibility of

relief *m* relief; **mettre en ~** *fig* highlight

relier connect (**à** to); *livre* bind

religieux, -euse 1 *adj* religious **2** *m* monk **3** *f* nun; **religion** *f* religion

reliure *f* binding

reluire shine

remanier *texte* re-work; POL reshuffle

remarquable remarkable

remarque *f* remark; **remarquer** notice; (*dire*) remark; **faire ~ qc à qn** point sth out to s.o.; **se faire ~** *d'un acteur* etc get o.s. noticed; *d'un écolier* get into trouble; *se différencier* be conspicuous

rembourrer stuff

remboursement *m* refund; *de dettes* repayment; **rembourser** *frais* refund, reimburse; *dettes, emprunt* pay back

remède *m* remedy; **remédier: ~ à** remedy

remerciement *m:* **~s** thanks; **remercier** thank (**de, pour** for); (*congédier*) dismiss

remettre put back; *vêtement* put on again; *peine* remit; *décision* postpone; (*ajouter*) add; **~ qc à qn** give sth to s.o.; **se ~ à qc** take sth up again; **se ~ à faire qc** start doing sth again; **se ~ de qc** recover from sth; **s'en ~ à qn** rely on s.o.

remise f (*hangar*) shed; *d'une lettre* delivery; *de peine* remission; COMM discount; *d'une décision* postponement; **à neuf** reconditioning; **~ en question** questioning

rémission f MÉD remission

remonte-pente m ski lift

remonter 1 v/i come/go up again; *dans une voiture* get back in; *de prix, température* go up again; *d'un avion, chemin* climb, rise **2** v/t *choses* bring/take back up; *rue, escalier* come/go back up; *montre* wind; TECH reassemble; *col* turn up; *stores* raise

remords mpl remorse

remorque f *véhicule* trailer; *câble* towrope; **remorquer** *voiture* tow

remplaçant, ~e m/f replacement; **remplacement** m replacement; **remplacer** replace (**par** with)

remplir fill (**de** with); *formulaire* fill out; *conditions* fulfill, Br fulfil; *tâche* carry out; **remplissage** m filling

remporter take away; *prix* win

remue-ménage m (*agitation*) commotion

remuer 1 v/t move (*aussi fig*);

sauce stir; *salade* toss; *terre* turn over **2** v/i move; **se ~** move; *fig* F get a move on F

rémunération f pay, remuneration; **rémunérer** pay

renaître REL be born again; *fig* be reborn

renard m fox

renchérir go up; **~ sur** outdo

rencontre f meeting; **aller à la ~ de** go and meet; **rencontrer** meet; *accueil* meet with; *difficulté* encounter; *amour* find; (*heurter*) hit; **se ~** meet

rendement m AGR yield; *d'un employé, d'une machine* output; *d'un placement* return

rendez-vous m appointment; *amoureux* date; *lieu* meeting place; **prendre ~** make an appointment

rendre 1 v/t give back; *salut, invitation* return; (*donner*) give; (*traduire*) render; (*vomir*) bring up; MIL surrender; **~ visite à** visit **2** v/i *de terre, d'un arbre* yield; **se ~ à un endroit** go; MIL surrender; **se ~ malade** make o.s. sick

rêne f rein

renfermer (*contenir*) contain; **se ~ dans le silence** withdraw into silence

renforcer reinforce

renfort m reinforcements pl; **à grand ~ de** with copious amounts of

renier *qn* disown

renifler sniff

renne *m* reindeer

renom *m* (*célébrité*) fame, renown; (*réputation*) reputation; **renommée** *f* fame

renoncement *m* renunciation (**à** of); **renoncer:** **~ à qc** give sth up; **~ à faire** give up doing

renouer 1 *v/t amitié* etc renew 2 *v/i:* **~ avec** get back in touch with; *après brouille* get back together with

renouveler renew; *demande, promesse* repeat; **se ~** (*se reproduire*) happen again; **renouvellement** *m* renewal

rénovation *f* renovation; *fig* (*modernisation*) updating

renseignement *m* piece of information (**sur** about); **~s** MIL information; intelligence; **prendre des ~s sur** find out about; **renseigner:** **~ qn sur qc** tell *ou* inform s.o. about sth; **se ~** find out

rentabilité *f* profitability; **rentable** cost-effective; *entreprise* profitable; **ce n'est pas ~** there's no money in it

rente *f revenu d'un bien privé* income; (*pension*) annuity; **versée à sa femme** etc allowance

rentrée *f* return; **~ des classes** beginning of the new school year; **~s** COMM takings

rentrer 1 *v/i* go/come in; *de*

nouveau go/come back in; *chez soi* go/come home; *dans un récipient* go in, fit; *de l'argent* come in; **~ dans** (*heurter*) collide with; *serrure, sac* go into; *responsabilités* be part of 2 *v/t* bring/take in; *voiture* put away; *ventre* pull in

renversement *m d'un régime* overthrow; **renverser** *image* reverse; (*mettre à l'envers*) upturn; (*faire tomber*) knock over; *liquide* spill; *gouvernement* overthrow

renvoi *m de personnel* dismissal; *d'un élève* expulsion; *d'une lettre* return; *dans un texte* cross-reference (**à** to); **renvoyer** (*faire retourner*) send back; *ballon* return; *personnel* dismiss; *élève* expel; *rencontre, décision* postpone

repaire *m* den

répandre spread; (*renverser*) spill; **se ~** spread; (*être renversé*) spill; **répandu** widespread

réparation *f* repair; (*compensation*) reparation; **en ~** being repaired; **réparer** repair; *fig* make up for

repartie *f* retort; **avoir de la ~** have a gift for repartee

repartir set off again; **~ de zéro** start again from scratch

répartir share out; *chargement* distribute; *en catégories* divide; **répartition** *f* dis-

tribution; *en catégories* division
repas *m* meal
repassage *m* ironing; **repasser 1** *v/i* come/go back again **2** *v/t linge* iron; *examen* take again
repentir 1: se ~ REL repent; **se ~ de** be sorry for **2** *m* penitence
répercussions *fpl* repercussions
repère *m* mark; (**point** *m* **de**) **~** landmark; **repérer** (*situer*) pinpoint; (*trouver*) find; (*marquer*) mark
répertoire *m* directory; THÉÂT repertoire
répéter repeat; THÉÂT rehearse; **répétition** *f* repetition; THÉÂT rehearsal
répit *m* respite
replacer put back, replace
repli *m* fold; *d'une rivière* bend; **replier** fold; *jambes* draw up; *journal* fold up; *manches* roll up; **se ~ sur soi-même** retreat into one's shell
répliquer retort; *d'un enfant* answer back
répondeur *m*: **~ automatique** answering machine; **répondre 1** *v/t* answer, reply **2** *v/i* answer; (*réagir*) respond; **~ à** answer, reply to; (*réagir à*) respond to; *besoin* meet; *attente* come up to; *signalement* match; **réponse** *f* answer; (*réaction*) response

reportage *m* report; **reporter** *m/f* reporter
repos *m* rest; **reposer 1** *v/t* (*remettre*) put back; *question* ask again; (*détendre*) rest; **se ~ rest 2** *v/i*: **~ sur** rest on
repoussant repulsive; **repousser 1** *v/t* (*dégoûter*) repel; (*différer*) postpone; *pousser en arrière*, MIL push back; (*rejeter*) reject **2** *v/i* grow again
reprendre 1 *v/t* take back; (*prendre davantage de*) take more; *ville* recapture; (*recommencer*) start again; (*corriger*) correct; *entreprise* take over (**à** from) **2** *v/i* (*recommencer*) start again; **se ~** (*se corriger*) correct o.s.; (*se maîtriser*) pull o.s. together
représailles *fpl* reprisals
représentant, ~e *m/f* representative; **représentation** *f* representation; *au théâtre* performance; **représenter** represent; THÉÂT perform; **se ~ qc** imagine sth
répression *f* repression; **mesures** *fpl* **de ~** crackdown (**contre** on)
réprimander reprimand
réprimer suppress
reprise *f de ville* recapture; *de marchandise* taking back; *de travail, de lutte* resumption; **à plusieurs ~s** on several occasions
repriser darn, mend

reproche *m* reproach; reprocher reproach; **~ qch à qn**
reproach s.o. for sth

reproduction *f* reproduction;
reproduire reproduce; **se ~**
happen again; BIOL repro-
duce

républicain, **~e** *m/f & adj* republican; république *f* republic

répugnant repugnant; répu-
gner: **~ à** be repelled by; **~
à faire** be reluctant to do

répulsion *f* repulsion
réputation *f* reputation
requérir require
requête *f* request
requin *m* shark
requis necessary
réseau *m* network
réservation *f* booking, reservation

réserve *f* reserve; (entrepôt)
storeroom; **sans ~** unreservedly; **sous ~ de** subject to

réserver reserve; *dans hôtel,
restaurant* book, reserve;
(mettre de côté) put aside;
~ qc à qn keep *ou* save sth
for s.o.

réservoir *m* tank; *lac etc* reservoir

résidence *f* residence; **~ universitaire** dormitory, *Br* hall
of residence; résider live; **~
dans** *fig* lie in

résidu *m* residue; MATH remainder

résigner resign; **se ~** resign
o.s. (*à* to)

résilier *contrat* cancel
résistance *f* resistance; (*endurance*) stamina; *d'un matériau* strength; **la Résistance** HIST the Resistance; résister resist; **~ à tentation,
personne** resist; **sécheresse**
withstand

résolu determined (**à faire** to
do); résolution *f* (*décision*)
resolution; (*fermeté*) determination; *d'un problème*
solving

résonner echo, resound
résoudre 1 *v/t problème* solve
2 *v/i:* **~ de faire, se ~ à faire**
decide to do

respect *m* respect; respecter
respect; **~ le(s) délai(s)** meet
the deadline; **se ~** have
some self-respect; *mutuelle-
ment* respect each other; **se
faire ~** command respect;
respectif, -ive respective;
respectueux, -euse re-
spectful

respiration *f* breathing; **retenir sa ~** hold one's breath; **~
artificielle** MÉD artificial respiration; respirer breathe

resplendir glitter

responsabilité *f* responsibility (**de** for); JUR liability;
responsable responsible
(**de** for)

ressaisir: **se ~** pull o.s. together

ressemblance *f* resem-
blance; ressembler: **~ à** resemble, be like; **se ~** resem-

ble each other, be like each other

ressemeler resole

ressentiment *m* resentment

ressentir feel; *se* ~ *de* still feel the effects of

resserrer tighten; *fig:* amitié strengthen

ressort *m* TECH spring; *fig* motive; (énergie) energy; (compétence) province; JUR jurisdiction

ressortir 1 come/go out again **2** (se détacher) stand out; *faire* ~ bring out; ~ *à* JUR fall within the jurisdiction of

ressource *f* resource

restant 1 *adj* remaining **2** *m* remainder

restaurant *m* restaurant

restauration *f* catering; ART restoration; ~ *rapide* fast food; **restaurer** restore

reste *m* rest, remainder; ~*s* CUIS leftovers; *du* ~, *au* ~ moreover; **rester** (subsister) be left, remain; (demeurer) stay, remain; *on en reste là* we'll stop there; *il reste du vin* there's some wine left

restituer (rendre) return; (reconstituer) restore; **restitution** *f* restitution

restreindre restrict

restriction *f* restriction; *sans* ~ unreservedly

résultat *m* result; **résulter** résult (*de* from)

résumé *m* summary

rétablir restore; *se* ~ recover

retard *m* lateness; *dans travail, paiement* delay; *avoir deux heures de* ~ be two hours late; *avoir du* ~ *sur qn* be behind s.o.; *être en* ~ be late; **retarder 1** *v/t* delay, hold up; *montre* put back **2** *v/i d'une montre* be slow; ~ *de cinq minutes* be five minutes slow; ~ *sur son temps fig* be behind the times

retenir *personne* keep; *argent* withhold; (rappeler) remember; *proposition* accept; (réserver) reserve; *se* ~ restrain o.s.

retentir sound; *du tonnerre* boom; ~ *sur* impact on; **retentissant** resounding (aussi fig)

retenu (réservé) reserved; (empêché) delayed

retenue *f sur salaire* deduction; *fig* (modération) restraint

réticence *f* (omission) omission; (hésitation) hesitation

retirer withdraw; *vêtement* take off; *promesse* take back; *profit* derive; ~ *qch de* remove sth from; *se* ~ withdraw; (prendre sa retraite) retire

retombées *fpl* fallout; **retomber** fall again; (tomber) land; *de cheveux, d'un rideau* fall; ~ *dans qc* sink back into sth

rétorsion POL: *mesure f de ~* retaliatory measure

retoucher *texte, vêtement* alter; *photographie* retouch

retour *m* return; *être de ~* be back; *bon ~!* have a good trip home!; **retourner 1** *v/i* return, go back; *~ sur ses pas* backtrack **2** *v/t matelas, tête* turn; *lettre* return; *vêtement* turn inside out; *se ~ au lit* turn over (*aussi* AUTO); (*tourner la tête*) turn (around)

retrait *m* withdrawal; *en ~* set back

retraite *f* retirement; (*pension*) retirement pension; MIL retreat; *prendre sa ~* retire; **retraité**, *~e m/f* pensioner, retired person

retrancher (*enlever*) remove, cut (*de* from); (*déduire*) deduct

rétrécir 1 *v/t* shrink; *fig* narrow **2** *v/i de tissu* shrink; *se ~* narrow

rétrograder 1 *v/t* demote **2** *v/i* retreat; AUTO downshift

rétrospectif, *-ive 1* *adj* retrospective **2** *f*: *rétrospective* retrospective

retrousser *manches* roll up

retrouver (*trouver*) find; *de nouveau* find again; (*rejoindre*) meet; *santé* regain; *se ~* meet; *se ~ seul* find o.s. alone

rétroviseur *m* AUTO rear-view mirror

réunion *f* meeting; POL reunion; **réunir** bring together; *pays* reunite; *documents* collect; *se ~* meet

réussi successful; **réussir 1** *v/i* succeed; *~ à faire* manage to do, succeed in doing **2** *v/t vie, projet* make a success of; *examen* be successful in; **réussite** *f* success; *aux cartes* solitaire, *Br aussi* patience

revanche *f* revenge; *en ~* on the other hand

rêve *m* dream

réveil *m* awakening; (*pendule*) alarm (clock); **réveiller** wake up; *fig* revive; *se ~* wake up

révélation *f* revelation; **révéler** reveal; *se ~ faux* prove to be false

revenant *m* ghost

revendeur, *-euse m/f* retailer

revendication *f* claim, demand; **revendiquer** claim

revendre resell

revenir come back, return (*à* to); *~ sur thème* go back to; *décision* go back on; *~ à qn d'une part* be due to s.o.; *~ de* évanouissement come around from; *étonnement* get over; *illusion* lose

revenu *m* income; *~s* revenue

rêver dream (*de*, *à* about)

réverbère *m* street lamp

rêverie *f* daydream

revers *m* back; *d'un pantalon* cuff, *Br* turn-up; *fig* (*échec*) reversal

revêtir *vêtement* put on; *forme, caractère* assume; *importance* take on

rêveur, -euse 1 *adj* dreamy 2 *m/f* dreamer

revirement *m*: ~ **d'opinion** sudden change in the public's attitude

réviser *texte* revise; *machine* service; **révision** *f* revision; AUTO service

révocation *f* revocation; *d'un dirigeant etc* dismissal

revoir 1 *v/t* see again; *texte* review; ÉDU review, *Br* revise 2 *m*: **au** ~! goodbye!

révolte *f* revolt; **révolter** revolt; **se** ~ rebel, revolt

révolution *f* revolution; **révolutionner** revolutionize

revolver *m* revolver

révoquer *fonctionnaire* dismiss; *contrat* revoke

revue *f* review; **passer en** ~ *fig* review

rez-de-chaussée *m* first floor, *Br* ground floor

rhubarbe *f* rhubarb

rhum *m* rum

rhumatismes *mpl* rheumatism

rhume *m* cold; ~ **des foins** hay fever

ricaner sneer; *bêtement* snigger

riche rich; *sol* fertile; *décoration* elaborate; **richesse** *f* wealth; *du sol* fertility

rictus *m* grimace

ride *f* wrinkle, line

rideau *m* drape, *Br* curtain

rider *peau* wrinkle; **se** ~ become wrinkled

ridicule 1 *adj* ridiculous 2 *m* ridicule; (*absurdité*) ridiculousness; **ridiculiser** ridicule; **se** ~ make a fool of o.s.

rien 1 *pron* nothing; *quelque chose* anything; **de** ~ *comme réponse* you're welcome; **ne** ... ~ nothing, not anything 2 *m* trifle; **en un** ~ **de temps** in no time

rigide rigid

rigole *f* (*conduit*) channel

rigoler F (*plaisanter*) joke; (*rire*) laugh

rigolo, -te F (*amusant*) funny

rigoureux, -euse rigorous; **rigueur** *f* rigor, *Br* rigour; **à la** ~ if absolutely necessary; **de** ~ compulsory

rincer rinse

riposte *f* riposte, response; *avec armes* return of fire; **riposter** reply, response; *avec armes* return fire

rire 1 *v/i* laugh (**de** about, at); (*s'amuser*) have fun; ~ **aux éclats** roar with laughter; ~ **de qn** laugh at s.o. 2 *m* laugh; ~**s** laughter

risque *m* risk; **à tes** ~**s et périls** at your own risk; **risqué** risky; *plaisanterie* risqué; **risquer** risk; ~ **de faire** risk doing; **se** ~ **dans** venture into

rituel, ~le *adj & m* ritual

rivage *m* shore

rival, ~e *m/f & adj* rival; **rivaliser** compete, vie; **rivalité** *f* rivalry

rive *f* d'un fleuve bank; d'une mer, d'un lac shore

riverain, ~e *m/f* resident

rivet *m* TECH rivet

rivière *f* river

riz *m* BOT rice

robe *f* dress; d'un juge robe; ~ **de chambre** robe, Br dressing gown

robinet *m* faucet, Br tap

robuste robust

roche *f* rock

rocher *m* rock; **rocheux**, **-euse** rocky

rôder prowl

rogne *f*: **être en ~** F be in a bad mood

rogner cut, trim

rognon *m* CUIS kidney

roi *m* king

rôle *m* role; (registre) roll; **à tour de ~** turn and turn about

roman *m* novel

romancier, **-ère** *m/f* novelist

romantique *m/f & adj* romantic; **romantisme** *m* romanticism

romarin *m* BOT rosemary

rompre *v/i* break; **~ avec** petit ami break it off with; tradition break with; habitude break 2 *v/t* break; négociations, fiançailles break off

ronce *f* BOT: **~s** brambles

rond, ~e 1 *adj* round; joues, personne plump; F (ivre) drunk 2 *adv*: **tourner ~** run smoothly 3 *m* figure circle *m* 4 *f*: **faire sa ronde** do one's rounds; de soldat, policier be on patrol; **à la ronde** around

rondelle *f* disk, Br disc; de saucisson slice; TECH washer

rondement (promptement) briskly; (carrément) frankly

rond-point *m* traffic circle, Br roundabout

ronflement *m* snoring; d'un moteur purr; **ronfler** snore; d'un moteur purr

ronger gnaw at; fig torment; **se ~ les ongles** bite one's nails; **rongeur** *m* zo rodent

ronronner purr

rosbif *m* CUIS roast beef

rose 1 *f* BOT rose 2 *m* couleur pink 3 *adj* pink

rosé ~ *m* rosé 2 *adj* pinkish

roseau *m* BOT reed

rosée *f* dew

rosier *m* rose bush

rossignol *m* zo nightingale

rot *m* F belch; **roter** F belch

rôti *m* roast; **rôtir** roast; **rôtisserie** *f* grill-room

rouage *m* cogwheel; **~s** d'une montre works; fig machinery

roue *f* wheel; **deux ~s** *m* two-wheeler; **quatre ~s motrices** all-wheel drive

roué crafty

rouer: **~ qn de coups** beat s.o. black and blue

rouge 1 *adj* red 2 *adv* fig: **voir ~** see red 3 *m* red; **~ à lèvres**

lipstick

rouge-gorge *m* robin (redbreast)

rougeole *f* MÉD measles *sg*

rougir go red; *d'une personne aussi* blush (**de** with); *de colère* flush (**de** with)

rouille *f* rust; **rouillé** rusty; **rouiller** rust; **se ~** rust; *fig* go rusty

rouleau *m* roller; *de pellicule etc* roll; CUIS rolling pin

rouler 1 *v/i* roll; *d'une voiture* travel; **~ sur qc** *d'une conversation* be about sth **2** *v/t* roll; **~ qn** F cheat s.o.

roulette *f* de meubles caster; *jeu* roulette

roumain, ~e 1 *adj* Romanian **2** *m* langue Romanian; **Roumain, ~e** *m/f* Romanian; **Roumanie: la ~** Romania

rouspéter F complain

rousseur *f*: **taches** *fpl* **de ~** freckles

route *f* road; (*parcours*) route; *fig* (*chemin*) path; **en ~** on the way; **se mettre en ~** set off; *fig* get under way; **faire ~ vers** be heading for

routier, -ère 1 *adj* road *atr* **2** *m* (*conducteur*) truck driver, *Br* long-distance lorry driver; *restaurant* truck stop, *Br aussi* transport café

routine *f* routine; **de ~** routine *atr*

roux, rousse *personne* red-haired; *cheveux* red

royal royal; *fig: pourboire, accueil* superb, right royal

royaume *m* kingdom; **le Royaume-Uni** the United Kingdom

R.-U. (= **Royaume-Uni**) UK (= United Kingdom)

ruban *m* ribbon; **~ adhésif** adhesive tape

rubéole *f* MÉD German measles *sg*

rubrique *f* heading

ruche *f* hive

rude *manières* uncouth; (*sévère*) harsh; *travail, lutte* hard

rudimentaire rudimentary; **rudiments** *mpl* rudiments

rue *f* street; **dans la ~** on the street

ruée *f* rush

ruelle *f* alley

rugby *m* rugby

rugir roar; *du vent* howl

rugueux, -euse rough

ruine *f* ruin; **ruiner** ruin

ruisseau *m* stream; (*caniveau*) gutter

ruisseler run

rumeur *f* hum; *de personnes* murmuring; (*nouvelle*) rumor, *Br* rumour

ruminer 1 *v/i* chew the cud, ruminate **2** *v/t fig*: **~ qch** mull sth over

rupture *f* breaking; *fig* split; *de négociations* breakdown; *de relations* breaking off; *de contrat* breach

ruse *f* ruse; **la ~** cunning; **rusé** crafty, cunning

russe 1 *adj* Russian **2** *m langue* Russian; **Russe** *m/f* Russian; **Russie:** *la* ~ Russia
rustique rustic

rustre *péj* **1** *adj* uncouth **2** *m* oaf
rythme *m* rhythm; (*vitesse*) pace; **rythmique** rhythmical

S

sa → **son**[1]
S.A. *f* (= **société anonyme**) Inc, *Br* plc
sable *m* sand; **sabler** sand; ~ **le champagne** break open the champagne
sablier *m* CUIS eggtimer
sabot *m* clog; ZO hoof
sabotage *m* sabotage; **saboter** sabotage; F *travail* make a mess of
sac *m* bag; *de pommes de terre* sack; ~ **de couchage** sleeping bag; ~ **à dos** backpack; ~ **à main** purse, *Br* handbag
saccadé *mouvements* jerky; *voix* breathless
saccager (*piller*) sack; (*détruire*) destroy
saccharine *f* saccharine
sachet *m* sachet; ~ **de thé** teabag
sacoche *f* bag; *de vélo* saddlebag
sacré sacred; F damn F
sacrement *m* REL sacrament
sacrifice *m* sacrifice; **sacrifier** sacrifice; **se** ~ sacrifice o.s.
sacrilège 1 *adj* sacrilegious **2** *m* sacrilege

sadique 1 *adj* sadistic **2** *m/f* sadist
safran *m* saffron
sagace shrewd; **sagacité** *f* shrewdness
sage 1 *adj* wise; *enfant* good **2** *m* sage, wise man; **sagefemme** *f* midwife; **sagesse** *f* wisdom; *d'un enfant* goodness
Sagittaire *m* ASTROL Sagittarius
saignant bleeding; CUIS rare; **saigner 1** *v/i* bleed **2** *v/t* *fig* bleed dry
saillant *pommettes* prominent; *fig* salient; **saillie** *f* ARCH projection; *fig* quip; **saillir** ARCH project
sain healthy; *gestion* sound; ~ **d'esprit** sane
saint, ~**e 1** *adj* holy **2** *m/f* saint; **sainteté** *f* holiness; **Saint-Sylvestre:** *la* ~ New Year's Eve
saisie *f* seizure; ~ **de données** INFORM data capture; **saisir** seize; *sens, intention* grasp; INFORM capture; **saisissant** striking; *froid* penetrating
saison *f* season; **saisonnier,**

-ère **1** *adj* seasonal **2** *m* ouvrier seasonal worker

salade *f* salad; **saladier** *m* salad bowl

salaire *m* *d'un ouvrier* wages *pl*; *d'un employé* salary; ~ **net** take-home pay

salarié, ~e 1 *adj* *travail* paid **2** *m/f* *ouvrier* wage-earner; *employé* salaried employee

salaud *m* P bastard P

sale *après le substantif* dirty; *devant le substantif* nasty

salé *eau* salt; CUIS salted; *histoire* daring; *prix* steep; **saler** salt

saleté *f* dirtiness; ~**s** *fig* (*grossièretés*) filthy remarks; F *choses sans valeur, nourriture* junk

salière *f* salt cellar

salir: ~ *qch* get sth dirty

salive *f* saliva

salle *f* room; ~ **d'attente** waiting room; ~ **d'eau** shower room; ~ **à manger** dining room

salon *m* living room; *d'un hôtel* lounge; (*foire*) show; ~ **de l'automobile** auto show, Br motor show; ~ **de thé** tea room

salope *f* P bitch; **saloperie** *f* F *chose sans valeur* piece of junk; (*bassesse*) dirty trick

salopette *f* dungarees *pl*

salubre healthy

saluer greet; MIL salute; ~ **qn (de la main)** wave to s.o.

salut *m* greeting; MIL salute;

(*sauvegarde*) safety; REL salvation; ~**!** F hi!; (*au revoir*) bye!

salutaire salutary

samedi *m* Saturday

sanction *f* sanction

sanctuaire *m* sanctuary

sandale *f* sandal

sandwich *m* sandwich

sang *m* blood; **sang-froid** *m* composure; **garder son** ~ keep one's cool; **tuer qn de** ~ kill s.o. in cold blood; **sanglant** bloodstained; *combat, mort* bloody

sanglot *m* sob; **sangloter** sob

sanguin blood *atr*; *tempérament* sanguine; **groupe** *m* ~ blood group

sanitaire sanitary

sans without; ~ **manger** without eating; ~ **balcon** without a balcony

sans-abri *m/f*: **les** ~ the homeless *pl*

sans-emploi *m*: **les** ~ the unemployed *pl*

santé *f* health; **à votre** ~**!** cheers!, your very good health!

saper undermine

sapeur-pompier *m* firefighter

saphir *m* sapphire

sapin *m* BOT fir

sarcasme *m* sarcasm; **sarcastique** sarcastic

sardine *f* sardine

sardonique sardonic

S.A.R.L. *f* (= **société à res-**

ponsabilité limitée) Inc, Br Ltd

satellite m satellite

satin m satin

satirique satirical

satisfaction f satisfaction; **satisfaire 1** v/i: **à 2** v/t satisfy; *attente* come up to; **satisfaisant** satisfactory; **satisfait** satisfied (**de** with)

saturer saturate

sauce f sauce

saucisse f sausage

saucisson m (dried) sausage

sauf¹ prép except; **avis contraire** unless you/I / *etc* hear to the contrary

sauf², sauve adj safe

sauf-conduit m safe-conduct

saugrenu ridiculous

saule m BOT willow; **pleureur** weeping willow

saumon m salmon

sauna m sauna

saupoudrer sprinkle (**de** with)

saut m jump; **faire un chez qn** fig drop in briefly on s.o.; **à l'élastique** bungee jumping; **en longueur** broad jump, Br long jump; **à la perche** pole vault

sauter 1 v/i jump; (*exploser*) blow up; *d'un fusible* blow; *d'un bouton* come off; **sur** *personne* pounce on; *occasion, offre* jump at; **cela saute aux yeux** it's obvious **2** v/t *fossé* jump (over); *mot, repas* skip

sauterelle f grasshopper

sautiller hop

sauvage 1 adj wild; (*insociable*) unsociable; (*primitif, barbare*) savage; *pas autorisé* unauthorized **2** m/f savage; (*solitaire*) unsociable person

sauvegarde f safeguard; INFORM back-up

sauver save; *personne en danger* save, rescue; *navire* salvage; **se run** away; F (*partir*) be off; (*déborder*) boil over

sauvetage m rescue; *de navire* salvaging; **sauveteur** m rescuer

sauveur m savior, Br saviour

savant 1 adj (*érudit*) learned; (*habile*) skillful, Br skilful **2** m scientist

saveur f taste

savoir 1 v/t & v/i know; **sais-tu nager?** can you swim?, do you know how to swim? **2** m knowledge

savoir-faire m expertise, knowhow

savoir-vivre m good manners pl

savon m soap

savourer savor, Br savour

savoureux, -euse tasty; *fig: récit* spicy

saxophone m saxophone, sax

scandale m scandal; **faire** cause a scandal; **faire tout un** make a scene; **scanda-**

liser scandalize; **se ~ de** be shocked by

scanner 1 *v/t* scan **2** *m* scanner

scaphandrier *m* diver

scarlatine *f* scarlet fever

sceau *m* seal; *fig (marque, signe)* stamp

scellé *m* official seal; **sceller** seal

scénario *m* scenario; *(script)* screenplay; **~ catastrophe** worst-case scenario

scène *f* scene *(aussi fig)*; *(plateau)* stage; **mettre en ~ pièce**, *film* direct; **présenter** stage; **~ de ménage** domestic argument

sceptique 1 *adj* skeptical, *Br* sceptical **2** *m* skeptic, *Br* sceptic

schéma *m* diagram; **schématiser** oversimplify

sciatique *f* sciatica

scie *f* saw; *fig* F bore

sciemment knowingly

science *f* science; *(connaissance)* knowledge; **scientifique 1** *adj* scientific **2** *m/f* scientist

scier saw; *branche etc* saw off

scinder *fig* split; **se ~** split up

scintiller sparkle

scission *f* split

scolaire school *atr*; *succès*, *échec* academic; **scolarité** *f* education, schooling

scooter *m* (motor) scooter

score *m* SP score; POL share of the vote

scorpion *m* ZO scorpion; ASTROL **Scorpion** Scorpio

scotch® *m* Scotch tape®, *Br* sellotape®

scrupule *m* scruple; **scrupuleux**, **-euse** scrupulous

scruter scrutinize

scrutin *m* ballot; **~ majoritaire** majority vote system; **~ proportionnel** proportional representation

sculpter sculpt; *pierre* carve; **sculpteur** *m* sculptor; **sculpture** *f* sculpture

SDF *m/f* (= **sans domicile fixe**) homeless person

se *réfléchi masculin* himself; *féminin* herself; *chose*, *animal* itself; *pluriel* themselves; *avec 'one'* oneself; *réciproque* each other; **cela ne ~ fait pas** that isn't done; **ils ~ lèvent à ...** they get up at ...

séance *f* session; *de cinéma* show, performance; **~ tenante** *fig* immediately

seau *m* bucket

sec, **sèche 1** *adj* dry; *fruits*, *légumes* dried; *(maigre)* thin; *réponse*, *ton* curt **2** *m*: **tenir au ~** keep in a dry place **3** *adv* *boire* neat, straight

sèche-cheveux *m* hair dryer; **sèche-linge** *m* clothes dryer; **sécher** dry; *d'un lac* dry up; **sécheresse** *f* dryness; *manque de pluie* drought; *de réponse*, *ton* curtness

second, ~e **1** *adj* second **2** *m* étage third floor; *Br* second floor; *(adjoint)* second in command **3** *f* second; *en train* second class; **secondaire** secondary; **seconder** *personne* assist

secouer shake; *poussière* shake off

secouriste *m/f* first-aider; **secours** *m* help; *matériel* aid; *au ~!* help!; **sortie** *f de ~* emergency exit; **premiers ~s** first aid

secousse *f* jolt; *électrique* shock; *tellurique* tremor

secret, -ète **1** *adj* secret **2** *m* secret; *(discrétion)* secrecy; *en ~* in secret

secrétaire 1 *m/f* secretary **2** *m* writing desk

secrétariat *m* secretariat; *profession* secretarial work

secte *f* REL sect

secteur *m* sector; *(zone)* area, district; ÉL mains *pl*

section *f* section; **sectionner** *(couper)* sever; *région etc* divide up

séculaire a hundred years old; *très ancien* centuries-old

séculier, -ère secular

sécurité *f* security; *(manque de danger)* safety; **Sécurité sociale** welfare, *Br* social security; **être en ~** be safe

sédatif *m* sedative

sédentaire sedentary; *population* settled

séduction *f* seduction; *fig (charme)* attraction; **séduire** seduce; *fig (charmer)* appeal to; *d'une personne* charm; **séduisant** appealing; *personne* attractive

ségrégation *f* segregation

seigle *m* AGR rye

seigneur *m* HIST the lord of the manor; REL: **le Seigneur** the Lord

sein *m* breast; *fig* bosom; *au ~ de* within

seize sixteen; **seizième** sixteenth

séjour *m* stay; *(salle f de) ~* living room; **séjourner** stay

sel *m* salt

sélection *f* selection; **sélectionner** select

selle *f* saddle; MÉD stool

selon according to; *~ moi* in my opinion; *c'est ~* it all depends

semaine *f* week; *à la ~* by the week; *en ~* during the week, on weekdays

semblable 1 *adj* similar; *tel* such; *~ à* similar, similar to **2** *m (être humain)* fellow human being

semblant *m* semblance; **faire ~ de faire** pretend to do

sembler seem

semelle *f* sole; *pièce intérieure* insole

semence *f* AGR seed

semer sow; *fig (répandre)* spread; *~ qn* F shake s.o. off

semestre *m* half-year

séminaire *m* seminar; REL seminary

semi-remorque *m* semi, *Br* articulated lorry

semonce *f* reproach

semoule *f* CUIS semolina

Sénat *m* POL Senate; **sénateur** *m* senator

sénile senile

sens *m* sense; *(direction)* direction; ~ **interdit** no entry; ~ **dessus dessous** upside down; ~ **de l'humour** sense of humor *ou Br* humour; *(rue f à)* ~ **unique** one-way street

sensation *f* feeling, sensation; *effet de surprise* sensation; *faire* ~ cause a sensation; **sensationnel**, ~**le** sensational

sensé sensible

sensibilité *f* sensitivity; **sensible** sensitive; *(notable)* appreciable; **sensiblement** appreciably; *plus ou moins* more or less

sensualité *f* sensuality; **sensuel**, ~**le** sensual

sentence *f* JUR sentence

sentier *m* path

sentiment *m* feeling; **sentimental** *vie* love *atr*; *péj* sentimental

sentinelle *f* MIL guard

sentir 1 *v/t* feel; *(humer)* smell; *(dégager une odeur de)* smell of; **se** ~ **bien** feel well **2** *v/i*: ~ **bon** smell good

séparable separable; **sépa-**

ration *f* separation; *(cloison)* partition; **séparatisme** *m* POL separatism; **séparé** separate; *époux* separated; **séparément** separately; **séparer** separate; **se** ~ separate

sept seven

septembre *m* September

septennat *m* term of office (of French President)

septentrional northern

septième seventh

septique septic

séquelles *fpl* MÉD after-effects; *fig* aftermath

séquence *f* sequence

serein calm

sérénité *f* serenity

série *f* series *sg*; *de casseroles, timbres* set; SP *(épreuve)* heat; *hors* ~ *numéro* special; *fabriquer en* ~ mass-produce

sérieux, **-euse 1** *adj* serious; *entreprise, employé* professional; *(consciencieux)* conscientious **2** *m* seriousness; *prendre au* ~ take seriously

seringue *f* MÉD syringe

serment *m* oath; *prêter* ~ take the oath

sermon *m* sermon

séropositif, **-ive** HIV-positive

serpent *m* snake; **serpenter** wind, meander

serpillière *f* floor cloth

serre *f* greenhouse; ~**s** ZO talons

serré tight; *pluie* heavy; *per-*

sonnes closely packed; *café* strong

serrer 1 *v/t* (*tenir*) clasp; *ceinture* tighten; *d'un vêtement* be too tight for **2** *v/i*: **se ~** (*s'entasser*) squeeze up; **se ~ contre qn** press against s.o.

serrure *f* lock; **serrurier** *m* locksmith

serveur *m dans un café* bartender, *Br* barman; *dans un restaurant* waiter; INFORM server

serveuse *f dans un café* bartender, *Br* barmaid; *dans un restaurant* server, waitress

serviable helpful

service *m* service; (*faveur*) favor, *Br* favour; *au tennis* service, serve; *d'une entreprise, d'un hôpital* department; **être de ~** be on duty; **rendre ~ à qn** do s.o. a favor; **mettre en ~** put into service; **hors ~** out of order

serviette *f* serviette; *de toilette* towel; *pour documents* briefcase; **~ hygiénique** sanitary napkin

servile servile

servir serve; (*être utile*) be useful; **~ à qn** be of use to s.o.; **~ à qch/à faire qch** be used for sth/for doing sth; **~ de qc** act as sth; **se ~ à table** help o.s. (**en** to); **se ~ de** (*utiliser*) use

ses → **son**[1]

seuil *m* doorstep; *fig* threshold

seul 1 *adj* alone; (*solitaire*) lonely; *devant le subst* only, sole **2** *adv* alone; **faire qch tout ~** do sth all by o.s. *ou* all on one's own

seulement only; **non ~ ... mais encore** *ou* **mais aussi** not only ... but also

sévère severe; **sévérité** *f* severity

sévices *mpl* abuse

sévir *d'une épidémie* rage; **~ contre qn** come down hard on s.o.; **~ contre qc** clamp down on sth

sexagénaire *m/f & adj* sixty-year old

sexe *m* sex; *organes* genitals *pl*; **sexiste** *m/f & adj* sexist; **sexualité** *f* sexuality; **sexuel, ~le** sexual

shampo(o)ing *m* shampoo

short *m* shorts *pl*

si 1 *conj* (*s'il, s'ils*) if; **~ bien que** with the result that **2** *adv* (*tellement*) so; *après négation* yes; **de ~ bonnes vacances** such a good vacation; **~ riche qu'il soit** (*subj*) however rich he may be; **tu ne veux pas? - mais ~!** you don't want to? - oh yes, I do

sida *m* MÉD Aids

sidéré F thunderstruck

siècle *m* century; *fig* (*époque*) age

siège *m* seat; *d'une entreprise* headquarters *pl*; MIL siege; **~**

social COMM head office; **siéger** sit; **~ à d'une entreprise** be headquartered in

sien: **le sien, la sienne, les siens, les siennes** *d'homme* his; *de femme* hers; *de chose, d'animal* its; *avec 'one'* one's

sieste f siesta, nap

sifflement m whistle; **siffler** whistle; *d'un serpent* hiss; **sifflet** m whistle; **coup** m **de ~** blow on the whistle

signal m signal; **~ d'alarme** alarm (signal); **signalement** m description; **signaler** *par un signal* signal; *(faire remarquer)* point out; *(dénoncer)* report; **se ~ par** distinguish o.s. by

signature f signature

signe m sign; **faire ~ à** gesture *ou* signal to s; *(contacter)* get in touch with; **~ de ponctuation** punctuation mark; **signer** sign

signet m bookmark

signification f meaning; **signifier** mean; **~ qch à qn** *(faire savoir)* notify s.o. of sth

silence m silence; **silencieux, -euse 1** *adj* silent **2** m *d'une arme* muffler, *Br* silencer

silhouette f outline, silhouette; *(figure)* figure

sillage m wake *(aussi fig)*

sillon m *dans un champ* furrow; *d'un disque* groove; **sil-**

lonner *(parcourir)* criss-cross

similaire similar; **similitude** f similarity

simple 1 *adj* simple **2** m *au tennis* singles *pl*; **simplicité** f simplicity

simplifier simplify

simulateur, -trice 1 m/f: **c'est un ~** he's pretending **2** m TECH simulator; **simulation** f simulation; **simuler** simulate

simultané simultaneous

sincère sincere; **sincérité** f sincerity

singe m monkey; **singer** ape; **singerie** f imitation; **~s** F antics

singulier, -ère 1 *adj* odd, strange **2** m GRAM singular

sinistre 1 *adj* sinister; *(triste)* gloomy **2** m disaster; **sinistré 1** *adj* stricken **2** m/f disaster victim

sinon *(autrement)* or else, otherwise; *(sauf)* except; *(si ce n'est)* if not

sinueux, -euse *route* winding; *ligne* squiggly; *explication* complicated

sinus m sinus; **sinusite** f sinusitis

sirène f siren

sirop m syrup

siroter sip

sismique seismic

sitcom m *ou* f sitcom

site m site; *(paysage)* area; **~ Web** website

sitôt 1 *adv:* **~ parti, il ...** as soon as he had left he ... **2** *conj:* **~ que** as soon as

situation *f* situation; *(emplacement, profession)* position; **situé** situated

six six; **sixième** sixth

skateboard *m* skateboard; **activité** skateboarding

sketch *m* sketch

ski *m* ski; *activité* skiing; **~ alpin** downhill (skiing); **~ de fond** cross-country (skiing); **~ nautique** water-skiing; **skier** ski; **skieur, -euse** *m/f* skier

slip *m* **de femme** panties *pl*; **d'homme** briefs; **~ de bain** swimming trunks *pl*

slogan *m* slogan

slovaque *adj* Slovak(ian); **Slovaque** *m/f* Slovak(ian)

slovène Slovene, Slovenian; **Slovène** *m/f* Slovene, Slovenian

smoking *m* tuxedo, *Br* dinner jacket

SMS *m* text (message)

S.N.C.F. *f* (= **Société nationale des chemins de fer français**) French national railroad company

sobre sober; *style* restrained

sociable sociable

social social; *COMM* company *atr*; **socialiser** socialize; **socialisme** *m* socialism; **socialiste** *m/f & adj* socialist

société *f* society; *firme* company; **~ anonyme** corpora-

tion, *Br* public limited company, plc

sociologie *f* sociology

socquette *f* anklet, *Br* ankle sock

soda *m* soda, *Br* fizzy drink; **un whisky ~** a whiskey and soda

sœur *f* sister; REL nun

sofa *m* sofa

soi oneself; **avec ~** with one; **ça va de ~** that goes without saying

soi-disant *inv* so-called

soie *f* silk

soif *f* thirst; **avoir ~** be thirsty

soigné *personne* well-groomed; *travail* careful; **soigner** look after, take care of; *d'un médecin* treat; **se ~** take care of o.s.; **soigneux, -euse** careful (**de** about)

soi-même oneself

soin *m* care; **~s** care; MÉD care, treatment; **prendre ~ de** look after, take care of; **être sans ~** be untidy

soir *m* evening; **le ~** in the evening; **soirée** *f* evening; *(fête)* party

soit¹ *adv* very well, so be it

soit² *conj* **~ ..., ~ ...** either ..., or ...; *(à savoir)* that is, ie

soixantaine *f* about sixty; **soixante** sixty; **soixante-dix** seventy

soja *m* BOT soy bean, *Br* soya

sol *m* ground; *(plancher)* floor; *(patrie)*, GÉOL soil

solaire solar

soldat *m* soldier

solde[1] *f* MIL pay

solde[2] *m* COMM balance; **~s marchandises** sale goods; *vente au rabais* sale; **solder compte** close, balance; *marchandises* sell off

sole *f* ZO sole

soleil *m* sun; *il y a du* **~** it's sunny; *coup de* **~** sunburn

solennel, **~le** solemn

solidaire: *être* **~ de qn** suport s.o.; **solidarité** *f* solidarity

solide 1 *adj* solid; *tissu* strong; *argument* sound; *personne* sturdy **2** *m* PHYS solid; **solidité** *f* solidity; *d'un matériau* strength; *d'un argument* soundness

solitaire 1 *adj* solitary **2** *m/f* loner **3** *m diamant* solitaire; **solitude** *f* solitude

sollicitation *f* plea; **solliciter** request; *attention* attract; *curiosité* arouse; **~ un emploi** apply for a job; **sollicitude** *f* solicitude

solstice *m* ASTR solstice

soluble soluble; *café m* **~** instant coffee

solution *f* solution

solvable solvent; *digne de crédit* creditworthy

sombre *couleur, salle* dark; *temps* overcast; *avenir, regard* somber, *Br* sombre

sommaire 1 *adj* brief; *exécution* summary **2** *m* summary

somme[1] *f* sum; *(quantité)* amount; **en ~**, **~ toute** in

short

somme[2] *m* nap, snooze

sommeil *m* sleep; *avoir* **~** be sleepy; **sommeiller** doze

sommelier *m* wine waiter

sommer: **~ qn de faire qc** order s.o. to do sth

sommet *m d'une montagne* summit, top; *d'un arbre, d'une tour* top; *fig* pinnacle; POL summit

sommier *m* mattress

somnambule *m/f* sleepwalker

somnifère *m* sleeping tablet

somnolence *f* drowsiness, sleepiness; **somnoler** doze

somptueux, **-euse** sumptuous; **somptuosité** *f* sumptuousness

son[1] *m*, *sa f*, *ses pl d'homme* his; *de femme* her; *de chose, d'animal* its; *avec 'one'* one's

son[2] *m* sound

sondage *m* probe; TECH drilling; **~ (d'opinion)** opinion poll, survey

sonde *f* probe; **sonder** MÉD probe; *personne, atmosphère* sound out

songe *m litt* dream; **songer**: **~ à (faire) qc** think about (doing) sth; **songeur**, **-euse** thoughtful

sonner 1 *v/i de cloches, sonnette* ring; *d'un réveil* go off; *d'un instrument, d'une voix* sound; *d'une horloge* strike; *midi a sonné* it has struck noon; **~ creux/faux**

fig ring hollow/false **2** *v/t cloches* ring; **sonnerie** *f de cloches* ringing; (*sonnette*) bell; **sonnette** *f* bell

sonore *voix* loud; *rire* resounding; *cuivres* sonorous; *onde, film* sound *atr*; **sonorité** *f* sound, tone; *d'une salle* acoustics *pl*

sophistiqué sophisticated

soporifique sleep-inducing, soporific

soprano **1** *f* soprano **2** *m* treble

sorcellerie *f* sorcery, witchcraft

sorcier *m* sorcerer; **sorcière** *f* witch

sordide filthy; *fig* sordid

sort *m* fate; (*condition*) lot; *tirer au ~* draw lots; *jeter un ~ à fig* cast a spell on

sorte *f* (*manière*) way; (*espèce*) sort, kind; *en quelque ~* in a way; *de* (*telle*) *~ que* and so

sortie *f* exit; (*promenade, excursion*) outing; *d'un livre* publication; *d'un disque* release; *d'une voiture* launch; TECH outlet; MIL sortie; (**sur**) *imprimante* printout

sortir 1 *v/i* come/go out; *pour se distraire* go out (**avec** with); *d'un livre, un disque* come out; *au loto* come up; *~ de endroit* leave; *accident, entretien* emerge from; (*provenir de*) come from **2** *v/t chose* bring/take out;

chien, personne take out; COMM bring out; F *bêtises* come out with **3**: *s'en ~ d'un malade* pull through

sot, ~te 1 *adj* silly, foolish **2** *m/f* fool; **sottise** *f* foolishness; *action/remarque* foolish thing to do/say

sou *m fig* penny; *être sans le ~* be penniless

souche *f d'un arbre* stump; *d'un carnet* stub

souci *m* worry, care; *sans ~* carefree; **soucier**: *se ~ de* worry about; **soucieux, -euse** anxious, concerned (*de* about)

soucoupe *f* saucer

soudain 1 *adj* sudden **2** *adv* suddenly

souder TECH weld; *fig* bring closer together

soudoyer bribe

souffle *m* breath; *d'une explosion* blast; *à bout de ~* breathless, out of breath; **souffler 1** *v/i du vent* blow; (*haleter*) puff; (*respirer*) breathe; (*reprendre son souffle*) get one's breath back **2** *v/t chandelle* blow out; ÉDU, *au théâtre* prompt; *~ qc à qn F* (*dire*) whisper sth to s.o.; (*enlever*) steal sth from s.o.

souffrance *f* suffering; **souffrant** unwell; **souffrir 1** *v/i* be in pain; *~ de* suffer from **2** *v/t* suffer

soufre *m* CHIM sulfur, *Br* sulphur

souhait m wish; **à vos ~s!** bless you!; **souhaitable** desirable; **souhaiter** wish for; **~ que** (+ subj) hope that

souiller dirty, soil; fig: réputation tarnish

soûl drunk

soulagement m relief; **soulager** relieve; **~ qn au travail** help s.o. out

soûler F: **~ qn** get s.o. drunk; **se ~** get drunk

soulèvement m uprising; **soulever** raise; enthousiasme arouse; protestations generate; **se ~** raise o.s.; (se révolter) rise up

souligner underline

soumettre pays, peuple subdue; à un examen submit (à to); (présenter) submit; **se ~ à** submit to; soumis peuple subject; (obéissant) submissive; **soumission** f submission; COMM tender

soupçon m suspicion; **un ~ de** a hint of; **soupçonner** suspect; **soupçonneux, -euse** suspicious

soupe f CUIS (thick) soup

souper 1 v/i have dinner ou supper 2 m dinner, supper

soupir m sigh; **soupirer** sigh

souple flexible; **souplesse** f flexibility

source f spring; fig source

sourcil m eyebrow

sourd deaf; voix low; douleur, bruit dull; colère repressed; **~-muet** deaf-and-dumb

souriant smiling

souricière f mousetrap; fig trap

sourire v/i & m smile

souris f mouse

sournois, ~e 1 adj underhanded **2** m/f underhanded person

sous under; **~ peu** soon; **~ la pluie** in the rain

souscription f subscription; **souscrire: ~ à** subscribe to (aussi fig); emprunt approve

sous-entendre imply; **sous-entendu 1** adj implied **2** m implication

sous-estimer underestimate

sous-jacent underlying

sous-louer sublet

sous-marin 1 adj underwater **2** m submarine

sous-sol m d'une maison basement

sous-titre m subtitle

soustraire MATH subtract (de from); fig: au regard de remove; à un danger protect (à from)

sous-traitance f sub-contracting

sous-vêtements mpl underwear

soutane f REL cassock

soute f MAR, AVIAT hold

soutenir support; pression withstand; fig: conversation keep going; opinion maintain; **~ que** maintain that;

se ~ support each other; **soutenu** *effort* sustained; *style* elevated

souterrain 1 *adj* underground, subterranean **2** *m* underground passage

soutien *m* support

soutien-gorge *m* brassiere, bra

souvenir 1: *se ~ de qn/qch* remember s.o./sth; *se ~ que* remember that **2** *m* memory; *objet* souvenir

souvent often; *le plus ~* most of the time

souverain, **~e** *m/f* sovereign

soyeux, **-euse** silky

spacieux, **-euse** spacious

spaghetti *mpl* spaghetti *sg*

sparadrap *m* Band-Aid®, *Br* Elastoplast®

spasme *m* MÉD spasm; **spasmodique** spasmodic

spatial spatial; ASTR space *atr*

spécial special; **spécialiser:** *se ~* specialize; **spécialiste** *m/f* specialist; **spécialité** *f* speciality

spécifier specify

spécifique specific

spécimen *m* specimen

spectacle *m* spectacle; *théâtre*, *cinéma* show, performance; **spectaculaire** spectacular

spectateur, **-trice** *m/f* (*témoin*) onlooker; SP spectator; *au théâtre* member of the audience

spectre *m* ghost; PHYS spectrum

spéculer speculate

spéléologie *f* caving

spermatozoïde *m* BIOL sperm

sperme *m* BIOL sperm

sphère *f* MATH sphere (*aussi fig*)

spirale *f* spiral

spirituel, **~le** spiritual; (*amusant*) witty

spiritueux *mpl* spirits

splendeur *f* splendor, *Br* splendour, magnificence; **splendide** splendid

sponsor *m* sponsor; **sponsoriser** sponsor

spontané spontaneous

sport 1 *m* sport; *faire du ~* do sport **2** *adj* *vêtements* casual *atr*

sportif, **-ive 1** *adj* *résultats*, *association* sports *atr*; *allure* sporty; (*fair-play*) sporting **2** *m* sportsman **3** *f* sportswoman

square *m* public garden

squash *m* SP squash

squatter squat; **squatteur**, **-euse** *m/f* squatter

squelette *m* skeleton

stabilisateur, **-trice 1** *adj* stabilizing **2** *m* stabilizer; **stabiliser** stabilize; **stabilité** *f* stability; **stable** stable

stade *m* SP stadium; *d'un processus* stage

stage *m* training period; (*cours*) training course; *pour professeur* teaching practice; (*expérience profession-nelle*) work placement; **stagiaire** *m/f* trainee

stagnant *eau* stagnant

stalle *f* *d'un cheval* box; **~s** REL stalls

stand *m* *de foire* booth, *Br* stand; *de kermesse* stall

standard *m* standard; TÉL switchboard

standardiser standardize

standardiste *m/f* TÉL (switchboard) operator

starter *m* AUTO choke

station *f* station; *de bus* stop; *de vacances* resort; **~ de taxis** cab stand, *Br* taxi rank; **~ thermale** spa

stationnement *m* parking; **stationner** park

station-service *f* gas station, *Br* petrol station

statistique 1 *adj* statistical **2** *f* statistic; *science* statistics *sg*

statue *f* statue

stature *f* stature

statut *m* status; **~s** *d'une société* statutes

stéréo *f* stereo

stéréotype *m* stereotype; **stéréotypé** stereotype

stérile sterile; **stériliser** sterilize; **stérilité** *f* sterility

steward *m* flight attendant, steward

stigmate *m* mark; **~s** REL stigmata

stimuler stimulate

stipulation *f* stipulation; **stipuler** stipulate

stock *m* stock; **stocker** stock; INFORM store

stoïque stoical

stop *m* stop; *écriteau* stop sign; (*feu* *m*) **~** AUTO brake light; **faire du ~** F hitchhike; **stopper** stop

store *m* *d'une fenêtre* shade, *Br* blind; *d'un magasin, d'une terrasse* awning

strapontin *m* tip-up seat

stratagème *m* stratagem

stratégie *f* strategy

stress *m* stress; **stressant** stressful; **stressé** stressed-out

strict strict; **le ~ nécessaire** the bare minimum

strident strident

strip-tease *m* strip(tease)

structure *f* structure

studieux, -euse studious

stupéfait stupefied; **stupéfiant 1** *adj* stupefying **2** *m* drug; **stupéfier** stupefy

stupeur *f* stupor

stupide stupid

style *m* style; **styliste** *m de mode, d'industrie* stylist

stylo *m* pen; **~ plume** fountain pen

suave *voix, goût* sweet

subalterne 1 *adj* junior **2** *m/f* junior, subordinate

subir (*endurer*) suffer; (*se soumettre volontairement à*) undergo

subit sudden

subjectif, -ive subjective

subjuguer *fig* captivate

sublime sublime

submerger submerge; *être submergé de* fig be buried in

subordonné, ~e adj & m/f subordinate; **subordonner** subordinate (*à* to)

subrepticement surreptitiously

subsidiaire subsidiary

subsistance f subsistence; **subsister** survive; *d'une personne aussi* live

substance f substance; **substantiel**, ~le substantial

substituer: ~ *X à Y* substitute X for Y

subterfuge m subterfuge

subtil subtle; **subtilité** f subtlety

subvenir: ~ *à* provide for

subvention f grant, subsidy; **subventionner** subsidize

subversif, -ive subversive

suc m: ~*s gastriques* gastric juices

succéder: ~ *à* follow; *personne* succeed; *se* ~ follow each other

succès m success

successeur m successor; **succession** f succession; JUR (*biens dévolus*) inheritance

succomber (*mourir*) die, succumb; ~ *à* succumb to

succulent succulent

succursale f COMM branch

sucer suck; **sucette** f *bonbon* lollipop; *de bébé* pacifier, Br dummy

sucre m sugar; **sucré** sweet; *au sucre* sugared; *péj* sugary; **sucrer** sweeten; *avec sucre* sugar; **sucreries** fpl sweet things

sud 1 m south; *au* ~ *de* (to the) south of **2** adj south; *hémisphère* southern

sud-américain, ~e South American; **Sud-Américain**, ~e m/f South American

sud-est m south-east

sud-ouest m south-west

Suède: *la* ~ Sweden; **suédois**, ~e **1** adj Swedish **2** m *langue* Swedish; **Suédois**, ~e m/f Swede

suer 1 v/i sweat **2** v/t sweat; fig (*dégager*) ooze; **sueur** f sweat

suffire be enough; *il suffit que tu le lui dises* (*subj*) all you have to do is tell her; *ça suffit!* that's enough!

suffisamment sufficiently, enough; ~ *intelligent* sufficiently intelligent, intelligent enough; ~ *de* ... enough ..., sufficient ...; **suffisance** f arrogance; **suffisant** sufficient, enough; (*arrogant*) arrogant

suffocant suffocating; fig breath-taking; **suffocation** f suffocation; **suffoquer** suffocate

suffrage m vote; ~ *universel* universal suffrage

suggérer suggest (*à* to); **suggestion** *f* suggestion

suicide *m* suicide; **suicider: se** ~ commit suicide

suinter *d'un mur* ooze

suisse Swiss; **Suisse** *m/f* Swiss **2 la Suisse** Switzerland

suite *f* pursuit; (*série*) series *sg*; (*continuation*) continuation; *d'un film, d'un livre* sequel; MUS, *appartement* suite; **la** ~ **de l'histoire** the rest of the story; ~**s** (*conséquences*) consequences; *d'un choc, d'une maladie* after-effects; *trois fois de* ~ three times in a row; *et ainsi de* ~ and so on; *par* ~ *de* as a result of; *tout de* ~ immediately

suivant, ~e 1 *adj* next, following **2** *m/f* next person; *au* ~*!* next! **3** *prép* (*selon*) according to **4** *conj:* ~ *que* depending on whether

suivi effort sustained; *relations* continuous; *argumentation* coherent

suivre 1 *v/t* follow; *cours* take **2** *v/i* follow; *à l'école* keep up; *faire* ~ *lettre* please forward; *à* ~ to be continued

sujet, ~te 1 *adj:* ~ *à* subject to **2** *m* subject; *au* ~ *de* on the subject of

sulfureux, -euse sultry

super 1 *adj* F great F, neat F **2** *m* essence premium

superbe superb

supercherie *f* hoax

superficie *f* fig surface; (*surface, étendue*) (surface) area; **superficiel, ~le** superficial

superflu 1 *adj* superfluous **2** *m* surplus

supérieur, ~e 1 *adj* higher; *étages, mâchoire* upper; (*meilleur, dans une hiérarchie*) superior (*aussi péj*) **2** *m/f* superior; **supériorité** *f* superiority

supermarché *m* supermarket

superposer stack; *couches* superimpose; *lits mpl* **superposés** bunk beds

superstitieux, -euse superstitious; **superstition** *f* superstition

superviser supervise

supplanter supplant

suppléant, ~e 1 *adj* acting **2** *m/f* stand-in, replacement; **suppléer:** ~ *à* make up for

supplément *m* supplement; *un* ~ *de* ... additional *ou* extra ...; **supplémentaire** additional

supplication *f* plea

supplice *m* torture; *fig* agony; **supplicier** torture

supplier: ~ *qn de faire* beg s.o. to do

support *m* support; **supportable** bearable; **supporter**[1] *v/t* TECH, ARCH support, hold up; *conséquences* take; *frais, douleur, personne* bear; *chaleur, alcool* tolerate; **sup-**

porter[2] *m* SP supporter, fan

supposer suppose; (*impliquer*) presuppose; **supposition** *f* supposition

suppression *f* suppression; **supprimer** *institution, impôt* abolish; *emplois* cut; *mot* delete; *concert* cancel

suprême supreme

sur on; *prendre qch ~ l'étagère* take sth off the shelf; *une fenêtre ~ la rue* a window looking onto the street; *tirer ~ qn* shoot at s.o.; *un film ~ ...* a movie on *ou* about ...; *un ~ dix* one out of ten

sûr sure; (*non dangereux*) safe; (*fiable*) reliable; *bien ~* of course; *à coup ~ il sera ...* he's bound to be ...

surcharge *f* overloading; (*poids excédentaire*) excess weight

surchauffer overheat

surclasser outclass

surcroît *m*: *un ~ de travail* extra work; *de ~, par ~* moreover

surdité *f* deafness

surdoué extremely gifted

surélever raise

sûrement surely

surenchère *f dans vente aux enchères* higher bid

surestimer overestimate

sûreté *f* safety; MIL security; *de jugement* soundness

surexciter overexcite

surexposer overexpose

surface *f* surface; *grande ~* COMM supermarket

surfait overrated

surfer surf; *~ sur Internet* surf the Net

surgelé 1 *adj* deep-frozen **2** *mpl*: *~s* frozen food

surgir suddenly appear; *d'un problème* crop up

sur-le-champ at once, straightaway

surlendemain *m* day after tomorrow

surligner highlight

surmener overwork; *se ~* overwork, overdo it F

surmonter dominate; *fig* overcome, surmount

surnaturel, ~le supernatural

surnom *m* nickname; **surnommer** nickname

surpasser surpass

surpeuplé *pays* overpopulated; *endroit* overcrowded

surplomber overhang

surplus *m* surplus; *au ~* moreover

surprenant surprising; **surprendre** surprise; *voleur* catch (in the act); *se ~ à faire qch* catch o.s. doing sth; **surpris** surprised; **surprise** *f* surprise

sursaut *m* jump, start; **sursauter** jump

sursis *m fig* reprieve, stay of execution; *peine avec ~* JUR suspended sentence

surtaxe *f* surcharge

surtout especially; (*avant*

tout) above all; **~ que** F especially since

surveillance *f* supervision; *par la police etc* surveillance; **surveillant, ~e** *m/f* supervisor; *de prison* guard; **surveiller** watch; *élèves, employés* supervise; **se ~** *comportement* watch one's step; *poids* watch one's figure

survenir *d'une personne* arrive unexpectedly; *d'un événement* happen; *d'un problème* come up, arise

survêtement *m* sweats *pl*, *Br* tracksuit

survie *f* survival; REL afterlife; **survivant, ~e 1** *adj* surviving **2** *m/f* survivor; **survivre: ~ à** survive

susceptible sensitive, touchy; **~ de faire qch** likely to do sth

susciter arouse

suspect (*équivoque*) suspicious; (*d'une qualité douteuse*) suspect; **~ de qc** suspected of sth; **suspecter** suspect

suspendre suspend; (*accrocher*) hang up; **suspendu** suspended

suspens: en ~ *personne* in suspense; *affaire* outstanding

suspense *m* suspense

suspension *f* suspension

suspicion *f* suspicion

svelte trim, slender

sweat(-shirt) *m* sweatshirt

syllabe *f* syllable

symbole *m* symbol; **symboliser** symbolize

symétrie *f* symmetry

sympathie *f* sympathy; (*amitié, inclination*) liking; **sympathique** nice, friendly; **sympathiser** get on

symphonie *f* symphony

symptôme *m* symptom

synagogue *f* synagogue

synchroniser synchronize

syndical labor *atr*, *Br* (trade) union *atr*

syndicat *m* (labor) union, *Br* (trade) union; **~ d'initiative** tourist information office

syndiqué unionized

synonyme 1 *adj* synonymous (**de** with) **2** *m* synonym

synthèse *f* synthesis; **synthétiseur** *m* MUS synthesizer

systématique systematic; **système** *m* system; **~ antidémarrage** immobilizer; **~ d'exploitation** INFORM operating system

T

ta → **ton²**

tabac *m* tobacco; **bureau** *m* **de ~** tobacco store, *Br* tobacconist's

table *f* table; **se mettre à ~** sit down to eat

tableau *m* **à l'école** board; (*peinture*) painting; *fig* picture; (*liste*) list; (*schéma*) table; **~ de bord** AVIAT instrument panel

tablette *f* shelf; **~ de chocolat** chocolate bar

tablier *m* apron

tabouret *m* stool

tache *f* stain

tâche *f* task

tacher stain

tâcher: ~ de faire try to do

tacheté stained

tacite tacit

taciturne taciturn

tact *m* tact; **avoir du ~** be tactful

tactique 1 *adj* tactical **2** *f* tactics *pl*

taie *f*: **~ (d'oreiller)** pillowslip

taille¹ *f* BOT pruning; **de la pierre** cutting

taille² *f* (*hauteur*) height; (*dimension*) size; ANAT waist

taille-crayon(s) *m* pencil sharpener

tailler BOT prune; *vêtement* cut out; *crayon* sharpen; *pierre* cut; **tailleur** *m* (*coutu-*

rier) tailor; *vêtement* (woman's) suit

taire: se ~ keep quiet (**sur** about); *s'arrêter de parler* stop talking; **tais-toi!** be quiet!, shut up!

talc *m* talc

talent *m* talent; **talentueux, -euse** talented

talon *m* heel; *d'un chèque* stub; **talonner** (*serrer de près*) follow close behind; (*harceler*) harass

talus *m* bank

tambour *m* MUS, TECH drum; **tambouriner** drum

Tamise: la ~ the Thames

tamiser sieve; *lumière* filter

tampon *m* **d'ouate** pad; *hygiène féminine* tampon; (*amortisseur*) buffer; (*cachet*) stamp; **tamponnement** *m* AUTO collision; **tamponner** *plaie* clean; (*cacheter*) stamp; AUTO collide with

tandis que while

tangente *f* MATH tangent

tangible tangible

tango *m* tango

tanière *f* lair, den (*aussi fig*)

tanné tanned; *peau* weatherbeaten; **tanner** tan; *fig F* pester

tant 1 *adv* so much; **~ de vin** so much wine; **~ d'erreurs** so many errors; **~ mieux** so much the better; **~ pis** too bad, tough **2** *conj:* **~ que** *temps* as long as; **en ~ que** *Français* as a Frenchman; **~ ... que ...** both ... and ...

tante *f* aunt

tantôt this afternoon; **à ~** see you soon; **~ ... ~ ...** now ... now ...

taon *m* horsefly

tapage *m* racket; *fig* fuss; **tapageur, -euse** (*voyant*) flashy, loud; (*bruyant*) noisy

tape *f* pat

taper 1 *v/t personne* hit; *table* bang on; (**à l'ordinateur**) F key, type **2** *v/i* hit; *à l'ordinateur* key; **~ sur les nerfs de qn** F get on s.o.'s nerves

tapir: *se* **~** crouch

tapis *m* carpet; *SP* mat; **~ roulant** TECH conveyor belt; *pour personnes* traveling *ou Br* travelling walkway; **~ de souris** mouse mat

tapisser *avec du papier peint* (wall)paper; **tapisserie** *f* tapestry; (*papier peint*) wallpaper

tapoter tap; *personne* pat

taquiner tease; **taquinerie** *f* teasing

tard 1 *adv* late; **plus ~** later (on); **au plus ~** at the latest **2** *m:* **sur le ~** late in life

tarder delay; **~ à faire** take a long time doing; **il me tarde de te revoir** I'm longing to see you again

tardif, -ive late

targuer: *se* **~** *de qc litt* pride o.s. on sth

tarif *m* rate; **~ unique** flat rate

tarir dry up (*aussi fig*); **se ~** dry up

tartan *m* tartan

tarte *f* tart; **tartelette** *f* tartlet

tartine *f* slice of bread; **~ de confiture** slice of bread and jam

tas *m* heap, pile; **un ~ de choses** heaps *pl ou* piles *pl* of things

tasse *f* cup; **une ~ de café** a cup of coffee; **une ~ à café** a coffee cup

tasser (*bourrer*) cram; **se ~** settle

tâter 1 *v/t* feel **2** *v/i* F: **~ de qc** try sth

tatillon, ~ne fussy

tâtons: *avancer à* **~** feel one's way forward

tatouage *m action* tattooing; *signe* tattoo

taudis *m* slum

taupe *f zo* mole

taureau *m* bull; *ASTROL* **Taureau** Taurus

taux *m* rate; **~ d'alcoolémie** blood alcohol level; **~ de change** exchange rate; **~ d'intérêt** interest rate

taxe *f* duty; (*impôt*) tax; **~ sur ou à la valeur ajoutée** sales tax, *Br* value added tax, VAT; **taxer** tax; **~ qn de qc** *fig* (*accuser*) tax s.o. with sth

taxi *m* taxi, cab

tchèque 1 *adj* Czech **2** *m lan-*

gue Czech; **Tchèque** *m/f* Czech

te you; *complément d'objet indirect* (to) you; *tu t'es coupé* you've cut yourself; *si tu ~ lèves à ...* if you get up at ...

technicien, **~ne** *m/f* technician

technique 1 *adj* technical **2** *f* technique

technologie *f* technology; **~ informatique** computer technology; **~ de pointe** high-tech; **technologique** technological

tee-shirt *m* T-shirt

teindre dye

teint, **~e 1** *adj* dyed **2** *m* complexion; **fond** *m* **de ~** foundation (cream) **3** *f* tint; *fig* tinge; **teinter** tint; *bois* stain; **teinture** *f action* dyeing; *produit* dye; PHARM tincture

tel, **~le** such; *une ~le surprise* such a surprise; *de ce genre a* surprise like that; *~(s)* ou *~le(s) que* such as, like

télé *f* F TV, tube F, *Br* telly F

télécharger INFORM download

télécommande *f* remote control

télécommunications *fpl* telecommunications

téléconférence *f* teleconference

téléguidage *m* remote control

téléobjectif *m* telephoto lens

télépathie *f* telepathy

téléphone *m* phone, telephone; **~ portable** cellphone, *Br* mobile (phone); **coup** *m* **de ~** (phone) call; **téléphoner 1** *v/i* phone, telephone; **~ à qn** call s.o., *Br aussi* phone s.o. **2** *v/t* phone, telephone; **téléphonique** phone *atr*; **appel** *m* **~** phone *ou* telephone call

téléréalité *f* reality TV

télescope *m* telescope; **télescoper** crash into; **se ~** crash

télésiège *m* chair lift

téléski *m* ski lift

téléspectateur, **-trice** *m/f* (TV) viewer

téléthon *m* telethon

télévision *f* television; **~ câblée** cable (TV)

tellement *adv; avec verbe* so much; *pas ~* not really; **~ de chance** so much good luck; **~ de filles** so many girls

téméraire reckless; **témérité** *f* recklessness

témoignage *m* JUR testimony, evidence; (*rapport*) account; *fig: d'estime* token; **témoigner** JUR testify, give evidence; **~ de** (*être le témoignage de*) show; **témoin** *m* witness; **être** (**le**) **~ de qch** witness sth

tempe *f* ANAT temple

tempérament *m* temperament; **à ~** in installments *ou Br* instalments

tenu

température f temperature;
avoir de la ~ have a fever,
Br aussi have a temperature
tempéré moderate
tempête f storm
temple m temple; *protestant*
church
temporaire temporary
temporel, ~le temporal
temporiser stall, play for
time
temps m time; *atmosphérique* weather; TECH stroke;
à ~ in time; **de ~ en ~** from
time to time; **il est ~ de partir** it's time to go; **il est ~ que
tu t'en ailles** (*subj*) it's time
you left; **en même ~** at the
same time; **par beau ~** in
good weather; **quel ~ fait-
-il?** what's the weather like?
tenace tenacious
tenailles fpl pincers
tendance f trend; (*disposition*) tendency; **avoir ~ à faire** have a tendency to do,
tend to do
tendon m ANAT tendon
tendre¹ **1** v/t *filet, ailes*
spread; *piège* set; *bras, main*
hold out; *muscles* tense; *corde* tighten; **~ qch à qn** hold
sth out to s.o.; **se ~ de rapports** become strained **2**
v/i: **~ à qch** strive for sth;
~ à faire qch tend to do sth
tendre² *adj* tender; *couleur*
soft
tendresse f tenderness
tendu *corde* tight; *fig* tense;

relations strained
ténèbres fpl darkness; **téné-
breux, -euse** dark
teneur f *d'une lettre* contents
pl; (*concentration*) content
tenir 1 v/t hold; (*maintenir*)
keep; *registre, promesse*
keep; *caisse* be in charge
of; *restaurant* run; *place* take
up; **~ à qc/qn** (*donner de
l'importance à*) value sth/
s.o.; *à un objet* be attached
to sth; **~ à faire qc** really
want to do sth; **cela ne tient
qu'à toi** (*dépend de*) it's entirely up to you **2** v/i hold; **~
dans** fit into 3: **se ~ d'un
spectacle** be held; (*être, se
trouver*) stand; **se ~ à qch**
hold on to sth; **s'en ~ à** confine o.s. to
tennis m tennis; *terrain* tennis
court; **~ pl** sneakers, *Br*
trainers; SP tennis shoes
ténor m MUS tenor
tension f tension; MÉD blood
pressure; **faire de la ~** F have
high blood pressure
tentacule m tentacle
tentant tempting; **tentation** f
temptation
tentative f attempt
tente f tent
tenter tempt; (*essayer*) attempt, try (**de faire** to do)
tenture f wallhanging
tenu: être ~ de faire qc be
obliged to do sth; **bien ~** well
looked after; **mal ~** badly
kept; *enfant* neglected

ténu fine; *espoir* slim

tenue f *de comptes* keeping; *de ménage* running; *(conduite)* behavior, *Br* behaviour; *du corps* posture; *(vêtements)* clothes pl; **~ de soirée** evening wear

tergiverser hum and haw

terme m *(fin)* end; *(échéance)* time limit; *(expression)* term; **à court/long ~** in the short/long term; *emprunt, projet* short-/long-term

terminaison f GRAM ending; **terminer** finish; **se ~** end; **se ~ par** end with; *d'un mot* end in

terminus m terminus

ternir tarnish

terrain m ground; GÉOL, MIL terrain; SP field; *un ~* a piece of land; **sur le ~** essai field atr; *essayer* in the field; **~ d'aviation** airfield; **~ à bâtir** building lot; **~ de jeu** play park; **véhicule m tout ~** 4x4, off-road vehicle

terrasse f terrace; **terrasser** *adversaire* fell

terre f *(sol, surface)* ground; *matière* earth, soil; *opposé à mer, propriété* land; *(monde)* earth, world; *pays, région* land, country; ÉL ground, *Br* earth; **à ~** *personne* down to earth; **à ou par ~** on the ground; **tomber par ~** fall down; **sur ~** on earth; **sur la ~** on the ground

terre-plein m: **~ central** me-

dian strip, *Br* central reservation

terrestre *animaux* land atr; REL earthly; TV terrestrial

terreur f terror

terrible terrible; F *(extraordinaire)* terrific; **c'est pas ~** it's not that good

terrien, **~ne 1** adj: **propriétaire m ~** landowner **2** m/f *(habitant de la Terre)* earthling

terrier m *de renard* earth; ZO terrier

terrifier terrify

territoire m territory

terroir m *viticulture* soil; **du ~** *(régional)* local

terroriser terrorize; **terrorisme** m terrorism; **terroriste** m/f & adj terrorist

tertre m mound

tes → **ton²**

test m test; **~ de résistance** endurance test

testament m JUR will; **Ancien/Nouveau Testament** REL Old/New Testament

tester test

testicule m testicle

tête f head; *(cheveux)* hair; *(visage)* face; SP header; **de ~ calculer** in one's head; *répondre* without looking anything up; **avoir la ~ dure** stubborn; **se casser la ~** fig rack one's brains; **n'en faire qu'à sa ~** do exactly as one likes; **tenir ~ à qn** stand up to s.o.; *péj* defy s.o.; **faire la ~** sulk; **il se paie ta ~** fig he's making a fool of you; **en ~** in the lead

tête-à-queue *m* AUTO spin; **tê-te-à-tête** *m* tête-à-tête; **en ~** in private

têtu obstinate

texte *m* text; **~s choisis** selected passages

textile *m* textile; **le ~ industrie** the textile industry, textiles *pl*

texto *m* text (message); **envoyer ~ à qn** send s.o. a text, text s.o.

texture *f* texture

T.G.V. *m* (= **train à grande vitesse**) high-speed train

thé *m* tea

théâtre *m* theater, *Br* theatre; *fig*: *cadre* scene

théière *f* teapot

thème *m* theme; ÉDU translation (into a foreign language)

théorie *f* theory; **théorique** theoretical

thérapeute *m/f* therapist; **thérapeutique 1** *f* (*thérapie*) therapy **2** *adj* therapeutic; **thérapie** *f* therapy

thermal thermal

thermomètre *m* thermometer

thermos *f ou m* thermos®

thèse *f* thesis

thon *m* tuna

thym *m* BOT thyme

tic *m* tic, twitch; *fig* habit

ticket *m* ticket; **~ de caisse** receipt

tiède warm; *péj* tepid, lukewarm (*aussi fig*); **tiédir** cool down; *devenir plus chaud* warm up

tien, ~ne: le tien, la tienne, les tiens, les tiennes yours

tiers, tierce 1 *adj* third; **le ~ monde** the Third World **2** *m* MATH third; JUR third party

tige *f* BOT stalk; TECH stem

tigre *m* tiger; **tigresse** *f* tigress

tilleul *m* BOT lime (tree); *boisson* lime-blossom tea

timbre *m* stamp; (*sonnette*) bell; (*son*) timbre; (*tampon*) stamp; **timbre-poste** *m* postage stamp

timide timid; **en société** shy

timoré timid

tintement *m* tinkle; *de clochettes* ringing; **tinter** *de verres* clink; *de clochettes* ring

tir *m* fire; *action*, SP shooting; **~ à l'arc** archery

tirage *m* à la loterie draw; PHOT print; TYP printing; (*exemplaires de journal*) circulation; *d'un livre* print run; COMM *d'un chèque* drawing; F (*difficultés*) trouble; **par un ~ au sort** by drawing lots

tirailler pull; **tiraillé entre** *fig* torn between

tire *f* P AUTO car, jeep P; **vol à la ~** pickpocketing

tiré *traits* drawn

tire-bouchon *m* corkscrew

tirelire *f* piggy bank

tirer 1 *v/t* pull; *chèque, ligne, conclusions* draw; *coup de fusil* fire; *oiseau, cible* fire at; PHOT, TYP *print*; *plaisir, satisfaction* derive 2 *v/i* pull (*sur* on); *avec arme* shoot (*sur* at); **à sa fin** draw to a close 3: *se ~ de situation difficile* get out of; *se ~* F take off

tiret *m* dash; (*trait d'union*) hyphen

tiroir *m* drawer

tisane *f* herbal tea

tisser weave; *d'une araignée* spin; *fig* hatch

tissu *m* fabric, material; BIOL tissue

titre *m* title; *d'un journal* headline; FIN security; **à ce ~** therefore; **à juste ~** rightly; **à ~ d'essai** on a trial basis; **au même ~** on the same basis

tituber stagger

titulaire *m/f d'un document, d'une charge* holder

toast *m* (*pain grillé*) piece of toast; *de bienvenue* toast

toboggan *m* slide; *rue* flyover

tocsin *m* alarm bell

toi you

toile *f de lin* linen; (*peinture*) canvas; **~ d'araignée** spiderweb, Br spider's web; **~ cirée** oilcloth; **~ de fond** backcloth; *fig* backdrop

toilette *f* (*lavage*) washing; (*mise*) outfit; (*vêtements*) clothes *pl*; **~s** toilet; **aller**

aux ~s go to the toilet; **faire sa ~** get washed

toi-même yourself

toiser *fig*: **~ qn** look s.o. up and down

toison *f de laine* fleece; (*cheveux*) mane of hair

toit *m* roof; **~ ouvrant** AUTO sun roof; **toiture** *f* roof

tôle *f* sheet metal; **~ ondulée** corrugated iron

tolérance *f aussi* TECH tolerance; **tolérant** tolerant; **tolérer** tolerate

tomate *f* tomato

tombe *f* grave

tombeau *m* tomb

tombée *f*: **à la ~ de la nuit** at nightfall

tomber fall; *de cheveux* fall out; *d'une colère* die down; *d'une fièvre, d'un prix, d'une demande* drop, fall; **~ malade** fall sick; **laisser ~** drop (*aussi fig*); **~ sur** MIL attack; (*rencontrer*) bump into; **~ d'accord** reach agreement

tome *m* volume

ton¹ *m* tone; MUS key; **il est de bon ~** it's the done thing

ton² *m*, **ta** *f*, **tes** *pl* your

tondeuse *f* lawnmower; *de coiffeur* clippers *pl*; AGR shears *pl*; **tondre** *mouton* shear; *haie* clip; *herbe* mow, cut; *cheveux* shave off

tonifier tone up

tonique 1 *m* tonic 2 *adj climat* bracing

tonitruant thunderous

tonne f (metric) ton

tonneau m barrel; MAR ton

tonner thunder; fig rage

tonnerre m thunder

tonton m F uncle

tonus m d'un muscle tone; (dynamisme) dynamism

toqué F mad (de about)

torche f flashlight, Br torch

torchon m dishtowel

tordre twist; linge wring; se ~ twist; se ~ le pied twist one's ankle

tornade f tornado

torpille f torpedo; **torpiller** torpedo (aussi fig)

torrent m torrent; fig: de larmes flood; d'injures torrent

torse m torso

tort m fault; (préjudice) harm; à ~ wrongly; à ~ et à travers wildly; avoir ~ be wrong (de faire to do); donner ~ à qn prove s.o. wrong; (désapprouver) blame s.o.; faire du ~ à hurt, harm

torticolis m MÉD stiff neck

tortiller twist; se ~ wriggle

tortue f tortoise; ~ de mer turtle

tortueux, -euse winding; fig tortuous; esprit, manœuvres devious

torture f torture; **torturer** torture

tôt early; (bientôt) soon; le plus ~ possible as soon as possible; au plus ~ at the soonest ou earliest; ~ ou

tard sooner or later

total 1 adj total **2** m total; au ~ in all; fig on the whole; **totalement** totally; **totaliser** total; **totalité** f: la ~ de all of; en ~ in full; **totalitaire** POL totalitarian

touchant touching

touche f touch; de clavier key; SP touchline; (remise en jeu) throw-in; pêche bite; être mis sur la ~ fig F be sidelined

toucher¹ v/t touch; but hit; (émouvoir) touch, move; (concerner) concern; (contacter) contact, get in touch with; argent get; réserves break into; d'une maison adjoin; ~ au but near one's goal; se ~ touch; de maisons, terrains adjoin

toucher² m touch

touffu dense, thick

toujours always; (encore) still; pour ~ for ever

toupet m F nerve

tour¹ f tower; (immeuble) high-rise

tour² m turn; (circonférence) circumference; (circuit) lap; (promenade) stroll, walk; (excursion, voyage) tour; (ruse) trick; TECH lathe; de potier wheel; à mon ~, c'est mon ~ it's my turn; en un ~ de main in no time at all

tourbe f matière peat

tourbillon m de vent whirlwind; *f d'eau* whirlpool

tourelle *f* turret

tourisme *m* tourism; ~ *écolo-gique* ecotourism; **touriste** *m/f* tourist

tourment *m litt* torture, torment

tourmente *f litt* storm

tourmenter torment; **se** ~ worry, torment o.s.

tournant 1 *adj* revolving **2** *m* turn; *fig* turning point

tournée *f* round; *d'un artiste* tour

tourner 1 *v/t* turn; *sauce* stir; *salade* toss; *difficulté* get around; *film* shoot; *bien tourné(e)* well-put **2** *v/i* turn; *du lait* turn; *j'ai la tête qui tourne* my head is spinning; *faire* ~ *clé* turn; *entreprise* run **3:** **se** ~ turn; **se** ~ *vers fig* turn to

tournesol *m* BOT sunflower

tournevis *m* screwdriver

tournoyer *d'oiseaux* wheel; *de feuilles* swirl

tournure *f (expression)* turn of phrase; *des événements* turn

tourterelle *f* turtledove

tous → **tout**

Toussaint: *la* ~ All Saints' Day

tousser cough

toussoter have a slight cough

tout *m*, **toute** *f*, **tous** *mpl*, **toutes** *fpl* **1** *adj* all; *(n'importe lequel)* any; ~ *Français* every Frenchman, all French-

men; **tous les deux jours** every two days; **tous les ans** every year **2** *pron sg* **tout** everything; *pl* **tous, toutes** all of us/them; *après* ~ after all; *facile comme* ~ F as easy as anything; *nous tous* all of us; **3** *adv* **tout** very, quite; ~ *comme un ...* it's just like a ...; ~ *nu* completely naked; *c'est* ~ *près d'ici* it's just nearby; *je suis* ~*e seule* I'm all alone; ~ *à fait* altogether; *oui,* ~ *à fait* yes, absolutely; ~ *de suite* straight away; ~ *pauvres qu'ils sont (ou soient) (subj)* however poor they are **4** *m* **tout** the whole lot, everything; *pas du* ~ not at all

toutefois however

toux *f* cough *m*

toxique 1 *adj* toxic **2** *m* poison

trac *m* nervousness; *pour un acteur* stage fright

traçabilité *f* traceablility

tracas *m:* **des** ~ worries; **tra-casser:** ~ *qn d'une chose* worry s.o.; *d'une personne* pester s.o.; **se** ~ worry

trace *f (piste)* track, trail; *(marque)* mark; *fig* impression; ~*s de sang,* poison traces; *des* ~*s de pas* footprints; *tracer plan* draw

trachée *f* windpipe, trachea

tractation *f péj:* ~*s* horsetrading

tracteur *m* tractor

tradition *f* tradition; traditionaliste *m/f & adj* traditionalist; traditionnel, *le* traditional

traducteur, -trice *m/f* translator; traduction *f* translation; traduire translate (**en** into); *fig* be indicative of; *se ~ par* result in

trafic *m* traffic; trafiquant *m* trafficker; *~ de drogue(s)* drug trafficker; trafiquer traffic in; *moteur* tinker with

tragédie *f* tragedy; tragique 1 *adj* tragic 2 *m* tragedy

trahir betray; trahison *f* betrayal; *crime* treason

train *m* train; *fig: de lois, décrets etc* series *sg*; *être en ~ de faire qc* be doing sth; *mettre en ~* set in motion; *au ~ où vont les choses* at the rate things are going; *~ d'atterrissage* undercarriage, landing gear; *~ de vie* lifestyle

traîner 1 *v/t* drag; *d'une voiture* pull, tow 2 *v/i de vêtements, livres* lie around; *d'une discussion* drag on; *dans les rues* hang around street corners 3: *se ~* drag o.s. along

train-train *m f: le ~ quotidien* the daily routine

traire milk

trait *m* (*ligne*) line; *du visage* feature; *de caractère* trait; *d'une œuvre, époque* feature, characteristic; *avoir ~*

à be about; *~ d'esprit* witticism; *~ d'union* hyphen

traite *f* COMM draft, bill of exchange; *d'une vache* milking; *d'une seule ~* in one go

traité *m* treaty

traitement *m* treatment; (*salaire*) pay; TECH, INFORM processing; traiter 1 *v/t* treat; TECH, INFORM process; *~ qn de menteur* call s.o. a liar 2 *v/i* (*négocier*) negotiate; *~ de qc* deal with sth

traître, *sse* 1 *m/f* traitor 2 *adj* treacherous

trajet *m* (*voyage*) journey; (*chemin*) way

trame *f fig: d'une histoire* background; *de la vie* fabric

tramway *m* streetcar, *Br* tram

tranchant 1 *adj* cutting 2 *m d'un couteau* cutting edge

tranche *f* (*morceau*) slice; (*bord*) edge; *~ d'âge* bracket

tranché *fig* clear-cut; *couleur* definite

tranchée *f* trench

trancher 1 *v/t* cut; *fig* settle 2 *v/i*: *~ sur* stand out against

tranquille quiet; (*sans inquiétude*) easy in one's mind; *laisse-moi ~!* leave me alone!; tranquillisant *m* tranquilizer, *Br* tranquillizer; tranquilliser: *~ qn* set s.o.'s mind at rest; tranquillité *f* quietness, peacefulness; *du sommeil* peacefulness; (*stabilité morale*) peace of mind

transaction f JUR compromise; COMM transaction

transatlantique 1 adj transatlantic **2** m bateau transatlantic liner; chaise deck chair

transcription f transcription; **transcrire** transcribe

transférer transfer; **transfert** m transfer; PSYCH transference

transformation f transformation; TECH processing; en rugby conversion; **transformer** transform; TECH process; appartement, en rugby convert

transfuge m defector

transfusion f: **~ (sanguine)** (blood) transfusion

transgénique genetically modified

transgresser loi break, transgress

transi: **~ (de froid)** frozen

transiger come to a compromise

transistor m transistor

transit m: **en ~** in transit

transition f transition

transmettre transmit; message, talen, maladie pass on; tradition, titre hand down; **transmissible**: **sexuellement ~** sexually transmitted; **transmission** f transmission; d'un message passing on; d'une tradition, d'un titre handing down; RAD, TV broadcast

transparence f transparency; **transparent** transparent

transpercer pierce; de l'eau, de la pluie go right through

transpiration f perspiration; **transpirer** perspire

transplant m transplant; **transplantation** f transplanting; MÉD transplant; **transplanter** transplant

transport m transport; **~s publics** mass transit, Br public transport; **transporter** transport, carry

transposer transpose

transversal cross atr

trapèze m trapeze

trappe f (ouverture) trapdoor

trapu stocky

traquer hunt

traumatiser PSYCH traumatize; **traumatisme** m MÉD, PSYCH trauma

travail m work; **être sans ~** be out of work; **travaux** (construction) construction work; **travailler 1** v/i work **2** v/t work on; d'une pensée trouble; **travailleur, -euse 1** adj hard-working **2** m/f worker

travers 1 adv: **de ~** crooked; marcher not straight; **en ~** across **2** prép: **à ~** qc, **au ~ de** qc through sth **3** m shortcoming

traversée f crossing; **traverser** rue, mer cross; forêt, crise go through; (percer) go right through

travesti 1 *adj pour fête* fancy-dress **2** *m* (*déguisement*) fancy dress; (*homosexuel*) transvestite; **travestir** *vérité* distort; **se** ~ dress up (**en** as a)

trébucher trip (**sur** over)

trèfle *m* BOT clover; *aux cartes* clubs *pl*

treize thirteen; **treizième** thirteenth

tremblant trembling, quivering; **tremblement** *m* trembling; ~ **de terre** earthquake; **trembler** tremble, shake (**de** with); *de la terre* shake

trémousser: se ~ wriggle

trempe *f* fig caliber, *Br* calibre

trempé soaked; *sol* saturated; **tremper** soak; *pain dans café etc* dunk; *pied dans l'eau* dip; *acier* harden; ~ **dans** *fig* be involved in

tremplin *m* springboard; *pour* ski jump; *fig* stepping stone

trentaine *f*: **une** ~ **de personnes** about thirty people *pl*; **trente** thirty; **trentième** thirtieth

trépied *m* tripod

trépigner stamp (one's feet)

très very; ~ **lu/visité** much read/visited

trésor *m* treasure; **Trésor** Treasury; **trésorier, -ère** *m/f* treasurer

tressaillir jump

tresse *f de cheveux* braid, *Br* plait

trêve *f* truce; ~ **de** ... that's enough ...; **sans** ~ without respite

tri *m* sort; **faire un** ~ **dans** *qc* sort sth out

triangle *m* triangle

tribord *m* MAR starboard

tribu *f* tribe

tribulations *fpl* tribulations

tribunal *m* court

tribune *f* platform; (*débat*) discussion; ~**s dans stade** bleachers, *Br* stands

tributaire: être ~ **de** be dependent on

tricher cheat; **tricheur, -euse** *m/f* cheat

tricolore: drapeau *m* ~ tricolor *ou Br* tricolour

tricot *m* knitting; *vêtement* sweater; **tricoter** knit

trier (*choisir*) pick through; (*classer*) sort

trimballer F hump F, lug

trimer F work like a dog F

trimestre *m* quarter; ÉDU trimester, *Br* term

trinquer (*porter un toast*) clink glasses; ~ **à** *fig* F toast, drink to

triomphe *m* triumph; **triompher** triumph (**de** over)

tripes *fpl* guts; CUIS tripe

triple triple; **triplés, -ées** *mpl, fpl* triplets

tripoter F *objet* play around with; *femme* feel up

triste sad; *temps, paysage* dreary; **tristesse** *f* sadness

trivial vulgar; *litt* (*banal*) trite

troc *m* barter

trognon *m d'un fruit* core; *d'un chou* stump

trois 1 *adj* three; **le ~ mai** May third; *Br* the third of May **2** *m* three; **troisième** third

trombe *f*: **des ~s d'eau** sheets of water; **en ~** *fig* at top speed

trombone *m* MUS trombone; *pour papiers* paper clip

trompe *f* MUS horn; *d'un éléphant* trunk

tromper deceive; *époux* be unfaithful to; *confiance* abuse; **se ~** be mistaken; **se ~ de numéro** get the wrong number; **tromperie** *f* deception

trompette 1 *f* trumpet **2** *m* trumpet player

trompeur, -euse deceptive; (*traître*) deceitful

tronc *m* BOT, ANAT trunk; *à l'église* collection box

tronçon *m* section

trône *m* throne

trop too; *avec verbe* too much; **~ de lait/gens** too much milk/too many people

tropical tropical; **tropique** *m* tropic

trot *m* trot; **aller au ~** trot; **trotter** *d'un cheval* trot; *d'une personne* run around

trottiner scamper

trottinette *f* scooter

trottoir *m* sidewalk, *Br* pavement

trou *m* hole; **~ de mémoire** lapse of memory

trouble 1 *adj eau, liquide* cloudy; *explication* unclear; *situation* murky **2** *m* (*désarroi*) trouble; (*émoi*) excitement; MÉD disorder; **~s** POL unrest; **trouble-fête** *m* party-pooper F

troubler *liquide* make cloudy; *silence, sommeil* disturb; *réunion* disrupt; (*inquiéter*) bother; **se ~** get flustered *d'un liquide* go cloudy

trouée *f* gap; **trouer** make a hole in

troupe *f* troop; *de comédiens* troupe

troupeau *m de vaches* herd; *de moutons* flock

trousse *f* kit; **être aux ~s de qn** *fig* be on s.o.'s heels; **~ de toilette** toilet bag

trousseau *m d'une mariée* trousseau; **~ de clés** bunch of keys

trouver find; *plan* come up with; (*rencontrer*) meet; **~ que** think that; **se ~** (*être*) be; **il se trouve que** it turns out that

truc *m* F (*chose*) thing, thingamajig F; (*astuce*) trick

truffe *f* BOT truffle; *d'un chien* nose; **truffé** with truffles; **~ de** *fig*: *citations* peppered with

truie *f* sow

truite *f* trout

truquage *m dans film* special

effect; *d'une photo* faking; truquer *élections, cartes* rig

tu you

tuba *m* snorkel; MUS tuba

tube *m* tube; F *(chanson)* hit

tuberculose *f* MÉD tuberculosis, TB

tuer kill; *fig (épuiser)* exhaust; *(peiner)* bother; **se ~** *(se suicider)* kill o.s.; *(trouver la mort)* be killed; **tue-tête: à ~** at the top of one's voice; **tueur** *m* killer

tulipe *f* tulip

tumeur *f* MÉD tumor, *Br* tumour

tumulte *m* uproar; *fig (activité)* hustle and bustle; **tumultueux, -euse** noisy; *passion* tumultuous, stormy

tunique *f* tunic

Tunisie: *la* **~** Tunisia; **tunisien, ~ne** Tunisian; **Tunisien, ~ne** *m/f* Tunisian

tunnel *m* tunnel

turbo-réacteur *m* AVIAT turbojet

turbulence *f* turbulence; *d'un élève* unruliness; **turbu-**

lent turbulent; *élève* unruly

turc, turque **1** *adj* Turkish **2** *m langue* Turkish; **Turc, Turque** *m/f* Turk

turf *m* SP horseracing; *terrain* racecourse

Turquie: *la* **~** Turkey

tutelle *f* JUR guardianship; *d'un état, d'une société* supervision, control; *fig* protection

tuteur, -trice **1** *m/f* JUR guardian **2** *m* BOT stake

tutoyer address as 'tu'

tuyau *m* pipe; *flexible* hose; F *(information)* tip; **~ d'arrosage** garden hose; **tuyauter** F: **~ qn** tip s.o. off

T.V.A. *f* (= **taxe sur** *ou* **à la valeur ajoutée**) sales tax, *Br* VAT (= value added tax)

type *m* type; F *(gars)* guy F; **contrat** *m* **~** standard contract

typhon *m* typhoon

typique typical *(de* of)

tyran *m* tyrant; **tyrannie** *f* tyranny; **tyranniser** tyrannize; *petit frère etc* bully

U

U.E. *f* (= **Union européenne**) EU (= European Union)

ulcère *m* MÉD ulcer; **ulcérer** *fig* aggrieve

ultérieur later, subsequent

ultimatum *m* ultimatum

ultime last

ultrason *m* PHYS ultrasound

ultraviolet, ~te *adj & m* ultraviolet

un, une **1** *article* a; *devant voyelle* an **2** *pron* one; **à la une** on the front page; **l'un des touristes** one of the tourists; *les uns avaient ...* some (of them) had ...; *elles s'aident les unes les autres* they help each other; *l'un et l'autre* both of them 3 *chiffre* one

unanime unanimous; **unanimité** *f* unanimity; *à l'~* unanimously

uni *pays* united; *surface* smooth; *tissu* solid(-colored), *Br* self-coloured); *famille* close-knit

unification *f* unification; **unifier** unite, unify

uniforme 1 *adj* uniform; *existence* unchanging **2** *m* uniform; **uniformité** *f* uniformity

unilatéral unilateral

union *f* union; *(cohésion)* unity; **Union européenne** European Union

unique *(seul)* single; *fils* only; *(extraordinaire)* unique; **uniquement** only

unir POL unite; *par moyen de communication* link; *couple* marry; *s'~* unite; *(se marier)* marry

unité *f* unit

univers *m* universe; *fig* world; **universel, ~le** universal

universitaire 1 *adj* university *atr* **2** *m* academic; **université** *f* university

uranium *m* CHIM uranium

urbain urban; **urbaniser** urbanize; **urbanisme** *m* town planning

urgence *f* urgency; *une ~* an emergency; *d'~* emergency *atr*; **urgent** urgent

urine *f* urine; **uriner** urinate

urne *f*: *aller aux ~s* go to the polls

usage *m* use; *(coutume)* custom; *linguistique* usage; *hors d'~* out of use; *à l'~ de qn* for use by s.o.; *d'~* customary; **usager** *m* user

usé worn; *vêtement, personne* worn-out; **user** *du gaz, de l'eau* use, consume; *vêtement* wear out; *yeux* ruin; *s'~* wear out; *personne* wear o.s. out; *~ de qc* use sth

usine *f* plant, factory; **usiner** machine

usité *mot* common

ustensile *m* tool; *~ de cuisine* kitchen utensil

usuel, ~le usual; *expression* common

usure *f* *(détérioration)* wear; *du sol* erosion

utérus *m* ANAT womb, uterus

utile useful; *en temps ~* in due course

utilisateur, -trice *m/f* user; *~ final* end user; **utilisation** *f* use; **utiliser** use

utilitaire utilitarian

utilité *f* usefulness, utility; *ça n'a aucune ~* it's no use whatever

V

vacance *f poste* opening, *Br* vacancy; **~s** vacation, *Br* holiday(s); **vacancier, -ère** *m/f* vacationer, *Br* holiday-maker

vacarme *m* din, racket

vaccin *m* vaccine; **vaccination** *f* vaccination; **vacciner** vaccinate

vache 1 *f* cow **2** *adj* F mean

vachement F *bon, content* damn F, *Br* bloody F; *changer, vieillir* one helluva lot F

vaciller *sur ses jambes* sway; *d'une flamme* flicker; *(hésiter)* vacillate

vagabond, ~e 1 *adj* wandering **2** *m/f* hobo, *Br* tramp

vagin *m* vagina

vague[1] *f* wave *(aussi fig)*; **~ de froid** cold snap

vague[2] **1** *adj* vague; *regard* faraway; **terrain** *m* **~** waste ground **2** *m* vagueness; **regarder dans le ~** stare into the middle distance

vaillant brave, valiant

vain vain; *mots* empty; **en ~** in vain

vaincre conquer; SP defeat; *fig: angoisse* overcome, conquer; *obstacle* overcome; **vaincu 1** *adj* conquered; SP defeated **2** *m* loser; **vainqueur** *m* winner, victor

vaisseau *m* ANAT, *litt (bateau)* vessel; **~ spatial** spaceship

vaisselle *f* dishes *pl*; **laver** *ou* **faire la ~** do *ou* wash the dishes

valable valid

valeur *f* value, worth; *d'une personne* worth; **~s** COMM securities; **sans ~** worthless; **mettre en ~** emphasize, highlight

valide *(sain)* fit; *passeport, ticket* valid; **valider** validate; *ticket* stamp; **validité** *f* validity

valise *f* bag, suitcase

vallée *f* valley

valoir be worth; *(coûter)* cost; **~ mieux** be better **(que** than**)**; **faire ~ droits** assert; *capital* make work; *(mettre en valeur)* emphasize

valoriser enhance the value of; *personne* enhance the image of

valse *f* waltz

vandale *m/f* vandal; **vandaliser** vandalize

vanille *f* vanilla

vanité *f (fatuité)* vanity; *(inutilité)* futility; **vaniteux, -euse** vain

vanne *f* sluice gate; F dig F

vantard, ~e 1 *adj* boastful **2** *m/f* boaster; **vanter** praise; **se ~ de qch** pride o.s. on sth

vapeur *f* vapor, *Br* vapour; **~**

(*d'eau*) steam; *cuire à la* ~ steam

vaporeux, **-euse** *paysage* misty; *tissu* filmy

vaporisateur *m* spray; **vaporiser** spray

varappe *f* rock-climbing

variable variable; *temps*, *humeur* changeable; **variante** *f* variant; **variation** *f* (*changement*) change; (*écart*) variation

varice *f* ANAT varicose vein

varicelle *f* MÉD chickenpox

varié varied; **varier** vary; **variété** *f* variety; ~**s** *spectacle* vaudeville, *Br* variety show

variole *f* MÉD smallpox

vase[1] *m* vase

vase[2] *f* mud; **vaseux**, **-euse** muddy; *F* (*nauséeux*) off-color, *Br* off-colour; *F explication* muddled

vasistas *m* fanlight

vaurien, ~**ne** *m/f* good-for-nothing

vautour *m* vulture

veau *m* calf; *viande* veal

vedette *f* star; (*bateau*) launch; *mettre en* ~ highlight

végétal **1** *adj* plant *atr*; *huile végétale* **2** *m* plant; **végétalien**, ~**ne** *m/f & adj* vegan

végétarien, ~**ne** *m/f & adj* vegetarian

végétation *f* vegetation; **végéter** vegetate

véhémence *f* vehemence; **véhément** vehement

véhicule *m* vehicle (*aussi fig*)

veille *f* previous day; *absence de sommeil* wakefulness; *à la* ~ *de* on the eve of; *veiller* stay up late; ~ *à faire qch* see to it that sth is done; ~ *sur qn* watch over s.o.

veinard, ~**e** *m/f* F lucky devil F; **veine** *f* vein; F luck

vélo *m* bike; *faire du* ~ go cycling; **vélomoteur** *m* moped

velours *m* velvet; ~ *côtelé* corduroy

velouté velvety; (*soupe*) creamy

velu hairy

venaison *f* venison

vendable saleable

vendange *f* grape harvest

vendeur *m* sales clerk, *Br* shop assistant; **vendeuse** *f* sales clerk, *Br* shop assistant; **vendre** sell; *fig* betray; *à* ~ for sale

vendredi *m* Friday; *Vendredi saint* Good Friday

vendu, ~**e** **1** *adj* sold **2** *m/f péj* traitor

vénéneux, **-euse** poisonous

vénérable venerable; **vénération** *f* veneration; **vénérer** revere

vénérien, ~**ne**: *maladie f* ~**ne** venereal disease

vengeance *f* vengeance; **venger** avenge (*qn de qc* s.o. for sth); *se* ~ *de qn* get one's revenge on s.o.; *se* ~ *de qc sur qn* get one's revenge for sth on s.o.

venimeux, -euse poisonous; **venin** *m* venom (*aussi fig*)

venir come; **à ~** to come; **où veut-il en ~?** what's he getting at?; **~ de** come from; **je viens de faire la vaisselle** I have just washed the dishes; **faire ~ médecin** send for

vent *m* wind; **coup *m* de ~** gust of wind; **il y a du ~** it's windy

vente *f* sale; *activité* selling; **~ à crédit** installment plan, *Br* hire purchase

venteux, -euse windy

ventilateur *m* ventilator; *électrique* fan; **ventilation** *f* ventilation; **ventiler** *pièce* air; *montant* break down

ventre *m* stomach; **~ à bière** beer belly

ventriloque *m* ventriloquist

venu, ~e 1 *adj*: **bien/mal ~** appropriate/inappropriate **2** *m/f*: **le premier ~, la première ~e** the first to arrive; **(n'importe qui)** anybody; **venue** *f* arrival

ver *m* worm; **~ de terre** earthworm; **~ à soie** silkworm

verbal verbal; **verbe** *m* verb

verdâtre greenish

verdict *m* verdict

verdir turn green

verdure *f* (*feuillages*) greenery; (*salade*) greens *pl*

verge *f* ANAT penis; (*baguette*) rod

verger *m* orchard

verglas *m* black ice

vergogne *f*: **sans ~** shameless; **avec verbe** shamelessly

véridique truthful

vérification *f* check; **vérifier** check; **se ~** turn out to be true

véritable real; *amour* true

vérité *f* truth; **en ~** actually; **à la ~** to tell the truth

vermeil, ~le bright red, vermillion

vermine *f* vermin

verni varnished; F lucky; **vernir** varnish; *céramique* glaze; **vernis** *m* varnish; *de céramique* glaze; **~ à ongle** nail polish, *Br aussi* nail varnish

verre *m* glass; **prendre un ~** have a drink; **~s de contact** contact lenses

verrerie *f* glassmaking; *fabrique* glassworks *sg*; *objets* glassware

verrière *f* (*vitrail*) stained-glass window; *toit* glass roof

verrou *m* bolt; **verrouillage** *m*: **~ central** AUTO central locking; **verrouiller** bolt; F lock up

verrue *f* wart

vers¹ *m* verse

vers² *prép* toward, *Br* towards; (*environ*) around

versant *m* slope

versatile changeable

Verseau *m* ASTROL Aquarius

versement *m* payment; **verser 1** *v/t* pour (out); *sang,* *larmes* shed; *argent à un compte* pay in; *intérêts, pension* pay **2** *v/i* (*basculer*) overturn

version *f* version; (*traduction*) translation

verso *m d'une feuille* back

vert 1 *adj* green; *fruit* unripe; *vin* too young; *fig: personne âgée* spry; *propos risqué* **2** *m* green; *les ~s* POL *mpl* the Greens

vertébral vertebral; **colonne** *f ~e* spine, spinal column; **vertèbre** *f* vertebra

vertical, ~e 1 *adj* vertical **2** *f* vertical (line)

vertige *m* vertigo, dizziness; *fig* giddiness; **un ~** a dizzy spell; **j'ai le ~** I feel dizzy

vertu *f* virtue; (*pouvoir*) property; **en ~ de** in accordance with; **vertueux, -euse** virtuous

verve *f* wit

vésicule *f* ANAT: **~ biliaire** gall bladder

vessie *f* ANAT bladder

veste *f* jacket

vestiaire *m de théâtre* checkroom, *Br* cloakroom; *d'un stade* locker room

vestibule *m* hall

vestiges *mpl* traces

veston *m* jacket, coat

vêtement *m* item of clothing, garment; **~s** clothes; (*industrie f du*) **~** clothing industry

vétérinaire 1 *adj* veterinary **2** *m/f* veterinarian, vet

vêtu dressed

vétuste *bâtiment* dilapidated, ramshackle

veuf 1 *adj* widowed **2** *m* widower

veuve 1 *adj* widowed **2** *f* widow

vexant humiliating; **vexation** *f* humiliation; **vexer: ~ qn** hurt s.o.'s feelings; **se ~** get upset

viable *projet*, BIOL viable

viaduc *m* viaduct

viager, -ère: rente f viagère life annuity

viande *f* meat

vibration *f* vibration; **vibrer** vibrate

vice *m* (*défaut*) defect; (*péché*) vice

vice-président *m* COMM, POL vice-president; *Br* COMM vice-chairman

vicié *air* stale

vicieux, -euse lecherous; *cercle* vicious

victime *f* victim

victoire *f* victory; SP win, victory; **victorieux, -euse** victorious

vidange *f* emptying, draining; AUTO oil change

vide 1 *adj* empty **2** *m* (*néant*) emptiness; *physique* vacuum; (*espace non occupé*) (empty) space; **avoir peur du ~** be afraid of heights

vidéo *adj & f* video **~-amateur** home movie; **vidéocassette** *f* video cassette

vide-ordures *m* rubbish chute

vider empty (out); F *personne* throw out; *cuis volaille* draw; *salle* vacate, leave; *se ~* empty; **videur** *m* F bouncer

vie *f* life; *moyens matériels* living; *à ~* for life; *être en ~* be alive; *coût de la ~* cost of living; *gagner sa ~* earn one's living

vieil → *vieux*

vieillard *m* old man; *les ~s* old people *pl*, the elderly *pl*

vieille → *vieux*

vieillesse *f* old age

vieillir 1 *v/t*: *~ qn* make s.o. older 2 *v/i d'une personne* get old, age; *d'un visage* age; *d'une théorie, d'un livre* become dated; *d'un vin* age, mature

viennoiseries *fpl croissants and similar types of bread*

vierge 1 *f* virgin; *Vierge* ASTROL Virgo 2 *adj* virgin; *feuille* blank

Viêt-nam: *le ~* Vietnam; **vietnamien, ~ne** 1 *adj* Vietnamese 2 *m langue* Vietnamese; **Vietnamien, ~ne** *m/f* Vietnamese

vieux, (*m vieil before a vowel or silent h*), **vieille** (*f*) 1 *adj* old 2 *m/f* old man/old woman; *les ~* old people *pl*, the aged *pl*

vif, vive 1 *adj* lively; (*en vie*) alive; *plaisir, satisfaction* great; *critique, douleur* sharp; *air* bracing; *froid* biting; *couleur* bright 2 *m à ~ plaie* open; *piqué au ~* cut to the quick; *le ~ du sujet* the heart of the matter; *avoir les nerfs à ~* be on edge

vigilance *f* vigilance; **vigilant** vigilant

vigile *m* (*gardien*) security man, guard

vigne *f* (*arbrisseau*) vine; (*plantation*) vineyard

vigneron, ~ne *m/f* wine grower

vignoble *m* plantation vineyard; *région* wine-growing area

vigoureux, -euse robust, vigorous; **vigueur** *f* vigor, *Br* vigour, robustness; *entrer en ~* come into force

V.I.H. *m* (= *Virus de l'Immunodéficience Humaine*) HIV (= human immunodeficiency virus)

vilain nasty; *enfant* naughty; (*laid*) ugly

villa *f* villa

village *m* village; **villageois, ~e** 1 *adj* village *atr* 2 *m/f* villager

ville *f* town; *grande city*; *aller en ~* go into town

vin *m* wine; *~ d'honneur* reception; *~ de pays* regional wine

vinaigre *m* vinegar

vinaigrette *f* salad dressing

vingt twenty; **vingtaine**: *une*

~ de personnes about twenty people *pl*; **vingtième** twentieth

viol *m* rape; *d'un lieu saint* violation; **violation** *f d'un traité* violation; *d'une église* desecration

violemment violently; *fig* intensely; **violence** *f* violence; *fig* intensity; **violent** violent; *fig* intense

violer *loi* break, *sexuellement* rape; *(profaner)* desecrate

violet, ~te *adj* violet

violette *f* BOT violet

violon *m* violin; *musicien* violinist

violoncelle *m* cello

virage *m de la route* curve, corner; *d'un véhicule* turn; *fig* change of direction; **virement** *m* COMM transfer; **virer 1** *v/i (changer de couleur)* change color *ou Br* colour; *d'un véhicule* corner **2** *v/t argent* transfer; **~ qn** F kick s.o. out

virginité *f* virginity

virgule *f* comma

viril male; *(courageux)* manly; **virilité** *f* manhood; *(vigueur sexuelle)* virility

virtuel, ~le *adj* virtual; *(possible)* potential

virulent virulent

virus *m* MÉD, INFORM virus

vis *f* screw; **escalier** *m* **à ~** spiral staircase

visa *m* visa

visage *m* face

vis-à-vis 1 *prép*: **~ de** opposite; *(envers)* toward, *Br* towards; *(en comparaison de)* compared with **2** *m* person sitting opposite; *(rencontre)* face-to-face meeting

viser 1 *v/t* aim at; *(s'adresser à)* be aimed at **2** *v/i* aim *(à at)*; **~ à faire** aim to do

viseur *m d'une arme* sights *pl*; PHOT viewfinder

visibilité *f* visibility; **visible** visible; *(évident)* clear

vision *f* sight; *(conception, apparition)* vision; **visionnaire** *m/f* & *adj* visionary

visite *f* visit; *d'une ville* tour; **rendre ~ à qn** visit s.o.; **avoir droit de ~** *d'un parent divorcé* have access; **~ de douane** customs inspection; **~ médicale** medical (examination); **visiter** visit; *(faire le tour de)* tour; *bagages* inspect; **visiteur, -euse** *m/f* visitor

vison *m* mink

visqueux, -euse viscous; *péj* slimy

visser screw

visuel, ~le visual; **champ** *m* **~** field of vision

vital vital; **vitalité** *f* vitality

vitamine *f* vitamin

vite fast, quickly; *(sous peu, bientôt)* soon; **~!** quick!; **vitesse** *f* speed; AUTO gear; **à toute ~** at top speed

viticulture *f* wine-growing

vitrage *m cloison* glass partition; *action* glazing; *ensem-*

ble de vitres windows *pl*

vitrail *m* stained-glass window

vitre *f* window (pane); *de voiture* window; **vitrer** glaze; **vitrier** *m* glazier

vitrine *f* (*étalage*) (store) window; *meuble* display cabinet

vivace hardy; *haine, amour* lasting; **vivacité** *f* liveliness, vivacity

vivant 1 *adj* alive; (*plein de vie*) lively; (*doué de vie*) living; *langue* modern **2** *m* living person; *de son ~* in his lifetime

vivement (*d'un ton vif*) sharply; (*vite*) briskly; *ému, touché* deeply

vivoter just get by

vivre **1** *v/i* live **2** *v/t* experience **3** *mpl: ~s* supplies

vocabulaire *m* vocabulary

vociférer shout

vodka *f* vodka

vœu *m* REL vow; (*souhait*) wish; *tous mes ~x!* best wishes!

voici here is *sg*, here are *pl*; *me ~!* here I am!; *le livre que ~* this book

voie *f* way; *de chemin de fer* track; *d'autoroute* lane; *en ~ de développement* developing; *être en ~ de guérison* be on the mend; *par ~ aérienne* by air; *par la ~ hiérarchique* through channels; *~ d'eau* leak; *~ express* expressway

voilà there is *sg*, there are *pl*; (*et*) *~!* there you are!; *en ~ assez!* that's enough!; *~ tout* that's all

voile 1 *m* veil **2** *f* MAR sail; SP sailing

voiler[1] *v/t* veil; *se ~ d'une femme* wear the veil; *du ciel* cloud over

voiler[2]: *se ~ du bois* warp; *d'une roue* buckle

voir see; *faire ~* show; *se ~* see each other; *cela se voit* that's obvious; *je ne peux pas le ~* I can't stand him

voisin, ~e 1 *adj* neighboring, *Br* neighbouring; (*similaire*) similar **2** *m/f* neighbor, *Br* neighbour; **voisinage** *m* neighborhood, *Br* neighbourhood; (*proximité*) vicinity

voiture *f* car; *d'un train* car, *Br* carriage; *en ~* by car; *~ de fonction* company car

voix *f* voice (*aussi* GRAM); POL vote; *à haute ~* in a loud voice, aloud; *à basse ~* in a low voice, quietly

vol[1] *m* theft; *~ à main armée* armed robbery

vol[2] *m* flight; *à ~ d'oiseau* as the crow flies; *au ~* in flight; *~ à voile* gliding

volaille *f* poultry; (*poulet etc*) bird

volant *m* AUTO (steering) wheel; SP shuttlecock; *d'un vêtement* flounce

volcan *m* volcano

volée f d'oiseaux flock; en tennis, de coups de feu volley; **à la ~** in mid-air

voler¹ v/t steal; **~ qch à qn** steal sth from s.o.

voler² v/i fly

volet m de fenêtre shutter; fig part; **trier sur le ~** fig handpick

voleur, -euse 1 adj thieving 2 m/f thief; **~ à l'étalage** shoplifter

volontaire 1 adj voluntary; (délibéré) deliberate; (décidé) headstrong 2 m/f volunteer

volonté f will; (souhait) wish; (fermeté) willpower; **de l'eau à ~** as much water as you like; **faire preuve de bonne ~** show willing

volontiers willingly, with pleasure

volt m ÉL volt; **voltage** m ÉL voltage

volte-face f about-turn (aussi fig)

volubilité f volubility

volume m volume; **volumineux, -euse** bulky

voluptueux, -euse voluptuous

vomir 1 v/i vomit, throw up 2 v/t bring up; fig spew out; **vomissement** m vomiting

vorace voracious

vos → votre

vote m vote; action voting; **voter** 1 v/i vote 2 v/t loi pass

votre, pl **vos** your

vôtre: le/la ~, les ~s yours

vouer dedicate (à to); **se ~ à** fig dedicate o.s. to

vouloir want; **il veut que tu partes** (subj) he wants you to leave; **je voudrais** I would like, I'd like; **je veux bien** I'd like to; **veuillez ne pas fumer** please do not smoke; **~ dire** mean; **en ~ à qn** have something against s.o.; **veux-tu te taire!** will you shut up!

voulu requisite; délibéré deliberate

vous sg et pl you; complément d'objet indirect, sg et pl (to) you; avec verbe pronominal yourself; pl yourselves; **~ ~ êtes coupé** you've cut yourself; **si ~ ~ levez à …** if you get up at …

vous-même, pl **vous-mêmes** yourself; pl yourselves

voûte f ARCH vault; **voûté** personne hunched; dos bent; ARCH vaulted

vouvoyer adress as 'vous'

voyage m trip, journey; en paquebot voyage; **~ d'affaires** business trip; **~ de noces** honeymoon; **~ organisé** package holiday; **voyager** travel; **voyageur, -euse** m/f traveler, Br traveller; par train, avion passenger; **~ de commerce** traveling ou Br travelling salesman

voyant, ~e 1 adj couleur garish 2 m (signal) light; 3 m/f

(*devin*) clairvoyant
voyelle *f* GRAM vowel
voyou *m* jeune lout
vrac *m*: **en** ~ COMM loose; *fig* jumbled together
vrai 1 *adj* (*après le subst*) true; (*devant le subst*) real, genuine; *ami* true **2** *m*: **à** ~ **dire, à dire** ~ to tell the truth; **vraiment** really
vraisemblable likely, probable; **vraisemblance** *f* likelihood, probability
vrombir throb

VTT *m* (= **vélo tout terrain**) mountain bike
vu in view of
vue *f* view; *sens, faculté* sight; **à première** ~ at first sight; **connaître qn de** ~ know s.o. by sight; **avoir la** ~ **basse** be shortsighted; **point** *m* **de** ~ viewpoint, point of view; **en** ~ **de faire** with a view to doing
vulgaire (*banal*) common; (*grossier*) common, vulgar
vulnérable vulnerable

W

wagon *m* car, *Br* carriage; *de marchandises* car, *Br* wagon; **wagon-lit** *m* sleeping car; **wagon-restaurant** *m* dining car
walkman *m* Walkman®

watt *m* ÉL watt
W.-C. *mpl* WC *sg*
week-end *m* weekend; **ce** ~ on the weekend
whisky *m* whiskey, *Br* whisky

X, Y

xénophobe xenophobic; **xénophobie** *f* xenophobia
xérès *m* sherry
y there; **on** ~ **va!** let's go!; **ça** ~ **est!** that's it!; **j'** ~ **suis** (*je comprends*) now I get it; ~

compris including; **j'** ~ **travaille** I'm working on it
yacht *m* yacht; **yachting** *m* yachting
yaourt *m* yoghurt
yeux *pl* → **œil**

Z

zapper channel-hop, *Br aussi* zap

zèbre *m* zebra

zèle *m* zeal; *faire du* ~ be overzealous; **zélé** zealous

zéro 1 *m* zero, *Br aussi* nought; SP *Br* nil; *fig* nonentity **2** *adj*: ~ *faute* no mistakes; *partir de* ~ start from nothing

zeste *m* peel, zest

zézayer lisp

zigouiller F bump off F

zigzag *m* zigzag; **zigzaguer** zigzag

zinc *m* zinc

zona *m* shingles *sg*

zone *f* area, zone; *péj* slums *pl*; ~ *euro* euro zone; ~ *industrielle* industrial park, *Br* industrial estate; ~ *interdite* prohibited area

zoo *m* zoo

zoologie *f* zoology; **zoologiste** *m/f* zoologist

zut! F blast!

English – French
Anglais – Français

A

a [ə] un(e)

abandon [ə'bændən] abandonner

abbreviate [ə'briːvɪeɪt] abréger; **abbreviation** abréviation *f*

abduct [əb'dʌkt] enlever

ability [ə'bɪlətɪ] capacité *f*; *skill* faculté *f*

able ['eɪbl] (*skillful*) compétent; **be ~ to do** pouvoir faire

abnormal [æb'nɔːrml] anormal

aboard [ə'bɔːrd] à bord

abolish [ə'bɑːlɪʃ] abolir; **abolition** abolition *f*

abort [ə'bɔːrt] suspendre; **abortion** MED avortement *m*; **have an ~** se faire avorter; **abortive** avorté

about [ə'baʊt] **1** *prep* (*concerning*) à propos de; *a book* **~** un livre sur; *talk* **~** parler de; *what's it* **~?** *of book, movie* de quoi ça parle? **2** *adv* (*roughly*) à peu près; **~** *noon* aux alentours de midi; **be ~ to do** (*be going to*) être sur le point de faire

above [ə'bʌv] au-dessus de; **on the floor ~** à l'étage du dessus

abrasive [ə'breɪsɪv] *personality* abrupt

abreast [ə'brest]: **three ~** les trois l'un à côté de l'autre; **keep ~ of** se tenir au courant de

abridge [ə'brɪdʒ] abréger

abroad [ə'brɔːd] à l'étranger

abrupt [ə'brʌpt] brusque

abscess ['æbsɪs] abcès *m*

absence ['æbsəns] absence *f*; **absent** absent; **absentee** absent(e) *m(f)*; **absenteeism** absentéisme *m*; **absent-minded** distrait

absolute ['æbsəluːt] absolu; **absolution** REL absolution *f*; **absolve** absoudre

absorb [əb'sɔːrb] absorber; **absorbent** absorbant; **absorbent cotton** coton *m* hydrophile; **absorbing** absorbant

abstain [əb'steɪn] *in vote* s'abstenir; **abstention** *in vote* abstention *f*

abstract ['æbstrækt] abstrait

absurd [əb'sɜːrd] absurde; **absurdity** absurdité *f*

abundance [ə'bʌndəns] abondance *f*; **abundant** abondant

abuse[1] [ə'bju:s] n verbal insultes fpl; physical violences fpl physiques; sexual sévices mpl sexuels; of power etc abus m

abuse[2] [ə'bju:z] v/t verbally insulter; physically maltraiter; sexually faire subir des sévices sexuels à; power etc abuser de

abysmal [ə'bɪzml] (very bad) lamentable

academic [ækə'demɪk] 1 n universitaire m/f 2 adj year: at school scolaire; at university universitaire; interests intellectuel; **academy** académie f

accelerate [ək'seləreɪt] accélérer; **acceleration** accélération f; **accelerator** accélérateur m

accent ['æksənt] accent m; **accentuate** accentuer

accept [ək'sept] accepter; **acceptable** acceptable; **acceptance** acceptation f

access ['ækses] 1 n accès m 2 v/t also COMPUT accéder à; **accessible** accessible

accessory [ək'sesərɪ] for wearing accessoire m; LAW complice m/f

accident ['æksɪdənt] accident m; by ~ par hasard; **accidental** accidentel; **accidentally** accidentellement

acclimate, **acclimatize** [ə'klaɪmət, ə'klaɪmətaɪz] s'acclimater

accommodate [ə'kɑ:mədeɪt] loger; needs s'adapter à; **accommodations** logement m

accompaniment [ə'kʌmpənɪmənt] MUS accompagnement m; **accompany** also MUS accompagner

accomplice [ə'kʌmplɪs] complice m/f

accomplished [ə'kʌmplɪʃt] accompli; **accomplishment** of task accomplissement m; (achievement) réussite f; (talent) talent m

accord [ə'kɔːrd] accord m; of one's own ~ de son plein gré

accordance [ə'kɔːrdəns]: in ~ with conformément à

according [ə'kɔːrdɪŋ]: ~ to selon; **accordingly** (consequently) par conséquent; (appropriately) en conséquence

account [ə'kaʊnt] financial compte m; (report) récit m; give an ~ of faire le récit de; on no ~ en aucun cas; on ~ of en raison de; take ... into ~ tenir compte de; **accountable**: be held ~ être tenu responsable; **accountant** comptable m/f; **accounts** comptabilité f

accumulate [ə'kjuːmjʊleɪt] 1 v/t accumuler 2 v/i s'accumuler; **accumulation** accumulation f

accuracy ['ækjʊrəsɪ] justesse f; **accurate** juste; **accurately** avec justesse

accusation [ækjuːˈzeɪʃn] accusation *f*; **accuse**: *~ s.o. of doing sth* accuser qn de faire qch; **accused** LAW accusé(e) *m(f)*; **accusing** accusateur

accustom [əˈkʌstəm]: *get ~ed to* s'accoutumer à

ace [eɪs] *in cards* as *m*; *tennis shot* ace *m*

ache [eɪk] **1** *n* douleur *f* **2** *v/i*: *my arm ~s* j'ai mal au bras

achieve [əˈtʃiːv] accomplir; **achievement** (*thing achieved*) accomplissement *m*; *of ambition* réalisation *f*

acid [ˈæsɪd] acide *m*

acknowledge [əkˈnɒlɪdʒ] reconnaître; *~ receipt of* accuser réception de; **acknowledg(e)ment** reconnaissance *f*; *of a letter* accusé *m* de réception

acoustics [əˈkuːstɪks] acoustique *f*

acquaint [əˈkweɪnt]: *be ~ed with* connaître; **acquaintance** *person* connaissance *f*

acquire [əˈkwaɪr] acquérir; **acquisition** acquisition *f*

acquit [əˈkwɪt] LAW acquitter; **acquittal** LAW acquittement *m*

acre [ˈeɪkər] acre *m* (4.047m²)

across [əˈkrɔːs] **1** *prep* de l'autre côté de; *walk ~ the street* traverser la rue; *~ Europe* all over dans toute l'Europe; *~ from* en face de **2** *adv*: *swim ~* traverser à la na-

ge; *10m ~* 10 m de large

act [ækt] **1** *v/i* (*take action*) agir; THEA faire du théâtre **2** *n* (*deed*) fait *m*; *of play* acte *m*; *in vaudeville* numéro *m*; (*law*) loi *f*

action [ˈækʃn] action *f*; *take ~* prendre des mesures

active [ˈæktɪv] actif *f*; **activist** POL activiste *m/f*; **activity** activité *f*

actor [ˈæktər] acteur *m*

actress [ˈæktrɪs] actrice *f*

actual [ˈæktʃuəl] véritable; **actually** [ˈæktʃuəlɪ] en fait; *expressing surprise* vraiment

acute [əˈkjuːt] *pain* intense; *sense* très développé

AD [eɪˈdiː] (= *anno domini*) apr. J.-C. (= après Jésus Christ)

ad [æd] → **advertisement**

adamant [ˈædəmənt]: *be ~ that ...* soutenir catégoriquement que ...

adapt [əˈdæpt] **1** *v/t* adapter **2** *v/i* of person s'adapter; **adaptability** faculté *f* d'adaptation; **adaptable** adaptable; **adaptation** *of play etc* adaptation *f*; **adapter** ELEC adaptateur *m*

add [æd] **1** *v/t* ajouter; MATH additionner **2** *v/i* of person faire des additions

◆ **add on** 15% etc ajouter

◆ **add up 1** *v/t* additionner **2** *v/i* avoir du sens

addict [ˈædɪkt] (*drug ~*) drogué(e) *m(f)*; *of TV program* *etc* accro *m/f*; **addicted** *to drugs* drogué; *to TV program etc* accro F; **addiction** *to drugs* dépendance *f* (**to** de); **addictive**: *be* ~ entraîner une dépendance

addition [ə'dɪʃn] MATH addition *f*; *to list* ajout *m*; *to company* recrue *f*; **in** ~ **to** en plus de; **additional** supplémentaire; **additive** additif *m*; **add-on** accessoire *m*

address [ə'dres] **1** *n* adresse *f* **2** *v/t letter* adresser; *audience* s'adresser à; **addressee** destinataire *m/f*

adequate ['ædɪkwət] (*sufficient*) suffisant; (*satisfactory*) satisfaisant; **adequately** suffisamment

◆ **adhere to** [əd'hɪr] adhérer à

adhesive [əd'hiːsɪv] adhésif *m*

adjacent [ə'dʒeɪsnt] adjacent *m*

adjective ['ædʒɪktɪv] adjectif *m*

adjoining [ə'dʒɔɪnɪŋ] attenant

adjourn [ə'dʒɜːrn] ajourner; **adjournment** ajournement *m*

adjust [ə'dʒʌst] ajuster; **adjustable** ajustable; **adjustment** ajustement *m*

ad lib [æd'lɪb] **1** *adj* improvisé **2** *v/i* improviser

administer [əd'mɪnɪstər] *country* administrer; **administration** administration *f*;

(*administrative work*) tâches *fpl* administratives; **administrative** administratif; **administrator** administrateur(-trice) *m(f)*

admirable ['ædmərəbl] admirable; **admiration** admiration *f*; **admire** admirer; **admirer** admirateur(-trice) *m(f)*; **admiring** admiratif; **admiringly** admirativement

admissible [əd'mɪsəbl] admis; **admission** (*confession*) aveu *m*; ~ **free** entrée *f* gratuite; **admit** *to a place*, (*accept*) admettre; (*confess*) avouer; **admittance**: **no** ~ entrée *f* interdite

adolescence [ædə'lesns] adolescence *f*; **adolescent 1** *adj* adolescent **2** *n* adolescent(e) *m(f)*

adopt [ə'dɑːpt] adopter; **adoption** adoption *f*

adorable [ə'dɔːrəbl] adorable; **adoration** adoration *f*; **adore** adorer

adrenalin [ə'drenəlɪn] adrénaline *f*

adult ['ædʌlt] **1** *adj* adulte **2** *n* adulte *m/f*; **adultery** adultère *m*

advance [əd'væns] **1** *n money* avance *f*; *in science etc* avancée *f*; MIL progression *f*; **in** ~ à l'avance; **payment in** ~ paiement *m* anticipé; **make** ~**s** (*progress*) faire des progrès; *sexually* faire des avances **2** *v/i* MIL, (*make progress*) avancer **3** *v/t theory, sum of money* avancer; *human knowledge, cause* faire avancer; **advanced** avancé

advantage [əd'vɑːntɪdʒ] avantage *m*; **take ~ of** *opportunity* profiter de; **advantageous** avantageux

adventure [əd'ventʃər] aventure *f*; **adventurous** aventureux

adverb ['ædvɜːrb] adverbe *m*

adversary ['ædvərsəri] adversaire *m/f*

adverse ['ædvɜːrs] adverse

advertise ['ædvərtaɪz] *product* faire de la publicité pour; *job* mettre une annonce pour; **advertisement** *for product* publicité *f*, pub *f*; *for job* annonce *f*; **advertiser** annonceur(-euse) *m(f)*; **advertising** publicité *f*

advice [əd'vaɪs] conseils *mpl*; **a bit of ~** un conseil; **advisable** conseillé; **advise** conseiller

advocate ['ædvəkeɪt] recommander

aerial ['eriəl] *Br* antenne *f*; **aerial photograph** photographie *f* aérienne

aerobics [e'roubɪks] aérobic *m*

aerodynamic [eroudaɪ'næmɪk] aérodynamique

aeroplane ['eroupleɪn] avion *m*

aerosol ['erəsɑːl] aérosol *m*

aesthetic *etc* → **esthetic** *etc*

affair [ə'fer] *(matter)* affaire *f*; *(love ~)* liaison *f*

affection [ə'fekʃn] affection *f*; **affectionate** affectueux; **affectionately** affectueusement

affirmative [ə'fɜːrmətɪv] affirmatif

affluence ['æfluəns] richesse *f*; **affluent** riche

afford [ə'fɔːrd]: **be able to ~ sth financially** pouvoir se permettre d'acheter qch

afloat [ə'flout] *boat* sur l'eau

afraid [ə'freɪd]: **be ~** avoir peur (**of** de); **I'm ~** *expressing regret* je crains

afresh [ə'freʃ]: **start ~** recommencer

Africa ['æfrɪkə] Afrique *f*

African ['æfrɪkən] **1** *adj* africain **2** *n* Africain(e) *m(f)*; **African-American 1** *adj* africain-américain(e) **2** *n* Afro-Américain(e) *m(f)*

after ['æftər] **1** *prep* après; **it's ten ~ two** il est deux heures dix **2** *adv (afterward)* après; **the day ~** le lendemain

afternoon [æftər'nuːn] après-midi *m*; **in the ~** l'après-midi; **this ~** cet après-midi; **good ~** bonjour

'after sales service service *m* après-vente; **aftershave** lotion *f* après-rasage; **afterward** ensuite

again [ə'geɪn] encore; **I never saw him ~** je ne l'ai jamais revu

against [əˈgenst] contre

age [eɪdʒ] âge *m*; **she's five years of ~** elle a cinq ans; **aged**: **~ 16** âgé de 16 ans; **age group** catégorie *f* d'âge; **age limit** limite *f* d'âge

agency [ˈeɪdʒənsɪ] agence *f*

agenda [əˈdʒendə] ordre *m* du jour

agent [ˈeɪdʒənt] COM agent *m*

aggravate [ˈægrəveɪt] faire empirer; (*annoy*) agacer

aggression [əˈgreʃn] agression *f*; **aggressive** agressif; **aggressively** agressivement

aghast [əˈgæst] horrifié

agile [ˈædʒəl] agile; **agility** agilité *f*

agitated [ˈædʒɪteɪtɪd] agité; **agitation** agitation *f*; **agitator** agitateur(-trice) *m(f)*

agnostic [ægˈnɒstɪk] agnostique *m/f*

ago [əˈgəʊ]: **two days ~** il y a deux jours; **long ~** il y a longtemps

agonize [ˈægənaɪz] se tourmenter (**over** sur); **agonizing** terrible; **agony** [ˈægənɪ] *mental* tourment *m*; *physical* grande douleur *f*

agree [əˈgriː] **1** *v/i* être d'accord; *of figures* s'accorder; (*reach agreement*) s'entendre **2** *v/t* **price** s'entendre sur; **agreeable** (*pleasant*) agréable; **agreement** accord *m*

agricultural [ægrɪˈkʌltʃərəl] agricole; **agriculture** agriculture *f*

ahead [əˈhed] devant; **plan/think ~** prévoir/penser à l'avance

aid [eɪd] **1** *n* aide *f* **2** *v/t* aider

aide [eɪd] aide *m/f*

Aids [eɪdz] sida *m*

ailing [ˈeɪlɪŋ] *economy* mal en point

ailment [ˈeɪlmənt] mal *m*

aim [eɪm] **1** *n* (*objective*) but *m* **2** *v/i in shooting* viser; **~ to do sth** essayer de faire qch **3** *v/t*: **be ~ed at** *of remark* viser; *of gun* être pointé sur; **aimless** [ˈeɪmlɪs] sans but

air [er] **1** *n* air *m*; **by ~** par avion; **in the open ~** en plein air **2** *v/t room* aérer; *views* exprimer; **airbag** airbag *m*; **air-conditioned** climatisé; **air-conditioning** climatisation *f*; **aircraft** avion *m*; **aircraft carrier** porte-avions *m inv*; **air force** armée *f* de l'air; **air hostess** hôtesse *f* de l'air; **airline** compagnie *f* aérienne; **airliner** avion *m* de ligne; **airmail**: **by ~** par avion; **airplane** avion *m*; **airport** aéroport *m*; **air terminal** aérogare *f*; **air-traffic controller** contrôleur(-euse) aérien(ne) *m(f)*

aisle [aɪl] *in airplane* couloir *m*; *in theater* allée *f*

ajar [əˈdʒɑːr]: **be ~** être entrouvert

alarm [əˈlɑːrm] **1** *n* (*fear*) inquiétude *f*; *device* alarme *f*;

(~ *clock*) réveil *m* **2** *v/t* alarmer; **alarming** alarmant; **alarmingly** de manière alarmante

album ['ælbəm] album *m*

alcohol ['ælkəhɒl] alcool *m*; **alcoholic 1** *adj drink* alcoolisé **2** *n* alcoolique *m/f*

alert [ə'lɜːrt] **1** *adj* vigilant **2** *n signal* alerte *f* **3** *v/t* alerter

alibi ['ælɪbaɪ] alibi *m*

alien ['eɪlɪən] **1** *adj* étranger (**to** à) **2** *n* étranger(-ère) *m(f)*; *from space* extra-terrestre *m/f*; **alienate** s'aliéner

align [ə'laɪn] aligner

alike [ə'laɪk] **1** *adj*: **be ~** se ressembler **2** *adv*: **old and young ~** les vieux comme les jeunes

alimony ['ælɪmənɪ] pension alimentaire

alive [ə'laɪv]: **be ~** être en vie

all [ɔːl] **1** *adj* tout **2** *pron* tout; **~ of us/them** nous/eux tous; **he ate ~ of it** il l'a mangé en entier; **for ~ I know** pour autant que je sache; **~ but him** (*except*) tous sauf lui **3** *adv*: **~ at once** (*suddenly*) tout d'un coup; (*at the same time*) tous ensemble; **~ but** (*nearly*) presque; **the better** encore mieux; **they're not at ~ alike** ils ne se ressemblent pas du tout; **not at ~!** pas du tout!; **two ~** *SP* deux à deux

allegation [ælɪ'geɪʃn] allégation *f*; **allege** alléguer; **alleged** supposé; **allegedly**

he ~ killed two women il aurait assassiné deux femmes

allegiance [ə'liːdʒəns] loyauté *f* (**to** à)

allergic [ə'lɜːrdʒɪk] allergique (**to** à)

alleviate [ə'liːvɪeɪt] soulager

alley ['ælɪ] ruelle *f*

alliance [ə'laɪəns] alliance *f*

allocate ['æləkeɪt] assigner; **allocation** [æləˈkeɪʃn] *action* assignation *f*; *amount allocated* part *f*

allot [ə'lɑːt] assigner

allow [ə'laʊ] (*permit*) permettre; (*calculate*) compter

♦ **allow for** prendre en compte

allowance [ə'laʊəns] *money* allocation *f*; (*pocket money*) argent *m* de poche

alloy ['ælɔɪ] alliage *m*

'**all-purpose** universel; *vehicle* tous usages; **all-round** général; *athlete* complet

♦ **allude to** [ə'luːd] faire allusion à

alluring [ə'luːrɪŋ] alléchant

all-wheel 'drive quatre roues motrices *fpl*; *vehicle* 4x4 *m*

ally ['ælaɪ] allié(e) *m(f)*

almond ['ɑːmənd] amande *f*

almost ['ɒːlməʊst] presque

alone [ə'ləʊn] seul

along [ə'lɒŋ] **1** *prep* le long de; **walk ~ this path** prenez ce chemin **2** *adv*: **bring ~** amener; **~ with** *in addition to* ainsi que

alongside [əlɒːŋ'saɪd] paral-

lel to à côté de; *in coopera-*
tion with aux côtés de
aloof [əˈluːf] distant
aloud [əˈlaʊd] à haute voix
alphabet [ˈælfəbət] alphabet
m; **alphabetical** alphabéti-
que
already [ɔːlˈredɪ] déjà
alright [ɔːlˈraɪt] (*permitted*)
permis; (*acceptable*) convenable; **be ~** (*in working order*) fonctionner; **she's ~**
not hurt elle n'est pas blessée; **everything is ~** tout va
bien
altar [ˈɔːltər] autel *m*
alter [ˈɔːltər] modifier; *person*
changer; **alteration** modification *f*
alternate 1 [ˈɔːltərneɪt] *v/i* alterner **2** [ˈɔːltərnət] *adj*: **on ~**
Mondays un lundi sur deux
alternative [ɔːlˈtɜːrnətɪv] **1**
adj alternatif **2** *n* alternative
f; **alternatively** sinon; **or ~** ou
bien
although [ɔːlˈðoʊ] bien que
(+*subj*), quoique (+*subj*)
altitude [ˈæltɪtuːd] altitude *f*
altogether [ɔːltəˈgeðər]
(*completely*) totalement; (*in
all*) en tout
altruism [ˈæltruːɪzm] altruisme *m*; **altruistic** altruiste
aluminum [əˈluːmənəm] aluminium [æljʊˈmɪnɪəm] alu-
minium *m*
always [ˈɔːlweɪz] toujours
a.m. [ˈeɪem] (= *ante meridi-*
em) du matin

amass [əˈmæs] amasser
amateur [ˈæmətər] *sp* amateur *m/f*; **amateurish** *at-*
tempt d'amateur; *painter*
sans talent
amaze [əˈmeɪz] étonner;
amazed étonné; **amaze-**
ment étonnement *m*;
amazing étonnant; (*very*
good) impressionnant;
amazingly étonnamment
ambassador [æmˈbæsədər]
ambassadeur(-drice) *m(f)*
amber [ˈæmbər]: **at ~** à l'orange
ambience [ˈæmbɪəns] ambiance *f*
ambiguity [æmbɪˈɡjuːɪtɪ]
ambiguïté *f*; **ambiguous**
ambigu
ambition [æmˈbɪʃn] ambition
f; **ambitious** ambitieux
ambivalent [æmˈbɪvələnt]
ambivalent
amble [ˈæmbl] déambuler
ambulance [ˈæmbjʊləns] ambulance *f*
ambush [ˈæmbʊʃ] **1** *n* embus-
cade *f* **2** *v/t* tendre une em-
buscade à
amend [əˈmend] modifier;
amendment modification *f*;
amends: **make ~** se racheter
amenities [əˈmiːnətɪz] facili-
tés *fpl*
America [əˈmerɪkə] (*United*
States) États-Unis *mpl*; *continent* Amérique *f*; **American**
1 *adj* américain **2** *n* Améri-
cain(e) *m(f)*

amicable ['æmɪkəbl] à l'amiable; amicably à l'amiable

ammunition [æmjʊ'nɪʃn] munitions *fpl*

amnesia [æm'ni:zɪə] amnésie *f*

amnesty ['æmnəstɪ] amnistie *f*

among(st) [ə'mʌŋ(st)] parmi

amoral [eɪ'mɔːrəl] amoral

amount [ə'maʊnt] quantité *f*; (*sum of money*) somme *f*
◆ amount to s'élever à; (*be equivalent to*) revenir à

amphibian [æm'fɪbɪən] amphibien *m*

ample ['æmpl] beaucoup de

amplifier ['æmplɪfaɪr] amplificateur *m*; amplify amplifier

amputate ['æmpjʊteɪt] amputer; amputation amputation *f*

amuse [ə'mju:z] (*make laugh*) amuser; (*entertain*) distraire; amusement (*merriment*) amusement *m*; (*entertainment*) divertissement *m*; amusement park parc *m* d'attractions; amusing amusant

an [æn] → *a*

anaemia *etc* → *anemia* *etc*

anaesthetic *etc* → *anesthetic* *etc*

analog ['ænəlɒg] analogique; analogy analogie *f*

analysis [ə'næləsɪs] PSYCH analyse *f*; analyst PSYCH analyste *m/f*; analytical analytique; analyze *also* PSYCH ana-

lyser

anarchy ['ænəkɪ] anarchie *f*

ancestor ['ænsestər] ancêtre *m/f*

anchor ['æŋkər] **1** *n* NAUT ancre *f*; TV présentateur(-trice) principal(e) *m(f)* **2** *v/i* NAUT ancrer

ancient ['eɪnʃənt] ancien; *Rome etc* antique

and [ænd] et

anemia [ə'ni:mɪə] anémie *f*; anemic anémique

anesthetic [ænəs'θetɪk] anesthésiant *m*

angel ['eɪndʒl] ange *m*

anger ['æŋgər] **1** *n* colère *f* **2** *v/t* mettre en colère

angle ['æŋgl] angle *m*

angry ['æŋgrɪ] *person* en colère; *mood, look* fâché

animal ['ænɪml] animal *m*

animated ['ænɪmeɪtɪd] animé; animated cartoon dessin *m* animé; animation animation *f*

animosity [ænɪ'mɒsətɪ] animosité *f*

ankle ['æŋkl] cheville *f*

annex ['æneks] **1** *n* annexe *f* **2** *v/t state* annexer

annihilate [ə'naɪəleɪt] anéantir; annihilation anéantissement *m*

anniversary [ænɪ'vɜːrsərɪ] anniversaire *m*

announce [ə'naʊns] annoncer; announcement annonce *f*; announcer [ə'naʊnsər] TV, RAD speaker *m*, speakrine

f

annoy [ə'nɔɪ] agacer; **annoyance** (anger) agacement m;
(nuisance) désagrément m;
annoying agaçant

annual ['ænuəl] annuel

annul [ə'nʌl] annuler; **annulment** annulation f

anonymous [ə'nɑːnɪməs]
anonyme

anorexia [ænə'reksɪə] anorexie f

another [ə'nʌðər] **1** adj autre
2 pron un(e) autre m(f); **they
know one ~** ils se connaissent

answer ['ænsər] **1** n réponse
f; (solution) solution f (to
à); **2** v/t répondre à **3** v/i répondre; **answerphone** répondeur m

ant [ænt] fourmi f

antagonism [æn'tægənɪzm]
antagonisme m; **antagonistic** hostile; **antagonize** provoquer

Antarctic [æn'tɑːrktɪk]: **the ~**
l'Antarctique m

antenatal [æntɪ'neɪtl] prénatal

antenna [æn'tenə] antenne f

antibiotic [æntaɪbaɪ'ɑːtɪk]
antibiotique m

anticipate [æn'tɪsɪpeɪt] prévoir; **anticipation** prévision f

antics ['æntɪks] singeries fpl

antidote ['æntɪdoʊt] antidote
m

antifreeze ['æntaɪfriːz] antigel m

antipathy [æn'tɪpəθɪ] antipathie f

antiquated ['æntɪkweɪtɪd]
antique

antique [æn'tiːk] antiquité f

antiseptic [æntaɪ'septɪk] **1**
adj antiseptique **2** n antiseptique m

antisocial [æntaɪ'soʊʃl] asocial, antisocial

antivirus program [æntaɪ
'vaɪrəs] COMPUT programme
m antivirus

anxiety [æŋ'zaɪətɪ] inquiétude f; **anxious** inquiet; (eager) soucieux

any ['enɪ] **1** adj: **are there ~
glasses?** est-ce qu'il y a
des verres?; **is there
bread/improvement?** est-ce
qu'il y a du pain/une amélioration?; **there isn't/aren't ~
...** il n'y a pas de ...; **have
you ~ idea at all?** est-ce
que vous avez une idée? **2**
pron: **do you have ~?** est-
ce que vous en avez?; **there
aren't/isn't ~ left** il n'y en a
plus; **~ of them could be
guilty** ils pourraient tous être
coupables

anybody ['enɪbɑːdɪ] quelqu'un; with negatives personne; no matter who n'importe
qui; **there wasn't ~ there** il
n'y avait personne

anyhow ['enɪhaʊ] (anyway)
enfin; (in any way) de quelque façon que ce soit

anyone ['enɪwʌn] → **anybody**

anything ['enɪθɪŋ] quelque chose; *with negatives* rien; **I didn't hear ~** je n'ai rien entendu **~ but ...** tout sauf ...

anyway ['enɪweɪ] → **anyhow**

anywhere ['enɪweər] quelque part; *with negative* nulle part; **I can't find it ~** je ne le trouve nulle part

apart [ə'pɑːrt] séparé; **~ from** (*except*) à l'exception de; (*in addition to*) en plus de

apartment [ə'pɑːrtmənt] appartement *m*; **apartment block** immeuble *m*

ape [eɪp] singe *m*

aperitif [ə'perɪtiːf] apéritif *m*

apologize [ə'pɑːlədʒaɪz] s'excuser (**to s.o.** auprès de qn); **apology** excuses *fpl*

appalling [ə'pɔːlɪŋ] scandaleux

apparatus [æpə'reɪtəs] appareils *mpl*

apparent [ə'pærənt] (*obvious*) évident; (*seeming*) apparent; **apparently** apparemment

appeal [ə'piːl] (*charm*) charme *m*; *for funds etc*, LAW appel *m*

◆ **appeal for** *calm etc* appeler à; *funds* demander

◆ **appeal to** (*be attractive to*) plaire à

appealing [ə'piːlɪŋ] séduisant

appear [ə'pɪr] apparaître; *in court* comparaître; (*seem*) paraître; **~ to be ...** avoir l'air d'être ...; **appearance**

apparition *f*; *in court* comparution *f*; (*look*) apparence *f*

appendicitis [əpendɪ'saɪtɪs] appendicite *f*

appendix [ə'pendɪks] MED, *of book etc* appendice *m*

appetite ['æpɪtaɪt] appétit *m*; **appetizer** *to drink* apéritif *m*; *to eat* amuse-gueule *m*; **appetizing** appétissant

applaud [ə'plɔːd] applaudir; **applause** applaudissements *mpl*

apple ['æpl] pomme *f*

appliance [ə'plaɪəns] appareil *m*

applicable [ə'plɪkəbl] applicable; **applicant** *for job* candidat(e) *m(f)*; **application** *for job* candidature *f*; *for passport etc* demande *f*; **apply 1** *v/t* appliquer **2** *v/i* of *rule, law* s'appliquer

◆ **apply for** *job* poser sa candidature pour; *passport etc* faire une demande de

◆ **apply to** (*contact*) s'adresser à; *of rules etc* s'appliquer à

appoint [ə'pɔɪnt] *to position* nommer; **appointment** *to position* nomination *f*; (*meeting*) rendez-vous *m*

appraisal [ə'preɪzl] évaluation *f*

appreciable [ə'priːʃəbl] considérable; **appreciate 1** *v/t* apprécier; (*acknowledge*) reconnaître **2** *v/i* FIN s'apprécier; **appreciative** *grateful* reconnaissant; *understanding* approbateur; *audience* réceptif

apprehensive [æprɪˈhensɪv] appréhensif

approach [əˈprəʊtʃ] **1** *n* approche *f* 2 (*proposal*) proposition *f* **2** *v/t* (*get near to*) approcher; (*contact*) faire des propositions à; *problem* aborder; **approachable** *person* d'un abord facile

appropriate [əˈprəʊprɪət] approprié

approval [əˈpruːvl] approbation *f*; **approve 1** *v/i* être d'accord **2** *v/t plan* approuver

approximate [əˈprɒksɪmət] approximatif; **approximately** approximativement

apricot [ˈeɪprɪkɑːt] abricot *m*

April [ˈeɪprəl] avril *m*

apt [æpt] *remark* pertinent; *aptitude* aptitude *f*

aquarium [əˈkweərɪəm] aquarium *m*

Arab [ˈærəb] **1** *adj* arabe **2** *n* Arabe *m/f*; **Arabic 1** *adj* arabe **2** *n* arabe *m*

arbitrary [ˈɑːrbɪtrəri] arbitraire

arbitrate [ˈɑːrbɪtreɪt] arbitrer; **arbitration** arbitrage *m*

arch [ɑːrtʃ] voûte *f*

archaeology *etc* → *archaeology etc*

archaic [ɑːrˈkeɪɪk] archaïque

archeological [ɑːrkɪəˈlɑːdʒɪkl] archéologique; **archeologist** archéologue *m/f*; ar-

cheology archéologie *f*

architect [ˈɑːrkɪtekt] architecte *m/f*; **architectural** architectural; **architecture** architecture *f*

archives [ˈɑːrkaɪvz] archives *fpl*

Arctic [ˈɑːrktɪk]: **the ~** l'Arctique *m*

ardent [ˈɑːrdənt] fervent

arduous [ˈɑːrdjuəs] ardu

area [ˈerɪə] *of city* quartier *m*; *of country* région *f*; *of research* domaine *m*; *of room* surface *f*; GEOM, *of land* superficie *f*; **area code** TELEC indicatif *m* régional

arena [əˈriːnə] SP arène *f*

Argentina [ɑːrdʒənˈtiːnə] Argentine *f*

Argentinian [ɑːrdʒənˈtɪnɪən] **1** *adj* argentin **2** *n* Argentin(e) *m(f)*

arguably [ˈɑːrɡjuəblɪ]: **it was ~ ...** on peut dire que ...; **argue** (*quarrel*) se disputer; (*reason*) argumenter; **argument** (*quarrel*) dispute *f*; (*discussion*) discussion *f*; (*reasoning*) argument *m*

arid [ˈærɪd] *land* aride

arise [əˈraɪz] *of situation* survenir

arithmetic [əˈrɪθmətɪk] arithmétique *f*

arm¹ [ɑːrm] *n* bras *m*

arm² [ɑːrm] *v/t* armer

armaments [ˈɑːrməmənts] armes *fpl*

'armchair fauteuil *m*

armed [ɑːrmd] armé; **armed forces** forces *fpl* armées; **armed robbery** vol *m* à main armée

'armpit aisselle *f*

arms [ɑːrmz] (*weapons*) armes *fpl*

army ['ɑːrmɪ] armée *f*

around [ə'raʊnd] **1** *prep* (*encircling*) autour de; **it's the corner** c'est juste à côté **2** *adv* (*in the area*) dans les parages; (*encircling*) autour; (*roughly*) à peu près; *with expressions of time* à environ

arouse [ə'raʊz] susciter; *sexually* exciter

arrange [ə'reɪndʒ] arranger; *furniture* disposer; *meeting etc* organiser; *time* fixer; *appointment* prendre; **I've d to meet her** j'ai prévu de la voir; **arrangement** (*agreement*), *music* arrangement *m*; *of furniture* disposition *f*; *flowers* composition *f*

arrears [ə'rɪərz] arriéré *m*

arrest [ə'rest] **1** *n* arrestation *f*; **be under** être en état d'arrestation **2** *v/t* arrêter

arrival [ə'raɪvl] arrivée *f*; **arrive** arriver

◆ **arrive at** arriver à

arrogance ['ærəɡəns] arrogance *f*; **arrogant** arrogant

arrow ['ærəʊ] flèche *f*

arson ['ɑːrsn] incendie *m* criminel

art [ɑːrt] art *m*

artery ['ɑːrtərɪ] artère *f*

'art gallery galerie *f* d'art

arthritis [ɑːr'θraɪtɪs] arthrite *f*

artichoke ['ɑːrtɪtʃoʊk] artichaut *m*

article ['ɑːrtɪkl] article *m*

articulate [ɑːr'tɪkjʊlət] *person* qui s'exprime bien

artificial [ɑːrtɪ'fɪʃl] artificiel

artillery [ɑːr'tɪlərɪ] artillerie *f*

artist ['ɑːrtɪst] artiste *m/f*; *artistic* artistique

'arts degree licence *f* de lettres

as [æz] **1** *conj* (*while, when*) alors que; (*because*) comme; (*like*) comme; **if** comme si; **usual** comme d'habitude **2** *adv*: **high** ... aussi haut que ...; **much that?** autant que ça?; **soon possible** aussi vite que possible **3** *prep* comme; **work a teacher** travailler comme professeur; **for** quant à; **from** *or* **of Monday** à partir de lundi

ash [æʃ] cendres *fpl*

ashamed [ə'ʃeɪmd] honteux; **be of** avoir honte de

'ash can poubelle *f*

ashore [ə'ʃɔːr] à terre; **go** débarquer

ashtray ['æʃtreɪ] cendrier *m*

Asia ['eɪʃə] Asie *f*; **Asian 1** *adj* asiatique **2** *n* Asiatique *m/f*; **Asian-American 1** *adj* américain(e) d'origine asiatique **2** *n* Américain(e) *m(f)* d'origine asiatique

aside [ə'saɪd] de côté; **move**

please poussez-vous, s'il vous plaît; **take s.o. ~** prendre qn à part; **~ from** à part

ask [æsk] demander; *question* poser; *(invite)* inviter; **~ s.o. for sth** demander qch à qn
♦ **ask after** *person* demander des nouvelles de
♦ **ask for** demander; *person* demander à parler à
♦ **ask out: he's asked me out** il m'a demandé de sortir avec lui

asleep [ə'sli:p] **be (fast) ~** être (bien) endormi; **fall ~** s'endormir

asparagus [ə'spærəgəs] asperges *fpl*

aspect ['æspekt] aspect *m*

aspirations [æspə'reɪʃnz] aspirations *fpl*

aspirin ['æsprɪn] aspirine *f*

ass[1] [æs] *(idiot)* idiot(e) *m(f)*

ass[2] [æs] *(butt)* cul *m*

assassin [ə'sæsɪn] assassin *m*; **assassinate** assassiner

assassination assassinat *m*

assault [ə'sɔ:lt] **1** *n* agression *f*; MIL attaque *f* **(on** contre) **2** *v/t* agresser

assemble [ə'sembl] **1** *v/t parts* assembler **2** *v/i of people* se rassembler; **assembly** POL assemblée *f*; *of parts* assemblage *m*; **assembly line** chaîne *f* de montage

assent [ə'sent] consentir

assertive [ə'sɜ:rtɪv] *person* assuré

assess [ə'ses] *situation* éva-

luer; *value* estimer; **assessment** *of situation* évaluation *f*; *of value* estimation *f*

asset ['æset] FIN actif *m*; atout *m*

assign [ə'saɪn] assigner; *assignment* mission *f*; EDU devoir *m*

assimilate [ə'sɪmɪleɪt] assimiler

assist [ə'sɪst] aider; **assistance** aide *f*; **assistant** assistant(e) *m(f)*; **assistant manager** sous-directeur *m*, sous-directrice *f*; *of department* assistant(e) *m(f)* du/de la responsable

associate 1 *v/t* [ə'səʊʃieɪt] associer **2** *n* [ə'səʊʃiət] *(colleague)* collègue *m/f*; **association** association *f*

assortment [ə'sɔ:rtmənt] assortiment *m*

assume [ə'su:m] *(suppose)* supposer; **assumption** supposition *f*

assurance [ə'ʃʊrəns] *(reassurance, confidence)* assurance *f*; **assure** *(reassure)* assurer

asthma ['æsmə] asthme *m*

astonish [ə'stɑ:nɪʃ] étonner; **astonishing** étonnant; **astonishment** étonnement *m*

astound [ə'staʊnd] stupéfier

astride [ə'straɪd] à califourchon sur

astrology [ə'strɑ:lədʒɪ] astrologie *f*

astronaut ['æstrənɔ:t] astro-

au pair

naute *m/f*
astronomer [ə'strɑːnəmər] astronome *m/f*; **astronomical** *price etc* astronomique; **astronomy** astronomie *f*
astute [ə'stuːt] fin
asylum [ə'saɪləm] *political,* *(mental ~)* asile *m*
at [æt] *with places* à; **~ Joe's** chez Joe; **~ 10 dollars** au prix de 10 dollars; **~ the age of 18** à l'âge de 18 ans; **~ 5 o'clock** à 5 heures; **be good/bad ~ ...** être bon/mauvais en ...
atheist ['eɪθɪɪst] athée *m/f*
athlete ['æθliːt] athlète *m/f*; **athletic** [æθ'letɪk] d'athlétisme; *(strong, sporting)* sportif; **athletics** athlétisme *m*
Atlantic [ət'læntɪk]: **the ~** l'Atlantique *m*
atlas ['ætləs] atlas *m*
ATM [eɪtiː'em](= **automatic teller machine**) distributeur *m* automatique (de billets)
atmosphere ['ætməsfɪr] atmosphère *f*
atom ['ætəm] atome *m*; **atomic** atomique
◆ **atone for** [ə'toʊn] racheter
atrocious [ə'troʊʃəs] atroce; **atrocity** atrocité *f*
at-'seat *TV* télévision que l'on regarde à sa place, par exemple en avion
attach [ə'tætʃ] attacher; **attachment** *to e-mail* fichier *m* joint
attack [ə'tæk] **1** *n* attaque *f* **2** *v/t* attaquer

attempt [ə'tempt] **1** *n* tentative *f* **2** *v/t* essayer
attend [ə'tend] assister à; *school* aller à
◆ **attend to** s'occuper de
attendance [ə'tendəns] présence *f*; **attendant** *in museum etc* gardien(ne) *m(f)*
attention [ə'tenʃn] attention *f*; **pay ~** faire attention; at- tentive attentif
attic ['ætɪk] grenier *m*
attitude ['ætɪtuːd] attitude *f*
attorney [ə'tɜːrni] avocat *m*
attract [ə'trækt] attirer; **at- traction** *of job, doing sth* at- trait *m*; *romantic* attirance *f*; *touristic* attraction *f*; **attrac- tive** *person* attirant; *idea, city* attrayant
auction ['ɔːkʃn] vente *f* aux enchères
audacity [ɔː'dæsəti] audace *f*
audible ['ɔːdəbl] audible
audience ['ɔːdɪəns] public *m*
audio ['ɔːdɪoʊ] audio; **audio- visual** audiovisuel
audit ['ɔːdɪt] **1** *n* audit *m* **2** *v/t* contrôler; *course* suivre en auditeur libre
audition [ɔː'dɪʃn] **1** *n* audition *f* **2** *v/i* passer une audition
auditor ['ɔːdɪtər] FIN audi- teur(-trice) *m(f)*
auditorium [ɔːdɪ'tɔːrɪəm] *of theater etc* auditorium *m*
August ['ɔːɡəst] août *m*
aunt [ænt] tante *f*
au pair [oʊ'per] jeune fille *f* au pair

aura ['ɔːrə] aura *f*

auspicious [ɔː'spiʃəs] favorable

austere [ɔː'stiːr] austère; **austerity** austérité *f*

Australia [ɔː'streiliə] Australie *f*; **Australian 1** *adj* australien **2** *n* Australien(ne) *m(f)*

Austria ['ɔːstriə] Autriche *f*; **Austrian 1** *adj* autrichien **2** *n* Autrichien(ne) *m(f)*

authentic [ɔː'θentik] authentique; **authenticity** authenticité *f*

author ['ɔːθər] auteur *m*

authoritarian [əθɔːri'teriən] autoritaire; **authoritative** *source* qui fait autorité; *person, manner* autoritaire; **authority** [ə'θɔːrəti] autorité *f*; (*permission*) autorisation *f*; **authorization** autorisation *f*; **authorize** autoriser

autistic [ɔː'tistik] autiste

autobiography [ɔːtəbai'ɑːgrəfi] autobiographie *f*

autocratic [ɔːtə'krætik] autocratique

autograph ['ɔːtəgræf] autographe *m*

automate ['ɔːtəmeit] automatiser; **automatic 1** *adj* automatique **2** *n car* automatique *f*; *gun* automatique *m*; **automatically** automatiquement; **automation** automatisation *f*

automobile ['ɔːtəmoubiːl] automobile *f*; **automobile**

industry industrie *f* automobile

autonomous [ɔː'tɑːnəməs] autonome

autopilot ['ɔːtoupailət] pilotage *m* automatique

autopsy ['ɔːtɑːpsi] autopsie *f*

autumn ['ɔːtəm] *Br* automne *m*

auxiliary [ɔːg'ziljəri] auxiliaire *f*

available [ə'veiləbl] disponible

avalanche ['ævəlænʃ] avalanche *f*

avenue ['ævənuː] avenue *f*; **explore all ~s** explorer toutes les possibilités

average ['ævərɪdʒ] **1** *adj* moyen **2** *n* moyenne *f*; **on ~** en moyenne

◆ **average out at** faire une moyenne de

averse [ə'vɜːrs] *not be ~ to* ne rien avoir contre; **aversion** aversion *f* (*to* pour)

avid ['ævid] avide

avocado [ɑːvə'kɑːdou] avocat *m*

avoid [ə'vɔid] éviter

await [ə'weit] attendre

awake [ə'weik] éveillé; *it's keeping me~* ça m'empêche de dormir

award [ə'wɔːrd] **1** *n* (*prize*) prix *m* **2** *v/t* décerner; *damages* attribuer; **awards ceremony** cérémonie *f* de remise des prix; EDU cérémonie *f* de remise des diplômes

aware [ə'weɪr]: **be ~ of sth** avoir conscience de qch; **become ~ of sth** prendre conscience de qch; **awareness** conscience *f*

away [ə'weɪ]: **be ~** être absent, ne pas être là; **walk ~** s'en aller; **look ~** tourner la tête; **it's 2 miles ~** c'est à 2 miles d'ici; **take sth ~ from s.o.** enlever qch à qn; **away game** SP match *m* à l'extérieur

awesome ['ɔːsəm] F (*terrific*) super *inv*

awful ['ɔːfəl] affreux

awkward ['ɔːkwərd] (*clumsy*) maladroit; (*difficult*) difficile; (*embarrassing*) gênant; **feel ~** se sentir mal à l'aise

ax, Br **axe** [æks] **1** *n* hache *f* **2** *v/t project* abandonner; *budget* faire des coupures dans; *job* supprimer

axle ['æksl] essieu *m*

B

baby ['beɪbɪ] bébé *m*; **baby--sit** faire du baby-sitting

bachelor ['bætʃələr] célibataire *m*

back [bæk] **1** *n of person, clothes* dos *m*; *of chair* dossier *m*; *of drawer* fond *m*; *of house* arrière *m*; SP arrière *m*; **in ~ (of the car)** à l'arrière (de la voiture); **at the ~ of the book** à la fin du livre; **~ to front** à l'envers **2** *adj door* de derrière; *wheels, legs* arrière *inv* **3** *adv*: **move ~** se reculer; **give sth ~ to s.o.** rendre qch à qn; **she'll be ~ tomorrow** elle sera de retour demain **4** *v/t* (*support*) soutenir; *car* faire reculer; *horse* miser sur

◆ **back down** faire marche arrière

◆ **back out** *of commitment* se dégager

◆ **back up 1** *v/t* (*support*) soutenir; *file* sauvegarder **2** *v/i in car* reculer

'**backache** mal *m* de dos; **backbone** colonne *f* vertébrale; **backdate** antidater; **backdoor** porte *f* arrière; **backer** bailleur *m* de fonds; *for artist, show* producteur (-trice) *m*(*f*); **background** *of picture* arrière-plan *m*; *social* milieu *m*; *of crime* contexte *m*; **his work** son expérience professionnelle; **backhand** *in tennis* revers *m*; **backing** (*support*) soutien *m*; MUS accompagnement *m*; **backing group** groupe *m* d'accompagnement; **backlash** répercussion(s) *f*(pl); **backlog** retard *m* (**of** dans); **backpack** sac *m* à dos; **back-**

packer randonneur(-euse) *m(f)*; **back seat** siège *m* arrière; **back streets** petites rues *fpl*; *poor area* quartiers *mpl* pauvres; **backstroke** SP dos *m* crawlé; **backtrack** retourner sur ses pas; **backup** (*support*) renfort *m*; COMPUT copie *f* de sauvegarde; **backyard** arrière-cour *f*

bacon ['beɪkn] bacon *m*

bacteria [bæk'tɪrɪə] bactéries *fpl*

bad [bæd] mauvais; *person* méchant; (*rotten*) avarié; **go ~** s'avarier; **it's not ~** c'est pas mal; **that's really too ~** (*shame*) c'est vraiment dommage

badge [bædʒ] insigne *f*

bad 'language grossièretés *fpl*; **badly** mal; *injured* grièvement; *damaged* sérieusement; **he ~ needs ...** il a grand besoin de ...

badminton ['bædmɪntən] badminton *m*

bad-tempered [bæd'tempərd] de mauvaise humeur

baffle ['bæfl] déconcerter; **be ~d** être perplexe

bag [bæg] sac *m*; (*piece of baggage*) bagage *m*

baggage ['bægɪdʒ] bagages *mpl*; **baggage check** contrôle *m* de bagages

baggy ['bægɪ] flottant; *fashionably* large

bail [beɪl] LAW caution *f*; **be**

out on ~ être en liberté provisoire sous caution

bait [beɪt] appât *m*

bake [beɪk] cuire au four; **baked potato** pomme *f* de terre au four; **baker** boulanger(-ère) *m(f)*; **bakery** boulangerie *f*

balance ['bæləns] **1** *n* équilibre *m*; (*remainder*) reste *m*; *of bank account* solde *m* **2** *v/t* mettre en équilibre **3** *v/i* rester en équilibre; *of accounts* équilibrer; **balanced** (*fair*) objectif; *diet, personality* équilibré; **balance sheet** bilan *m*

balcony ['bælkənɪ] balcon *m*

bald [bɔːld] chauve; **balding** qui commence à devenir chauve

ball [bɔːl] *for soccer etc* ballon *m*; *for tennis, golf* balle *f*

ballad ['bæləd] ballade *f*

ballet ['bæleɪ] ballet *m*; **ballet dancer** danceur(-euse) *m(f)* de ballet

'ball game match *m* de baseball

ballistic missile [bə'lɪstɪk] missile *m* balistique

balloon [bə'luːn] *child's* ballon *m*; *for flight* montgolfière *f*

ballot ['bælət] **1** *n* vote *m* **2** *v/t members* faire voter; **ballot box** urne *f*

'ballpark terrain *m* de baseball; **ballpark figure** chiffre *m* en gros; **ballpoint (pen)**

stylo *m* bille

balls [bɔːlz] V **couilles** *fpl*

bamboo [bæm'buː] **bambou** *m*

ban [bæn] **1** *n* **interdiction** *f* **2** *v/t* **interdire**

banal [bə'næl] **banal**

banana [bə'nænə] **banane** *f*

band [bænd] MUS **orchestre** *m*; *pop* **groupe** *m*; *of material* **bande** *f*

bandage ['bændɪdʒ] **1** *n* **bandage** *m* **2** *v/t* **faire un bandage à**

'**Band-Aid**® **sparadrap** *m*

bandit ['bændɪt] **bandit** *m*

bandy ['bændɪ] *legs* **arqué**

bang [bæŋ] **1** *n* **noise boum** *m*; (*blow*) **coup** *m* **2** *v/t* **door claquer**; (*hit*) **cogner**

bangle ['bæŋgl] **bracelet** *m*

bangs [bæŋz] **frange** *f*

banisters ['bænɪstərz] **rampe** *f*

banjo ['bændʒou] **banjo** *m*

bank¹ [bæŋk] *of river* **bord** *m*, **rive** *f*

bank² [bæŋk] FIN **banque** *f*
◆ **bank on compter sur**

'**bank account compte** *m* **en banque**; **banker banquier** (-ière) *m(f)*; **banker's card carte** *f* **d'identité bancaire**; **banking banque** *f*; **bank loan emprunt** *m* **bancaire**; **bank manager**² **directeur** (-trice) *m(f)* **de banque**; **bank rate taux** *m* **bancaire**; **bankroll financer**; **bankrupt en faillite**; **go ~ faire faillite**;

bankruptcy faillite *f*

banner ['bænər] **bannière** *f*

banquet ['bæŋkwɪt] **banquet** *m*

baptism ['bæptɪzm] **baptême** *m*; **baptize baptiser**

bar¹ [bɑːr] *n of iron, chocolate* **barre** *f*; *for drinks, counter* **bar** *m*

bar² [bɑːr] *v/t* **exclure**

barbaric [bɑːr'bærɪk] **barbare**

barbecue ['bɑːrbɪkjuː] **1** *n* **barbecue** *m* **2** *v/t* **cuire au barbecue**

barbed 'wire [bɑːrbd] **fil** *m* **barbelé**

barber ['bɑːrbər] **coiffeur** *m*

'**bar code code** *m* **barre**

bare [ber] **nu**; *room, shelves* **vide**; **barefoot: be ~ être pieds nus**; **bare-headed tête nue**; **barely à peine**

bargain ['bɑːrgɪn] **1** *n* (*deal*) **marché** *m*; (*good buy*) **bonne affaire** *f* **2** *v/i* **marchander**
◆ **barge into se heurter contre**; (*enter noisily*) **faire irruption dans**

baritone ['bærɪtoun] **baryton** *m*

bark¹ [bɑːrk] **1** *n of dog* **aboiement** *m* **2** *v/i* **aboyer**

bark² [bɑːrk] *of tree* **écorce** *f*

barn [bɑːrn] **grange** *f*

barometer [bə'rɑːmɪtər] *also fig* **baromètre** *m*

barracks ['bærəks] MIL **caserne** *f*

barrel ['bærəl] **tonneau** *m*

barren ['bærən] *land* stérile

barrette [bə'ret] barrette *f*

barricade [bærɪ'keɪd] barricade *f*

barrier ['bærɪər] barrière *f*

'bar tender barman *m*, barmaid *f*

barter ['bɑːrtər] **1** *n* troc *m* **2** *v/t* troquer (**for** contre)

base [beɪs] **1** *n* base *f* **2** *v/t* baser (**on** sur); *baseball* baseball *m*; *ball* ballon *m* de baseball; **baseball cap** casquette *f* de baseball; **baseboard** plinthe *f*; **basement** sous-sol *m*

basic ['beɪsɪk] (*rudimentary*) rudimentaire; (*fundamental*), *salary* de base; **basically** au fond

basin ['beɪsn] *for washing dishes* bassine *f*; *in bathroom* lavabo *m*

basis ['beɪsɪs] base *f*; *of argument* fondement *m*

bask [bæsk] se dorer

basket ['bæskɪt] panier *m*; **basketball** *game* basket (-ball) *m*; *ball* ballon *m* de basket

bass [beɪs] basse *f*; **double ~** contrebasse *f*; **~ guitar** basse *f*

bastard ['bæstərd] salaud(e) *m(f)*

bat¹ [bæt] **1** *n for baseball* batte *f*; *for table tennis* raquette *f* **2** *v/i in baseball* batter

bat² [bæt] *animal* chauve-souris *f*

batch [bætʃ] *of students, data* lot *m*; *of bread* fournée *f*

bath [bæθ] (~*tub*) baignoire *f*

bathe [beɪð] (*have a bath*) se baigner

'bathrobe peignoir *m*; **bathroom** salle *f* de bains; *toilet* toilettes *fpl*; **bath towel** serviette *f* de bain; **bathtub** baignoire *f*

batter ['bætər] *for cakes, pancakes etc* pâte *f* lisse; *in baseball* batteur *m*; **battered** *wife, children* battu

battery ['bætərɪ] pile *f*; MOT batterie *f*

battle ['bætl] **1** *n* bataille *f*; *fig* lutte *f* **2** *v/i against illness etc* se battre, lutter; **battleship** cuirassé *m*

bawl [bɔːl] (*shout, weep*) brailler

bay [beɪ] (*inlet*) baie *f*

BC [biː'siː] (= *before Christ*) av. J.-C.

be [biː] ◇ être; **~ 15** avoir 15 ans; **it's me** c'est moi; **how much is…?** combien coûte …?; **there is/are** il y a; **how are you?** comment ça va? ◇ **has the mailman been?** est-ce que le facteur est passé?; **I've never been to Japan** je ne suis jamais allé au Japon ◇ *tags:* **that's right, isn't it?** c'est juste, n'est-ce pas?; **she's American, isn't she?** elle est américaine, n'est-ce pas?

◇ *passive*: **he was killed** il a été tué; **it hasn't been decided** on n'a encore rien décidé

beach [biːtʃ] plage *f*; **beachwear** vêtements *mpl* de plage

beads [biːdz] collier *m* de perles

beak [biːk] bec *m*

beam [biːm] **1** *n in ceiling etc* poutre *f* **2** *v/i (smile)* rayonner

bean [biːn] haricot *m*; *of coffee* grain *m*

bear¹ [ber] *n animal* ours *m*

bear² [ber] **1** *v/t weight* porter; *costs* prendre en charge; *(tolerate)* supporter; **bearable** supportable

beard [bɪrd] barbe *f*

beat [biːt] **1** *n of heart* battement *m*; *of music* mesure *f* **2** *v/i of heart* battre; *of rain* s'abattre **3** *v/t in competition,* *(hit)* battre; *(pound)* frapper
◆ **beat up** tabasser

beaten ['biːtən]: **off the ~ track** à l'écart; **beating** *physical* raclée *f*; **beat-up** déglingué

beautiful ['bjuːtəful] beau; **beautifully** admirablement; **beauty** beauté *f*

beaver ['biːvər] castor *m*

because [bɪ'kɑːz] parce que; **~ of** à cause de

become [bɪ'kʌm] devenir; **what's ~ of her?** qu'est-elle devenue?; **becoming** seyant

bed [bed] *also of sea* lit *m*; *of*
flowers parterre *m*; **go to ~** aller se coucher; **bedding** literie *f*; **bedridden** cloué au lit; **bedroom** chambre *f* (à coucher); **bedtime** heure *f* du coucher

bee [biː] abeille *f*

beech [biːtʃ] hêtre *m*

beef [biːf] bœuf *m*; **beefburger** steak *m* haché

beep [biːp] **1** *n* bip *m* **2** *v/i* faire bip

beer [bɪr] bière *f*

beet [biːt] betterave *f*

beetle ['biːtl] coléoptère *m*, cafard *m*

before [bɪ'fɔːr] **1** *prep* avant; **~ signing it** avant de le signer; **~ a vowel** devant une voyelle **2** *adv* auparavant; *(already)* déjà; **the week/day ~** la semaine/le jour d'avant **3** *conj* avant que (+*subj*); **I had a coffee ~ I left** j'ai pris un café avant de partir; **beforehand** à l'avance

befriend [bɪ'frend] se lier d'amitié avec

beg [beg] **1** *v/i* mendier **2** *v/t*: **~ s.o. to do sth** prier qn de faire qch; **beggar** mendiant (e) *m (f)*

begin [bɪ'gɪn] *v/i* commencer; **beginner** débutant(e) *m(f)*; **beginning** début *m*

behalf [bɪ'hɑːf]: **in** or **on ~ of** de la part de

behave [bɪ'heɪv] se comporter; **~ (yourself)!** sois sage!; **behavior,** *Br* **behaviour**

comportement *m*

behind [bɪ'haɪnd] **1** *prep* derrière; **be ~ ...** (*responsible for, support*) être derrière ... **2** *adv* (*at the back*) à l'arrière; *leave, stay* derrière; **be ~ in match** être derrière

beige [beɪʒ] beige

being ['biːɪŋ] (*creature*) être *m*; (*existence*) existence *f*

belated [bɪ'leɪtɪd] tardif

belch [beltʃ] **1** *n* éructation *f*, rot *m* **2** *v/i* éructer, roter

Belgian ['beldʒən] **1** *adj* belge **2** *n* Belge *m/f*; **Belgium** Belgique *f*

belief [bɪ'liːf] conviction *f*; REL *also* croyance *f*; *in person* foi *f* (**in** en); believe croyance

◆ **believe in** *God, person* croire en; *sth* croire à; *cacher* la vérité aux gens

believer [bɪ'liːvər] *in God* croyant(e) *m(f)*; *in sth* partisan(e) *m(f)* (**in** de)

bell [bel] *on bike, door* sonnette *f*; *in church* cloche *f*; *in school:* electric sonnerie *f*; **bellhop** groom *m*

belligerent [bɪ'lɪdʒərənt] belligérant

bellow ['beloʊ] brailler; *of bull* beugler

belly ['belɪ] *of person* ventre *m*; *fat* bedaine *f*; *of animal* panse *f*

◆ **belong to** *of object* appartenir à; *club, organization* faire partie de

belongings [bɪ'lɒːŋɪŋz] affaires *fpl*

beloved [bɪ'lʌvɪd] bien-aimé

below [bɪ'loʊ] **1** *prep* au-dessous de **2** *adv* en bas, au-dessous; *in text* en bas; **10 degrees ~** moins dix

belt [belt] ceinture *f*

benchmark ['bentʃmɑːrk] référence *f*

bend [bend] **1** *n* tournant *m* **2** *v/t head* baisser; *arm, knees* plier; *metal, plastic* tordre **3** *v/i of road* tourner; *of person* se pencher

◆ **bend down** se pencher

beneath [bɪ'niːθ] **1** *prep* sous **2** *adv* (au-)dessous

benefactor ['benɪfæktər] bienfaiteur(-trice) *m(f)*

beneficial [benɪ'fɪʃl] bénéfique

benefit ['benɪfɪt] **1** *n* bénéfice *m* **2** *v/t* bénéficier à **3** *v/i* bénéficier (**from** de)

benevolent [bɪ'nevələnt] bienveillant

benign [bɪ'naɪn] doux; MED bénin

bequeath [bɪ'kwiːð] léguer; **bequest** legs *m*

beret ['bereɪ] béret *m*

berry ['berɪ] baie *f*

berth [bɜːrθ] couchette *f*; *for ship* mouillage *m*

beside [bɪ'saɪd] à côté de; **be ~ o.s.** être hors de soi; **that's ~ the point** c'est hors de propos

besides [bɪ'saɪdz] **1** *adv* d'ailleurs **2** *prep* (*apart from*) à part

biological

best [best] **1** *adj* meilleur **2** *adv* le mieux; **I like her ~** c'est elle que j'aime le plus **3** *n*: **do one's ~** faire de son mieux; **the ~** le mieux; **the ~** (*outstanding thing or person*) le (la) meilleur(e) *m(f)*; **all the ~!** meilleurs vœux!; best before date date *f* limite de consommation; best man *at wedding* garçon *m* d'honneur

bet [bet] **1** *n* pari *m* **2** *v/t & v/i* parier; **you ~!** évidemment!

betray [bɪ'treɪ] trahir; betrayal trahison *f*

better ['betər] **1** *adj* meilleur; **get ~** s'améliorer; **he's ~ in health** il va mieux **2** *adv* mieux; **I'd really ~not** je ne devrais vraiment pas; **I like her ~** je l'aime plus; better--off (*richer*) plus aisé

between [bɪ'twiːn] entre

beware [bɪ'wer]: **~ of** attention à

bewilder [bɪ'wɪldər] confondre; bewilderment confusion *f*

beyond [bɪ'jɑːnd] au-delà de

bias ['baɪəs] parti *m* pris, préjugé *m*; bias(s)ed partial, subjectif

Bible ['baɪbl] Bible *f*; biblical biblique

bicentennial [baɪsen'tenɪəl] bicentenaire *m*

bicker ['bɪkər] se chamailler

bicycle ['baɪsɪkl] bicyclette *f*

bid [bɪd] **1** *n at auction* enchè-

re *m*; (*attempt*) tentative *f*; *in takeover* offre *f* **2** *v/i at auction* faire une enchère; bidder enchérisseur(-euse) *m(f)*

biennial [baɪ'enɪəl] biennal

big [bɪg] **1** *adj* grand; *sum of money, mistake* gros; **my ~ brother/sister** mon grand frère/ma grande sœur **2** *adv*: **talk ~** se vanter

bigamist ['bɪgəmɪst] bigame *f*

'bighead crâneur(-euse) *m(f)*

bigot ['bɪgət] fanatique *m/f*, sectaire *m*

bike [baɪk] vélo *m*; (*motorbike*) moto *f*; biker ['baɪkər] motard(e) *m(f)*

bikini [bɪ'kiːni] bikini *m*

bilingual [baɪ'lɪŋgwəl] bilingue

bill [bɪl] facture *f*; *money* billet *m* (de banque); POL projet *m* de loi; (*poster*) affiche *f*; billboard panneau *m* d'affichage; billfold portefeuille *m*

billion ['bɪljən] milliard *m*

bin [bɪn] *for storage* boîte *f*

bind [baɪnd] (*connect*) unir; (*tie*) attacher; LAW (*oblige*) obliger; binding *agreement* obligatoire

binoculars [bɪ'nɑːkjələrz] jumelles *fpl*

biodegradable [baɪoʊdɪ-'greɪdəbl] biodégradable

biographer [baɪ'ɑːgrəfər] biographe *m/f*; biography biographie *f*

biological [baɪoʊ'lɑːdʒɪkl]

biologique; **biology** biologie f

bird [bɜːrd] oiseau m

biro® ['baɪroʊ] Br stylo m bille

birth [bɜːrθ] naissance f; (labor) accouchement m; **give ~ to** child donner naissance à; **date of ~** date f de naissance; **birth certificate** acte m de naissance; **birth control** contrôle m des naissances; **birthday** anniversaire m **happy ~!** bon anniversaire!

biscuit ['bɪskɪt] biscuit m

bisexual ['baɪseksjʊəl] **1** adj bisexuel **2** n bisexuel(le) m(f)

bishop ['bɪʃəp] évêque m

bit [bɪt] (piece) morceau m; (part: of book) passage m; (part: of garden, road) partie f; COMPUT bit m; **a ~ of** (a little) un peu de

bitch [bɪtʃ] **1** n dog chienne f; F: woman garce f **2** v/i F (complain) rouspéter

bite [baɪt] **1** of dog, snake morsure f; of flea, mosquito piqûre f; of food morceau m **2** v/t & v/i of dog, snake, person mordre; of flea, mosquito piquer

bitter ['bɪtər] taste, person amer

black [blæk] **1** adj noir; tea nature; future sombre **2** n color noir m; person Noir(e) m(f)

◆ **black out** (faint) s'évanouir

'blackboard tableau m noir;

black coffee café m noir; **black economy** économie f souterraine; **black eye** œil m poché; **blacklist** liste f noire; **blackmail 1** n chantage m **2** v/t faire chanter; **black market** marché m noir; **blackness** noirceur f; **blackout** ELEC panne f d'électricité; MED évanouissement m

bladder ['blædər] vessie f

blade [bleɪd] of knife lame f; of propeller ailette f; of grass brin m

blame [bleɪm] **1** n responsabilité f **2** v/t: **~ s.o. for sth** reprocher qch à qn

bland [blænd] fade

blank [blæŋk] **1** adj paper, tape vierge; look vide **2** n (empty space) espace m vide; **blank check**, Br **blank cheque** chèque m en blanc

blanket ['blæŋkɪt] couverture f

blast [blæst] **1** n (explosion) explosion f; (gust) rafale f **2** v/t tunnel etc percer (à l'aide d'explosifs); **~!** mince!; **blast-off** lancement m

blatant ['bleɪtənt] flagrant; person éhonté

blaze [bleɪz] **1** n (fire) incendie m **2** v/i of fire flamber

blazer ['bleɪzər] blazer m

bleach [bliːtʃ] **1** n for clothes eau f de Javel; for hair décolorant m **2** v/t hair décolorer

bleak [bliːk] countryside désolé; weather morne; future

sombre

bleary-eyed ['blɪrɪaɪd] aux yeux troubles

bleat [bliːt] *of sheep* bêler

bleed [bliːd] saigner; **bleeding** saignement *m*

bleep [bliːp] **1** *n* bip *m* **2** *v/i* faire un bip

blemish ['blemɪʃ] tache *f*

blend [blend] **1** *n* mélange *m* **2** *v/t* mélanger; **blender** *machine* mixeur *m*

bless [bles] bénir; **~ you!** *in response to sneeze* à vos souhaits!; **blessing** bénédiction *f*

blind [blaɪnd] **1** *adj* aveugle; **~ corner** virage *m* masqué **2** *v/t of sun* aveugler; **blind alley** impasse *f*; **blind date** rendez-vous *m* arrangé; **blindfold 1** *n* bandeau *m* sur les yeux **2** *v/t* bander les yeux à; **blinding** *light* aveuglant; *headache* terrible; **blindly** sans rien voir; *fig* aveuglément; **blind spot** *in road* angle *m* mort

blink [blɪŋk] *of person* cligner des yeux; *of light* clignoter

blizzard ['blɪzərd] tempête *f* de neige

bloc [blɑːk] POL bloc *m*

block [blɑːk] **1** *n* bloc *m*; *buildings* pâté *m* de maisons; *(blockage)* obstruction *f m*; **it's three ~s away** c'est à trois rues d'ici **2** *v/t* bloquer; **blockage** obstruction *f*; **blockbuster** *movie* film *m*

à grand succès; *novel* roman *m* à succès; **block letters** capitales *fpl*

blond [blɑːnd] blond; **blonde** *woman* blonde *f*

blood [blʌd] sang *m*; **blood donor** donneur(-euse) *m(f)* de sang; **blood group** groupe *m* sanguin; **'blood poisoning** empoisonnement *m* du sang; **blood pressure** tension *f* (artérielle); **blood sample** prélèvement *m* sanguin; **bloodshed** carnage *m*; **without ~** sans effusion de sang; **bloodshot** injecté de sang; **bloodstained** taché de sang; **blood test** test *m* sanguin; **bloodthirsty** sanguinaire

bloom [bluːm] *also fig* fleurir

blossom ['blɑːsəm] **1** *n* fleur *f* **2** *v/i* fleurir; *fig* s'épanouir

blot [blɑːt] tache *f*

◆ **blot out** effacer

blouse [blauz] chemisier *m*

blow[1] [bloʊ] *n also fig* coup *m*

blow[2] [bloʊ] **1** *v/t* souffler; **~ one's whistle** donner un coup de sifflet **2** *v/i of wind, person* souffler; *of whistle* retentir; *of fuse* sauter; *of tire* éclater

◆ **blow out 1** *v/t candle* souffler **2** *v/i of candle* s'éteindre

◆ **blow over 1** *v/t* renverser **2** *v/i se* renverser; *(pass)* passer

◆ **blow up 1** *v/t with explosives* faire sauter; *balloon* gonfler; *photograph* agrandir **2** *v/i* of boiler etc sauter, exploser

'blow-dry sécher (au sèche-cheveux); **blow-out** of tire éclatement *m*

blue [bluː] bleu; *movie* porno; **blueberry** myrtille *f*; **blue chip** de premier ordre; **blues** MUS blues *m*; **have the ~** avoir le cafard

bluff [blʌf] **1** *n* (deception) bluff *m* **2** *v/i* bluffer

blunder ['blʌndər] **1** *n* gaffe *f* **2** *v/i* faire une gaffe

blunt [blʌnt] émoussé; person franc; **bluntly** franchement

blur [bləːr] **1** *n* masse *f* confuse **2** *v/t* brouiller

◆ **blurt out** [bləːrt] lâcher

blush [blʌʃ] **1** *n* rougissement *m* **2** *v/i* rougir; **blusher** cosmetic rouge *m*

blustery ['blʌstərɪ] à bourrasques

BO [biː'ou] (= body odor) odeur *f* corporelle

board [bɔːrd] **1** *n* of wood planche *f*; cardboard carton *m*; for game plateau *m* de jeu; for notices panneau *m*; **~ (of directors)** conseil *m* d'administration; **on~** à bord **2** *v/t* plane, ship monter à bord de; train, bus monter dans **3** *v/i* of passengers embarquer; on train, bus monter (à bord)

◆ **board up** windows condamner

boarder ['bɔːrdər] pension-naire *m/f*; EDU interne *m/f*; **board game** jeu *m* de société; **boarding card** carte *f* d'embarquement; **boarding school** internat *m*, pensionnat *m*; **board meeting** réunion *f* du conseil d'administration; **board room** salle *f* du conseil

boast [boust] se vanter (**about** de)

boat [bout] bateau *m*; small, for leisure canot *m*

bodily ['bɑːdɪlɪ] **1** *adj* corporel **2** *adv*: **they ~ ejected him** ils l'ont saisi à bras-le-corps et l'ont mis dehors **body** corps *m*; **dead** cadavre *m*; **bodyguard** garde *m* du corps; **bodywork** MOT carrosserie *f*

bogus ['bougəs] faux

boil¹ [bɔɪl] *n* (swelling) furoncle *m*

boil² [bɔɪl] **1** *v/t* faire bouillir **2** *v/i* bouillir

◆ **boil down to** se ramener à

boiler ['bɔɪlər] chaudière *f*

boisterous ['bɔɪstərəs] bruyant

bold [bould] **1** *adj* courageux; text en caractères gras **2** *n* print caractères *mpl* gras

bolster ['boulstər] confidence soutenir

bolt [boult] **1** *n* (metal pin) boulon *m*; on door verrou *m* **2** *adv*: **~ upright** tout droit **3** *v/t* (fix with bolts) boulonner; close verrouiller **4** *v/i* (run off) décamper; of horse s'emballer

bomb [bɑːm] **1** n bombe f **2** v/t MIL bombarder; of terrorist faire sauter; **bombard** [bɑːmˈbɑːrd] also fig bombarder; **bomb attack** attaque f à la bombe; **bomber airplane** bombardier m; terrorist poseur m(f) de bombes; **bomb scare** alerte f à la bombe; **bombshell**: *come as a ~* faire l'effet d'une bombe

bond [bɑːnd] **1** n (tie) lien m; FIN obligation f **2** v/i of glue se coller

bone [boʊn] os m; in fish arête f

bonnet [ˈbɑːnɪt] Br of car capot m

bonus [ˈboʊnəs] money prime f; (something extra) plus m

boob [buːb] P (breast) nichon m

booboo [ˈbuːbuː] F bêtise f

book [bʊk] **1** n livre m **2** v/t seat réserver; ticket prendre; of policeman donner un P.V. à; **bookcase** bibliothèque f; **booked up** complet; perso complètement pris; **bookie** F bookmaker m; **booking** réservation f; **bookkeeper** comptable m

'bookkeeping comptabilité f; **booklet** livret m; **bookmaker** bookmaker m; **books** (accounts) comptes mpl; **bookseller** libraire m/f; **book-**store librairie f

boom[1] [buːm] **1** n boum m **2** v/i of business aller très fort

boom[2] [buːm] n noise boum m

boost [buːst] **1** n: *give sth a ~* stimuler qc **2** v/t stimuler

boot [buːt] botte f; for climbing, football chaussure f

◆ **boot up** COMPUT **1** v/i démarrer **2** v/t faire démarrer

booth [buːð] at market tente f (de marché); at fair baraque f; at trade fair stand m; in restaurant alcôve f

booze [buːz] boisson f (alcoolique)

border [ˈbɔːrdər] **1** n frontière f; (edge) bordure f **2** v/t country avoir une frontière avec

◆ **border on** avoir une frontière avec; (be almost) friser

bore[1] [bɔːr] v/t hole percer

bore[2] [bɔːr] **1** n person raseur(-euse) m(f) **2** v/t ennuyer

bored [bɔːrd] ennuyé; *be ~* s'ennuyer; **boredom** ennui m; **boring** ennuyeux, chiant

born [bɔːrn]: *be ~* être né

borrow [ˈbɑːroʊ] emprunter

bosom [ˈbʊzm] poitrine f

boss [bɑːs] patron(-onne) m(f)

◆ **boss around** donner des ordres à

bossy [ˈbɑːsɪ] autoritaire

botanical [bəˈtænɪkl] botanique

botch [bɑːtʃ] bâcler

both [bəʊθ] **1** *adj & pron* les deux; **~ of them** tous(-tes) *m(f)* les deux **2** *adv:* **~ ... and ...** à la fois ... et ...

bother ['bɒðər] **1** *n* problèmes *mpl* **2** *v/t* (*disturb*) déranger; (*worry*) ennuyer **3** *v/i* s'inquiéter (**with** de)

◆ **bother** *up* feelings réprimer

bottle ['bɒtl] bouteille *f*; *for medicines* flacon *m*; *for baby* biberon *m*

'bottle bank conteneur *m* à verre; **bottled water** eau *f* en bouteille; **bottleneck** rétrécissement *m*; *in production* goulet *m* d'étranglement; **bottle-opener** ouvre-bouteilles *m inv*

bottom ['bɒtəm] **1** *adj* du bas **2** *n of drawer, pan, garden* fond *m*; (*underside*) dessous *m*; (*lowest part*) bas *m*; *of street* bout *m*; (*buttocks*) derrière *m*

◆ **bottom out** se stabiliser

bottom 'line *financial* résultat *m*; (*real issue*) la question principale

boulder ['bəʊldər] rocher *m*

bounce [baʊns] **1** *v/t* ball faire rebondir **2** *v/i of ball* rebondir; *on sofa etc* sauter; *of check* être refusé; **bouncer** videur *m*

bound¹ [baʊnd] *adj:* **be ~ to do sth** (*sure to*) aller forcément faire qch

bound² [baʊnd] *adj:* **be ~ for** *of ship* être à destination de

bound³ [baʊnd] *n* (*jump*) bond *m*

boundary ['baʊndərɪ] frontière *f*

bouquet [bʊ'keɪ] bouquet *m*

bourbon ['bɜːrbən] bourbon *m*

bout [baʊt] MED accès *m*; *in boxing* match *m*

bow¹ [baʊ] **1** *n as greeting* révérence *f* **2** *v/i* faire une révérence **3** *v/t head* baisser

bow² [bəʊ] (*knot*) nœud *m*; MUS archet *m*; *for archery* arc *m*

bow³ [baʊ] *of ship* avant *m*

bowels ['baʊəlz] intestins *mpl*

bowl¹ [bəʊl] *n* bol *m*; *for soup etc* assiette *f* creuse; *for serving salad etc* saladier *m*; *for washing dishes* cuvette *f*

bowl² [bəʊl] *v/i* jouer au bowling

bowling ['bəʊlɪŋ] bowling *m*; **bowling alley** bowling *m*

bow 'tie [bəʊ] (nœud *m*) papillon *m*

box¹ [bɑːks] *n container* boîte *f*; *on form* case *f*

box² [bɑːks] *v/i* boxer

boxer ['bɑːksər] boxeur *m*; **boxing** boxe *f*; **boxing glove** gant *m* de boxe; **boxing match** match *m* de boxe

'box number boîte *f* postale; **box office** bureau *m* de location

boy [bɔɪ] garçon *m*; (*son*) fils *m*

boycott ['bɔɪkɑːt] **1** *n* boycott

m **2** *v/t* boycotter

'**boyfriend** petit ami *m*; *younger* copain *m*

bra [brɑː] soutien-gorge *m*

bracelet ['breɪslɪt] bracelet *m*

bracket ['brækɪt] *for shelf support m* (d'étagère)

brag [bræg] se vanter (**about** de)

braid [breɪd] *in hair* tresse *f*; *trimming* galon *m*

braille [breɪl] braille *m*

brain [breɪn] ANAT cerveau *m*; **brainless** écervelé; **brains** cerveau *m*; **brain** surgeon neurochirurgien(ne) *m(f)*; **brain tumor**, *Br* **brain tumour** tumeur *f* au cerveau; **brainwash** conditionner

brake [breɪk] **1** *n* frein *m* **2** *v/i* freiner

branch [brɑːntʃ] *of tree, company* branche *f*

brand [brænd] **1** *n* marque *f* **2** *v/t*: **be ~ed a liar** être étiqueté comme voleur; **brand image** image *f* de marque

brandish ['brændɪʃ] brandir

brand 'leader marque *f* dominante; **brand name** nom *m* de marque; **brand-new** flambant neuf

brandy ['brændɪ] brandy *m*

brassière [brə'zɪr] soutien-gorge *m*

brat [bræt] garnement *m*

brave [breɪv] courageux; **bravery** courage *m*

brawl [brɔːl] **1** *n* bagarre *f* **2** *v/i* se bagarrer

Brazil [brə'zɪl] Brésil *m*; **Brazilian 1** *adj* brésilien **2** *n* Brésilien(ne) *m(f)*

breach [briːtʃ] (*violation*) violation *f*; *in party* désaccord *m*; **breach of contract** rupture *f* de contrat

bread [bred] pain *m*

breadth [bredθ] largeur *m*; *of knowledge* étendue *f*

'**breadwinner** soutien *m* de famille

break [breɪk] **1** *n* fracture *f*; (*rest*) repos *m*; *in relationship* séparation *f* **2** *v/t* casser; *rules, law, promise* violer; *news* annoncer; *record* battre **3** *v/i* se casser; *of news, storm* éclater

◆ **break down 1** *v/i of vehicle, machine* tomber en panne; *of talks* échouer; *in tears* s'effondrer; *mentally* faire une dépression **2** *v/t door* défoncer; *figures* détailler

◆ **break even** rentrer dans ses frais

◆ **break in** (*interrupt*) interrompre qn; *of burglar* s'introduire par effraction

◆ **break up 1** *v/t into parts* décomposer; *fight* interrompre **2** *v/i of ice* se briser; *of couple, band* se séparer; *of meeting* se dissoudre

breakable ['breɪkəbl] cassable; **breakage** casse *f*; **breakdown** *of talks* échec *m*; (*nervous ~*) dépression *f* (nerveuse); *of figures* détail

m

breakfast ['brekfəst] petit déjeuner *m*; **have ~** prendre son petit déjeuner; **break-in** cambriolage *m*; **break-through** percée *f*; **breakup** of partnership échec *m*

breast [brest] of woman sein *m*; **breastfeed** allaiter; **breaststroke** brasse *f*

breath [breθ] souffle *m*; **out of ~** à bout de souffle

breathe [bri:ð] respirer

◆ **breathe in** inspirer

◆ **breathe out** expirer

breathing ['bri:ðɪŋ] respiration *f*

breathtaking ['breθteɪkɪŋ] à vous couper le souffle

breed [bri:d] **1** *n* race *f* **2** *v/t* animals élever; plants, also fig cultiver **3** *v/i* of animals se reproduire; **breeding** of animals élevage *m*; of person éducation *f*

breeze [bri:z] brise *f*; **breezy** venteux

brew [bru:] **1** *v/t* beer brasser **2** *v/i* couver; **brewery** brasserie *f*

bribe [braɪb] **1** *n* pot-de-vin *m* **2** *v/t* soudoyer; **bribery** corruption *f*

brick [brɪk] brique *m*

bride [braɪd] about to be married (future) mariée *f*; married jeune mariée *f*; **bride-groom** about to be married (futur) marié *m*; married jeune marié *m*; **bridesmaid** de-moiselle *f* d'honneur

bridge [brɪdʒ] **1** *n* pont *m*; of ship passerelle *f* **2** *v/t* gap combler

bridle ['braɪdl] bride *f*

brief[1] [bri:f] *adj* bref, court

brief[2] [bri:f] **1** *n* (mission) instructions *fpl* **2** *v/t*: **~ s.o. on sth** (give information) informer qn de qch

'briefcase serviette *f*; **briefing session** séance *f* d'information; instructions instructions *fpl*; **briefly** brièvement; (to sum up) en bref; **briefs** slip *m*

bright [braɪt] color vif; smile radieux; future brillant; (sunny) clair; (intelligent) intelligent; **brightly** smile d'un air radieux; colored vivement; **shine ~** resplendir

brilliance ['brɪljəns] of person esprit *m* lumineux; of color vivacité *f*; of sunshine etc resplendissant; (very good) génial; (very intelligent) brillant

brim [brɪm] of container, hat bord *m*

bring [brɪŋ] object apporter; person, peace amener; hope, happiness donner

◆ **bring back** (return) ramener; (re-introduce) réintroduire; **it brought back memories of ... childhood** ça m'a rappelé ...

◆ **bring down** also fig: government faire tomber; air-

plane abattre; *price* faire baisser
◆ **bring on** *illness* donner
◆ **bring out** (*produce*) sortir
◆ **bring up** *child* élever; *subject* soulever; (*vomit*) vomir
brink [brɪŋk] bord *m*
brisk [brɪsk] vif; (*businesslike*) énergique; *trade* florissant
bristles ['brɪslz] *on chin* poils *mpl* raides; (*of brush* poils *mpl*
Britain ['brɪtn] Grande-Bretagne; **British 1** *adj* britannique **2** *npl*: **the** ~ les Britanniques
brittle ['brɪtl] fragile
broad [brɔːd] **1** *adj* large; *smile* grand; (*general*) général; **in** ~ **daylight** en plein jour **2** *n* F gonzesse *f*; **broadcast 1** *n* émission *f* **2** *v/t* transmettre; **broadcaster** présentateur(-trice) *m(f)* (*radio/télé*); **broad jump** saut *m* en longueur; **broadly**: ~ **speaking** en gros; **broadminded** large d'esprit
broccoli ['brɑːkəlɪ] brocoli(s) *m(pl)*
brochure ['brouʃər] brochure *f*
broil [brɔɪl] griller; **broiler** *on stove* grill *m*; *chicken* poulet *m* à rôtir
broke [brouk] fauché; **broken** cassé; *home* brisé; **broker** courtier *m*
bronchitis [brɑːŋ'kaɪtɪs] bronchite *f*

bronze [brɑːnz] bronze *m*
brooch [broutʃ] broche *f*
brothel ['brɑːθl] bordel *m*
brother ['brʌðər] frère *m*; **brother-in-law** beau-frère *m*; **brotherly** fraternel
brow [brau] (*forehead*) front *m*; *of hill* sommet *m*
brown [braun] **1** *adj* marron *inv*; (*tanned*) bronzé **2** *n* marron *m*; **brownie** brownie *m*
brown paper 'bag sac *m* en papier kraft
browse [brauz] *in store* flâner; COMPUT surfer; ~ **through a book** feuilleter un livre; **browser** COMPUT navigateur *m*
bruise [bruːz] bleu *m*; *on fruit* meurtrissure *f*
brunette [bruː'net] brune *f*
brush [brʌʃ] **1** *n* brosse *f*; (*conflict*) accrochage *m* **2** *v/t* brosser; (*touch lightly*) effleurer
◆ **brush aside** *person* mépriser; *remark, criticism* écarter
◆ **brush up** réviser
brusque [brusk] brusque
brutal ['bruːtl] brutal; **brutality** brutalité *f*; **brutally** brutalement; **brute** brute *f*
bubble ['bʌbl] bulle *f*
buck¹ [bʌk] *n* F (*dollar*) dollar *m*
buck² [bʌk] *v/i of horse* ruer
bucket ['bʌkɪt] seau *m*
buckle¹ ['bʌkl] **1** *n* boucle *f* **2** *v/t belt* boucler
buckle² ['bʌkl] *v/i of metal* dé-

former

bud [bʌd] BOT bourgeon *m*

buddy ['bʌdɪ] copain *m*, copine *f*; *form of address* mec

budge [bʌdʒ] **1** *v/t (move)* déplacer **2** *v/i (move)* bouger

budget ['bʌdʒɪt] budget *m*

buff [bʌf] passionné(e) *m(f)*

buffalo ['bʌfələʊ] buffle *m*

buffer ['bʌfər] RAIL, COMPUT, *fig* tampon *m*

buffet ['bʊfeɪ] *meal* buffet *m*

bug [bʌg] **1** *n (insect)* insecte *m*; *(virus)* virus *m*; COMPUT bogue *f*; *(spying device)* micro *m* **2** *v/t room, telephone* mettre sur écoute; F *(annoy)* énerver

buggy ['bʌgɪ] *for baby* poussette *f*

build [bɪld] **1** *n of person* carrure *f* **2** *v/t* construire

◆ **build up 1** *v/t strength* développer; *relationship* construire **2** *v/i* s'accumuler; *fig* s'intensifier

builder ['bɪldər] constructeur(-trice) *m(f)*; *building* bâtiment *m*; *activity* construction *f*

'**building site** chantier *m*; **building society** *Br* caisse *f* d'épargne-logement; **building trade** (industrie *f* du) bâtiment *m*; **build-up** accumulation *f*; **give s.o./sth a big ~** faire beaucoup de battage autour de qn/qch; **built-in** encastré; *flash* incorporé

bulb [bʌlb] BOT bulbe *m*; *(light*

~*)* ampoule *f*

bulge [bʌldʒ] **1** *n* gonflement *m*, saillie *f* **2** *v/i* être gonflé, faire saillie

'**bulky** ['bʌlkɪ] encombrant; *sweater* gros

bull [bʊl] *animal* taureau *m*; **bulldozer** ['bʊldəʊzər] bulldozer *m*

bullet ['bʊlɪt] balle *f*

bulletin ['bʊlɪtɪn] bulletin *m*

'**bulletin board** tableau *m* d'affichage; COMPUT serveur *m* télématique

'**bullet-proof** protégé contre les balles; *vest* pare-balles

'**bull's-eye** mille *m*; **hit the ~** *also fig* mettre dans le mille; **bullshit** merde *f* V, conneries *fpl* P

bully ['bʊlɪ] **1** *n* brute *f* **2** *v/t* brimer; **bullying** brimades *fpl*

bum [bʌm] **1** *n* F *(worthless person)* bon à rien *m*; *(tramp)* clochard *m* **2** *v/t*: **can I ~ a cigarette?** est-ce que je peux vous taper une cigarette?

bump [bʌmp] **1** *n* bosse *f* **2** *v/t* se cogner; **bumper** MOT pare-chocs *mpl*; **bumpy** *road* cahoteux; **we had a ~ flight** nous avons été secoués pendant le vol

bunch [bʌntʃ] *of people* groupe *m*; *of keys* trousseau *m*; *of grapes* grappe *f*; *of flowers* bouquet *m*; **thanks a ~** merci beaucoup

bungle ['bʌŋgl] bousiller

bunk [bʌŋk] couchette *f*

buoy [bɔɪ] NAUT bouée *f*; **buoyant** *mood* jovial; *economy* prospère

burden ['bɜːrdn] **1** *n* fardeau *m* **2** *v/t*: **~ s.o. with sth** accabler qn de qch

bureau ['bjʊroʊ] bureau *m*; **bureaucrat** bureaucrate *m/f*; **bureaucratic** bureaucratique

burger ['bɜːrgər] steak *m* hâché; *in roll* hamburger *m*

burglar ['bɜːrglər] cambrioleur(-euse) *m(f)*; **burglar alarm** alarme *f* antivol; **burglarize** cambrioler; **burglary** cambriolage *m*

burial ['berɪəl] enterrement *m*

burn [bɜːrn] **1** *n* brûlure *f* **2** *v/t* & *v/i* brûler

◆ **burn down 1** *v/t* incendier **2** *v/i* être réduit en cendres

burp [bɜːrp] **1** *n* rot *m* **2** *v/i* roter

burst [bɜːrst] **1** *n in pipe* trou *m* **2** *adj* tire creuvé **3** *v/t* & *v/i* crever; *of pipe* éclater; **~ into tears** fondre en larmes; **~ out laughing** éclater de rire

bus [bʌs] (auto)bus *m*; *long distance* (auto)car *m*

bush [bʊʃ] buisson *m*

bushy ['bʊʃɪ] *beard* touffu

business ['bɪznɪs] commerce *m*; *(company)* entreprise *f*; *(work)* travail *m*; *(sector)* secteur *m*; *(matter)* affaire *f*; **on ~** en déplacement (professionnel); **mind your own ~!** occupe-toi de tes affaires!; **business card** carte *f* de visite; **business class** classe *f* affaires; **businesslike** sérieux; **businessman** homme *m* d'affaires; **business meeting** réunion *f* d'affaires; **business school** école *f* de commerce; **business studies** *course* études *fpl* de commerce; **business trip** voyage *m* d'affaires; **businesswoman** femme *f* d'affaires

'bus station gare *f* routière; **bus stop** arrêt *m* d'autobus

bust[1] [bʌst] *n of woman* poitrine *f*

bust[2] [bʌst] F *(broken)* cassé

'bust-up F brouille *f*; **busty** à la poitrine plantureuse

busy ['bɪzɪ] *person*, TELEC occupé; *day, life* bien rempli; *street, shop* plein de monde; **busybody** curieux(-se) *m(f)*

but [bʌt] **1** *conj* mais **2** *prep*: **all ~ him** tous sauf lui; **the last ~ one** l'avant-dernier; **~ for you** si tu n'avais pas été là; **nothing ~ the best** rien que le meilleur

butcher ['bʊtʃər] boucher (-ère) *m(f)*

butt [bʌt] **1** *n of cigarette* mégot *m*; F *(backside)* cul *m* **2** *v/t* donner un coup de tête à

butter ['bʌtər] beurre *m*; **butterfly** *also swimming* papillon *m*

buttocks ['bʌtəks] fesses *fpl*

button ['bʌtn] bouton m; (badge) badge m

buy [baɪ] acheter

◆ **buy out** COM racheter la part de

buyer ['baɪr] acheteur(-euse) m (f)

buzz [bʌz] **1** n bourdonnement m **2** v/i of insect bourdonner; buzzer sonnerie f

by [baɪ] to show agent par; (near, next to) près de; (no later than) pour; mode of transport en; ~ **bus** en bus; ~ **day** le jour; ~ **my watch** selon ma montre; ~ **o.s.** tout seul

bye(-bye) [baɪ] au revoir

'**bypass** road déviation f; MED pontage m (coronarien); by-product sous-produit m; bystander spectateur(-trice) m(f)

C

cab [kæb] taxi m; of truck cabine f; cab driver chauffeur m de taxi

cabin ['kæbɪn] of plane, ship cabine f; cabin attendant male steward m; female hôtesse f (de l'air); cabin crew équipage m

cabinet ['kæbɪnɪt] furniture meuble m (de rangement); POL cabinet m; display ~ vitrine f

cable ['keɪbl] câble m; cable car téléphérique m; on rail funiculaire m; cable television (télévision f par) câble m

'**cab stand** station f de taxis

cactus ['kæktəs] cactus m

cadaver [kə'dævər] cadavre m

caddie ['kædɪ] in golf caddie m

Caesarean Br → **Cesarean**

café ['kæfeɪ] café m; cafeteria cafétéria f

caffeine ['kæfiːn] caféine f

cage [keɪdʒ] cage f; **cagey** évasif

cake [keɪk] gâteau m

calculate ['kælkjuleɪt] (work out) évaluer; in arithmetic calculer; **calculating** calculateur; **calculation** calcul m; **calculator** calculatrice f

calendar ['kæləndər] calendrier m

calf[1] [kæf] (young cow) veau m

calf[2] [kæf] of leg mollet m

caliber, Br **calibre** ['kælɪbər] of gun calibre m

call [kɔːl] **1** n appel m; (phone ~ also) coup m de téléphone **2** v/t on phone appeler; be ~**ed** ... s'appeler ... **3** v/i on phone appeler; (visit) passer

◆ **call back 1** v/t rappeler **2** v/i

on phone rappeler; (make another visit) repasser

◆ **call for** (collect) venir chercher; (demand, require) demander

◆ **call off** annuler

caller ['kɔːlər] on phone personne f qui appelle; (visitor) visiteur m

callous ['kæləs] dur

calm [kɑːm] **1** adj calme, tranquille **2** n calme m

◆ **calm down 1** v/t calmer **2** v/i se calmer

calmly ['kɑːmlɪ] calmement

calorie ['kælərɪ] calorie f

camcorder ['kæmkɔːrdər] caméscope m

camera ['kæmərə] appareil m photo; TV caméra f; **cameraman** cadreur m, caméraman m

camouflage ['kæməflɑːʒ] **1** n camouflage m **2** v/t camoufler

camp [kæmp] **1** n camp m **2** v/i camper

campaign [kæm'peɪn] **1** n campagne f **2** v/i faire campagne

camper ['kæmpər] person campeur m; vehicle camping-car m; **camping** camping m; **campsite** (terrain m de) camping m

campus ['kæmpəs] campus m

can[1] [kæn] v/aux pouvoir; ~ **you hear me?** tu m'entends?; ~ **she swim?** sait-elle nager?; ~ **I help you?** est-ce

que je peux t'aider?

can[2] [kæn] n for food boîte f; for drinks canette f; of paint bidon m

Canada ['kænədə] Canada m; **Canadian 1** adj canadien **2** n Canadien m

canal [kə'næl] canal m

cancel ['kænsl] annuler; **cancellation** annulation f

cancer ['kænsər] cancer m

candid ['kændɪd] franc

candidacy ['kændɪdəsɪ] candidature f; **candidate** candidat m

candle ['kændl] bougie f; in church cierge m

candor, Br **candour** ['kændər] franchise f

candy ['kændɪ] (sweet) bonbon m; (sweets) bonbons mpl

cane [keɪn] (tige f de) bambou m

canister ['kænɪstər] boîte f (métallique); for gas, spray bombe f

canned [kænd] en conserve, en boîte; (recorded) enregistré

cannot ['kænɑːt] = **can not**

canny ['kænɪ] (astute) rusé

canoe [kə'nuː] canoë m

'can opener ouvre-boîte m

can't [kænt] = **can not**

canteen [kæn'tiːn] in factory cantine f

canvas ['kænvəs] toile f

canyon ['kænjən] canyon m

cap [kæp] hat bonnet m; with peak casquette f; of soldier, *policeman* képi *m*

capability [keɪpə'bɪlətɪ] capacité *f*; **capable** capable

capacity [kə'pæsətɪ] capacité *f*

capital ['kæpɪtl] *of country* capitale *f*; *letter* majuscule *f*; *money* capital *m*; **capitalism** capitalisme *m*; **capitalist 1** *adj* capitaliste **2** *n* capitaliste *m/f*; **capital punishment** peine *f* capitale

capsize [kæp'saɪz] chavirer

capsule ['kæpsəl] *of medicine* gélule *f*; *(space* ~*)* capsule *f* spatiale

captain ['kæptɪn] capitaine *m*; *of aircraft* commandant *m* de bord

caption ['kæpʃn] légende *f*

captivate ['kæptɪveɪt] captiver, fasciner; **captive** captif; **captivity** captivité *f*; **capture 1** *n of city* prise *f*; *of person, animal* capture *f* **2** *v/t person, animal* capturer; *city, building* prendre; *market share* conquérir

car [kɑːr] voiture *f*, automobile *f*; *of train* wagon *m*, voiture *f*; **by** ~ en voiture

carbon monoxide [kɑːrbənmən'ɑːksaɪd] monoxyde *m* de carbone

carbureter, carburetor [kɑːrbu'retər] carburateur *m*

carcass ['kɑːrkəs] carcasse *f*

card [kɑːrd] carte *f*; **cardboard box** carton *m*

cardiac ['kɑːrdɪæk] cardiaque

cardinal ['kɑːrdɪnl] REL cardinal *m*

care [ker] **1** *n of baby, pet* garde *f*; *of the elderly, sick* soins *mpl*; *(medical* ~*)* soins *mpl* médicaux; *(worry)* souci *m*; **take** ~ **of** → **c/o**; **take** ~ *(be cautious)* faire attention; **take** ~ **of** s'occuper de **2** *v/i* se soucier; **I don't** ~! ça m'est égal!
◆ **care about** s'intéresser à
◆ **care for** *(look after)* s'occuper de

career [kə'rɪr] carrière *f*

careful ['kerfl] *(cautious)* prudent; *(thorough)* méticuleux; **(be)** ~! *(fais)* attention!; **carefully** *(with caution)* prudemment; *worded etc* soigneusement; **careless** négligent; *work* négligé; **carelessly** négligemment

caress [kə'res] caresser

'car ferry (car-)ferry *m*, transbordeur *m*

cargo ['kɑːrgoʊ] cargaison *f*

caricature ['kærɪkətʃər] caricature *f*

carnival ['kɑːrnɪvl] fête *f* foraine; *with processions etc* carnaval *m*

carpenter ['kɑːrpɪntər] charpentier *m*; *for smaller objects* menuisier *m*

carpet ['kɑːrpɪt] tapis *m*; *fitted* moquette *f*

'car phone téléphone *m* de voiture; **carpool** faire du co-voiturage; **car rental** location *f* de voitures

carrier ['kærɪər] *company* entreprise *f* de transport; *of disease* porteur(-euse) *m(f)*

carrot ['kærət] carotte *f*

carry ['kærɪ] **1** *v/t* porter; *of ship, bus etc* transporter **2** *v/i of sound* porter

♦ **carry on 1** *v/i* (*continue*) continuer (**with sth** qch) **2** *v/t business* exercer

♦ **carry out** *survey etc* faire; *orders etc* exécuter

cart [kɑːrt] charrette *f*

carton ['kɑːrtn] carton *m*; *of cigarettes* cartouche *f*

cartoon [kɑːr'tuːn] dessin *m* humoristique; *on TV* dessin *m* animé; (*strip ~*) BD *f*, bande *f* dessinée

carve [kɑːrv] *meat* découper; *wood* sculpter

case¹ [keɪs] *for eyeglasses, camera* étui *m*; *for gadget* pochette *f*; *of wine etc* caisse *f*; *Br* (*suitcase*) valise *f*

case² [keɪs] (*instance*), MED cas *m*; *for police* affaire *f*; LAW procès *m*; **in ~** . au cas où ...; **in any ~** en tout cas

cash [kæʃ] **1** *n* (*money*) argent *m*; (*coins and notes*) (argent *m*) liquide *m* **2** *v/t check* toucher; **cash desk** caisse *f*; **cash flow** COM trésorerie *f*; **I've got ~ problems** j'ai des problèmes d'argent; **cashier** *in store etc* caissier(-ère) *m(f)*; **cashpoint** *Br* distributeur *m* automatique (de billets); **cash register** caisse *f*

enregistreuse

casino [kə'siːnou] casino *m*

casket ['kæskɪt] (*coffin*) cercueil *m*

casserole ['kæsəroul] *meal* ragoût *m*; *container* cocotte *f*

cassette [kə'set] cassette *f*; **cassette player** lecteur *m* de cassettes

cast [kæst] **1** *n of play* distribution *f*; (*mold*) moule *m* **2** *v/t doubt* jeter; *metal* couler

cast iron fonte *f*

castle ['kæsl] chateau *m*

casual ['kæʒuəl] (*chance*) fait au hasard; (*offhand*) désinvolte; (*not formal*) décontracté; **casually** *dressed* de manière décontractée; *say* de manière désinvolte; **casualty** victime *f*

cat [kæt] chat(te) *m(f)*

catalog, *Br* **catalogue** ['kætəlɔːg] catalogue *m*

catalyst ['kætəlɪst] catalyseur *m*

catastrophe [kə'tæstrəfɪ] catastrophe *f*; **catastrophic** catastrophique

catch [kætʃ] **1** *n* prise *f* (au vol); *of fish* pêche *f*; (*lock: on door*) loquet *m*; (*problem*) entourloupette *f* **2** *v/t ball, prisoner, dog, illness* attraper; (*get on: bus, train*) prendre; (*hear*) entendre; **catching** *also fig* contagieux; **catchy** facile à retenir

categoric [kætə'gɔːrɪk] catégorique; **category** catégorie *f*

caterer ['keɪtərər] traiteur *m*

cathedral [kə'θiːdrl] cathédrale *f*

Catholic ['kæθəlɪk] **1** *adj* catholique **2** *n* catholique *m/f*; **Catholicism** catholicisme *m*

catty ['kætɪ] méchant

cause [kɔːz] **1** *n* cause *f*; (*grounds*) raison *f* **2** *v/t* causer

caution ['kɔːʃn] **1** *n* (*carefulness*) prudence *f* **2** *v/t* (*warn*) avertir; **cautious** prudent; **cautiously** prudemment

cave [keɪv] caverne *f*, grotte *f*

cavity ['kævətɪ] cavité *f*

CD [siː'diː] (= *compact disc*) CD *m* (= compact-disc *m*, disque *m* compact)

C'D player lecteur *m* de CD; **CD-ROM** CD-ROM *m*

cease [siːs] cesser

'cease-fire cessez-le-feu *m*

ceiling ['siːlɪŋ] plafond *m*

celebrate ['selɪbreɪt] **1** *v/i* faire la fête **2** *v/t* fêter; *Christmas, event* célébrer; **celebrated** célèbre; **celebration** fête *f*; *of event, wedding* célébration *f*; **celebrity** célébrité *f*

cell [sel] *for prisoner, of spreadsheet,* BIO cellule *f*

cellar ['selər] cave *f*

cello ['tʃelou] violoncelle *m*

cell phone, cellular phone ['seljuːlər] (téléphone *m*) portable *m*

cement [sɪ'ment] ciment *m*

cemetery ['semətərɪ] cimetière *m*

censor ['sensər] censurer

census ['sensəs] recensement *m*

cent [sent] cent *m*

centenary [sen'tiːnərɪ] centenaire *m*

center ['sentər] **1** *n* centre *m* **2** *v/t* centrer

centigrade ['sentɪgreɪd] centigrade

centimeter, *Br* **centimetre** ['sentɪmiːtər] centimètre *m*

central ['sentrəl] central

central 'heating chauffage *m* central; **centralize** centraliser; **central locking** MOT verrouillage *m* centralisé

centre *Br* → **center**

century ['sentʃərɪ] siècle *m*

CEO [siːiː'ou] (= *Chief Executive Officer*) directeur *m* général

ceramic [sɪ'ræmɪk] en céramique

cereal ['sɪrɪəl] céréale *f*; (*breakfast ~*) céréales *fpl*

ceremonial [serɪ'mounɪəl] **1** *adj* de cérémonie **2** *n* cérémonial *m*; **ceremony** cérémonie *f*

certain ['sɜːrtn] (*sure*) certain, sûr; (*particular*) certain; **certainly** certainement; **certainty** certitude *f*

certificate [sər'tɪfɪkət] certificat *m*

certified public accountant ['sɜːrtɪfaɪd] expert *m* comptable; **certify** certifier

Cesarean [sɪˈzerɪən] césarienne *f*

CFO [siːefˈou] (= **chief financial officer**) directeur *m* financier

chain [tʃeɪn] **1** *n also of stores etc* chaîne *f* **2** *v/t:* ~ **sth. to sth** enchaîner qch à qch

chair [tʃer] **1** *n* chaise *f*; (*arm*~) fauteuil *m*; *at university* chaire *f* **2** *v/t meeting* présider; **chair lift** télésiège *m*; **chairman** président *m*; **chairmanship** présidence *f*; **chairperson** président(e) *m(f)*

chalk [tʃɔːk] craie *f*

challenge [ˈtʃælɪndʒ] **1** *n* défi *m*, challenge *m* **2** *v/t* (*defy*) défier; (*call into question*) mettre en doute; ~ **s.o. to a game** proposer à qn de faire une partie; **challenger** challenger *m*; **challenging** *job, undertaking* stimulant

Chamber of 'Commerce Chambre *f* de commerce

champagne [ʃæmˈpeɪn] champagne *m*

champion [ˈtʃæmpɪən] **1** *n* SP, *of cause* champion(ne) *m(f)* **2** *v/t cause* être le (la) champion(ne) *m(f)* de; **championship** *event* championnat *m*; *title* titre *m* de champion(ne)

chance [tʃæns] (*possibility*) chances *fpl*; (*opportunity*) occasion *f*; (*luck*) hasard *m*; **by** ~ par hasard; **take a** ~

prendre un risque

change [tʃeɪndʒ] **1** *n* changement *m*; (*money*) monnaie *f*; **for a** ~ pour changer un peu **2** *v/t* changer; *bankbill* faire la monnaie sur **3** *v/i* changer; (*put on different clothes*) se changer; **changeover** changement *m*; **changing room** SP vestiaire *m*; *in shop* cabine *f* d'essayage

channel [ˈtʃænl] *on TV, radio* chaîne *f*; (*waterway*) chenal *m*

chant [tʃænt] **1** *n* slogans *mpl* scandés; REL chant *m* **2** *v/i of crowds etc* scander des slogans; REL psalmodier

chaos [ˈkeɪɑs] chaos *m*; **chaotic** chaotique

chapel [ˈtʃæpl] chapelle *f*

chapter [ˈtʃæptər] chapitre *m*

character [ˈkærɪktər] caractère *m*; (*person*) personne *f*; *in book* personnage *m*; **characteristic 1** *n* caractéristique *f* **2** *adj* caractéristique; **characterize** caractériser

charge [tʃɑːrdʒ] **1** *n* (*fee*) frais *mpl*; LAW accusation *f*; **free of** ~ gratuit; **be in** ~ être responsable **2** *v/t sum of money* faire payer; LAW inculper (**with** de); *battery* charger; **can you** ~ **it?** (*put on account*) pouvez-vous le mettre sur mon compte? **3** *v/i* (*attack*) charger; **charge account** compte *m*; **charge card** carte *f* de paiement

charitable ['tʃærɪtəbl] charitable; **charity** charité *f*; (*organization*) organisation *f* caritative

charm [tʃɑːrm] **1** *n also on bracelet* charme *m* **2** *v/t* (*delight*) charmer; **charming** charmant

charred [tʃɑːrd] carbonisé

chart [tʃɑːrt] diagramme *m*; (*map*) carte *f*

'charter flight (vol *m*) charter *m*

chase [tʃeɪs] **1** *n* poursuite *f* **2** *v/t* poursuivre

◆ **chase away** *v/t* chasser

chassis ['ʃæsɪ] *of car* châssis *m*

chat [tʃæt] **1** *n* causette *f* **2** *v/i* causer; **chatline** chat *m* téléphonique; **chat room** chat *m*

chatter ['tʃætər] **1** *n* bavardage *m* **2** *v/i* (*talk*) bavarder; **my teeth were ~ing** je claquais des dents

chauffeur ['ʃoʊfər] chauffeur *m*

chauvinist ['ʃoʊvɪnɪst] (*male ~*) machiste *m*

cheap [tʃiːp] bon marché, pas cher; (*nasty*) méchant; (*mean*) pingre

cheat [tʃiːt] **1** *n person* tricheur(-euse) *m(f)* **2** *v/t* tromper **3** *v/i* tricher

check¹ [tʃek] **1** *adj shirt* à carreaux **2** *n* carreaux *m*

check² [tʃek] *n* FIN chèque *m*; *in restaurant etc* addition *f*

check³ [tʃek] **1** *n to verify sth* contrôle *m*, vérification *f* **2** *v/t* vérifier; *with a ~mark* cocher; *coat etc* mettre au vestiaire **3** *v/i* vérifier

◆ **check in** *v/i at airport* faire enregistrer; *at hotel* s'inscrire

◆ **check out 1** *v/i of hotel* régler sa note **2** *v/t* (*look into*) enquêter sur; *club etc* essayer

◆ **check up on** se renseigner sur

'checkbook carnet *m* de chèques; **checked** *material* à carreaux

checkered ['tʃekərd] *pattern* à carreaux; *career* varié

'check-in (**counter**) enregistrement *m*; **checking account** compte *m* courant; **checklist** liste *f* (de contrôle); **check mark**: *put a ~ against sth* cocher qch; **check-out** caisse *f*; **checkpoint** contrôle *m*; **checkroom** *for coats* vestiaire *m*; *for baggage* consigne *f*; **checkup** *medical* examen *m* médical; *dental* examen *m* dentaire

cheek [tʃiːk] *on face* joue *f*

cheer [tʃɪr] **1** *n* hourra *m* **2** *v/t* acclamer **3** *v/i* pousser des hourras

◆ **cheer up 1** *v/i* reprendre courage; *cheer up!* courage! **2** *v/t* remonter le moral à

cheerful ['tʃɪrfl] gai, joyeux; **cheering** acclamations *fpl*; **cheerleader** meneuse *f* de ban

cheese [tʃiːz] fromage *m*

chef [ʃef] chef *m* (de cuisine)

chemical ['kemɪkl] **1** *adj* chimique **2** *n* produit *m* chimique; **chemist** *in laboratory* chimiste *m/f*; *Br* pharmacien(ne) *m(f)*; **chemistry** chimie *f*

chemotherapy [kiːmouˈθerəpɪ] chimiothérapie *f*

cheque [tʃek] *Br* → **check²**

chess [tʃes] (jeu *m* d'échecs *mpl*; **play ~** jouer aux échecs

chest [tʃest] poitrine *f*; (box) coffre *m*, caisse *f*

chew [tʃuː] mâcher; *of rat* ronger; **chewing gum** chewing-gum *m*

chick [tʃɪk] poussin *m*; F *girl* nana

chicken ['tʃɪkɪn] poulet *m*

chief [tʃiːf] **1** *n* chef *m* **2** *adj* principal; **chiefly** principalement

child [tʃaɪld] enfant *m/f*; **childhood** enfance *f*; **childish** puéril; **childlike** enfantin

children ['tʃɪldrən] *pl* → **child**

Chile ['tʃɪli] Chili *m*; **Chilean 1** *adj* chilien **2** *n* Chilien(ne) *m(f)*

◆ **chill out** se relaxer

chilly ['tʃɪli] *also fig* froid

chimney ['tʃɪmnɪ] cheminée *f*

chin [tʃɪn] menton *m*

China ['tʃaɪnə] Chine *f*

china ['tʃaɪnə] **1** *n* porcelaine *f* **2** *adj* en porcelaine

Chinese [tʃaɪˈniːz] **1** *adj* chinois **2** *n language* chinois *m*; *person* Chinois(e) *m(f)*

chip [tʃɪp] **1** *n damage* brèche *f*; *in gambling* jeton *m*; COMPUT puce *f*; **~s** (*potato ~s*) chips *mpl*; *Br* pommes frites *fpl* **2** *v/t damage* ébrécher

chipmunk tamia *m* rayé

chisel ['tʃɪzl] ciseau *m*, burin *m*

chlorine ['klɔːriːn] chlore *m*

chocolate ['tʃɑːkələt] chocolat *m*

choice [tʃɔɪs] **1** *n* choix *m*; **I had no ~** je n'avais pas le choix **2** *adj* (*top quality*) de choix

choir ['kwaɪr] chœur *m*

choke [tʃouk] **1** *v/i* s'étrangler **2** *v/t* (*strangle*) étrangler

cholesterol [kəˈlestərɒl] cholestérol *m*

choose [tʃuːz] choisir; **choosey** difficile

chop [tʃɑːp] **1** *n of meat* côtelette *f* **2** *v/t* couper

◆ **chop down** *tree* abattre

chore [tʃɔːr] **~s** travaux *mpl* domestiques

choreography [kɔːriˈɑːgrəfɪ] chorégraphie *f*

chorus ['kɔːrəs] *singers* chœur *m*; *of song* refrain *m*

Christ [kraɪst] Christ *m*; **~!** mon Dieu!

christen ['krɪsn] baptiser

Christian ['krɪstʃən] **1** *n* chrétien(ne) *m(f)* **2** *adj* chrétien; **Christianity** christianisme *m*

Christmas ['krɪsməs] Noël *m*;
Merry ~! Joyeux Noël!;
Christmas card carte *f* de
Noël; **Christmas Day** jour
m de Noël; **Christmas Eve**
veille *f* de Noël; **Christmas
present** cadeau *m* de Noël;
Christmas tree arbre *m* de
Noël

chronic ['krɑːnɪk] chronique

chubby ['tʃʌbɪ] potelé

chuck [tʃʌk] lancer

chuckle ['tʃʌkl] **1** *n* petit rire
m **2** *v/i* rire tout bas

chunk [tʃʌŋk] gros morceau *m*

church [tʃɜːrtʃ] église *f*;
church service office *m*;
churchyard cimetière *m* (autour d'une église)

chute [ʃuːt] *for garbage* vide-
-ordures *m*; *for escape* toboggan *m*

cigar [sɪ'gɑːr] cigare *m*

cigarette [sɪgə'ret] cigarette
f; **cigarette lighter** briquet *m*

cinema ['sɪnəmə] *Br* cinéma
m

circle ['sɜːrkl] **1** *n* cercle *m* **2**
v/i of plane tournoyer

circuit ['sɜːrkɪt] circuit *m*;
(lap) tour *m* (de circuit); **circuit board** COMPUT plaquette
f; **circular** ['sɜːrkjələr] **1** *n*
circulaire *f* **2** *adj* circulaire;
circulate ['sɜːrkjuleɪt] **1** *v/i*
circuler **2** *v/t memo* faire circuler; **circulation** circulation
f; *of newspaper* tirage *m*

circumstances ['sɜːrkəm-
stænsɪz] circonstances *fpl*;

financial situation *f* finan-
cière

circus ['sɜːrkəs] cirque *m*

cistern ['sɪstərn] réservoir *m*;
of WC réservoir *m* de chasse
d'eau

citizen ['sɪtɪzn] citoyen(ne)
m(f); **citizenship** citoyenneté *f*

city ['sɪtɪ] (grande) ville *f*

city 'center, *Br* **city 'centre**
centre-ville *m*; **city hall** hôtel
m de ville

civic ['sɪvɪk] municipal; *pride,
responsibilities* civique

civil ['sɪvl] civil; *(polite)* poli;
civil ceremony mariage *m*
civil; **civil engineer** ingénieur *m* des travaux publics

civilian [sɪ'vɪljən] civil(e)
m(f); **civilization** civilisation
f; **civilize** civiliser; **civil
rights** droits *mpl* civils; **civil
servant** fonctionnaire *m/f*;
civil service fonction *f* publique, administration *f*; **civil
war** guerre *f* civile

claim [kleɪm] **1** *n (request)* demande *f*; *(assertion)* affirmation *f* **2** *v/t (ask for as a right)*
demander, réclamer; *(assert)*
affirmer; *lost property* réclamer; **claimant** ['kleɪmənt]
demandeur(-euse) *m(f)*

clam [klæm] palourde *f*, clam
m

clammy ['klæmɪ] moite

clamp [klæmp] *fastener* pince
f, crampon *m*

◆ **clamp down on** sévir con-

clerk

tre

clandestine [klæn'destɪn]
clandestin

clap [klæp] (*applaud*) applaudir

clarification [klærɪfɪ'keɪʃn]
clarification *f*; **clarify** clarifier; **clarity** clarté *f*

clash [klæʃ] **1** *n between people* affrontement *m* **2** *v/i* s'affronter; *of colors* détonner;
of events tomber en même
temps

clasp [klæsp] **1** *n* agrafe *f* **2** *v/t
in hand* serrer

class [klæs] *n* (*lesson*) cours
m; (*group of people, category*) classe *f*; *the ~ of 2002* la
promo(tion) 2002 **2** *v/t* classer

classic ['klæsɪk] **1** *adj* classique **2** *n* classique *m*; **classical music** classique *m*; **classification** classification *f*; **classified information** secret;
petite annonce f; **classify**
classifier; **classroom** salle *f*
de classe; **classy** F *restaurant
etc* chic *inv*; *person* classe

clause [klɔːz] (*in agreement*)
clause *f*; GRAM proposition *f*

claustrophobia [klɔːstrə-
'fəʊbɪə] claustrophobie *f*

claw [klɔː] *of cat* griffe *f*; *of
lobster* pince *f*

clay [kleɪ] argile *f*, glaise *f*

clean [kliːn] **1** *adj* propre **2**
adv (*completely*) complète-
ment **3** *v/t* nettoyer; **cleaner**

male agent m de propreté; *female femme f* de ménage;
(*dry~*) teinturier(-ère) *m(f)*

cleanse [klenz] *skin* nettoyer;
cleanser *for skin* démaquillant *m*

clear [klɪr] **1** *adj voice, photo*
net; *to understand, sky, water*
clair; *conscience* tranquille **2**
v/t roads etc dégager; *place*
(faire) évacuer; *table* débarrasser; *ball* dégager; (*acquit*)
innocenter; (*authorize*) autoriser **3** *v/i of sky* se dégager;
of mist se dissiper; *of face*
s'éclairer

◆ **clear out 1** *v/t closet* vider **2**
v/i ficher le camp

◆ **clear up 1** *v/i in room etc*
ranger; *of weather's* s'éclaircir;
of illness disparaître **2** *v/t* (*tidy*) ranger; *problem* résou-
dre

clearance [klɪrəns] (*space*)
espace *m* (libre); (*authorization*) autorisation *f*; **clearance sale** liquidation *f*;
clearing clairière *f*; **clearly**
speak, see clairement; *hear*
distinctement; (*evidently*)
manifestement

cleavage ['kliːvɪdʒ] décolleté
m

clench [klentʃ] serrer

clergy ['klɜːrdʒɪ] clergé *m*;
clergyman écclésiastique
m; *Protestant* pasteur *m*

clerk [klɜːrk] *administrative*
employé(e) *m(f)* de bureau;
in store vendeur(-euse) *m(f)*

clever ['klevər] intelligent; *gadget* ingénieux; *(skillful)* habile

click [klɪk] **1** *n* COMPUT clic *m* **2** *v/i* cliqueter

◆ **click on** COMPUT cliquer sur

client ['klaɪənt] client(e) *m(f)*; *clientele* clientèle *f*

climate ['klaɪmət] *also fig* climat *m*

climax ['klaɪmæks] point *m* culminant

climb [klaɪm] **1** *n up mountain* ascension *f* **2** *v/t* monter sur; *mountain* escalader **3** *v/i* monter; **climber** alpiniste *m/f*

clinch [klɪntʃ] *deal* conclure

cling [klɪŋ] *of clothes* coller

◆ **cling to** s'accrocher à

clingy ['klɪŋɪ] *person* collant

clinic ['klɪnɪk] clinique *f*; **clinical** clinique

clip[1] [klɪp] **1** *n fastener* pince *f*; *for hair* barrette *f* **2** *v/t*: **~ sth to sth** attacher qch à qch

clip[2] [klɪp] **1** *n (extract)* extrait *m* **2** *v/t hair, grass* couper; **clipping** *from press* coupure *f* (de presse)

clock [klɑːk] horloge *f*; **clock radio** radio-réveil *m*; **clockwise** dans le sens des aiguilles d'une montre

clone [kloʊn] **1** *n* clone *m* **2** *v/t* cloner; **cloning** clonage *m*

close[1] [kloʊs] **1** *adj family, friend* proche **2** *adv* près; **~ at hand, ~ by** tout près; **~ to** près de

close[2] [kloʊz] *v/t* fermer

closed-circuit 'television télévision *f* en circuit fermé; **close-knit** très uni; **closely** *listen* attentivement; *watch* de près; *cooperate* étroitement

closet ['klɑːzɪt] armoire *f*, placard *m*

close-up ['kloʊsʌp] gros plan *m*

closing date ['kloʊzɪŋ] date *f* limite

closure ['kloʊzər] fermeture *f*

clot [klɑːt] **1** *n of blood* caillot *m* **2** *v/i of blood* coaguler

cloth [klɑːθ] *tissu m; for drying* torchon *m; for washing* lavette *f*

clothes [kloʊðz] vêtements *mpl*; **clothing** vêtements *mpl*

cloud [klaʊd] nuage *m*; **cloudless** sans nuages; **cloudy** nuageux

clout [klaʊt] *fig (influence)* influence *f*

clove of 'garlic [kloʊv] gousse *f* d'ail

clown [klaʊn] *also pej* clown *m*

club [klʌb] club *m; weapon* massue *f*

clue [kluː] indice *m*

clumsiness ['klʌmzɪnɪs] maladresse *f*; **clumsy** maladroit

cluster ['klʌstər] groupe *m*

clutch [klʌtʃ] **1** *n* MOT embrayage *m* **2** *v/t* étreindre

◆ **clutch at** s'agripper à

c/o (**= care of**) chez

Co. (= *Company*) Cie (= Compagnie)

coach [kəʊtʃ] **1** *n* (*trainer*) entraîneur(-euse) *m(f)*; *Br* (*bus*) (auto)car *m* **2** *v/t* SP entraîner; **coaching** entraînement *m*

coagulate [kəʊˈægjʊleɪt] *of blood* coaguler

coal [kəʊl] charbon *m*

coalition [kəʊəˈlɪʃn] coalition *f*

'coalmine mine *f* de charbon

coarse [kɔːrs] *fabric* rugueux; *hair* épais; (*vulgar*) grossier; **coarsely** (*vulgarly*), *ground* grossièrement

coast [kəʊst] côte *f*; **coastal** côtier; **coastguard** gendarmerie *f* maritime; *person* gendarme *m* maritime; **coastline** littoral *m*

coat [kəʊt] **1** *n* veston *m*; (*over~*) pardessus *m*; *of animal* pelage *m*; *of paint etc* couche *f* **2** *v/t* (*cover*) couvrir (**with** de); **coathanger** cintre *m*; **coating** couche *f*

coax [kəʊks] cajoler

cocaine [kəˈkeɪn] cocaïne *f*

cock [kɑːk] *chicken* coq *m*; *any male bird* (oiseau *m*) mâle *m*; **cockpit** *of plane* poste *m* de pilotage, cockpit *m*; **cockroach** cafard *m*; **cocktail** cocktail *m*

cocoa [ˈkəʊkəʊ] cacao *m*

coconut [ˈkəʊkənʌt] noix *m* de coco; **coconut palm** cocotier *m*

code [kəʊd] code *m*; *in ~* codé

coeducational [kəʊedʊˈkeɪʃnl] mixte

coerce [kəʊˈɜːrs] forcer

coexist [kəʊɪɡˈzɪst] coexister; **coexistence** coexistence *f*

coffee [ˈkɑːfɪ] café *m*; **coffee maker** machine *f* à café; **coffee pot** cafetière *f*; **coffee shop** café *m*

cohabit [kəʊˈhæbɪt] cohabiter

coherent [kəʊˈhɪrənt] cohérent

coil [kɔɪl] *of rope* rouleau *m*; *of snake* anneau *m*

coin [kɔɪn] pièce *f* (de monnaie)

coincide [kəʊɪnˈsaɪd] coïncider; **coincidence** coïncidence *f*

Coke® [kəʊk] coca® *m*

cold [kəʊld] **1** *adj* froid; *I'm ~* j'ai froid; *it's ~* of weather il fait froid **2** *n* froid *m*; MED rhume *m*; **cold-blooded** à sang froid; *murder* commis de sang-froid; **coldly** froidement; **coldness** froideur *f*; **cold sore** bouton *m* de fièvre

collaborate [kəˈlæbəreɪt] collaborer; **collaboration** collaboration *f*; **collaborator** collaborateur(-trice) *m(f)*

collapse [kəˈlæps] s'effondrer; *of building* s'écrouler; **collapsible** pliant

collar [ˈkɑːlər] col *m*; *for dog* collier *m*

colleague [ˈkɑːliːg] collègue
m/f
collect [kəˈlekt] 1 v/t person,
cleaning etc aller/venir chercher; as hobby collectionner;
(gather together) recueillir 2
v/i (gather together) s'assembler; **collect call** communication f en PCV; **collection**
collection f; in church collecte f; **collective** collectif; **collector** collectionneur(-euse)
m(f)
college [ˈkɑːlɪdʒ] université f
collide [kəˈlaɪd] se heurter;
collision collision f
colon [ˈkəʊlən] punctuation
deux-points mpl
colonel [ˈkɜːrnl] colonel m
colonial [kəˈləʊnɪəl] colonial;
colonize coloniser; **colony**
colonie f
color [ˈkʌlər] couleur f; **color-
-blind** daltonien; **colored**
person de couleur; **colorful**
also fig coloré
colossal [kəˈlɑːsl] colossal
colour Br → **color**
colt [kəʊlt] poulain m
column [ˈkɑːləm] architectural, of text colonne f; **columnist** chroniqueur(-euse)
m(f)
coma [ˈkəʊmə] coma m
comb [kəʊm] 1 n peigne m 2
v/t peigner; area passer au
peigne fin
combat [ˈkɑːmbæt] 1 n combat m 2 v/t combattre
combination [kɑːmbɪˈneɪʃn]

also of safe combinaison f;
combine 1 v/t combiner; in-
gredients mélanger 2 v/i se
combiner
come [kʌm] venir; of train,
bus arriver
◆ **come across** (find) tomber sur
◆ **come along** (come too) venir (aussi); (turn up) arriver;
(progress) avancer
◆ **come back** revenir
◆ **come down** descendre; in
price etc baisser; of rain,
snow tomber
◆ **come for** (attack) attaquer;
(to collect) venir chercher
◆ **come forward** se présenter
◆ **come from** venir de
◆ **come in** entrer; of train, in
race arriver; of tide monter
◆ **come in for** criticism recevoir
◆ **come off** of handle etc se
détacher
◆ **come out** sortir; of results
être communiqué; of sun,
product apparaître; of stain
partir
◆ **come to** 1 v/t (reach) arriver à; **that comes to $70**
fait 70 $ 2 v/i (regain con-
sciousness) revenir à soi
◆ **come up** monter; of sun se
lever
'comeback retour m, come-
-back m
comedian [kəˈmiːdɪən] (comic) comique m/f; pej pitre
m/f; **comedy** comédie f

comfort ['kʌmfərt] **1** n confort m; (consolation) réconfort m **2** v/t réconforter; **comfortable** confortable; **be ~** of person être à l'aise

comic ['kɑːmɪk] **1** n to read bande f dessinée; (comedian) comique m/f **2** adj comique; **comical** comique; **comic book** bande f dessinée, BD f; **comics** bandes fpl dessinées; **comic strip** bande f dessinée

comma ['kɑːmə] virgule f

command [kə'mænd] **1** n (order) ordre m; MIL commandement m **2** v/t commander

commandeer [kɑːmən'dɪr] réquisitionner

commander [kə'mændər] commandant(e) m(f); **commander-in-chief** commandant(e) m(f) en chef

commemorate [kə'meməreɪt] commémorer

commence [kə'mens] commencer

commendable [kə'mendəbl] louable; **commendation** for bravery éloge m

comment ['kɑːment] **1** n commentaire m **2** v/t: **~ on** commenter; **commentary** commentaire m; **commentator** commentateur(-trice) m(f)

commerce ['kɑːmɜːrs] commerce m; **commercial 1** adj commercial **2** n (ad) publicité f; **commercial break** page f de publicité; **commercial-**

ize commercialiser

commission [kə'mɪʃn] (payment, committee) commission f; (job) commande f

commit [kə'mɪt] crime commettre; money engager; **commitment** in relationship engagement m; (responsibility) responsabilité f; **committee** comité m

commodity [kə'mɑːdəti] marchandise f

common ['kɑːmən] courant; species etc commun; (shared) commun; **have sth in ~ with s.o.** avoir qch en commun; **commonly** communément; **common sense** bon sens m

commotion [kə'mouʃn] agitation f

communal [kəm'juːnl] en commun

communicate [kə'mjuːnɪkeɪt] communiquer; **communication** communication f; **communicative** communicatif

Communion [kə'mjuːnjən] REL communion f

Communism ['kɑːmjunɪzəm] communisme m; **Communist 1** adj communiste **2** n communiste m/f

community [kə'mjuːnəti] communauté f

commute [kə'mjuːt] **1** v/i faire la navette (pour aller travailler) **2** v/t LAW commuer

compact 1 adj [kəm'pækt] compact **2** n ['kɑːmpækt]

MOT petite voiture f

companion [kəm'pænjən] compagnon m

company ['kʌmpəni] COM société f; (companionship) compagnie f; (guests) invités mpl

comparable ['kɑːmpərəbl] comparable; **comparative** comparativement; **compare** comparer; **comparison** comparaison f

compartment [kəm'pɑːrtmənt] compartiment m

compass ['kʌmpəs] compas m

compassion [kəm'pæʃn] compassion f; **compassionate** compatissant

compatibility [kəmpætə'biliti] compatibilité f; **compatible** compatible

compel [kəm'pel] obliger

compensate ['kɑːmpənseit] 1 v/t dédommager 2 v/i: **~ for** compenser; **compensation** (money) dédommagement m; (reward) compensation f; (comfort) consolation f

compete [kəm'piːt] être en compétition; (take part) participer (**in** à)

competence ['kɑːmpitəns] compétence f; **competent** person compétent, capable; piece of work (très) satisfaisant

competition [kɑːmpə'tiʃn] (contest) concours m; SP

compétition f; (competing, competitors) concurrence f; **competitive** compétitif; price, offer concurrentiel; **competitiveness** COM compétitivité f; of person esprit m de compétition; **competitor** concurrent m

complacent [kəm'pleisənt] complaisant, suffisant

complain [kəm'plein] se plaindre; **complaint** plainte f; IN SHOP réclamation f; MED maladie f

complementary [kɑːmpli'mentəri] complémentaire

complete [kəm'pliːt] 1 adj complet; (finished) terminé 2 v/t task, building etc terminer, achever; form remplir; **completely** complètement; **completion** achèvement m

complex ['kɑːmpleks] 1 adj complexe 2 n building, PSYCH complexe m; **complexion** facial teint m; **complexity** complexité f

compliance [kəm'plaiəns] conformité f

complicate ['kɑːmplikeit] compliquer; **complicated** compliqué; **complication** complication f

complimentary [kɑːmpli'mentəri] élogieux, flatteur; (free) gratuit

comply [kəm'plai] obéir; **~ with ...** se conformer à

component [kəm'pounənt] composant m

compose [kəm'pəʊz] composer; **composed** (*calm*) calme; **compose** mus composer *m*; **composition** composition *f*; **composure** calme *m*

compound ['kɑːmpaʊnd] chem composé *m*

comprehend [kɑːmprɪ'hend] comprendre; **comprehension** compréhension *f*; **comprehensive** complet

compress [kəm'pres] comprimer; *information* condenser

comprise [kəm'praɪz] comprendre; (*make up*) constituer; **be ~d of** se composer de

compromise ['kɑːmprəmaɪz] **1** *n* compromis *m* **2** *v/i* trouver un compromis **3** *v/t* compromettre

compulsion [kəm'pʌlʃn] psych compulsion *f*; **compulsive** *behavior* compulsif; *reading* captivant; **compulsory** obligatoire

computer [kəm'pjuːtər] ordinateur *m*; **computer game** jeu *m* informatique; **computerize** informatiser; **computer science** informatique *f*; **computing** informatique *f*

comrade ['kɑːmreɪd] camarade *m/f*; **comradeship** camaraderie *f*

conceal [kən'siːl] cacher; **concealment** dissimulation *f*

conceit [kən'siːt] vanité *f*; **conceited** vaniteux

conceivable [kən'siːvəbl] concevable; **conceive** *of woman* concevoir

concentrate ['kɑːnsəntreɪt] **1** *v/i* se concentrer **2** *v/t* *energies* concentrer; **concentration** concentration *f*

concept ['kɑːnsept] concept *m*; **conception** *of child* conception *f*

concern [kən'sɜːrn] **1** *n* (*anxiety, care*) inquiétude *f*, souci *m*; (*business*) affaire *f*; (*company*) entreprise *f* **2** *v/t* (*involve*) concerner; (*worry*) préoccuper; **concerned** (*anxious*) inquiet; (*caring, involved*) concerné; **concerning** concernant, au sujet de

concert ['kɑːnsərt] concert *m*; **concerted** concerté

concession [kən'seʃn] concession *f*

concise [kən'saɪs] concis

conclude [kən'kluːd] conclure; **~ sth from sth** déduire qch de qch; **conclusion** conclusion *f*; **conclusive** concluant

concrete ['kɑːnkriːt] **1** *n* béton *m* **2** *adj* concret

concussion [kən'kʌʃn] commotion *f* cérébrale

condemn [kən'dem] condamner; **condemnation** condamnation *f*

condescend [kɑːndɪ'send]

daigner (**to do**) faire); **condescending** condescendant

condition [kən'dɪʃn] **1** *n* (*state, requirement*) condition *f*; MED maladie *f* **2** *v/t* PSYCH conditionner; **conditioning** PSYCH conditionnement *m*

condo ['kɑːndou] *building* immeuble *m* (en copropriété); *apartment* appart *m*

condolences [kən'doulənsɪz] *fpl* condoléances *fpl*

condom ['kɑːndəm] préservatif *m*

condominium [kɑːndə'mɪniəm] → **condo**

condone [kən'doun] excuser

conduct ['kɑːndʌkt] **1** *n* (*behavior*) conduite *f* **2** *v/t* [kən'dʌkt] (*carry out*) mener; ELEC conduire; MUS diriger; **conducted tour** visite *f* guidée; **conductor** MUS chef *m* d'orchestre; *on train* chef *m* de train

cone [koun] cône *m*; *for ice cream* cornet *m*; *of pine tree* pomme *f* de pin

conference ['kɑːnfərəns] conférence *f*; *discussion* réunion *f*; **conference room** salle *f* de conférences

confess [kən'fes] **1** *v/t* avouer, confesser **2** *v/i* *also to police* avouer; REL se confesser; **confession** confession *f*

confide [kən'faɪd] **1** *v/t* confier **2** *v/i*: **in s.o.** (*trust*) faire confiance à qn; **confidence** confiance *f*; (*in self*) assurance *f*; **confident** (*self-assured*) sûr de soi; (*convinced*) confiant; **confidential** confidentiel; **confidently** avec assurance

confine [kən'faɪn] (*imprison*) enfermer; (*restrict*) limiter; **confined** *space* restreint

confirm [kən'fɜːrm] confirmer; **confirmation** confirmation *f*

confiscate ['kɑːnfɪskeɪt] confisquer

conflict ['kɑːnflɪkt] **1** *n* conflit *m* **2** *v/i* [kən'flɪkt] être en conflit; *of dates* coïncider

confront [kən'frʌnt] (*face*) affronter; (*tackle*) confronter; **confrontation** confrontation *f*; (*clash, dispute*) affrontement *m*

confuse [kən'fjuːz] (*muddle*) compliquer; *person* embrouiller; **~ s.o. with s.o.** confondre qn avec qn; **confused** *person* désorienté; *ideas, situation* confus; **confusing** déroutant; **confusion** confusion *f*

congestion [kən'dʒestʃn] *on roads* encombrement *m*

congratulate [kən'grætuleɪt] féliciter (**on** pour); **congratulations** félicitations *fpl*

congregate ['kɑːŋgrɪgeɪt] se rassembler; REL assemblée *f*

Congress ['kɑːŋgres] le Congrès; **Congressional** du

Congrès; **Congressman**
membre *m* du Congrès; **Con-**
gresswoman membre *m* du
Congrès
conjecture [kən'dʒektʃər]
conjecture *f*
con man ['kɑːnmæn] escroc
m, arnaqueur *m*
connect [kə'nekt] raccorder,
relier; TELEC passer; (*link*)
associer; *to power supply*
brancher; **connected: be**
well-~ avoir des relations;
be ~ with être lié à; **connec-**
tion *in wiring* branchement
m, connexion *f*; *causal etc*
rapport *m*; *when traveling*
correspondance *f*; (*personal
contact*) relation *f*
connoisseur [kɑːnə'sɜːr]
connaisseur *m*, connaisseuse
f
conquer ['kɑːŋkər] conquérir; *fear etc* vaincre; **con-**
queror conquérant *m*; **con-**
quest conquête *f*
conscience ['kɑːnʃəns] conscience *f*; **conscientious**
consciencieux; **conscien-**
tiousness conscience *f*
conscious ['kɑːnʃəs] conscient; (*deliberate*) délibéré;
consciously (*knowingly*)
consciemment; (*delibera-*
tely) délibérément; **con-**
sciousness conscience *f*;
lose/regain ~ perdre/repren-
dre connaissance
consecutive [kən'sekjutɪv]
consécutif

consensus [kən'sensəs] consensus *m*
consent [kən'sent] **1** *n* con-
sentement *m* **2** *v/i* consentir
(**to** à)
consequence ['kɑːn-
sɪkwəns] conséquence *f*;
consequently par conséquent
conservation [kɑːnsər'veɪʃn]
protection *f*; **conservation-**
ist écologiste *m/f*; **conserva-**
tive conservateur; *clothes*
classique; *estimate* prudent;
conserve 1 *n* (*jam*) confiture
f **2** *v/t* *energy* économiser
consider [kən'sɪdər] considérer; (*show regard for*) prendre en compte; **considera-**
ble considérable; **consider-**
ably considérablement; **con-**
siderate attentionné; **con-**
siderately gentiment; **con-**
sideration (*thought*) réflexion *f*; (*factor*) facteur
m; (*thoughtfulness, concern*)
attention *f*; *take sth into ~*
prendre qch en considéra-
tion

◆ **consist of** [kən'sɪst] consister en
consistency [kən'sɪstənsɪ]
(*texture*) consistance *f*; (*un-
changingness*) constance *f*;
(*logic*) cohérence *f*; **consist-**
ent (*unchanging*) constant;
logically etc cohérent
consolidate [kən'sɑːlɪdeɪt]
consolider
conspicuous [kən'spɪkjuəs]

voyant; **look** ~ se faire remarquer

conspiracy [kən'spɪrəsɪ] conspiration f; **conspirator** conspirateur(-trice) m(f); conspire conspirer

constant ['kɑːnstənt] constant; **constantly** constamment

constipated ['kɑːnstɪpeɪtɪd] constipé; **constipation** constipation f

constitute ['kɑːnstɪtuːt] constituer; **constitution** constitution f; **constitutional** POL constitutionnel

constraint [kən'streɪnt] (restriction) contrainte f

construct [kən'strʌkt] construire; **construction** construction f; (trade) bâtiment m; **constructive** constructif

consul ['kɑːnsl] consul m; **consulate** consulat m

consult [kən'sʌlt] consulter; **consultancy** company cabinet-conseil m; (advice) conseil m; **consultant** consultant m; **consultation** consultation f

consume [kən'suːm] consommer; **consumer** consommateur m; **consumption** consommation f

contact ['kɑːntækt] **1** n contact m **2** v/t contacter; **contact lens** lentille f de contact

contagious [kən'teɪdʒəs] contagieux

contain [kən'teɪn] contenir;

container récipient m; COM conteneur m, container m

contaminate [kən'tæmɪneɪt] contaminer; **contamination** contamination f

contemporary [kən'tempərerɪ] **1** adj contemporain **2** n contemporain m

contempt [kən'tempt] mépris m; **contemptible** méprisable; **contemptuous** méprisant

contender [kən'tendər] in sport prétendant m; in competition concurrent m; POL candidat m

content¹ ['kɑːntent] n contenu m

content² [kən'tent] **1** adj content **2** v/t: ~ **o.s. with** se contenter de

contented [kən'tentɪd] satisfait; **contentment** contentement m

contents ['kɑːntents] contenu m

contest¹ ['kɑːntest] n (competition) concours m; in sport compétition f; (struggle for power) lutte f

contest² [kən'test] leadership etc disputer; (oppose) contester; ~ **an election** se présenter à une élection

contestant [kən'testənt] concurrent m

context ['kɑːntekst] contexte m

continent ['kɑːntɪnənt] continent m; **continental** continental

continual [kən'tɪnʊəl] continuel; **continually** continuellement; **continuation** continuation f; *of story* suite f; **continue** continuer; **continuous** continu; **continuously** continuellement

contort [kən'tɔ:rt] *face* tordre; **~ one's body** se contorsionner

contraception [kɑ:ntrə'sepʃn] contraception f; **contraceptive** contraceptif m

contract¹ ['kɑ:ntrækt] *n* contrat m

contract² [kən'trækt] **1** *v/i* (*shrink*) se contracter **2** *v/t illness* contracter

contractor [kən'træktər] entrepreneur m

contractual [kən'træktʊəl] contractuel

contradict [kɑ:ntrə'dɪkt] contredire; **contradiction** contradiction f; **contradictory** contradictoire

contrary¹ ['kɑ:ntrərɪ] **1** *adj* contraire; **~ to ...** contrairement à ... **2** *n*: **on the ~** au contraire

contrary² [kən'trerɪ] *adj* (*perverse*) contrariant

contrast ['kɑ:ntræst] **1** *n* contraste m **2** *v/t* mettre en contraste **3** *v/i* contraster; **contrasting** contrastant; *views* opposé

contravene [kɑ:ntrə'vi:n] enfreindre

contribute [kən'trɪbju:t] **1** contribuer (**to** à); *to magazine* collaborer (**to** à) **2** *v/t money, suggestion* donner, apporter; **contribution** contribution f; *to political party, church* don m; *contributor of money* donateur m; *to magazine* collaborateur(-trice) m(f)

control [kən'troʊl] **1** *n* contrôle m; **be in ~ of** contrôler **2** *v/t* contrôler; *company* diriger

controversial [kɑ:ntrə'vɜ:rʃl] controversé; **controversy** controverse f

convenience [kən'vi:nɪəns] commodité f; **at your ~** à votre convenance; **convenience store** magasin m de proximité; **convenient** commode, pratique

convent ['kɑ:nvənt] couvent m

convention [kən'venʃn] (*tradition*) conventions fpl; (*conference*) convention f; **conventional** conventionnel; *person* conformiste

conversation [kɑ:nvər'seɪʃn] conversation f; **conversational** de conversation

conversion [kən'vɜ:rʃn] conversion f; *of building* aménagement m; **convert 1** *n* converti m **2** *v/t* convertir; *building* aménager; **convertible** *car* (voiture f) décapotable f

convey [kən'veɪ] (*transmit*) transmettre; (*carry*) trans-

porter; **conveyor belt** convoyeur *m*, tapis *m* roulant
convict 1 [ˈkɑːnvɪkt] *n* détenu *m* **2** [kənˈvɪkt] *v/t* LAW déclarer coupable; **conviction** LAW condamnation *f*; *(belief)* conviction *f*
convince [kənˈvɪns] convaincre
convoy [ˈkɑːnvɔɪ] convoi *m*
cook [kuk] **1** *n* cuisinier(-ière) *m(f)* **2** *v/t meal* préparer; *food* faire cuire **3** *v/i* faire la cuisine; *of food* cuire; **cookbook** livre *m* de cuisine; **cookery** cuisine *f*; **cookie** cookie *m*; **cooking** cuisine *f*
cool [kuːl] **1** *n*: **keep one's ∼** garder son sang-froid **2** *adj* frais; *dress* léger; *(calm)* calme; *(unfriendly)* froid; P *(great)* cool **3** *v/i* refroidir; *of tempers* se calmer; *of interest* diminuer **4** *v/t*: **∼ it** on se calme
◆ **cool down 1** *v/i* refroidir; *of weather* se rafraîchir; *of tempers* se calmer **2** *v/t food* (faire) refroidir; *fig* calmer
cooperate [kouˈɑːpəreɪt] coopérer; **cooperation** coopération *f*; **cooperative 1** *n* COM coopérative *f* **2** *adj* coopératif
coordinate [kouˈɔːrdɪneɪt] coordonner; **coordination** coordination *f*
cop [kɑːp] F flic *m* F
cope [koup] se débrouiller; **∼**

with ... faire face à ...
copier [ˈkɑːpiər] *machine* photocopieuse *f*
copper [ˈkɑːpər] cuivre *m*
copy [ˈkɑːpɪ] **1** *n* copie *f*; *of book* exemplaire *m* **2** *v/t* copier; *(photocopy)* photocopier
cord [kɔːrd] *(string)* corde *f*; *(cable)* fil *m*, cordon *m*
cordon [ˈkɔːrdn] cordon *m*
cords [kɔːrdz] *pants* pantalon *m* en velours (côtelé)
core [kɔːr] **1** *n of fruit*, problem cœur *m*; *of party* noyau *m* **2** *adj issue* fondamental
cork [kɔːrk] *in bottle* bouchon *m*; *material* liège *m*; **corkscrew** tire-bouchon *m*
corn [kɔːrn] *grain* maïs *m*
corner [ˈkɔːrnər] **1** *n* coin *m*; *in road* virage *m*, tournant *m*; *in soccer* corner *m*; **on the ∼** *of street* au coin **2** *v/t person* coincer; **∼ the market** accaparer le marché **3** *v/i of driver, car* prendre le/les virage(s)
coronary [ˈkɑːrəneri] **1** *adj* coronaire **2** *n* infarctus *m* (du myocarde)
coroner [ˈkɑːrənər] coroner *m*
corporal [ˈkɔːrpərəl] caporal *m*; **corporal punishment** châtiment *m* corporel
corporate [ˈkɔːrpərət] COM d'entreprise; **corporation** *(business)* société *f*, entreprise *f*

corpse [kɔːrps] cadavre *m*, corps *m*

corral [kəˈræl] corral *m*

correct [kəˈrekt] **1** *adj* correct; *the ~ answer* la bonne réponse; *that's ~* c'est exact **2** *v/t* corriger; **correction** correction *f*; **correctly** correctement

correspond [karɪˈspaːnd] correspondre (*to* à); **correspondence** correspondance *f*; **correspondent** correspondant(e) *m(f)*

corridor [ˈkɔːrɪdər] couloir *m*

corroborate [kəˈraːbəreɪt] corroborer

corrosion [kəˈrouʒn] corrosion *f*

corrupt [kəˈrʌpt] **1** *adj also* COMPUT corrompu; MORALS, YOUTH dépravé **2** *v/t* corrompre; **corruption** corruption *f*

cosmetic [kaːzˈmetɪk] cosmétique; *fig* esthétique; **cosmetics** cosmétiques *mpl*; **cosmetic surgery** chirurgie *f* esthétique

cosmopolitan [kaːzməˈpaːlɪtən] cosmopolite

cost [kaːst] **1** *n also fig* coût *m* **2** *v/t* coûter; *how much does it ~?* combien ça coûte?

'cost-effective rentable; **cost of living** coût *m* de la vie

costume [ˈkaːstuːm] *for actor* costume *m*

cosy *Br* → **cozy**

cot [kaːt] (*camp-bed*) lit *m* de camp; *Br for child* lit *m* d'enfant

cottage [ˈkaːtɪdʒ] cottage *m*

cotton [ˈkaːtn] **1** *n* coton *m* **2** *adj* en coton; **cotton candy** barbe *f* à papa; **cotton wool** *Br* coton *m* hydrophile, ouate *f*

couch [kautʃ] canapé *m*; **couch potato** téléphage *m/f*

cough [kaːf] **1** *n* toux *f* **2** *v/i* tousser; **cough medicine**, **cough syrup** sirop *m* contre la toux

could [kʊd]: *~ I have my key?* pourrais-je avoir ma clef?; *~ you help me?* pourrais-tu m'aider?; *you ~ be right* vous avez peut-être raison; *you ~ have warned me!* tu aurais pu me prévenir!

council [ˈkaunsl] (*assembly*) conseil *m*, assemblée *f*; **councilor** conseiller *m*

counsel [ˈkaunsl] **1** *n* (*advice*) conseil *m*; (*lawyer*) avocat *m* **2** *v/t* conseiller; **counseling**, *Br* **counselling** aide *f* (psychological); **counselor**, *Br* **counsellor** (*adviser*) conseiller *m*; LAW maître *m*

count [kaunt] **1** *n* compte *m* **2** *v/t & v/i* compter

◆ **count on** compter sur

'countdown compte *m* à rebours

counter [ˈkauntər] *in shop*, *café* comptoir *m*; *in game* pion *m*

'counteract neutraliser, contrecarrer; **counter-attack 1**

n contre-attaque *f* **2** *v/i* contre-attaquer; **counterclockwise** dans le sens inverse des aiguilles d'une montre; **counterespionage** contre-espionnage *m*; **counterfeit 1** *v/t* contrefaire **2** *adj* faux; **counterpart** *person* homologue *m/f*; **counterproductive** contre-productif

countless ['kaʊntlɪs] innombrable

country ['kʌntrɪ] pays *m*; *as opposed to town* campagne *f*

county ['kaʊntɪ] comté *m*

coup [kuː] POL coup *m* d'État; *fig* beau coup *m*

couple ['kʌpl] *(two people)* couple *m*; **a ~ of** *(a pair)* deux; *(a few)* quelques

courage ['kʌrɪdʒ] courage *m*; **courageous** courageux

courier ['kʊrɪər] *(messenger)* coursier *m*; *with tourist party* guide *m/f*

course [kɔːrs] *of lessons* cours *m(pl)*; *of meal* plat *m*; *of ship, plane* route *f*; *for sports* piste *f*; *for golf* terrain *m*; **of ~** bien sûr; **of ~ not** bien sûr que non

court [kɔːrt] LAW tribunal *m*, cour *f*; FOR TENNIS court *m*; *for basketball* terrain *m*; **take s.o. to ~** faire un procès à qn; **court case** affaire *f*, procès *m*

courtesy ['kɜːrtəsɪ] courtoisie *f*

'courthouse palais *m* de justi-

ce, tribunal *m*; **courtroom** salle *f* d'audience; **courtyard** cour *f*

cousin ['kʌzn] cousin(e) *m(f)*

cover ['kʌvər] **1** *n protective* housse *f*; *of book, magazine* couverture *f*; *(shelter)* abri *m*; *(insurance)* couverture *f*, assurance *f* **2** *v/t* couvrir

◆ **cover up 1** *v/t* couvrir; *scandal* dissimuler **2** *v/i* cacher la vérité

coverage ['kʌvərɪdʒ] *by media* couverture *f* (médiatique)

covert ['koʊvɜːrt] secret, clandestin

'cover-up black-out *m inv*

cow [kaʊ] vache *f*

coward ['kaʊərd] lâche *m/f*; **cowardice** lâcheté *f*

'cowboy cow-boy *m*

co-worker ['koʊwɜːrkər] collègue *m/f*

cozy ['koʊzɪ] confortable, douillet

crab [kræb] crabe *m*

crack [kræk] **1** *n* fissure *f*; *in cup, glass* fêlure *f*; *in voice* vanne *f* **2** *v/t cup, glass* fêler; *nut* casser; *(solve)* résoudre; *code* décrypter **3** *v/i* se fêler; **crack (cocaine)** crack *m*; **cracked** *cup* fêlé; **cracker** *to eat* cracker *m*

cradle ['kreɪdl] berceau *m*

craft¹ [kræft] NAUT embarcation *f*

craft² *(trade)* métier *m*; *weaving, pottery etc* artisanat *m*

(*craftsmanship*) art *m*;
craftsman (*artisan*) artisan *m*; **crafty** malin, rusé

crag [kræg] (*rock*) rocher *m* escarpé

cram [kræm] fourrer; *food* enfourner; *people* entasser

cramps [kræmps] crampe *f*

crane [kreɪn] **1** *n* (*machine*) grue *f* **2** *v/t*: **~ one's neck** tendre le cou

crank [kræŋk] *person* allumé *m*; **cranky** (*bad-tempered*) grognon

crash [kræʃ] **1** *n* noise fracas *m*; *accident* accident *m*; COM faillite *f*; *of stock exchange* krach *m*; COMPUT plantage *m* **2** *v/i* s'écraser; *of car* avoir un accident; *of market* s'effondrer; COMPUT se planter **3** *v/t* car avoir un accident avec; **crash course** cours *m* intensif; **crash diet** régime *m* intensif; **crash helmet** casque *m*; **crash-land** atterrir en catastrophe

crate [kreɪt] caisse *f*

crater ['kreɪtər] cratère *m*

crave [kreɪv] avoir très envie de; **craving** envie *f* (irrépressible)

crawl [krɔːl] **1** *n in swimming* crawl *m* **2** *v/i on belly* ramper; *on hands and knees* marcher à quatre pattes; (*move slowly*) se traîner

crayon ['kreɪɑːn] crayon *m* de couleur

craze [kreɪz] engouement *m*

the latest **~** la dernière mode; **crazy** crazy fou

creak [kriːk] craquer, grincer; **creaky** qui craque, grinçant

cream [kriːm] **1** *n* crème *f*; *color* crème *m* **2** *adj* crème inv

crease [kriːs] **1** *n* pli *m* **2** *v/t accidentally* froisser

create [kriːˈeɪt] créer; **creation** création *f*; **creative** créatif; **creator** créateur(-trice) *m(f)*

creature ['kriːtʃər] *animal m*; (*person*) créature *f*

credibility [kredəˈbɪlətɪ] crédibilité *f*; **credible** crédible

credit ['kredɪt] crédit *m*; (*honor*) honneur *m*, mérite *m*; **creditable** honorable; **credit card** carte *f* de crédit; **credit limit** limite *f* de crédit; **creditor** créancier *m*; **creditworthy** solvable

creep [kriːp] **1** *n pej* sale type *m* **2** *v/i* se glisser (*in silence*); (*move slowly*) avancer lentement; **creepy** F flippant F

cremate [krɪˈmeɪt] incinérer; **cremation** incinération *f*, crémation *f*

crest [krest] crête *f*

crevice ['krevɪs] fissure *f*

crew [kruː] *of ship, airplane* équipage *m*; **crew cut** cheveux *mpl* en brosse

crib [krɪb] *for baby* lit *m* d'enfant

crime [kraɪm] crime *m*; **criminal 1** *n* criminel *m* **2** *adj* criminel; (*shameful*) honteux

crimson ['krɪmzn] cramoisi

cripple ['krɪpl] **1** *n* handicapé(e) *m(f)* **2** *v/t person* estropier; *fig* paralyser

crisis ['kraɪsɪs] crise *f*

crisp [krɪsp] *weather* vivifiant; *lettuce, apple* croquant; *bacon, toast* croustillant; **crisps** *Br* chips *fpl*

criterion [kraɪ'tɪrɪən] critère *m*

critic ['krɪtɪk] critique *m*; **critical** critique; **criticism** critique *f*; **criticize** critiquer

crocodile ['krɑːkədaɪl] crocodile *m*

crony ['krəʊnɪ] pote *m* , copain *m*

crook [krʊk] escroc *m*; **crooked** de travers; *streets* tortueux; (*dishonest*) malhonnête

crop [krɑːp] **1** *n* culture *f*; (*harvest*) récolte *f* **2** *v/t hair, photo* couper

◆ **crop up** surgir

cross [krɑːs] **1** *adj* (*angry*) fâché **2** *n* croix *f* **3** *v/t* (*go across*) traverser; ~ **o.s.** REL se signer **4** *v/i* (*go across*) traverser; *of lines* se croiser

◆ **cross off, cross out** rayer

'crosscheck 1 *n* recoupement *m* **2** *v/t* vérifier par recoupement; **cross-examine** LAW faire subir un contre-interrogatoire à; **cross-eyed** qui louche; **crossing** NAUT traversée *f*; **crossroads** *also*

fig carrefour *m*; **crosswalk** passage *m* (pour) piétons; **crossword** (**puzzle**) mots *mpl* croisés

crotch [krɑːtʃ] entrejambe *m*

crouch [kraʊtʃ] s'accroupir

crowd [kraʊd] foule *f*; *at sports event* public *m*; **crowded** bondé, plein (de monde)

crown [kraʊn] *also on tooth* couronne *f*

crucial ['kruːʃl] crucial

crucifix ['kruːsɪfɪks] crucifix *m*; **crucifixion** *of Christ* crucifixion *f*; **crucify** REL crucifier; *fig* assassiner

crude [kruːd] **1** *adj* (*vulgar*) grossier; (*unsophisticated*) rudimentaire **2** *n*: ~ (**oil**) pétrole *m* brut

cruel [kruːəl] cruel; **cruelty** cruauté *f*

cruise [kruːz] **1** *n* croisière *f* **2** *v/i of people* faire une croisière; *of car* rouler (à une vitesse de croisière); *of plane* voler (à une vitesse de croisière)

crumb [krʌm] miette *f*

crumble ['krʌmbl] *of bread* s'émietter; *of stonework* s'effriter; *fig: of opposition etc* s'effondrer

crumple ['krʌmpl] **1** *v/t* (*crease*) froisser **2** *v/i* (*collapse*) s'écrouler

crush [krʌʃ] **1** *n* (*crowd*) foule *f* **2** *v/t* écraser; (*crease*) froisser

crust [krʌst] *on bread* croûte *f*

crutch [krʌtʃ] *for injured person* béquille *f*

cry [kraɪ] **1** *n* (*call*) cri *m* **2** *v/i* (*weep*) pleurer

◆ **cry out** crier

cryptic [ˈkrɪptɪk] énigmatique

crystal [ˈkrɪstl] cristal *m*

cube [kjuːb] cube *m*; **cubic** cubique; **~ meter** mètre cube

cubicle [ˈkjuːbɪkl] (*changing room*) cabine *f*

cuddle [ˈkʌdl] câliner

cue [kjuː] *for actor etc* signal *m*; *for pool* queue *f*

cuff [kʌf] *of shirt* poignet *m*; *of pants* revers *m*; (*blow*) gifle *f*

culminate [ˈkʌlmɪneɪt] **~ in** se terminer par; **culmination** apogée *f*

culprit [ˈkʌlprɪt] coupable *m/f*

cult [kʌlt] (*sect*) secte *f*

cultivate [ˈkʌltɪveɪt] *land, person* cultiver; **cultivated** *person* cultivé; **cultivation** *of land* culture *f*

cultural [ˈkʌltʃərəl] culturel; **culture** culture *f*; **cultured** cultivé

cumulative [ˈkjuːmjʊlətɪv] cumulatif

cunning [ˈkʌnɪŋ] **1** *n* ruse *f* **2** *adj* rusé

cup [kʌp] tasse *f*; (*trophy*) coupe *f*

cupboard [ˈkʌbərd] placard *m*

curb [kɜːrb] **1** *n of street* bord *m* du trottoir; *on powers etc* frein *m* **2** *v/t* réfréner

cure [kjʊr] **1** *n* MED remède *m* **2** *v/t* MED guérir; *meat* saurer

curiosity [kjʊrɪˈɑːsətɪ] curiosité *f*; **curious** curieux

curl [kɜːrl] **1** *n in hair* boucle *f*; *of smoke* volute *f* **2** *v/t hair* boucler; (*wind*) enrouler **3** *v/i of hair* boucler; *of leaf, paper etc* se gondoler

◆ **curl up** se pelotonner

curly [ˈkɜːrlɪ] *hair* bouclé; *tail* en tire-bouchon

currency [ˈkʌrənsɪ] monnaie *f*; **foreign ~** devise *f* étrangère; **current 1** *n in sea*, ELEC courant *m* **2** *adj* actuel; **current affairs** actualité *f*

curse [kɜːrs] **1** *n* (*spell*) malédiction *f*; (*swearword*) juron *m* **2** *v/t* maudire **3** *v/i* (*swear*) jurer

cursor [ˈkɜːrsər] COMPUT curseur *m*

cursory [ˈkɜːrsərɪ] superficiel

curt [kɜːrt] abrupt

curtain [ˈkɜːrtn] *also* THEA rideau *m*

curve [kɜːrv] **1** *n* courbe *f* **2** *v/i* (*bend*) s'incurver; *of road* faire une courbe

cushion [ˈkʊʃn] **1** *n* coussin *m* **2** *v/t blow, fall* amortir

custody [ˈkʌstədɪ] *of children* garde *f*; **in ~** LAW en détention

custom [ˈkʌstəm] coutume *f*; COM clientèle *f*; **customer** client *m*; **customer service** service *m* clientèle

customs [ˈkʌstəmz] douane

f; **customs officer** douanier *m*

cut [kʌt] **1** *n with knife, scissors* entaille *f*; (*injury*) coupure *f*; (*of garment, hair*) coupe *f*; (*reduction*) réduction *f* **2** *v/t* couper; (*reduce*) réduire; **get one's hair ~** se faire couper les cheveux

◆ **cut down 1** *v/t tree* abattre **2** *v/i on smoking etc* réduire

◆ **cut off** couper; (*isolate*) isoler

◆ **cut up** *meat etc* découper

cutback réduction *f*

cute [kjuːt] *in appearance* mignon; (*clever*) malin

'**cutoff date** date *f* limite; **cut--price** à prix *m* réduit; **cut--throat** *competition* acharné; **cutting 1** *n from newspaper* coupure *f* **2** *adj remark* blessant

cyber... ['saɪbər] cyber...

cycle ['saɪkl] **1** *n* vélo *m*; *of events* cycle *m* **2** *v/i* aller en vélo; **cycling** cyclisme *m*; **cyclist** cycliste *m/f*

cylinder ['sɪlɪndər] *in engine* cylindre *m*; **cylindrical** cylindrique

cynic ['sɪnɪk] cynique *m/f*; **cynical** cynique; **cynicism** cynisme *m*

Czech [tʃek] **1** *adj* tchèque; **the ~ Republic** la République tchèque **2** *n person* Tchèque *m/f*; *language* tchèque *m*

D

DA [diːˈeɪ] (= *district attorney*) procureur *m*

◆ **dabble in** toucher à

dad [dæd] papa *m*

daily ['deɪlɪ] **1** *n paper* quotidien *m* **2** *adj* quotidien

'**dairy products** produits *mpl* laitiers

dam [dæm] *for water* barrage *m*

damage ['dæmɪdʒ] **1** *n* dommage(s) *m(pl)*; *to reputation* préjudice *m* **2** *v/t* endommager; *fig: reputation* nuire à; **damages** LAW dommages--intérêts *mpl*; **damaging** préjudiciable

damn [dæm] F **1** *interj* zut **2** *adj* sacré **3** *adv* (*very*) vachement F; **damning** *evidence, report* accablant

damp [dæmp] humide

dance [dæns] **1** *n* danse *f*; *social event* bal *m* **2** *v/i* danser; **dancer** danseur(-euse) *m(f)*; **dancing** danse *f*

Dane [deɪn] Danois(e) *m(f)*

danger ['deɪndʒər] danger *m*; **dangerous** dangereux

dangle ['dæŋgl] **1** *v/t* balancer **2** *v/i* pendre

Danish ['deɪnɪʃ] **1** *adj* danois **2** *n language* danois *m*

Danish (pastry) feuilleté *m*

(sucré)

dare [der] **1** *v/i* oser; ~ **to do sth** oser faire qch **2** *v/t*: ~ **s.o. to do sth** défier qn de faire qch; *daring* audacieux

dark [dɑ:rk] **1** *n* noir **2** *adj room* sombre, noir; *hair* brun; *eyes, color, clothes* foncé; *dark glasses* lunettes *fpl* noires; *darkness* obscurité *f*

darling [ˈdɑ:rlɪŋ] chéri(e) *m(f)*

dart [dɑ:rt] **1** *n for game* fléchette *f* **2** *v/i* se précipiter

dash [dæʃ] **1** *n punctuation* tiret *m*; *a* ~ *of* un peu de **2** *v/i* se précipiter **3** *v/t hopes* anéantir; *dashboard* tableau *m* de bord

data [ˈdeɪtə] données *fpl*; *database* base *f* de données

date¹ [deɪt] *fruit* datte *f*

date² [deɪt] date *f*; *meeting, person* rendez-vous *m*; *out of* ~ *clothes* démodé; *passport* périmé; *up to* ~ *information* à jour; *style* à la mode; *dated* démodé

daughter [ˈdɔ:tər] fille *f*; *daughter-in-law* belle-fille *f*

dawn [dɔ:n] *also fig* aube *f*

day [deɪ] jour *m*; *stressing duration* journée *f*; *the* ~ *after* le lendemain; *the* ~ *after tomorrow* après-demain; *the* ~ *before* la veille; *the* ~ *before yesterday* avant-hier; *in those* ~*s* en ce temps-là, à l'époque; *the other* ~ (*recently*) l'autre jour; *day-*

break aube *f*, point *m* du jour; *daydream* **1** *n* rêverie *f*; *day spa* spa *m* urbain

dazed [deɪzd] *by news* hébété; *by blow* étourdi

dazzle [ˈdæzl] éblouir

dead [ded] **1** *adj mort*; *battery* à plat; *the phone's* ~ il n'y a pas de tonalité **2** *adv* F (*very*) très; ~ *beat*, ~ *tired* crevé **3** *npl*: *the* ~ les morts *mpl*; *dead end street* impasse *f*; *dead heat* arrivée *f* ex æquo; *deadline date f* limite; *for newspaper* heure *f* de clôture; *meet the* ~ respecter le(s) délai(s); *deadlock in talks* impasse *f*; *deadly* mortel

deaf [def] sourd; *deafening* assourdissant; *deafness* surdité *f*

deal [di:l] **1** *n* accord *m*, marché *m*; *a great* ~ *of* beaucoup de **2** *v/t cards* distribuer

♦ *deal in* COM être dans le commerce de; *drugs* dealer

♦ *deal with* (*handle*) s'occuper de; (*do business with*) traiter avec; (*be about*) traiter de

dealer [ˈdi:lər] marchand *m*; (*drug* ~) dealer *m*, dealeuse *f*; *large-scale* trafiquant *m* de drogue; *dealing* (*drug* ~) trafic *m* de drogue; *dealings* (*business*) relations *fpl*

dear [dɪr] cher *m*; *Dear Sir* Monsieur

death [deθ] mort *f*; **death toll** nombre *m* de morts

debatable [dɪ'beɪtəbl] discutable; **debate 1** *n* débat *m* **2** *v/i* débattre **3** *v/t* débattre de

debit ['debɪt] **1** *n* débit *m* **2** *v/t account* débiter; *amount* porter au débit; **debit card** carte *f* bancaire

debris [də'briː] débris *mpl*

debt [det] dette *f*; **be in ~** être endetté; **debtor** débiteur *f*

debug [diː'bʌg] COMPUT déboguer

decade ['dekeɪd] décennie *f*

decadent ['dekədənt] décadent

decaffeinated [dɪ'kæfɪneɪtɪd] décaféiné

decay [dɪ'keɪ] **1** *n* détérioration *f*; *in wood, plant* pourriture *f*; *in teeth* carie *f* **2** *v/i of wood, plant* pourrir; *of civilization* tomber en décadence; *of teeth* se carier

deceased [dɪ'siːst]: **the ~** le défunt/la défunte

deceit [dɪ'siːt] duplicité *f*; **deceitful** fourbe; **deceive** tromper

December [dɪ'sembər] décembre *m*

decency ['diːsənsɪ] décence *f*; **decent** *person* correct, honnête; *salary* correct, décent; *meal, sleep* bon

deception [dɪ'sepʃn] tromperie *f*; **deceptive** trompeur

decide [dɪ'saɪd] décider; de-

cided (*definite*) décidé; *views* arrêté; *improvement* net

decimal ['desɪml] décimale *f*

decipher [dɪ'saɪfər] déchiffrer

decision [dɪ'sɪʒn] décision *f*; **decisive** décidé; (*crucial*) décisif

deck [dek] *of ship* pont *m*; *of cards* jeu *m* (de cartes)

declaration [deklə'reɪʃn] déclaration *f*; **declare** déclarer

decline [dɪ'klaɪn] **1** *n* baisse *f*, *of civilization, health* déclin *m* **2** *v/t invitation* décliner; **~ to comment** refuser de commenter **3** *v/i* (*refuse*) refuser; (*decrease*) baisser; *of health* décliner

decode [diː'koud] décoder

décor ['deɪkɔːr] décor *m*

decorate ['dekəreɪt] *room* refaire; *with paint* peindre; *with paper* tapisser; (*adorn*) soldier décorer; **decoration** décoration *f*; **decorator** (*interior ~*) décorateur *m* (d'intérieur)

decoy ['diːkɔɪ] appât *m*, leurre *m*

decrease [*'diːkriːs*] **1** *n* baisse *f*, diminution *f*; *in size* réduction *f* **2** *v/t & v/i* diminuer

dedicate ['dedɪkeɪt] *book etc* dédicacer; **dedicated** dévoué; **dedication** *in book* dédicace *f*; *to cause, work* dévouement *m*

deduce [dɪ'duːs] déduire

deduct [dɪ'dʌkt] déduire

(from de); **deduction** *from salary* prélèvement *m*; *(conclusion)* déduction *f*

deed [di:d] *(act)* acte *m*; LAW acte *m* (notarié)

deep [di:p] profond; *voice* grave; *color* intense; **deepen 1** *v/t* creuser 2 *v/i* devenir plus profond; *of mystery* s'épaissir; **deep freeze** congélateur *m*

deer [dɪr] cerf *m*; *female* biche *f*

deface [dɪ'feɪs] abîmer

defamation [defə'meɪʃn] diffamation *f*; **defamatory** diffamatoire

defeat [dɪ'fi:t] **1** *n* défaite *f* **2** *v/t* battre

defect ['di:dekt] défaut *m*; **defective** défectueux

defence *Br* → **defense**

defend [dɪ'fend] défendre; *decision* justifier; **defendant** défenseur *m*, défenderesse *f*; *in criminal case* accusé(e) *m(f)*; **defense** défense *f*; **defenseless** sans défense; **Defense Secretary** POL ministre de la Défense; **defensive 1** *n*: **go on (to) the ~** se mettre sur la défensive **2** *adj* défensif

deference ['defərəns] déférence *f*

defiance [dɪ'faɪəns] défi *m*; **defiant** [dɪ'faɪənt] provocant; *look* de défi

deficiency [dɪ'fɪʃənsɪ] manque *m*; MED carence *f*

deficit ['defɪsɪt] déficit *m*

define [dɪ'faɪn] définir

definite ['defɪnɪt] définitif; *improvement* net; *(certain)* catégorique; **definitely** sans aucun doute; **~ not** certainement pas!

definition [defɪ'nɪʃn] définition *f*

deformity [dɪ'fɔ:rmətɪ] difformité *f*

defrost [di:'frɒst] *food* décongeler; *fridge* dégivrer

defuse [di:'fju:z] *bomb, situation* désamorcer

defy [dɪ'faɪ] défier; *superiors* braver

degrading [dɪ'greɪdɪŋ] dégradant

degree [dɪ'gri:] degré *m*; *from university* diplôme *m*

dehydrated [di:haɪ'dreɪtɪd] déshydraté

deign [deɪn]: **~ to** daigner

dejected [dɪ'dʒektɪd] déprimé

delay [dɪ'leɪ] **1** *n* retard *m* **2** *v/t* retarder; **be ~ed** être en retard **3** *v/i* tarder

delegate ['delɪgət] **1** *n* délégué(e) *m(f)* *v/t* déléguer; **delegation** délégation *f*

delete [dɪ'li:t] effacer; *(cross out)* rayer; **deletion** *act* effacement *m*; *that deleted* rature *f*

deliberate 1 [dɪ'lɪbərət] *adj* délibéré **2** [dɪ'lɪbəreɪt] *v/i* délibérer; *(reflect)* réfléchir; **deliberately** délibérément, exprès

delicate ['delɪkət] délicat

delicatessen [delɪkə'tesn] traiteur m; épicerie f fine

delicious [dɪ'lɪʃəs] délicieux

delight [dɪ'laɪt] joie f, plaisir m; **delighted** ravi; **delightful** charmant

deliver [dɪ'lɪvər] livrer; *letters* distribuer; *parcel etc* remettre; *message* transmettre; *baby* mettre au monde; *speech* faire; **delivery** of goods livraison f; of mail distribution f; of baby accouchement m; of speech débit m; **delivery date** date f de livraison

de luxe [də'lʌks] de luxe; *model* haut de gamme *inv*

demand [dɪ'mænd] **1** n also COM demande f; of terrorist, unions etc revendication f; **in ~** demandé **2** v/t exiger; *pay rise etc* réclamer; **demanding** job éprouvant; *person* exigeant

demo ['deməu] (*protest*) manif f; of video etc démo f

democracy [dɪ'mɑːkrəsɪ] démocratie f; **democrat** démocrate m/f; **democratic** démocratique

demolish [dɪ'mɑːlɪʃ] *building, argument* démolir; **demolition** démolition f

demonstrate ['demənstreɪt] **1** v/t démontrer; *machine etc* faire une démonstration de **2** v/i *politically* manifester; **demonstration** dé-

monstration f; (*protest*) manifestation f; **demonstrator** (*protester*) manifestant(e) m(f)

demoralized [dɪ'mɔːrəlaɪzd] démoralisé; **demoralizing** démoralisant

demote [diː'məut] rétrograder

den [den] *room* antre m

denial [dɪ'naɪəl] of accusation démenti m, dénégation f; of request refus m

denim ['denɪm] jean m

Denmark ['denmɑːrk] le Danemark

denomination [dɪnɑːmɪ'neɪʃn] of money coupure f; *religious* confession f

dense [dens] (*thick*) dense; **density** ['densɪtɪ] densité f

dent [dent] **1** n bosse f **2** v/t bosseler

dental ['dentl] dentaire

dented ['dentɪd] bosselé

dentist ['dentɪst] dentiste m/f; **dentures** dentier m

Denver boot ['denvər] sabot m de Denver

deny [dɪ'naɪ] *charge* nier; *right, request* refuser

deodorant [diː'əudərənt] déodorant m

department [dɪ'pɑːrtmənt] of company service m; of university département m; of government ministère m; of store rayon m; **Department of State** ministère m des Affaires étrangères; **depart-**

ment store grand magasin *m*

departure [dɪ'pɑːtʃər] départ *m*; *from standard etc* entorse *f* (**from** à); **departure lounge** salle *f* d'embarquement; **departure time** heure *f* de départ

depend [dɪ'pend] dépendre; **that ~s** cela dépend; **dependence, dependency** dépendance *f*

depict [dɪ'pɪkt] représenter

deplorable [dɪ'plɔːrəbl] déplorable; **deplore** déplorer

deploy [dɪ'plɔɪ] (*use*) faire usage de; (*position*) déployer

deport [dɪ'pɔːrt] expulser; **deportation** expulsion *f*

deposit [dɪ'pɑːzɪt] **1** *n in bank* dépôt *m*; *on purchase* acompte *m*; *security* caution *f*; *of mineral* gisement *m* **2** *v/t money, object* déposer; **deposition** LAW déposition *f*

depot [depou] *for storage* dépôt *m*, entrepôt *m*

depreciation [dɪpriːʃɪ'eɪʃn] FIN dépréciation *f*

depress [dɪ'pres] *person* déprimer; **depressed** déprimé; **depressing** déprimant; **depression** MED, *meteorological* dépression *f*; *economic* crise *f*, récession *f*

deprivation [deprɪ'veɪʃn] privation(s) *f(pl)*; **deprive**: **~ s.o. of sth** priver qn de qch; **deprived** défavorisé

depth [depθ] profondeur *f*; *of color* intensité *f*; **in ~** en profondeur

deputy ['depjʊtɪ] adjoint(e) *m(f)*; *of sheriff* shérif *m* adjoint

derail [dɪ'reɪl]: **be ~ed** *of train* dérailler

derelict ['derəlɪkt] délabré

deride [dɪ'raɪd] se moquer de; **derision** dérision *f*; **derisory** dérisoire

derivative [dɪ'rɪvətɪv] (*not original*) dérivé

derive [dɪ'raɪv] tirer (**from** de); **be ~d from** dériver de

dermatologist [dɜːrmə'tɑːlədʒɪst] dermatologue *m/f*

derogatory [dɪ'rɑːgətɔːrɪ] désobligeant; *term* péjoratif

descendant [dɪ'sendənt] descendant(e) *m(f)*; **descent** descente *f*; (*ancestry*) descendance *f*

describe [dɪ'skraɪb] décrire; **description** description *f*; *of criminal* signalement *m*

desegregate [diː'segrəgeɪt] supprimer la ségrégation dans

desert[1] ['dezərt] *n* désert *m*

desert[2] [dɪ'zɜːrt] **1** *v/t* abandonner **2** *v/i of soldier* déserter; **deserted** désert; **deserter** MIL déserteur *m*; **desertion** abandon *m*; MIL désertion *f*

deserve [dɪ'zɜːrv] mériter

design [dɪ'zaɪn] **1** *n* (*subject*) design *m*; (*style*) style *m*; (*drawing, pattern*) dessin *m*

2 v/t (draw) dessiner; building, car concevoir

designate ['dezɪgneɪt] person désigner

designer [dɪ'zaɪnər] designer m/f; of car, ship concepteur(-trice) m/f; of clothes styliste m/f; **designer clothes** vêtements mpl de marque

desirable [dɪ'zaɪrəbl] souhaitable; sexually, change désirable; house beau; **desire** désir m

desk [desk] bureau m; in hotel réception f; **desk clerk** réceptionniste m/f; **desktop publishing** publication f assistée par ordinateur

desolate ['desələt] place désolé

despair [dɪ'sper] **1** n désespoir m; **in ~** désespéré **2** v/i désespérer (**of** de); **desperate** ['desperət] désespéré; **be ~ for sth** avoir très envie de qch; **desperation** désespoir m; **in ~** en désespoir de cause

despicable [dɪs'pɪkəbl] méprisable; **despise** mépriser

despite [dɪ'spaɪt] malgré, en dépit de

dessert [dɪ'zɜːrt] dessert m

destination [destɪ'neɪʃn] destination f

destroy [dɪ'strɔɪ] détruire; **destroyer** NAUT destroyer m; **destruction** destruction f; **destructive** power destructeur; **a ~ child** un enfant qui casse tout

detach [dɪ'tætʃ] détacher; **detached** (objective) neutre; **detachment** (objectivity) neutralité f

detail [dɪ'teɪl] détail m; **detailed** détaillé

detain [dɪ'teɪn] (hold back) retenir; as prisoner détenir; **detainee** détenu(e) m(f); **political ~** prisonnier m politique

detect [dɪ'tekt] déceler; of device détecter; **detection** of criminal découverte f; of smoke etc détection f; **detective** inspecteur m de police; **detector** détecteur m

détente ['deɪtɑːnt] POL détente f

deter [dɪ'tɜːr] dissuader

detergent [dɪ'tɜːrdʒənt] détergent m

deteriorate [dɪ'tɪriəreɪt] se détériorer

determination [dɪtɜːrmɪ'neɪʃn] (resolution) détermination f; **determine** (establish) déterminer; **determined** déterminé, résolu; effort délibéré

detest [dɪ'test] détester; **detestable** détestable

detour ['diːtʊr] détour m; (diversion) déviation f

devaluation [diːvæljʊ'eɪʃn] dévaluation f; **devalue** dévaluer

devastate ['devəsteɪt] dévaster; fig: person anéantir

develop [dɪ'veləp] **1** v/t *film,
business* développer; *site*
aménager; *technique, vaccine* mettre au point; *illness*
attraper **2** v/i (*grow*) se développer; **developing country**
pays *m* en voie de développement; **development** *of film,
business* développement *m*;
of site aménagement *m*;
(*event*) événement *m*; *of
technique, vaccine* mise *f* au
point

device [dɪ'vaɪs] (*tool*) appareil *m*

devil ['devl] diable *m*; **a little ~**
un petit monstre

devise [dɪ'vaɪz] concevoir

devote [dɪ'vəʊt] consacrer;
devoted *son enc* dévoué (**to**
à); **devotion** dévouement *m*

devour [dɪ'vaʊər] dévorer

devout [dɪ'vaʊt] pieux

diabetes [daɪə'biːtiːz] diabète *m*; **diabetic** diabétique *m/f*

diagnose ['daɪəgnəʊz] diagnostiquer; **diagnosis** diagnostic *m*

diagonal [daɪ'ægənl] diagonal; **diagonally** en diagonale

diagram ['daɪəgræm] diagramme *m*

dial ['daɪl] **1** *n* cadran *m* **2** v/i
TELEC faire le numéro **3** v/t
TELEC *number* composer

dialog, *Br* **dialogue** ['daɪə-
lɒːg] dialogue *m*

'dial tone tonalité *f*

diameter [daɪ'æmɪtər] diamètre *m*

diamond ['daɪmənd] diamant
m; *shape* losange *m*

diaper ['daɪpər] couche *f*

diaphragm ['daɪəfræm] dia-
phragme *m*

diarrhea, *Br* **diarrhoea**
[daɪə'riːə] diarrhée *f*

diary ['daɪrɪ] journal *m*; *for
appointments* agenda *m*

dice [daɪs] *m*; *pl* dés *mpl*

dictate [dɪk'teɪt] dicter; **dictator** POL dictateur *m*; **dictatorship** dictature *f*

dictionary ['dɪkʃənerɪ] dictionnaire *m*

die [daɪ] mourir

♦ **die down** *of storm* se calmer; *of excitement* s'apaiser

♦ **die out** disparaître

diet ['daɪət] **1** *n* (*regular food*)
alimentation *f*; *to lose
weight, for health* régime *m*
2 v/i faire un régime

differ ['dɪfər] différer; (*disagree*) différer; **difference** différence *f*; **different** différent;
differently différemment

difficult ['dɪfɪkəlt] difficile;
difficulty difficulté *f*

dig [dɪg] creuser

digest [daɪ'dʒest] digérer; *information* assimiler; **digestion** digestion *f*

digit ['dɪdʒɪt] chiffre *m*; **digital** numérique; **digital
camera** appareil *m* photo numérique; **digital photo** photo *f*
numérique

dignified ['dɪgnɪfaɪd] digne;
dignity dignité *f*

dilapidated [dɪˈlæpɪdeɪtɪd] délabré

dilemma [dɪˈlemə] dilemme m

dilute [daɪˈluːt] diluer

dim [dɪm] **1** adj room, prospects sombre; light faible; outline vague; (stupid) bête **2** v/i of lights baisser

dime [daɪm] (pièce f de) dix cents mpl

dimension [daɪˈmenʃn] dimension f

diminish [dɪˈmɪnɪʃ] diminuer

din [dɪn] brouhaha m

dine [daɪn] dîner

dinghy [ˈdɪŋɪ] small yacht dériveur m; rubber boat canot m pneumatique

dining car [ˈdaɪnɪŋ] RAIL wagon-restaurant m; **dining room** salle f à manger; in hotel salle f de restaurant

dinner [ˈdɪnər] dîner m; at midday déjeuner m; gathering repas m; **dinner party** dîner m, repas m

dip [dɪp] **1** n for food sauce f (dans laquelle on trempe des aliments); in road inclinaison f **2** v/i of road s'incliner

diploma [dɪˈploʊmə] diplôme m

diplomacy [dɪˈploʊməsɪ] also (tact) diplomatie f; **diplomat** diplomate m/f; **diplomatic** diplomatique; (tactful) diplomate

direct [daɪˈrekt] **1** adj direct **2**

v/t to a place indiquer (**to sth** qch); play mettre en scène; movie réaliser; attention diriger

direction [daɪˈrekʃn] direction f; of movie réalisation f; **~s** (instructions) indications fpl; for use mode m d'emploi; for medicine instructions fpl; **ask for ~s** to a place demander son chemin; **directly** (straight) directement; (soon) dans très peu de temps; (immediately) immédiatement; **director** of company directeur(-trice) m(f); of movie réalisateur(-trice) m(f); of play metteur(-euse) m(f) en scène; **directory** répertoire m (d'adresses); TELEC annuaire m (des téléphones)

dirt [dɜːrt] saleté f; **dirty 1** adj sale; (pornographic) cochon **2** v/t salir

disability [dɪsəˈbɪlətɪ] infirmité f; **disabled** handicapé

disadvantage [dɪsədˈvæntɪdʒ] désavantage m; **disadvantaged** défavorisé

disagree [dɪsəˈgriː] of person ne pas être d'accord; **disagreeable** désagréable

disagreement désaccord m; (argument) dispute f

disappear [dɪsəˈpɪr] disparaître; **disappearance** disparition f

disappoint [dɪsəˈpɔɪnt] décevoir; **disappointing** décevant; **disappointment** déception f

disapproval [dɪsə'pruːvl] dés- approbation f; **disapprove** désapprouver; **~ of actions** désapprouver; **s.o.** ne pas aimer; **disapproving** désapprobateur

disarm [dɪs'ɑːrm] désarmer; **disarmament** désarmement m

disaster [dɪ'zæstər] désastre m; **disastrous** désastreux

disband [dɪs'bænd] **1** v/t disperser **2** v/i se disperser

disbelief [dɪsbə'liːf] incrédulité f

disc [dɪsk] disque m; CD CD m

discard [dɪ'skɑːrd] old clothes etc se débarrasser de; boyfriend abandonner

disciplinary [dɪsɪ'plɪnərɪ] disciplinaire; **discipline** discipline f

'disc jockey disc-jockey m

disclaim [dɪs'kleɪm] nier; **disclose** [dɪs'kloʊz] révéler

disco ['dɪskoʊ] discothèque f; type of dance, music disco m

discomfort [dɪs'kʌmfərt] gêne f; **be in ~** être incommodé

disconcert [dɪskən'sɜːrt] déconcerter

disconnect [dɪskə'nekt] hose détacher; electrical appliance débrancher; supply, phones couper

discontent [dɪskən'tent] mécontentement m

discontinue [dɪskən'tɪnuː]

product arrêter; bus service supprimer

discotheque ['dɪskətek] discothèque f

discount ['dɪskaʊnt] remise f

discourage [dɪs'kʌrɪdʒ] décourager

discover [dɪ'skʌvər] découvrir; **discovery** découverte f

discredit [dɪs'kredɪt] discréditer

discreet [dɪ'skriːt] discret

discrepancy [dɪ'skrepənsɪ] divergence f

discretion [dɪ'skreʃn] discrétion f

discriminate [dɪ'skrɪmɪneɪt] **~ against** pratiquer une discrimination contre; **discriminating** avisé; **discrimination** sexual etc discrimination f

discuss [dɪ'skʌs] discuter de; of article traiter de; **discussion** discussion f

disease [dɪ'ziːz] maladie f

disembark [dɪsəm'bɑːrk] débarquer

disentangle [dɪsən'tæŋgl] démêler

disfigure [dɪs'fɪgər] défigurer

disgrace [dɪs'greɪs] **1** n honte f **2** v/t faire honte à; **disgraceful** honteux

disguise [dɪs'gaɪz] **1** n déguisement m **2** v/t déguiser; fear, anxiety dissimuler

disgust [dɪs'gʌst] **1** n dégoût m **2** v/t dégoûter; **disgusting** dégoûtant

dish [dɪʃ] plat m; **~es** vaisselle f

disheartening [dɪsˈhɑːrtnɪŋ] décourageant

dishonest [dɪsˈɑːnɪst] malhonnête; **dishonesty** malhonnêteté f

dishonor [dɪsˈɑːnər] déshonneur m; **dishonorable** dishonorant

dishonour etc Br → **dishonor** etc

disillusion [dɪsɪˈluːʒn] désillusionner; **disillusionment** désillusion f

disinfect [dɪsɪnˈfekt] désinfecter; **disinfectant** désinfectant m

disinherit [dɪsɪnˈherɪt] déshériter

disintegrate [dɪsˈɪntəɡreɪt] se désintégrer; of marriage se désagréger

disjointed [dɪsˈdʒɔɪntɪd] décousu

disk [dɪsk] also COMPUT disque m; floppy disquette f; **disk drive** COMPUT lecteur m de disque/disquette; **diskette** disquette f

dislike [dɪsˈlaɪk] **1** n aversion f **2** v/t ne pas aimer

dislocate [ˈdɪsləkeɪt] disloquer

disloyalty [dɪsˈlɔɪəltɪ] déloyauté f

dismal [ˈdɪzməl] weather morne; prospect sombre; person (sad) triste; person (negative) lugubre; failure lamentable

dismantle [dɪsˈmæntl] object démonter; organization démanteler

dismay [dɪsˈmeɪ] consternation f

dismiss [dɪsˈmɪs] employee renvoyer; suggestion rejeter; idea écarter; **dismissal** of employee renvoi m

disobedience [dɪsəˈbiːdɪəns] désobéissance f; **disobedient** désobéissant; **disobey** désobéir à

disorganized [dɪsˈɔːrɡənaɪzd] désorganisé

disoriented [dɪsˈɔːrɪəntʌd] désorienté

disparaging [dɪˈspærɪdʒɪŋ] désobligeant

disparity [dɪˈspærətɪ] disparité f

dispassionate [dɪˈspæʃənət] impartial, objectif

dispatch [dɪˈspætʃ] (send) envoyer

disperse [dɪˈspɜːrs] se disperser

display [dɪˈspleɪ] **1** n of paintings etc exposition f; of emotion, in store window étalage m; COMPUT affichage m **2** v/t emotion montrer; at exhibition, for sale exposer; COMPUT afficher

displease [dɪsˈpliːz] déplaire à; **displeasure** mécontentement m

disposable [dɪˈspouzəbl] jetable; **disposal** of waste élimination f; (sale) cession f

***put sth at s.o.'s* ~** mettre qch
à la disposition de qn
◆ **dispose of** [dɪ'spəʊz] (*get rid of*) se débarrasser de

disprove [dɪs'pruːv] réfuter

dispute [dɪ'spjuːt] **1** *n* contestation *f*; *between two countries* conflit *m*; *industrial* ~ conflit *m* social **2** *v/t* contester; (*fight over*) se disputer

disqualification [dɪskwɒlɪfɪ'keɪʃn] disqualification *f*; **disqualify** disqualifier

disregard [dɪsrə'gɑːrd] **1** *n* indifférence *f* (*à l'égard de*) **2** *v/t* ne tenir aucun compte de

disreputable [dɪs'repjʊtəbl] peu recommandable

disrespect [dɪsrə'spekt] manque *m* de respect, irrespect *m*; **disrespectful** irrespectueux

disrupt [dɪs'rʌpt] perturber; **disruption** perturbation *f*

dissatisfaction [dɪssætɪs'fækʃn] mécontentement *m*; **dissatisfied** mécontent

dissident ['dɪsɪdənt] dissident(e) *m(f)*

dissolve [dɪ'zɒlv] **1** *v/t* dissoudre **2** *v/i* se dissoudre

distance ['dɪstəns] distance *f*; *in the* ~ au loin; **distant** éloigné; *fig* (*aloof*) distant

distaste [dɪs'teɪst] dégoût *m*; **distasteful** désagréable

distinct [dɪ'stɪŋkt] (*clear*) net; (*different*) distinct; **distinctive** distinctif; **distinctly** dis-

tinctement; (*decidedly*) vraiment

distinguish [dɪ'stɪŋgwɪʃ] distinguer; ~ ***between X and Y*** distinguer X de Y; **distinguished** distingué

distort [dɪ'stɔːrt] déformer

distract [dɪ'strækt] *person* distraire; *attention* détourner; **distraught** [dɪ'strɔːt] angoissé

distress [dɪ'stres] **1** *n* douleur *f* **2** *v/t* (*upset*) affliger; **distressing** pénible

distribute [dɪ'strɪbjuːt] *also* COM distribuer; **distribution** *also* COM distribution *f*; *of wealth* répartition *f*; **distributor** COM distributeur *m*

district ['dɪstrɪkt] *of town* quartier *m*; *of country* région *f*; **district attorney** procureur *m*

distrust [dɪs'trʌst] méfiance *f*

disturb [dɪ'stɜːrb] (*interrupt*) déranger; (*upset*) inquiéter; **disturbance** (*interruption*) dérangement *m*; ~**s** (*civil unrest*) troubles *mpl*; **disturbed** perturbé; *mentally* dérangé; **disturbing** perturbant

disused [dɪs'juːzd] désaffecté

ditch [dɪtʃ] **1** *n* fossé *m* **2** *v/t* F (*get rid of*) se débarrasser de; *boyfriend, plan* laisser tomber

dive [daɪv] **1** *n* plongeon *m*; *underwater* plongée *f*; *of* *plane* (vol *m*) piqué *m*; F *bar etc* bouge *m* **2** *v/i* plonger; *underwater* faire de la plongée sous-marine; *of plane* descendre en piqué; **diver** plongeur(-euse) *m(f)*

diverge [daɪˈvɜːrdʒ] diverger

diversification [daɪvɜːrsɪfɪˈkeɪʃn] COM diversification *f*; **diversify** COM se diversifier

diversion [daɪˈvɜːrʃn] *for traffic* déviation *f*; *to distract attention* diversion *f*; **divert** *traffic* dévier; *attention* détourner

divide [dɪˈvaɪd] (*share*) partager; MATH, *country, family* diviser

dividend [ˈdɪvɪdend] FIN dividende *m*

diving [ˈdaɪvɪŋ] *from board* plongeon *m*; *underwater* plongée *f* (sous-marine); **diving board** plongeoir *m*

division [dɪˈvɪʒn] division *f*

divorce [dɪˈvɔːrs] **1** *n* divorce *m* **2** *v/t* divorcer de **3** *v/i* divorcer; **divorced** divorcé(e); **divorcee** divorcé(e) *m(f)*

divulge [daɪˈvʌldʒ] divulguer

DIY [diːaɪˈwaɪ] (= *do-it-yourself*) bricolage *m*

dizziness [ˈdɪzɪnɪs] vertige *m*; **dizzy**: *feel* ~ avoir un vertige des vertiges

DJ [ˈdiːdʒeɪ] (= *disc jockey*) D.J. *m/f* (= disc-jockey)

DNA [diːenˈeɪ] (= *deoxyribonucleic acid*) AND *m* (= acide *m* désoxyribonucléique)

do [duː] **1** *v/t* faire; ~ *one's hair* se coiffer **2** *v/i* (*be suitable, enough*) aller; *that will* ~*!* ça va!; ~ *well in health, of business* aller bien; (*be successful*) réussir; *well done!* (*congratulations!*) bien!; *how* ~*you*~*?* enchanté

◆ **do away with** supprimer

◆ **do up** *building* rénover; *street* refaire; (*fasten*), *coat etc* fermer; *laces* faire

◆ **do with**: *I could do with ...* j'aurais bien besoin de ...

◆ **do without** *v/i* s'en passer **2** *v/t* se passer de

docile [ˈdəʊsaɪl] docile

dock¹ [dɒk] **1** *n* NAUT bassin *m* **2** *v/i of ship* entrer au bassin; *of spaceship* s'arrimer

dock² [dɒk] *n* LAW banc *m* des accusés

doctor [ˈdɒktər] MED docteur *m*, médecin *m*; *form of address* docteur; **doctorate** doctorat *m*

doctrine [ˈdɒktrɪn] doctrine *f*

document [ˈdɒkjʊmənt] document *m*; **documentary** documentaire *m*; **documentation** documentation *f*

dodge [dɒdʒ] *blow, person* éviter; *question* éluder

dog [dɒg] **1** *n* chien *m* **2** *v/t of bad luck* poursuivre

dogma [ˈdɒgmə] dogme *m*; **dogmatic** dogmatique

'dog tag MIL plaque *f* d'identification; **dog-tired** F crevé

do-it-yourself [duːɪtjərˈself]

bricolage m

doldrums ['dooldrəmz]: *be in the ~ of economy* être dans le marasme; *of person* avoir le cafard

doll [dɑːl] *also F woman* poupée f

dollar ['dɑːlər] dollar m

dolphin ['dɑːlfɪn] dauphin m

dome [doʊm] *of building* dôme m

domestic [də'mestɪk] *chores* domestique; *news item* national; *policy* intérieur; **domestic flight** vol m intérieur

dominant ['dɑːmɪnənt] dominant; **dominate** dominer; **domination** domination f; **domineering** dominateur

donate [doʊ'neɪt] faire don de; **donation** don m

donkey ['dɑːŋkɪ] âne m

donor ['doʊnər] *of money* donateur(-trice) *m(f)*; MED donneur(-euse) *m(f)*

donut ['doʊnʌt] beignet m

doom [duːm] *(fate)* destin m; *(ruin)* ruine f; **doomed** *project* voué à l'échec

door [dɔːr] porte f; *of car* portière f; **doorbell** sonnette f; **doorman** portier m; **doorway** embrasure f de porte

dope [doʊp] **1** *n (drugs)* drogue f; *(idiot)* idiot(e) *m(f)* **2** *v/t* doper

dormant ['dɔːrmənt]: ~ *volcano* volcan m en repos

dormitory ['dɔːrmɪtɔːrɪ] résidence f universitaire; *Br* dortoir m

dose [doʊs] dose f

dot [dɑːt] point m

double ['dʌbl] **1** *n* double m; *of film star* doublure f **2** *adj* double **3** *adv* deux fois (plus); ~ *the size* deux fois plus grand **4** *v/t & v/i* doubler; **double bed** grand lit m; **doublecheck** revérifier; **double-click** double-cliquer; **doublecross** trahir; **doublepark** stationner en double file; **double room** chambre f pour deux personnes; **doubles** *in tennis* double m

doubt [daʊt] **1** *n* doute m; *be in ~* être incertain; *no ~ (probably)* sans doute **2** *v/t* douter de; **doubtful** *look* douteux; *be ~ of person* avoir des doutes; **doubtless** sans aucun doute

dough [doʊ] pâte f

dove [dʌv] colombe f

down [daʊn] **1** *adv (downward)* en bas, vers le bas; ~ *there* en bas; *$200 ~ (as deposit)* 200 dollars d'acompte; ~ *south* dans le sud; *be ~ of price, numbers* être en baisse; *(not working)* être en panne; F *(depressed)* être déprimé **2** *prep (along)* le long de; *run ~ the stairs* descendre les escaliers en courant; *it's just ~ the street* c'est à deux pas; **down-and-out** clochard(e) *m(f)*; **download** COMPUT **1** *v/t* télécharger **2** *n* fichier m téléchargé;

downmarket *Br* bas de gamme; **down payment** paiement *m* au comptant; **downplay** minimiser; **downpour** averse *f*; **downscale** bas de gamme; **downside** *(disadvantage)* inconvénient *m*; **downsize** *car etc* réduire la taille de; *company* réduire les effectifs de; **downstairs 1** *adj* neighbors etc d'en bas **2** *adv* en bas; **down-town 1** *adj* du centre-ville **2** *adv* en ville

doze [dəʊz] sommeiller

dozen [ˈdʌzn] douzaine *f*

draft [dræft] **1** *n of air* courant *m* d'air; *of document* brouillon *m*; MIL conscription *f*; ~ **beer** bière *f* à la pression **2** *v/t* document faire le brouillon de; MIL appeler; **draft dodger** réfractaire *m*; **draftsman** dessinateur(-trice) *m(f)*

drag [dræg] **1** *v/t* traîner, tirer; *(search)* draguer **2** *v/i of time* se traîner; *of show, movie* traîner en longueur

drain [dreɪn] **1** *n pipe* tuyau *m* d'écoulement; *under street* égout *m* **2** *v/t oil* vidanger; *vegetables* égoutter; *land* drainer; *glass, tank* vider; *(exhaust: person)* épuiser; **drainage** *(drains)* système *m* d'écoulement des eaux usées; *of water from soil* drainage *m*; **drainpipe** tuyau *m* d'écoulement

drama [ˈdrɑːmə] drame *m*; **dramatic** dramatique; *scenery* spectaculaire; **dramatist** dramaturge *m/f*; **dramatize** *story* adapter (**for** pour); *fig* dramatiser

drapes [dreɪps] rideaux *mpl*

drastic [ˈdræstɪk] radical; *measures also* drastique

draught [dræft] *Br* → **draft**

draw [drɔː] **1** *n in competition* match *m* nul; *in lottery* tirage *m* (au sort); *(attraction)* attraction *f* **2** *v/t picture* dessiner; *(pull)*, *in lottery, gun* tirer; *(attract)* attirer; *(lead)* emmener; *from bank account* retirer **3** *v/i of artist* dessiner; *in competition* faire match nul

◆ **draw back 1** *v/i (recoil)* reculer **2** *v/t (pull back)* retirer; *drapes* ouvrir

◆ **draw out** *wallet, from bank* retirer

◆ **draw up 1** *v/t document* rédiger; *chair* approcher **2** *v/i of vehicle* s'arrêter

'drawback désavantage *m*, inconvénient *m*

drawer [drɔːr] *of desk* tiroir *m*

drawing [ˈdrɔːɪŋ] dessin *m*

drawl [drɔːl] voix *f* traînante

dread [dred] ~ **doing** redouter de faire; **dreadful** épouvantable

dream [driːm] **1** *n* rêve *m* **2** *v/t* rêver (**about, of** de)

◆ **dream up** inventer

dreary [ˈdrɪrɪ] morne

dress [dres] **1** *n for woman* robe *f*; (*clothing*) tenue *f* **2** *v/t person* habiller; *wound* panser; **get ~ed** s'habiller **3** *v/i* s'habiller

◆ **dress up** s'habiller chic; (*wear a disguise*) se déguiser (**as** en)

'dress circle premier balcon *m*; **dresser** (*dressing table*) coiffeuse *f*; *in kitchen* buffet *m*; **dressing** *for salad* assaisonnement *m*; *for wound* pansement *m*; **dress rehearsal** (répétition *f*) générale *f*

dribble ['drɪbl] *of person* baver; *of water* dégouliner; SP dribbler

dried [draɪd] *fruit etc* sec

drier [draɪr] → **dryer**

drift [drɪft] *of snow* s'amonceler; *of ship* être à la dérive; (*go off course*) dériver; *of person* aller à la dérive; **drifter** personne qui vit au jour le jour

drill [drɪl] **1** *n tool* perceuse *f*; *exercise*, MIL exercice *m* **2** *v/t hole* percer **3** *v/i for oil* forer; MIL faire l'exercice

drily ['draɪlɪ] *say* d'un ton pince-sans-rire

drink [drɪŋk] **1** *n* boisson *f*; **can I have a ~ of water** est-ce que je peux avoir de l'eau? **2** *v/t & v/i* boire; **I don't ~** je ne bois pas; **drinkable** buvable; *water* potable

drinker ['drɪŋkər] buveur(-eu-

se) *m(f)*; **drinking water** eau *f* potable

drip [drɪp] **1** *n liquid* goutte *f*; MED goutte-à-goutte *m*, perfusion *f* **2** *v/i* goutter

drive [draɪv] **1** *n outing* promenade *f* (en voiture); (*energy*) dynamisme *m*; COMPUT unité *f*, lecteur *m*; (*campaign*) campagne *f* **2** *v/t vehicle* conduire; (*be owner of*) avoir; (*take in car*) amener; TECH actionner **3** *v/i* conduire; **~ to work** aller au travail en voiture; **drive-in** *movie theater* drive-in

drivel ['drɪvl] bêtises *fpl*

driver ['draɪvər] conducteur (-trice) *m(f)*; *of truck* camionneur(-euse) *m(f)*; COMPUT pilote *m*; **driver's license** permis *m* de conduire

'driveway allée *f*; **drive-thru** drive-in *m inv*

drizzle ['drɪzl] **1** *n* bruine *f* **2** *v/i* bruiner

drop [drɑːp] **1** *n* goutte *f*; *in price, temperature* chute *f* **2** *v/t object* faire tomber; *bomb* lancer; *person from car* déposer; *person from team* écarter; (*stop seeing*), *charges, subject* laisser tomber; (*give up*) arrêter **3** *v/i* tomber

◆ **drop in** (*visit*)

◆ **drop off** *v/t person, goods* déposer **2** *v/i* (*fall asleep*) s'endormir; (*decline*) diminuer

◆ **drop out** (*withdraw*) se retirer (**of** de); *of school* abandonner (**of sth** qch)

drought [draʊt] sécheresse *f*

drown [draʊn] se noyer

drug [drʌg] **1** *n* MED médicament *m*; *illegal* drogue *f* **2** *v/t* droguer; **drug addict** toxicomane *m/f*; **drug dealer** dealer *m*, dealeuse *f*; *large-scale* trafiquant(e) *m(f)* de drogue; **druggist** pharmacien(ne) *m(f)*; **drugstore** drugstore *m*; **drug trafficking** trafic *m* de drogue

drum [drʌm] MUS tambour *m*; *container* tonneau *m*; **~s** batterie *f*; **drumstick** MUS baguette *f* de tambour

drunk [drʌŋk] **1** *n* ivrogne *m/f*; *habitually* alcoolique *m/f* **2** *adj* ivre, soûl; **get ~** se soûler; **drunk driving** conduite *f* en état d'ivresse

dry [draɪ] **1** *adj* sec **2** *v/t clothes* faire sécher; *dishes, eyes* essuyer **3** *v/i* sécher; **dryclean** nettoyer à sec; **dry cleaner** pressing *m*; **dryer** *machine* sèche-linge *m*

dual [ˈdu:əl] double

dub [dʌb] *movie* doubler

dubious [ˈdu:brəs] douteux; *I'm still ~ about ...* j'ai encore des doutes quant à ...

duck [dʌk] **1** *n* canard *m*; *female* cane *f* **2** *v/i* se baisser

dud [dʌd] F *(false bill)* faux *m*

due [du:] *(owed)* dû; *the rent is ~ tomorrow* il faut payer le loyer demain

dull [dʌl] *weather* sombre; *sound, pain* sourd; *(boring)* ennuyeux

duly [ˈdu:lɪ] *(as expected)* comme prévu; *(properly)* dûment, comme il se doit

dumb [dʌm] *(mute)* muet; F *(stupid)* bête

dump [dʌmp] **1** *n for garbage* décharge *f*; *(unpleasant place)* trou *m*; *house, hotel* taudis *m* **2** *v/t (deposit)* déposer; *(throw away)* jeter; *(leave)* laisser; *waste* déverser

dune [du:n] dune *f*

duplex (apartment) [ˈdu:pleks] duplex *m*

duplicate [ˈdu:plɪkət] double *m*

durable [ˈdʊrəbl] *material* résistant

during [ˈdʊrɪŋ] pendant

dusk [dʌsk] crépuscule *m*

dust [dʌst] **1** *n* poussière *f* **2** *v/t* épousseter; **duster** chiffon *m* (à poussière); **dustpan** pelle *f* à poussière; **dusty** poussiéreux

duty [ˈdu:tɪ] devoir *m*; *(task)* fonction *f*; *on goods* droit(s) *m(pl)*; **be on ~** être de service; **dutyfree** hors taxe

DVD [di:vi:ˈdi:] (= *digital versatile disk*) DVD *m*; **DVD-ROM** DVD-ROM *m*

dwarf [dwɔ:rf] **1** *n* nain(e) *m(f)* **2** *v/t* rapetisser

dwindle [ˈdwɪndl] diminuer

dye [daɪ] **1** *n* teinture *f* **2** *v/t*

teindre
dying ['daɪɪŋ] *person* mourant; *industry* moribond; *tradition* qui se perd
dynamic [daɪ'næmɪk] dynamique; **dynamism** dynamis-

me *m*
dynasty ['daɪnəstɪ] dynastie *f*
dyslexic [dɪs'leksɪk] **1** *adj* dyslexique **2** *n* dyslexique *m/f*

E

each [iːtʃ] **1** *adj* chaque **2** *adv* chacun; **they're $1.50 ~** ils coûtent $1.50 chacun, ils coûtent 1,50 $ pièce **3** *pron* chacun(e) *m(f)*; **~ of them** chacun(e) d'entre eux(elles) *m(f)*; **we know ~ other** nous nous connaissons
eager ['iːgər] désireux; *look* avide; **be ~ to do sth** désirer vivement faire qch; **eagerly** avec empressement; *wait* impatiemment; **eagerness** empressement *m*
eagle ['iːgl] aigle *m*; **eagle-eyed**: **be ~** avoir des yeux d'aigle
ear[1] [ɪr] oreille *f*
ear[2] [ɪr] *of corn* épi *m*
'**earache** mal *m* d'oreilles
early ['ɜːrlɪ] **1** *adv* (*not late*) tôt; (*ahead of time*) en avance **2** *adj* *stages, Romans* premier; *arrival* en avance; *retirement* anticipé; *music* ancien; (*in the near future*) prochain; (*in*) **~ October** début octobre; **have an ~ supper** dîner tôt *or* de bonne heure; **early bird**: **be an ~** (*early rising*

er) être matinal
earmark ['ɪrmɑːrk] réserver
earn [ɜːrn] gagner; *interest* rapporter
earnest ['ɜːrnɪst] sérieux
earnings ['ɜːrnɪŋz] salaire *m*; *of company* profits *mpl*
'**earphones** écouteurs *mpl*;
earring boucle *f* d'oreille
earth [ɜːrθ] terre *f*; *earthenware* poterie *f*; *earthly* terrestre; **it's no ~ use doing that** F ça ne sert strictement à rien de faire cela; **earthquake** tremblement *m* de terre; **earth-shattering** stupéfiant
ease [iːz] **1** *n* facilité *f*; **feel at ~** se sentir à l'aise **2** *v/t pain, mind* soulager; *suffering, shortage* diminuer **3** *v/i of pain* diminuer
easel ['iːzl] chevalet *m*
easily ['iːzəlɪ] facilement; (*by far*) de loin
east [iːst] **1** *n* est *m* **2** *adj* est *inv*; *wind* d'est **3** *adv travel* vers l'est
Easter ['iːstər] Pâques *fpl*;
Easter Day (jour *m* de) Pâ-

ques *m*; **Easter egg** œuf *m* de Pâques

easterly ['i:stərli] *wind* de l'est; *direction* vers l'est

Easter Monday lundi *m* de Pâques

eastern ['i:stərn] de l'est; (*oriental*) oriental; **easterner** habitant(e) *m(f)* de l'Est des États-Unis

Easter Sunday (jour *m* de) Pâques *m*

eastward ['i:stwərd] vers l'est

easy ['i:zi] facile; (*relaxed*) tranquille; **easy chair** fauteuil *m*; **easy-going** accommodant

eat [i:t] manger

◆ **eat out** manger au restaurant

eatable ['i:təbl] mangeable

eavesdrop ['i:vzdrɑ:p] écouter de façon indiscrète (**on s.o.** qn)

ebb [eb] *of tide* descendre

e-book ['i:buk] livre *m* électronique; **e-business** commerce *m* électronique

eccentric [ik'sentrik] **1** *adj* excentrique **2** *n* original(e) *m(f)*; **eccentricity** excentricité *f*

echo ['ekou] **1** *n* écho *m* **2** *v/i* faire écho **3** *v/t words* répéter; *views* se faire l'écho de

eclipse [i'klips] **1** *n* éclipse *f* **2** *v/t fig* éclipser

ecological [i:kə'lɑ:dʒikl] écologique; **ecologically** écologiquement; **ecologically**

friendly écologique; **ecologist** écologiste *m/f*; **ecology** écologie *f*

economic [i:kə'nɑ:mik] économique; **economical** (*cheap*) économique; (*thrifty*) économe; **economics** économie *f*; *financial aspects* aspects *mpl* économiques; **economist** économiste *m/f*; **economize** économiser

◆ **economize on** économiser

economy [i'kɑ:nəmi] économie *f*; **economy class** classe *f* économique

ecosystem ['i:kousistm] écosystème *m*; **ecotourism** tourisme *m* écologique

ecstasy ['ekstəsi] extase *f*; **ecstatic** extatique

eczema ['eksmə] eczéma *m*

edge [edʒ] **1** *n* bord *m*; **on ~** énervé **2** *v/i* (*move slowly*) se faufiler; **edgewise**: *I couldn't get a word in ~* je n'ai pas pu en placer une *F*; **edgy** énervé

edible ['edibl] comestible

edit ['edit] *text* mettre au point; *book* préparer pour la publication; *newspaper* diriger; *TV program* réaliser; *film* monter; **edition** édition *f*; **editor** *of text, book* rédacteur(-trice) *m(f)*; *of newspaper* rédacteur(-trice) *m(f)* en chef; *of TV program* réalisateur(-trice) *m(f)*; *of film* monteur(-euse) *m(f)*; **edito-**

rial 1 *adj* de la rédaction **2** *n* éditorial *m*

educate ['edʒəkeɪt] instruire (**about** sur); **she was ~d in France** elle a fait sa scolarité en France; **educated** instruit; **education** éducation *f*; *as subject* pédagogie *f*; **educational** scolaire; *(informative)* instructif

eerie ['ɪrɪ] inquiétant

effect [ɪ'fekt] effet *m*; **effective** *(efficient)* efficace; *(striking)* frappant

effeminate [ɪ'femɪnət] efféminé

efficiency [ɪ'fɪʃənsɪ] efficacité *f*; *in motel* chambre *f* avec coin-cuisine; **efficient** efficace; **efficiently** efficacement

effort ['efərt] effort *m*; **effortless** aisé, facile

e.g. [i:'dʒiː] ex; *spoken* par example

egg [eg] œuf *m*; **eggcup** coquetier *m*; **egghead** F intello *m/f* F; **eggplant** aubergine *f*

ego ['iːgoʊ] PSYCH ego *m*; **egocentric** égocentrique; **egoism** égoïsme *m*; **egoist** égoïste *m/f*

eiderdown ['aɪdərdaʊn] *(quilt)* édredon *m*

eight [eɪt] huit; **eighteen** dix-huit; **eighteenth** dix-huitième; **eighth** huitième; **eightieth** quatre-vingtième; **eighty** quatre-vingts; **~-two/four** *etc* quatre-vingt-deux/-quatre *etc*

either ['iːðər] **1** *adj* l'un ou l'autre; *(both)* chaque **2** *pron* l'un(e) ou l'autre **3** *adv*: **I won't go ~** je n'irai pas non plus **4** *conj*: **~ ... or** soit ... soit ...; *with negative* ni ... ni ...

eject [ɪ'dʒekt] **1** *v/t* éjecter **2** *v/i from plane* s'éjecter

◆ **eke out** [iːk] suppléer à l'insuffisance de; **eke out a living** vivoter

el [el] métro *m* aérien

elaborate 1 [ɪ'læbərət] *adj* compliqué **2** *v/i* [ɪ'læbəreɪt] donner des détails (**on** sur)

elapse [ɪ'læps] (se) passer

elastic [ɪ'læstɪk] **1** *adj* élastique **2** *n* élastique *m*; **elasticated** élastique

elated [ɪ'leɪtɪd] transporté (de joie); **elation** exultation *f*

elbow ['elboʊ] coude *m*

elder ['eldər] **1** *adj* aîné(e) *m(f)*; **elderly 1** *adj* âgé **2** *npl*: **the ~** les personnes *fpl* âgées; **eldest 1** *adj* aîné **2** *n*: **the ~** l'aîné(e) *m(f)*

elect [ɪ'lekt] élire; **elected** élu; **election** élection *f*; **election campaign** campagne *f* électorale; **election day** jour *m* des élections; **electorate** électorat *m*

electric [ɪ'lektrɪk] *also fig* électrique; **electrical** électrique; **electric chair** chaise *f* électrique; **electrician** électricien(ne) *m(f)*; **electricity** électricité *f*; **electrify** électrifier; *fig* électriser

electrocute [ɪ'lektrəkjuːt] électrocuter

electron [ɪ'lektrɑːn] electron *m*; **electronic** électronique; **electronics** électronique *f*

elegance ['elɪgəns] élégance *f*; **elegant** élégant

element ['elɪmənt] élément *m*; **elementary** élémentaire; **elementary schoo** école *f* primaire

elephant ['elɪfənt] éléphant *m*

elevate ['elɪveɪt] élever; **elevated railroad** métro *m* aérien; **elevation** (*altitude*) altitude *f*; **elevator** ascenseur *m*

eleven [ɪ'levn] onze; **eleventh** onzième

eligible ['elɪdʒəbl]: **be ~ to do sth** avoir le droit de faire qch

eliminate [ɪ'lɪmɪneɪt] éliminer; **elimination** élimination *f*

élite [eɪ'liːt] **1** *n* élite *f* **2** *adj* d'élite

eloquence ['eləkwəns] éloquence *f*; **eloquent** éloquent

else [els]: **anything ~?** autre chose?; **nothing ~** rien d'autre; **no one ~** personne d'autre; **everyone ~ is going** tous les autres y vont; **someone ~** quelqu'un d'autre; **something ~** autre chose; **let's go somewhere ~** allons autre part; **or ~** sinon; **elsewhere** ailleurs

elude [ɪ'luːd] (*escape from*) échapper à; (*avoid*) éviter

elusive insaisissable

emaciated [ɪ'meɪsɪeɪtɪd] émacié

e-mail ['iːmeɪl] **1** *n* e-mail *m*, courrier *m* électronique **2** *v/t person* envoyer un e-mail à; **e-mail address** adresse *f* e-mail, adresse *f* électronique

emancipation [ɪmænsɪ'peɪʃn] émancipation *f*

embalm [ɪm'bɑːm] embaumer

embankment [ɪm'bæŋkmənt] *of river* berge *f*; RAIL remblai *m*

embargo [em'bɑːrgəʊ] embargo *m*

embark [ɪm'bɑːrk] (s')embarquer

embarrass [ɪm'bærəs] gêner, embarrasser; **embarrassed** gêné, embarrassé; **embarrassing** gênant, embarrassant; **embarrassment** gêne *f*, embarras *m*

embassy ['embəsɪ] ambassade *f*

embezzle [ɪm'bezl] détourner; **embezzlement** détournement *m* de fonds

emblem ['embləm] emblème *m*

embodiment [ɪm'bɑːdɪmənt] personnification *f*; **embody** personnifier

embrace [ɪm'breɪs] **1** *n* étreinte *f* **2** *v/t* (*hug*) serrer dans les bras, étreindre; (*take in*) embrasser **3** *v/i of two people se* serrer dans les bras, s'étreindre

embroider [ɪmˈbrɔɪdər] broder; *fig* enjoliver

embryo [ˈembrɪou] embryon *m*; **embryonic** *fig* embryonnaire

emerald [ˈemərəld] émeraude *f*

emerge [ɪˈmɜːrdʒ] sortir; *from mist, of truth* surgir

emergency [ɪˈmɜːrdʒənsɪ] urgence *f*; **emergency exit** sortie *f* de secours; **emergency landing** atterrissage *m* forcé; **emergency services** services *mpl* d'urgence

emigrate [ˈemɪɡreɪt] émigrer; **emigration** émigration *f*

Eminence [ˈemɪnəns] REL: **His ~** son Éminence; **eminent** éminent

emission [ɪˈmɪʃn] *of gases* émission *f*; **emit** émettre

emotion [ɪˈmouʃn] émotion *f*; **emotional** *problems* émotionnel, affectif; *(full of emotion)* ému; *reunion* émouvant

emphasis [ˈemfəsɪs] accent *m*; **emphasize** *syllable* accentuer; *fig* souligner; **emphatic** catégorique

empire [ˈempaɪr] *also fig* empire *m*

employ [ɪmˈplɔɪ] employer; **employee** employé(e) *m(f)*; **employer** employeur(-euse) *m(f)*; **employment** *(jobs)* emplois *mpl*; *(work)* emploi

m

emptiness [ˈemptɪnɪs] vide *m*; **empty 1** *adj* vide; *promises* vain **2** *v/t* vider **3** *v/i* *of room, street* se vider

emulate [ˈemjuleɪt] imiter

enable [ɪˈneɪbl] permettre

enchanting [ɪnˈtʃæntɪŋ] ravissant

encircle [ɪnˈsɜːrkl] encercler

enclose [ɪnˈklouz] *in letter* joindre; *area* entourer; **enclosure** *with letter* pièce *f* jointe

encore [ˈɑːŋkɔːr] bis *m*

encounter [ɪnˈkaʊntər] **1** *n* rencontre *f* **2** *v/t* *person* rencontrer; *problem, resistance* affronter

encourage [ɪnˈkʌrɪdʒ] encourager; **encouragement** encouragement *m*; **encouraging** encourageant

encyclopedia [ɪnsaɪkləˈpiːdɪə] encyclopédie *f*

end [end] **1** *n* *(conclusion, purpose)* fin *f*; *(extremity)* bout *m*; **in the ~** à la fin **2** *v/t* terminer, finir **3** *v/i* se terminer, finir

◆ **end up** finir

endanger [ɪnˈdeɪndʒər] mettre en danger; **endangered species** espèce *f* en voie de disparition

endeavor, *Br* **endeavour** [ɪnˈdevər] **1** *n* effort *m* **2** *v/i* essayer (**to do sth** de faire qch)

endemic [ɪnˈdemɪk] endémique

ending ['endɪŋ] fin f; GRAM terminaison f; **endless** sans fin

endorse [ɪn'dɔːrs] candidacy appuyer; product associer son image à; **endorsement** of candidacy appui m; of product association f de son image à

end 'product produit m fini

endurance [ɪn'dʊrəns] of person endurance f; of car résistance f; **endure 1** v/t endurer **2** v/i (last) durer; **enduring** durable

enemy ['enəmɪ] ennemi(e) m(f)

energetic [enərdʒetɪk] also fig énergique; **energy** énergie f; **energy supply** alimentation f en énergie

enforce [ɪn'fɔːrs] mettre en vigueur

engage [ɪn'geɪdʒ] **1** v/t (hire) engager **2** v/i of machine part s'engrener; **engaged** to be married fiancé; Br TELEC occupé; **get ~** se fiancer; **engagement** to be married fiançailles fpl; MIL engagement m; **engagement ring** bague f de fiançailles

engine ['endʒɪn] moteur m; **engineer** ingénieur m/f; NAUT, RAIL mécanicien(ne) m(f); **engineering** ingénierie f

England ['ɪŋglənd] Angleterre f; **English 1** adj anglais **2** n language anglais m; **the**

~ les Anglais mpl; **Englishman** Anglais m; **Englishwoman** Anglaise f

engrave [ɪn'greɪv] graver; **engraving** gravure f

engrossed [ɪn'groust]: ~ **in** absorbé dans

engulf [ɪn'gʌlf] engloutir

enhance [ɪn'hæns] flavor rehausser; reputation accroître; performance améliorer; enjoyment augmenter

enigma [ɪ'nɪgmə] énigme f

enjoy [ɪn'dʒɔɪ] aimer; ~ **o.s.** s'amuser; ~**I said to s.o. eating** bon appétit!; **enjoyable** agréable; **enjoyment** plaisir m

enlarge [ɪn'lɑːrdʒ] agrandir; **enlargement** agrandissement m

enlighten [ɪn'laɪtn] éclairer

enlist [ɪn'lɪst] MIL enrôler

enmity ['enmɪtɪ] inimitié f

enormous [ɪ'nɔːrməs] énorme

enough [ɪ'nʌf] **1** adj assez de **2** pron assez; **will $50 be ~?** est-ce que $50 suffiront?; **that's ~** ça suffit **3** adv assez; **big ~** assez grand

enquire [ɪn'kwaɪr] etc → **inquire** etc

enroll, Br **enrol** [ɪn'roʊl] s'inscrire

en suite (bathroom) ['ɒːnswiːt] salle f de bains attenante

ensure [ɪn'ʃʊər] assurer; ~ **that ...** s'assurer que ...

entail [ɪn'teɪl] entraîner

entangle [ɪn'tæŋgl] *in rope* empêtrer

enter ['entər] **1** *v/t room, house* entrer dans; *competition* entrer en; COMPUT entrer **2** *v/i* entrer; *in competition* s'inscrire **3** *n* COMPUT touche *f* entrée

enterprise ['entərpraɪz] *(initiative)* (esprit *m* d')initiative *f*; *(venture)* entreprise *f*; **enterprising** entreprenant

entertain [entər'teɪn] *(amuse)* amuser; *(consider: idea)* envisager; **entertainer** artiste *m/f* de variété; **entertaining** amusant, divertissant; **entertainment** divertissement *m*

enthusiasm [ɪn'θuːzɪæzəm] enthousiasme *m*; **enthusiast** enthousiaste *m/f*; **enthusiastic** enthousiaste; **enthusiastically** avec enthousiasme

entire [ɪn'taɪr] entier; **entirely** entièrement

entitle [ɪn'taɪtl]: ~ *s.o.* **to sth** donner à qn droit à qch; **be ~d to** avoir droit à

entrance ['entrəns] entrée *f*

entranced [ɪn'trænst] enchanté

'**entrance exam(ination)** examen *m* d'entrée

entrant ['entrənt] inscrit(e) *m(f)*

entrepreneur [ɑːntrəprə'nɜːr] entrepreneur(-euse) *m(f)*; **entre-** neurial *skills* d'entrepreneur

entrust [ɪn'trʌst] confier

entry ['entrɪ] entrée *f*; *for competition: person* participant(e) *m(f)*; **entryphone** interphone *m*

envelop [ɪn'veləp] envelopper

envelope ['envəloup] enveloppe *f*

enviable ['envɪəbl] enviable; **envious** envieux; **be ~ of s.o.** envier qn

environment [ɪn'vaɪrənmənt] environnement *m*; **environmental** écologique; **environmentalist** écologiste *m/f*; **environmentally friendly** écologique; **environs** environs *mpl*

envisage [ɪn'vɪzɪdʒ] envisager

envoy ['envɔɪ] envoyé(e) *m(f)*

envy ['envɪ] **1** *n* envie *f* **2** *v/t*: ~ *s.o.* **sth** envier qch à qn

epic ['epɪk] **1** *n* épopée *f*; *movie* film *m* à grand spectacle **2** *adj journey* épique

epicenter, *Br* **epicentre** ['episentər] épicentre *m*

epidemic [epɪ'demɪk] *also fig* épidémie *f*

episode ['epɪsoud] épisode *m*

epitaph ['epɪtæf] épitaphe *f*

equal ['iːkwl] **1** *adj* égal; **be ~ to task** être à la hauteur de **2** *n* égal *m* **3** *v/t* égaler; **equality** égalité *f*; **equalize 1** *v/t* égaliser **2** *v/i Br* SP égaliser; **equalizer** *Br* SP but *m* égalisateur; **equally** *divide* de manière égale; *qualified, intelligent* tout aussi; **equal rights** égalité *f* des droits

equation [ɪ'kweɪʒn] MATH équation *f*

equator [ɪ'kweɪtər] équateur *m*

equip [ɪ'kwɪp] équiper; **equipment** équipement *m*

equity ['ekwətɪ] FIN capitaux *mpl* propres

equivalent [ɪ'kwɪvələnt] **1** *adj* équivalent **2** *n* équivalent *m*

era ['ɪrə] ère *f*

eradicate [ɪ'rædɪkeɪt] éradiquer

erase [ɪ'reɪz] effacer

erect [ɪ'rekt] **1** *adj* droit **2** *v/t* ériger, élever; **erection** *of building, penis* érection *f*

ergonomic [ɜːrgou'nɑ:mɪk] ergonomique

erode [ɪ'roud] éroder; *fig: power* miner; *rights* supprimer progressivement; **erosion** érosion *f*; *fig: of rights* suppression *f* progressive

errand ['erənd] commission *f*

erratic [ɪ'rætɪk] *performance, course* irrégulier; *driving* capricieux; *behavior* changeant

error ['erər] erreur *f*

erupt [ɪ'rʌpt] *of volcano* entrer en éruption; *of violence* éclater; *of person* exploser F; **eruption** *of volcano* éruption *f*; *of violence* explosion *f*

escalate ['eskəleɪt] s'intensifier; **escalation** intensifica-

tion *f*; **escalator** escalier *m* mécanique, escalator *m*

escape [ɪ'skeɪp] **1** *n* *of prisoner* évasion *f*; *of animal, gas* fuite *f* **2** *v/i* s'échapper

escort ['eskɔ:rt] **1** *n* cavalier (-ière) *m(f)*; *(guard)* escorte *f* **2** *v/t* [ɪ'skɔ:rt] *socially* accompagner; *(act as guard to)* escorter

especially [ɪ'speʃlɪ] particulièrement

espionage ['espɪənɑ:ʒ] espionnage *m*

espresso (**coffee**) [es'presou] expresso *m*

essay ['eseɪ] *at school* rédaction *f*; *at university* dissertation *f*; *by writer* essai *m*

essential [ɪ'senʃl] essentiel

establish [ɪ'stæblɪʃ] *company* fonder; *(create, determine)* établir; **establishment** *firm, shop etc* établissement *m*

estate [ɪ'steɪt] *land* propriété *f*; *of dead person* biens *mpl*

esthetic [ɪs'θetɪk] esthétique

estimate ['estɪmət] **1** *n* estimation *f*; *from builder etc* devis *m* **2** *v/t* estimer

estuary ['estʃəwerɪ] estuaire *m*

etc [et'setrə] (= *et cetera*) etc.

eternal [ɪ'tɜ:rnl] éternel; **eternity** éternité *f*

ethical ['eθɪkl] *problem* éthique; *(morally right)* moral; **ethics** éthique *f*

ethnic ['eθnɪk] ethnique

EU [i:'ju:] (= *European Un-*

***ion*) U.E. *f* (= Union *f* euro-péenne)

euphemism ['juːfəmɪzm] eu-phémisme *m*

euro ['jʊrəʊ] FIN euro *m*

Europe ['jʊrəp] Europe *f*; **European 1** *adj* européen **2** *n* Européen(ne) *m(f)*

euthanasia [juːθəˈneɪzɪə] eu-thanasie *f*

evacuate [ɪˈvækjʊeɪt] *(clear people from)* faire évacuer; *(leave)* évacuer

evade [ɪˈveɪd] éviter; *question* éluder

evaluate [ɪˈvæljʊeɪt] évaluer; **evaluation** évaluation *f*

evaporate [ɪˈvæpəreɪt] *also fig* s'évaporer; **evaporation** évaporation *f*

evasion [ɪˈveɪʒn] fuite *f*; **eva-sive** évasif

eve [iːv] veille *f*

even ['iːvn] **1** *adj breathing* ré-gulier; *distribution* égal; *(lev-el)* plat; *surface* plan; *num-ber* pair; **get ~ with ...** pren-dre sa revanche sur ... **2** *adv* même; **~ bigger** encore plus grand; **not ~** pas même; **so** quand même; **~ if** même si **3** *v/t*: **~ the score** égaliser

evening ['iːvnɪŋ] soir *m*; **in the ~** le soir; **this ~** ce soir; **good ~** bonsoir; **evening class** cours *m* du soir; **eve-ning dress** *for woman* robe *f* du soir; *for man* tenue *f* de soirée

evenly ['iːvnlɪ] *(regularly)* de

manière égale; *breathe* régu-lièrement

event [ɪˈvent] événement *m*; SP épreuve *f*; **eventful** mou-vementé

eventually [ɪˈventʃʊəlɪ] fina-lement

ever ['evər] jamais; **have you ~ been to Japan?** est-ce que tu es déjà allé au Japon?; **for ~** pour toujours; **since** de-puis lors; **~ since we ...** depuis le jour où nous ...; **ever-lasting** éternel

every ['evrɪ]: **~ day** tous les jours, chaque jour; **~ one of ...** chacun de ...; **~body** → **everyone**; **every-day** de tous les jours; **every-one** tout le monde; **~ who ...** tous ceux qui ...; **everything** tout; **everywhere** partout; *(wherever)* partout où

evict [ɪˈvɪkt] expulser

evidence ['evɪdəns] preuve(s) *f(pl)*; LAW témoignage *m*; **give ~** témoigner; **evident** évident; **evidently** *(clearly)* à l'évidence; *(apparently)* de toute évidence

evil ['iːvl] **1** *adj* mauvais **2** *n* mal *m*

evolution [iːvəˈluːʃn] évolu-tion *f*; **evolve** évoluer

ex [eks] F *wife, husband* ex *m/f* F

exact [ɪgˈzækt] exact; **exact-ing** exigeant; **exactly** exacte-ment

exaggerate [ɪgˈzædʒəreɪt]

exagérer; **exaggeration** exagération *f*

exam [ɪg'zæm] examen *m*; **examination** examen *m*; **examine** examiner

example [ɪg'zæmpl] exemple *m*; **for** ~ par exemple

excavate ['ekskəveɪt] (*dig*) excaver; *of archeologist* fouiller; **excavation** excavation *f*; *archeological* fouille(s) *f(pl)*

exceed [ɪk'siːd] dépasser; *authority* outrepasser; **exceedingly** extrêmement

excel [ɪk'sel] **1** *v/i* exceller (**at** en) **2** *v/t*: ~ **o.s.** se surpasser; **excellence** excellence *f*; **excellent** excellent

except [ɪk'sept] sauf; ~ **for** à l'exception de; **exception** exception *f*; **exceptional** exceptionnel

excerpt ['eksɜːrpt] extrait *m*

excess [ɪk'ses] **1** *n* excès *m* **2** *adj*: ~ **water** excédent *m* d'eau; **excessive** excessif

exchange [ɪks'tʃeɪndʒ] **1** *n* échange *m* **2** *v/t* échanger; **exchange rate** FIN cours *m* du change

excite [ɪk'saɪt] (*make enthusiastic*) enthousiasmer; **excited** excité; **get** ~ s'exciter; **excitement** excitation *f*; **exciting** passionnant

exclaim [ɪk'skleɪm] s'exclamer; **exclamation** exclamation *f*; **exclamation point** point *m* d'exclamation

exclude [ɪk'skluːd] exclure; **excluding** excluant; **exclusive** *hotel* huppé; *rights, interview* exclusif

excuse [ɪk'skjuːs] **1** *n* excuse *f* **2** *v/t* [ɪk'skjuːz] excuser; (*forgive*) pardonner; ~ **me** excusez-moi

ex-directory *Br*: **be** ~ être sur liste rouge

execute ['eksɪkjuːt] *criminal, plan* exécuter; **execution** *of criminal, plan* exécution *f*; **executive** cadre *m*

exempt [ɪg'zempt] exempt

exercise ['eksərsaɪz] **1** *n* exercice *m* **2** *v/t muscle* exercer; *dog* promener; *caution, restraint* user de **3** *v/i* prendre de l'exercice

exhale [eks'heɪl] exhaler

exhaust [ɪg'zɔːst] **1** *n fumes* gaz *m* d'échappement; *pipe* tuyau *m* d'échappement **2** *v/t* (*tire, use up*) épuiser; **exhausted** (*tired*) épuisé; **exhausting** épuisant; **exhaustion** épuisement *m*; **exhaustive** exhaustif

exhibit [ɪg'zɪbɪt] **1** *n in exhibition* objet *m* exposé **2** *v/t of artist* exposer; (*give evidence of*) montrer; **exhibition** exposition *f*; *of bad behavior* étalage *m*; *of skill* démonstration *f*

exhilarating [ɪg'zɪləreɪtɪŋ] *weather* vivifiant; *sensation* grisant

exile ['eksaɪl] **1** *n* exil *m*; *per-*

son exilé(e) *m(f)* **2** *v/t* exiler

exist [ɪgˈzɪst] exister; ~ **on** subsister avec; **existence** existence *f*; **be in** ~ exister; **existing** existant

exit [ˈeksɪt] **1** *n* sortie *f* **2** *v/i* COMPUT sortir

exonerate [ɪgˈzɑːnəreɪt] (*clear*) disculper

exotic [ɪgˈzɑːtɪk] exotique

expand [ɪkˈspænd] **1** *v/t* étendre **2** *v/i of population* s'accroître; *of business, city* se développer; *of metal, gas* se dilater; **expanse** étendue *f*; **expansion** *of population* accroissement *m*; *of business, city* développement *m*; *of metal, gas* dilatation *f*

expect [ɪkˈspekt] **1** *v/t also ba-by* attendre; (*suppose*) penser; (*demand*) exiger **2** *v/i*: **be ~ing** attendre un bébé; **I** ~ **so** je pense que oui; **~pectant mother** future maman *f*; **expectation** attente *f*, espérance *f*

expedition [ekspɪˈdɪʃn] expédition *f*

expel [ɪkˈspel] expulser

expendable [ɪkˈspendəbl] *person* pas indispensable

expenditure [ɪkˈspendɪtʃər] dépenses *fpl* (**on** de)

expense [ɪkˈspens] dépense *f*; **expenses** frais *mpl*; **ex-pensive** cher

experience [ɪkˈspɪrɪəns] **1** *n* expérience *f* **2** *v/t pain, plea-sure* éprouver; *difficulty* con-

naître; **experienced** expéri-menté

experiment [ɪkˈsperɪmənt] **1** *n* expérience *f* **2** *v/i* faire des expériences; **experimental** expérimental

expert [ˈekspɜːrt] **1** *adj* expert **2** *n* expert(e) *m(f)*; **expertise** savoir-faire *m*

expiration date [ˈekspɪˈreɪʃn] date *f* d'expiration; **expire** expirer; **expiry** expiration *f*; **expiry date** *Br* date *f* d'expi-ration

explain [ɪkˈspleɪn] expliquer; **explanation** explication *f*; **explanatory** explicatif

explicit [ɪkˈsplɪsɪt] *instructions* explicite

explode [ɪkˈsploʊd] **1** *v/i of bomb, fig* exploser **2** *v/t bomb* faire exploser

exploit[1] [ˈeksplɔɪt] *n* exploit *m*

exploit[2] [ɪkˈsplɔɪt] *v/t person, resources* exploiter; **exploitation** [eksplɔɪˈteɪʃn] *of person* exploitation *f*

exploration [ekspləˈreɪʃn] ex-ploration *f*; **explore** *country, possibility* explorer; **explorer** explorateur(-trice) *m(f)*

explosion [ɪkˈsploʊʒn] *also in population* explosion *f*; **ex-plosive** explosif *m*

export [ˈekspɔːrt] **1** *n* exporta-tion *f* **2** *v/t also* COMPUT ex-porter; **exporter** exporta-teur(-trice) *m(f)*

expose [ɪkˈspoʊz] (*uncover*)

mettre à nu; *scandal* dévoiler; *person* démasquer; **~ X to Y** exposer X à Y; **exposure** exposition *f*; MED effets *mpl* du froid; *of dishonest behavior* dénonciation *f*; PHOT pose *f*; *in media* couverture *f*

express [ɪk'spres] **1** *adj* (*fast*) express; (*explicit*) explicite **2** *n* *train* express *m* **3** *v/t* exprimer; **expression** expression *f*; **expressive** expressif; **expressly** (*explicitly*) expressément; (*deliberately*) exprès; **expressway** voie *f* express

expulsion [ɪk'spʌlʃn] expulsion *f*

extend [ɪk'stend] **1** *v/t* *house, garden* agrandir; *search* étendre (**to** à); *runway, contract, visa* prolonger **2** *v/i* *of garden* s'étendre; **extension** *to house* agrandissement *m*; *of contract, visa* prolongation *f*; TELEC poste *m*; **extensive** *search, knowledge* vaste, étendu; *damage* considérable; **extent** étendue *f*, ampleur *f*; **to a certain ~** jusqu'à un certain point

exterior [ɪk'stɪriər] **1** *adj* extérieur **2** *n* *of building* extérieur *m*; *of person* dehors *mpl*

exterminate [ɪk'stɜːrmɪneɪt] exterminer

external [ɪk'stɜːrnl] extérieur

extinct [ɪk'stɪŋkt] *species* disparu; **extinction** *of species* extinction *f*; **extinguish** *fire,*

cigarette éteindre; **extinguisher** extincteur *m*

extortion [ɪk'stɔːrʃn] extortion *f*

extra ['ekstrə] **1** *n* extra *m* **2** *adj* (*spare*) de rechange; (*additional*) en plus; **be ~** (*cost more*) être en supplément **3** *adv* ultra-

extract[1] ['ekstrækt] *n* extrait *m*

extract[2] [ɪk'strækt] extraire; *tooth also* arracher; *information* arracher; **extraction** extraction *f*

extradite ['ekstrədaɪt] extrader; **extradition** extradition *f*

extramarital [ekstrə'mærɪtl] extraconjugal

extraordinary [ɪkstrə'ɔːrdɪnerɪ] extraordinaire

extra 'time *Br* SP prolongation(s) *f(pl)*

extravagance [ɪk'strævəgəns] dépenses *fpl* extravagantes; *single act* dépense *f* extravagante; **extravagant** *person* dépensier; *price* exorbitant; *claim* excessif

extreme [ɪk'striːm] **1** *n* extrême *m* **2** *adj* extrême; **extremely** extrêmement; **extremist** extrémiste *m/f*

extrovert ['ekstrəvɜːrt] **1** *n* extraverti(e) *m(f)* **2** *adj* extraverti

exuberant [ɪg'zuːbərənt] exubérant

eye [aɪ] **1** *n* œil *m* **2** *v/t* regarder; **eye-catching** accrocheur; **eyeglasses** lunettes *fpl*; **eyeliner** eye-liner *m*;

eyeshadow ombre *f* à paupières; **eyesight** vue *f*; **eyewitness** témoin *m* oculaire

F

fabric ['fæbrɪk] tissu *m*

fabulous ['fæbjʊləs] fabuleux

façade [fə'sɑːd] façade *f*

face [feɪs] **1** *n* visage *m*, figure *f* **2** *v/t person, sea* faire face à

◆ **face up to** *bully* affronter; *responsibilities* faire face à

'facecloth gant *m* de toilette; **facelift** lifting *m*

facial ['feɪʃl] soin *m* du visage

facilitate [fə'sɪlɪteɪt] faciliter; **facilities** *of school, town etc* installations *fpl*; *(equipment)* équipements *mpl*

fact [fækt] fait *m*; **in ~, as a matter of ~** en fait

faction ['fækʃn] faction *f*

factor ['fæktər] facteur *m*

faculty ['fækltɪ] faculté *f*

fad [fæd] lubie *f*

fade [feɪd] *of colors* passer; **faded** *color* passé

fag [fæg] *pej* F *(homosexual)* pédé *m* F

fail [feɪl] **1** *v/i* échouer **2** *v/t exam* être refusé à; **failing** défaut *m*, faiblesse *f*; **failure** échec *m*

faint [feɪnt] **1** *adj* faible, léger **2** *v/i* s'évanouir; **faintly** légèrement

fair¹ [fer] *(fun~)*, COM foire *f*

fair² [fer] *hair* blond; *complexion* blanc

fairly ['ferlɪ] *treat* équitablement; *(quite)* assez; **fairness** *of treatment* équité *f*

faith [feɪθ] *also* REL foi *f*; **faithful** fidèle; **faithfully** fidèlement

fake [feɪk] **1** *n (article m)* faux *m* **2** *adj* faux; *suicide attempt* simulé **3** *v/t (forge)* falsifier; *(feign)* feindre; *suicide, kidnap* simuler

fall¹ *in season* automne *m*

fall² [fɔːl] **1** *v/i* tomber; *of prices* baisser **2** *n* chute *f*; *in price, temperature* baisse *f*

◆ **fall behind** prendre du retard

◆ **fall for** *person* tomber amoureux de; *(be deceived by)* se laisser prendre à

◆ **fall through** *of plans* tomber à l'eau

fallible ['fæləbl] faillible

false [fɔːls] faux; **false start** *in race* faux départ *m*; **false teeth** fausses dents *fpl*; **falsify** falsifier

fame [feɪm] célébrité *f*

familiar [fə'mɪljər] familier; **be ~ with sth** bien connaître qch; **familiarity** *with subject etc* (bonne) connaissance *f* (**with** de); **familiarize**: **~ o.s. with** se familiariser avec

family ['fæməlɪ] famille *f*; **family doctor** médecin *m* de famille; **family planning clinic** centre *m* de planning familial; **family tree** arbre *m* généalogique

famine ['fæmɪn] famine *f*

famous ['feɪməs] célèbre

fan[1] [fæn] *n in sport* fana *m/f* F; *of singer, band* fan *m/f*

fan[2] [fæn] **1** *n electric* ventilateur *m*; *handheld* éventail *m* **2** *v/t*: **~ o.s.** s'éventer

fanatical [fə'nætɪkl] fanatique; **fanaticism** fanatisme *m*

fantasize ['fæntəsaɪz] fantasmer (**about** sur); **fantastic** fantastique; **fantasy** *hopeful* rêve *m*; *unrealistic, sexual* fantasme *m*

fanzine ['fænziːn] fanzine *m*

far [fɑːr] loin; (*much*) bien; **~ away** très loin; **as ~ as the corner** jusqu'au coin

farce [fɑːrs] farce *f*

fare [fer] *for ticket* prix *m* du billet; *for taxi* prix *m*

Far 'East Extrême-Orient *m*

farewell [fer'wel] adieu *m*

farfetched [fɑːr'fetʃt] tiré par les cheveux

farm [fɑːrm] ferme *f*; **farmer** fermier(-ière) *m(f)*; **farming** agriculture *f*; **farmworker** ouvrier(-ière) *m(f)* agricole; **farmyard** cour *f* de ferme

far-'off lointain, éloigné; **far-sighted** prévoyant; *visually* hypermétrope; **farther** plus loin; **farthest** le plus loin

fascinate ['fæsɪneɪt] fasciner; **fascinating** fascinant; **fascination** fascination *f*

fascism ['fæʃɪzm] fascisme *m*; **fascist 1** *n* fasciste *m/f* **2** *adj* fasciste

fashion ['fæʃn] mode *f*; (*manner*) manière *f*, façon *f*; **in ~** à la mode; **out of ~** démodé; **fashionable** à la mode; **fashionably** à la mode; **fashion-conscious** au courant de la mode; **fashion designer** créateur(-trice) *m(f)* de mode; **fashion show** défilé *m* de mode

fast[1] [fæst] **1** *adj* rapide; **be ~** *of clock* avancer **2** *adv* vite; **be ~ asleep** dormir à poings fermés

fast[2] [fæst] *n* (*not eating*) jeûne *m*

fasten ['fæsn] **1** *v/t* attacher; *lid, window* fermer **2** *v/i of dress etc* s'attacher; **fastener** ['fæsnər] *for dress* agrafe *f*; *for lid* fermeture *f*

fast 'food fast-food *m*; **fast lane** voie *f* rapide; **fast train** train *m* rapide

fat [fæt] **1** *adj* gros **2** *n on meat* gras *m*; *for baking* graisse *f*

fatal ['feɪtl] *also error* fatal; **fatality** *accident* mortel; **fatally** fatalement; **~ injured** mortellement blessé fate [feɪt] destin *m*

'fat free sans matières grasses; *yoghurt etc* 0%

father ['fɑːðər] père *m*; fatherhood paternité *f*; father-in-law beau-père *m*; fatherly paternel

fatigue [fə'tiːg] fatigue *f*

fatten ['fætn] *animal* engraisser; fatty **1** *adj* adipeux **2** *n* F *person* gros(se) *m(f)*

faucet ['fɔːsɪt] robinet *m*

fault [fɔːlt] *(defect)* défaut *m*; **it's your/my ~** c'est de ta/ma faute; faultless impeccable; faulty défectueux

favor ['feɪvər] **1** *n* faveur *f*; **do s.o. a ~** rendre (un) service à qn **2** *v/t (prefer)* préférer; favorable favorable; favorite **1** *n person* préféré(e) *m(f)*; *food* plat *m* préféré; *in race* **2** *adj* préféré; favoritism favoritisme *m*

favour *Br* → **favor**

fax [fæks] **1** *n* fax *m* **2** *v/t* faxer

fear [fɪr] **1** *n* peur *f* **2** *v/t* avoir peur de; fearless sans peur; fearlessly sans peur

feasibility study [fiːzə'bɪlətɪ] étude *f* de faisabilité; feasible faisable

feast [fiːst] festin *m*

feat [fiːt] exploit *m*

feather ['feðər] plume *f*

feature ['fiːtʃər] *on face* trait *m*; *of city, building, style* caractéristique *f*; *article in paper* chronique *f*; feature film long métrage *m*

February ['februərɪ] février *m*

federal ['fedərəl] fédéral; federation fédération *f*

fed 'up F: **be ~ with** en avoir ras-le-bol de F

fee [fiː] *of lawyer, doctor etc* honoraires *mpl*; *for membership* frais *mpl*

feeble ['fiːbl] faible

feed [fiːd] nourrir; feedback réactions *fpl*

feel [fiːl] **1** *v/t (touch)* toucher; *(sense)* sentir; *pain, pleasure* ressentir; *(think)* penser **2** *v/i*: **it ~s like silk** on dirait de la soie; **do you ~ like a drink?** est-ce que tu as envie de boire quelque chose?

◆ feel up to se sentir capable de

feeler ['fiːlər] *of insect* antenne *f*; feeling sentiment *m*; *(sensation)* sensation *f*

fellow 'citizen concitoyen(ne) *m(f)*

felony ['felənɪ] crime *m*

felt [felt] feutre *m*; felt tip stylo *m* feutre

female ['fiːmeɪl] **1** *adj* femelle; *relating to people* féminin **2** *n* femelle *f*; *person* femme *f*

feminine ['femɪnɪn] **1** *adj* féminin **2** *n* GRAM féminin *m*; feminism féminisme *m*; feminist **1** *n* féministe *m/f* **2** *adj* féministe

fence [fens] barrière *f*, clôture *f*

fender ['fendər] MOT aile *f*

fermentation [fɜːrmen'teɪʃn]

fermentation f

ferocious [fəˈrouʃəs] féroce

ferry [ˈferɪ] ferry m

fertile [ˈfɜːrtl] fertile; fertility fertilité f; fertilize féconder; fertilizer for soil engrais m

fervent [ˈfɜːrvənt] fervent

fester [ˈfestər] of wound suppurer

festival [ˈfestɪvl] festival m; festive de fête; festivities festivités fpl

fetal [ˈfiːtl] fœtal

fetch [fetʃ] (go and ~) aller chercher (from à); (come and ~) venir chercher (from à); price atteindre

fetus [ˈfiːtəs] fœtus m

feud [fjuːd] querelle f

fever [ˈfiːvər] fièvre f; feverish also fig fiévreux

few [fjuː] 1 adj (not many) peu de; a ~ quelques; quite a ~, a good ~ (a lot) beaucoup de 2 pron (not many) peu; a ~ quelques-un(e)s m(f); quite a ~, a good ~ beaucoup; fewer moins de

fiancé [fɪˈɑːnseɪ] fiancé m; fiancée fiancée f

fiber [ˈfaɪbər] fibre f; fiberglass n fibre f de verre; fiber optics fibres fpl optiques

fibre Br → fiber

fickle [ˈfɪkl] inconstant

fiction [ˈfɪkʃn] romans mpl; (made-up story) fiction f; fictional de roman; fictitious fictif

fiddle [ˈfɪdl] 1 n (violin) violon

m 2 v/i: ~ around with tripoter 3 v/t accounts, results truquer

fidgety [ˈfɪdʒɪtɪ] remuant

field [fiːld] champ m; for sport terrain m; (competitors in race) concurrent(e)s m(f)pl; fielder in baseball joueur m de champ

fierce [fɪrs] animal féroce; wind, storm violent; fiercely also fig violemment

fiery [ˈfaɪrɪ] ardent, fougueux

fifteen [fɪfˈtiːn] quinze; fifteenth quinzième; fifth cinquième; fiftieth cinquantième; fifty cinquante; fifty-fifty moitié-moitié

fight [faɪt] 1 n combat m; (argument) dispute f; for survival etc lutte f 2 v/t enemy, person combattre; in boxing se battre contre; injustice lutter contre 3 v/i se battre; (argue) se disputer; fighter combattant(e) m(f); airplane avion m de chasse; (boxer) boxeur m; fighting physical combat m; verbal dispute f

figure [ˈfɪɡjər] 1 n (digit) chiffre m; of person ligne f; (form, shape) figure f 2 v/t F (think) penser:

◆ figure on F (plan) compter

◆ figure out comprendre; calculation calculer

file¹ [faɪl] 1 n of documents dossier m; COMPUT fichier m 2 v/t documents classer

file² [faɪl] for wood etc lime f

'file cabinet classeur *m*
fill [fɪl] remplir; *tooth* plomber; *prescription* préparer
◆ fill in *form* remplir; *hole* boucher
◆ fill out 1 *v/t form* remplir 2 *v/i* (*get fatter*) grossir
fillet ['fɪlɪt] filet *m*
filling ['fɪlɪŋ] 1 *n in sandwich* garniture *f; in tooth* plombage *m* 2 *adj food* nourrissant; filling station station-service *f*
film [fɪlm] 1 *n* pellicule *f;* (*movie*) film *m* 2 *v/t* filmer; film-maker réalisateur(-trice) *m(f)* de films; film star star *f* de cinéma
filter ['fɪltər] 1 *n* filtre *m* 2 *v/t* filtrer
filth ['fɪlθ] saleté; *filthy sale: language etc* obscène
final ['faɪnl] 1 *adj* dernier, décision définitif, irrévocable 2 *n* SP finale *f;* finale apothéose *f;* finalist finaliste *m/f;* finalize finaliser, mettre au point; finally finalement, enfin
finance ['faɪnæns] 1 *n* finance *f;* (*funds*) financement *m* 2 *v/t* financer; financial financier; financially financièrement; financier financier(-ière) *m(f)*
find [faɪnd] trouver
◆ find out découvrir; (*enquire about*) se renseigner sur
findings ['faɪndɪŋz] *of report*

constatations *fpl*
fine¹ [faɪn] *day* beau; (*good*) bon, excellent; *distinction* subtil; *line* fin; **how's that? – that's** ~ que dites-vous de ça? – c'est bien
fine² [faɪn] 1 *n* amende *f* 2 *v/t* condamner à une amende de $5.000
finger ['fɪŋgər] 1 *n* doigt *m* 2 *v/t* toucher; fingerprint empreinte *f* digitale
finicky ['fɪnɪkɪ] *person* tatillon; *design* alambiqué
finish ['fɪnɪʃ] 1 *v/t* finir, terminer 2 *v/i* finir 3 *n of product* finition *f; of race* arrivée *f*
◆ finish with *boyfriend etc* en finir avec
fire ['faɪr] 1 *n* feu *m;* (*blaze*) incendie *m;* (*electric, gas*) radiateur *m;* **be on ~** être en feu; **set ~ to sth** mettre le feu à qch 2 *v/i* (*shoot*) tirer 3 *v/t* F (*dismiss*) virer F; fire alarm signal *m* d'incendie; firearm arme *f* à feu; firecracker pétard *m;* fire department sapeurs-pompiers *mpl;* fire engine *esp Br* voiture *f* de pompiers; fire escape *ladder* échelle *f* de secours; *stairs* escalier *m* de secours; fire extinguisher extincteur *m* (d'incendie); fire fighter pompier *m;* fireplace cheminée *f;* fire station caserne *f* de pompiers; fire truck voiture *f* de pompiers; firework pièce *f* d'artifice; **~s**

(*display*) feu *m* d'artifice
firm[1] [fɜːrm] *adj* ferme
firm[2] [fɜːrm] *n* COM firme *f*
first [fɜːrst] **1** *adj* premier **2** *n* premier(-ière) *m(f)* **3** *adv* arrive, finish le/la premier(-ière) *m(f)*; (*beforehand*) d'abord; **at ~** au début; **first aid** premiers secours *mpl*; **first class 1** *adj* ticket de première classe; (*very good*) de première qualité **2** *adv* travel en première classe; **first floor** rez-de-chaussée *m*; Br premier étage *m*; **First Lady** première dame *f*; **firstly** premièrement; **first name** prénom *m*; **first night** première *f*; **first-rate** de premier ordre
fiscal ['fɪskl] fiscal; **fiscal year** année *f* fiscale
fish [fɪʃ] **1** *n* poisson *m* **2** *v/i* pêcher; **fisherman** pêcheur *m*; **fishing** pêche *f*; **fishing boat** bateau *m* de pêche; **fish stick** bâtonnet *m* de poisson; **fishy** F (*suspicious*) louche
fist [fɪst] poing *m*
fit[1] [fɪt] *n* MED crise *f*, attaque *f*
fit[2] [fɪt] *adj* physically en forme; morally digne
fit[3] [fɪt] **1** *v/t* of clothes aller à; (*install, attach*) poser; **it doesn't ~ me any more** je ne rentre plus dedans **2** *v/i* of clothes aller
fitness ['fɪtnɪs] physical (bonne) forme *f*; **fitting** approprié; **fittings** installations *fpl*

five [faɪv] cinq
fix [fɪks] **1** *n* (*solution*) solution *f* **2** *v/t* (*attach*) attacher; (*repair*) réparer; *meeting etc* arranger; *lunch* préparer; *dishonestly: match etc* truquer; **fixed** fixe; **fixings** garniture *f*
flab [flæb] *on body* graisse *f*; **flabby** *muscles etc* mou
flag[1] [flæg] *n* drapeau *m*; NAUT pavillon *m*
flag[2] [flæg] *v/i* (*tire*) faiblir
flagpole mât *m* (de drapeau)
flagrant ['fleɪgrənt] flagrant
flair [fler] (*talent*) flair *m*; **have a natural ~ for** avoir un don pour
flake [fleɪk] *of snow* flocon *m*; *of plaster* écaille *f*
flamboyant [flæm'bɔɪənt] extravagant; **flamboyantly** avec extravagance
flame [fleɪm] flamme *f*
flammable ['flæməbl] inflammable
flank [flæŋk] **1** *n* flanc *m* **2** *v/t*: **be ~ed by** être flanqué de
flap [flæp] **1** *n of envelope, pocket* rabat *m* **2** *v/t wings* battre **3** *v/i of flag etc* battre
◆ **flare up** [fler] *of violence, rash* éclater; *of fire* s'enflammer; (*get very angry*) s'emporter
flash [flæʃ] **1** *n of light* éclair *m*; PHOT flash *m*; **in a ~** F en un rien de temps; **~ of lightning** éclair *m* **2** *v/i of light* clignoter; **flashback** *in movie* flash-back *m*; **flashlight** lam-

pe *f* de poche; PHOT flash *m*; flashy *pej* voyant

flask [flæsk] (*hip ~*) fiole *f*

flat[1] [flæt] **1** *adj* plat; *beer* éventé; *battery, tire* à plat; *bémol* **2** *adv* MUS trop bas **3** *n* pneu *m* crevé

flat[2] [flæt] *n Br* (*apartment*) appartement *m*

flatly ['flætlɪ] *deny* catégoriquement; **flat rate** tarif *m* unique; **flatten** *land,* road aplanir; *by bombing, demolition* raser

flatter ['flætər] flatter; **flatterer** flatteur(-euse) *m(f)*; **flattering** *comments* flatteur; *color, clothes* avantageux; **flattery** flatterie *f*

flavor ['fleɪvər] **1** *n* goût *m*; *of ice cream* parfum *m* **2** *v/t food* assaisonner; **flavoring** arôme *m*

flavour *Br* → **flavor**

flaw [flɔː] défaut *m*; **flawless** parfait

flee [fliː] s'enfuir

fleet [fliːt] NAUT flotte *f*; *of vehicles* parc *m*

fleeting ['fliːtɪŋ] *visit etc* très court

flesh [fleʃ] *also of fruit* chair *f*

flex [fleks] *muscles* fléchir; **flexibility** flexibilité *f*; **flexible** flexible; **flextime** horaire *m* à la carte

flicker ['flɪkər] vaciller

flier ['flaɪr] (*circular*) prospectus *m*

flight [flaɪt] *in airplane* vol *m*;

(*fleeing*) fuite *f*; **~** (**of stairs**) escalier *m*; **flight attendant** *male* steward *m*; *female* hôtesse *f* de l'air; **flight path** trajectoire *f* de vol; **flight recorder** enregistreur *m* de vol; **flight time** *departure* heure *f* de vol; *duration* durée *f* de vol; **flighty** frivole

flimsy ['flɪmzɪ] *furniture* fragile; *dress, material* léger; *excuse* faible

flinch [flɪntʃ] tressaillir

flipper ['flɪpər] nageoire *f*

flirt [flɜːrt] **1** *v/i* flirter **2** *n* flirteur(-euse) *m(f)*; **flirtatious** flirteur

float [flout] *also* FIN flotter

flock [flɑːk] **1** *n of sheep* troupeau *m* **2** *v/i* venir en masse

flood [flʌd] **1** *n* inondation *f* **2** *v/t of river* inonder; **flooding** inondation(s) *f(pl)*

'floodlight projecteur *m*; **flood waters** inondations *fpl*

floor [flɔːr] sol *m*; *wooden* plancher *m*; (*story*) étage *m*

flop [flɑːp] **1** *v/i* s'écrouler; F (*fail*) faire un bide F **2** *n* F (*failure*) bide *m* F; **floppy** (**disk**) disquette *f*

florist ['flɔːrɪst] fleuriste *m/f*

flour ['flaʊr] farine *f*

flourish ['flʌrɪʃ] *of plants* fleurir; *fig* prospérer; **flourishing** *business* fleurissant, prospère

flow [flou] **1** *v/i of river* couler; *of electric current* passer; *of traffic* circuler; *of work* se dérouler **2** *n of river* cours *m*; *of information* circulation *f*; **flowchart** organigramme *m*

flower ['flaur] **1** *n* fleur *f* **2** *v/i* fleurir

flu [flu:] grippe *f*

fluctuate ['flʌktʃueit] fluctuer; **fluctuation** fluctuation *f*

fluency ['flu:ənsi] *in a language* maîtrise *f* (**in** de); **fluent** *person* qui s'exprime avec aisance; **he speaks ~ Spanish** il parle couramment l'espagnol; **fluently** couramment; *in own language* avec aisance

fluid ['flu:ɪd] fluide *m*

flunk [flʌŋk] F *subject* rater

flush [flʌʃ] **1** *v/t:* **~ the toilet** tirer la chasse d'eau **2** *v/i* (*go red*) rougir

flutter ['flʌtər] *of bird* voleter; *of wings* battre; *of flag* s'agiter; *of heart* palpiter

fly[1] [flai] *n* (*insect*) mouche *f*

fly[2] [flai] *n on pants* braguette *f*

fly[3] [flai] **1** *v/i* voler; *in airplane* prendre l'avion; *of flag* flotter **2** *v/t airplane* piloter, voler; *airline* voyager par; (*transport by air*) envoyer par avion

♦ **fly past** *of time* filer

flying ['flaiɪŋ]: **I hate ~** je déteste prendre l'avion

foam [foum] *on sea* écume *f*; *on drink* mousse *f*; **foam rubber** caoutchouc *m* mous-

se

focus ['foukəs] *of attention* centre *m*; PHOT mise *f* au point

♦ **focus on** se concentrer sur; PHOT mettre au point sur

fodder ['fɑːdər] fourrage *m*

fog [fɑːg] brouillard *m*; **foggy** brumeux

foil[1] [fɔil] *n silver* feuille *f* d'aluminium

foil[2] [fɔil] *v/t* (*thwart*) faire échouer

fold [fould] **1** *v/t paper etc* plier; **~ one's arms** croiser les bras **2** *v/i of business* fermer (*ses portes*) **3** *n in cloth etc* pli *m*

♦ **fold up 1** *v/t* plier **2** *v/i of chair, table* se (re)plier

folder ['fouldər] *for documents* chemise *f*; COMPUT dossier *m*; **folding** pliant

foliage ['fouliɪdʒ] feuillage *m*

folk [fouk] (*people*) gens *mpl*; **folk music** folk *m*; **folk singer** chanteur(-euse) *m(f)* de folk

follow ['fɑːlou] **1** *v/t also* (*understand*) suivre **2** *v/i logically* s'ensuivre

♦ **follow up** *inquiry* donner suite à

follower ['fɑːlouər] *of politician etc* partisan(e) *m(f)*; *of football team* supporteur (-trice) *m(f)*; **following 1** *adj* suivant **2** *n people* partisans *mpl*

fond [fɑːnd] (*loving*) aimant;

memory agréable; *be ~ of* beaucoup aimer

fondle ['fɒndl] caresser

fondness ['fɒndnɪs] *for s.o.* tendresse *f*; *for sth* penchant *m*

font [fɑnt] *for printing* police *f*; *in church* fonts *mpl* baptismaux

food [fuːd] nourriture *f*; **French ~** la cuisine française; **food poisoning** intoxication *f* alimentaire

fool [fuːl] **1** *n* idiot(e) *m(f)* **2** *v/t* berner; **foolhardy** téméraire; **foolish** idiot, bête; **foolproof** à toute épreuve

foot [fʊt] *also measurement* pied *m*; *of animal* patte *f*; **put one's ~ in it** F mettre les pieds dans le plat F; **footage** séquences *fpl*; **football** football *m* américain; *(soccer)* football *m* F; *(ball)* ballon *m* de football; **football player** joueur(-euse) *m(f)* de football américain; *soccer* joueur(-euse) *m(f)* de football; **foothills** contreforts *mpl*; **footnote** note *f* (de bas de page); **footpath** sentier *m*; **footprint** trace *f* de pas; **footstep** pas *m*

for [fər], [fɔːr] pour; *a train ~ ...* un train à destination de ...; *what is this ~?* pour quoi est-ce que c'est fait?; *what ~?* pourquoi?; *~ three days* pendant trois jours; *it lasted ~ three days* ça a duré trois

jours; *I've been waiting ~ an hour* j'attends depuis une heure

forbid [fər'bɪd] interdire; **forbidden** interdit; **forbidding** menaçant

force [fɔːrs] **1** *n* force *f*; **come into ~** *of law etc* entrer en vigueur **2** *v/t* door, lock forcer; **~ s.o. to do sth** forcer qn à faire qch; **forced** forcé; **forced landing** atterrissage *m* forcé; **forceful** argument, speaker puissant; character énergique

forceps ['fɔːrseps] MED forceps *m*

forcibly ['fɔːrsəblɪ] restrain par force

foreboding [fər'boʊdɪŋ] pressentiment *m*; **forecast 1** *n* of results pronostic *m*; of weather prévisions *fpl* **2** *v/t* result pronostiquer; future, weather prévoir; **forefathers** ancêtres *mpl*; **forefinger** index *m*; **foreground** premier plan *m*; **forehead** front *m*

foreign [ˈfɑrən] étranger; **foreign affairs** affaires *fpl* étrangères; **foreign body** corps *m* étranger; **foreign currency** devises *fpl* étrangères; **foreigner** étranger (-ère) *m(f)*; **foreign exchange** devises *fpl* étrangè-

'foreman chef *m* d'équipe; **foremost 1** *adv* (*uppermost*) le plus important **2** *adj* (*lead-*

ing) premier

forensic 'medicine [fə'rensɪk] médecine f légale; **forensic scientist** expert m légiste

'forerunner *person* prédécesseur m; *thing* ancêtre m/f; **foresee** prévoir; **foresight** prévoyance f

forest [fɒrɪst] forêt f; **forestry** sylviculture f

fore'tell prédire

forever [fə'revər] toujours

'foreword avant-propos m

forfeit [fɔːrfɪt] (*lose*) perdre; (*give up*) renoncer à

forge [fɔːrdʒ] contrefaire; **forgery** *bank bill* faux billet m; *document* faux m; *signature* contrefaçon f

forget [fər'get] oublier; **forgetful: you're so ~** tu as vraiment mauvaise mémoire

forgive [fər'gɪv] **1** *v/t:* **~ s.o. sth** pardonner qch à qn **2** *v/i* pardonner; **forgiveness** pardon m

fork [fɔːrk] fourchette f; *for gardening* fourche f; *in road* embranchement m

form [fɔːrm] **1** *n* (*shape*) forme f; *document* formulaire m **2** *v/t* former; *friendship* développer; *opinion* se faire **3** *v/i* (*take shape, develop*) se former; **formal** *language* soutenu; *dress* de soirée; *manner, reception* cérémonieux; *recognition etc* officiel; **formality** *of language*

caractère m soutenu; *of occasion* cérémonie f; **it's just a ~** c'est juste une formalité; **formally** *speak* cérémonieusement; *recognized* officiellement

format [fɔːrmæt] **1** *v/t* formater **2** *n* format m

formation [fɔːr'meɪʃn] formation f

former [fɔːrmər] ancien; **the ~** le premier, la première; **formerly** autrefois

formidable [fɔːrmɪdəbl] redoutable

formula [fɔːrmjʊlə] MATH, CHEM formule f; *fig* recette f

fort [fɔːrt] MIL fort m

forthcoming [fɔːrθkʌmɪŋ] (*future*) futur; *personality* ouvert

'forthright franc

fortieth [fɔːrtɪθ] quarantième

fortnight [fɔːrtnaɪt] *Br* quinze jours *mpl*, quinzaine f

fortress [fɔːrtrɪs] MIL forteresse f

fortunate [fɔːrtʃnət] *decision* heureux; **be ~** avoir de la chance; **fortunately** heureusement; **fortune** *(fate)* destin m; *(luck)* chance f; *(lot of money)* fortune f

forty [fɔːrtɪ] quarante

forward [fɔːrwərd] **1** *adv* en avant **2** *adj pej: person* effronté **3** *n sp* avant m **4** *v/t letter* faire suivre; **forward-looking** moderne

fossil ['fɒsɪl] fossile *m*

foster ['fɒstər] *child* servir de famille d'accueil à; *attitude, belief* encourager

foul [faʊl] **1** *n* SP faute *f* **2** *adj smell* infect; *weather* sale **3** *v/t* SP commettre une faute contre

found [faʊnd] *school etc* fonder; **foundation** *of theory etc* fondement *m*; (*organization*) fondation *f*; **foundations** *of building* fondations *fpl*; **founder** fondateur(-trice) *m(f)*

fountain ['faʊntɪn] fontaine *f*; *with vertical spout* jet *m* d'eau

four [fɔːr] quatre; **four-star** *hotel etc* quatre étoiles; **fourteen** quatorze; **fourteenth** quatorzième; **fourth** quatrième; **four-wheel drive** MOT quatre-quatre *m*

fox [fɒks] **1** *n* renard *m* **2** *v/t* (*puzzle*) mystifier

foyer ['fɔɪər] hall *m* d'entrée

fraction ['frækʃn] fraction *f*; **fractionally** très légèrement

fracture ['fræktʃər] **1** *n* fracture *f* **2** *v/t* fracturer

fragile ['frædʒaɪl] fragile

fragment ['frægmənt] fragment *m*

fragrance ['freɪgrəns] parfum *m*; **fragrant** parfumé

frail [freɪl] frêle, fragile

frame [freɪm] **1** *n* *of picture, bicycle* cadre *m*; *of window* châssis *m*; *of eyeglasses* mon-

ture *f* **2** *v/t picture* encadrer; F *person* monter un coup contre; **framework** structure *f*; **within the ~ of** dans le cadre de

France [fræns] France *f*

franchise ['fræntʃaɪz] *for business* franchise *f*

frank [fræŋk] franc; **frankly** franchement; **frankness** franchise *f*

frantic ['fræntɪk] frénétique

fraternal [frə'tɜːrnl] fraternel

fraud [frɔːd] fraude *f*; *person* imposteur *m*; **fraudulent** frauduleux

frayed [freɪd] *cuffs* usé

freak [friːk] **1** *n* (*unusual event*) phénomène *m* étrange; (*two-headed animal etc*) monstre *m*; F (*strange person*) taré(e) *m(f)*F **2** *adj storm* anormalement violent

free [friː] **1** *adj* libre; *no cost* gratuit **2** *v/t prisoners* libérer; **freedom** liberté *f*; **free enterprise** libre entreprise *f*; **free kick** *in soccer* coup *m* franc; **freelance** indépendant, **free-lance** *inv*; **freely** *admit* volontiers; **free speech** libre parole *f*; **freeway** autoroute *f*

freeze [friːz] **1** *v/t* congeler; *bank account* bloquer; **~ a video** faire un arrêt sur image **2** *v/i of water* geler; **freeze-dried** lyophilisé; **freezer** congélateur *m*;

freezing 1 *adj* glacial **2** *n*: **10 below ~** 10 degrés au-dessous de zéro

freight [freɪt] fret *m*; **freighter** *ship*cargo *m*; *airplane* avion-cargo *m*

French [frentʃ] **1** *adj* français **2** *n language* français *m*; **the ~** les Français *mpl*; **French fries** frites *fpl*; **Frenchman** Français *m*; **Frenchwoman** Française *f*

frenzied ['frenzid] *attack, activity* forcené; *mob* déchaîné; **frenzy** frénésie *f*

frequency ['friːkwənsɪ] *also of radio* fréquence *f*

frequent[1] *adj* fréquent

frequent[2] [frɪ'kwent] *v/t bar etc* fréquenter

frequently ['friːkwəntlɪ] fréquemment

fresh [freʃ] frais; *start* nouveau; *sheets* propre; (*impertinent*) insolent; **fresh air** air *m* frais

◆ **freshen up 1** *v/i* se rafraîchir **2** *v/t paintwork* rafraîchir

freshly ['freʃlɪ] fraîchement

freshman étudiant(e) *m(f)* de première année; **freshwater** d'eau douce

fret [fret] *v/i* s'inquiéter

friction ['frɪkʃn] friction *f*

Friday ['fraɪdeɪ] vendredi *m*

fridge [frɪdʒ] frigo *m* F

friend [frend] ami(e) *m(f)*; **friendliness** amabilité *f*; **friendly** amical; *hotel, city* sympathique; *argument* entre amis; **friendship** amitié *f*

fries [fraɪz] frites *fpl*

fright [fraɪt] peur *f*; **frighten** faire peur à; **be ~ed** avoir peur (**of** de); **frightening** effrayant

frill [frɪl] *on dress etc*, (*extra*) falbala *m*

fringe [frɪndʒ] frange *f*; *of city* périphérie *f*; *of society* marge *f*; **fringe benefits** avantages *mpl* sociaux

frisk [frɪsk] fouiller

◆ **fritter away** ['frɪtər] *time, fortune* gaspiller

frivolity [frɪ'vɑːlətɪ] frivolité *f*; **frivolous** frivole

frizzy ['frɪzɪ] *hair* crépu

frog [frɑːg] grenouille *f*; **frogman** homme-grenouille *m*

from [frɑːm] ♦ **9 to 5** (*o'clock*) de 9 heures à 5 heures; **~ the 18th century** à partir du XVIIIe siècle; **~ today on** à partir d'aujourd'hui; **~ here to there** d'ici à là(-bas); **I am ~ New Jersey** je viens du New Jersey; **tired ~ the journey** fatigué par le voyage; **it's ~ overeating** c'est d'avoir trop mangé

front [frʌnt] **1** *n of building* façade *f*, devant *m*; *of book* devant *m*; (*cover organization*) façade *f*; MIL, *of weather* front *m*; **in ~** devant; **in ~** *in a race* en tête; **in ~ of** devant **2** *adj wheel, seat* avant **3** *v/t TV program* présenter; **front door** porte *f* d'entrée

frontier ['frʌntɪr] *also fig*

frontière f

'**front line** MIL front m; **front page** of newspaper une f; **front-wheel drive** traction f avant

frost [frɒst] gel m; **frostbite** gelure f; **frosting** on cake glaçage m; **frosty** also fig glacial

froth [frɒθ] écume f, mousse f

frown [fraʊn] froncer les sourcils

frozen ['frəʊzn] gelé; food surgelé

fruit [fruːt] fruit m; collective fruits mpl; **fruitful** discussions etc fructueux; **fruit juice** jus m de fruit; **fruit salad** salade f de fruits

frustrate ['frʌstreɪt] person frustrer; plans contrarier; **frustrating** frustrant; **frustration** frustration f

fry [fraɪ] (faire) frire; **frypan** poêle f (à frire)

fuck [fʌk] V baiser V; ∼ **you!** putain! V

fuel ['fjʊəl] **1** n carburant m **2** v/t fig entretenir

fugitive ['fjuːdʒətɪv] fugitif (-ive) m(f)

fulfill, Br **fulfil** [fʊl'fɪl] dreams réaliser; task accomplir; contract remplir; **fulfillment**, Br **fulfilment** of contract etc exécution f; moral, spiritual accomplissement m

full [fʊl] plein (**of** de); hotel, account complet; **pay in** ∼ tout payer; **full moon** pleine

lune f; **full stop** Br point m; **full-time** à plein temps; **fully** complètement; describe en détail

fumble ['fʌmbl] catch mal attraper

fumes [fjuːmz] s fumée f

fun [fʌn] **1** n amusement m; **it was great** ∼ on s'est bien amusé; **have** ∼**!** amuse-toi bien! **2** adj F marrant F

function ['fʌŋkʃn] **1** n fonction f; (reception etc) réception f **2** v/i fonctionner; ∼ **as** faire fonction de; **functional** fonctionnel

fund [fʌnd] **1** n fonds m **2** v/t project etc financer

fundamental [fʌndə'mentl] fondamental; **fundamentalist** fondamentaliste m/f; **fundamentally** fondamentalement

funding ['fʌndɪŋ] (money) financement m

funeral ['fjuːnərəl] enterrement m; **funeral home** établissement m de pompes funèbres

fungus ['fʌŋgəs] champignon m; mold moisissure f

funnies ['fʌnɪz] F pages fpl drôles; **funnily** (oddly) bizarrement; (comically) comiquement; ∼ **enough** chose curieuse; **funny** (comical) drôle; (odd) bizarre, curieux

fur [fɜːr] fourrure f

furious ['fjʊrɪəs] furieux

furnace ['fɜːrnɪs] four(neau)

m

furnish ['fɜːrnɪʃ] *room* meubler; *(supply)* fournir; **furniture meubles** *mpl*; *a piece of ~* un meuble

further ['fɜːrðər] **1** *adj* supplémentaire; *(more distant)* plus éloigné **2** *adv* walk, drive plus loin **3** *v/t cause etc* faire avancer, promouvoir; **furthermore** de plus, en outre

furtive ['fɜːrtɪv] furtif

fury ['fjʊrɪ] fureur *f*

fuse [fjuːz] **1** *n* ELEC fusible *m*, plomb *m* F **2** *v/i* ELEC: *the*

lights have ~d les plombs ont sauté **3** *v/t* ELEC faire sauter; **fusebox boîte** *f* à fusibles

fusion ['fjuːʒn] fusion *f*

fuss [fʌs] agitation *f*; **fussy** *person* difficile; *design etc* trop compliqué

futile ['fjuːtɪl] futile; **futility** futilité *f*

future ['fjuːtʃər] **1** *n* avenir *f*; GRAM futur *m* **2** *adj* futur; **futuristic design** futuriste

fuzzy ['fʌzɪ] *hair* crépu; *(out of focus)* flou

G

gadget ['gædʒɪt] gadget *m*

gag [gæg] **1** *n* bâillon *m*; *(joke)* gag *m* **2** *v/t also fig* bâillonner

gain [geɪn] acquérir; *victory* remporter; *advantage, sympathy* gagner

gala ['gælə] gala *m*

galaxy ['gæləksɪ] galaxie *f*

gale [geɪl] tempête *f*

gallery ['gælərɪ] *for art, in theater* galerie *f*

gallon ['gælən] gallon *m* (0,785l, en GB 0,546l)

gallop ['gæləp] galoper

gamble ['gæmbl] jouer; **gambler joueur(-euse)** *m(f)*; **gambling** jeu *m*

game [geɪm] *also in tennis* jeu *m*; *have a ~ of tennis* faire une partie de tennis

gang [gæŋ] gang *m*; *of friends* bande *f*; **gangster** gangster *m*; **gangway** passerelle *f*

gap [gæp] trou *m*; *in time* intervalle *m*; *between personalities* fossé *m*

gape [geɪp] rester bouche bée; **gaping** *hole* béant

garage ['gɜːrɑːʒ] garage *m*

garbage ['gɑːrbɪdʒ] ordures *fpl*; *(fig: nonsense)* bêtises *fpl*; **garbage can** poubelle *f*; **garbage truck** benne *f* à ordures

garbled ['gɑːrbld] *message* confus

garden ['gɑːrdn] jardin *m*; **gardening** jardinage *m*

garish ['gerɪʃ] criard

garlic ['gɑːrlɪk] ail *m*

garment ['gɑːrmənt] vêtement *m*

garnish ['gɑːrnɪʃ] garnir (**with** de)

gas [gæs] gaz *m*; (*gasoline*) essence *f*

gash [gæʃ] entaille *f*

gasket ['gæskɪt] joint *m* d'étanchéité

gasoline ['gæsəliːn] essence *f*

gasp [gæsp] **1** *n in surprise* hoquet *m*; *with exhaustion* halètement *m* **2** *v/i with exhaustion* haleter; **with surprise** pousser une exclamation de surprise

'**gas pedal** accélérateur *m*; **gas pump** pompe *f* (à essence); **gas station** station-service *f*

gate [geɪt] *also at airport* porte *f*; **gateway** entrée *f*; *also fig* porte *f*

gather ['gæðər] **1** *v/t facts* recueillir; **~ speed** prendre de la vitesse **2** *v/i of crowd* s'assembler; **gathering** (*group of people*) assemblée *f*

gaudy ['gɔːdɪ] voyant

gauge [geɪdʒ] **1** *n jauge f* **2** *v/t pressure* jauger; *opinion* mesurer

gaunt [gɔːnt] émacié

gawky ['gɔːkɪ] gauche

gawp [gɔːp] F rester bouche bée (**at** devant)

gay [geɪ] gay

gaze [geɪz] **1** *n regard m* (fixe) **2** *v/i* regarder fixement

gear [gɪr] (*equipment*) équipement *m*; *in vehicles* vitesse *f*;

gearbox MOT boîte *f* de vitesses; **gear shift** MOT levier *m* de vitesse

gel [dʒel] *for hair, shower* gel *m*

gem [dʒem] pierre *f* précieuse; *fig* perle *f*

gender ['dʒendər] genre *m*

gene [dʒiːn] gène *m*

general ['dʒenrəl] **1** *n* MIL général(e) *m(f)* **2** *adj* général; **generalization** généralisation *f*; **generalize** généraliser; **generally** généralement; **~ speaking** de manière générale

generate ['dʒenəreɪt] produire; **generation** génération *f*; **generator** générateur *m*

generosity [dʒenə'rɑːsətɪ] générosité *f*; **generous** généreux

genetic [dʒɪ'netɪk] génétique; **genetically** génétiquement; **genetically engineered** transgénique; **genetically modified** génétiquement modifié; **genetic engineering** génie *m* génétique; **genetic fingerprint** empreinte *f* génétique; **genetics** génétique *f*

genial ['dʒiːnjəl] agréable

genitals ['dʒenɪtlz] organes *mpl* génitaux

genius ['dʒiːnjəs] génie *m*

genocide ['dʒenəsaɪd] génocide *m*

gentle ['dʒentl] doux; *breeze* léger; **gentleman** monsieur

m; **he's a real ~** c'est un vrai
gentleman; **gentleness** douceur *f*; **gently** doucement;
blow légèrement

genuine ['dʒenuɪn] authentique; **genuinely** vraiment,
sincèrement

geographical [dʒɪə'græfɪkl]
géographique; **geography**
géographie *f*

geological [dʒɪə'lɒ:dʒɪkl]
géologique; **geologist** géologue *m/f*; **geology** géologie
f

geometric, geometrical
[dʒɪə'metrɪk(l)] géométri-
que; **geometry** géométrie *f*

geriatric [dʒerɪ'ætrɪk] **1** *adj*
gériatrique **2** *n* patient(e)
m(f) gériatrique

germ [dʒɜːrm] *also of idea etc*
germe *m*

German ['dʒɜːrmən] **1** *adj* allemand **2** *n person* Alle-
mand(e) *m(f)*; *language* allemand *m*; **German shepherd**
berger *m* allemand; **Germany** Allemagne *f*

gesture ['dʒestʃər] *also fig*
geste *m*

get [get] *(obtain)* obtenir;
(buy) acheter; *(fetch)* aller
chercher; *(receive: letter)* recevoir; *(receive: knowledge,
respect etc)* acquérir; *(catch:
bus, train etc)* prendre; *(understand)* comprendre; *(become)* devenir; **when we ~
home** quand nous arrivons
chez nous; **~ old/tired** vieil-

lir/se fatiguer; **~ sth done**
(by s.o. else) faire faire qch;
~ s.o. to do sth faire faire
qch à qn; **~ one's hair cut**
se faire couper les cheveux;
~ sth ready préparer qch;
have got avoir; **have got
to** devoir; **I have got to
study** je dois étudier, il faut
que j'étudie (subj); **~ to
know** commencer à bien
connaître

◆ **get at** *(criticize)* s'en prendre à; *(imply, mean)* vouloir
dire

◆ **get by** *(pass)* passer; *financially* s'en sortir

◆ **get down 1** *v/i from ladder
etc* descendre; *(duck)* se
baisser **2** *v/t (depress)* déprimer

◆ **get in 1** *v/i of train, plane*
arriver; *(come home)* ren-
trer; *to car* entrer **2** *v/t to suitcase etc* rentrer

◆ **get into** *house* entrar dans;
car monter dans

◆ **get off 1** *v/i from bus etc*
descendre; *(finish work)* finir; *(not be punished)* s'en tirer **2** *v/t (remove)* enlever

◆ **get on 1** *v/i to bike, bus*
monter; *(be friendly)* s'entendre; *(advance: of time)*
se faire tard; *(become old)*
prendre de l'âge; *(progress:
of book)* avancer **2** *v/t* **get
on the bus** monter dans le
bus

◆ **get out 1** *v/i of car, prison*

etc sortir; **get out!** va-t-en! **2**
v/t nail, stain enlever; *gun,*
pen sortir

◆ **get through** *on telephone*
obtenir la communication

◆ **get up 1** *v/i* se lever **2** *v/t*
(climb: hill) monter

'getaway car voiture utilisée
pour s'enfuir; **get-together**
réunion *f*

ghastly ['gæstlı] horrible

ghetto ['getou] ghetto *m*

ghost [goust] fantôme *m*,
spectre *m*; **ghostly** spectral

ghoul [gu:l] personne *f* morbide

giant ['dʒaɪənt] **1** *n* géant(e)
m(f) **2** *adj* géant

gibberish ['dʒɪbərɪʃ] F charia-
bia *m*

gibe [dʒaɪb] moquerie *f*

giddiness ['gɪdɪnɪs] vertige
m; **giddy**: *feel* ~ avoir le vertige

gift [gɪft] cadeau *m*; *talent* don
m; **gift card** carte *f* cadeau;
gifted doué·e; **giftwrap**: ~ *sth*
faire un paquet-cadeau

gig [gɪg] F concert *m*

gigabyte ['gɪgəbaɪt] COMPUT
gigaoctet *m*

gigantic [dʒaɪ'gæntɪk] gigantesque

giggle ['gɪgl] **1** *v/i* glousser **2** *n*
gloussement *m*

gimmick ['gɪmɪk] truc F

gin [dʒɪn] gin *m*; ~ *and tonic*
gin *m* tonic

gipsy ['dʒɪpsɪ] gitan·e *m(f)*

girder ['gɜːrdər] poutre *f*

girl [gɜːrl] (jeune) fille *f*; **girl-**
friend *of boy* petite amie *f*;
younger also copine *f*; *of girl*
amie *f*, *younger also* copine
f; **girlish** de jeune fille

gist [dʒɪst] essence *f*

give [gɪv] donner; *present* offrir; *(supply: electricity etc)*
fournir; *talk, lecture* faire;
cry, groan pousser

◆ **give away** *as present* donner; *(betray)* trahir

◆ **give back** rendre

◆ **give in 1** *v/i (surrender)* se
rendre **2** *v/t (hand in)* remettre

◆ **give onto** *(open onto)* donner sur

◆ **give out 1** *v/t leaflets etc*
distribuer **2** *v/i of supplies,*
strength s'épuiser

◆ **give up 1** *v/t smoking etc*
arrêter de **2** *v/i (stop making*
effort) abandonner

◆ **give way** *of bridge etc*
s'écrouler

give-and-'take concessions
fpl mutuelles

gizmo ['gɪzmou] F truc *m*

glad [glæd] heureux; **gladly**
volontiers, avec plaisir

glamor [glæmər] éclat *m*, fascination *f*; **glamorize** donner
un aspect séduisant à; **glam-**
orous séduisant, fascinant;
job prestigieux; **glamour** *Br*
→ *glamor*

glance [glæns] **1** *n* regard *m* **2**
v/i jeter un regard, lancer un
coup d'œil

gland [glænd] glande f

glare [gler] **1** n of sun, lights éclat m (éblouissant) **2** v/i of sun, lights briller d'un éclat éblouissant

♦ **glare at** lancer un regard furieux à

glaring ['glerɪŋ] mistake flagrant

glass [glæs] material, for drink verre m; **glasses** lunettes fpl

glazed [gleɪzd] expression vitreux

gleam [gli:m] **1** n lueur f **2** v/i luire

glee [gli:] joie f; **gleeful** joyeux

glib [glɪb] désinvolte; **glibly** avec désinvolture

glide [glaɪd] glisser; of bird, plane planer; **glider** planeur m; **gliding** sport vol m à voile

glimpse [glɪmps] **1** n: **catch a ~ of** ... entrevoir **2** v/t entrevoir

glint [glɪnt] **1** n lueur f **2** v/i of light, eyes luire

glisten ['glɪsn] of light luire; of water miroiter; of silk chatoyer

glitter ['glɪtər] of light, jewels briller, scintiller

gloat [gloʊt] jubiler

♦ **gloat over** se réjouir de

global ['gloʊbl] (worldwide) mondial; (without exceptions) global; **globalization** mondialisation f; **global warming** réchauffement m

de la planète; **globe** globe m

gloom [glu:m] (darkness) obscurité f; (mood) tristesse f; **gloomy** sombre

glorious ['glɔ:rɪəs] weather magnifique; victory glorieux; **glory** gloire f

gloss [glɑ:s] (shine) brillant m; (general explanation) glose f; **glossary** glossaire f; **glossy 1** adj paper glacé **2** n magazine magazine m de luxe

glove [glʌv] gant m; **glove compartment** boîte f à gants

glow [gloʊ] **1** n of light lueur f; of fire rougeoiement m; in cheeks couleurs fpl **2** v/i of light luire; of fire rougeoyer; of cheeks être rouge; **glowing** description élogieux

glucose ['glu:koʊs] glucose m

glue [glu:] **1** n colle f **2** v/t coller

glum [glʌm] morose

glut [glʌt] surplus m

glutton ['glʌtn] glouton(ne) m(f)

gnaw [nɔ:] bone ronger

go [goʊ] aller; (leave) partir; (work, function) marcher, fonctionner; (come out: of stain etc) s'en aller; (cease: of pain etc) disparaître; (match: of colors etc) aller ensemble; **hamburger to ~** hamburger à emporter

♦ **go away** of person s'en aller, partir; of rain cesser;

pain, clouds partir
◆ **go back** (*return*) retourner; (*date back*) remonter (**to** à)
◆ **go by** *of car, time* passer
◆ **go down** descendre; *of sun* se coucher
◆ **go in** *to room, house* entrer; *of sun* se cacher; (*fit: of part etc*) s'insérer
◆ **go off** (*leave*) partir; *of bomb* exploser; *of gun* partir; *of alarm* se déclencher
◆ **go on** (*continue*) continuer; (*happen*) se passer
◆ **go out** *of person* sortir; *of light, fire* s'éteindre
◆ **go over** (*check*) revoir
◆ **go through** *hard times* traverser; *illness* subir; (*check*) revoir; (*read through*) lire en entier
◆ **go under** (*sink*) couler; *of company* faire faillite
◆ **go up** (*climb*) monter; *of prices* augmenter
◆ **go without 1** *v/t food etc* se passer de **2** *v/i* s'en passer
'**go-ahead 1** *n* feu vert *m* **2** *adj* (*enterprising, dynamic*) entreprenant, dynamique
goal [gəʊl] *in sport*, (*objective*) but *m*; **goalkeeper** gardien *m* de but; **goal kick** remise *f* en jeu; **goalpost** poteau *m* de but
goat [gəʊt] chèvre *m*
gobble ['gɑ:bl] dévorer
gobbledygook ['gɑ:bldɪgu:k] F charabia *m* F
'**go-between** intermédiaire

m/f
god [gɑ:d] dieu *m*; **thank God!** Dieu merci!
'**godchild** filleul(e) *m(f)*; **godfather** *also in mafia* parrain *m*; **godmother** marraine *m*
gofer ['gəʊfər] F coursier(-ière) *m(f)*
goggles ['gɑ:gl] lunettes *fpl*
goings-on [gəʊɪŋz'ɑ:n] activités *fpl*
gold [gəʊld] **1** *n* or *m* **2** *adj* en or; *ingot* d'or; **golden** *sky* doré; *hair also* d'or; **golden wedding** noces *fpl* d'or; **gold medal** médaille *f* d'or; **gold mine** *fig* mine *f* d'or
golf [gɑ:lf] golf *m*; **golf ball** balle *f* de golf; **golf club** *organization, stick* club *m* de golf; **golf course** terrain *m* de golf; **golfer** golfeur(-euse) *m(f)*
good [gʊd] bon; *weather*, *child* sage; **goodbye** au revoir; **good-for-nothing** *n* bon(ne) *m(f)* à rien; **Good Friday** Vendredi *m* saint; **good-humored**, *Br* **good-humoured** jovial; **good-looking** beau; **good-natured** bon, au bon naturel; **goodness** *moral* bonté *f*; *of fruit etc* bonnes choses *fpl*; **goods** COM marchandises *fpl*; **goodwill** bonne volonté *f*
goof [gu:f] F gaffer F
goose [gu:s] oie *f*; **goose bumps** chair *f* de poule

gorgeous ['gɔːrdʒəs] magnifique, superbe

gospel ['gɑːspl] évangile m

gossip ['gɑːsɪp] **1** n potins mpl; malicious commérages mpl; person commère f **2** v/i bavarder; maliciously faire des commérages; **gossip column** échos mpl

gourmet ['gʊrmeɪ] gourmet m

govern ['gʌvərn] gouverner; **government** gouvernement m; **governor** gouverneur m

gown [gaʊn] robe f; wedding dress robe f de mariée; of academic, judge toge f; of surgeon blouse f

grab [græb] saisir; food avaler

grace [greɪs] of dancer etc grâce f; before meals bénédicité m; **graceful** gracieux; **gracious** person bienveillant; style élégant

grade [greɪd] **1** n (quality) qualité f; EDU classe f; (mark) note f **2** v/t classer; school work noter; **grade crossing** passage m à niveau; **grade school** école f primaire

gradient ['greɪdɪənt] pente f

gradual ['grædʒʊəl] graduel; **gradually** peu à peu, progressivement

graduate 1 ['grædʒʊət] n diplômé(e) m(f) **2** ['grædʒʊeɪt] v/i obtenir son diplôme (from de); **graduation** obtention f du diplôme

graffiti [grə'fiːtiː] graffitis mpl; single graffiti m

graft [græft] **1** n BOT, MED greffe f; F (corruption) corruption f **2** v/t BOT, MED greffer

grain [greɪn] bere m; of rice etc, in wood grain m

gram [græm] gramme m

grammar ['græmər] grammaire f; **grammatical** grammatical

grand [grænd] **1** adj grandiose; F (very good) génial **2** n F ($1000) mille dollars mpl; **grandchild** petit-fils m, petite-fille f; **granddaughter** petite-fille f; **grandeur** grandeur f; **grandfather** grand-père m; **grand jury** grand jury m; **grandmother** grand-mère f; **grandparents** grands-parents mpl; **grand piano** piano m à queue; **grandson** petit-fils m

granite ['grænɪt] granit m

grant [grænt] **1** n money subvention f **2** v/t wish, visa accorder

granule ['grænuːl] grain m

grape [greɪp] grain m de) raisin m; **some ~s** du raisin; **grapefruit juice** jus m de pamplemousse

graph [græf] graphique m, courbe f; **graphic 1** adj (vivid) très réaliste **2** n COMPUT graphique m

◆ **grapple with** ['græpl] attacker en venir aux prises avec; problem etc s'attaquer à

grasp [græsp] **1** *n physical* prise *f*; *mental* compréhension *f* **2** *v/t physically* saisir; (*understand*) comprendre

grass [græs] herbe *f*; **grasshopper** sauterelle *f*; **grass roots** *people* base *f*; **grassy** ['græsɪ] herbeux, herbu

grate¹ [greɪt] *n* metal grille *f*

grate² [greɪt] **1** *v/t in cooking* râper **2** *v/i*: ~ **on the ear** faire mal aux oreilles

grateful ['greɪtfʊl] reconnaissant; **gratefully** avec reconnaissance

gratify ['grætɪfaɪ] satisfaire

grating ['greɪtɪŋ] **1** *n* grille *f* **2** *adj sound, voice* grinçant

gratitude ['grætɪtuːd] gratitude *f*, reconnaissance *f*

grave¹ [greɪv] *n* tombe *f*

grave² [greɪv] *adj* grave

gravel ['grævl] gravier *m*

gravestone pierre *f* tombale; **graveyard** cimetière *m*

gravity ['grævətɪ] PHYS, *of situation* gravité *f*

gray [greɪ] gris; **gray-haired** aux cheveux gris

graze¹ [greɪz] *v/i of cow etc* paître

graze² [greɪz] **1** *v/t arm etc* écorcher **2** *n* écorchure *f*

grease [griːs] *for cooking* graisse *f*; *for car* lubrifiant *m*; **greasy** *adj*; (*covered in grease*) graisseux

great [greɪt] grand; *mistake, sum* gros; F (*very good*) su-

per F; **Great Britain** Grande-Bretagne *f*; **greatly** beaucoup; **not ~ different** pas très différent; **greatness** grandeur *f*

Greece [griːs] Grèce *f*

greed [griːd] *for money* avidité *f*; *for food also* gourmandise *f*; **greedily** avec avidité; **greedy** *for money* avide; *for food also* gourmand

Greek [griːk] **1** *n* Grec(que) *m(f)*; *language* grec *m* **2** *adj* grec

green [griːn] vert; **green beans** haricots *mpl* verts; **green belt** ceinture *f* verte; **green card** (*work permit*) permis *m* de travail; **greenhouse effect** effet *m* de serre; **greens** légumes *mpl* verts

greet [griːt] saluer; (*welcome*) accueillir; **greeting** salut *m*

grenade [grɪ'neɪd] grenade *f*

grey [greɪ] *Br* → **gray**

grid [grɪd] grille *f*; **gridiron** SP terrain *m* de football; **gridlock** *in traffic* embouteillage *m*

grief [griːf] chagrin *m*, douleur *f*; **grief-stricken** affligé; **grievance** grief *m*; **grieve** être affligé; ~ **for s.o.** pleurer qn

grill [grɪl] **1** *n on window* grille *f* **2** *v/t* (*interrogate*) mettre sur la sellette

grille [grɪl] grille *f*

grim [grɪm] sinistre, sombre

grimace ['grɪməs] grimace f

grime [graɪm] crasse f; **grimy** crasseux

grin [grɪn] **1** n (large) sourire m **2** v/i sourire

grind [graɪnd] coffee moudre; meat hacher

grip [grɪp] saisir, serrer; **gripping** prenant, captivant

gristle ['grɪsl] cartilage m

grit [grɪt] **1** n for roads gravillon m **2** v/t: ~ **one's teeth** grincer des dents; **gritty** F réaliste

groan [grəʊn] **1** n gémissement m **2** v/i gémir

groceries ['grəʊsərɪz] provisions fpl; **grocery store** épicerie f l'épicerie

groggy ['grɑːgɪ] F groggy F

groin [grɔɪn] ANAT aine f

groom [gruːm] **1** n for bride marié m; for horse palefrenier(-ère) m(f) **2** v/t horse panser; (train, prepare) préparer

groove [gruːv] rainure f; on record sillon m

grope [grəʊp] **1** v/i in the dark tâtonner **2** v/t sexually peloter F

gross [grəʊs] (coarse, vulgar) grossier; exaggeration gros; FIN brut

ground [graʊnd] **1** n sol m, terre f; for football etc, fig terrain; (reason) motif m; ELEC terre f **2** v/t ELEC mettre une prise de terre à; **grounding** in subject bases fpl;

groundless sans fondement; **ground meat** viande f hachée; **groundwork** travail m préparatoire

group [gruːp] **1** n groupe m **2** v/t grouper

groupie ['gruːpɪ] F groupie f F

grouse [graʊs] **1** n F rouspéter F **2** v/i F plainte f

grovel ['grɑːvl] fig ramper (**to** devant)

grow [grəʊ] **1** v/i grandir; of plants, hair pousser; of number augmenter; of business se développer; (become) devenir **2** v/t flowers faire pousser

◆ **grow up** of person devenir adulte; of city se développer

growl [graʊl] **1** n grognement m **2** v/i grogner

'**grown-up 1** n adulte m/f **2** adj adulte

growth [grəʊθ] of person, company croissance f; (increase) augmentation f; MED tumeur f

grudge [grʌdʒ] rancune f; **grudging** accordé à contre-cœur; person plein de ressentiment; **grudgingly** à contre-cœur

grueling, Br **gruelling** ['gruːəlɪŋ] épuisant

gruff [grʌf] bourru, revêche

grumble ['grʌmbl] ronchonner; **grumbler** grognon(ne) m(f)

grunt [grʌnt] **1** n grognement m **2** v/i grogner

guarantee [gærən'tiː] **1** n garantie f **2** v/t garantir; **guarantor** garant(e) m(f)

guard [gɑːrd] **1** n gardien(ne) m(f); MIL garde f **2** v/t garder; **guard dog** chien m de garde; **guarded** reply prudent; **guardian** LAW tuteur(-trice) m(f)

guerrilla [gə'rɪlə] guérillero m; **guerrilla warfare** guérilla f

guess [ges] **1** n conjecture f **2** v/t answer deviner **2** v/i deviner; I ~ so je crois; **guesswork** conjecture(s) f(pl)

guest [gest] invité(e) m(f); in hotel hôte m/f; **guestroom** chambre f d'amis

guidance ['gaɪdəns] conseils mpl; **guide 1** n person guide m/f; book guide m **2** v/t guider; **guidebook** guide m; **guided missile** missile m téléguidé; **guided tour** visite f guidée; **guidelines** directives fpl

guilt [gɪlt] culpabilité f; **guilty** also LAW coupable

guinea pig ['gɪnɪpɪg] also fig cobaye m

guitar [gɪ'tɑːr] guitare f; **guitarist** guitariste m/f

gulf [gʌlf] golfe m; fig gouffre m

gull [gʌl] mouette f; bigger goéland m

gullet ['gʌlɪt] ANAT gosier m

gullible ['gʌlɪbl] crédule

gulp [gʌlp] **1** n of drink gorgée

f **2** v/i in surprise dire en s'étranglant

◆ **gulp down** drink avaler à grosses gorgées; food avaler à grosses bouchées

gum¹ [gʌm] in mouth gencive f

gum² [gʌm] (glue) colle f; (chewing gum) chewing-gum m

gun [gʌn] arme f à feu; pistol pistolet m; revolver revolver m; rifle fusil m; cannon canon m

◆ **gun down** abattre

gunfire coups mpl de feu; **gunman** homme m armé; **gunshot** coup m de feu; **gunshot wound** blessure f par balle

gurgle ['gɜːrgl] of baby gazouiller; of drain gargouiller

guru ['guːruː] fig gourou m

gush [gʌʃ] of liquid jaillir

gust [gʌst] rafale f, coup m de vent

gusto ['gʌstəu]: **with ~** avec enthousiasme

gusty ['gʌstɪ] weather très venteux

gut [gʌt] **1** n intestin m; F (stomach) bide m **2** v/t (destroy) ravager; **guts** F (courage) cran m F; **gutsy** F (brave) qui a du cran F

gutter ['gʌtər] on sidewalk caniveau m; on roof gouttière f

guy [gaɪ] F type m F

guzzle ['gʌzl] food engloutir; drink avaler

gym [dʒɪm] *sports club* club *m* de gym; *in school* gymnase *m*; *activity* gym(nastique) *f*; **gymnast** gymnaste *m/f*; **gymnastics** gymnastique *f*

gynecology, *Br* **gynaecology** [gaɪnɪˈkɒlədʒɪ] gynécologie

gypsy [ˈdʒɪpsɪ] gitan(e) *m(f)*

H

habit [ˈhæbɪt] habitude *f*

habitable [ˈhæbɪtəbl] habitable; **habitat** habitat *m*

habitual [həˈbɪtjʊəl] habituel; *smoker, drinker* invétéré

hacker [ˈhækər] COMPUT pirate *m* informatique

hackneyed [ˈhæknɪd] rebattu

haemorrhage *Br →* **hemorrhage**

haggard [ˈhægərd] hagard, égaré

haggle [ˈhægl] chipoter

hail [heɪl] grêle *f*

hair [her] cheveux *mpl*; *single* cheveu *m*; *on body* poils *mpl*; *single* poil *m*; **hairbrush** brosse *f* à cheveux; **haircut** coupe *f* de cheveux; **have a ~** se faire couper les cheveux; **'hairdo** coiffure *f*; **hairdresser** coiffeur(-euse) *m(f)*; **hairdryer** sèche-cheveux *m*; **hairpin** épingle *f* à cheveux; **hairpin curve** virage *m* en épingle à cheveux; **hair-raising** horrifique; **hair remover** crème *f* épilatoire; **hairsplitting** ergotage *m*; **hairstyle** coiffure *f*; **hairstylist** coiffeur(-euse) *m(f)*; **hairy** *arm*,

animal poilu; F *(frightening)* effrayant

half [hæf] **1** *n* moitié *f*; **~ past ten** dix heures et demie; **~ an hour** une demi-heure **2** *adj* demi; **at ~ price** à moitié prix **3** *adv* à moitié; **half-hearted** tiède; **half time** SP mi-temps *f*; halfway **1** *adj*: **reach the ~ point** être à la moitié **2** *adv in space, distance* à mi-chemin

hall [hɔːl] *(large room)* salle *f*; *(hallway in house)* vestibule *m*

Hallowe'en [hæloʊˈwiːn] halloween *f*

halo [ˈheɪloʊ] auréole *f*

halt [hɔːlt] **1** *v/i* faire halte, s'arrêter **2** *v/t* arrêter

halve [hæv] couper en deux; *input, costs* réduire de moitié

ham [hæm] jambon *m*; **hamburger** hamburger *m*

hammer [ˈhæmər] **1** *n* marteau *m* **2** *v/i* marteler; **~ at the door** frapper à la porte à coups redoublés

hammock [ˈhæmək] hamac *m*

hamper[1] [ˈhæmpər] *n for food* pannier *m*

hamper[2] [ˈhæmpər] *v/t (ob-*

struct) entraver, gêner

hand [hænd] **1** *n* main *f*; *of clock* aiguille *f*; *(worker)* ouvrier(-ère) *m(f)*; **at ~, to ~ thing** sous la main; **at ~ person** à disposition; **on the one ~ ..., on the other ~** d'une part ..., d'autre part; **on your right ~** sur votre droite; **give s.o. a ~** donner un coup de main à qn

◆ **hand down** transmettre

◆ **hand out** distribuer

◆ **hand over** donner; *to authorities* livrer

'**handbag** *Br* sac *m* à main; **hand baggage** bagages *mpl* à main; **handcuff** menotter; **handcuffs** menottes *fpl*

handicap ['hændɪkæp] handicap *m*; **handicapped** handicapé; **handiwork** object ouvrage *m*

handkerchief ['hæŋkərtʃɪf] mouchoir *m*

handle ['hændl] **1** *n of door, suitcase* poignée *f*; *of knife, pan* manche *m* **2** *v/t goods* manier, manipuler; *case, deal* s'occuper de; **handlebars** guidon *m*

'**hand luggage** bagages *m* à main; **handmade** fait (à la) main; **hands-free** mains libres; **handshake** poignée *f* de main

handsome ['hænsəm] beau

'**handwriting** écriture *f*; **handwritten** écrit à la main;

handy *device* pratique

hang ['hæŋ] **1** *v/t person* pendre **2** *v/t of dress, hair* tomber

◆ **hang on** *(wait)* attendre

◆ **hang up** TELEC raccrocher

hangar ['hæŋər] hangar *m*

hanger ['hæŋər] *for clothes* cintre *m*

'**hang glider** *person* libériste *m/f*; *device* deltaplane *m*; **hang gliding** deltaplane *m*; **hangover** gueule *f* de bois

hankie, hanky ['hæŋkɪ] F mouchoir *m*

haphazard [hæp'hæzərd] au hasard

happen ['hæpn] se passer, arriver

happily ['hæpɪlɪ] gaiement; *spend* volontiers; *(luckily)* heureusement; **happiness** bonheur *m*; **happy** heureux; **happy-go-lucky** insouciant

harass [hə'ræs] harceler; **harassed** surmené; **harassment** harcèlement *m*

harbor, *Br* **harbour** ['hɑːrbər] **1** *n* port *m* **2** *v/t criminal* héberger; *grudge* entretenir

hard [hɑːrd] **1** *adj* dur; *facts* brut; *evidence* concret **2** *adv work* dur; *rain, pull, push* fort; **try ~** faire tout son possible; **hardback** livre *m* cartonné; **hard-boiled** *egg* dur; **hard copy** copie *f* sur papier; **hard core** *pornography* (pornographie *f*) hard *m*; **hard currency** monnaie *f* forte; **hard disk** disque *m*

dur; **harden 1** v/t durcir **2** v/i
of glue, attitude se durcir;
hard hat casque m; (construction worker) ouvrier m
du bâtiment; **hardheaded**
réaliste; **hardhearted** au
cœur dur; **hard line** ligne f
dure; **hardliner** due(e) m(f)
hardly ['hɑːrdlɪ] à peine; see
s.o. etc presque pas
hardness ['hɑːrdnɪs] dureté f;
(difficulty) difficulté f; **hard-
ship** privation f; **hardware**
COMPUT hardware m, maté-
riel m; **hardware store** quincaillerie f; **hard-working** travailleur; **hardy** robuste
harm [hɑːrm] **1** n mal m **2** v/t
faire du mal à; non-physical-
ly nuire à; **harmful substance**
nocif; influence nuisible;
harmless inoffensif
harmonious [hɑːrˈmoʊnɪəs]
harmonieux; **harmonize**
s'harmoniser; **harmony** harmonie f
harsh [hɑːrʃ] words dur; color
criard; light cru; **harshly** durement
harvest ['hɑːrvɪst] moisson f
hash browns [hæʃ] pommes
de terre fpl sautées; **hash
mark** caractère m #, dièse f
haste [heɪst] hâte f; **hastily** à
la hâte; **hasty** hâtif, précipité
hat [hæt] chapeau m
hatch [hætʃ] for serving guichet m; on ship écoutille f
◆ **hatch out** éclore
hatchet ['hætʃɪt] hachette f;

bury the ~ enterrer la hache
de guerre
hate [heɪt] **1** n haine f **2** v/t détester, haïr; **hatred** haine f
haul [hɔːl] **1** n of fish coup m
de filet **2** v/t (pull) tirer, traîner; **haulage** transports mpl
(routiers)
haunch [hɔːntʃ] of person
hanche f; of animal arrière-
-train m
haunt [hɔːnt] hanter; **this
place is** ~ed ce lieu est hanté
have [hæv] **1** v/t (own) avoir;
breakfast, lunch prendre; ~
(got) to devoir; **you don't** ~
to do it tu n'es pas obligé
de le faire; **do I** ~ **to pay?**
est-ce qu'il faut payer?; **I'll
** ~ **it sent to you** je vous le ferai envoyer; **I had my hair
cut** je me suis fait couper
les cheveux **2** v/aux (past
tense): ~ **you seen her?**
l'as-tu vue?; **they** ~ **arrived**
ils sont arrivés
◆ **have on** (wear) porter
haven ['heɪvn] fig havre m
hawk [hɔːk] also fig faucon m
hay [heɪ] foin m; **hay fever**
rhume m des foins
hazard ['hæzərd] danger m;
hazard lights MOT feux mpl
de détresse; **hazardous** dangereux
haze [heɪz] brume f; **hazy**
view brumeux; image flou;
memories vague
he [hiː] il; **there** ~ **is** le voilà
head [hed] **1** n tête f; (boss,

leader) chef *m/f*; *Br : of school* directeur(-trice) *m(f)*; *on beer* mousse *f* **2** *v/t* (*lead*) être à la tête de; *ball* jouer de la tête

◆ **head for** se diriger vers

'**headache** mal *m* de tête; **headband** bandeau *m*; **header** *in soccer* (coup *m* de) tête *f*; *in document* en-tête *m*; **headhunter** COM chasseur *m* de têtes; **heading** *in list* titre *m*; **headlamp** phare *m*; **headline** *in newspaper* (gros) titre *m*; **head office** *of company* bureau *m* central; **head-on 1** *adv crash* de front **2** *adj* frontal; **headphones** écouteurs *mpl*; **headquarters** quartier *m* général; **headrest** appui-tête *m*; **headroom** *under bridge* hauteur *f* limite; *in car* hauteur *f* au plafond; **headscarf** foulard *m*; **headstrong** entêté; **head waiter** maître *m* d'hôtel; **heady** *wine etc* capiteux

heal [hiːl] guérir

health [helθ] santé *f*; **health food store** magasin *m* d'aliments diététiques; **health insurance** assurance *f* maladie; **healthy** *person* en bonne santé; *food, lifestyle, economy* sain

heap [hiːp] tas *m*

hear [hɪr] entendre

◆ **hear from** (*have news from*) avoir des nouvelles de

hearing ['hɪrɪŋ] ouïe *f*; LAW audience *f*; **hearing aid** appareil *m* acoustique, audiophone *m*

hearse [hɜːrs] corbillard *m*

heart [hɑːrt] *also fig* cœur *m*; **know sth by ~** connaître qch par cœur; **heart attack** crise *f* cardiaque; **heartbreaking** navrant; **heartbroken: be ~** avoir le cœur brisé; **heartburn** brûlures *fpl* d'estomac

hearth [hɑːrθ] foyer *m*, âtre *f*

heartless ['hɑːrtlɪs] insensible, cruel; **hearty** *appetite* gros; *meal* copieux; *person* jovial

heat [hiːt] chaleur *f*

◆ **heat up** réchauffer

heated ['hiːtɪd] *pool* chauffé; *discussion* passionné; **heater** radiateur *m*; *in car* chauffage *m*; **heating** chauffage *m*; **heatproof**, **heat-resistant** résistant à la chaleur; **heatwave** vague *f* de chaleur

heave [hiːv] (*lift*) soulever

heaven ['hevn] ciel *m*; **heavenly** *F* divin

heavy ['hevɪ] *also food, loss* lourd; *cold* grand; *rain, accent* fort; *traffic, smoker, bleeding* gros; **heavy-duty** très résistant; **heavyweight** SP poids lourd

hectic ['hektɪk] agité

hedge [hedʒ] haie *f*

heel [hiːl] talon *m*; **heel bar** talon-minute *m*

hefty ['heftɪ] gros; *person also*

costaud

height [haɪt] *of person* taille *f*; *of building* hauteur *f*; *of airplane* altitude *f*; **heighten** *tension* renforcer

heir [er] héritier *m*; **heiress** héritière *f*

helicopter ['helɪkɑːptər] hélicoptère *m*

hell [hel] enfer *m*; **what the ~ are you doing?** F mais enfin qu'est-ce que tu fais?; **go to ~!** F va te faire foutre! P

hello [həˈloʊ] bonjour; TELEC allô

helmet ['helmɪt] casque *m*

help [help] **1** *n* aide *f* **2** *v/t* aider; **~ o.s. to food** se servir; **I can't ~ it** je ne peux pas m'en empêcher; **helper** aide *m/f*, assistant(e) *m(f)*; **helpful** *advice* utile; *person* serviable; **helping** *of food* portion *f*; **helpless** (*unable to cope*) sans défense; (*powerless*) impuissant; **helplessness** impuissance *f*

hem [hem] *of dress etc* ourlet *m*

hemisphere ['hemɪsfɪr] hémisphère *m*

'hemline ourlet *m*

hemorrhage ['hemərɪdʒ] **1** *n* hémorragie *f* **2** *v/i* faire une hémorragie

hen [hen] poule *f*; **hen party** soirée *f* entre femmes

hepatitis [hepəˈtaɪtɪs] hépatite *f*

her [hɜːr] **1** *adj* son, sa; *pl* ses **2** *pron object* la; *before vowel* l'; *indirect object* lui, à elle; *with prep* elle; **I know ~** je la connais; **I gave ~ a dollar** je lui ai donné un dollar; **this is for ~** c'est pour elle; **who? – ~** qui? – elle

herb [ɜːrb] herbe *f*; **herb(al) tea** tisane *f*

herd [hɜːrd] troupeau *m*

here [hɪr] ici; **in ~, over ~** ici; **~'s to you!** *as toast* à votre santé!; **~ you are** *giving sth* voilà

hereditary [həˈredɪteri] héréditaire; **heredity** hérédité *f*; **heritage** héritage *m*

hero [ˈhɪroʊ] héros *m*; **heroic** héroïque; **heroically** héroïquement

heroin [ˈheroʊɪn] héroïne *f*

heroine [ˈheroʊɪn] héroïne *f*

heroism [ˈheroʊɪzm] héroïsme *f*

herpes [ˈhɜːrpiːz] herpès *m*

hers [hɜːrz] le sien, la sienne; *pl* les siens, les siennes; **it's ~** c'est à elle

herself [hɜːrˈself] elle-même; *reflexive* se; *after prep* elle; **she hurt ~** elle s'est blessée

hesitant [ˈhezɪtənt] hésitant; **hesitantly** avec hésitation; **hesitate** hésiter; **hesitation** hésitation *f*

heterosexual [hetəroʊˈsekʃuəl] hétérosexuel

hi [haɪ] salut

hibernate [ˈhaɪbərneɪt] hiberner

hiccup ['hɪkʌp] hoquet *m*; (*minor problem*) hic *m* F

hidden ['hɪdn] caché

hide¹ [haɪd] **1** *v/t* cacher **2** *v/i* se cacher

hide² [haɪd] *n of animal* peau *f*; *as product* cuir *m*

hide-and-'seek cache-cache *m*; **hideaway** cachette *f*

hideous ['hɪdɪəs] affreux, horrible

hiding ['haɪdɪŋ] (*beating*) rossée *f*; **hiding place** cachette *f*

hierarchy ['haɪrɑːrkɪ] hiérarchie *f*

high [haɪ] **1** *adj* haut; *salary, price, rent, temperature* élevé; *wind* fort; *speed* grand; *on drugs* défoncé F **2** *n* MOT quatrième *f*; cinquième *f*; *in statistics* pointe *f*; EDU collège *m*, lycée *m*; **highbrow** intellectuel; **highchair** chaise *f* haute; **high-class** de première class; **high-frequency** de haute fréquence; **high-grade** *ore* à haute teneur; ~ **gasoline** supercarburant *m*; **high-handed** arbitraire; **high-heeled** à hauts talons; **high jump** saut *m* en hauteur; **high-level** à haut niveau; **highlight 1** *n* (*main event*) point *m* marquant; *in hair* reflets *mpl*, mèches *fpl* **2** *v/t with pen* surligner; COMPUT mettre en relief; **highlighter** *pen* surligneur *m*; **highly** *desirable, likely* fort, très; **think ~ of s.o.** pen-

ser beaucoup de bien de qn; **high performance** *drill, battery* haute performance; **high-pitched** aigu; **high point** *of career* point *m* culminant; **high-powered** *engine* très puissant; *intellectual* très compétent; **high pressure** *weather* anticyclone *m*; **high-pressure** TECH à haute pression; *salesman* de choc; *job, lifestyle* dynamique; **high school** collège *m*, lycée *m*; **high-strung** nerveux, très sensible; **high tech 1** *n* technologie *f* de pointe, high-tech *m* **2** *adj* de pointe, high-tech; **highway** grande route *f*

hijack ['haɪdʒæk] **1** *v/t* détourner **2** *n* détournement *m*; **hijacker** *of plane* pirate *m* de l'air; *of bus* pirate *m* de la route

hike¹ [haɪk] **1** *n* randonnée *f* à pied **2** *v/i* marcher à pied

hike² [haɪk] *n in prices* hausse *f*

hiker ['haɪkər] randonneur (-euse) *m(f)*; **hiking** randonnée *f* (pédestre)

hilarious [hɪ'lerɪəs] hilarant, désopilant

hill [hɪl] colline *f*; (*slope*) côte *f*; **hilltop** sommet *m* de la colline; **hilly** montagneux; *road* vallonné

hilt [hɪlt] poignée *f*

him [hɪm] *object* le; *before vowel* l'; *indirect object, with prep* lui; **I know ~** je le connais; **I gave ~ a dollar** je lui ai donné un dollar; **this is for ~** c'est pour lui; **who? – him** qui? – lui; **himself** lui-même; *reflexive* se; *after prep* lui; **he hurt ~** il s'est blessé

hinder ['hɪndər] gêner, entraver; **~ s.o. from doing sth** empêcher qn de faire qch; **hindrance** obstacle m

hinge [hɪndʒ] charnière f

hint [hɪnt] (*clue*) indice m; (*piece of advice*) conseil m; (*suggestion*) allusion f; *of red, sadness etc* soupçon m

hip [hɪp] hanche f; **hip pocket** poche f revolver

hire ['haɪr] louer

his [hɪz] **1** *adj* son, sa; *pl* ses **2** *pron* le sien, la sienne; *pl* les siens, les siennes; **it's ~** c'est à lui

Hispanic [hɪ'spænɪk] **1** n Hispano-Américain(e) *m(f)* **2** *adj* hispano-américain

hiss [hɪs] siffler

historian [hɪ'stɔːrɪən] historien(ne) *m(f)*; **historic** historique; **historical** historique; **history** histoire f

hit [hɪt] **1** *v/t* frapper; (*collide with*) heurter; **he was ~ by a bullet** il a été touché par une balle **2** n (*blow*) coup m; MUS, (*success*) succès m; *on website* visiteur m

hitch [hɪtʃ] **1** n (*problem*) ani-croche f, accroc m **2** *v/t* atta-

cher; **hitchhike** faire du stop; **hitchhiker** auto-stoppeur (-euse) *m(f)*

'hitman tueur m à gages; **hit--or-miss** aléatoire

HIV [eɪtʃaɪ'viː] (= **human immunodeficiency virus**) V.I.H. m (= Virus de l'Immunodéficience Humaine); **people with ~** les séropositifs

hive [haɪv] *for bees* ruche f

HIV-positive séropositif

hoard [hɔːrd] **1** n réserves *fpl* **2** *v/t money* amasser; *in times of shortage* faire des réserves de

hoarse [hɔːrs] rauque

hoax [hoʊks] canular m

hobble ['hɑːbl] boitiller

hobby ['hɑːbɪ] hobby m

hockey ['hɑːkɪ] (*ice hockey*) hockey m (sur glace)

hog [hɑːg] (*pig*) cochon m

hoist [hɔɪst] **1** n palan m **2** *v/t* hisser

hold [hoʊld] **1** *v/t in hand* tenir; (*support, keep in place*) soutenir; *passport, license, prisoner* détenir; (*contain*) contenir; *job, post* occuper; **~ the line** TELEC ne quittez pas! **2** n *in ship* cale f; *in plane* soute f; **take ~ of sth** saisir qch

◆ **hold back** *crowds* contenir; *facts* retenir

◆ **hold out 1** *v/t* hand tendre; *prospect* offrir **2** *v/i* *of supplies* durer; (*survive*) tenir (bon)

◆ **hold up** hand lever; *bank etc* attaquer; (*make late*) retenir

holder ['hoʊldər] (*container*) boîtier *m*; *of passport, ticket, record* détenteur(-trice) *m(f)*; **holding company** holding *m*; **holdup** (*robbery*) hold-up *m*; (*delay*) retard *m*

hole [hoʊl] trou *m*

holiday ['hɑːlədeɪ] jour *m* de congé; *Br*: *period* vacances *fpl*

hollow ['hɑːloʊ] creux; *promise* faux

holocaust ['hɑːləkɔːst] holocauste *m*

hologram ['hɑːləgræm] hologramme *m*

holster ['hoʊlstər] holster *m*

holy ['hoʊlɪ] saint; **Holy Spirit** Saint-Esprit *m*

home [hoʊm] **1** *n* maison *f*; (*native country, town*) patrie *f*; *for old people* maison *f* de retraite; **at ~** chez moi/lui *etc*; (*in own country*) dans mon/son *etc* pays; SP à domicile; **make o.s. at ~** faire comme chez soi **2** *adv* à la maison, chez soi; (*in own country*) dans son pays; (*in own town*) dans sa ville; **go ~** rentrer; **home address** adresse *f* personnelle; **home banking** services *mpl* télématiques (ban-

caires); **homecoming** retour *m* (à la maison); **home computer** ordinateur *m* familial; **home game** match *m* à domicile; **homeless 1** *adj* sans abri **2** *npl*: **the ~** les sans-abri *mpl*, les S.D.F. *mpl* (sans domicile fixe); **homeloving** casanier; **homely** (*homelike*) simple, comme à la maison; (*not good-looking*) sans beauté; **homemade** fait (à la) maison; **home page** COMPUT page *f* d'accueil; **homesick**: **be ~** avoir le mal du pays; **home town** ville *f* natale; **homeward** *to own house* vers la maison; *to own country* vers son pays; **homework** EDU devoirs *mpl*

homicide ['hɑːmɪsaɪd] homicide *m*; *department* homicides *mpl*

homophobia [hoʊmə'foʊbɪə] homophobie *f*

homosexual [hoʊmə'sekʃʊəl] **1** *adj* homosexuel **2** *n* homosexuel(le) *m(f)*

honest ['ɑːnɪst] honnête; **honestly** honnêtement; **~!** vraiment!; **honesty** honnêteté *f*

honey ['hʌnɪ] miel *m*; F (*darling*) chéri(e) *m(f)*; **honeymoon** lune *f* de miel

honk [hɑːŋk] horn klaxonner

honor ['ɑːnər] **1** *n* honneur *f* **2** *v/t* honorer; **honorable** honorable; **honour** *Br* → **honor**

hood [hʊd] *over head* capuche *f*; *over cooker* hotte *f*; *over car* capot *m*; F (*gangster*) truand *m*

hook [hʊk] *to hang clothes on* patère *f*; *for fishing* hameçon *m*; **off the ~** TELEC décroché; **hooked** accro F; **be ~ on sth** être accro de qch; **hooker** F putain *f* P; *in rugby* talonneur *m*

hoot [huːt] **1** *v/t horn* donner un coup de **2** *v/i of car* klaxonner; *of owl* huer

hop [hɑːp] sauter, sautiller

hope [hoʊp] **1** *n* espoir *m* **2** *v/i* espérer; **I ~ so** je l'espère, j'espère que oui **2** *v/t*: **~ that** espérer que; **hopeful** plein d'espoir; (*promising*) prometteur; **hopefully** *say, wait* avec espoir; (*I/we hope*) avec un peu de chance; **hopeless** *position* sans espoir, désespéré; (*useless: person*) nul

horizon [həˈraɪzn] horizon *m*; **horizontal** horizontal

hormone [ˈhɔːrmoʊn] hormone *f*

horn [hɔːrn] *of animal* corne *f*; MOT klaxon *m*

hornet [ˈhɔːrnɪt] frelon *m*

horny [ˈhɔːrnɪ] F *sexually* excité

horrible [ˈhɑːrɪbl] horrible, affreux; **horrify** horrifier; **horrifying** horrifiant; **horror** horreur *f*

horse [hɔːrs] cheval *m*; **horse race** course *f* de chevaux;

horseshoe fer *m* à cheval

horticulture horticulture *f*

hose [hoʊz] tuyau *m*

hospitable [ˈhɑːspɪtəbl] hospitalier

hospital [ˈhɑːspɪtl] hôpital *m*; **hospitality** hospitalité *f*

host [hoʊst] *at party* hôte *m/f*; *of TV program* présentateur(-trice) *m(f)*

hostage [ˈhɑːstɪdʒ] otage *m*; **hostage taker** preneur(-euse) *m(f)* d'otages

hostel [ˈhɑːstl] *for students* foyer *m*; (*youth* ~) auberge *f* de jeunesse

hostess [ˈhoʊstɪs] hôtesse *f*

hostile [ˈhɑːstl] hostile; **hostility** hostilité *f*; **hostilities** hostilités

hot [hɑːt] chaud; (*spicy*) épicé, fort; **I'm ~** j'ai chaud; **it's ~** *weather* il fait chaud; **hot dog** hot-dog *m*

hotel [hoʊˈtel] hôtel *m*

hour [ˈaʊr] heure *f*

house [haʊs] maison *f*; **at your ~** chez vous; **housebreaking** cambriolage *m*; **household** ménage *m*; **household name** nom *m* connu de tous; **housekeeper** femme *f* de ménage; **House of Representatives** Chambre *f* des Représentants; **housewarming** (*party*) pendaison *f* de crémaillère; **housewife** femme *f* au foyer; **housework** travaux *mpl* domestiques; **housing**

logement *m*; TECH boîtier *m*
hovel ['hɒvl] taudis *m*
hover ['hɒːvər] planer
how [haʊ] comment; **~ are you?** comment allez-vous?; **~ about a drink?** et si on allait prendre un pot?; **~ much?** combien?; **~ much is it?** *cost* combien ça coûte?; **~ many?** combien?; **~ often?** tous les combien?; **~ sad!** comme c'est triste!; however cependant; **~ big they are** qu'ils soient grands ou non
howl [haʊl] hurler
hub [hʌb] *of wheel* moyeu *m*; **hubcap** enjoliveur *m*
◆ **huddle together** ['hʌdl] se blottir les uns contre les autres
hug [hʌg] serrer dans ses bras
huge [hjuːdʒ] énorme
hull [hʌl] coque *f*
hum [hʌm] fredonner
human ['hjuːmən] **1** *n* être humain *m*; **2** *adj* humain; **human being** être *m* humain
humane [hjuːˈmeɪn] humain, plein d'humanité
humanitarian [hjuːmænɪˈterɪən] humanitaire
humanity [hjuːˈmænətɪ] humanité *f*; **human race** race *f* humaine; **human resources** ressources *fpl* humaines
humble ['hʌmbl] modeste
humdrum ['hʌmdrʌm] monotone, banal

humid ['hjuːmɪd] humide; **humidifier** humidificateur *m*; **humidity** humidité *f*
humiliate [hjuːˈmɪlɪeɪt] humilier; **humiliating** humiliant; **humiliation** humiliation *f*; **humility** humilité *f*
humor ['hjuːmər] humour *m*; (*mood*) humeur *f*; **sense of ~** sens *m* de l'humour; **humorous** drôle; **humour** *Br* → **humor**
hunch [hʌntʃ] (*idea*) intuition *f*, pressentiment *m*
hundred ['hʌndrəd] cent *m*; **hundredth** centième
hunger ['hʌŋgər] faim *f*
hung-over: **be ~** avoir la gueule de bois F
hungry ['hʌŋgrɪ] affamé; **I'm ~** j'ai faim
hunk [hʌŋk] gros morceau *m*; F *man* beau mec F
hunt [hʌnt] **1** *n chasse f* (**for** à); *for new leader, missing child etc* recherche *f* (**for** de) **2** *v/t* chasser; **hunter** chasseur (-euse) *m(f)*; **hunting** chasse *f*
hurdle ['hɜːrdl] SP haie *f*; *fig* obstacle *m*
hurl [hɜːrl] lancer, jeter
hurray [hʊˈreɪ] hourra
hurricane ['hʌrɪkən] ouragan *m*
hurried ['hʌrɪd] précipité; **hurry 1** *n* hâte *f*; **be in a ~** être pressé **2** *v/i* se dépêcher
◆ **hurry up 1** *v/i* se dépêcher; **hurry up!** dépêchez-vous! **2**

v/t presser

hurt [hɜːrt] **1** *v/i* faire mal **2** *v/t* faire mal à; *emotionally* blesser

husband ['hʌzbənd] mari *m*

hush [hʌʃ] silence *m*

◆ **hush up** *scandal etc* étouffer

husky ['hʌskɪ] *voice* rauque

hut [hʌt] cabane *f*, hutte *f*

hybrid ['haɪbrɪd] hybride *m*

hydrant ['haɪdrənt] prise *f* d'eau; *(fire ~)* bouche *f* d'incendie

hydraulic [haɪ'drɒlɪk] hydraulique

hydroelectric [haɪdroʊɪ'lektrɪk] hydroélectrique

hydrogen ['haɪdrədʒən] hydrogène *m*

hygiene ['haɪdʒiːn] hygiène *f*; **hygienic** hygiénique

hymn [hɪm] hymne *m*

hype [haɪp] battage *m* publicitaire

hyperactive [haɪpər'æktɪv] hyperactif; **hypersensitive** hypersensible; **hypertext** COMPUT hypertexte *m*

hypnosis [hɪp'noʊsɪs] hypnose *f*; **hypnotize** hypnotiser

hypocrisy [hɪ'pɑːkrəsɪ] hypocrisie *f*; **hypocrite** hypocrite *m/f*; **hypocritical** hypocrite

hypothesis [haɪ'pɑːθəsɪs] hypothèse *f*; **hypothetical** hypothétique

hysterectomy [hɪstə'rektəmɪ] hystérectomie *f*

hysteria [hɪ'stɪrɪə] hystérie *f*; **hysterical** hystérique; F *(very funny)* à mourir de rire F; **hysterics** crise *f* de nerfs; *laughter* fou rire *m*

I

I [aɪ] je; *before vowel* j'; **here ~ am** me voici

ice [aɪs] glace *f*; *on road* verglas *m*; **icebox** glacière *f*; **ice cream** glace *f*; **ice cube** glaçon *m*; **iced** *drink* glacé; **ice hockey** hockey *m* sur glace; **ice rink** patinoire *f*; **ice skate** patin *m* (à glace); **ice skating** patinage *m* (sur glace)

icon ['aɪkɑːn] symbole *m*; COMPUT icône *f*

icy ['aɪsɪ] gelé; *welcome* glacial

ID [aɪ'diː] (= *identity*) identité *f*

idea [aɪ'diːə] idée *f*; **ideal** idéal; **idealistic** idéaliste

identical [aɪ'dentɪkl] identique; **identification** identification *f*; *(papers etc)* papiers *mpl* d'identité; **identify** identifier; **identity** identité *f*; **~ card** carte *f* d'identité

ideological [aɪdɪə'lɑːdʒɪkl] idéologique; **ideology** idéologie *f*

idiomatic [ɪdɪə'mætɪk] (*natural*) idiomatique

idiot ['ɪdɪət] idiot(e) *m(f)*; **idiotic** idiot, bête

idle ['aɪdl] **1** *adj* (*not working*) inoccupé; (*lazy*) paresseux; *threat* oiseux; *machinery* non utilisé **2** *v/i of engine* tourner au ralenti

idol ['aɪdl] idole *f*; **idolize** idolâtrer

if [ɪf] si

ignite [ɪg'naɪt] mettre le feu à; **ignition** *in car* allumage *m*; ~ **key** clef *f* de contact

ignorance ['ɪgnərəns] ignorance *f*; **ignorant** ignorant; (*rude*) grossier; **ignore** ignorer

ill [ɪl] malade; **fall ~, be taken ~** tomber malade

illegal [ɪ'liːgl] illégal

illegible [ɪ'ledʒəbl] illisible

illegitimate [ɪlɪ'dʒɪtɪmət] *child* illégitime

illicit [ɪ'lɪsɪt] illicite

illiterate [ɪ'lɪtərət] illettré

illness ['ɪlnɪs] maladie *f*

illogical [ɪ'lɒdʒɪkl] illogique

ill-treat maltraiter

illuminating [ɪ'luːmɪneɪtɪŋ] *remarks etc* éclairant

illusion [ɪ'luːʒn] illusion *f*

illustrate ['ɪləstreɪt] illustrer; **illustration** illustration *f*; **illustrator** illustrateur(-trice) *m(f)*

image ['ɪmɪdʒ] image *f*

imaginary [ɪ'mædʒɪnərɪ] imaginaire; **imagination** imagination *f*; **imaginative** imaginatif; **imagine** imaginer; **you're imagining things** tu te fais des idées

IMF [aɪem'ef] (= **International Monetary Fund**) F.M.I. *m* (= Fonds *m* Monétaire International)

imitate ['ɪmɪteɪt] imiter; **imitation** imitation *f*

immaculate [ɪ'mækjʊlət] impeccable

immature [ɪmə'tʊr] immature

immediate [ɪ'miːdɪət] immédiat; **immediately** immédiatement

immense [ɪ'mens] immense

immerse [ɪ'mɜːrs] immerger, plonger

immigrant ['ɪmɪgrənt] immigrant(e) *m(f)*; **immigrate** immigrer; **immigration** immigration *f*

imminent ['ɪmɪnənt] imminent

immobilize [ɪ'moʊbɪlaɪz] immobiliser

immoderate [ɪ'mɑːdərət] immodéré

immoral [ɪ'mɒrəl] immoral; **immorality** immoralité *f*

immortal [ɪ'mɔːrtl] immortel; **immortality** immortalité *f*

immune [ɪ'mjuːn] *to illness* immunisé (**to** contre); *from ruling* exempt (**from** de); **immune system** MED système *m* immunitaire; **immunity** immunité *f*; *from ruling* exemption *f*

impact ['ɪmpækt] impact m
impair [ɪm'per] affaiblir
impartial [ɪm'pɑːrʃl] impartial
impassable [ɪm'pæsəbl] *road* impraticable
impassioned [ɪm'pæʃnd] *speech, plea* passionné
impatience [ɪm'peɪʃəns] impatience *f*; **impatient** impatient
impatiently impatiemment
impeccable [ɪm'pekəbl] impeccable
impede [ɪm'piːd] gêner, empêcher; **impediment** *obstacle* obstacle *m*; **speech** ~ défaut *m* d'élocution
impending [ɪm'pendɪŋ] imminent
imperative [ɪm'perətɪv] **1** *adj* impératif **2** *n* GRAM impératif *m*
imperfect [ɪm'pɜːrfekt] **1** *adj* imparfait **2** *n* GRAM imparfait *m*
impersonal [ɪm'pɜːrsənl] impersonnel; **impersonate** *as a joke* imiter; *illegally* se faire passer pour
impertinence [ɪm'pɜːrtɪnəns] impertinence *f*; **impertinent** impertinent
impervious [ɪm'pɜːrvɪəs]: ~ **to** insensible à
impetuous [ɪm'petʃʊəs] impétueux
impetus ['ɪmpətəs] *of campaign etc* force *f*, élan *m*
implement ['ɪmplɪmənt] **1** *n*

instrument *m*, outil *m* **2** *v/t* ['ɪmplɪment] appliquer
implicate ['ɪmplɪkeɪt] impliquer; **implication** implication *f*
implore [ɪm'plɔːr] implorer
imply [ɪm'plaɪ] impliquer; (*suggest*) suggérer
impolite [ɪmpə'laɪt] impoli
import ['ɪmpɔːrt] **1** *n* importation *f* **2** *v/t* importer
importance [ɪm'pɔːrtəns] importance *f*; **important** important
importer [ɪm'pɔːrtər] importateur(-trice) *m(f)*
impose [ɪm'pəʊz] *tax* imposer; **imposing** imposant
impossibility [ɪmpɑːsɪ'bɪlɪtɪ] impossibilité *f*; **impossible** impossible
impotence ['ɪmpətəns] impuissance *f*; **impotent** impuissant
impractical [ɪm'præktɪkəl] dénué de sens pratique
impress [ɪm'pres] impressionner; **impression** impression *f*; (*impersonation*) imitation *f*; **impressive** impressionnant
imprint ['ɪmprɪnt] *of credit card* empreinte *f*
imprison [ɪm'prɪzn] emprisonner; **imprisonment** emprisonnement *m*
improbable [ɪm'prɑːbəbl] improbable
improve [ɪm'pruːv] **1** *v/t* améliorer **2** *v/i* s'améliorer; im-

provement amélioration *f*

improvize ['ɪmprəvaɪz] improviser

impudent ['ɪmpjʊdənt] impudent

impulse ['ɪmpʌls] impulsion *f*; **impulsive** impulsif

in [ɪn] **1** *prep* dans; *with time* en; ~ **Rouen** à Rouen; ~ **1999** en 1999; ~ **the morning** le matin; ~ **the summer** l'été; ~ **August** en août, au mois d'août; ~ **two hours** *from now* dans deux heures; *over period of* en deux heures; ~ **English** en anglais; ~ **yellow** en jaune; ~ **crossing the road** en traversant la route **2** *adv* (*at home, in the building etc*) là; (*arrived: train*) arrivé; (*in its position*) dedans; ~ **here** ici **3** *adj* (*fashionable, popular*) à la mode

inability [ɪnə'bɪlɪtɪ] incapacité *f*

inaccurate [ɪn'ækjʊrət] inexact

inadequate [ɪn'ædɪkwət] insuffisant, inadéquat

inadvisable [ɪnəd'vaɪzəbl] peu recommandé

inanimate [ɪn'ænɪmət] inanimé

inappropriate [ɪnə'prəʊprɪət] peu approprié

inaudible [ɪn'ɔːdəbl] inaudible

inaugural [ɪ'nɔːgjʊrəl] *speech* inaugural; **inaugurate** inaugurer

inborn ['ɪnbɔːrn] inné

inc. (= *incorporated*) S.A. *f* (= Société *f* Anonyme)

incalculable [ɪn'kælkjʊləbl] *damage* incalculable

incapable [ɪn'keɪpəbl] incapable

incentive [ɪn'sentɪv] encouragement *m*, stimulation *f*

incessant [ɪn'sesnt] incessant; **incessantly** sans arrêt

incest ['ɪnsest] inceste *m*

inch [ɪntʃ] pouce *m*

incident ['ɪnsɪdənt] incident *m*; **incidental** fortuit; ~ **expenses** frais *mpl* accessoires; **incidentally** soit dit en passant

incision [ɪn'sɪʒn] incision *f*; **incisive** incisif

incite [ɪn'saɪt] inciter

inclination [ɪnklɪ'neɪʃn] (*liking*) penchant *m*; (*tendency*) tendance *f*

inclose, inclosure → **enclose, enclosure**

include [ɪn'kluːd] inclure, comprendre; **including** y compris; ~ **service** service compris; **inclusive 1** *adj* ~ **price** tout compris **2** *prep*: ~ **of** en incluant **3** *adv* tout compris; *from Monday to Thursday* ~ du lundi au jeudi inclus

incoherent [ɪnkəʊ'hɪrənt] incohérent

income ['ɪnkəm] revenu *m*; **income tax** impôt *m* sur le revenu

incomparable [ɪnˈkɑːmpərəbl] incomparable

incompatibility [ɪnkəmpætɪˈbɪlɪtɪ] incompatibilité f; **incompatible** incompatible

incompetence [ɪnˈkɑːmpɪtəns] incompétence f; **incompetent** incompétent

incomplete [ɪnkəmˈpliːt] incomplet

incomprehensible [ɪnkɑːmprɪˈhensɪbl] incompréhensible

inconceivable [ɪnkənˈsiːvəbl] inconcevable

inconsiderate [ɪnkənˈsɪdərət] *action* inconsidéré; **be ~ of** *person* manquer d'égards

inconsistent [ɪnkənˈsɪstənt] incohérent; *person* inconstant

inconspicuous [ɪnkənˈspɪkjuəs] discret

inconvenience [ɪnkənˈviːnɪəns] inconvénient m; **inconvenient** *time* inopportun; *place, arrangement* peu commode

incorporate [ɪnˈkɔːrpəreɪt] incorporer

incorrect [ɪnkəˈrekt] incorrect

increase 1 [ɪnˈkriːs] *v/t & v/i* augmenter **2** [ˈɪnkriːs] augmentation f; **increasing** croissant; **increasingly** de plus en plus

incredible [ɪnˈkredɪbl] incroyable

incur [ɪnˈkɜːr] *costs* encourir; *debts* contracter; *s.o.'s anger* s'attirer

incurable [ɪnˈkjurəbl] *also fig* incurable

indecent [ɪnˈdiːsnt] indécent

indecisive [ɪndɪˈsaɪsɪv] *argument* peu concluant; *person* indécis; **indecisiveness** indécision f

indeed [ɪnˈdiːd] (*in fact*) vraiment; (*yes, agreeing*) en effet; **very much ~** beaucoup

indefinable [ɪndɪˈfaɪnəbl] indéfinissable

indefinite [ɪnˈdefɪnɪt] indéfini; **indefinitely** indéfiniment

indelicate [ɪnˈdelɪkət] délicat

independence [ɪndɪˈpendəns] indépendance f; **Independence Day** fête f de l'Indépendance; **independent** indépendant

indescribable [ɪndɪˈskraɪbəbl] indescriptible; (*very bad*) inqualifiable

index [ˈɪndeks] *for book* index m

India [ˈɪndɪə] Inde f; **Indian 1** *adj* indien **2** *n also American* Indien(ne) m(f)

indicate [ˈɪndɪkeɪt] **1** *v/t* indiquer **2** *v/i when driving* mettre ses clignotants; **indication** indication f, signe m

indict [ɪnˈdaɪt] accuser

indifference [ɪnˈdɪfrəns] indifférence f; **indifferent** indifférent; (*mediocre*) médiocre

indigestion [ɪndɪ'dʒestʃn] indigestion *f*

indignant [ɪn'dɪgnənt] indigné; **indignation** indignation *f*

indirect [ɪndɪ'rekt] indirect; **indirectly** indirectement

indiscreet [ɪndɪ'skriːt] indiscret

indiscriminate [ɪndɪ'skrɪmɪnət] aveugle; *accusations* à tort et à travers

indispensable [ɪndɪ'spensəbl] indispensable

indisposed [ɪndɪ'spouzd] (*not well*) indisposé

indisputable [ɪndɪ'spjuːtəbl] incontestable

indistinct [ɪndɪ'stɪŋkt] indistinct

indistinguishable [ɪndɪ'stɪŋwɪʃəbl] indifférenciable

individual [ɪndɪ'vɪdʒuəl] **1** *n* individu *m* **2** *adj* (*separate*) particulier; (*personal*) individuel; **individually** individuellement

indoctrinate [ɪn'dɑːktrɪneɪt] endoctriner

Indonesia [ɪndə'niːʒə] Indonésie *f*; **Indonesian 1** *adj* indonésien **2** *n person* Indonésien(ne) *m(f)*

indoor ['ɪndɔːr] *activities, games* d'intérieur; *sport* en salle; *arena* couvert; **indoors** à l'intérieur; (*at home*) à la maison

indorse → **endorse**

indulgent [ɪn'dʌldʒənt] (*not strict enough*) indulgent

industrial [ɪn'dʌstrɪəl] industriel; **industrial dispute** conflit *m* social; **industrialist** industriel(le) *m(f)*; **industrious** travailleur; **industry** industrie *f*

ineffective [ɪnɪ'fektɪv] inefficace

inefficient [ɪnɪ'fɪʃənt] inefficace

inept [ɪ'nept] inepte

inequality [ɪnɪ'kwɑːlɪtɪ] inégalité *f*

inescapable [ɪnɪ'skeɪpəbl] inévitable

inevitable [ɪn'evɪtəbl] inévitable; **inevitably** inévitablement

inexcusable [ɪnɪk'skjuːzəbl] inexcusable

inexhaustible [ɪnɪg'zɔːstəbl] inépuisable

inexpensive [ɪnɪk'spensɪv] bon marché, pas cher

inexperienced [ɪnɪk'spɪriənst] inexpérimenté

inexplicable [ɪnɪk'splɪkəbl] inexplicable

infallible [ɪn'fælɪbl] infaillible

infamous ['ɪnfəməs] infâme

infancy ['ɪnfənsɪ] *of person* petite enfance *f*; *of state, institution* débuts *mpl*; **infant** petit(e) enfant *m(f)*; **infantile** *pej* infantile

infantry ['ɪnfəntrɪ] infanterie *f*

infect [ɪn'fekt] contaminer;

become ~ed of wound s'infecter; **infection** contamination f; (disease), of wound infection f; **infectious** disease infectieux; laughter contagieux

infer [ɪnˈfɜːr] **~ X from Y** déduire X de Y

inferior [ɪnˈfɪərər] inférieur; **inferiority** infériorité f; **inferiority complex** complexe m d'infériorité

infertile [ɪnˈfɜːtl] stérile; **infertility** stérilité f

infidelity [ɪnfɪˈdelɪtɪ] infidélité f

infinite [ˈɪnfɪnət] infini; **infinitive** infinitif m

infinity [ɪnˈfɪnətɪ] infinité f; MATH infini m

inflammable [ɪnˈflæməbl] inflammable; **inflammation** MED inflammation f

inflatable [ɪnˈfleɪtəbl] dinghy gonflable; **inflate** tire, dinghy gonfler; **inflation** inflation f; **inflationary** inflationniste

inflexible [ɪnˈfleksɪbl] attitude, person inflexible

inflict [ɪnˈflɪkt] infliger (**on** à)

influence [ˈɪnfluəns] **1** n influence f **2** v/t influencer; **influential** influent

inform [ɪnˈfɔːrm] **1** v/t informer **2** v/i: **~ on** dénoncer

informal [ɪnˈfɔːrməl] meeting, agreement non-officiel; form of address familier; conversation, dress simple; **informality** of meeting, agreement caractère m non officiel; of form of address familiarité f; of conversation, dress simplicité f

informant [ɪnˈfɔːrmənt] informateur(-trice) m(f); **information** renseignements mpl; **information technology** informatique f; **informative** instructif; **informer** dénonciateur(-trice) m(f)

infra-red [ɪnfrəˈred] infrarouge

infrastructure [ˈɪnfrəstrʌktʃər] infrastructure f

infrequent [ɪnˈfriːkwənt] rare

infuriate [ɪnˈfjʊrɪeɪt] rendre furieux; **infuriating** exaspérant

ingenious [ɪnˈdʒiːnɪəs] ingénieux

ingot [ˈɪŋgət] lingot m

ingratitude [ɪnˈgrætɪtuːd] ingratitude f

ingredient [ɪnˈgriːdɪənt] for cooking ingrédient m; for success recette f

inhabit [ɪnˈhæbɪt] habiter; **inhabitant** habitant(e) m(f)

inhale [ɪnˈheɪl] **1** v/t inhaler **2** v/i when smoking avaler la fumée

inherit [ɪnˈherɪt] hériter; **inheritance** héritage m

inhibited [ɪnˈhɪbɪtɪd] inhibé; **inhibition** inhibition f

inhospitable [ɪnhɑˈspɪtəbl] inhospitalier

inhuman [ɪnˈhjuːmən] inhumain

initial [ɪˈnɪʃl] **1** *adj* initial **2** *n* initiale *f* **3** *v/t* (*write initials on*) parapher; **initially** au début; **initiate** *procedure* lancer; *person* initier; **initiation** lancement *m*; *of person* initiation *f*; **initiative** initiative *f*

inject [ɪnˈdʒekt] injecter; **injection** injection *f*

injure [ˈɪndʒər] blesser; **injury** blessure *f*

injustice [ɪnˈdʒʌstɪs] injustice *f*

ink [ɪŋk] encre *f*

inland [ˈɪnlənd] intérieur

in-laws [ˈɪnlɔːz] belle-famille *f*

inmate [ˈɪnmeɪt] *of prison* détenu(e) *m(f)*; *of mental hospital* interné(e) *m(f)*

inn [ɪn] auberge *f*

innate [ɪˈneɪt] inné

inner [ˈɪnər] *courtyard* intérieur; *thoughts* intime; *ear* interne

innocence [ˈɪnəsəns] innocence *f*; **innocent** innocent

innocuous [ɪˈnɑːkjuəs] inoffensif

innovation [ɪnəˈveɪʃn] innovation *f*; **innovative** innovant; **innovator** innovateur(-trice) *m(f)*

inoculate [ɪˈnɑːkjuleɪt] inoculer; **inoculation** inoculation *f*

inoffensive [ɪnəˈfensɪv] inoffensif

'in-patient patient(e) hospitalisé(e) *m(f)*

input [ˈɪnput] **1** *n into project etc* apport *m*, contribution *f*; COMPUT entrée *f* **2** *v/t into project* apporter; COMPUT entrer

inquest [ˈɪnkwest] enquête *f* (**into** sur)

inquire [ɪnˈkwaɪr] se renseigner; **inquiry** demande *f* de renseignements; ***government ~*** enquête *f* officielle

inquisitive [ɪnˈkwɪzɪtɪv] curieux

insane [ɪnˈseɪn] fou

insanitary [ɪnˈsænɪterɪ] insalubre

insanity [ɪnˈsænɪtɪ] folie *f*

inscription [ɪnˈskrɪpʃn] inscription *f*

insect [ˈɪnsekt] insecte *m*; **insecticide** insecticide *m*

insecure [ɪnsɪˈkjʊr] *be ~ not safe* ne pas se sentir en sécurité; *not sure of self* manquer d'assurance; **insecurity** *psychological* manque *m* d'assurance

insensitive [ɪnˈsensɪtɪv] insensible (*to* à)

insert 1 [ˈɪnsɜːrt] *n in magazine etc* encart *m* **2** [ɪnˈsɜːrt] *v/t* insérer

inside [ɪnˈsaɪd] **1** *n* intérieur *m*; **~ out** à l'envers **2** *prep* à l'intérieur de; **~ of 2 hours** en moins de 2 heures **3** *adv* à l'intérieur **4** *adj*: **~ information** informations *fpl* internes; **~ lane** SP couloir *m* intérieur

inside pocket poche *f* intérieure; **insider** initié(e) *m(f)*; **insider trading** FIN délit *m* d'initié; **insides** (*stomach*) ventre *m*

insignificant [ɪnsɪg'nɪfɪkənt] insignifiant

insincere [ɪnsɪn'sɪr] peu sincère; **insincerity** manque *f* de sincérité

insinuate [ɪn'sɪnjʊeɪt] insinuer

insist [ɪn'sɪst] insister (**on** sur); **insistent** insistant

insolent ['ɪnsələnt] insolent

insolvent [ɪn'sɑːlvənt] insolvable

insomnia [ɪn'sɑːmnɪə] insomnie *f*

inspect [ɪn'spekt] *work, tickets, baggage* contrôler; *factory, school* inspecter; **inspection** *of work, tickets, baggage* contrôle *m*; *of factory, school* inspection *f*; **inspector** *in factory* inspecteur(-trice) *m(f)*

inspiration [ɪnspə'reɪʃn] inspiration *f*; **inspire** inspirer

instability [ɪnstə'bɪlɪtɪ] instabilité *f*

install [ɪn'stɔːl] installer; **installation** installation *f*; **installment, Br instalment** *of story etc* épisode *m*; (*payment*) versement *m*; **installment plan** vente *f* à crédit

instance ['ɪnstəns] (*example*) exemple *m*; **for ~** par exemple

instant ['ɪnstənt] **1** *adj* instantané **2** *n* instant *m*; **instantaneous** instantané; **instant coffee** café *m* soluble; **instantly** immédiatement

instead [ɪn'sted] à la place; **~ of me** à ma place; **~ of going home** au lieu de rentrer à la maison

instinct ['ɪnstɪŋkt] instinct *m*; **instinctive** instinctif

institute ['ɪnstɪtuːt] **1** *n* institut *m*; (*special home*) établissement *m* **2** *v/t new law, inquiry* instituer; **institution** institution *f*

instruct [ɪn'strʌkt] (*order*) donner; (*teach*) instruire; **instruction** instruction *f*; **~s for use** mode *m* d'emploi; **instructive** instructif; **instructor** moniteur(-trice) *m(f)*

instrument ['ɪnstrʊmənt] instrument *m*

insubordinate [ɪnsə'bɔːrdɪneɪt] insubordonné

insufficient [ɪnsə'fɪʃnt] insuffisant

insulate ['ɪnsəleɪt] ELEC, *against cold* isoler; **insulation** isolation *f*; *material* isolement *m*

insulin ['ɪnsəlɪn] insuline *f*

insult 1 ['ɪnsʌlt] *n* insulte *f* **2** [ɪn'sʌlt] *v/t* insulter

insurance [ɪn'ʃʊrəns] assurance *f*; **insurance company** compagnie *f* d'assurance; **insurance policy** police *f* d'as-

surance; **insurance premium** prime *f* d'assurance; **insure** assurer

insurmountable [ɪnsər-
'maʊntəbl] insurmontable

intact [ɪn'tækt] (*not damaged*) intact

integrate ['ɪntɪgreɪt] intégrer;
integrity (*honesty*) intégrité
f

intellect ['ɪntəlekt] intellect
m; **intellectual 1** *adj* intellectuel **2** *n* intellectuel(le) *m(f)*

intelligence [ɪn'telɪdʒəns] intelligence *f*; (*information*)
renseignements *mpl*; **intelligent** intelligent

intelligible [ɪn'telɪdʒəbl] intelligible

intend [ɪn'tend] *v/i*: ~ **to do
sth** avoir l'intention de

intense [ɪn'tens] intense; *personality* passionné; **intensify
1** *v/t* intensifier **2** *v/i of pain,
fighting* s'intensifier; **intensity** intensité *f*; **intensive** intensif; **intensive care** MED
service *m* de soins intensifs

intention [ɪn'tenʃn] intention
f; **intentional** intentionnel;
intentionally délibérément

interaction [ɪntər'ækʃn] interaction *f*; **interactive** interactif

intercept [ɪntər'sept] intercepter

interchange ['ɪntərtʃeɪndʒ] *of
highways* échangeur *m*; **interchangeable** interchangeable

intercom ['ɪntərkɑːm] interphone *m*

intercourse ['ɪntərkɔːrs] *sexual* rapports *mpl*

interdependent [ɪntərdɪ-
'pendənt] interdépendant

interest ['ɪntrəst] **1** *n* intérêt
m; *financial* intérêt(s) *m(pl)*
2 *v/t* intéresser; **interested**
intéressé; **interesting** intéressant; **interest rate** taux
m d'intérêt

interface ['ɪntərfeɪs] **1** *n* interface *f* **2** *v/i* avoir une interface

interfere [ɪntər'fɪr] se mêler
(**with** de); **interference** inge-
rence *f*; *on radio* interféren-
ce *f*

interior [ɪn'tɪrɪər] **1** *adj* intérieur **2** *n* intérieur *m*; **interior
design** design *m* d'inté-
rieurs; **interior designer** designer *m/f* d'intérieurs

interlude ['ɪntərluːd] intermè-
de *m*

intermediary [ɪntər'miːdɪeɪr]
intermédiaire *m/f*; **intermediate** *level* intermédiaire;
course (de niveau) moyen

intermission [ɪntər'mɪʃn] *in
theater* entracte *m*

internal [ɪn'tɜːrnl] interne;
trade intérieur; **internally** *in
organization* en interne;
not to be taken ~ à usage externe; **Internal Revenue
(Service)** direction *f* générale des) impôts *mpl*

international [ɪntər'næʃnl]

international; **internationally** internationalement

Internet [ˈɪntərnet] Internet *m*; **on the ~** sur Internet

interpret [ɪnˈtɜːrprɪt] interpréter; **interpretation** interprétation *f*; **interpreter** interprète *m/f*

interrogate [ɪnˈterəgeɪt] interroger; **interrogation** interrogatoire *m*; **interrogator** interrogateur(-trice) *m(f)*

interrupt [ɪntəˈrʌpt] interrompre; **interruption** interruption *f*

intersect [ɪntərˈsekt] **1** *v/t* couper, croiser **2** *v/i* s'entrecouper, s'entrecroiser; **intersection** *of roads* carrefour *m*

interstate [ˈɪntərsteɪt] autoroute *f*

interval [ˈɪntərvl] intervalle *m*; *in theater* entracte *m*

intervene [ɪntərˈviːn] intervenir; **intervention** intervention *f*

interview [ˈɪntərvjuː] **1** *n* interview *f*; *for job* entretien *m* **2** *v/t for job* faire passer un entretien à; **interviewer** interviewer(-euse) *m(f)*; *for job* personne *f* responsable d'un entretien

intimate [ˈɪntəmət] intime

intimidate [ɪnˈtɪmɪdeɪt] intimider; **intimidation** intimidation *f*

into [ˈɪntʊ] dans; *translate ~ English* traduire en anglais;

be ~ sth F (*like*) aimer qch; *politics etc* être engagé dans qch

intolerable [ɪnˈtɑːlərəbl] intolérable; **intolerant** intolérant

intoxicated [ɪnˈtɑːksɪkeɪtɪd] ivre

intravenous [ɪntrəˈviːnəs] intraveineux

intricate [ˈɪntrɪkət] compliqué, complexe

intrigue [ˈɪntriːg] *n* intrigue *f* **2** [ɪnˈtriːg] *v/t* intriguer; **intriguing** intrigant

introduce [ɪntrəˈduːs] *new technique etc* introduire; *~ s.o. to s.o.* présenter qn à qn; **introduction** *to person* présentations *fpl*; *in book, of new techniques* introduction *f*

intrude [ɪnˈtruːd] déranger; **intruder** intrus(e) *m(f)*; **intrusion** intrusion *f*

intuition [ɪntuˈɪʃn] intuition *f*

invade [ɪnˈveɪd] envahir

invalid[1] [ɪnˈvælɪd] *adj* non valable

invalid[2] [ˈɪnvəlɪd] *n* MED invalide *m/f*

invalidate [ɪnˈvælɪdeɪt] *claim, theory* invalider

invaluable [ɪnˈvæljʊbl] inestimable

invariably [ɪnˈveɪrɪəblɪ] (*always*) invariablement

invasion [ɪnˈveɪʒn] invasion *f*

invent [ɪnˈvent] inventer; **invention** invention *f*; **inventive** inventif; **inventor** inven-

teur(-trice) *m(f)*
inventory ['ɪnvəntɔʊrɪ] inventaire *m*
invert [ɪn'vɜːrt] inverser
invest [ɪn'vest] investir
investigate [ɪn'vestɪɡeɪt] *crime* enquêter sur; *scientific phenomenon* étudier; **investigation** *of crime* enquête *f*; *in science* étude *f*
investment [ɪn'vestmənt] investissement *m*; **investor** investisseur *m*
invincible [ɪn'vɪnsəbl] invincible
invisible [ɪn'vɪzɪbl] invisible
invitation [ɪnvɪ'teɪʃn] invitation *f*; **invite** inviter
invoice ['ɪnvɔɪs] **1** *n* facture *f* **2** *v/t customer* facturer
involuntary [ɪn'vɑːləntərɪ] involontaire
involve [ɪn'vɑːlv] *work* nécessiter; *expense* entraîner; *(concern)* concerner; **what does it ~?** qu'est-ce que cela implique?; **involved** *(complex)* compliqué; **involvement** *in project, crime etc* participation *f*; *in politics* engagement *m*
invulnerable [ɪn'vʌlnərəbl] invulnérable
inward ['ɪnwərd] **1** *adj* intérieur **2** *adv* vers l'intérieur; **inwardly** intérieurement
IQ [aɪ'kjuː] (= **intelligence quotient**) Q.I. *m* (= Quotient *m* intellectuel)
Iran [ɪ'rɑːn] Iran *m*; **Iranian**

adj iranien **2** *n* Iranien(ne) *m(f)*
Iraq [ɪ'ræːk] Iraq *m*; **Iraqi 1** *adj* irakien **2** *n* Irakien(ne) *m(f)*
Ireland ['aɪrlənd] Irlande *f*; **Irish 1** *adj* irlandais **2** *npl:* **the ~** les Irlandais
iron ['aɪərn] **1** *n* fer *m*; *for clothes* fer *m* à repasser **2** *v/t shirts etc* repasser
ironic(al) [aɪ'rɑːnɪk(l)] ironique
'ironing board planche *f* à repasser
irony ['aɪrənɪ] ironie *f*
irrational [ɪ'ræʃənl] irrationnel
irreconcilable [ɪrekən'saɪləbl] *people* irréconciliable; *positions* inconciliable
irregular [ɪ'reɡjʊlər] irrégulier
irrelevant [ɪ'reləvənt] hors de propos
irreplaceable [ɪrɪ'pleɪsəbl] irremplaçable
irrepressible [ɪrɪ'presəbl] *sense of humor* à toute épreuve; *person* qui ne se laisse pas abattre
irresistible [ɪrɪ'zɪstəbl] irrésistible
irresponsible [ɪrɪ'spɑːnsəbl] irresponsable
irreverent [ɪ'revərənt] irrévérencieux
irrevocable [ɪ'revəkəbl] irrévocable
irrigate ['ɪrɪɡeɪt] irriguer; **irrigation** irrigation *f*

irritable ['ırıtəbl] irritable; irritate irriter; irritating irri-
tant; irritation irritation f
Islam ['ızlɑ:m] religion islam
m; peoples, civilization Islam
m; Islamic islamique
island ['aılənd] île f
isolate ['aısəleıt] isoler; isolated isolé; isolation isolement m
ISP [aıes'pi:] (= Internet service provider) fournisseur
m Internet
Israel ['ızreıl] Israël m; Israeli
1 adj israélien 2 n person Is-
raélien(ne) m(f)
issue ['ıʃu:] 1 n (matter) question f, problème m; of magazine numéro m 2 v/t supplies
distribuer; coins, warning
émettre; passport délivrer
IT [aı'ti:] (= information technology) informatique f
it [ıt] as subject il, elle; as object le, la; ~'s through there
c'est par là; give ~ to him

donne-le lui; on top of ~ dessus; let's talk about ~ par-
lons-en; ~'s raining il pleut;
~'s me/him c'est moi/lui;
that's ~! (that's right) c'est
ça!; (finished) c'est fini!
Italian [ı'tæljən] 1 adj italien 2
n person Italien(ne) m(f);
language italien m
italics [ı'tælıks] italique m
Italy ['ıtəlı] Italie f
itch [ıtʃ] 1 n démangeaison f 2
v/i: it ~es ça me démange
item ['aıtəm] article m; on
agenda point m; ~ of news
nouvelle f; itemize invoice
détailler
itinerary [aı'tınərerı] itinéraire m
its [ıts] son, sa; pl ses
it's [ıts] → it is, it has
itself [ıt'self] reflexive se;
stressed lui-même; elle-même; by ~ (automatically)
tout(e) seul(e)

J

jab [dʒæb]:~ a stick into s.o.
donner un coup de bâton à
qn
jack [dʒæk] MOT cric m; in
cards valet m
jacket ['dʒækıt] veste f; of
book couverture f
'jackpot jackpot m
jagged ['dʒægıd] découpé
jail [dʒeıl] prison f

jam¹ [dʒæm] n for bread confiture f
jam² [dʒæm] 1 n MOT embouteillage m; F (difficulty) pétrin m F 2 v/t (ram) fourrer;
(cause to stick) bloquer;
broadcast brouiller 3 v/i
(stick) se bloquer
janitor ['dʒænıtər] concierge
m/f

January ['dʒænjʊerɪ] janvier m

Japan [dʒə'pæn] Japon m; **Japanese 1** adj japonais **2** n person Japonais(e) m(f); language japonais m; **the ~** les Japonais mpl

jar [dʒɑːr] container pot m

jargon ['dʒɑːrgən] jargon m

jaw [dʒɔː] mâchoire f

jaywalker ['dʒeɪwɔːkər] piéton(ne) m(f) imprudent(e)

jazz [dʒæz] jazz m

jealous ['dʒeləs] jaloux; **jealousy** jalousie f

jeans [dʒiːnz] jean m

jeep [dʒiːp] jeep f

jeer [dʒɪr] **1** n raillerie f; of crowd huée f **2** v/i of crowd huer

Jello® ['dʒeloʊ] gelée f

jelly ['dʒelɪ] jam confiture f; **jellyfish** méduse f

jeopardize ['dʒepərdaɪz] mettre en danger

jerk¹ [dʒɜːrk] **1** n saccade f **2** v/t tirer d'un coup sec

jerk² [dʒɜːrk] n F couillon m F

jerky ['dʒɜːrkɪ] movement saccadé

Jesus ['dʒiːzəs] Jésus

jet [dʒet] (airplane) avion m à réaction, jet m; of water jet m; (nozzle) jet m; **jetlag** (troubles mpl dus au) décalage m horaire

jettison ['dʒetɪsn] jeter par-dessus bord; fig abandonner

jetty ['dʒetɪ] jetée f

Jew [dʒuː] Juif(-ive) m(f)

jewel ['dʒuːəl] bijou m; fig : person perle f; **jeweler**, Br **jeweller** bijoutier(-ère) m(f); **jewelry**, Br **jewellery** bijoux mpl

Jewish ['dʒuːɪʃ] juif

jigsaw (puzzle) ['dʒɪgsɔː] puzzle m

jilt [dʒɪlt] laisser tomber

jingle ['dʒɪŋgl] **1** n song jingle m **2** v/i of keys, coins cliqueter

jinx [dʒɪŋks] person porte-malheur m/f; **there's a ~ on this project** ce projet porte malheur

jittery ['dʒɪtərɪ] F nerveux

job [dʒɑːb] travail m; **jobless** sans travail

jockey ['dʒɑːkɪ] jockey m

jog [dʒɑːg] as exercise faire du footing or jogging; **jogger** person joggeur(-euse) m(f); **jogging** jogging m

john [dʒɑːn] F (toilet) petit coin m F

join [dʒɔɪn] **1** n joint m **2** v/i of roads, rivers se rejoindre; (become a member) devenir membre **3** v/t (connect) relier; person, of road rejoindre; club devenir membre de

◆ **join in** participer

joint [dʒɔɪnt] ANAT articulation f; in woodwork joint m; of meat rôti m; **joint account** compte m joint; **joint venture** entreprise f commune

joke [ʒoʊk] **1** n plaisanterie f,

blague f F; (*practical* ~) tour m **2** v/i plaisanter; **joker** farceur(-euse) m(f), blagueur (-euse) m(f) F; *in cards* joker m; **jokingly** en plaisantant

jostle ['dʒɑːsl] bousculer

journal ['dʒɜːrnl] (*magazine*) revue f; (*diary*) journal m; **journalism** journalisme m; **journalist** journaliste m/f

journey ['dʒɜːrnɪ] voyage m; *across town etc* trajet m

joy [dʒɔɪ] joie f

jubilant ['dʒuːbɪlənt] débordant de joie; **jubilation** jubilation f

judge [dʒʌdʒ] **1** n juge m/f **2** v/t juger; *measurement, age* estimer **3** v/i juger; (*judgment*) jugement m; (*opinion*) avis m; **Judg(e)ment Day** le Jugement dernier

judicial [dʒuː'dɪʃl] judiciaire

juggle ['dʒʌgl] *also fig* jongler avec

juice [dʒuːs] jus m; **juicy** juteux; *gossip* croustillant

July [dʒuː'laɪ] juillet m

jumbo (**jet**) ['dʒʌmbou] jumbo-jet m; **jumbo-sized** F géant

jump [dʒʌmp] **1** n saut m; (*increase*) bond m **2** v/i sauter; *in surprise* sursauter; (*increase*) faire un bond **3** v/t *fence etc* sauter; F (*attack*) attaquer; ~ **the lights** griller un feu (rouge)

◆ **jump at** *opportunity* sauter sur

jumper ['dʒʌmpər] *dress* robe-chasuble f; **jumpy** nerveux

June [dʒuːn] juin m

jungle ['dʒʌŋgl] jungle f

junior ['dʒuːnjər] **1** adj subalterne; (*younger*) plus jeune **2** n *in rank* subalterne m/f; **she is ten years my** ~ elle est ma cadette de dix ans; **junior high** collège m

junk [dʒʌŋk] camelote f F; **junk food** cochonneries fpl; **junkie** F drogué(e) m(f); **junk mail** prospectus mpl

jurisdiction [dʒʊrɪs'dɪkʃn] LAW juridiction f

juror ['dʒʊrər] juré(e) m(f); **jury** jury m

just [dʒʌst] **1** adj *cause* juste **2** adv (*barely, only*) juste; ~ **as intelligent** tout aussi intelligent; **I've** ~ **seen her** je viens de la voir; ~ **about** (*almost*) presque; **I was** ~ **about to leave when** ... j'étais sur le point de partir quand ...; ~ **now** (*a few moments ago*) tout à l'heure; (*at this moment*) en ce moment

justice ['dʒʌstɪs] justice f

justifiable [dʒʌstɪ'faɪəbl] justifiable; **justifiably** à juste titre; **justification** justification f; **justify** *also text* justifier

justly ['dʒʌstlɪ] (*fairly*) de manière juste; (*rightly*) à juste titre

◆ **jut out** [dʒʌt] être en saillie

juvenile ['dʒuːvənəl] *crime* juvénile; *court pour enfants*; *pej* puéril; **juvenile delin-quent** mineur(e) délin-quant(e) *m(f)*

K

k [keɪ] (= *kilobyte*) Ko *m* (= kilo-octet *m*); (= *thousand*) mille
keel [kiːl] NAUT quille *f*
keen [kiːn] (*intense*) vif
keep [kiːp] **1** *v/t* garder; (*detain*) retenir; *in specific place* mettre; *family* entretenir; *dog etc* avoir; *bees, cattle* élever; *promise* tenir; **~ sth from s.o.** cacher qch à qn; **~ s.o. from doing sth** empêcher qn de faire qch; **~ trying!** essaie encore!; **don't ~ interrupting!** arrête de m'interrompre tout le temps! **2** *v/i* (*remain*) rester; *of food, milk* se conserver
♦ **keep back** (*hold in check*) retenir; *information* cacher
♦ **keep down** *costs etc* réduire; *food* garder
♦ **keep to** *path* rester sur; *rules* s'en tenir à
♦ **keep up 1** *v/i when walking, running etc* suivre; **keep up with** aller au même rythme que **2** *v/t pace, payments* continuer; *bridge, pants* soutenir
'**keepsake** souvenir *m*
kennel ['kenl] niche *f*; **kennels** chenil *m*
kerosene ['kerəsiːn] AVIA ké-

rosène *m*; *for lamps* pétrole *m* (lampant)
ketchup ['ketʃʌp] ketchup *m*
kettle ['ketl] bouilloire *f*
key [kiː] **1** *n* clef *f*, clé *f*; COMPUT, MUS touche *f* **2** *adj* (*vital*) clef *inv*, clé *inv* **3** *v/t & v/i* COMPUT taper
♦ **key in** *data* taper
'**keyboard** COMPUT, MUS clavier *m*; **keyboarder** COMPUT claviste *m/f*; **keycard** carte-clef *f*; **keyed-up** tendu; **keyring** porte-clefs *m*
kick [kɪk] **1** *n* coup *m* de pied **2** *v/t* donner un coup de pied dans **3** *v/i of horse* ruer
♦ **kick around** *ball* taper dans; F (*discuss*) débattre
♦ **kick off** donner le coup d'envoi; F (*start*) démarrer
♦ **kick out** mettre à la porte; **be kicked out of the company** être mis à la porte de la société
'**kickback** F (*bribe*) dessous-de-table *m* F
'**kickoff** SP coup *m* d'envoi
kid [kɪd] **1** *n* F (*child*) gamin(e) *m(f)* **2** *v/t* F taquiner **3** *v/i* F plaisanter
kidnap ['kɪdnæp] kidnapper; **kidnap(p)er** kidnappeur (-euse) *m(f)*; **kidnap(p)ing**

kidnapping *m*

kidney ['kɪdnɪ] ANAT rein *m*; *in cooking* rognon *m*

kill [kɪl] *also time* tuer; **killer** (*murderer*) tueur(-euse) *m(f)*; **killing** meurtre *m*

kiln [kɪln] four *m*

kilo ['kiːlou] kilo *m*; **kilobyte** kilo-octet *m*; **kilogram** kilogramme *m*; **kilometer**, *Br* **kilometre** kilomètre *m*

kind[1] [kaɪnd] *adj* gentil

kind[2] [kaɪnd] *n* (*sort*) sorte *f*, genre *m*; (*make, brand*) marque *f*; **~ of sad/strange** F plutôt triste/bizarre

kind-hearted [kaɪnd'haːrtɪd] bienveillant, bon; **kindly** gentil, bon; **kindness** bonté *f*, gentillesse *f*

king [kɪŋ] roi *m*; **kingdom** royaume *m*

kinky ['kɪŋkɪ] F bizarre

kiosk ['kiːɑːsk] kiosque *m*

kiss [kɪs] **1** *n* baiser *m* **2** *v/t* embrasser **3** *v/i* s'embrasser

kit [kɪt] (*equipment*) trousse *f*; *for assembly* kit *m*

kitchen ['kɪtʃɪn] cuisine *f*

kitten ['kɪtn] chaton(ne) *m(f)*

kitty ['kɪtɪ] *money* cagnotte *f*

klutz [klʌts] F (*clumsy person*) empoté(e) *m(f)*

knack [næk] **have the ~ of doing** avoir le chic pour faire; **there's a ~ to it** il y a un truc F

knee [niː] genou *m*; **kneecap** rotule *f*

kneel [niːl] s'agenouiller

'knee-length à la hauteur du genou

knife [naɪf] couteau *m*

knit [nɪt] tricoter; **knitwear** tricot *m*

knob [nɑːb] *on door* bouton *m*; *of butter* noix *f*

knock [nɑːk] **1** *n on door*, (*blow*) coup *m* **2** *v/t* (*hit*) frapper; *knee etc* se cogner; F (*criticize*) débiner F **3** *v/i on door* frapper

◆ **knock down** renverser; *wall, building* abattre; F (*reduce the price of*) solder

◆ **knock out** assommer; *boxer* mettre knock-out; *power lines etc* détruire; (*eliminate*) éliminer

◆ **knock over** renverser

'knockout *in boxing* knock-out *m*

knot [nɑːt] **1** *n* nœud *m* **2** *v/t* nouer

know [nou] **1** *v/t* savoir; *person, place, language* connaître; (*recognize*) reconnaître **2** *v/i* savoir; **~ about sth** être au courant de qch; **know-how** F savoir-faire *m*; **knowing** *smile* entendu; **knowingly** (*wittingly*) sciemment; *smile etc* d'un air entendu; **know-it-all** F je-sais-tout *m/f*; **knowledge** savoir *m*; *of a subject* connaissance(s) *f(pl)*; **to the best of my ~** autant que je sache

knuckle ['nʌkl] articulation *f* du doigt

Koran [kɔˈræn] Coran *m*
Korea [kəˈriːə] Corée *f*; **Korean 1** *adj* coréen **2** *n* Coréen(ne) *m(f)*; *language* coréen *m*

kosher [ˈkouʃər] REL casher *inv*; F réglo *inv* F
kudos [ˈkjuːdɑːs] prestige *m*

L

lab [læb] labo *m*
label [ˈleɪbl] **1** *n* étiquette *f* **2** *v/t also fig* étiqueter
labor [ˈleɪbər] *also in pregnancy* travail *m*
laboratory [ˈlæbrətɔːrɪ] laboratoire *m*
labored [ˈleɪbərd] *style, speech* laborieux; **laborer** travailleur *m* manuel; **laborious** laborieux; **labor union** syndicat *m*
labour *Br* → **labor**
lace [leɪs] dentelle *f*; *for shoe* lacet *m*
lack [læk] **1** *n* manque *m* **2** *v/t* manquer de **3** *v/i*: **be ~ing** manquer
lacquer [ˈlækər] laque *f*
ladder [ˈlædər] échelle *f*
laden [ˈleɪdn] chargé (**with** de)
ladies room [ˈleɪdiːz] toilettes *fpl* (pour dames)
lady [ˈleɪdɪ] dame *f*; **ladybug** coccinelle *f*; **ladylike** distingué
lager [ˈlɑːgər] *Br* bière *f* blonde
laidback [leɪdˈbæk] relax F
lake [leɪk] lac *m*
lamb [læm] agneau *m*
lame [leɪm] boîteux; *excuse*

mauvais,
laminated [ˈlæmɪneɪtɪd] *flooring, paper* stratifié; *wood* contreplaqué; *with plastic* plastifié; **~ glass** verre *m* feuilleté
lamp [læmp] lampe *f*; **lamppost** réverbère *m*; **lampshade** abat-jour *m inv*
land [lænd] **1** *n* terre *f*; *(country)* pays *m*; **by ~** par (voie de) terre **2** *v/t of airplane* faire atterrir; *job* décrocher F **3** *v/i of airplane* atterrir; *of ball* tomber; *landing of airplane* atterrissage *m*; *(top of staircase)* palier *m*; **landing strip** piste *f* d'atterrissage; **landlady** propriétaire *f*; *of rented room* loueuse *f*; *Br of bar* patronne *f*; **landlord** propriétaire *m*; *of rented room* loueur *m*; *Br of bar* patron *m*; **landmark** point *m* de repère; **be a ~ in** *fig* faire date dans; **land owner** propriétaire *m* foncier; **landscape 1** *n* paysage *m* **2** *adv* print en format paysage; **landslide** glissement *m* de terrain; **landslide victory** victoire *f* écrasante

lane [leɪn] *in country* petite route *f* (de campagne); *(alley)* ruelle *f*; **мот sole** *f*

language ['læŋgwɪdʒ] langue *f*; *(style, code etc)* langage *m*; **language lab** laboratoire *m* de langues

lap¹ [læp] *of track* tour *m*

lap² [læp] *of water* clapotis *m*

lap³ [læp] *of person* genoux *mpl*

lapel [lə'pel] revers *m*

lapse [læps] **1** *n (mistake)* erreur *f*; *in behavior* écart *m* (de conduite); *of time* intervalle *m* **2** *v/i* expirer

laptop ['læptɑːp] comput portable *m*

larceny ['lɑːrsənɪ] vol *m*

larder ['lɑːrdər] garde-manger *m inv*

large [lɑːrdʒ] grand; *sum of money, head* gros; **largely** *(mainly)* en grande partie

laryngitis [lærɪn'dʒaɪtɪs] laryngite *f*

laser ['leɪzər] laser *m*; **laser printer** imprimante *f* laser

lash¹ [læʃ] *v/t with whip* fouetter

lash² [læʃ] *n (eyelash)* cil *m*

last¹ [læst] **1** *adj (newest)*; **~ night** hier soir **2** *adv* arrive, leave en dernier; **at ~** enfin

last² [læst] *v/i* durer; **lasting** durable; **lastly** pour finir

late [leɪt] **1** *adj (behind time)* en retard; *in day* tard; **it's getting ~** il se fait tard **2** *adv* arrive, leave tard; **lately**

récemment; **later** plus tard; **latest** dernier

Latin A'merica Amérique *f* latine; **Latin American 1** *n* Latino-Américain *m* **2** *adj* latino-américain

latitude ['lætɪtuːd] *also (freedom)* latitude *f*

latter ['lætər] dernier

laugh [læf] **1** *n* rire *m* **2** *v/i* rire ◆ **laugh at** rire de; *(mock)* se moquer de

laughter ['læftər] rires *mpl*

launch [lɔːntʃ] **1** *n boat* vedette *f*; *of rocket, product* lancement *m*; *of ship* mise *f* à l'eau **2** *v/t rocket, product* lancer; *ship* mettre à l'eau

launder ['lɔːndər] *clothes, money* blanchir; **laundromat** laverie *f* automatique; **laundry** *place* blanchisserie *f*; *clothes* lessive *f*

lavatory ['lævətərɪ] W.-C. *mpl*

lavish ['lævɪʃ] somptueux

law [lɔː] loi *f*; *subject* droit *m*; **be against the ~** être contraire à la loi; **law-abiding** respectueux des lois; **law court** tribunal *m*; **lawful** légal; **wife, child** légitime; **lawless** anarchique

lawn [lɔːn] pelouse *f*; **lawn mower** tondeuse *f* (à gazon)

'lawsuit procès *m*; **lawyer** avocat *m*

lax [læks] laxiste; *security* relâché

laxative ['læksətɪv] laxatif *m*

lay [leɪ] (*put down*) poser; *eggs* pondre; V *sexually* s'envoyer V

♦ **lay off** *workers* licencier; *temporarily* mettre au chômage technique

♦ **lay out** *objects* disposer; *page* faire la mise en page de

layer ['leɪr] couche *f*

'**layman** REL laïc *m*; *fig* profane *m*

'**lay-out** agencement *m*; *of page* mise *f* en page

lazy ['leɪzɪ] *person* paresseux; *day* tranquille

lb (= **pound**) livre *f*

lead[1] [liːd] **1** *v/t* mener; *company* être à la tête de **2** *v/i in race, competition* mener; (*provide leadership*) diriger

lead[2] [liːd] *for dog* laisse *f*

lead[3] [led] *substance* plomb *m*; **leaded** *gas* au plomb

leader ['liːdər] *of state* dirigeant *m*; *in race* leader *m*; *of group* chef *m*; **leadership** *of party etc* direction *f*

lead-free ['ledfriː] *gas* sans plomb

leading ['liːdɪŋ] *runner* en tête (de la course); *company, product* premier; **leading-edge** *company, technology* de pointe

leaf [liːf] feuille *f*

♦ **leaf through** feuilleter

leaflet ['liːflət] dépliant *m*

league [liːg] ligue *f*

leak [liːk] **1** *n also of information* fuite *f* **2** *v/i of pipe* fuir;

of boat faire eau **3** *v/t information* divulguer

lean[1] [liːn] **1** *v/i* (*be at an angle*) pencher; **~ against sth** s'appuyer contre qch **2** *v/t* appuyer

lean[2] [liːn] *adj meat* maigre

leap [liːp] **1** *n* saut *m* **2** *v/i* sauter; **leap year** année *f* bissextile

learn [lɜːrn] apprendre; **learner** apprenant(e) *m(f)*; **learning** (*knowledge*) savoir *m*; *act* apprentissage *m*

lease [liːs] **1** *n for apartment* bail *m*; *for equipment* location *f* **2** *v/t* louer

♦ **lease out** louer

leash [liːʃ] *for dog* laisse *f*

least [liːst] **1** *adj* (*slightest*) (le ou la) moindre; *smallest quantity of* le moins de **2** *adv* (le) moins **3** *n* le moins; **at ~** au moins

leather ['leðər] **1** *n* cuir *m* **2** *adj* de cuir

leave [liːv] **1** *n* (*vacation*) congé *m* **2** *v/t* quitter; *food, scar, memory* laisser; (*forget, leave behind*) oublier; **~ sth alone** ne pas toucher à qch; **~ s.o. alone** laisser qn tranquille; **be left** rester **2** *v/i of person, plane etc* partir

♦ **leave behind** *intentionally* laisser; (*forget*) oublier

♦ **leave out** omettre; (*not put away*) ne pas ranger

leaving party ['liːvɪŋ] soirée *f* d'adieu

lecture ['lektʃər] **1** *n* conférence *f*; *at university* cours *m* **2** *v/i at university* donner des cours; **lecturer** conférencier *m*; *at university* maître *m* de conférences

ledge [ledʒ] *of window* rebord *m*; *on rock face* saillie *f*; **ledger** COM registre *m* de comptes

left [left] **1** *adj* gauche **2** *n also* POL gauche *f*; **on/to the ~** à gauche **3** *adv turn, look* à gauche; **left-hand** gauche; **left-handed** gaucher; **left luggage (office)** *Br* consigne *f*; **left-overs** *food* restes *mpl*; **left-wing** POL de gauche

leg [leg] jambe *f*; *of animal* patte *f*; *of table etc* pied *m*

legacy ['legəsɪ] héritage *m*, legs *m*

legal ['liːgl] *(allowed)* légal; *relating to the law* juridique; **legal adviser** conseiller (-ère) *m(f)* juridique; **legality** légalité *f*; **legalize** légaliser

legend ['ledʒənd] légende *f*; **legendary** légendaire

legible ['ledʒəbl] lisible

legislate ['ledʒɪsleɪt] légiférer; **legislation** *(laws)* législation *f*; **legislative** législatif; **legislature** POL corps *m* législatif

legitimate [lɪ'dʒɪtɪmət] légitime

'leg room place *f* pour les jambes

leisure ['liːʒər] loisir *m*; *(free time)* temps *m* libre; **leisurely** tranquille

lemon ['lemən] citron *m*; **lemonade** citronnade *f*; *carbonated* limonade *f*

lend [lend] prêter

length [leŋθ] longueur *f*; *(piece: of material)* pièce *f*; *of piping, road* tronçon *m*; **at ~** *describe, explain* en détail; *(eventually)* finalement; **lengthen** *sleeve etc* allonger; *contract* prolonger; **lengthy** long

lenient ['liːnɪənt] indulgent

lens [lenz] *of microscope* lentille *f*; *of eyeglasses* verre *m*; *of camera* objectif *m*; *of eye* cristallin *m*

Lent [lent] REL Carême *m*

leotard ['liːoʊtɑːrd] justaucorps *m*

lesbian ['lezbɪən] **1** *n* lesbienne *f* **2** *adj* lesbien

less [les] **1** *adv* moins; **~ than $200** moins de 200 dollars **2** *adj money, salt* moins de; **lessen 1** *v/t* réduire **2** *v/i* diminuer

lesson ['lesn] leçon *f*; *at school* cours *m*

let [let] *(allow)* laisser; *Br house* louer; **~'s stay here** restons ici; **~ go of sth** lâcher qch

◆ **let down** *hair* détacher; *blinds* baisser; *(disappoint)* décevoir

◆ **let in** *to house* laisser entrer

◆ **let out** *from room, building* laisser sortir; *jacket etc* agrandir; *groan,yell* laisser échapper; *Br* (*rent*) louer

◆ **let up** (*stop*) s'arrêter

lethal ['liːθl] mortel

lethargic [lɪ'θɑːrdʒɪk] léthargique; **lethargy** léthargie *f*

letter ['letər] *of alphabet, in mail* lettre *f*; **letterbox** *Br* boîte *f* aux lettres; **letterhead** (*heading*) en-tête *m*; (*headed paper*) papier *m* à en-tête

lettuce ['letɪs] laitue *f*

leukemia [luː'kiːmɪə] leucémie *f*

level ['levl] **1** *adj surface* plat; *in competition* à égalité **2** *n* niveau *m*; *on scale, in hierarchy* échelon *m*; **on the ~** *F* (*honest*) réglo *F*; **level-headed** pondéré

lever ['levər] levier *m*; **leverage** effet *m* de levier; (*influence*) poids *m*

levy ['levɪ] *taxes* lever

liability [laɪə'bɪlətɪ] (*responsibility*) responsabilité *f*; (*likeliness*) disposition *f* (**to** à); **liable** responsable (**for** de); **be ~ to** (*likely*) être susceptible de

◆ **liaise with** [lɪ'eɪz] assurer la liaison avec

liaison [lɪ'eɪzɑːn] (*contacts*) communication(s) *f*

liar [laɪr] menteur(-euse) *m(f)*

libel ['laɪbl] **1** *n* diffamation *f* **2** *v/t* diffamer

liberal ['lɪbərəl] large d'esprit;

portion etc généreux; POL libéral

liberate ['lɪbəreɪt] libérer; **liberated** libéré; **liberation** libération *f*; **liberty** liberté *f*

librarian [laɪ'brerɪən] bibliothécaire *m/f*; **library** bibliothèque *f*

Libya ['lɪbɪə] Libye *f*; **Libyan 1** *adj* libyen **2** *n* Libyen(ne) *m(f)*

lice [laɪs] *pl → louse*

licence ['laɪsns] *Br → license 1 n*

license ['laɪsns] **1** *n* permis *m* **2** *v/t company* accorder une licence à (**to do** pour faire); **be ~d** *equipment* être autorisé; **license number** numéro *m* d'immatriculation; **license plate** *of car* plaque *f* d'immatriculation

lick [lɪk] lécher

lid [lɪd] couvercle *m*

lie[1] [laɪ] **1** *n* (*untruth*) mensonge *m* **2** *v/i* mentir

lie[2] [laɪ] *v/i of person* (*lie down*) s'allonger; (*be lying down*) être allongé; *of object* être; (*be situated*) être, se trouver

◆ **lie down** se coucher

lieutenant [luː'tenənt] lieutenant *m*

life [laɪf] vie *f*; **life expectancy** espérance *f* de vie; **lifeguard** maître nageur *m*; **life imprisonment** emprisonnement *m* à vie; **life insurance** assurance-vie *f*; **life jacket** gilet *m* de sauvetage; **lifeless** *body* inanimé; *personality* mou; *town* mort; **lifelike** réaliste; **lifelong** de toute une vie; **life-sized** grandeur nature; **life support** (équipement *m* de) maintien *m* artificiel; **life-threatening** *illness* extrêmement grave; **lifetime** vie *f*; *in my* ~ de mon vivant

lift [lɪft] **1** *v/t* soulever **2** *v/i of fog* se lever **3** *n Br* (*elevator*) ascenseur *m*; *give s.o. a* ~ *in car* emmener qn en voiture; **lift-off** *of rocket* décollage *m*

ligament ['lɪɡəmənt] ligament *m*

light¹ [laɪt] **1** *n* lumière *f*; *do you have a* ~? vous avez du feu? **2** *v/t fire, cigarette* allumer; (*illuminate*) éclairer **3** *adj* (*not dark*) clair

light² [laɪt] *adj* (*not heavy*) léger

◆ **light up 1** *v/t* éclairer **2** *v/i* (*start to smoke*) s'allumer une cigarette

'light bulb ampoule *f*

lighten¹ ['laɪtn] *color* éclaircir

lighten² ['laɪtn] *load* alléger

lighter ['laɪtər] *for cigarettes* briquet *m*; **light-headed** étourdi; **lighting** éclairage *m*; **lightness** *of room, color* clarté *f*; *in weight* légèreté *f*; **lightning** éclair *m*, foudre *f*; **lightweight** *in boxing* poids *m* léger; **light year** année-lumière *f*

like¹ [laɪk] **1** *prep* comme; *be*

~ *s.o./sth* ressembler à qn/qch; *what is she* ~? comment est-elle?; *it's not* ~ *him* not his character ça ne lui ressemble pas **2** *conj* F (*as*) comme; ~ *I said* comme je l'ai dit

like² [laɪk] *v/t* aimer; *I* ~ *it* ça me plaît (bien); *I* ~ *Susie* j'aime bien Susie; *romantically* Susie me plaît (bien); *I would* ~ ... je voudrais, j'aimerais ...; *I would* ~ *to leave* je voudrais *or* j'aimerais partir; *would you* ~ ...? voulez-vous...?; *would you* ~ *to* ...? as-tu envie de ...?; ~ *to do sth* aimer faire qch; *if you* ~ si vous voulez; **likeable** agréable, plaisant; **likelihood** probabilité *f*; **likely** probable; **likeness** ressemblance *f*; **likewise** de même, aussi; **liking** *for person* affection *f*; *for sth* penchant *m*

limb [lɪm] membre *m*

lime¹ [laɪm] *fruit* citron *m* vert; *tree* limettier *m*

lime² [laɪm] *substance* chaux *f*

limit ['lɪmɪt] **1** *n* limite *f* **2** *v/t* limiter; **limitation** limitation *f*; **limited company** *Br* société *f* à responsabilité limitée

limousine ['lɪməziːn] limousine *f*

limp¹ [lɪmp] *adj* mou

limp² [lɪmp] **1** *n* claudication *f*; *he has a* ~ il boite **2** *v/i* boiter

line¹ [laɪn] *n* ligne *f*; RAIL voie

f; of people file *f; of trees* rangée *f; of poem* vers *m; **stand in ~** faire la queue

line² [laɪn] *v/t with material* recouvrir, garnir; *clothes* doubler

linear ['lɪnɪər] linéaire

linen ['lɪnɪn] *material* lin *m; (sheets etc)* linge *m*

liner ['laɪnər] *ship* paquebot *m* de grande ligne

linesman ['laɪnzmən] SP juge *m* de touche; *tennis* juge *m* de ligne

linger ['lɪŋgər] *of person* s'attarder; *of pain* persister

lingerie ['længərɪ] lingerie *f*

linguist ['lɪŋgwɪst] linguiste *m;* **linguistic** linguistique

lining ['laɪnɪŋ] *of clothes* doublure *f; of brakes, pipes* garniture *f*

link [lɪŋk] **1** *n* lien *m; in chain* maillon *m* **2** *v/t* lier, relier

lion ['laɪən] lion *m*

lip [lɪp] lèvre *f*

liposuction ['lɪpoʊsʌkʃən] liposuccion *f*

'lipread lire sur les lèvres; **lipstick** rouge *m* à lèvres

liqueur [lɪ'kjʊr] liqueur *f*

liquid ['lɪkwɪd] **1** *n* liquide *m* **2** *adj* liquide; **liquidate** liquider; **liquidation** liquidation *f;* **go into ~** entrer en liquidation; **liquidity** FIN liquidité *f;* **liquidize** passer au mixeur; **liquidizer** mixeur *m*

liquor ['lɪkər] alcool *m;* **liquor store** magasin *m* de vins et spiritueux

lisp [lɪsp] **1** *n* zézaiement *m* **2** *v/i* zézayer

list [lɪst] **1** *n* liste *f* **2** *v/t* faire la liste de; *(enumerate)* énumérer

listen ['lɪsn] écouter

◆ **listen to** écouter

listener ['lɪsnər] *to radio* auditeur(-trice) *m(f)*

listless ['lɪstlɪs] amorphe

liter ['liːtər] litre *m*

literal ['lɪtərəl] littéral; **literally** littéralement

literary ['lɪtərerɪ] littéraire; **literature** littérature *f; about a product* documentation *f*

litre ['liːtər] *Br* → **liter**

litter ['lɪtər] détritus *mpl*, ordures *fpl; of animal* portée *f*

little ['lɪtl] **1** *adj* petit **2** *n* peu *m;* **a ~ wine** un peu de vin **3** *adv* peu; **a ~ bigger** un peu plus gros

live¹ [lɪv] *v/i* vivre

live² [laɪv] *adj broadcast* en direct; *bomb* non désamorcé

◆ **live up to** être à la hauteur de

livelihood ['laɪvlɪhʊd] gagne-pain *m inv;* **liveliness** vivacité *f;* **lively** *person, city* plein de vie; *party* animé; *music* entraînant

liver ['lɪvər] foie *m*

livestock ['laɪvstɑːk] bétail *m*

livid ['lɪvɪd] *(angry)* furieux

living ['lɪvɪŋ] **1** *adj* vivant **2** *n* vie *f;* **living room** salle *f* de séjour

lizard ['lɪzərd] lézard *m*

load [loud] **1** *n* charge *f* **2** *v/t* charger

loaf [louf]: *a ~ of bread* un pain

♦ **loaf around** F traîner

loafer ['loufər] *shoe* mocassin *m*

loan [loun] **1** *n* prêt *m* **2** *v/t*: *~ s.o. sth* prêter qch à qn

loathe [louð] détester; **loathing** dégoût *m*

lobby ['lɑːbɪ] *in hotel* hall *m*; *in theater* vestibule *m*; POL lobby *m*

lobe [loub] *of ear* lobe *m*

lobster ['lɑːbstər] homard *m*

local ['loukl] **1** *adj* local; **local call** TELEC appel *m* local; **local elections** élections *fpl* locales; **local government** autorités *f* locales; **locality** endroit *m*; **localize** localiser; **locally** *live, work* dans le quartier, dans la région; **local time** heure *f* locale

locate [lou'keɪt] *new factory etc* établir; (*identify position of*) localiser; *be ~d* se trouver; **location** emplacement *m*; (*identifying position of*) localisation *f*; *on ~ movie* en extérieur

lock[1] [lɑːk] *n of hair* mèche *f*

lock[2] [lɑːk] **1** *n on door* serrure *f* **2** *v/t door* fermer à clef

♦ **lock up** *in prison* mettre sous les verrous

locker ['lɑːkər] casier *m*; **locker room** vestiaire *m*

locust ['loukəst] locuste *f*, sauterelle *f*

lodge [lɑːdʒ] **1** *v/t complaint* déposer **2** *v/i of bullet* se loger

lofty ['lɑːftɪ] *heights* haut; *ideals* élevé

log [lɑːg] bûche *f*; (*written record*) journal *m* de bord

♦ **log in** se connecter (*to* à)

♦ **log off** se déconnecter

♦ **log on** se connecter (*to* à)

♦ **log out** se déconnecter

log 'cabin cabane *f* en rondins

logic ['lɑːdʒɪk] logique *f*; **logical** logique; **logically** logiquement

logistics [lə'dʒɪstɪks] logistique *f*

logo ['lougou] logo *m*, sigle *m*

loiter ['lɔɪtər] traîner

lollipop ['lɑːlɪpɑːp] sucette *f*

London ['lʌndən] Londres

loneliness ['lounlɪnɪs] *of person* solitude *f*; *of place* isolement *m*; **lonely** *person* seul, solitaire; *place* isolé; **loner** solitaire *m/f*

long[1] [lɑːŋ] **1** *adj* long; *it's a ~ way* c'est loin **2** *adv* longtemps; *how ~ will it take?* combien de temps cela va-t-il prendre?; *he no ~er works here* il ne travaille plus ici; *so ~ as* (*provided*) pourvu que; *so ~!* à bientôt!

long[2] [lɑːŋ] *v/i*: *~ for sth* avoir très envie de qch; *be ~ing to*

do sth avoir très envie de faire qch

long-'distance *phonecall* longue distance; *race* de fond; *flight* long-courrier; **longevity** longévité *f*; **longing** désir *m*, envie *f*; **longitude** longitude *f*; **long jump** saut *m* en longueur; **long-range missile** à longue portée; *forecast* à long terme; **long-sleeved** à manches longues; **long-standing** de longue date; **long-term** à long terme; *unemployment* de longue durée

loo [lu:] *Br* F toilettes *fpl*

look [lʊk] **1** *n* (*appearance*) air *m*; (*glance*) coup *m* d'œil, regard *m*; **~s** (*beauty*) beauté *f* **2** *v/i* regarder; (*search*) chercher, regarder; (*seem*) avoir l'air

◆ **look after** s'occuper de

◆ **look ahead** *fig* regarder en avant

◆ **look around** jeter un coup d'œil

◆ **look at** regarder; (*examine*) examiner; (*consider*) envisager

◆ **look back** regarder derrière soi

◆ **look down on** mépriser

◆ **look for** chercher

◆ **look into** (*investigate*) examiner

◆ **look onto** *garden etc* donner sur

◆ **look out** *of window etc* regarder dehors; (*pay attention*) faire attention

◆ **look over** *house, translation* examiner

◆ **look through** *magazine, notes* parcourir, feuilleter

◆ **look up 1** *v/i from paper etc* lever les yeux; (*improve*) s'améliorer **2** *v/t word, phone number* chercher; (*visit*) passer voir

◆ **look up to** (*respect*) respecter

'lookout *person* sentinelle *f*; **be on the ~ for** être à l'affût de

loop [lu:p] boucle *f*; **loophole** *in law* lacune *f*

loose [lu:s] *knot* lâche; *connection, screw* desserré; *clothes* ample; *morals* relâché; *wording* vague; **~ change** petite monnaie *f*; **loosely** *worded* de manière approximative; **loosen** desserrer

loot [lu:t] **1** *n* butin *m* **2** *v/i* se livrer au pillage; **looter** pilleur(-euse) *m(f)*

lop-sided [lɒp'saɪdɪd] déséquilibré, disproportionné

Lord [lɔ:rd] (*god*) Seigneur *m*

lorry ['lɒrɪ] *Br* camion *m*

lose [lu:z] **1** *v/t* perdre **2** *v/i* SP perdre; *of clock* retarder; **loser** perdant(-e) *m(f)*

loss [lɒs] perte *f*

lost [lɒst] perdu; **lost-and-found**, *Br* **lost property** (**office**) (bureau *m* des) objets *mpl* trouvés

lot [lɑːt]: **a ~ (of)**, **~s (of)** beaucoup (of)

lotion ['ləʊʃn] lotion f

lottery ['lɑːtərɪ] loterie f

loud [laʊd] *music, voice* fort; *noise* grand; *color* criard; **loudspeaker** haut-parleur m

louse [laʊs] pou m; **lousy** F minable F , mauvais

lout [laʊt] rustre m

lovable ['lʌvəbl] sympathique, adorable; **love 1** n amour m; *in tennis* zéro m; **fall in ~** tomber amoureux **(with** de); **make ~** faire l'amour **(to** avec) **2** v/t aimer; *wine, music* adorer; **love affair** aventure f; **lovely** beau; *house, wife* ravissant; *character* charmant; *meal* délicieux; **lover** *man* amant m; *woman* maîtresse f; *person in love* amoureux(-euse) m(f); **loving** affectueux; **lovingly** avec amour

low [ləʊ] **1** *adj* bas; *quality* mauvais **2** n *in weather* dépression f; *in statistics* niveau m bas; **lowbrow** peu intellectuel; **low-calorie** hypocalorique; **low-cut** *dress* décolleté; **lower** baisser; **to the ground** faire descendre; **low-fat** allégé; **lowkey** discret, mesuré

loyal ['lɔɪəl] fidèle, loyal; **loyally** fidèlement; **loyalty** loyauté f

lozenge ['lɑːzɪndʒ] *shape* losange m; *tablet* pastille f

Ltd (= **limited**) *company* à responsabilité limitée

lubricant ['luːbrɪkənt] lubrifiant m; **lubricate** lubrifier; **lubrication** lubrification f

lucid ['luːsɪd] *(clear)* clair; *(sane)* lucide

luck [lʌk] chance f; **good ~!** bonne chance!; **luckily** heureusement; **lucky** *person* chanceux; *number* porte-bonheur *inv*; *coincidence* heureux; **you were ~** tu as eu de la chance

lucrative ['luːkrətɪv] lucratif

ludicrous ['luːdɪkrəs] ridicule

lug [lʌg] F traîner

luggage ['lʌgɪdʒ] bagages *mpl*

lukewarm ['luːkwɔːrm] *also fig* tiède

lull [lʌl] *in storm, fighting* accalmie f; *in conversation* pause f

lumber ['lʌmbər] *(timber)* bois m de construction

luminous ['luːmɪnəs] lumineux

lump [lʌmp] *of sugar* morceau m; *(swelling)* grosseur f; **lump sum** forfait m; **lumpy** *liquid, sauce* grumeleux; *mattress* défoncé

lunacy ['luːnəsɪ] folie f

lunar ['luːnər] lunaire

lunatic ['luːnətɪk] fou m, folle f

lunch [lʌntʃ] déjeuner m; **have ~** déjeuner; **lunch box** panier-repas m; **lunch**

break pause-déjeuner f;
lunchtime heure f du déjeuner, midi m
lung [lʌŋ] poumon m
lurch [lɜːrtʃ] *of person* tituber;
of ship tanguer
lure [lʊr] **1** n appât m **2** v/t attirer
lurid ['lʊrɪd] *color* cru; *details* choquant

lurk [lɜːrk] *of person* se cacher
lush [lʌʃ] *vegetation* luxuriant
lust [lʌst] désir m
luxurious [lʌgˈʒʊriəs]
luxueux; **luxuriously** luxueusement; **luxury 1** n luxe
m **2** adj de luxe
lynch [lɪntʃ] lyncher
lyrics ['lɪrɪks] paroles fpl

M

ma'am [mæm] madame
machine [məˈʃiːn] machine f;
machine gun mitrailleuse f;
machinery machines fpl
machismo [məˈkɪzmoʊ] machisme m
macho ['mætʃoʊ] macho inv;
~ type macho m
macro ['mækroʊ] COMPUT macro f
mad [mæd] (*insane*) fou; F (*angry*) furieux; **madden** (*infuriate*) exaspérer; **maddening** exaspérant; **madhouse** fig maison f de fous; **madman** fou m; **madness** folie f
Madonna [məˈdɑːnə] Madone f
Mafia ['mɑːfɪə]: **the ~** la Mafia
magazine [mægəˈziːn] *printed* magazine m
Magi ['meɪdʒaɪ] REL: **the ~** les Rois mpl mages
magic ['mædʒɪk] **1** adj magique **2** n magie f; **magical** magique; **magician** *performer*

prestidigitateur(-trice) m(f)
magnanimous [mægˈnænɪməs] magnanime
magnet ['mægnɪt] aimant m;
magnetic *also fig* magnétique; **magnetism** *also fig* magnétisme m
magnificence [mægˈnɪfɪsəns] magnificence f; **magnificent** magnifique
magnify ['mægnɪfaɪ] grossir;
difficulties exagérer; **magnifying glass** loupe f
magnitude ['mægnɪtuːd] ampleur f
maid [meɪd] *servant* domestique f; *in hotel* femme f de chambre
maiden name ['meɪdn] nom m de jeune fille
mail [meɪl] **1** n courrier m,
poste f **2** v/t *letter* poster;
mailbox boîte f aux lettres;
mailing list fichier m d'adresses; **mailman** facteur m; **mailshot** mailing m, pu-

blipostage *m*

maim [meɪm] estropier, mutiler

main [meɪn] principal; **main course** plat *m* principal; **mainframe** ordinateur *m* central; **mainly** principalement; **main road** route *f* principale; **main street** rue *f* principale

maintain [meɪn'teɪn] *peace, law and order* maintenir; *speed* soutenir; *relationship, machine, building* entretenir; *innocence, guilt* affirmer; **maintenance** *of machine, building* entretien *m*; *Br money* pension *f* alimentaire; *of law and order* maintien *m*

majestic [məˈdʒestɪk] majestueux

major [ˈmeɪdʒər] **1** *adj* (*significant*) important, majeur **2** *n* MIL commandant *m*

◆ **major in** se spécialiser en

majority [məˈdʒɑːrətɪ] *also* POL majorité *f*

make [meɪk] **1** *n* (*brand*) marque *f* **2** *v/t* faire; (*manufacture*) fabriquer; (*earn*) gagner; *decision* prendre; **3 and 3 ~ 6** 3 et 3 font 6; **~ it** (*catch bus, train*) arriver à temps; (*come*) venir; (*succeed*) réussir; (*survive*) s'en sortir; **what time do you ~ it?** quelle heure as-tu?; **~ believe** prétendre; **~ do with** se contenter de, faire avec;

what do you ~ of it? qu'en dis-tu?; **~ s.o. do sth** (*force to*) forcer qn à faire qch; (*cause to*) faire faire qch à qn; **~ s.o. happy/angry** rendre qn heureux/furieux

◆ **make out** *list, check* faire; (*see*) distinguer; (*imply*) prétendre

◆ **make up 1** *v/i of woman, actor* se maquiller; *after quarrel* se réconcilier **2** *v/t story* inventer; *face* maquiller; (*constitute*) constituer

◆ **make up for** compenser

'make-believe: **it's just ~** c'est juste pour faire semblant

maker [ˈmeɪkər] (*manufacturer*) fabricant *m*; **makeshift** de fortune; **make-up** (*cosmetics*) maquillage *m*

maladjusted [mælə'dʒʌstɪd] inadapté

male [meɪl] **1** *adj* masculin; *animal* mâle **2** *n* (*man*) homme *m*; *animal, bird* mâle *m*; **male chauvinism** machisme *m*; **male chauvinist pig** macho *m*

malevolent [məˈlevələnt] malveillant

malfunction [mæl'fʌŋkʃn] **1** *n* mauvais fonctionnement *m*, défaillance *f* **2** *v/i* mal fonctionner

malice [ˈmælɪs] méchanceté *f*, malveillance *f*; **malicious** [məˈlɪʃəs] méchant, malveillant

malignant [məˈlɪgnənt] *tumor* malin

mall [mɔːl] (*shopping ~*) centre *m* commercial

malnutrition [mælnuːˈtrɪʃn] malnutrition *f*

maltreat [mælˈtriːt] maltraiter; **maltreatment** mauvais traitement *m*

mammal [ˈmæml] mammifère *m*

man [mæn] **1** *n* (*pl* **men** [men]) homme *m*; (*humanity*) l'homme *m*; (*in checkers*) pion *m* **2** *v/t* telephones être de permanence à; *front desk* être de service à

manage [ˈmænɪdʒ] **1** *v/t* *business* diriger; *money* gérer; *bags* porter; *~* **to ...** réussir à ... **2** *v/i* (*cope*) se débrouiller; **manageable** gérable; *vehicle* maniable; *task* faisable; **management** (*managing*) gestion *f*, direction *f*; (*managers*) direction *f*; **management consultant** conseiller(-ère) *m(f)* en gestion; **manager** directeur(-trice) *m(f)*; *of store, restaurant, hotel* gérant(e) *m(f)*; *of department* responsable *m/f*; *of singer, band, team* manageur(-euse) *m(f)*; **managerial** de directeur, de gestionnaire; **managing director** directeur(-trice) *m(f)* général(e)

mandate [ˈmændeɪt] mandat *m*; **mandatory** obligatoire

maneuver [məˈnuːvər] **1** *n* manœuvre *f* **2** *v/t* manœuvrer

mangle [ˈmæŋgl] (*crush*) broyer

manhandle [ˈmænhændl] *person* malmener; *object* déplacer manuellement

manhood [ˈmænhʊd] (*maturity*) âge *m* d'homme; (*virility*) virilité *f*; **manhunt** chasse *f* à l'homme

mania [ˈmeɪnɪə] (*craze*) manie *f*; **maniac** F fou *m*, folle *f*

manicure [ˈmænɪkjʊr] manucure *f*

manifest [ˈmænɪfest] **1** *adj* manifeste **2** *v/t* manifester

manipulate [məˈnɪpjʊleɪt] manipuler; **manipulation** manipulation *f*; **manipulative** manipulateur

mankind humanité *f*; **manly** viril; **man-made** synthétique

manner [ˈmænər] *of doing sth* manière *f*, façon *f*; (*attitude*) comportement *m*; **manners** manières *fpl*

manoeuvre [məˈnuːvər] *Br* → **maneuver**

'**manpower** main-d'œuvre *f*

manual [ˈmænjuəl] **1** *adj* manuel **2** *n* manuel *m*; **manually** manuellement

manufacture [mænjuˈfæktʃər] **1** *n* fabrication *f* **2** *v/t* *equipment* fabriquer; **manufacturer** fabricant *m*; **manufacturing** *industry* industrie *f*

manure [məˈnʊr] fumier *m*

manuscript [ˈmænjuskrɪpt] manuscrit *m*

many ['menɪ] **1** *adj* beaucoup de; **~ times** bien des fois; **too ~ problems** trop de problèmes; **as ~ as possible** autant que possible **2** *pron* beaucoup; **a great ~, a good ~** un bon nombre; **how ~ do you need?** combien en veux-tu?

map [mæp] carte *f*; *of town* plan *m*

maple ['meɪpl] érable *m*

mar [mɑːr] gâcher

marathon ['mærəθən] *race* marathon *m*

marble ['mɑːrbl] *material* marbre *m*

March [mɑːrtʃ] mars *m*

march [mɑːrtʃ] **1** *n also (demonstration)* marche *f* **2** *v/i* marcher au pas; *in protest* défiler; **marcher** manifestant(e) *m(f)*

Mardi Gras ['mɑːrdɪgrɑː] mardi *m* gras

margin ['mɑːrdʒɪn] *of page*, COM marge *f*; **marginal** *(slight)* léger; **marginally** *(slightly)* légèrement

marihuana, marijuana [mærɪ'hwɑːnə] marijuana *f*

marina [mə'riːnə] port *m* de plaisance

marine [mə'riːn] **1** *adj* marin **2** *n* MIL marine *m*

marital ['mærɪtl] conjugal; **marital status** situation *f* de famille

maritime ['mærɪtaɪm] maritime

mark [mɑːrk] **1** *n* marque *f*; *(stain)* tache *f*; *(sign, token)* signe *m*; *(trace)* trace *f*; *Br* EDU note *f* **2** *v/t* marquer; *(stain)* tacher; *Br* EDU noter **3** *v/i of fabric* se tacher; **marked** *(definite)* marqué; **marker** *(highlighter)* marqueur *m*

market ['mɑːrkɪt] **1** *n* marché *m* **2** *v/t* commercialiser; **marketable** commercialisable; **market economy** économie *f* de marché; **marketing** marketing *m*; **market leader** *product* produit *m* vedette; *company* leader *m* du marché; **market place** *in town* place *f* du marché; *for commodities* marché *m*; **market research** étude *f* de marché; **market share** part *f* du marché

mark-up ['mɑːrkʌp] majoration *f*

marriage ['mærɪdʒ] mariage *m*; **marriage certificate** acte *m* de mariage; **married** marié; *be ~ to* être marié à; **married life** vie *f* conjugale; **marry** épouser, se marier avec; *of priest* marier; **get married** se marier

marsh [mɑːrʃ] *Br* marais *m*

marshal ['mɑːrʃl] *in police* chef *m* de la police; *in security service* membre *m* du service d'ordre

martial 'law loi *f* martiale

martyr ['mɑːrtər] *also fig* mar-

tyr(e) *m(f)*
marvel ['mɑːrvl] merveille *f*;
marvelous, *Br* **marvellous** merveilleux

Marxism ['mɑːrksɪzm]
marxisme *m*; **Marxist 1** *adj*
marxiste **2** *n* marxiste *m/f*

mascara [mæ'skærə] mascara *m*

mascot ['mæskət] mascotte *f*

masculine ['mæskjulɪn] *also*
GRAM masculin; **masculinity** masculinité *f*

mash [mæʃ] *n* réduire en purée

mask [mæsk] **1** *n* masque *m* **2** *v/t feelings* masquer

masochism ['mæsəkɪzm]
masochisme *m*; **masochist** masochiste *m/f*

mass[1] [mæs] **1** *n* (*great amount*) masse *f*; **~es of** F des tas de F **2** *v/i* se masser

mass[2] [mæs] *n* REL messe *f*

massacre ['mæsəkər] **1** *n also fig* F massacre *m* **2** *v/t also fig* F massacrer

massage ['mæsɑːʒ] **1** *n* massage *m* **2** *v/t* masser; *figures* manipuler

massive ['mæsɪv] énorme;
heart attack grave

mass 'media médias *mpl*;
mass-produce fabriquer en série; **mass production** fabrication *f* en série

mast [mæst] *of ship* mât *m*;
for radio signal pylône *m*

master ['mæstər] **1** *n of dog* maître *m*; *of ship* capitaine *m* **2** *v/t* maîtriser; **master**

bedroom chambre *f* principale; **master key** passe-partout *m inv*; **masterly** magistral; **mastermind 1** *n* cerveau *m* **2** *v/t* organiser; **masterpiece** chef-d'œuvre *m*; **master's (degree)** maîtrise *f*; **mastery** maîtrise *f*

mat [mæt] *for floor* tapis *m*;
for table napperon *m*

match[1] [mætʃ] *n for cigarette* allumette *f*

match[2] [mætʃ] **1** *n* (*competition*) match *m*, partie *f* **2** *v/t* (*be the same as*) être assorti à; (*equal*) égaler **3** *v/i of colors, patterns* aller ensemble;
matching assorti; **match stick** allumette *f*

mate [meɪt] *n of animal* mâle *m*, femelle *f*; NAUT second *m* **2** *v/i* s'accoupler

material [mə'tɪrɪəl] **1** *n* (*fabric*) tissu *m*; (*substance*) matériau *m*, matière *f* **2** *adj* matériel; **materialism** matérialisme *m*; **materialist** matérialiste *m/f*; **materialistic** matérialiste; **materialize** (*appear*) apparaître; (*happen*) se concrétiser

maternal [mə'tɜːrnl] maternel; **maternity** maternité *f*;
maternity leave congé *m* de maternité

math [mæθ] maths *fpl*; **mathematical** mathématique *f*;
mathematician mathématicien(ne) *m(f)*; **maths** *Br* →
math

matinée ['mætɪneɪ] matinée f

matriarch ['meɪtrɪɑːrk] femme f chef de famille

matrimony ['mætrəmoʊnɪ] mariage m

matt [mæt] mat

matter ['mætər] **1** n (affair) affaire f, question f; PHYS matière f; **what's the ~?** qu'est-ce qu'il y a? **2** v/i importer; **it doesn't ~** cela ne fait rien; **matter-of-fact** impassible

mattress ['mætrɪs] matelas m

mature [mə'tjʊr] **1** adj mûr **2** v/i of person mûrir; of insurance policy arriver à échéance; **maturity** maturité f

maximize ['mæksɪmaɪz] maximiser; **maximum 1** adj maximal, maximum **2** n maximum m

May [meɪ] mai m

may [meɪ] ◇ possibility: **it ~ rain** il va peut-être pleuvoir; **it ~ not happen** cela n'arrivera peut-être pas
◇ permission: pouvoir; **~ I help?** puis-je aider?

maybe ['meɪbɪ] peut-être

mayo, mayonnaise ['meɪoʊ, meɪə'neɪz] mayonnaise f

mayor ['meɪər] maire m

maze [meɪz] labyrinthe m

MB (= **megabyte**) Mo (= mégaoctet)

MBA [embɪ'eɪ] (= **master of business administration**) MBA m

MD [em'diː] (= **Doctor of Med-**

icine) docteur m en médecine; (= **managing director**) DG m (= directeur général)

me [miː] me; before vowel m'; after prep moi; **he knows ~** il me connaît; **she gave ~ a dollar** elle m'a donné un dollar; **it's for ~** c'est pour moi; **it's ~** c'est moi

meadow ['medoʊ] pré m

meager, Br **meagre** ['miːgər] maigre

meal [miːl] repas m; **enjoy your ~!** bon appétit!

mean¹ [miːn] adj with money avare; (nasty) mesquin

mean² [miːn] v/t (signify) signifier, vouloir dire; **be ~t for** être destiné à; of remark être adressé à; meaning of word sens m; meaningful (comprehensible) compréhensible; (constructive) significatif; glance éloquent; meaningless sentence etc dénué de sens; gesture insignifiant

means [miːnz] financial moyens mpl; (way) moyen m; **by all ~** (certainly) bien sûr; **by ~ of** au moyen de

meantime ['miːntaɪm] entre-temps

measles ['miːzlz] rougeole f

measure ['meʒər] **1** n (step) mesure f **2** v/t & v/i mesurer ◆ measure up to être à la hauteur de

measurement ['meʒərmənt] action mesure f; (dimension)

dimension *f*; **measuring tape** mètre *m* ruban

meat [miːt] viande *f*; **meatball** boulette *f* de viande

mechanic [mɪˈkænɪk] mécanicien(ne) *m(f)*; **mechanical** *device etc also* machinal; **mechanical engineer** ingénieur *m* mécanicien; **mechanically** mécaniquement; *do sth* machinalement; **mechanism** mécanisme *m*; **mechanize** mécaniser

medal [ˈmedl] médaille *f*; **medalist**, *Br* **medallist** médaillé *m*

meddle [ˈmedl] se mêler (**in** de)

media [ˈmiːdɪə]: **the ~** les médias *mpl*; **media coverage** couverture *f* médiatique

median strip [miːdɪənˈstrɪp] terre-plein *m* central

'media studies études *fpl* de communication

mediate [ˈmiːdɪeɪt] arbitrer; **mediation** médiation *f*; **mediator** médiateur(-trice) *m(f)*

medical [ˈmedɪkl] **1** *adj* médical **2** *n* visite *f* médicale; **medicated** pharmaceutique, traitant; **medication** médicaments *mpl*; **medicinal** médicinal

medicine *science* médecine *f*; (*medication*) médicament *m*

medieval [medɪˈiːvl] médiéval

mediocre [miːdɪˈoʊkər] médiocre; **mediocrity** *of work etc* médiocrité *f*; *person* médiocre *m/f*

meditate [ˈmedɪteɪt] méditer; **meditation** méditation *f*

Mediterranean [medɪtəˈreɪnɪən] **1** *adj* méditerranéen **2** *n*: **the ~** la Méditerranée

medium [ˈmiːdɪəm] **1** *adj* (*average*) moyen; *steak* à point **2** *n* *in size* taille *f* moyenne; (*vehicle*) moyen *m*; (*spiritualist*) médium *m*

medley [ˈmedlɪ] (*assortment*) mélange *m*

meet [miːt] **1** *v/t* rencontrer; (*be introduced to*) faire la connaissance de; (*collect*) (aller/venir) chercher; *in competition* affronter; *of eyes* croiser; (*satisfy*) satisfaire **2** *v/i* se rencontrer; *by appointment* se retrouver; *of committee etc* se réunir **3** *n* SP rencontre *f*; **meeting** *by accident* rencontre *f*; *in business, of committee* réunion *f*; **he's in a ~** il est en réunion

megabyte [ˈmeɡəbaɪt] COMPUT méga-octet *m*

mellow [ˈmeloʊ] **1** *adj* doux **2** *v/i of person* s'adoucir

melodious [mɪˈloʊdɪəs] mélodieux

melodramatic [melədrəˈmætɪk] mélodramatique

melody [ˈmelədɪ] mélodie *f*

melon [ˈmelən] melon *m*

melt [melt] **1** *v/i* fondre **2** *v/t*

faire fondre; **melting pot** *fig* creuset *m*

member ['membər] membre *m*; **Member of Congress** membre *m* du Congrès; **membership** adhésion *f*; *number of members* membres *mpl*

membrane ['membreɪn] membrane *f*

memento [me'mentou] souvenir *m*

memo ['memou] note *f* (de service)

memoirs ['memwɑːrz] mémoires *fpl*

memorable ['memərəbl] mémorable

memorial [mɪ'mɔːrɪəl] **1** *adj* commémoratif **2** *n* mémorial *m*; **Memorial Day** *jour commémoration des soldats américains morts à la guerre*

memorize ['meməraɪz] apprendre par cœur; **memory** mémoire *f*; *sth remembered* souvenir *m*

men [men] *pl* → **man**

menace ['menɪs] **1** *n* menace *f*; *person* danger *m* **2** *v/t* menacer; **menacing** menaçant

mend [mend] réparer; *clothes* raccommoder

menial ['miːnɪəl] subalterne

menopause ['menoupɔːz] ménopause *f*

'men's room toilettes *fpl* pour hommes

menstruate ['menstrueɪt] avoir ses règles

mental ['mentl] mental; *abili-ty, powers* intellectuel; *health, suffering* moral; F (*crazy*) malade F; **mental hospital** hôpital *m* psychiatrique; **mental illness** maladie *f* mentale; **mentality** mentalité *f*; **mentally** (*inwardly*) intérieurement; *calculate etc* mentalement

mention ['menʃn] **1** *n* mention *f* **2** *v/t* mentionner; **don't ~ it** (*you're welcome*) il n'y a pas de quoi!

mentor ['mentɔːr] mentor *m*

menu ['menjuː] *also* COMPUT menu *m*

mercenary ['mɜːrsɪnerɪ] **1** *adj* intéressé **2** *n* MIL mercenaire *m*

merchandise ['mɜːrtʃəndaɪz] marchandises *fpl*

merchant ['mɜːrtʃənt] négociant *m*, commerçant *m*

merciful ['mɜːrsɪfl] clément; *God* miséricordieux; **mercifully** (*thankfully*) heureusement; **merciless** impitoyable; **mercy** clémence *f*, pitié *f*

mere [mɪr] simple; **merely** simplement, seulement

merge [mɜːrdʒ] *of two lines etc* se rejoindre; *of companies* fusionner; **merger** COM fusion *f*

merit ['merɪt] **1** *n* mérite *m* **2** *v/t* mériter

mesh [meʃ] *of net* maille(s) *f(pl)*; *of grid* grillage *m*

might

mess [mes] (*untidiness*) désordre *m*, pagaille *f*; (*trouble*) gâchis *m*

message ['mesɪdʒ] *also of movie etc* message *m*

messenger ['mesɪndʒər] (*courier*) messager *m*

messy ['mesɪ] *room* en désordre; *person* désordonné; *job* salissant; *divorce* pénible

metabolism [mə'tæbəlɪzm] métabolisme *m*

metal ['metl] **1** *adj* en métal **2** *n* métal *m*; **metallic** métallique; *paint* métallisé

metaphor ['metəfər] métaphore *f*

meteor ['miːtɪɔːr] météore *m*; **meteoric** *fig* fulgurant; **meteorite** météorite *m* or *f*

meteorological [miːtɪərə-'lɑːdʒɪkl] météorologique; **meteorologist** météorologiste *m/f*; **meteorology** météorologie *f*

meter¹ ['miːtər] *for gas, electricity* compteur *m*; (*parking* ~) parcmètre *m*

meter² ['miːtər] *unit of length* mètre *m*

method ['meθəd] méthode *f*; **methodical** méthodique

meticulous [mə'tɪkjuləs] méticuleux

metre ['miːtə(r)] *Br* → **meter²**

metropolis [mə'trɑːpəlɪs] métropole *f*; **metropolitan** citadin; *area* urbain

mew [mjuː] → **miaow**

Mexican ['meksɪkən] **1** *adj*

mexicain **2** *n* Mexicain(e) *m(f)*; **Mexico** Mexique *m*

miaow [mɪau] **1** *n* miaou *m* **2** *v/i* miauler

mice [maɪs] *pl* → **mouse**

microchip puce *f*; **microclimate** microclimat *m*; **microcosm** microcosme *m*; **microorganism** micro-organisme *m*; **microphone** microphone *m*; **microprocessor** microprocesseur *m*; **microscope** microscope *m*; **microscopic** microscopique; **microwave oven** micro-ondes *m inv*

midday ['mɪddeɪ] midi *m*

middle ['mɪdl] **1** *adj* du milieu **2** *n* milieu *m*; **be in the** ~ **of doing sth** être en train de faire qch; **middle-aged** entre deux âges; **middle-class** bourgeois; **middle class(es)** classe(s) moyenne(s) *f(pl)*; **Middle East** Moyen-Orient *m*; **middleman** intermédiaire *m*; **middle name** deuxième prénom *m*; **middleweight** *boxer* poids moyen *m*

midfielder [mɪd'fiːldər] *in soccer* milieu *m* de terrain

midget ['mɪdʒɪt] miniature

midnight ['mɪdnaɪt] minuit *m*; **midsummer** milieu *m* de l'été; **midweek** en milieu de semaine; **Midwest** Middle West *m*; **midwife** sage-femme *f*; **midwinter** milieu *m* de l'hiver

might¹ [maɪt] *v/aux*: **I** ~ **be late** je serai peut-être en retard; **you** ~ **have told me!**

vous auriez pu m'avertir!

might² [maɪt] *n* (*power*) puissance *f*

mighty ['maɪtɪ] **1** *adj* puissant **2** *adv* F (*extremely*) vachement F, très

migraine ['miːgreɪn] migraine *f*

migrant worker ['maɪgrənt] travailleur *m* itinérant; **migrate** migrer; **migration** migration *f*

mike [maɪk] F micro *m*

mild [maɪld] doux; *taste* léger; **mildly** doucement; *spicy* légèrement; **mildness** douceur *f*; *of taste* légèreté *f*

mile [maɪl] mile *m*; **milestone** *fig* événement *m* marquant, jalon *m*

militant ['mɪlɪtənt] **1** *adj* militant **2** *n* militant(e) *m*(*f*)

military ['mɪlɪtrɪ] **1** *adj* militaire **2** *n*: **the** ~ l'armée *f*

militia [mɪ'lɪʃə] milice *f*

milk [mɪlk] **1** *n* lait *m* **2** *v/t* traire; **milk chocolate** chocolat *m* au lait; **milkshake** milk-shake *m*

mill [mɪl] *for grain* moulin *m*; *for textiles* usine *f*

millennium [mɪ'lenɪəm] millénaire *m*

milligram ['mɪligræm] milligramme *m*

millimeter, *Br* **millimetre** ['mɪlimiːtər] millimètre *m*

million ['mɪljən] million *m*

millionaire [mɪljə'ner] millionnaire *m/f*

mime [maɪm] mimer

mimic ['mɪmɪk] **1** *n* imitateur(-trice) *m*(*f*) **2** *v/t* imiter

mince [mɪns] hacher

mind [maɪnd] **1** *n* esprit *m*; **bear** *or* **keep sth in** ~ ne pas oublier qch; **change one's** ~ changer d'avis; **make up one's** ~ se décider; **have sth on one's** ~ être préoccupé par qch; **keep one's** ~ **on sth** se concentrer sur qch **2** *v/t* (*look after*) surveiller; (*heed*) faire attention à; **I don't** ~ **what he thinks** il peut penser ce qu'il veut, cela m'est égal; **do you** ~ **if I smoke?** cela ne vous dérange pas si je fume?; ~ **the step!** attention à la marche! **3** *v/i*: ~*I* (*be careful*) fais attention!; (*never mind*) peu importe!; **I don't** ~ cela m'est égal; **mind-boggling** ahurissant; **mindless** *violence* gratuit

mine¹ [maɪn] *pron* le mien *m*, la mienne *f*; *pl* les miens *m*, les miennes; **it's** ~ c'est à moi

mine² [maɪn] *n for coal etc* mine *f*

mine³ [maɪn] **1** *n explosive* mine *f* **2** *v/t* miner; **minefield** MIL champ *m* de mines; *fig* poudrière *f*; **miner** mineur *m*

mineral ['mɪnərəl] minéral *m*; **mineral water** eau *f* minérale

'minesweeper NAUT dragueur *m* de mines

mingle ['mɪŋgl] *of sounds* se

miserly

mélanger; *at party* se mêler (aux gens)

mini ['mɪnɪ] *skirt* minijupe *f*

miniature ['mɪnɪtʃər] miniature

minimal ['mɪnɪməl] minime; **minimalism** minimalisme *m*; **minimize** réduire au minimum; (*downplay*) minimiser; **minimum 1** *adj* minimal, minimum **2** *n* minimum *m*

mining ['maɪnɪŋ] exploitation *f* minière

'**miniskirt** minijupe *f*

minister ['mɪnɪstər] POL, REL ministre *m*; **ministerial** ministériel

mink [mɪŋk] vison *m*

minor ['maɪnər] **1** *adj* mineur; *pain* léger **2** *n* LAW mineur(e) *m(f)*; **minority** minorité *f*

mint [mɪnt] *herb* menthe *f*; *chocolate* chocolat *m* à la menthe; *hard candy* bonbon *m* à la menthe

minus ['maɪnəs] **1** *n* (~ *sign*) moins *m* **2** *prep* moins

minuscule ['mɪnəskjuːl] minuscule

minute¹ ['mɪnɪt] *n of time* minute *f*

minute² [maɪ'nuːt] *adj* (*tiny*) minuscule; (*detailed*) minutieux

'**minute hand** ['mɪnɪt] grande aiguille *f*

minutely [maɪ'nuːtlɪ] (*in detail*) minutieusement; (*very slightly*) très légèrement

minutes ['mɪnɪts] *of meeting* procès-verbal *m*

miracle ['mɪrəkl] miracle *m*; **miraculous** miraculeux; **miraculously** par miracle

mirror ['mɪrər] **1** *n* miroir *m*; MOT rétroviseur *m* **2** *v/t* refléter

misanthropist [mɪ'zænθrəpɪst] misanthrope *m/f*

misbehave [mɪsbə'heɪv] se conduire mal

misbehavior, *Br* **misbehaviour** mauvaise conduite *f*

miscalculate [mɪs'kælkjuleɪt] mal calculer; **miscalculation** erreur *f* de calcul; *fig* mauvais calcul *m*

miscarriage ['mɪskærɪdʒ] MED fausse couche *f*

miscellaneous [mɪsə'leɪnɪəs] divers; *collection* varié

mischief ['mɪstʃɪf] (*naughtiness*) bêtises *fpl*; **mischievous** (*naughty*) espiègle; (*malicious*) malveillant

misconception [mɪskən'sepʃn] idée *f* fausse

misconduct [mɪs'kɑːndʌkt] mauvaise conduite *f*

misconstrue [mɪskən'struː] mal interpréter

misdemeanor, *Br* **misdemeanour** [mɪsdə'miːnər] délit *m*

miser ['maɪzər] avare *m/f*

miserable ['mɪzrəbl] (*unhappy*) malheureux; *weather, performance* épouvantable

miserly ['maɪzrlɪ] avare; *sum* dérisoire

misery ['mɪzərɪ] (*unhappiness*) tristesse *f*; (*wretchedness*) misère *f*

misfire [mɪs'faɪr] *of scheme* rater; *of joke* tomber à plat

misfit ['mɪsfɪt] *in society* marginal(e) *m(f)*

misfortune [mɪs'fɔːrt∫ən] malheur *m*, malchance *f*

misguided [mɪs'gaɪdɪd] malavisé, imprudent

mishandle [mɪs'hændl] *situation* mal gérer

misinform [mɪsɪn'fɔːrm] mal informer

misinterpret [mɪsɪn'tɜːrprɪt] mal interpréter; misinterpretation mauvaise interprétation *f*

misjudge [mɪs'dʒʌdʒ] mal juger

mislay [mɪs'leɪ] égarer

mislead [mɪs'liːd] induire en erreur, tromper; misleading trompeur

mismanage [mɪs'mænɪdʒ] mal gérer; mismanagement mauvaise gestion *f*

misprint ['mɪsprɪnt] faute *f* typographique

mispronounce [mɪsprə'naʊns] mal prononcer; mispronunciation mauvaise prononciation *f*

misread [mɪs'riːd] *word, figures* mal lire; *situation* mal interpréter

misrepresent [mɪsreprɪ'zent] présenter sous un faux jour

miss¹ [mɪs]: **Miss Smith** mademoiselle Smith; **~!** mademoiselle!

miss² [mɪs] **1** *n* SP coup *m* manqué **2** *v/t* manquer, rater; *bus, train etc*, (*not notice*) rater; **I ~ you** tu me manques **3** *v/i* rater son coup

misshapen [mɪs'∫eɪpən] déformé; *person, limb* difforme

missile ['mɪsaɪl] *mil* missile *m*; *stone etc* projectile *m*

missing ['mɪsɪŋ]: **be ~** *have disappeared* avoir disparu; *member of school party*, *one of a set etc* ne pas être là

mission ['mɪ∫n] mission *f*

misspell [mɪs'spel] mal orthographier

mist [mɪst] brume *f*

mistake [mɪ'steɪk] **1** *n* erreur *f*, faute *f*; **make a ~** faire une erreur, se tromper **2** *v/t* se tromper de; **~ s.o./sth for s.o./sth** prendre qn/qch pour qn/qch d'autre; mistaken erroné, faux; **be ~** faire erreur, se tromper

mister ['mɪstər] → **Mr**

mistress ['mɪstrɪs] maîtresse *f*

mistrust [mɪs'trʌst] **1** *n* méfiance *f* **2** *v/t* se méfier de

misunderstand [mɪsʌndər'stænd] mal comprendre; misunderstanding malentendu *m*

misuse **1** [mɪs'juːs] *n* mauvais usage *m* **2** [mɪs'juːz] *v/t* faire mauvais usage de; *word* employer à tort

mitigating circumstances ['mɪtɪgeɪtɪŋ] *circonstances fpl* atténuantes

mitt [mɪt] *in baseball* gant *m*; *mitten* moufle *f*

mix [mɪks] **1** *n* mélange *m*; *in cooking: ready to use* préparation *f* **2** *v/t* mélanger; *cement* malaxer **3** *v/i socially* être sociable

◆ **mix up** confondre; *get out of order* mélanger; *be mixed up in* être mêlé à; *mixed economy, school, races* mixte; *reactions* mitigé; *mixer for food* mixeur *m*; *drink* boisson non-alcoolisée que l'on mélange avec certains alcools; *mixture* mélange *m*; *medicine* mixture *f*; *mix-up* confusion *f*

moan [moʊn] **1** *n of pain* gémissement *m* **2** *v/i in pain* gémir

mob [mɑːb] **1** *n* foule *f* **2** *v/t* assaillir

mobile ['moʊbəl] **1** *adj* mobile; *be ~ have car* être motorisé **2** *n for decoration* mobile *m*; *Br phone* portable *m*; **mobile home** mobile home *m*; **mobile phone** *Br* téléphone *m* portable; **mobility** mobilité *f*

mobster ['mɑːbstər] *gangster m*

mock [mɑːk] **1** *adj* faux, feint **2** *v/t* se moquer de; **mockery** (*derision*) moquerie *f*; (*travesty*) parodie *f*

mode [moʊd] mode *m*

model ['mɑːdl] **1** *adj employee, husband* modèle; *boat, plane* modèle réduit *inv* **2** *n* (*miniature*) maquette *f*; (*pattern*) modèle *m*; (*fashion ~*) mannequin *m* **3** *v/i for designer* être mannequin; *for artist, photographer* poser

modem ['moʊdəm] modem *m*

moderate 1 ['mɑːdərət] *adj also* POL modéré **2** ['mɑːdərət] *n* POL modéré *m* **3** ['mɑːdəreɪt] *v/t* modérer; **moderately** modéré; **moderation** (*restraint*) modération *f*

modern ['mɑːdərn] moderne; **modernization** modernisation *f*; **modernize 1** *v/t* moderniser **2** *v/i* se moderniser

modest ['mɑːdɪst] modeste; *wage, amount* modique; *modesty of apartment* simplicité *f*; *of wage* modicité *f*; (*lack of conceit*) modestie *f*

modification [mɑːdɪfɪ'keɪʃn] modification *f*; **modify** modifier

module ['mɑːdʒuːl] module *m*

moist [mɔɪst] humide; **moisten** humidifier; **moisture** humidité *f*; **moisturizer** *for skin* produit *m* hydratant

molasses [mə'læsɪz] mélasse *f*

mold¹ [moʊld] *n on food* moisi *m*, moisissure(s) *f(pl)*

mold² [moʊld] **1** *n* moule *m* **2**

v/t clay modeler; *character* façonner

moldy ['mǝʊldɪ] *food* moisi

molecule ['mɒlɪkjuːl] molécule *f*

molest [mǝ'lest] *child, woman* agresser (sexuellement)

mollycoddle ['mɒlɪkɒdl] F dorloter

molten ['mǝʊltǝn] en fusion

mom [mɑːm] F maman *f*

moment ['mǝʊmǝnt] *instant m,* moment *m;* **at the ~** en ce moment; **momentarily** *(for a moment)* momentanément; *(in a moment)* dans un instant; **momentary** ce moment; **momentous** capital

momentum [mǝ'mentǝm] élan *m*

monarch ['mɒnǝrk] monarque *m*

monastery ['mɒnǝstrɪ] monastère *m;* **monastic** monastique

Monday ['mʌndeɪ] lundi *m*

monetary ['mɒnǝterɪ] monétaire

money ['mʌnɪ] argent *m;* **money belt** sac *m* banane; **money market** marché *m* monétaire; **money order** mandat *m* postal

mongrel ['mʌŋgrǝl] bâtard *m*

monitor ['mɒnɪtǝr] 1 *n* COMPUT moniteur *m* 2 *v/t* surveiller, contrôler

monk [mʌŋk] moine *m*

monkey ['mʌŋkɪ] singe *m;* F

child polisson *m;* **monkey wrench** clef *f* anglaise

monolog, Br **monologue** ['mɒnǝlɒg] monologue *m*

monopolize [mǝ'nɒpǝlaɪz] exercer un monopole sur; *fig* monopoliser; **monopoly** monopole *m*

monotonous [mǝ'nɒtǝnǝs] monotone; **monotony** monotonie *f*

monster ['mɒnstǝr] monstre *m;* **monstrosity** horreur *f*

month [mʌnθ] mois *m;* **monthly 1** *adj* mensuel **2** *adv* mensuellement **3** *n magazine* mensuel *m*

monument ['mɒnjumǝnt] monument *m*

mood [muːd] *(frame of mind)* humeur *f;* *(bad ~)* mauvaise humeur *f;* *of meeting, country* état *m* d'esprit; **moody** *changing moods* lunatique; *(bad-tempered)* maussade

moon [muːn] lune *f;* **moonlight** clair *m* de lune; **moonlit** éclairé par la lune

moor [mʊr] *boat* amarrer

moose [muːs] orignal *m*

mop [mɒp] **1** *n for floor* balai *m* lave-sol; *for dishes* éponge *f* à manche **2** *v/t floor* laver; *eyes, face* éponger, essuyer

◆ **mop up** éponger; MIL balayer

moral ['mɒrǝl] **1** *adj* moral **2** *n of story* morale *f;* **~s** moralité *f*

morale [mǝ'ræl] moral *m*

morality [məˈrælətɪ] moralité f

morbid [ˈmɔːrbɪd] morbide

more [mɔːr] **1** *adj* plus de; *some ~ tea?* encore un peu de thé?; *there's no ~ coffee* il n'y a plus de café; *~ and ~ students* de plus en plus d'étudiants **2** *adv* plus; *~ important*, plus important; *~ and ~* de plus en plus; *~ or less* plus ou moins; *once ~* une fois de plus; *I don't live there any ~* je n'habite plus là-bas **3** *pron* plus; *do you want some ~?* est-ce que tu en veux encore *or* davantage?; *a little ~* un peu plus; *moreover* de plus

morgue [mɔːrg] morgue f

morning [ˈmɔːrnɪŋ] matin m; *in the ~* le matin; *(tomorrow)* demain matin; *tomorrow ~* demain matin; *good ~* bonjour

moron [ˈmɔːrɑːn] F crétin m

morphine [ˈmɔːrfiːn] morphine f

mortal [ˈmɔːrtl] **1** *adj* mortel **2** *n* mortel m; *mortality* condition f mortelle; *(death rate)* mortalité f

mortar [ˈmɔːrtər] MIL, *cement* mortier m

mortgage [ˈmɔːrgɪdʒ] **1** *n* prêt m immobilier; *on own property* hypothèque f **2** *v/t* hypothéquer

mosaic [moʊˈzeɪk] mosaïque f

Moscow [ˈmɑːskaʊ] Moscou

Moslem [ˈmʊzlɪm] **1** *adj* musulman **2** *n* Musulman(e) m(f)

mosque [mɒsk] mosquée f

mosquito [mɑːsˈkiːtoʊ] moustique m

moss [mɑːs] mousse f

most [moʊst] **1** *adj* la plupart de **2** *adv* *(very)* extrêmement, très; *play, swim, eat etc* le plus; *the ~ beautiful* le plus beau; *~ of all* surtout **3** *pron*: *~ of* la plupart de; *at (the) ~* au maximum; *make the ~ of* profiter au maximum de; *mostly* surtout

motel [moʊˈtel] motel m

moth [mɑːθ] papillon m de nuit

mother [ˈmʌðər] **1** *n* mère f **2** *v/t* materner; *motherhood* maternité f; *Mothering Sunday → Mother's Day*; *mother-in-law* belle-mère f; *motherly* maternel; *Mother's Day* la fête des Mères; *mother tongue* langue f maternelle

motif [moʊˈtiːf] motif m

motion [ˈmoʊʃn] **1** *n* *(movement)* mouvement m; *(proposal)* motion f; *motionless* immobile

motivate [ˈmoʊtɪveɪt] motiver; *motivation* motivation f; *motive for crime* mobile m

motor [ˈmoʊtər] moteur m; *motorbike* moto f; *motorcycle* moto f; *motorcyclist* motocycliste *m/f*; **motor home** camping-car *m*; **motor mechanic** mécanicien(ne) *m(f)*; **motor racing** course *f* automobile; **motor vehicle** véhicule *m* à moteur

motto ['mɒtəʊ] devise *f*

mould *etc Br* → **mold** *etc*

mound [maʊnd] (*hillock*) monticule *m*; (*pile*) tas *m*

mount [maʊnt] **1** *n* (*mountain*) mont *m*; (*horse*) monture *f* **2** *v/t steps, photo* monter; *horse, bicycle* monter sur; *campaign* organiser **3** *v/i* monter

◆ **mount up** s'accumuler

mountain ['maʊntɪn] montagne *f*; **mountaineer** alpiniste *m/f*; **mountaineering** alpinisme *m*; **mountainous** montagneux

mourn [mɔːrn] pleurer; **mourner** parent/ami *m* du défunt; **mournful** triste, mélancolique

mouse [maʊs] (*pl* **mice** [maɪs]) *also* COMPUT souris *f*; **mouse mat** tapis *m* de souris

moustache *Br* → **mustache**

mouth [maʊθ] bouche *f*; *of animal* gueule *f*; *of river* embouchure *f*; **mouthful** *of food* bouchée *f*; *of drink* gorgée *f*; **mouthpiece** *of instrument* embouchure *f*; (*spokesperson*) porte-parole *m inv*; **mouthwash** bain *m* de bouche; **mouthwatering** alléchant

move [muːv] **1** *n* mouvement *m*; *in chess etc* coup *m*; (*step, action*) action *f*; (*change of house*) déménagement *m* **2** *v/t object* déplacer; *limbs* bouger; (*transfer*) transférer; *emotionally* émouvoir; ~ **house** déménager **3** *v/i* bouger; (*transfer*) être transféré

◆ **move around** bouger, remuer; *from place to place* bouger, déménager

◆ **move in** emménager

movement ['muːvmənt] *also organization, MUS* mouvement *m*; **movers** déménageurs *mpl*

movie ['muːvɪ] film *m*; **go to a/the ~s** aller au cinéma; **moviegoer** amateur *m* de cinéma, cinéphile *m/f*; **movie theater** cinéma *m*

moving ['muːvɪŋ] *parts* mobile; *emotionally* émouvant

mow [moʊ] *grass* tondre; **mower** tondeuse *f* (à gazon)

mph [empiː'eɪtʃ] (= *miles per hour*) miles à l'heure

Mr ['mɪstər] Monsieur, M.

Mrs ['mɪsɪz] Madame, Mme

Ms [mɪz] Madame, Mme

much [mʌtʃ] **1** *adj* beaucoup de; **so ~ money** tant d'argent; **as ... as ...** autant (de)... que... **2** *adv* beaucoup; **very ~** beaucoup; **too ~** trop **3** *pron* beaucoup; **nothing ~** pas grand-chose; **as ~ as ...** autant que...

mud [mʌd] boue f

muddle ['mʌdl] **1** n (mess) désordre m; (confusion) confusion f **2** v/t embrouiller

muddy ['mʌdɪ] boueux

muffin ['mʌfɪn] muffin m

muffle ['mʌfl] étouffer; muffler MOT silencieux m

mug¹ [mʌg] n for coffee chope f; F (face) gueule f F

mug² [mʌg] v/t (attack) agresser

mugger ['mʌgər] agresseur m; mugging agression f; muggy lourd, moite

mule [mjuːl] animal mulet m, mule f; slipper mule f

multicultural [mʌltɪ'kʌltʃərəl] multiculturel; multilateral POL multilatéral; multimedia **1** adj multimédia **2** n multimédia m; multinational **1** adj multinational **2** n COM multinationale f

multiple ['mʌltɪpl] multiple; multiple sclerosis sclérose f en plaques

multiplex ['mʌltɪpleks] (cinéma m) multiplex m

multiplication [mʌltɪplɪ-'keɪʃn] multiplication f; multiply **1** v/t multiplier **2** v/i se multiplier

multitasking [mʌltɪ'tæskɪŋ] multitâche f; for persons multiplicité f des tâches

mumble ['mʌmbl] **1** n marmonnement m **2** v/t & v/i marmonner

munch [mʌntʃ] mâcher

municipal [mjuː'nɪsɪpl] mu-

nicipal

mural ['mjʊrəl] peinture f murale

murder ['mɜːrdər] **1** n meurtre m **2** v/t person assassiner; song massacrer; murderer meurtrier(-ière) m(f)

murky ['mɜːrkɪ] also fig trouble

murmur ['mɜːrmər] **1** n murmure m **2** v/t murmurer

muscle ['mʌsl] muscle m; muscular pain musculaire; person musclé

museum [mjuː'zɪəm] musée m

mushroom ['mʌʃrʊm] **1** n champignon m **2** v/i fig proliférer

music ['mjuːzɪk] musique f; in written form partition f; musical **1** adj musical; person musicien **2** n comédie f musicale; musician musicien(ne) m(f)

mussel ['mʌsl] moule f

must [mʌst] **1** v/aux ◇ necessity devoir; I ~ be on time je dois être à l'heure, il faut que je sois (subj) à l'heure; I ~n't be late je ne dois pas être en retard, il ne faut pas que je sois en retard

◇ probability devoir; it ~ be about 6 o'clock il doit être environ six heures

mustache [mə'stæʃ] moustache f

mustard ['mʌstərd] moutarde f

musty ['mʌstɪ] *room* qui sent le renfermé; *smell* de renfermé

mutilate ['mju:tɪleɪt] mutiler

mutiny ['mju:tɪnɪ] **1** *n* mutinerie *f* **2** *v/i* se mutiner

mutter ['mʌtər] marmonner

mutual ['mju:tʃʊəl] (*reciprocal*) mutuel; (*common*) commun

muzzle ['mʌzl] **1** *n of animal* museau *m*; *for dog* muselière *f* **2** *v/t*: **~ the press** bâillonner la presse

my [maɪ] mon *m*, ma *f*; *pl* mes; **myself** moi-même; *reflexive* me; *before vowel* m'; *after prep* moi; **I hurt ~** je me suis blessé

mysterious [mɪ'stɪrɪəs] mystérieux; **mysteriously** mystérieusement; **mystery** mystère *m*; **mystify** rendre perplexe; *of tricks* mystifier

myth [mɪθ] *also fig* mythe *m*; **mythical** mythique

N

nag [næg] **1** *v/i of person* faire des remarques continuelles **2** *v/t* harceler; **nagging** *pain* obsédant; **I have this ~ doubt that ...** je n'arrive pas à m'empêcher de penser que ...

nail [neɪl] *for wood* clou *m*; *on finger, toe* ongle *m*; **nail polish** vernis *m* à ongles; **nail polish remover** dissolvant *m*

naive [naɪ'iːv] naïf

naked ['neɪkɪd] nu

name [neɪm] **1** *n* nom *m*; **what's your ~?** comment vous appelez-vous? **2** *v/t* appeler; *namely* à savoir; **namesake** homonyme *m/f*

nanny ['nænɪ] nurse *f*

nap [næp] sieste *f*

napkin ['næpkɪn] (*table ~*) serviette *f* (de table); (*sanitary~*) serviette *f* hygiénique

narcotic [nɑːr'kɑːtɪk] stupéfiant *m*

narrate [nə'reɪt] raconter

narrative **1** *adj poem, style* narratif **2** *n* (*story*) récit *m*; **narrator** narrateur(-trice) *m(f)*

narrow ['nærou] étroit; *victory* serré; **narrowly** *win* de justesse; *escape* de peu; **narrow-minded** étroit d'esprit

nasty ['næstɪ] *person, thing to say* méchant; *smell* nauséabond; *weather, cut, wound, disease* mauvais

nation ['neɪʃn] nation *f*; **national 1** *adj* national **2** *n* national *m*, ressortissant *m*; **national anthem** hymne *m* national; **national debt** dette *f* publique; **nationalism** nationalisme *m*; **nationality** nationalité *f*; **nationalize** in-

dustry etc nationaliser

native ['neɪtɪv] **1** *adj* natal **2** *n* natif(-ive) *m(f)*; *(tribesman)* indigène *m*; **Native American 1** *adj* américain **2** *n* Amérindien(ne) *m(f)*

NATO ['neɪtəʊ] (= **North Atlantic Treaty Organization**) OTAN *f* (= Organisation du traité de l'Atlantique Nord)

natural ['nætʃrəl] naturel; **naturalist** naturaliste *m/f*; **naturalize**: *become* ⁓*d* se faire naturaliser; **naturally** *(of course)* bien entendu; *behave, speak* naturellement, avec naturel; *(by nature)* de nature; **nature** réserve *f*; nature reserve réserve *f* naturelle

naughty ['nɔːtɪ] vilain; *photograph , word etc* coquin

nausea ['nɔːzɪə] nausée *f*; **nauseate** *fig* écœurer; **nauseating** écœurant; **nauseous**: *feel* ⁓ avoir la nausée

nautical ['nɔːtɪkl] nautique, marin

naval ['neɪvl] naval, maritime; *history* de la marine

navel ['neɪvl] nombril *m*

navigate ['nævɪgeɪt] *also* COMPUT naviguer; *in car* diriger; **navigation** navigation *f*; *in car* indications *fpl*; **navigator** navigateur *m*

navy ['neɪvɪ] marine *f*; **navy blue 1** *adj* bleu marine *inv* **2** *n* bleu *m* marine

near [nɪr] **1** *adv* près; *come* ⁓*er* approche-toi **2** *prep* près de **3** *adj* proche; *in the ~ future* dans un proche avenir; **nearby** tout près; **nearly** presque; *I ~ lost it* j'ai failli le perdre; **near-sighted** myope

neat [niːt] *room, desk* bien rangé; *person* ordonné; *in appearance* soigné; *whiskey etc* sec; *solution* ingénieux; F *(terrific)* super *inv* F

necessarily ['nesəsərəlɪ] nécessairement, forcément; **necessary** nécessaire; *it is ~ to ...* il faut ...; **necessity** nécessité *f*

neck [nek] cou *m*; *of clothing* col *m*; **necklace** collier *m*; **neckline** *of dress* encolure *f*; **necktie** cravate *f*

née [neɪ] née

need [niːd] **1** *n* besoin *m*; *if ~ be* si besoin est; *in ~* dans le besoin **2** *v/t* avoir besoin de; *you don't ~ to wait* vous n'êtes pas obligés d'attendre; *I ~ to talk to you* il faut que je te parle

needle ['niːdl] aiguille *f*; **needlework** travaux *mpl* d'aiguille

needy ['niːdɪ] nécessiteux

negative ['negətɪv] négatif

neglect [nɪ'glekt] **1** *n* négligence *f*; *state* abandon *m* **2** *v/t* négliger; **neglected** négligé

negligence ['neglɪdʒəns] négligence *f*; **negligent** négligent; **negligible** *quantity* négligeable

negotiable [nɪˈgouʃəbl] négociable; **negotiate 1** *v/i* négocier **2** *v/t deal* négocier; *obstacles* franchir; *bend in road* négocier, prendre; **negotiation** négociation *f*; **negotiator** négociateur(-trice) *m(f)*

neighbor [ˈneɪbər] voisin(e) *m(f)*; **neighborhood** *in town* quartier *m*; **neighboring** *house, state* voisin; **neighborly** aimable

neighbour *etc Br* → **neighbor** *etc*

neither [ˈniːðər] **1** *adj*: **~ player** aucun(e) des deux joueurs **2** *pron* ni l'un ni l'autre **3** *adv*: **~ … nor …** ni … ni … **4** *conj*: **~ do/can I** moi non plus

neon light [ˈniːɑːn] néon *m*

nephew [ˈnefjuː] neveu *m*

nerve [nɜːrv] nerf *m*; *(courage)* courage *m*; *(impudence)* culot *m* F; **nerve-racking** angoissant, éprouvant; **nervous** nerveux; **nervous breakdown** dépression *f* nerveuse; **nervousness** nervosité *f*; **nervy** *(fresh)* effronté, culotté F

nest [nest] nid *m*

net[1] [net] *n for fishing, tennis etc* filet *m*; *Internet* Net *m*

net[2] [net] *adj price etc* net

nettle [ˈnetl] ortie *f*

'network *also* COMPUT réseau *m*

neurologist [nʊˈrɑːlədʒɪst] neurologue *m/f*

neurosis [nʊˈrousɪs] névrose *f*; **neurotic** névrosé, obsédé

neuter [ˈnuːtər] *animal* castrer; **neutral 1** *adj* neutre **2** *n gear* point *m* mort; **neutrality** neutralité *f*; **neutralize** neutraliser

never [ˈnevər] jamais; **I've ~ been to New York** je ne suis jamais allé à New York; **nevertheless** néanmoins

new [nuː] nouveau; *(not used)* neuf; **newborn** nouveau-né; **newcomer** nouveau venu *m*, nouvelle venue *f*; **newly** *(recently)* récemment, nouvellement; **newly-weds** jeunes mariés *mpl*

news [nuːz] nouvelle*s* *f(pl)*; *on TV, radio* informations *fpl*; **newscast** TV journal *m* télévisé; **newscaster** TV présentateur(-trice) *m(f)*; **news flash** flash *m* d'information; **newspaper** journal *m*; **newsreader** TV *etc* présentateur(-trice) *m(f)*; **news report** reportage *m*; **newsstand** kiosque *m* à journaux; **newsvendor** vendeur(-euse) *m(f)* de journaux

'New Year nouvel an *m*; **Happy ~!** Bonne année!; **New Year's Day** jour *m* de l'an; **New Year's Eve** la Saint-Sylvestre

next [nekst] **1** *adj* prochain; **the ~ month** le mois suivant

2 *adv* (*after*) ensuite, après; **~ to** à côté de; **next-door 1** *adj* **neighbor** f d'à côté **2** *adv* à côté; **next of kin** parent *m* le plus proche

nibble ['nɪbl] *cheese* grignoter; *ear* mordiller

nice [naɪs] agréable; *person also* sympathique; *house, hair* beau; **that's very ~ of you** c'est très gentil de votre part; **nicely** *written, presented* bien; (*pleasantly*) agréablement

niche [niːʃ] *in market* créneau *m*; (*special position*) place f

nick [nɪk] (*cut*) coupure f

nickel ['nɪkl] MIN nickel *m*; *coin* pièce f de cinq cents

nickname surnom *m*

niece [niːs] nièce f

night [naɪt] nuit f; (*evening*) soir *m*; **11 o'clock at ~** onze heures du soir; **during the ~** pendant la nuit; **good-~** going to bed bonne nuit; *leaving office, friends' house etc* bonsoir; **nightcap** *drink* boisson f du soir; **nightclub** boîte f de nuit; **nightdress** chemise f de nuit; **night flight** vol *m* de nuit; **night life** vie f nocturne; **nightly 1** *adj* de toutes les nuits; *in evening* de tous les soirs **2** *adv* toutes les nuits; *in evening* tous les soirs; **nightmare** *also fig* cauchemar *m*; **night porter** gardien *m* de nuit; **night school** cours *mpl* du soir; **night shift**

équipe f de nuit; **nightshirt** chemise f de nuit (d'homme); **nightspot** boîte f de nuit); **nighttime**: **at ~, in the ~** la nuit

nimble ['nɪmbl] agile; *mind* vif

nine [naɪn] neuf; **nineteen** dix-neuf; **nineteenth** dix-neuvième; **ninetieth** quatre-vingt-dixième; **ninety** quatre-vingt-dix; **ninth** neuvième

nip [nɪp] (*pinch*) pincement *m*; (*bite*) morsure f

nipple ['nɪpl] mamelon *m*

nitrogen ['naɪtrədʒn] azote *m*

no [nou] **1** *adv* non **2** *adj* aucun, pas de; **there's ~ coffee left** il ne reste plus de café; **I have ~ money** je n'ai pas d'argent; **~ smoking** défense de fumer

noble ['noubl] noble

nobody ['noubədɪ] personne; **~ knows** personne ne le sait; **there was ~ at home** il n'y avait personne

no-brainer [nou'breɪnər] jeu *m* d'enfant; **the math test was a ~** le devoir de maths était super facile

nod [nɑːd] **1** *n* signe *m* de tête **2** *v/i* faire un signe de tête

noise [nɔɪz] bruit *m*; **noisy** bruyant; **be ~** *of person* faire du bruit

nominal ['nɑːmɪnl] nominal; (*token*) symbolique

nominate ['nɑːmɪneɪt] (*ap-*

point) nommer; **nomination** (*appointment*) nomination *f*; (*person proposed*) candidat *m*; **nominee** candidat *m*

nonalco'holic non alcoolisé

noncommissioned 'officer ['nɑːnkəmɪʃnd] sous-officier *m*

noncommittal [nɑːnkə'mɪtl] évasif

nondescript ['nɑːndɪskrɪpt] quelconque; *color* indéfinissable

none [nʌn] aucun(e); **there is/ are ~ left** il n'en reste plus

nonentity [nɑːn'entətɪ] être *m* insignifiant

non'existent inexistant

non'fiction ouvrages *mpl* non littéraires

noninter'ference non-ingérence *f*

noninter'vention non-intervention *f*

no-'nonsense *approach* pragmatique

non'payment non-paiement *m*

nonpol'luting non polluant

non'resident non-résident *m*; *in hotel* client *m* de passage

nonre'turnable non remboursable

nonsense ['nɑːnsəns] absurdité(s) *f(pl)*; **don't talk ~** ne raconte pas n'importe quoi

non'smoker non-fumeur (-euse) *m(f)*

non'standard non standard *inv*; *use of word* impropre

non'stop 1 *adj flight, train* direct; *chatter* incessant **2** *adv fly, travel* sans escale; *chatter, argue* sans arrêt

non'union non syndiqué

non'violence non-violence *f*; **nonviolent** non-violent

noodles ['nuːdlz] nouilles *fpl*

noon [nuːn] midi *m*

no-one → **nobody**

noose [nuːs] nœud *m* coulant

nor [nɔːr] ni; **~ do I** moi non plus

norm [nɔːrm] norme *f*; **normal** normal; **normality** normalité *f*; **normally** normalement

north [nɔːrθ] **1** *n* nord *m* **2** *adj* nord *inv*; *wind* du nord **3** *adv travel* vers le nord; **North America** Amérique *f* du Nord; **North American 1** *adj* nord-américain **2** *n* Nord-Américain(e) *m(f)*; **northeast** nord-est *m*; **northerly** *wind* du nord; *direction* vers le nord; **northern** du nord; **northerner** habitant *m* du Nord; **North Korea** Corée *f* du Nord; **North Korean 1** *adj* nord-coréen **2** *n* Nord-Coréen(ne) *m(f)*; **North Pole** pôle *m* Nord; **northward** *travel* vers le nord; **northwest** nord-ouest *m*

nose [nouz] nez *m*

◆ **nose around** F fouiner

nostalgia [nɑː'stældʒə] nostalgie *f*; **nostalgic** nostalgique

nostril ['nɑːstrəl] narine f

nosy ['nouzɪ] F curieux

not [nɑːt] pas; **~ now** pas maintenant; **~ there** pas là; **~ a lot** pas beaucoup **with** verbs ne … pas; **it's ~ allowed** ce n'est pas permis; **he didn't help** il n'a pas aidé

notable ['noutəbl] notable

notch [nɑːtʃ] entaille f

note [nout] MUS, written note f; (short letter) mot m; **notebook** carnet m; COMPUT ordinateur m bloc-notes; **noted** célèbre; **notepad** bloc-notes m; **notepaper** papier m à lettres

nothing ['nʌθɪŋ] rien; **she said ~** elle n'a rien dit; **~ but** rien que; **~ much** pas grand-chose; **for ~** (for free) gratuitement; (for no reason) pour un rien

notice ['noutɪs] **1** n on bulletin board, in street affiche f; (advance warning) préavis m; in newspaper avis m; **to leave job** démission f; **to leave house** préavis m; **at short ~** dans un délai très court; **until further ~** jusqu'à nouvel ordre; **hand in one's ~** to employer donner sa démission; **take no ~ of** ne pas faire attention à **2** v/t remarquer; **noticeable** visible

notify ['noutɪfaɪ]: **~ s.o. of sth** signaler qch à qn

notion ['nouʃn] idée f

notorious [nou'tɔːrɪəs] notoire

noun [naun] substantif m, nom m

nourishing ['nʌrɪʃɪŋ] nourrissant; **nourishment** nourriture f

novel ['nɑːvl] roman m; **novelist** romancier(-ière) m(f); **novelty** nouveauté f

November [nou'vembər] novembre m

novice ['nɑːvɪs] (beginner) novice m, débutant m

now [nau] maintenant; **~ and again, ~ and then** de temps à autre; **by ~** maintenant; **nowadays** aujourd'hui, de nos jours

nowhere ['nouwer] nulle part; **it's ~ near finished** c'est loin d'être fini

nuclear ['nuːklɪər] nucléaire; **nuclear energy** énergie f nucléaire; **nuclear power** énergie f nucléaire; POL puissance f nucléaire; **nuclear power station** centrale f nucléaire; **nuclear reactor** réacteur m nucléaire; **nude** [nuːd] **1** adj nu **2** n painting nu m; **in the ~** tout nu

nudge [nʌdʒ] person donner un coup de coude à; parked car pousser (un peu)

nudist ['nuːdɪst] nudiste m/f

nuisance ['nuːsns] peste f, plaie f F; event, task ennui m; **make a ~ of o.s.** être embêtant F

null and 'void [nʌl] nul et non avenu

numb [nʌm] engourdi; *emotionally* insensible

number ['nʌmbər] **1** *n* nombre *m*; *symbol* chiffre *m*; *of hotel room, phone ~ etc* numéro *m* **2** *v/t* (*put a ~ on*) numéroter

numeral ['nu:mərəl] chiffre *m*

numerous ['nu:mərəs] nombreux

nun [nʌn] religieuse *f*

nurse [nɜːrs] infirmier(-ière) *m(f)*; **nursery** maternelle *f*; *for plants* pépinière *f*; **nurs-ery rhyme** comptine *f*; **nurs-ery school** école *f* maternelle; **nursing profession** *f* d'infirmier; **nursing home** *for old people* maison *f* de retraite

nut [nʌt] (*walnut*) noix *f*; (*Brazil*) noix *f* du Brésil; (*hazelnut*) noisette *f*; (*peanut*) cacahuète *f*; *for bolt* écrou *m*; **nutcrackers** casse-noisettes *m inv*

nutrient ['nu:trɪənt] élément *m* nutritif; **nutrition** nutrition *f*; **nutritious** nutritif

nuts [nʌts] F (*crazy*) fou

O

oar [ɔːr] aviron *m*, rame *f*

oasis [oʊ'eɪsɪs] *also fig* oasis *f*

oath [oʊθ] LAW serment *m*; (*swearword*) juron *m*

oats [oʊts] *npl* avoine *f*

obedience [oʊ'biːdɪəns] obéissance *f*; **obedient** obéissant; **obediently** docilement

obese [oʊ'biːs] obèse; **obesity** obésité *f*

obey [oʊ'beɪ] obéir à

obituary [oʊ'bɪtʃuerɪ] nécrologie *f*

object[1] ['ɑːbdʒɪkt] *n* (*thing*) objet *m*; (*aim*) objectif *m*; GRAM complément *m* d'objet

object[2] [əb'dʒekt] *v/i* protester; *if nobody ~s* si personne n'y voit d'objection

objection [əb'dʒekʃn] objection *f*; **objectionable** (*unpleasant*) désagréable; **objective 1** *adj* objectif **2** *n* objectif *m*; **objectively** objectivement; **objectivity** objectivité *f*

obligation [ɑːblɪ'ɡeɪʃn] obligation *f*; **obligatory** obligatoire; **obliging** serviable, obligeant

oblique [ə'bliːk] **1** *adj* *reference* indirect; *line* oblique **2** *n in punctuation* barre *f* oblique

obliterate [ə'blɪtəreɪt] *city* détruire; *memory* effacer

oblivion [ə'blɪvɪən] oubli *m*

oblong ['ɑːblɑːŋ] **1** *adj* oblong **2** *n* rectangle *m*

obscene [əb'si:n] obscène; *salary, poverty* scandaleux; **obscenity** obscénité *f*

obscure [əb'skjur] obscur; *village* inconnu; **obscurity** obscurité *f*

observant [əb'zɜ:rvnt] observateur; **observation** observation *f*; **observe** observer; **observer** observateur(-trice) *m(f)*

obsess [əb'ses]: **be ~ed with** être obsédé par; **obsession** obsession *f* (**with** de)

obsolete ['ɑ:bsəli:t] obsolète

obstacle ['ɑ:bstəkl] *also fig* obstacle *m*

obstetrician [ɑ:bstə'trɪʃn] obstétricien(ne) *m(f)*; **obstetrics** obstétrique *f*

obstinacy ['ɑ:bstɪnəsɪ] entêtement *m*, obstination *f*; **obstinate** obstiné

obstruct [əb'strʌkt] *road* bloquer, obstruer; *investigation* entraver; *police* gêner; **obstruction** *on road etc* obstacle *m*; **obstructive** *behavior* qui met des bâtons dans les roues; *tactics* obstructionniste

obtain [əb'teɪn] obtenir; **obtainable** *products* disponible

obtuse [əb'tu:s] *fig* obtus

obvious ['ɑ:bvɪəs] évident, manifeste; **obviously** manifestement; *~!* évidemment!

occasion [ə'keɪʒn] occasion *f*; **occasional** occasionnel; **occasionally** de temps en temps, occasionnellement

occupant ['ɑ:kjupənt] occupant(e) *m(f)*; **occupation** (*job*) métier *m*; *of country* occupation *f*; **occupy** occuper

occur [ə'kɜ:r] avoir lieu, se produire; (*event*) fait *m*; **occurrence** fait *m*

ocean ['ouʃn] océan *m*

o'clock [ə'klɑ:k]: **at five ~** à cinq heures

October [ɑ:k'toubər] octobre *m*

odd [ɑ:d] (*strange*) bizarre; (*not even*) impair; **oddball** F original *m*; **odds and ends** petites choses *fpl*, bricoles *fpl*; **odds-on**: **the ~ favorite** le grand favori

odometer [ou'dɑ:mətər] odomètre *m*

odor, *Br* **odour** ['oudər] odeur *f*

of [ɑ:v] de; **the name ~ the street/hotel** le nom de la rue/de l'hôtel; **the color ~ the paper** la couleur du papier; **five minutes ~ ten** dix heures moins cinq; **die ~ cancer** mourir d'un cancer; **love ~ money** l'amour de l'argent

off [ɑ:f] **1** *prep*: **~ the main road** *away from* en retrait de la route principale; *near* près de la route principale; **$20 ~ the price** 20 dollars de réduction **2** *adv*: **be ~** *of light, TV, machine* être éteint; *of brake* être des-

serré; *of lid* ne pas être mis;
not at work ne pas être là;
canceled être annulé; **we're**
~ tomorrow leaving nous
partons demain; **take a day**
~ prendre un jour de congé;
it's 3 miles ~ c'est à 3 miles;
it's a long way ~ c'est loin **3**
adj: **the ~ switch** le bouton
d'arrêt

offence *Br* → offense

offend [ə'fend] (*insult*) offenser; **offender** LAW délin-
quant(e) *m(f)*; **offense** LAW
minor infraction *f*; *serious*
délit *m*; **take ~ at sth** s'offenser de qch; **offensive 1** *adj*
behavior, remark offensant;
smell repoussant **2** *n* MIL offensive *f*

offer ['ɑːfər] **1** *n* offre *f* **2** *v/t*
offrir

off'hand *attitude* désinvolte

office ['ɑːfɪs] bureau *m*; (*position*) fonction *f*; **officer** MIL
officier *m*; *in police* agent
m de police; **official 1** *adj* officiel **2** *n* civil servant etc
fonctionnaire *m/f*; **officially**
officiellement; (*strictly
speaking*) en théorie; **offi-
cious** trop zélé

'off-line *work* hors connexion;
go ~ se déconnecter

'off-peak *rates* en période
creuse

'off-season basse saison *f*

'offset *losses* compenser

'offshore offshore

'offside SP hors jeu

'offspring progéniture *f*

'off-the-record officieux

often ['ɑːfn] souvent; **how ~
do you go there?** vous y allez tous les combien?

oil [ɔɪl] **1** *n* huile *f*; *petroleum*
pétrole *m* **2** *v/t* lubrifier, huiler; **oil change** vidange *f*; **oil**
company compagnie *f* pé-
trolière; **oilfield** champ *m*
pétrolifère; **oil painting**
peinture *f* à l'huile; **oil refinery** raffinerie *f* de pétrole; **oil**
rig *at sea* plate-forme *f* de forage; **on land** tour *f* de forage;
oil slick marée *f* noire; **oil**
tanker *ship* pétrolier *m*;
oil well puits *m* de pétrole;
oily graisseux

ointment ['ɔɪntmənt] pom-
made *f*

ok [ou'keɪ]: **can I? – ~** je peux?
– d'accord; **is it ~ with you if
...?** ça te dérange si ...?;
does that look ~? est-ce
que ça va?; **that's ~ by me**
ça me va; **are you ~?** (*well,
not hurt*) ça va?

old [ould] vieux; (*previous*)
ancien; **how ~ is he?** quel
âge a-t-il?; **old age** vieillesse
f; **old-fashioned** démodé

olive ['ɑːlɪv] olive *f*; **olive oil**
huile *f* d'olive

Olympic Games [ə'lɪmpɪk]
Jeux *mpl* Olympiques

omelet, *Br* omelette ['ɑːmlət]
omelette *f*

ominous ['ɑːmɪnəs] inquiétant

omission [ou'mɪʃn] omission
f; **omit** [ou'mɪt] omettre

on [ɑːn] **1** *prep* sur; ~ *the table*
sur la table; ~ *the bus* dans le
bus; ~ *the third floor* au
deuxième étage; ~ *TV* à la télé; ~ *Sunday* dimanche; ~
Sundays le dimanche; ~
the 1st of ... le premier...;
this is ~ *me* (*I'm paying*)
c'est moi qui paie; *have
you any money* ~ *you?* as-tu
de l'argent sur toi?; ~ *his arrival* à son arrivée; ~ *his departure* au moment de son
départ; ~ *hearing this* en en-
tendant ceci 2 *adj be* ~ *of
light, TV, computer etc* être
allumé; *of brake* être serré;
of lid être mis; *of program:
being broadcast* passer; *of
meeting etc:* be scheduled to
happen avoir lieu; *what's* ~
tonight? on TV etc qu'est-ce
qu'il y a ce soir?; (*what's
planned?*) qu'est-ce qu'on
fait ce soir?; *you're* ~ (*I accept*) c'est d'accord; ~ *you
go* (*go ahead*) vas-y; *talk* ~
continuer à parler; *and so
*~ et ainsi de suite; ~ *and* ~
talk etc pendant des heures
3 *adj:* *the* ~ *switch* le bouton
marche

once [wʌns] **1** *adv* (*one time*)
une fois; (*formerly*) autrefois; ~ *again,* ~ *more* encore
une fois; *at* ~ (*immediately*)
tout de suite **2** *conj* une fois
que; ~ *you have finished*

une fois que tu auras terminé

one [wʌn] **1** *n number* un *m* **2**
adj un(e); ~ *day* un jour **3**
pron: ~ *is bigger than the
other* l'un(e) est plus
grand(e) que l'autre; *which
~?* lequel/laquelle?; ~ *by
~, enter, deal with* un(e) à la fois;
the little ~*s* les petits *mpl;* *I
for* ~ pour ma part; *what
can* ~ *say?* qu'est-ce qu'on
peut dire?; *one-parent family* famille *f* monoparentale;
oneself: *hurt* ~ se faire
mal; *for* ~ pour soi or soi-même; *do sth by* ~ faire qch
tout seul; *one-way street*
rue *f* à sens unique; *one-
-way ticket* aller *m* simple

onion ['ʌnjən] oignon *m*

'on-line en ligne; *go* ~ *to* se
connecter à; *on-line bank-
ing* (services *mpl* de) banque
f en ligne; *on-line dating*
rencontres *fpl* en ligne; *on-
-line shopping* shopping *m*
en ligne

onlooker ['ɑːnlʊkər] specta-
teur(-trice) *m(f)*

only ['oʊnlɪ] **1** *adv* seulement;
he's ~ *six* il n'a que six ans **2**
adj unique

'onset début *m*

on-the-job 'training formation *f* sur le tas

opaque [ou'peɪk] *glass* opaque

open ['oʊpən] **1** *adj* ouvert; *in
the* ~ *air* en plein air **2** *v/t* ouvrir **3** *v/i of shop, flower* s'ou-

vrir; **open-air** *meeting, concert* en plein air; *pool* découvert; **open day** journée *f* portes ouvertes; **open-ended** *contract* etc flexible; **opening** *in wall* etc ouverture *f*; *of film, novel* etc début *m*; *(job)* poste *m* (vacant); **openly** (*honestly, frankly*) ouvertement; **open-minded** à l'esprit ouvert, ouvert; **open ticket** billet *m* ouvert

opera ['ɒpərə] opéra *m*; **opera house** opéra *m*; **opera singer** chanteur(-euse) *m(f)* d'opéra

operate ['ɒpəreɪt] **1** *v/i of company* opérer; *of airline, bus service* circuler; *of machine* fonctionner; MED opérer **2** *v/t machine* faire marcher

◆ **operate on** MED opérer

'**operating room** MED salle *f* d'opération; **operating system** COMPUT système *m* d'exploitation; **operation** MED opération *f* (chirurgicale); *of machine* fonctionnement *m*; **have an ~** MED se faire opérer; **operator** *of machine* opérateur(-trice) *m(f)*; *(tour ~)* tour-opérateur *m*, voyagiste *m*; TELEC standardiste *m/f*

opinion [ə'pɪnjən] opinion *f*; **opinion poll** sondage *m* d'opinion

opponent [ə'pəunənt] adversaire *m/f*

opportunist [ɑːpər'tuːnɪst] opportuniste *m/f*; **opportunity** occasion *f*

oppose [ə'pəuz] s'opposer à; **be ~d to** être opposé à

opposite ['ɑːpəzɪt] **1** *adj* opposé; *meaning* contraire **2** *adv* en face; **the house ~** la maison d'en face **3** *prep* en face de; **opposite 'number** homologue *m/f*

opposition [ɑːpə'zɪʃn] opposition *f*

oppress [ə'pres] *people* opprimer; **oppressive** *rule* oppressif; *weather* oppressant

optician [ɑːp'tɪʃn] opticien (-ne) *m(f)*

optimism ['ɑːptɪmɪzəm] optimisme *m*; **optimist** optimiste *m/f*; **optimistic** optimiste *m/f*; **optimistically** avec optimisme

optimum ['ɑːptɪməm] optimal

option ['ɑːpʃn] option *f*; **optional** facultatif

or [ɔːr] ou; **~ else!** sinon ...

oral ['ɔːrəl] *exam* oral; *hygiene* dentaire

orange ['ɔːrɪndʒ] **1** *adj color* orange *inv* **2** *n fruit* orange *f*; *color* orange *m*; **orange juice** jus *m* d'orange

orator ['ɔːrətər] orateur(-trice) *m(f)*

orbit ['ɔːrbɪt] **1** *n of earth* orbite *f* **2** *v/t the earth* décrire une orbite autour de

orchard ['ɔːrtʃərd] verger *m*

orchestra [ˈɔːrkəstrə] orchestre *m*

orchid [ˈɔːrkɪd] orchidée *f*

ordain [ɔːrˈdeɪn] ordonner

ordeal [ɔːrˈdiːl] épreuve *f*

order [ˈɔːrdər] **1** *n* ordre *m*; *for goods, in restaurant* commande *f*; **an ~ of fries** une portion de frites; **in ~ to** pour; **out of ~** *(not functioning)* hors service; **out of ~** *(not in sequence)* pas dans l'ordre **2** *v/t* *(put in sequence, proper layout)* ranger; *goods, meal* commander; **~ s.o. to do sth** ordonner à qn de faire qch **3** *v/i in restaurant* commander; **orderly 1** *adj lifestyle* bien réglé **2** *n in hospital* aide-soignant *m*

ordinarily [ɔːrdɪˈnerɪlɪ] *(as a rule)* d'habitude; **ordinary** ordinaire

ore [ɔːr] minerai *m*

organ [ˈɔːrgən] ANAT organe *m*; MUS orgue *m*; **organic** *food, fertilizer* biologique; **organically grown** biologiquement; **organism** organisme *m*

organization [ɔːrgənaɪˈzeɪʃn] organisation *f*; **organize** organiser; **organizer** *person* organisateur(-trice) *m(f)*

Orient [ˈɔːrɪənt] Orient *m*; **Oriental** oriental

origin [ˈɔːrɪdʒɪn] origine *f*; **original 1** *adj (not copied)* original; *(first)* d'origine, initial **2** *n painting etc* original

m; **originality** originalité *f*; **originally** à l'origine; *(at first)* au départ; **originate 1** *v/t idea* être à l'origine de **2** *v/i of idea, belief* émaner *(from* de); *of family* être originaire *(from* de)

ornamental [ɔːrnəˈmentl] décoratif

ornate [ɔːrˈneɪt] *architecture* chargé; *prose style* fleuri

orphan [ˈɔːrfn] orphelin(e) *m(f)*

orthodox [ˈɔːrθədɑːks] orthodoxe

orthopedic [ɔːrθəˈpiːdɪk] orthopédique

ostensibly [ɑːˈstensəblɪ] en apparence

ostentatious [ɑːstenˈteɪʃəs] prétentieux, tape-à-l'œil *inv*

ostracize [ˈɑːstrəsaɪz] frapper d'ostracisme

other [ˈʌðər] **1** *adj* autre; **the ~ day** *(recently)* l'autre jour; **every ~ day** un jour sur deux; **~ people** d'autres **2** *n:* **the ~** l'autre *m/f*

otherwise [ˈʌðərwaɪz] **1** *conj* sinon **2** *adv (differently)* autrement

ought [ɔːt]: **I/you ~ to know** je/tu devrais le savoir; **you ~ to have done it** tu aurais dû le faire

ounce [aʊns] once *f*

our [ˈaʊər] notre; *pl* nos; **ours** le nôtre, la nôtre; *pl* les nôtres; **it's ~** c'est à nous; **ourselves** nous-mêmes; *reflex-*

ive nous; *after prep* nous; **we enjoyed** nous nous sommes amusé(e)s

oust [aust] *from office* évincer

out [aut]: **be~** *of light, fire* être éteint; *of flower* être en fleur; *of sun* briller; *(not at home, not in building)* être sorti; *of calculations* être faux; *(be published)* être sorti; *of secret* être connu; *(no longer in competition)* être éliminé; *(no longer in fashion)* être passé de mode; **~ here in Dallas** ici à Dallas; **(get) ~!** dehors!; **(get) ~ of my room!** sors de ma chambre!; **that's ~!** hors de question!; **he's ~ to win** *(fully intends to)* il est bien décidé à gagner; **outbreak** *of war* déclenchement *m*; *of violence* éruption *f*

'outcast exclu(e) *m(f)*

'outcome résultat *m*

'outcry tollé *m*

out'dated démodé

out'do surpasser

out'door *activities* de plein air; *life* au grand air; *toilet* extérieur; **outdoors** dehors

outer ['autər] *wall etc* extérieur

'outfit *(clothes)* tenue *f*, ensemble *m*; *(company, organization)* boîte *f* F

out'last durer plus longtemps que

'outlet *of pipe* sortie *f*; for

sales point m de vente; ELEC prise *f* de courant

'outline 1 *n* silhouette *f*; *of plan, novel* esquisse *f* **2** *v/t plans* ébaucher

out'live survivre à

'outlook *(prospects)* perspective *f*

out'number être plus nombreux que

out of ◇ *motion* de, hors de; **run ~ the house** sortir de la maison en courant
◇ *position:* **20 miles ~ Detroit** à 32 kilomètres de Détroit
◇ *cause* par; **~ jealousy** par jalousie
◇ *without:* **we're ~ gas** nous n'avons plus d'essence
◇ *from a group* sur; **5 ~ 10** 5 sur 10

out-of-'date dépassé; *(expired)* périmé

'output 1 *n of factory* production *f*, rendement *m*; COMPUT sortie *f* **2** *v/t (produce)* produire

'outrage 1 *n feeling* indignation *f*; *act* outrage *m* **2** *v/t* faire outrage à; **outrageous** *acts* révoltant; *prices* scandaleux

'outright 1 *adj winner* incontesté **2** *adv kill* sur le coup; *refuse* catégoriquement

'outset début *m*

out'shine éclipser

'outside 1 *adj* extérieur **2** *adv* dehors, à l'extérieur **3** *prep* of l'extérieur de; (*apart from*) en dehors de **4** *n of building, case etc* extérieur *m*

'out**size** *clothing* grande taille

'out**skirts** *of town* banlieue *f*

out'**smart** → **outwit**

'out**source** externaliser

out'**standing** exceptionnel, remarquable; FIN impayé

out**stretched** ['aʊtstretʃt] *hands* tendu

outward ['aʊtwərd] *appearance* extérieur; ~ *journey* voyage *m* aller; **outwardly** en apparence

out'**weigh** l'emporter sur

out'**wit** se montrer plus malin que

oval ['əʊvl] ovale

oven ['ʌvn] four *m*

over ['əʊvər] **1** *prep* (*above*) au-dessus de; (*across*) de l'autre côté de; (*more than*) plus de; (*during*) pendant; **she walked ~ the street** elle traversa la rue; **travel all ~ Brazil** voyager à travers le Brésil; **we're ~ the worst** le pire est passé; **~ and above** en plus de **2** *adv*: **be ~** (*finished*) être fini; (*left*) rester; **there were just 6 ~** il n'en restait que 6; **~ in Japan** au Japon; **~ here** ici; **~ there** là-bas; **it hurts all ~** ça fait mal partout; **painted white all ~** peint tout en blanc; **it's all ~** c'est fini; **~ and again** maintes et maintes fois; **do sth ~** (*again*) refaire

qch; **overall** *measure* en tout; (*in general*) dans l'ensemble; **overalls** bleu *m* de travail

over'**awe** impressionner, intimider

over'**balance** *of person* perdre l'équilibre

over'**bearing** dominateur

over'**cast** *sky* couvert

over'**charge** faire payer trop cher à

'over**coat** pardessus *m*

over'**come** *difficulties* surmonter

over'**crowded** *city* surpeuplé; *train* bondé

over'**do** (*exaggerate*) exagérer; *in cooking* trop cuire; over'**done** *meat* trop cuit

over'**dose** dose *f*

'over**draft** découvert *m*; **have an ~** être à découvert; over'**draw** *account* mettre à découvert

over**dressed** trop habillé

over'**estimate** surestimer

overex'**pose** surexposer

'over**flow**[1] *n pipe* trop-plein *m inv*

over'**flow**[2] *v/i of water* déborder

over'**haul** *engine etc* remettre à neuf; *plans* remanier

over**head 1** *adj* au-dessus *m* **2** *n* FIN frais *mpl* généraux

over'**hear** entendre (par hasard)

over'**heated** *room* surchauffé; *engine* qui chauffe

overjoyed [əʊvər'dʒɔɪd] ravi,

enchanté

'**overland 1** *adj transport par
terre* **2** *adv travel* par voie
de terre

over'**lap** *of tiles, periods etc* se
chevaucher; *of theories* se re-
couper

over'**load** surcharger

over'**look** *of tall building etc*
surplomber, dominer; *of
window* donner sur; *(not
see)* laisser passer

'**overly** ['ouvrlɪ] trop

'**overnight** *travel* la nuit; *fig:
change etc* du jour au lendemain

'**overpass** pont *m*

over'**power** *physically* maîtriser

over**priced** [ouvər'praɪst]
trop cher

over**rated** [ouvə'reɪtɪd] surfait

over'**ride** *decision etc* annuler;
technically forcer; over**riding** *concern* principal

over'**rule** *decision* annuler

over'**seas** à l'étranger

over'**see** superviser

over'**shadow** *fig* éclipser

'**oversight** omission *f*

over'**sleep** se réveiller en retard

over'**state** exagérer; over-
statement exagération *f*

over'**take** *also Br* MOT dépasser

over'**throw**[1] *v/t government*
renverser

'**overthrow**[2] *n of government*
renversement *m*

'**overtime 1** *n* SP temps *m* supplémentaire **2** *adv*: **work ~**
faire des heures supplémen-
taires

over'**turn 1** *v/t also government* renverser **2** *v/i of vehicle* se retourner

'**overview** vue *f* d'ensemble

overwhelming [ouvər'welm-
ɪŋ] *feeling* irrépressible; *relief* énorme; *majority* écrasant

over'**work 1** *n* surmenage *m* **2**
v/i se surmener

owe [ou] devoir (**s.o.** à qn);
owing to à cause de

owl [aul] hibou *m*, chouette *f*

own[1] [oun] *v/t* posséder

own[2] [oun] *pron*: **an apartment of my ~** un appartement à moi; **on my/his ~** tout
seul

◆ **own up** avouer

owner ['ounər] propriétaire
m/f; ownership possession
f, propriété *f*

oxygen ['ɑːksɪdʒən] oxygène
m

oyster ['ɔɪstər] huître *f*

ozone ['ouzoun] ozone *m*;
ozone layer couche *f* d'ozone

P

PA [piːˈeɪ] (= *personal assistant*) secrétaire *m/f*

pace [peɪs] (*step*) pas *m*; (*speed*) allure *f*; **pacemaker** MED stimulateur *m* cardiaque, pacemaker *m* SP lièvre *m*

Pacific [pəˈsɪfɪk]: **the ~ (Ocean)** le Pacifique, l'océan *m* Pacifique

pacifier [ˈpæsɪfaɪər] *for baby* sucette *f*; **pacifism** pacifisme *m*; **pacifist** pacifiste *m/f*; **pacify** calmer, apaiser

pack [pæk] **1** *n* (*back~*) sac *m* à dos; *of cereal, cigarettes etc* paquet *m*; *of cards* jeu *m* **2** *v/t item of clothing etc* mettre dans ses bagages; *goods* emballer; **~ one's bag** faire sa valise **3** *v/i* faire ses bagages; **package 1** *n* (*parcel*) paquet *m*; *of offers etc* forfait *m* **2** *v/t in packs* conditionner; *idea, project* présenter; **packaging** *of product* conditionnement *m*; *material* emballage *m*; *of idea* présentation *f*; **packet** paquet *m*

pact [pækt] pacte *m*

pad¹ [pæd] **1** *n protective* tampon *m* de protection; *over wound* tampon *m*; *for writing* bloc *m* **2** *v/t with material* rembourrer; *speech, report* délayer

pad² [pæd] *v/i* (*move quietly*) marcher à pas feutrés

padding [ˈpædɪŋ] *material* rembourrage *m*; *in speech etc* remplissage *m*

paddle [ˈpædl] **1** *n for canoe* pagaie *f* **2** *v/i in canoe* pagayer

paddock [ˈpædək] paddock *m*

padlock [ˈpædlɑːk] cadenas *m*

page¹ [peɪdʒ] *n of book etc* page *f*

page² [peɪdʒ] (*call*) (faire) appeler

pager [ˈpeɪdʒər] pager *m*, radiomessageur *m*; *for doctor* bip *m*

paid em'ployment travail *m* rémunéré

pain [peɪn] douleur *f*; **be in ~** souffrir; **painful** *arm, leg etc* douloureux; (*distressing*) pénible; (*laborious*) difficile; **painfully** (*extremely, acutely*) terriblement; **painkiller** analgésique *m*; **painstaking** minutieux

paint [peɪnt] **1** *n* peinture *f* **2** *v/t* peindre; **paintbrush** pinceau *m*; **painter** peintre *m*; **painting** *activity* peinture *f*; *picture* tableau *m*; **paintwork** peinture *f*

pair [per] paire *f*; *of people, animals* couple *m*; **a ~ of pants** un pantalon

pajamas [pə'dʒɑːməz] pyjama m

Pakistan [pækɪ'stɑːn] Pakistan m; **Pakistani 1** adj pakistanais **2** n Pakistanais(e) m(f)

pal [pæl] F (friend) copain m, copine f

palace ['pælɪs] palais m

palate ['pælət] ANAT, fig palais m

palatial [pə'leɪʃl] somptueux

pale [peɪl] pâle; **go ~** pâlir

Palestine ['pæləstaɪn] Palestine f; **Palestinian 1** adj palestinien **2** n Palestinien(ne) m(f)

pallet ['pælɪt] palette f

pallor ['pælər] pâleur f

palm [pɑːm] of hand paume f

palm tree palmier m

paltry ['pɔːltrɪ] dérisoire

pamper ['pæmpər] gâter

pamphlet ['pæmflɪt] for information brochure f; political tract m

pan [pæn] casserole f; for frying poêle f

pancake ['pænkeɪk] crêpe f

pandemonium [pændɪ'məʊnɪəm] désordre m

pane [peɪn]: **a ~ of glass** un carreau

panel ['pænl] panneau m; people comité m; on TV program invités mpl

paneling, Br **panelling** lambris m

panic ['pænɪk] **1** n panique f **2** v/i paniquer; **panic-stricken**

affolé, pris de panique

panorama [pænə'rɑːmə] panorama m; **panoramic** panoramique

pant [pænt] of person haleter

panties ['pæntɪz] culotte f

pantihose → pantyhose

pants [pænts] pantalon m

pantyhose ['pæntɪhəʊz] collant m

papal ['peɪpl] papal

paparazzi [pæpə'rætsiː] paparazzi m/f

paper ['peɪpər] **1** n papier m; (news~) journal m; (wall~) papier m peint; academic article m, exposé m; (examination ~) épreuve f; **~s** (documents) documents mpl; (identity ~s) papiers mpl **2** adj (made of ~) en papier **3** v/t room tapisser; **paperback** livre m de poche; **paper clip** trombone m; **paperwork** tâches fpl administratives

parachute ['pærəʃuːt] **1** n parachute m **2** v/i sauter en parachute **3** v/t troops, supplies parachuter

parade [pə'reɪd] **1** n (procession) défilé m **2** v/i of soldiers défiler; showing off parader

paradise ['pærədaɪs] REL, fig paradis m

paradox ['pærədɒks] paradoxe m; **paradoxical** paradoxal; **paradoxically** paradoxalement

paragraph ['pærəgræf] paragraphe *m*

parallel ['pærəlel] **1** *n* parallèle *f*; GEOG, *fig* parallèle *m* **2** *adj also fig* parallèle **3** *v/t* (*match*) égaler

paralysis [pə'rælǝsɪs] *also fig* paralysie *f*; **paralyze** paralyser

paramedic [pærə'medɪk] auxiliaire *m/f* médical(e)

parameter [pǝ'ræmɪtǝr] paramètre *m*

paramilitary [pærǝ'mɪlɪterɪ] **1** *adj* paramilitaire **2** *n* membre *m* d'une organisation paramilitaire

paranoia [pærǝ'nɔɪǝ] paranoïa *f*; **paranoid** paranoïaque

paraphrase ['pærǝfreɪz] paraphraser

parasite ['pærǝsaɪt] *also fig* parasite *m*

parasol ['pærǝsɑːl] parasol *m*

paratrooper ['pærǝtruːpǝr] parachutiste *m*, para *m* F

parcel ['pɑːrsl] colis *m*, paquet *m*

pardon ['pɑːrdn] **1** *n* LAW grâce *f*; **I beg your ~?** (*what did you say?*) comment?; (*I'm sorry*) je vous demande pardon **2** *v/t* pardonner; LAW gracier; **~ me?** pardon?

parent ['perǝnt] père *m*; mère *f*; **my ~s** mes parents; **parental** parental; **parent company** société *f* mère

parent-'teacher association association *f* de parents

d'élèves

parish ['perɪʃ] paroisse *f*

park[1] [pɑːrk] *n* parc *m*

park[2] [pɑːrk] MOT **1** *v/t* garer *m* **2** *v/i* stationner, se garer; **parking** MOT stationnement *m*; **parking brake** frein *m* à main; **parking garage** parking *m* couvert; **parking lot** parking *m*; **parking meter** parcmètre *m*; **parking ticket** contravention *f*

parliament ['pɑːrlǝmǝnt] parlement *m*

parole [pǝ'roʊl] **1** *n* libération *f* conditionnelle **2** *v/t* mettre en liberté conditionnelle

parrot ['pærǝt] perroquet *m*

part [pɑːrt] **1** *n* partie *f*; *of machine* pièce *f*; *in movie* rôle *m*; *in hair* raie *f*; **take ~ in** participer à, prendre part à **2** *adv* (*partly*) en partie **3** *v/i of two people* se quitter, se séparer; **partial** (*incomplete*) partiel; **partially** partiellement

participant [pɑːr'tɪsɪpǝnt] participant(e) *m(f)*; **participate** participer (*in* à); **participation** participation *f*

particular [pǝr'tɪkjǝlǝr] particulier; (*fussy*) à cheval (**about** sur), exigeant; **particularly** particulièrement

partition [pɑːr'tɪʃn] (*screen*) cloison *f*; *of country* partage *m*, division *f*

partly ['pɑːrtlɪ] en partie

partner ['pɑːrtnǝr] partenaire

m; COM associé *m*; *in relationship* compagnon(ne) *m(f)*; **partnership** COM, *in relationship* association *f*; *in particular activity* partenariat *m*

'part-time à temps partiel

party ['pɑːrtɪ] **1** *n (celebration)* fête *f*; *for adults in the evening also* soirée *f*; POL parti *m*; *(group of people)* groupe *m* **2** *v/i* F faire la fête

pass [pæs] **1** *n for entry* laissez-passer *m inv*; SP passe *f*; *in mountains* col *m* **2** *v/t (go past)* passer devant; *another car* doubler, dépasser; *competitor* dépasser; *(go beyond)*; *(approve)* approuver; **~ an exam** réussir (à) un examen **3** *v/i of time* passer; *in exam* être reçu; SP faire une passe; *(go away)* passer

♦ **pass away** *(euph: die)* s'éteindre

♦ **pass on 1** *v/t information, book* passer **2** *v/i (euph: die)* s'éteindre

♦ **pass out** *(faint)* s'évanouir

♦ **pass up** *opportunity* laisser passer

passable ['pæsəbl] *road* praticable; *(acceptable)* passable

passage ['pæsɪdʒ] *(corridor)* couloir *m*; *from book, of time* passage *m*

passenger ['pæsɪndʒər] passager(-ère) *m(f)*

passer-by [pæsər'baɪ] passant(e) *m(f)*

passion ['pæʃn] passion *f*;

passionate *lover* passionné; *(fervent)* fervent, véhément

passive ['pæsɪv] **1** *adj* passif **2** *n* GRAM passif *m*; **passive smoking** tabagisme *m* passif

'passport passeport *m*; **passport control** contrôle *m* des passeport; **password** mot *m* de passe

past [pæst] **1** *adj (former)* passé; **the ~ few days** ces derniers jours *2 n* passé *m*; **in the ~** autrefois **3** *prep* après; **it's ~ 7 o'clock** il est plus de 7 heures; **it's half ~ two** il est deux heures et demie **4** *adv:* **run ~** passer en courant

pasta ['pɑːstə] pâtes *fpl*

paste [peɪst] **1** *n (adhesive)* colle *f* **2** *v/t (stick)* coller

pastime ['pæstaɪm] passetemps *m inv*

past par'ticiple GRAM participe *m* passé

pastry ['peɪstrɪ] *for pie* pâte *f*; *small cake* pâtisserie *f*

'past tense GRAM passé *m*

pasty ['peɪstɪ] *complexion* blafard

pat [pæt] **1** *n* petite tape *f* **2** *v/t* tapoter

patch [pætʃ] **1** *n on clothing* pièce *f*; *(period of time)* période *f*; *(area)* tache *f*; **go through a bad ~** traverser une mauvaise passe **2** *v/t clothing* rapiécer

♦ **patch up** *(repair)* rafistoler F; *quarrel* régler

patchy ['pætʃɪ] inégal

patent ['peɪtnt] **1** *adj (obvious)* manifeste **2** *n for invention* brevet *m* **3** *v/t invention* breveter

paternal [pə'tɜːrnl] paternel; **paternalism** paternalisme *m*; **paternalistic** paternaliste; **paternity** paternité *f*

path [pæθ] chemin *m*; *surfaced* allée *f*; *fig* voie *f*

pathetic [pə'θetɪk] touchant; *F (very bad)* pathétique

pathological [pæθə'lɑːdʒɪkl] pathologique

patience ['peɪʃns] patience *f*; **patient 1** *adj* patient **2** *n* patient *m*; **patiently** patiemment

patio ['pætɪou] *Br* patio *m*

patriot ['peɪtrɪət] patriote *m/f*; **patriotic** *person* patriote; *song* patriotique; **patriotism** patriotisme *m*

patrol [pə'troul] **1** *n* patrouille *f* **2** *v/t streets, border* patrouiller dans/à; **patrol car** voiture *f* de police; **patrolman** agent *m* de police; **patrol wagon** fourgon *m* cellulaire

patron ['peɪtrən] *of store, movie theater* client(e) *m(f)*; *of artist, charity etc* protecteur(-trice) *m(f)*; **patronize** *person* traiter avec condescendance; **patronizing** condescendant; **patron saint** patron(ne) *m(f)*

pattern ['pætərn] *on fabric* motif *m*; *for sewing* patron *m*; *(model)* modèle *m*; *in events* scénario *m*

paunch [pɔːntʃ] ventre *m*

pause [pɔːz] **1** *n* pause *f* **2** *v/i* faire une pause **3** *v/t tape* mettre en mode pause

pave [peɪv] paver; *(roadway)* chaussée *f*; *Br (sidewalk)* trottoir *m*

paw [pɔː] **1** *n* patte *f* **2** *v/t* F tripoter

pawn [pɔːn] *in chess, fig* pion *m*

pay [peɪ] **1** *n* paye *f*, salaire *m* **2** *v/t* payer; ~ **attention** faire attention **3** *v/i* payer; *(be profitable)* être rentable; ~ **for** *purchase* payer

◆ **pay back** rembourser; *(get revenge on)* faire payer à

◆ **pay off 1** *v/t debt* rembourser; *(corrupt official* acheter **2** *v/i (be profitable)* être rentable

◆ **pay up** payer

payable ['peɪəbl] payable; **pay check**, *Br* **pay cheque** chèque *m* de paie; **payday** jour *m* de paie; **payee** bénéficiaire *m/f*; **payment** paiement *m*; **pay phone** téléphone *m* public

PC [piː'siː] (= *personal computer*) P.C. *m*; (= *politically correct*) politiquement correct

pea [piː] petit pois *m*

peace [piːs] paix *f*; **peaceful** paisible, tranquille; *demonstration* pacifique; **peace-**

fully paisiblement

peach [piːtʃ] pêche f

peak [piːk] **1** n of mountain pic m; fig apogée f **2** v/i culminer; **peak hours** of electricity consumption heures fpl pleines; of traffic heures fpl de pointe

peanut ['piːnʌt] cacahuète f; **get paid ~s** F être payé trois fois rien; **peanut butter** beurre m de cacahuètes

pear [per] poire f

pearl [pɜːrl] perle f

pecan ['piːkæn] pécan m

peck [pek] **1** n (bite) coup m de bec; (kiss) bise f (rapide) **2** v/t (bite) donner un coup de bec à; (kiss) embrasser rapidement

peculiar [pɪˈkjuːljər] (strange) bizarre; **peculiarity** bizarrerie f; (special feature) particularité f

pedal ['pedl] **1** n of bike pédale f **2** v/i pédaler; **he ~ed off home** il est rentré chez lui à vélo

peddle ['pedl] drugs faire du trafic de

pedestrian [pɪˈdestrɪən] piéton(ne) m(f)

pediatric [piːdɪˈætrɪk] pédiatrique; **pediatrician** pédiatre m/f; **pediatrics** pédiatrie f

pedicure ['pedɪkjʊr] soins mpl des pieds

pedigree ['pedɪgriː] **1** adj avec pedigree **2** n of dog, racehorse pedigree m; of person

arbre m généalogique

pee [piː] v/i F faire pipi F

peek [piːk] **1** n coup m d'œil (furtif) **2** v/i jeter un coup d'œil, regarder furtivement

peel [piːl] **1** n peau f **2** v/t fruit, vegetables éplucher, peler **3** v/i of nose, shoulders peler; of paint s'écailler

peep [piːp] → **peek**

peephole judas m

peer[1] [pɪr] (equal) pair m; of same age group personne f du même âge

peer[2] [pɪr] v/i regarder

peg [peg] for hat, coat patère f; for tent piquet m; **off the ~** de confection

pejorative [pɪˈdʒɑːrətɪv] péjoratif

pellet ['pelɪt] boulette f; for gun plomb m

pen[1] [pen] stylo m

pen[2] [pen] (enclosure) enclos m

pen[3] [pen] → **penitentiary**

penalize ['piːnəlaɪz] pénaliser

penalty ['penltɪ] sanction f; JUR peine f; fine amende f; SP pénalisation f; soccer penalty m; **penalty area** soccer surface f de réparation; **penalty clause** LAW clause f pénale; **penalty kick** soccer penalty m

pencil ['pensɪl] crayon m (de bois); **pencil sharpener** taille-crayon m inv

pendant ['pendənt] necklace pendentif m

penetrate ['penɪtreɪt] pénétrer; **penetration** pénétration *f*

penguin ['peŋgwɪn] manchot *m*

penicillin [penɪ'sɪlɪn] pénicilline *f*

peninsula [pə'nɪnsʊlə] presqu'île *f*

penitence ['penɪtəns] pénitence *f*, repentir *m*; **penitentiary** pénitencier *m*

'**pen name** nom *m* de plume

pennant ['penənt] fanion *m*

penniless ['penɪlɪs] sans le sou

'**pen pal** correspondant(e) *m(f)*

pension ['penʃn] retraite *f*, pension *f*

◆ **pension off** mettre à la retraite

pensive ['pensɪv] pensif

Pentagon ['pentəgɑːn]: *the ~* le Pentagone

pentathlon [pen'tæθlən] pentathlon *m*

penthouse ['penthaʊs] penthouse *m*, appartement *m* luxueux (édifié sur le toit d'un immeuble)

pent-up ['pentʌp] refoulé

penultimate [pe'nʌltɪmət] avant-dernier

people ['piːpl] gens *mpl*; (*race*, *tribe*) peuple *m*; **10 ~** 10 personnes; *the ~* le peuple; **~ say** ... on dit...

pepper ['pepər] *spice* poivre *m*; *vegetable* poivron *m*; pep-

permint *candy* bonbon *m* à la menthe; *flavoring* menthe *f* poivrée

per [pɜːr] par; **~ annum** par an

perceive [pər'siːv] percevoir

percent [pər'sent] pour cent; **percentage** pourcentage *m*

perceptible [pər'septəbl] perceptible; **perceptibly** sensiblement; **perception** perception *f*; (*insight*) perspicacité *f*; **perceptive** perspicace

percolate ['pɜːrkəleɪt] *of coffee* passer; **percolator** cafetière *f* à pression

perfect 1 ['pɜːrfɪkt] *adj* parfait **2** ['pɜːrfɪkt] *n* GRAM passé *m* composé **3** [pər'fekt] *v/t* perfectionner; **perfection** perfection *f*; **perfectionist** perfectionniste *m/f*; **perfectly** parfaitement; (*totally*) tout à fait

perforated ['pɜːrfəreɪtɪd] perforé; **~ line** pointillé *m*

perform [pər'fɔːrm] **1** *v/t* (*carry out*) exécuter; *of actor etc* jouer **2** *v/i of actor, musician, dancer* jouer; *of machine* fonctionner; **performance** *by actor, musician etc* interprétation *f*; (*event*) représentation *f*; *of employee, company etc* résultats *mpl*; *of machine* performances *fpl*; rendement *m*; **performer** interprète *m/f*

perfume ['pɜːrfjuːm] parfum *m*

perfunctory [pər'fʌŋktərɪ]

sommaire

perhaps [pər'hæps] peut-être

peril ['perəl] péril *m*

perimeter [pə'rɪmɪtər] périmètre *m*

period ['pɪrɪəd] période *f*; *(menstruation)* règles *fpl*; *punctuation mark* point *m*; **periodic** périodique; **periodical** périodique *m*

peripheral [pə'rɪfərəl] **1** *adj (not crucial)* secondaire **2** *n* COMPUT périphérique *m*; **periphery** périphérie *f*

perish ['perɪʃ] *of rubber* se détériorer; *of person* périr; **perishable** *food* périssable

perjure ['pɜːrdʒər]: ~ **o.s.** faire un faux témoignage; **perjury** faux témoignage *m*

perm [pɜːrm] **1** *n* permanente *f* **2** *v/t*: **have one's hair ~ed** se faire faire une permanente

permanent ['pɜːrmənənt] permanent; *address* fixe; **permanently** en permanence

permeate ['pɜːrmɪeɪt] *also fig* imprégner

permissible [pər'mɪsəbl] permis; **permission** permission *f*; **permissive** permissif; **permit 1** *n* permis *m* **2** *v/t* permettre (**s.o. to do** à qn de faire)

perpendicular [pɜːrpən'dɪkjʊlər] perpendiculaire

perpetual [pər'petʃuəl] perpétuel; **perpetually** perpétuellement

perplex [pər'pleks] laisser perplexe; **perplexity** perplexité *f*

persecute ['pɜːrsɪkjuːt] persécuter; **persecution** persécution *f*; **persecutor** persécuteur(-trice) *m(f)*

perseverance [pɜːrsɪ'vɪrəns] persévérance *f*; **persevere** persévérer

persist [pər'sɪst] persister; **persistent** *person* tenace, têtu; *questions* incessant; *rain, unemployment etc* persistant; **persistently** *(continually)* continuellement

person ['pɜːrsn] personne *f*; **personal** personnel; **personal computer** ordinateur *m* individuel; **personality** personnalité *f*; **personally** personnellement; *come, intervene* en personne; **personal organizer** organiseur *m*, agenda *m* électronique; *in book form* agenda *m*; **personal stereo** baladeur *m*; **personify** *of person* personnifier

personnel [pɜːrsə'nel] *(employees)* personnel *m*; *department* service *m* du personnel

perspective [pər'spektɪv] *in art* perspective *f*; **get sth into** ~ relativiser qch

perspiration [pɜːrspɪ'reɪʃn] transpiration *f*; **perspire** transpirer

persuade [pər'sweɪd] *person*

persuader; **persuasion** persuasion *f*; **persuasive** *person* persuasif; *argument* convaincant

perturb [pər'tɜːrb] perturber; **perturbing** perturbant

pervasive [pər'veɪsɪv] *influence, ideas* envahissant

perversion [pər'vɜːrʃn] *sexual* perversion *f*; **pervert** *sexual* pervers(e) *m(f)*

pessimism ['pesɪmɪzm] pessimisme *m*; **pessimist** pessimiste *m/f*; **pessimistic** pessimiste

pest [pest] parasite *m*; F *person* peste *f*

pester ['pestər] harceler

pesticide ['pestɪsaɪd] pesticide *m*

pet [pet] **1** *n animal* animal *m* domestique; *(favorite)* chouchou *m* F **2** *adj* préféré, favori **3** *v/t animal* caresser **4** *v/i of couple* se peloter F

petite [pə'tiːt] menu

petition [pə'tɪʃn] pétition *f*

petrify ['petrɪfaɪ] pétrifier

petrochemical [petrou'kemɪkl] pétrochimique

petrol ['petrl] *Br* essence *f*

petroleum [pɪ'trouliəm] pétrole *m*

petting ['petɪŋ] pelotage *m* F

petty ['petɪ] *person, behavior* mesquin; *details* insignifiant

pew [pjuː] banc *m* d'église

pharmaceutical [fɑːrmə'suːtɪkl] pharmaceutique; **pharmaceuticals** produits *mpl* pharmaceutiques

pharmacist ['fɑːrməsɪst] pharmacien(ne) *m(f)*; **pharmacy** *store* pharmacie *f*

phase [feɪz] phase *f*

phenomenal [fə'nɑːmɪnl] phénoménal; **phenomenon** phénomène *m*

philanthropic [fɪlən'θrɑːpɪk] *person* philanthrope; *action* philanthropique; **philanthropist** philanthrope *m/f*; **philanthropy** philanthropie *f*

Philippines ['fɪlɪpiːnz]: **the ~** les Philippines *fpl*

philosopher [fɪ'lɑːsəfər] philosophe *m/f*; **philosophical** philosophique; *attitude etc* philosophe; **philosophy** philosophie *f*

phobia ['foubiə] phobie *f* (**about** de)

phone [foun] **1** *n* téléphone *m* **2** *v/t* téléphoner à **3** *v/i* téléphoner; **phone book** annuaire *m*; **phone booth** cabine *f* téléphonique; **phonecall** coup *m* de fil *or* de téléphone; **phone card** télécarte *f*; **phone number** numéro *m* de téléphone

phon(e)y ['founɪ] F faux

photo ['foutou] photo *f*; **photocopier** photocopieuse *f*; **photocopy 1** *n* photocopie *f* **2** *v/t* photocopier; **photogenic** photogénique; **photograph 1** *n* photographie *f* **2** *v/t* photographier; **photog-**

rapher photographe *m/f*;
photography photographie
f

phrase [freɪz] **1** *n* expression
f; *in grammar* syntagme *m*
2 *v/t* formuler

physical ['fɪzɪkl] **1** *adj* physique **2** *n* MED visite *f* médicale; **physically** physiquement

physician [fɪ'zɪʃn] médecin
m

physicist ['fɪzɪsɪst] physicien(ne) *m(f)*; **physics** physique *f*

physiotherapist [fɪzɪəʊ'θerəpɪst] kinésithérapeute *m/f*;
physiotherapy kinésithérapie *f*

physique [fɪ'ziːk] physique *m*

pianist ['pɪənɪst] pianiste *m/f*;
piano piano *m*

pick [pɪk] (*choose*) choisir;
flowers, fruit cueillir

◆ **pick up 1** *v/t* prendre;
phone décrocher; *from ground* ramasser; (*collect*)
passer prendre; *information*
recueillir; *in car* prendre; *in sexual sense* lever F; *language, skill* apprendre; *illness* attraper; (*buy*) acheter
2 *v/i of business, economy* reprendre; *of weather* s'améliorer

picket ['pɪkɪt] **1** *n of strikers*
piquet *m* de grève **2** *v/t*: ~ *a factory* faire le piquet de
grève devant une usine

'**pickpocket** voleur *m* à la tire,

pickpocket *m*

pick-up (truck) ['pɪkʌp] pick-up *m*, camionnette *f*

picky ['pɪkɪ] F difficile

picnic ['pɪknɪk] **1** *n* pique-nique *m* **2** *v/i* pique-niquer

picture ['pɪktʃər] **1** *n* (*photo*)
photo *f*; (*painting*) tableau
m; (*illustration*) image *f*;
(*movie*) film *m* **2** *v/t* imaginer

picturesque [pɪktʃə'resk] pittoresque

pie [paɪ] tarte *f*; *with top* tourte *f*

piece [piːs] morceau *m*; (*component*) pièce *f*; *in board game* pion *m*; *a ~ of advice*
un conseil; *take to ~s* démonter

◆ **piece together** *broken plate* recoller; *evidence* regrouper

piecemeal ['piːsmiːl] petit à
petit

pier [pɪr] *Br at seaside* jetée *f*

pierce [pɪrs] (*penetrate*) transpercer; *ears* percer; **piercing**
noise, eyes perçant; *wind* pénétrant

pig [pɪg] cochon *m*, porc *m*;
(*unpleasant person*) porc *m*

pigeon ['pɪdʒɪn] pigeon *m*; **pigeonhole** casier *m*

pigheaded [pɪg'hedɪd] obstiné; **pigpen** *also fig* porcherie
f

pile [paɪl] *of books, plates etc*
pile *f*; *of sand etc* tas *m*; *a ~ of work* F un tas de boulot F

◆ **pile up 1** *v/i of work, bills*

s'accumuler **2** v/t empiler

'pile-up MOT carambolage m

pilfering ['pɪlfərɪŋ] chardage m F

pill [pɪl] pilule f

pillar ['pɪlər] pilier m

pillow ['pɪloʊ] oreiller m; **pillowcase** taie f d'oreiller

pilot ['paɪlət] **1** n AVIA, NAUT pilote m **2** v/t airplane piloter

pimp [pɪmp] maquereau m, proxénète m

pimple ['pɪmpl] bouton m

PIN [pɪn] (= **personal identification number**) code m confidentiel

pin [pɪn] **1** n for sewing épingle f; in bowling quille f; (badge) badge m; fiche f **2** v/t (hold down) clouer; (attach) épingler

◆ **pin up** notice accrocher

pincers ['pɪnsərz] of crab pinces fpl; tool tenailles fpl

pinch [pɪntʃ] **1** n pincement m; of salt etc pincée f **2** v/t pincer **3** v/i of shoes serrer

pine [paɪn] tree, wood pin m; **pineapple** ananas m

pink [pɪŋk] rose

pinnacle ['pɪnəkl] fig apogée f

'pinpoint indiquer précisément; find identifier; **pins and needles** fourmillements mpl; **pin-up** (girl) pin-up f inv

pioneer [paɪə'nɪr] **1** n fig pionnier(-ière) m(f) **2** v/t lancer; **pioneering** work innovateur

pious ['paɪəs] pieux

pip [pɪp] Br of fruit pépin m

pipe [paɪp] **1** n tuyau m; for smoking pipe f **2** v/t transporter par tuyau; **pipeline** for oil oléoduc m; for gas gazoduc m

pirate ['paɪrət] **1** n pirate m **2** v/t software pirater

pissed [pɪst] P (annoyed) en rogne F; Br P (drunk) bourré

pistol ['pɪstl] pistolet m

piston ['pɪstən] piston m

pit [pɪt] (hole) fosse f; (coalmine) mine f

pitch¹ [pɪtʃ] n ton m

pitch² [pɪtʃ] **1** v/i in baseball lancer **2** v/t tent planter; ball lancer

pitcher¹ ['pɪtʃər] in baseball lanceur m

pitcher² ['pɪtʃər] container pichet m

pitfall ['pɪtfɔːl] piège m

pitiful ['pɪtɪfl] pitoyable; **pitiless** impitoyable

pittance ['pɪtns] somme f dérisoire

pity ['pɪti] n pitié f; **what a ~!** quel dommage! **2** v/t person avoir pitié de

pizza ['piːtsə] pizza f

placard ['plækɑːrd] pancarte f

place [pleɪs] **1** n endroit m; in race, competition place f; (seat) place f; **at my/his ~** chez moi/lui; **in ~ of** à la place de; **take ~** avoir lieu **2** v/t (put) mettre, poser; order passer

placid ['plæsɪd] placide

plagiarism ['pleɪdʒərɪzm] plagiat *m*; **plagiarize** plagier

plain¹ [pleɪn] *n* plaine *f*

plain² [pleɪn] **1** *adj* (*clear, obvious*) clair, évident; (*not ornate*) simple; (*not patterned*) uni; (*not pretty*) ordinaire; (*blunt*) franc **2** *adv* tout simplement; **plainly** (*clearly*) manifestement; (*bluntly*) franchement; (*simply*) simplement; **plain-spoken** direct

plaintive ['pleɪntɪv] plaintif

plan [plæn] **1** *n* plan *m*, projet *m*; (*drawing*) plan *m* **2** *v/t* (*prepare*) organiser, planifier; (*design*) concevoir **3** *v/i* faire des projets

plane¹ [pleɪn] AVIA avion *m*

plane² [pleɪn] *tool* rabot *m*

planet ['plænɪt] planète *f*

plank [plæŋk] *of wood* planche *f*; *fig: of policy* point *m*

planning ['plænɪŋ] organisation *f*, planification *f*

plant¹ [plænt] **1** *n* BOT plante *f* **2** *v/t* planter

plant² [plænt] (*factory*) usine *f*; (*equipment*) installation *f*, matériel *m*

plantation [plæn'teɪʃn] plantation *f*

plaque [plæk] *on wall* plaque *f*; *on teeth* plaque *f* dentaire

plaster ['plɑːstər] **1** *n* plâtre *m* **2** *v/t* wall, ceiling plâtrer

plastic ['plæstɪk] **1** *adj* en plastique **2** *n* plastique *m*;

plastic money cartes *fpl* de crédit; **plastic surgeon** spécialiste *m* en chirurgie esthétique; **plastic surgery** chirurgie *f* esthétique

plate [pleɪt] *for food* assiette *f*; (*sheet of metal*) plaque *f*

plateau ['plætoʊ] plateau *m*

platform ['plætfɔːrm] (*stage*) estrade *f*; *of railroad station* quai *m*; *fig: political* plate-forme *f*

platinum ['plætɪnəm] **1** *adj* en platine **2** *n* platine *m*

platonic [plə'tɑːnɪk] platonique

platoon [plə'tuːn] *of soldiers* section *f*

plausible ['plɔːzəbl] plausible

play [pleɪ] **1** *n* jeu *m*; *in theater, on TV* pièce *f* **2** *v/i* jouer **3** *v/t* *musical instrument* jouer de; *piece of music* jouer; *game* jouer à; *opponent* jouer contre; (*perform: Macbeth etc*) jouer

◆ **play around** F (*be unfaithful*) coucher à droite et à gauche

◆ **play down** minimiser

player ['pleɪr] SP joueur(-euse) *m(f)*; (*musician*) musicien (-ne) *m(f)*; (*actor*) acteur (-trice) *m(f)*; **playful** enjoué; **playground** aire *f* de jeu; **playing card** carte *f* à jouer; **playwright** dramaturge *m/f*

plaza ['plɑːzə] *for shopping* centre *m* commercial

plc [piːel'siː] *Br* (= **public lim-**

ited company S.A. f (= société anonyme)

plea [pli:] appel

plead [pli:d]: ~ **guilty/not guilty** plaider coupable/non coupable; ~ **with** supplier

pleasant ['pleznt] agréable

please [pli:z] **1** adv s'il vous plaît, s'il te plaît; ~ **do** je vous en prie **2** v/t plaire &; ~ **yourself** comme tu veux; **pleased** content, heureux; ~ **to meet you** enchanté; **pleasing** agréable; **pleasure** plaisir m; **with** ~ avec plaisir

pleat [pli:t] in skirt pli m

pledge [pledʒ] **1** n (promise) promesse f; as guarantee gage m; **Pledge of Allegiance** serment m d'allégeance **2** v/t (promise) promettre; money mettre en gage

plentiful ['plentɪfl] abondant; **be** ~ abonder; **plenty** (abundance) abondance f; ~ **of** beaucoup de

pliable ['plaɪəbl] flexible

pliers ['plaɪərz] pinces fpl

plight [plaɪt] détresse f

plod [plɑːd] (walk) marcher d'un pas lourd

plot¹ [plɑːt] of land parcelle f

plot² [plɑːt] **1** n (conspiracy) complot m; of novel intrigue f **2** v/t & v/i comploter

plotter ['plɑːtər] conspirateur(-trice) m(f); COMPUT traceur m

plow, Br **plough** [plaʊ] **1** n charrue f **2** v/t & v/i labourer

♦ **plow back** profits réinvestir

pluck [plʌk] chicken plumer; ~ **one's eyebrows** s'épiler les sourcils

plug [plʌg] **1** n for sink, bath bouchon m; electrical prise f; (spark ~) bougie f **2** v/t hole boucher; new book etc faire de la pub pour F

♦ **plug in** brancher

plumage ['plu:mɪdʒ] plumage m

plumber ['plʌmər] plombier m; **plumbing** plomberie f

plummet ['plʌmɪt] of airplane plonger, piquer; of share prices dégringoler

plump [plʌmp] person, chicken dodu; hands, feet potelé; face, cheek rond

plunge [plʌndʒ] **1** n plongeon m; in prices chute f **2** v/i tomber; of prices chuter **3** v/t plonger; knife enfoncer; **plunging** neckline plongeant

plural ['plʊrəl] pluriel m

plus [plʌs] **1** prep plus **2** adj plus de **3** n sign signe m plus; (advantage) plus m **4** conj (moreover, in addition) en plus

plush [plʌʃ] luxueux

plywood ['plaɪwʊd] contreplaqué m

PM [pi:'em] Br (= Prime Minister) Premier ministre

p.m. [pi:'em] (= post meridiem) afternoon de l'après-midi; evening du soir

pneumonia [nuːˈməʊnɪə] pneumonie f

poach¹ [pəʊtʃ] cook pocher

poach² [pəʊtʃ] salmon etc braconner

poached egg [pəʊtʃtˈeg] œuf m poché

P.O. Box [piːˈəʊbɑːks] boîte f postale, B.P. f

pocket [ˈpɑːkɪt] 1 n poche f 2 adj (miniature) de poche 3 v/t empocher; pocketbook purse pochette f; (billfold) portefeuille m; book livre m de poche; pocket calculator calculatrice f de poche

podium [ˈpəʊdɪəm] estrade f; for winner podium m

poem [ˈpəʊɪm] poème m; poet poète m, poétesse f; poetic poétique; poetry poésie f

poignant [ˈpɔɪnjənt] poignant

point [pɔɪnt] 1 n of pencil, knife pointe f; in competition, exam point m; (purpose) objet m; (moment) moment m; in argument, discussion point m; in decimals virgule f; that's beside the ~ là n'est pas la question; be on the ~ of doing sth être sur le point de faire qch; get to the ~ en venir au fait; the ~ is ... le fait est (que)...; there's no ~ in waiting ça ne sert à rien d'attendre 2 v/i montrer (du doigt)

♦ point out sights montrer; advantages etc faire remarquer

♦ point to with finger montrer du doig; fig (indicate) indiquer

pointed [ˈpɔɪntɪd] remark acerbe, mordant; pointer for teacher baguette f; (hint) conseil m; (sign, indication) indice m; pointless inutile; point of view point m de vue

poise [pɔɪz] assurance f, aplomb m; poised person posé

poison [ˈpɔɪzn] 1 n poison m 2 v/t empoisonner; poisonous snake, spider venimeux; plant vénéneux

poke [pəʊk] 1 n coup m 2 v/t (prod) pousser; (stick) enfoncer

♦ poke around F fouiner F

poker [ˈpəʊkər] card game poker m

polar [ˈpəʊlər] polaire

pole¹ [pəʊl] of wood, metal perche f

pole² [pəʊl] of earth pôle m

police [pəˈliːs] police f; police car voiture f de police; policeman gendarme m; criminal policier m; police state État m policier; police station gendarmerie f; for criminal matters commissariat m; policewoman femme f gendarme; criminal femme f policier

policy¹ [ˈpɑːləsɪ] politique f

policy² [ˈpɑːləsɪ] (insurance ~) police f (d'assurance)

polio [ˈpəʊlɪəʊ] polio f

polish ['pɑːlɪʃ] **1** *n for furniture* cire *f*; *for shoes* cirage *m*; *for metal* produit *m* lustrant; (*nail ~*) vernis *m* (à ongles) **2** *v/t* faire briller, lustrer; *shoes* cirer; *speech* parfaire; **polished** *performance* impeccable

polite [pə'laɪt] poli; **politely** poliment; **politeness** politesse *f*

political [pə'lɪtɪkl] politique; **politically correct** politiquement correct; **politician** politicien *m*, homme *m*/femme *f* politique; **politics** politique *f*

poll [poʊl] **1** *n* (*survey*) sondage *m*; **go to the ~s** (*vote*) aller aux urnes **2** *v/t people* faire un sondage auprès de; *votes* obtenir

pollen ['pɑːlən] pollen *m*

pollster ['poʊlstər] sondeur *m*

pollutant [pə'luːtənt] polluant *m*; **pollute** polluer; **pollution** pollution *f*

'**polo shirt** polo *m*

polyester [pɑːlɪ'estər] polyester *m*

polystyrene [pɑːlɪ'staɪriːn] polystyrène *m*

polyunsaturated [pɑːlɪʌn'sætʃəreɪtɪd] polyinsaturé

pond [pɑːnd] étang *m*; *artificial* bassin *m*

pontiff ['pɑːntɪf] pontife *m*

pony ['poʊni] poney *m*; **ponytail** queue *f* de cheval

pool¹ [puːl] (*swimming ~*) piscine *f*; *of water, blood* flaque

f

pool² [puːl] *game* billard *m* américain

pool³ [puːl] **1** *n* (*common fund*) caisse *f* commune **2** *v/t resources* mettre en commun

'**pool hall** salle *f* de billard; **pool table** table *f* de billard

poop [puːp] F caca *m* F

pooped [puːpt] F crevé F

poor [pʊr] **1** *adj* pauvre; *quality etc* médiocre, mauvais **2** *npl*: **the ~s** les pauvres *mpl*; **poorly 1** *adj* (*unwell*) malade **2** *adv* mal

pop¹ [pɑːp] MUS pop *f*

pop² [pɑːp] F (*father*) papa *m*

'**popcorn** pop-corn *m*

pope [poʊp] pape *m*

Popsicle® ['pɑːpsɪkl] glace *f* à l'eau

popular ['pɑːpjələr] populaire; **popularity** popularité *f*

populate ['pɑːpjəleɪt] peupler; **population** population *f*

porch [pɔːrtʃ] porche *m*

pork [pɔːrk] porc *m*

porn [pɔːrn] F porno F; **pornographic** pornographique; **pornography** pornographie *f*

port¹ [pɔːrt] *n* port *m*

port² [pɔːrt] *adj* (*left-hand*) de bâbord

portable ['pɔːrtəbl] **1** *adj* portable, portatif **2** *n* COMPUT portable *m*; *TV* téléviseur

m portable *or* portatif
porter ['pɔːrtər] (*doorman*) portier *m*

portion ['pɔːrʃn] partie *f*, part *f*; *of food* portion *f*

portrait ['pɔːrtreɪt] **1** *n* portrait *m* **2** *adv print* en mode portrait, à la française; **portray** *of artist* représenter; *of actor* interpréter; *of author* décrire

Portugal ['pɔːrtʃəgl] le Portugal; **Portuguese 1** *adj* portugais **2** *n person* Portugais(e) *m(f)*; *language* portugais *m*

pose [pouz] **1** *n* attitude *f* **2** *v/i for artist* poser; ~ **as** se faire passer pour **3** *v/t problem* poser; *threat* constituer

position [pə'zɪʃn] **1** *n* position *f* **2** *v/t* placer

positive ['pɑːzətɪv] positif; **be ~** (*sure*) être sûr; **positively** vraiment

possess [pə'zes] posséder; **possession** possession *f*; **possessive** possessif

possibility [pɑːsə'bɪlətɪ] possibilité *f*; **possible** possible; **possibly** (*perhaps*) peut-être

post¹ [poust] **1** *n of wood, metal* poteau *m* **2** *v/t notice* afficher; *profits* enregistrer

post² [poust] **1** *n* (*place of duty*) poste *m* **2** *v/t soldier, employee* affecter; *guards* poster

post³ [poust] *Br* **1** *n* (*mail*) courrier *m* **2** *v/t letter* poster

postage ['poustɪdʒ] affranchissement *m*; **postage stamp** *fml* timbre *m*; **postal** postal; **postcard** carte *f* postale; **postdate** postdater

poster ['poustər] poster *m*, affiche *f*

postgraduate ['poustgrædʒuət] étudiant(e) *m(f)* de troisième cycle

posthumous ['pɑːstʃəməs] posthume

posting ['poustɪŋ] (*assignment*) affectation *f*

postmark cachet *m* de la poste

post-mortem [poust'mɔːrtəm] autopsie *f*

post office poste *f*

postpone [poust'poun] remettre (à plus tard), reporter; **postponement** report *m*

pot¹ [pɑːt] *for cooking* casserole *f*; *for coffee* cafetière *f*; *for tea* théière *f*; *for plant* pot *m*

pot² [pɑːt] F (*marijuana*) herbe *f*

potato [pə'teɪtou] pomme *f* de terre; **potato chips**, *Br* **potato crisps** chips *fpl*

potent ['poutənt] puissant

potential [pə'tenʃl] **1** *adj* potentiel **2** *n* potentiel *m*; **potentially** potentiellement

pothole *in road* nid-de-poule *m*

potter ['pɑːtər] potier(-ière) *m(f)*; **pottery** poterie *f*; *items* poteries *fpl*

pouch [pautʃ] *bag* petit sac *m*

poultry ['pəʊltrɪ] volaille f
pound[1] [paʊnd] *weight* livre f (0,453kg)
pound[2] [paʊnd] *n for strays, cars* fourrière f
pound[3] [paʊnd] *v/i of heart* battre (la chamade)
pour [pɔːr] **1** *v/t liquid* verser **2** *v/i: it's ~ing (with rain)* il pleut à verse
♦ **pour out** *liquid* verser; *troubles* déballer F
poverty ['pɑːvərtɪ] pauvreté f
powder ['paʊdər] **1** *n* poudre f **2** *v/t: ~ one's face* se poudrer le visage
power ['paʊər] **1** *n (strength)* puissance f, force f; *(authority)* pouvoir m; *(energy)* énergie f; *(electricity)* courant m; **power drill** perceuse f; **power failure** panne f d'électricité; **powerful** puissant; **powerless** impuissant; **power line** ligne f électrique; **power outage** coupure f de courant; **power station** centrale f électrique; **power steering** direction f assistée
PR [piːˈɑːr] (= **public relations**) relations fpl publiques
practical ['præktɪkl] pratique; **practically** d'une manière pratique; *(almost)* pratiquement
practice ['præktɪs] **1** *n* pratique f, *training also* entraînement m; *(rehearsal)* répétition f; *(custom)* coutume f **2** *v/i* s'entraîner **3** *v/t* travail-

ler; *law, medicine* exercer
practise Br → **practice** *v/i & v/t*
prairie ['prerɪ] prairie f
praise [preɪz] **1** *n* louange f, éloge m **2** *v/t* louer; **praiseworthy** méritoire, louable
pray [preɪ] prier; **prayer** prière f
preach [priːtʃ] prêcher; **preacher** pasteur m
precaution [prɪˈkɔːʃn] précaution f; **precautionary measure** préventif, de précaution
precede [prɪˈsiːd] précéder; **precedent** précédent m; **preceding** précédent
precious ['preʃəs] précieux
precise [prɪˈsaɪs] précis; **precisely** précisément; **precision** précision f
preconceived ['priːkənsiːvd] *idea* préconçu
precondition [priːkənˈdɪʃn] condition f requise
predator ['predətər] prédateur m; **predatory** prédateur
predecessor ['priːdɪsesər] prédécesseur m
predicament [prɪˈdɪkəmənt] situation f délicate
predict [prɪˈdɪkt] prédire, prévoir; **prediction** prédiction f
predominant [prɪˈdɑːmɪnənt] prédominant; **predominantly** principalement
prefabricated [priːˈfæbrɪkeɪtɪd] préfabriqué
preface ['prefɪs] préface f

prefer [prɪ'fɜ:r] préférer; **preferable** préférable; **preferably** de préférence; **preference** préférence f; **preferential** préférentiel

pregnancy ['pregnənsɪ] grossesse f **2 pregnant** enceinte; *animal* pleine

prehistoric [pri:hɪs'tɒrɪk] *also fig* préhistorique

prejudice ['predʒʊdɪs] **1** n (*bias*) préjugé m **2** v/t *person* influencer; *chances* compromettre; **prejudiced** partial

preliminary [prɪ'lɪmɪnerɪ] préliminaire

premarital [pri:'mærɪtl] *sex* avant le mariage

premature [prɪ:mə'tʊr] prématuré

premier ['premɪr] POL Premier ministre m

première ['premɪer] première f

premises ['premɪsɪz] locaux mpl

premium ['pri:mɪəm] *in insurance* prime f

prenatal [pri:'neɪtl] prénatal

preoccupied [prɪ'ɒ:kjupaɪd] préoccupé

preparation [prepə'reɪʃn] préparation f; **~s** préparatifs mpl; **prepare** [prɪ'per] **1** v/t préparer; **be ~d to do sth** *willing, ready* être prêt à faire qch **2** v/i se préparer

preposition [prepə'zɪʃn] préposition f

prerequisite [pri:'rekwɪzɪt]

condition f préalable

prescribe [prɪ'skraɪb] *of doctor* prescrire; **prescription** MED ordonnance f

presence ['prezns] présence f; **in the ~ of** en présence de

present¹ ['preznt] **1** adj (*current*) actuel; **be ~** être présent **2** n: **the ~** *also* GRAM le présent

present² ['preznt] n (*gift*) cadeau m

present³ [prɪ'zent] v/t *award, bouquet* remettre; *program* présenter

presentation [prezn'teɪʃn] présentation f; **present-day** actuel; **presenter** présentateur(-trice) m(f); **presently** (*at the moment*) à présent; (*soon*) bientôt

preservative [prɪ'zɜ:rvətɪv] conservateur m; **preserve 1** n (*domain*) domaine m **2** v/t *standards, peace etc* maintenir; *wood etc* préserver; *food* conserver

preside [prɪ'zaɪd] *at meeting* présider; **presidency** présidence f; **president** POL président(e) m(f); *of company* président-directeur m général, PDG m; **presidential** présidentiel

press [pres] **1** n: **the ~** la presse **2** v/t *button* appuyer sur; *hand* serrer; *grapes, olives* presser; *clothes* repasser; **pressing** pressant; **pressure 1** n pression f **2** v/t faire pression sur

prestige [pre'sti:ʒ] prestige *m*; **prestigious** prestigieux

presumably [prɪ'zu:məblɪ] sans doute; **presume** présumer; **presumption** *of innocence, guilt* présomption *f*

presuppose [pri:sə'pouz] présupposer

pre-tax [pri:'tæks] avant impôts

pretence *Br* → **pretense**

pretend [prɪ'tend] **1** *v/t* prétendre **2** *v/i* faire semblant; **pretense** semblant *m*; *under the* **~** *of cooperation* sous prétexte de coopération; **pretentious** prétentieux

pretext ['pri:tekst] prétexte *m*

pretty ['prɪtɪ] **1** *adj* joli **2** *adv* (*quite*) assez

prevail [prɪ'veɪl] (*triumph*) prévaloir, l'emporter; **prevailing** *wind* dominant; *opinion* prédominant; (*current*) actuel

prevent [prɪ'vent] empêcher; *disease* prévenir; **~** *s.o.* (*from*) *doing sth* empêcher qn de faire qch; **prevention** prévention *f*; **preventive** préventif

preview ['pri:vju:] **1** *n* avant-première *f* **2** *v/t* voir en avant-première

previous ['pri:vɪəs] (*earlier*) antérieur; (*the one before*) précédent; **previously** auparavant, avant

prey [preɪ] proie *f*

price [praɪs] **1** *n* prix *m* **2** *v/t* COM fixer le prix de; **priceless** sans prix

prick¹ [prɪk] **1** *n* pain piqûre *f* **2** *v/t* (*jab*) piquer

prick² [prɪk] V (*penis*) bite *f* V; *person* con *m* F

prickle ['prɪkl] *on plant* épine *f*, piquant *m*; **prickly** *beard, plant* piquant; (*irritable*) irritable

pride [praɪd] fierté *f*; (*self-respect*) amour-propre *m*, orgueil *m*

priest [pri:st] prêtre *m*

primarily [praɪ'merɪlɪ] principalement; **primary 1** *adj* principal **2** *n* POL (*élection f*) primaire *f*

prime 'minister Premier ministre *m*

primitive ['prɪmɪtɪv] primitif; *conditions* rudimentaire

prince [prɪns] prince *m*; **princess** princesse *f*

principal ['prɪnsəpl] **1** *adj* principal **2** *n* of school directeur(-trice) *m(f)*; **principally** principalement

principle ['prɪnsəpl] principe *m*; *on* **~** par principe; *in* **~** en principe

print [prɪnt] **1** *n* *in book etc* texte *m*; (*photograph*) épreuve *f*; *out of* **~** épuisé **2** *v/t* imprimer; (*use block capitals*) écrire en majuscules; **printer** ['prɪntər] *person* imprimeur *m*; *machine* imprimante *f*; **printout** impression *f*

prior ['praɪr] **1** *adj* préalable, antérieur **2** *prep*: **~ to** avant

prioritize (*put in order of priority*) donner un ordre de priorité à; (*give priority to*) donner la priorité à; **priority** priorité *f*

prison ['prɪzn] prison *f*; **prisoner** prisonnier(-ière) *m(f)*; **take s.o. ~** faire prisonnier; **prisoner of war** prisonnier(-ière) *m(f)* de guerre

privacy ['prɪvəsɪ] intimité *f*; **private 1** *adj* privé; *letter* personnel; *secretary* particulier **2** *n* MIL simple soldat *m*; **privately** *talk to s.o.* en privé; (*inwardly*) intérieurement; **~ owned** privé

privilege ['prɪvɪlɪdʒ] privilège *m*; **privileged** privilégié

prize [praɪz] **1** *n* prix *m* **2** *v/t* priser, faire (grand) cas de; **prizewinner** gagnant *m*; **prizewinning** gagnant

probability [prɑːbə'bɪlətɪ] probabilité *f*; **probable** probable; **probably** probablement

probation [prə'beɪʃn] *in job* période *f* d'essai; LAW probation *f*

probe [proʊb] **1** *n* (*investigation*) enquête *f*; *scientific* sonde *f* **2** *v/t* sonder; (*investigate*) enquêter sur

problem ['prɑːbləm] problème *m*; **no ~** pas de problème; *it doesn't worry me* c'est pas grave

procedure [prə'siːdʒər] procédure *f*; **proceed** (*go: of people*) se rendre; *of work etc* avancer, se dérouler; **proceedings** (*events*) événements *mpl*; **proceeds** bénéfices *mpl*

process ['prɑːses] **1** *n* processus *m* **2** *v/t* *food, raw materials* transformer; *data, application* traiter; **procession** procession *f*; **processor** processeur *m*

prod [prɑːd] **1** *n* (petit) coup *m* **2** *v/t* donner un (petit) coup à, pousser

prodigy ['prɑːdɪdʒɪ]: prodige *m*; (*child*) **~** enfant *m/f* prodige

produce¹ ['prɑːduːs] *n* produits *mpl* (agricoles)

produce² [prə'duːs] *v/t* produire; (*bring about*) provoquer; (*bring out*) sortir

producer [prə'duːsər] producteur *m*; *of play, movie, TV program* producteur *m*; **product** produit *m*; **production** production *f*; **productive** productif; **productivity** productivité *f*

profess [prə'fes] prétendre; **profession** profession *f*; **professional 1** *adj* professionnel **2** *n* (*doctor, lawyer etc*) personne *f* qui exerce une profession libérale; *not amateur* professionnel(le) *m(f)*; **professionally** *play sport* professionnellement;

(*well, skillfully*) de manière professionnelle

professor [prə'fesər] professeur *m*

proficient [prə'frɪʃnt] excellent, compétent

profile ['proufaɪl] profil *m*

profit ['prɑːfɪt] **1** *n* bénéfice *m*, profit *m* **2** *v/i*: ~ **from** profiter de; **profitability** rentabilité *f*; **profitable** rentable

profound [prə'faund] profond

prognosis [prɑːg'nousɪs] MED pronostic *m*

program ['prougræm] **1** *n* programme *m*; on radio, TV émission *f* **2** *v/t* programmer; **programme** *Br* → **program**; **programmer** programmeur(-euse) *m(f)*

progress ['prɑːgres] *n* progrès *m(pl)* **2** [prə'gres] *v/i* (*in time*) avancer; (*move on*) passer à; (*make* ~) faire des progrès, progresser; **progressive** (*enlightened*) progressiste; (*which progresses*) progressif; **progressively** progressivement

prohibit [prə'hɪbɪt] défendre, interdire; **prohibitive** *prices* prohibitif

project[1] ['prɑːdʒekt] *n* projet *m*; EDU étude *f*; (*housing area*) cité *f* (H.L.M.)

project[2] [prə'dʒekt] **1** *v/t figures, sales* prévoir; *movie* projeter **2** *v/i* (*stick out*) faire saillie

projection [prə'dʒekʃn] (*forecast*) projection *f*, prévision *f*; **projector** *for slides* projecteur *m*

prolog, *Br* **prologue** ['proulɑːg] prologue *m*

prolong [prə'lɔːŋ] prolonger

prominent ['prɑːmɪnənt] *nose, chin* proéminent; *visually* voyant; (*significant*) important

promiscuity [prɑːmɪ'skjuːɪtɪ] promiscuité *f*; **promiscuous** dévergondé

promise ['prɑːmɪs] **1** *n* promesse *f* **2** *v/t & v/i* promettre; **promising** prometteur

promote [prə'mout] *employee, idea* promouvoir; COM *also* faire la promotion de; **promoter** *of sports event* organisateur *m*; **promotion** promotion *f*

prompt [prɑːmpt] **1** *adj* (*on time*) ponctuel; (*speedy*) prompt **2** *v/t* (*cause*) provoquer; *actor* souffler à; **promptly** (*on time*) ponctuellement; (*immediately*) immédiatement

prone [proun]: *be* ~ *to* être sujet à

pronoun ['prounaun] pronom *m*

pronounce [prə'nauns] prononcer

pronto ['prɑːntou] F illico (*presto*) F

pronunciation [prənʌnsɪ'eɪʃn] prononciation *f*

proof [pru:f] preuve *f*; *of book* épreuve *f*

prop [prɑ:p] THEA accessoire *m*

♦ **prop up** soutenir

propaganda [prɑ:pə'gændə] propagande *f*

propel [prə'pel] propulser; **propeller** hélice *f*

proper ['prɑ:pər] *(real)* vrai; *(correct)* bon, correct; *(fitting)* convenable; **properly** *(correctly)* correctement; *(fittingly also)* convenablement; **property** propriété *f*

proportion [prə'pɔ:rʃn] proportion *f*; **proportional** proportionnel

proposal [prə'pouzl] proposition *f*; *of marriage* demande *f* en mariage; **propose 1** *v/t (suggest)* proposer; **~ to do sth** *(plan)* se proposer de faire qch **2** *v/i (make offer of marriage)* faire sa demande en mariage (**to** à); **proposition 1** *n* proposition *f* **2** *v/t woman* faire des avances à

proprietor [prə'praiətər] propriétaire *m*

prosecute ['prɑ:sɪkju:t] LAW poursuivre (en justice); **prosecution** LAW poursuites *fpl* (judiciaires); *lawyers* accusation *f*

prospect ['prɑ:spekt] *(chance, likelihood)* chance(s) *f(pl)*; *(thought of something in the future)* perspective *f*; **~s** perspectives *fpl*

(d'avenir); **prospective** potentiel

prosper ['prɑ:spər] prospérer; **prosperity** prospérité *f*; **prosperous** prospère

prostitute ['prɑ:stɪtu:t] prostituée *f*; *male* **~** prostitué *m*; **prostitution** prostitution *f*

protect [prə'tekt] protéger; **protection** protection *f*; **protective** protecteur; **protector** protecteur(-trice) *m(f)*

protein ['prouti:n] protéine *f*

protest ['proutest] **1** [pə'-test] *n* protestation *f*; *(demonstration)* manifestation *f* **2** [prə'test] *v/t (object to)* protester contre **3** [prə'test] *v/i* protester; *(demonstrate)* manifester

Protestant ['prɑ:tɪstənt] **1** *adj* protestant **2** *n* protestant(e) *m(f)*

protester [prə'testər] manifestant(e) *m(f)*

prototype ['proutətaip] prototype *m*

protrude [prə'tru:d] *of eyes, ear* être saillant; *from pocket etc* sortir; **protruding** saillant; *ears* décollé; *chin* avancé; *teeth* en avant

proud [praud] fier; **proudly** fièrement, avec fierté

prove [pru:v] prouver

proverb ['prɑ:vɜ:rb] proverbe *m*

provide [prə'vaid] fournir; **~d that** *(on condition that)* pourvu que (+*subj*), à condition que (+*subj*)

province ['prɒvɪns] province *f*; **provincial** *also pej* provincial; *city* de province

provision [prə'vɪʒn] (*supply*) fourniture *f*; *of services* prestation *f*; *in a law, contract* disposition *f*; **provisional** provisoire

provocation [prɒvə'keɪʃn] provocation *f*; **provocative** provocant; **provoke** provoquer

prowl [praʊl] *of tiger etc* chasser; *of burglar* rôder; **prowler** rôdeur(-euse) *m(f)*

proximity [prɒk'sɪmətɪ] proximité *f*

proxy ['prɒksɪ] (*authority*) procuration *f*; *person* mandataire *m/f*

prudence ['pruːdns] prudence *f*; **prudent** prudent

pry [praɪ] être indiscret

PS [piːes] (= **postscript**) P.-S. *m*

pseudonym ['suːdənɪm] pseudonyme *m*

psychiatric [saɪkɪ'ætrɪk] psychiatrique; **psychiatrist** psychiatre *m/f*; **psychiatry** psychiatrie *f*

psychoanalysis [saɪkouən'æləsɪs] psychanalyse *f*; **psychoanalyst** psychanalyste *m/f*; **psychoanalyze** psychanalyser

psychological [saɪkə'lɒdʒɪkl] psychologique; **psychol-**

ogist psychologue *m/f*

psychology [saɪ'kɒlədʒɪ] psychologie *f*

psychopath ['saɪkoupæθ] psychopathe *m/f*

psychosomatic [saɪkousə'mætɪk] psychosomatique

pub [pʌb] *Br* pub *m*

public ['pʌblɪk] **1** *adj* public **2** *n*: **the ~** le public

publication [pʌblɪ'keɪʃn] publication *f*

public 'holiday jour *m* férié

publicity [pʌb'lɪsətɪ] publicité *f*; **publicize** (*make known*) faire connaître, rendre public; COM faire de la publicité pour

publicly ['pʌblɪklɪ] en public, publiquement

'public school école *f* publique; *Br* école privée (du secondaire)

publish ['pʌblɪʃ] publier; **publisher** éditeur(-trice) *m(f)*; maison *f* d'édition; **publishing** édition *f*; **publishing company** maison *f* d'édition

puff [pʌf] **1** *n of wind* bourrasque *f*; *of smoke* bouffée *f* **2** *v/i* (*pant*) souffler, haleter; **puffy** *eyes, face* bouffi

pull [pʊl] **1** *n on rope* coup *m*; F (*appeal*) attrait *m*; F (*influence*) influence *f* **2** *v/t* tirer; *tooth* arracher; *muscle* se déchirer **3** *v/i* tirer

◆ **pull ahead** *in race, competition* prendre la tête

◆ **pull down** (*lower*) baisser; (*demolish*) démolir

◆ **pull in** *of bus, train* arriver

◆ **pull up 1** *v/t* (*raise*) remonter; *plant* arracher **2** *v/i of car etc* s'arrêter

pulley ['pʊlɪ] poulie *f*

pulsate [pʌl'seɪt] *of heart, blood* battre; *of rhythm* vibrer

pulse [pʌls] pouls *m*

pulverize ['pʌlvəraɪz] pulvériser

pump [pʌmp] **1** *n* pompe *f* **2** *v/t* pomper

pumpkin ['pʌmpkɪn] potiron *m*

pun [pʌn] jeu *m* de mots

punch [pʌntʃ] **1** *n blow* coup *m* de poing; *implement* perforeuse *f* **2** *v/t with fist* donner un coup de poing à; *hole* percer; *ticket* composter

punctual ['pʌŋktʃʊəl] ponctuel; **punctuality** ponctualité *f*

punctuation [pʌŋktʃʊ'eɪʃn] ponctuation *f*

puncture ['pʌŋktʃər] **1** *n* piqûre *f* **2** *v/t* percer, perforer

punish ['pʌnɪʃ] punir; **punishing** *pace, schedule* éprouvant, épuisant; **punishment** punition *f*

puny ['pjuːnɪ] *person* chétif

pup [pʌp] chiot *m*

pupil¹ ['pjuːpl] *of eye* pupille *f*

pupil² ['pjuːpl] (*student*) élève *m/f*

puppet ['pʌpɪt] *also fig* marionnette *f*

purchase¹ ['pɜːrtʃəs] **1** *n* achat *m* **2** *v/t* acheter

purchase² ['pɜːrtʃəs] *n* (*grip*) prise *f*

purchaser ['pɜːrtʃəsər] acheteur(-euse) *m(f)*

pure [pjʊr] pur; *white* immaculé; **purely** purement

purge [pɜːrdʒ] **1** *n* POL purge *f* **2** *v/t* POL épurer

purify ['pjʊrɪfaɪ] *water* épurer

puritan ['pjʊrɪtən] puritain *m(f)*

purity ['pjʊrɪtɪ] pureté *f*

purpose ['pɜːrpəs] (*aim, object*) but *m*; on ~ exprès; **purposely** exprès

purr [pɜːr] *of cat* ronronner

purse [pɜːrs] (*pocketbook*) sac *m* à main; *Br for money* porte-monnaie *m inv*

pursue [pər'suː] poursuivre; **pursuer** poursuivant(e) *m(f)*; **pursuit** poursuite *f*; (*activity*) activité *f*

push [pʊʃ] **1** *n* (*shove*) poussée *f* **2** *v/t* (*shove, pressure*) pousser; *button* appuyer sur; F *drugs* revendre, trafiquer **3** *v/i* pousser; **pusher** F *of drugs* dealer(-euse) *m(f)*; **push-up**: *do* ~*s* faire des pompes; **pushy** F qui se met en avant

puss, pussy (*cat*) [pʊs, 'pʊsɪ (kæt)] F minou *m*

put [pʊt] mettre; *question* poser; ~ *the cost at* estimer le prix à

◆ **put across** *idea etc* faire comprendre
◆ **put aside** *money, work* mettre de côté
◆ **put away** *in closet etc* ranger; *in institution* enfermer; *in prison* emprisonner; F (*consume*) s'enfiler F; *animal* faire piquer
◆ **put back** (*replace*) remettre
◆ **put down** poser; *deposit* verser; *rebellion* réprimer; (*belittle*) rabaisser
◆ **put forward** *idea etc* soumettre, suggérer
◆ **put in for** (*apply for*) demander
◆ **put off** *light, TV* éteindre; (*postpone*) repousser; (*deter*) dissuader; (*repel*) dégoûter
◆ **put on** *light, TV* allumer; *music, jacket etc* mettre; (*perform*) monter; *accent etc* prendre
◆ **put out** *hand* tendre; *fire, light* éteindre
◆ **put together** (*assemble*) monter; (*organize*) organiser
◆ **put up** *hand* lever; *person* héberger; (*erect*) ériger; *prices* augmenter; *poster* accrocher; *money* fournir
◆ **put up with** supporter, tolérer
putty ['pʌtɪ] mastic *m*
puzzle ['pʌzl] **1** *n* (*mystery*) énigme *f*, mystère *m*; *game* jeu *m*, casse-tête *m*; (*jigsaw* ~) puzzle *m* **2** *v/t* laisser perplexe; **puzzling** curieux
PVC [piːviːˈsiː] (= *polyvinyl chloride*) P.V.C. *m* (= polychlorure de vinyle)
pyjamas *Br* → **pajamas**
pylon ['paɪlən] pylône *m*

Q

quadrangle ['kwaːdræŋgl] *figure* quadrilatère *m*; *courtyard* cour *f*
quadruped ['kwaːdruped] quadrupède *m*
quail [kweɪl] flancher
quaint [kweɪnt] *cottage* pittoresque; (*eccentric: ideas etc*) curieux
quake [kweɪk] **1** *n* (*earthquake*) tremblement *m* de terre **2** *v/i* of earth, with fear tremble

qualification [kwaːlɪfɪˈkeɪʃn] *from university etc* diplôme *m*; *qualified* doctor, engineer etc qualifié; (*restricted*) restreint; **qualify 1** *v/t of degree, course etc* qualifier; *remark etc* nuancer **2** *v/i* (*get degree etc*) obtenir son diplôme; *in competition* se qualifier
quality ['kwaːlətɪ] qualité *f*; **quality control** contrôle *m* de qualité
quandary ['kwaːndərɪ] di-

lemme *m*

quantify [ˈkwɒːntɪfaɪ] quantifier

quantity [ˈkwɒːntətɪ] quantité *f*

quarantine [ˈkwɒːrəntiːn] quarantaine *f*

quarrel [ˈkwɒːrəl] **1** *n* dispute *f*, querelle *f* **2** *v/i* se disputer

quarry¹ [ˈkwɒːrɪ] *in hunt* gibier *m*

quarry² [ˈkwɒːrɪ] *for mining* carrière *f*

quart [kwɒːrt] quart *m* de gallon *(0,946 litre)*

quarter [ˈkwɒːrtər] quart *m*; *25 cents* vingt-cinq cents *mpl*; *part of town* quartier *m*; **a ~ of an hour** un quart d'heure; **a ~ of 5** cinq heures moins le quart; **a ~ after 5** cinq heures et quart; **quarterfinal** quart *m* de finale; **quarterfinalist** quart de finaliste *m*, quart-finaliste *m*; **quarterly 1** *adj* trimestriel **2** *adv* trimestriellement; **quarters** MIL quartiers *mpl*; **quartet** MUS quatuor *m*

quartz [kwɒːrts] quartz *m*

quash [kwɒʃ] *rebellion* réprimer, écraser; *court decision* casser, annuler

quaver [ˈkweɪvər] **1** *n in voice* tremblement *m* **2** *v/i of voice* trembler

queasy [ˈkwiːzɪ] nauséeux; **feel ~** avoir la nausée

queen [kwiːn] reine *f*

queer [kwɪr] *(peculiar)* bizar-re

quell [kwel] réprimer

quench [kwentʃ] *thirst* étancher, assouvir; *flames* éteindre

query [ˈkwɪrɪ] **1** *n* question *f* **2** *v/t (express doubt about)* mettre en doute; *(check)* vérifier

quest [kwest] quête *f*

question [ˈkwestʃn] **1** *n* question *f* **2** *v/t person* questionner, interroger; *(doubt)* mettre en question; **questionable** contestable; **questioning 1** *adj look* interrogateur *m* **2** *n* interrogatoire *m*; **question mark** point *m* d'interrogation; **questionnaire** questionnaire *m*

queue [kjuː] *Br* **1** *n* queue *f* **2** *v/i* faire la queue

quibble [ˈkwɪbl] chipoter, chercher la petite bête

quick [kwɪk] rapide; **be ~!** fais vite!; **quickly** vite, rapidement; **quickwitted** à l'esprit vif

quiet [ˈkwaɪət] *street, life* tranquille; *music* doux; *engine* silencieux; *voice* bas; **~!** silence!; **quietly** doucement, sans bruit; *(unassumingly, peacefully)* tranquillement; **quietness** calme *m*, tranquillité *f*

quilt [kwɪlt] *on bed* couette *f*

quinine [ˈkwɪniːn] quinine *f*

quip [kwɪp] **1** *n* trait *m* d'esprit **2** *v/i* plaisanter

quirk [kwɜːrk] manie *f*, lubie *f*

f; **quirky** bizarre, excentrique

quit [kwɪt] **1** *v/t job* quitter **2** *v/i (leave job)* démissionner; COMPUT quitter

quite [kwaɪt] *(fairly)* assez; *(completely)* tout à fait; **~ a lot** pas mal, beaucoup

quiver ['kwɪvər] trembler

quiz [kwɪz] **1** *n on TV* jeu *m* télévisé; *on radio* jeu *m* ra-diophonique; *at school* interrogation *f* **2** *v/t* interroger

quota ['kwoʊtə] quota *m*

quotation [kwoʊ'teɪʃn] *from author* citation *f*; *price* devis *m*; **quotation marks** guillemets *mpl*; **quote 1** *n from author* citation *f*; *price* devis *m*; *(quotation mark)* guillemet *m*; **in ~s** entre guillemets **2** *v/t text* citer; *price* proposer

R

rabbit ['ræbɪt] lapin *m*

rabble ['ræbl] cohue *f*, foule *f*; **rabble-rouser** agitateur(-trice) *m(f)*

rabies ['reɪbiːz] rage *f*

raccoon [rə'kuːn] raton *m* laveur

race¹ [reɪs] *n of people* race *f*

race² [reɪs] **1** *n* SP course *f* **2** *v/i (run fast)* courir à toute vitesse **3** *v/t*: **I'll ~ you** le premier arrivé a gagné

'racecourse champ *m* de courses, hippodrome *m*; **racehorse** cheval *m* de course; **race riot** émeute *f* raciale; **racetrack** *for cars* circuit *m*, piste *f*; *for horses* hippodrome *m*

racial ['reɪʃl] racial

racing ['reɪsɪŋ] course *f*

racism ['reɪsɪzm] racisme *m*; **racist 1** *adj* raciste **2** *n* raciste *m/f*

rack [ræk] **1** *n for bags on train* porte-bagages *m inv*; *for CDs* range-CD *m inv* **2** *v/t*: **~ one's brains** se creuser la tête

racket¹ ['rækɪt] SP raquette *f*

racket² ['rækɪt] *(noise)* vacarme *m*; *criminal activity* escroquerie *f*

radar ['reɪdɑːr] radar *m*

radiance ['reɪdɪəns] éclat *m*; **radiant smile** radieux; **radiate** *of heat, light* irradier, rayonner; **radiation** *nuclear* radiation *f*; **radiator** radiateur *m*

radical ['rædɪkl] **1** *adj* radical **2** *n* POL radical(e) *m(f)*; **radicalism** POL radicalisme *m*; **radically** radicalement

radio ['reɪdɪoʊ] radio *f*; **radio-active** radioactif; **radioactivity** radioactivité *f*; **radio alarm** radio-réveil *m*; **radiographer** radiologue *m/f*; **radiography** radiographie *f*;

radio station station f de radio

radius ['reɪdɪəs] rayon m

raft [ræft] radeau m

rafter ['ræftər] chevron m

rag [ræg] for cleaning etc chiffon m

rage [reɪdʒ] 1 n colère f, rage f 2 v/i of storm faire rage

ragged ['rægɪd] edge irrégulier; appearance négligé; clothes en loques

raid [reɪd] 1 n by troops, FIN raid m; by robbers hold-up m 2 v/t of troops attaquer; of police faire une descente dans; of robbers attaquer; fridge faire une razzia dans; raider (robber) voleur m

rail [reɪl] on track rail m; (hand~) rampe f; for towel porte-serviettes m inv; by ~ en train; railings around park etc grille f; railroad chemin m de fer; track voie f ferrée; railroad station gare f; railway Br chemin m de fer; track voie f ferrée

rain [reɪn] 1 n pluie f 2 v/i pleuvoir; it's ~ing il pleut; rainbow arc-en-ciel m; raincheck: can I take a ~ on that? F peut-on remettre cela à plus tard?; raincoat imperméable m; raindrop goutte f de pluie; rainfall précipitations fpl; rain forest forêt f tropicale (humide); rainproof fabric imperméable; rainstorm pluie f torrentielle; rainy pluvieux

raise [reɪz] 1 n in salary augmentation f (de salaire) 2 v/t shelf etc surélever; offer augmenter; children élever; question soulever; money rassembler

rake [reɪk] for garden râteau m

rally ['rælɪ] (meeting, reunion) rassemblement m; MOT rallye m; in tennis échange m

RAM [ræm] COMPUT (= random access memory) RAM f, mémoire f vive

ram [ræm] 1 n bélier m 2 v/t ship, car heurter, percuter

ramble ['ræmbl] 1 n walk randonnée f 2 v/i walk faire de la randonnée; when speaking discourir; (talk incoherently) divaguer; rambling 1 adj speech décousu 2 n walking randonnée f; in speech digression f

ramp [ræmp] rampe f (d'accès), passerelle f; for raising vehicle pont m élévateur

rampant ['ræmpənt] inflation galopant

rampart ['ræmpɑːrt] rempart m

ramshackle ['ræmʃækl] délabré

ranch [ræntʃ] ranch m; rancher éleveur m/f de ranch; ranchhand employé m de ranch

rancid ['rænsɪd] rance

rattlesnake

rancor, Br **rancour** ['ræŋkər] rancœur f

R & D [ɑːrən'diː] (= *research and development*) R&D f (= recherche et développement)

random ['rændəm] **1** adj aléatoire, au hasard; **~ sample** échantillon m pris au hasard **2** n: **at ~** au hasard

range [reɪndʒ] **1** n of products gamme f; of gun portée f; of airplane autonomie f; of voice, instrument registre m; of mountains chaîne f; **at close ~** de très près **2** v/i: **~ from X to Y** aller de X à Y; **ranger** garde m forestier

rank [ræŋk] **1** n MIL grade m; in society rang m **2** v/t classer ♦ **rank among** compter parmi

ransack ['rænsæk] searching fouiller; plundering saccager

ransom ['rænsəm] money rançon f

rap [ræp] **1** n at door etc petit coup m sec; MUS rap m **2** v/t table etc taper sur

rape[1] [reɪp] **1** n viol m **2** v/t violer

rape[2] [reɪp] n BOT colza m

rapid ['ræpɪd] rapide; **rapidity** rapidité f; **rapidly** rapidement; **rapids** rapides mpl

rapist ['reɪpɪst] violeur m

rare [rer] rare; steak saignant, bleu; **rarely** rarement; **rarity** rareté f

rash[1] [ræʃ] n MED éruption f (cutanée)

rash[2] [ræʃ] adj action, imprudent, impétueux; **rashly** sans réfléchir

rat [ræt] rat m

rate [reɪt] taux m; (price) tarif m; (speed) rythme m; **at this ~** (at this speed) à ce rythme; (carrying on like this) si ça continue comme ça; **at any ~** en tout cas

rather ['ræðər] (fairly, quite) plutôt; **I would ~ stay here** je préférerais rester ici

ratification [rætɪfɪ'keɪʃn] of treaty ratification f; **ratify** ratifier

ratings ['reɪtɪŋz] indice m d'écoute

ratio ['reɪʃɪoʊ] rapport m, proportion f

ration ['ræʃn] **1** n ration f **2** v/t supplies rationner

rational ['ræʃənl] rationnel; **rationality** rationalité f; **rationalization** rationalisation f; **rationalize 1** v/t rationaliser **2** v/i (se) chercher des excuses; **rationally** rationnellement

rattle ['rætl] **1** n of bottles, chains cliquetis m; in engine bruit m de ferraille; toy hochet m **2** v/t chains etc entrechoquer **3** v/i faire du bruit; of engine faire un bruit de ferraille; of crates s'entrechoquer; of chains cliqueter; **rattlesnake** serpent m à sonnette

raucous ['rɔːkəs] bruyant

rave [reɪv] **1** *n party* rave *f*, rave-party *f* **2** *v/i* délirer; ~ *about sth* (*be very enthusiastic*) s'emballer pour qch

ravenous ['rævənəs] affamé

ravine [rə'viːn] ravin *m*

raw [rɔː] *meat, vegetable* cru; *sugar, iron* brut; **raw materials** *fpl* matières *fpl* premières

ray [reɪ] rayon *m*

razor ['reɪzər] rasoir *m*; **razor blade** lame *f* de rasoir

re [riː] COM en référence à

reach [riːtʃ] **1** *n*: **within** ~ à portée; **out of** ~ hors de portée **2** *v/t* atteindre; *destination* arriver à; *decision* parvenir à

react [rɪ'ækt] réagir; **reaction** réaction *f*; **reactionary 1** *adj* POL réactionnaire **2** *n* POL réactionnaire *m/f*; **reactor** *nuclear* réacteur *m*

read [riːd] lire
◆ **read out** *aloud* lire à haute voix

readable ['riːdəbl] lisible; **reader** *person* lecteur(-trice) *m(f)*

readily ['redɪlɪ] *admit, agree* volontiers, de bon cœur

reading ['riːdɪŋ] *activity* lecture *f*; *from meter etc* relevé *m*

readjust [riːə'dʒʌst] **1** *v/t* régler (de nouveau) **2** *v/i to conditions* se réadapter (**to** à)

ready ['redɪ] (*prepared, willing*) prêt; **get sth** ~ préparer qch; **ready cash** (argent *m*)

liquide *m*; **ready-made** *stew etc* cuisiné; *solution* tout trouvé; **ready-to-wear** de confection; ~ *clothing* prêt-à-porter *m*

real [riːl] *not imaginary* réel; *not fake* vrai; **real estate** immobilier *m*, biens *mpl* immobiliers; **real estate agent** agent *m* immobilier; **realism** réalisme *m*; **realist** réaliste *m/f*; **realistic** réaliste; **realistically** de façon réaliste; **reality** réalité *f*; **realize** se rendre compte de; FIN réaliser; **really** vraiment; **real time** COMPUT temps *m* réel; **real-time** COMPUT en temps réel

realtor ['riːltər] agent *m* immobilier; **realty** immobilier *m*

reappear [riːə'pɪr] réapparaître

reappearance réapparition *f*

rear [rɪr] **1** *adj* arrière *inv*, de derrière **2** *n* arrière *m*

rearm [riː'ɑːrm] réarmer

rearrange [riːə'reɪndʒ] *flowers* réarranger; *furniture* déplacer; *schedule, meetings* réorganiser

rear-view 'mirror rétroviseur *m*, rétro *m* F

reason ['riːzn] **1** *n* (*cause*) faculty raison *f*; **reasonable** raisonnable; **reasonably** *act, behave* raisonnablement; (*quite*) relativement; **reasoning** raisonnement *m*

reassure [riːə'ʃʊr] rassurer;

reassuring rassurant
rebate ['ri:beɪt] (*refund*) remboursement *m*
rebel 1 ['rebl] *n* rebelle *m/f* **2** [rɪ'bel] *v/i* se rebeller; **rebellion** rébellion *f*; **rebellious** rebelle; **rebelliousness** esprit *m* de rébellion
rebound [rɪ'baʊnd] *of ball etc* rebondir
rebuild ['ri:bɪld] reconstruire
recall [rɪ'kɔːl] *goods, ambassador* rappeler; (*remember*) se rappeler
recap ['ri:kæp] récapituler
recapture [ri:'kæptʃər] reprendre
recede [rɪ'siːd] *of flood waters* baisser
receipt [rɪ'siːt] *for purchase* reçu *m* (**for** de), ticket *m* de caisse; **~s** FIN recette(s) *f(pl)*; **receive** recevoir; **receiver** TELEC combiné *m*; *for radio* (poste *m*) récepteur *m*; **receivership**: **be in ~** être en liquidation judiciaire
recent ['ri:snt] récent; **recently** récemment
reception [rɪ'sepʃn] réception *f*; (*welcome*) accueil *m*; **reception desk** réception *f*; **receptionist** réceptionniste *m/f*; **receptive**: **be ~ to sth** être réceptif à qch
recess ['ri:ses] *in wall etc* renfoncement *m*, recoin *m*; EDU récréation *f*; *of legislature* vacances *fpl* judiciaires; **recession** *economic* récession *f*

recharge [ri:'tʃɑːrdʒ] *battery* recharger
recipe ['resəpɪ] recette *f*
recipient [rɪ'sɪpɪənt] *of parcel etc* destinataire *m/f*; *of payment* bénéficiaire *m/f*
reciprocal [rɪ'sɪprəkl] réciproque
recite [rɪ'saɪt] *poem* réciter; *details, facts* énumérer
reckless ['reklɪs] imprudent; **recklessly** imprudemment
reckon ['rekən] (*think, consider*) penser
♦ **reckon on** compter sur
reclaim [rɪ'kleɪm] *land from sea* gagner sur la mer; *lost property* récupérer
recline [rɪ'klaɪn] s'allonger; **recliner** *chair* chaise *f* longue, relax *m*
recluse [rɪ'kluːs] reclus *m*
recognition [rekəg'nɪʃn] reconnaissance *f*; **recognizable** reconnaissable; **recognize** reconnaître
recoil [rɪ'kɔɪl] reculer
recollect [rekə'lekt] se souvenir de; **recollection** souvenir *m*
recommend [rekə'mend] recommander; **recommendation** recommandation *f*
recompense ['rekəmpens] compensation *f*, dédommagement *m*
reconcile ['rekənsaɪl] réconcilier; *differences* concilier; *facts* faire concorder; **reconciliation** réconciliation *f*; *of*

differences, facts conciliation *f*

recondition [riːkənˈdɪʃn] refaire, remettre à neuf

reconnaissance [rɪˈkɒnɪsəns] MIL reconnaissance *f*

reconsider [riːkənˈsɪdər] **1** *v/t* reconsidérer **2** *v/i* reconsidérer la question

reconstruct [riːkənˈstrʌkt] reconstruire; *crime* reconstituer

record¹ [ˈrekərd] *n* MUS disque *m*; SP *etc* record *m*; *written document etc* rapport *m*; *in database* article *m*, enregistrement *m*; **~s** (*archives*) archives *fpl*, dossiers *mpl*; **have a criminal ~** avoir un casier judiciaire

record² [rɪˈkɔːrd] *v/t electronically* enregistrer; *in writing* consigner

'record-breaking qui bat tous les records; **record holder** recordman *m*, recordwoman *f*

recording [rɪˈkɔːrdɪŋ] enregistrement *m*

recount [rɪˈkaʊnt] (*tell*) raconter

re-count [ˈriːkaʊnt] **1** *n of votes* recompte *m* **2** *v/t* recompter

recoup [rɪˈkuːp] *financial losses* récupérer

recover [rɪˈkʌvər] **1** *v/t* retrouver **2** *v/i from illness* se remettre; *of business* reprendre; **recovery** *of sth lost* ré-

cupération *f*; *from illness* rétablissement *m*

recreation [rekrɪˈeɪʃn] récréation *f*; **recreational** *done for pleasure* de loisirs

recruit [rɪˈkruːt] **1** *n* recrue *f* **2** *v/t* recruter; **recruitment** recrutement *m*

rectangle [ˈrektæŋgl] rectangle *m*; **rectangular** rectangulaire

rectify [ˈrektɪfaɪ] rectifier

recuperate [rɪˈkuːpəreɪt] récupérer

recur [rɪˈkɜːr] *of error, event* se reproduire; *of symptoms* réapparaître; **recurrent** récurrent

recycle [riːˈsaɪkl] recycler; **recycling** recyclage *m*

red [red] **1** *adj* rouge **2** *n*: **in the ~** FIN dans le rouge; **Red Cross** Croix-Rouge *f*

redecorate [riːˈdekəreɪt] refaire

redeem [rɪˈdiːm] *debt* rembourser; *sinners* racheter

redevelop [riːdɪˈveləp] *part of town* réaménager

'redhead roux *m*, rousse *f*; **red light** *for traffic* feu *m* rouge; **red light district** quartier *m* chaud; **red meat** viande *f* rouge; **redneck** F plouc *m* F; **red tape** F paperasserie *f*

reduce [rɪˈduːs] réduire; **reduction** réduction *f*

reek [riːk] empester (**of sth** qch)

reel [riːl] *of film, thread* bobine f

re-e'lect réélire; **re-election** réélection f

re-'entry of spacecraft rentrée f

ref [ref] F arbitre m
♦ **refer to** faire allusion à; dictionary etc se reporter à
referee [refə'riː] SP arbitre m; for job: personne m qui donne des références; **reference** (allusion) allusion f; for job référence f; (~ number) (numéro m de) référence f; **reference book** ouvrage m de référence; **reference number** numéro m de référence
referendum [refə'rendəm] référendum m
refill ['riːfɪl] remplir
refine [rɪ'faɪn] oil, sugar raffiner; technique affiner; **refinement** to process, machine perfectionnement m; **refinery** raffinerie f
reflect [rɪ'flekt] 1 v/t refléter 2 v/i (think) réfléchir; **reflection** also fig reflet m; (consideration) réflexion f
reflex ['riːfleks] in body réflexe m
reform [rɪ'fɔːrm] 1 n réforme f 2 v/t réformer; **reformer** réformateur(-trice) m(f)
refresh [rɪ'freʃ] rafraîchir; of sleep, rest reposer; of meal redonner des forces à; **refreshing** drink rafraîchissant; experience agréable; **refreshments** rafraîchisse-

ments mpl
refrigerate [rɪ'frɪdʒəreɪt] réfrigérer; **refrigerator** réfrigérateur m
refuel [riː'fjuːəl] 1 v/t airplane ravitailler 2 v/i of airplane se ravitailler (en carburant)
refuge ['refjuːdʒ] refuge m; take ~ from storm etc se réfugier; **refugee** réfugié(e) m(f)
refund 1 ['riːfʌnd] n remboursement m 2 [rɪ'fʌnd] v/t rembourser
refusal [rɪ'fjuːzl] refus m; **refuse** refuser; ~ **to do sth** refuser de faire qch
regain [rɪ'ɡeɪn] control, territory, the lead reprendre; composure retrouver
regard [rɪ'ɡɑːrd] 1 n: **with ~ to** en ce qui concerne; (kind) ~s cordialement; **with no ~ for** sans égard pour 2 v/t: ~ **as** considérer comme; **regarding** en ce qui concerne; **regardless** quand même; ~ **of** sans se soucier de
regime [reɪ'ʒiːm] (government) régime m
regiment ['redʒɪmənt] régiment m
region ['riːdʒən] région f; **regional** régional
register ['redʒɪstər] 1 n registre m 2 v/t birth, death déclarer; vehicle immatriculer; letter recommander; emotion exprimer 3 v/i for a course s'inscrire; with police se déclarer (with à); **regis-**

tered letter lettre *f* recommandée; **registration of birth, death** déclaration *f*; *of vehicle* immatriculation *f*; *for a course* inscription *f*

regret [rɪ'gret] **1** *v/t* regretter **2** *n* regret *m*; **regretful** plein de regrets; **regrettable** regrettable

regular ['regjʊlər] **1** *adj* régulier; *(normal)* normal **2** *n* *at bar etc* habitué(e) *m(f)*; **regularity** régularité *f*; **regularly** régulièrement

regulate ['regjʊleɪt] régler; *expenditure* contrôler; **regulation** *(rule)* règlement *m*

rehabilitate [ri:hə'bɪlɪteɪt] *ex-criminal* réinsérer; *disabled person* rééduquer

rehearsal [rɪ'hɜ:rsl] répétition *f*; **rehearse** répéter

reign [reɪn] **1** *n* règne *m* **2** *v/i* régner

reimburse [ri:ɪm'bɜ:rs] rembourser

reinforce [ri:ɪn'fɔ:rs] renforcer; *argument* étayer; **reinforced concrete** béton *m* armé; **reinforcements** MIL renforts *mpl*

reinstate [ri:ɪn'steɪt] *person in office* réintégrer, rétablir dans ses fonctions; *paragraph etc* réintroduire

reject [rɪ'dʒekt] rejeter; **rejection** rejet *m*

relapse ['ri:læps] MED rechute *f*

related [rɪ'leɪtɪd] *by family* apparenté; *events, ideas etc* associé; **relation** *in family* parent(e) *m(f)*; *(connection)* rapport *m*, relation *f*; **relationship** relation *f*; *sexual* liaison *f*; **relative 1** *adj* relatif **2** *n* parent(e) *m(f)*; **relatively** relativement

relax [rɪ'læks] **1** *v/i* se détendre; *~!* du calme! **2** *v/t muscle* relâcher; **relaxation** détente *f*, relaxation *f*; **relaxed** détendu, décontracté; **relaxing** reposant, relaxant

relay [rɪ'leɪ] *message* transmettre; *radio, TV signals* relayer, retransmettre **2** *n* ['ri:leɪ]: *~* *(race)* (course *f* de) relais *m*

release [rɪ'li:s] **1** *n from prison* libération *f*; *of CD, movie etc* sortie *f*; *CD, record* nouveauté *f* **2** *v/t prisoner* libérer; *CD, record, movie* sortir; *parking brake* desserrer; *information* communiquer

relegate ['relɪgeɪt] reléguer

relent [rɪ'lent] se calmer; *of person* s'adoucir; **relentless** *(determined)* acharné; *rain etc* incessant

relevance ['reləvəns] pertinence *f*; **relevant** pertinent

reliability [rɪlaɪə'bɪlɪtɪ] fiabilité *f*; **reliable** fiable; **reliance** [rɪ'laɪəns] confiance *f* (**on** en); *CD equipment* dépendance *f* (**on** vis-à-vis de)

relic ['relɪk] relique *f*

relief [rɪ'li:f] soulagement *m*;

relieve *pain* soulager; (*take over from*) relayer, relever

religion [rɪˈlɪdʒən] religion *f*; **religious** religieux; *person* croyant

relinquish [rɪˈlɪŋkwɪʃ] abandonner

relish [ˈrelɪʃ] **1** *n sauce* relish *f*; (*enjoyment*) délectation *f* **2** *v/t idea, prospect* se réjouir de

relive [riːˈlɪv] revivre

relocate [riːləˈkeɪt] *of business* se réimplanter; *of employee* être muté

reluctance [rɪˈlʌktəns] réticence *f*; **reluctant** réticent; **be ~ to do sth** hésiter à faire qch

◆ **rely on** [rɪˈlaɪ] compter sur; **rely on s.o. to do sth** compter sur qn pour faire qch

remain [rɪˈmeɪn] rester; **~ silent** garder le silence; **remainder** *also* MATH reste *m*; **remaining** restant; **the ~ refugees** le reste des réfugiés; **remains** *of body* restes *mpl*

remake [ˈriːmeɪk] *of movie* remake *m*, nouvelle version *f*

remark [rɪˈmɑːrk] **1** *n* remarque *f* **2** *v/t* (*comment*) faire remarquer; **remarkable** remarquable; **remarkably** remarquablement

remarry [riːˈmærɪ] se remarier

remedy [ˈremədɪ] MED, *fig* remède *m*

remember [rɪˈmembər] **1** *v/t* se souvenir de, se rappeler

2 *v/i* se souvenir

remind [rɪˈmaɪnd]: **~ s.o. to do sth** rappeler à qn de faire qch; **~ X of Y** rappeler Y à X; **~ s.o. of sth** (*bring to their attention*) rappeler qch à qn; **reminder** rappel *m*

reminisce [remɪˈnɪs] évoquer le passé

remission [rɪˈmɪʃn] MED rémission *f*; **go into ~** *of patient* être en sursis

remnant [ˈremnənt] vestige *m*, reste *m*

remorse [rɪˈmɔːrs] remords *m*; **remorseless** impitoyable; *demands* incessant

remote [rɪˈmout] *village* isolé; *possibility* vague; *ancestor* lointain; **remote control** télécommande *f*; **remotely** *related, connected* vaguement

removable [rɪˈmuːvəbl] amovible; **removal** enlèvement *m*; *of demonstrators* expulsion *f*; *of doubt* dissipation *f*; **remove** enlever; *demonstrators* expulser; *doubt* dissiper

rename [riːˈneɪm] rebaptiser; *file* renommer

rendez-vous [ˈrɑːndeɪvuː] rendez-vous *m*

renew [rɪˈnuː] *contract* renouveler; *discussion* reprendre; **renewal** *of contract etc* renouvellement *m*; *of discussion* reprise *f*

renounce [rɪˈnauns] renoncer à

renovate ['renəveɪt] rénover; renovation rénovation f

rent [rent] 1 n loyer m; for ~ à louer 2 v/t louer; rental for apartment loyer m; for TV, car location f; rental car voiture f de location; rent-free sans payer de loyer

reopen [riː'əupn] 1 v/t rouvrir; negotiations reprendre 2 v/i of store etc rouvrir

reorganization [riːɔːɡənaɪ-'zeɪʃn] réorganisation f; reorganize réorganiser

repaint [riː'peɪnt] repeindre

repair [rɪ'per] 1 v/t réparer 2 n réparation f; repairman réparateur m

repatriate [riː'pætrɪeɪt] rapatrier; repatriation rapatriement m

repay [riː'peɪ] rembourser; repayment remboursement m

repeal [rɪ'piːl] law abroger

repeat [rɪ'piːt] 1 v/t répéter 2 n TV program etc rediffusion f; repeatedly à plusieurs reprises

repel [rɪ'pel] repousser; (disgust) dégoûter; repellent 1 adj repoussant, répugnant 2 n (insect ~) répulsif m

repercussions [riːpər'kʌʃnz] répercussions fpl

repertoire ['repərtwɑːr] répertoire m

repetition [repɪ'tɪʃn] répétition f; repetitive répétitif

replace [rɪ'pleɪs] (put back) remettre; (take the place of) remplacer; replacement person remplaçant m; product produit m de remplacement; replacement part pièce f de rechange

replay ['riːpleɪ] 1 n recording relecture f, replay m; match nouvelle rencontre f, replay m 2 v/t match rejouer

replenish [rɪ'plenɪʃ] container, supplies remplir (de nouveau); supplies refaire

replica ['replɪkə] réplique f

reply [rɪ'plaɪ] 1 n réponse f 2 v/t & v/i répondre

report [rɪ'pɔːrt] 1 n (account) rapport m, compte-rendu m; in newspaper bulletin m 2 v/t facts rapporter; to authorities déclarer 3 v/i (present o.s.) se présenter; reporter reporter m/f

repossess [riːpə'zes] COM reprendre possession de

represent [reprɪ'zent] représenter; representative 1 adj (typical) représentatif 2 n représentant(e) m(f)

repress [rɪ'pres] réprimer; repression POL répression f; repressive POL répressif

reprieve [rɪ'priːv] 1 n LAW sursis m; fig also répit m 2 v/t prisoner accorder un sursis à

reprimand ['reprɪmænd] réprimander

reprint ['riːprɪnt] 1 n réimpression f 2 v/t réimprimer

reprisal [rɪ'praɪzl] représailles

fpl

reproach [rɪ'prəʊtʃ] **1** *n* reproche *m* **2** *v/t:* **~ s.o. for sth** reprocher qch à qn; **reproachful** réprobateur

reproduce [riːprə'djuːs] **1** *v/t* reproduire **2** *v/i* BIO se reproduire; **reproduction** reproduction *f*

reproductive reproducteur

reptile ['reptaɪl] reptile *m*

republic [rɪ'pʌblɪk] république *f*; **Republican 1** *adj* républicain **2** *n* Républicain(e) *m(f)*

repulsive [rɪ'pʌlsɪv] repoussant

reputable ['repjʊtəbl] de bonne réputation; **reputation** réputation *f*

request [rɪ'kwest] **1** *n* demande *f*; **on ~** sur demande **2** *v/t* demander

require [rɪ'kwaɪr] (*need*) avoir besoin de; **required** (*necessary*) requis; **requirement** (*need*) besoin *m*, exigence *f*; (*condition*) condition *f* (requise)

requisition [rekwɪ'zɪʃn] réquisitionner

re-route [riː'ruːt] *airplane etc* dérouter

rerun ['riːrʌn] **1** *n of TV program* rediffusion *f* **2** *v/t tape* repasser

reschedule [riː'skedjuːl] changer l'heure/la date de

rescue ['reskjuː] **1** *n* sauvetage *m* **2** *v/t* sauver, secourir

research [rɪ'sɜːtʃ] recherche *f*; **research and development** recherche *f* et développement; **researcher** chercheur(-euse) *m(f)*

resemblance [rɪ'zembləns] ressemblance *f*; **resemble** ressembler à

resent [rɪ'zent] ne pas aimer; *person also* en vouloir à; **resentful** plein de ressentiment; **resentment** ressentiment *m* (**of** par rapport à)

reservation [rezər'veɪʃn] réservation *f*; *mental, (special area)* réserve *f*; **reserve 1** *n* (*store, aloofness*) réserve *f*; SP remplaçant(e) *m(f)* **2** *v/t seat, judgment* réserver; **reserved** *table, manner* réservé

reservoir ['rezərvwɑːr] *for water* réservoir *m*

residence ['rezɪdəns] *fml: house etc* résidence *f*; (*stay*) séjour *m*; **resident** résident(e) *m(f)*; *on street* riverain(e) *m(f)*; *in hotel* client(e) *m(f)*; **residential** résidentiel

residue ['rezɪdjuː] résidu *m*

resign [rɪ'zaɪn] **1** *v/t position* démissionner de; **~ o.s. to** se résigner à **2** *v/i from job* démissionner; **resignation** *from job* démission *f*; *mental* résignation *f*

resilient [rɪ'zɪliənt] *personality* fort; *material* résistant

resist [rɪ'zɪst] **1** *v/t* résister à; *new measures* s'opposer à **2** *v/i* résister; **resistance** résistance *f*; resistant *material* résistant

resolution [rezə'luːʃn] résolution *f*

resort [rɪ'zɔːt] *place* lieu *m* de vacances; *at seaside* station *f* balnéaire; *for health cures* station *f* thermale; *as a last* ∼ en dernier ressort

◆ resort to avoir recours à, recourir à

◆ resound with [rɪ'zaʊnd] résonner de

resounding [rɪ'zaʊndɪŋ] *success, victory* retentissant

resource [rɪ'sɔːs] ressource *f*; resourceful ingénieux

respect [rɪ'spekt] 1 *n* respect *m*; *in this/that* ∼ à cet égard; *in many* ∼s à bien des égards 2 *v/t* respecter; respectability respectabilité *f*; respectable respectable; respectful respectueux; respectful respectif; respectively respectivement

respiration [respɪ'reɪʃn] respiration *f*; respirator MED respirateur *m*

respond [rɪ'spɒnd] répondre; (*react also*) réagir; response réponse *f*; (*reaction also*) réaction *f*,

responsibility [rɪspɒnsɪ'bɪlətɪ] responsabilité *f*; responsible responsable (*for* de); *a* ∼ *job* un poste à responsabilités

rest¹ [rest] 1 *n* repos *m*; *during walk, work* pause *f* 2 *v/i*

se reposer 3 *v/t* (*lean, balance*) poser

rest² [rest]: *the* ∼ *objects* le reste; *people* les autres

restaurant ['restərɒnt] restaurant *m*

restful ['restfl] reposant; rest home maison *f* de retraite; restless agité; restlessly nerveusement

restoration [restə'reɪʃn] *of building* restauration *f*; restore *building etc* restaurer; (*bring back*) restituer; *confidence* redonner

restrain [rɪ'streɪn] retenir; restraint (*moderation*) retenue *f*

restrict [rɪ'strɪkt] restreindre; *I'll* ∼ *myself to ...* je me limiterai à ...; restriction restriction *f*

'rest room toilettes *fpl*

result [rɪ'zʌlt] résultat *m*; *as a* ∼ *of this* par conséquent

resume [rɪ'zuːm] reprendre

résumé ['rezʊmeɪ] *of career* curriculum vitæ *m inv*, C.V. *m inv*

resumption [rɪ'zʌmpʃn] reprise *f*

resurface [riː'sɜːfɪs] 1 *v/t roads* refaire (le revêtement de) 2 *v/i* (*reappear*) refaire surface

Resurrection [rezə'rekʃn] REL Résurrection *f*

retail ['riːteɪl] 1 *adv*: *sell sth* ∼ vendre qch au détail 2 *v/i*: ∼ *at* se vendre à; retailer détail-

lant(e) *m(f)*
retain [rɪ'teɪn] conserver; **re-
tainer** FIN provision *f*
retaliate [rɪ'tælɪeɪt] riposter,
se venger; **retaliation** riposte
f
rethink [riː'θɪŋk] repenser
reticence ['retɪsns] réserve *f*;
reticent réservé
retire [rɪ'taɪr] *from work* prendre sa retraite; **retired** à la retraite; **retirement** retraite *f*;
retiring réservé
retort [rɪ'tɔːrt] **1** *n* réplique *f* **2**
v/t répliquer
retract [rɪ'trækt] *claws, undercarriage* rentrer; *statement*
retirer
're-train se recycler
retreat [rɪ'triːt] **1** *v/i also* MIL
battre en retraite **2** *n* MIL,
place retraite *f*
retrieve [rɪ'triːv] récupérer
retroactive [retrou'æktɪv]
law etc rétroactif; **retroac-
tively** rétroactivement, par
rétroaction
retrograde ['retrəgreɪd] ré-
trograde
retrospective [retrə'spektɪv]
rétrospective *f*
return [rɪ'tɜːrn] **1** *n* retour *m*;
(*profit*) bénéfice *m*; ~ (*ticket*)
Br aller *m* retour; **many happy ~s (of the day)** bon anniversaire; *in* ~ **for** en échange
de; contre **2** *v/t* (*give back*)
rendre; (*send back*) renvoyer; (*put back*) remettre
3 *v/i* (*go back*) retourner;

(*come back*) revenir
reunification [riːjuːnɪfɪ-
'keɪʃn] réunification *f*
reunion [riː'juːnjən] réunion
f; **reunite** réunir; *country*
réunifier
reusable [riː'juːzəbl] réutili-
sable; **reuse** réutiliser
◆ **rev up** [rev] *engine* emballer
revaluation [riːvæljuː'eɪʃn]
réévaluation *f*
reveal [rɪ'viːl] révéler; (*make
visible*) dévoiler; **revealing**
remark révélateur; *dress* sug-
gestif; **revelation** révélation
f
revenge [rɪ'vendʒ] vengeance
f; **take one's** ~ se venger
revenue ['revənuː] revenu *m*
reverberate [rɪ'vɜːrbəreɪt] *of
sound* retentir, résonner
revere [rɪ'vɪr] révérer; **rever-
ence** déférence *f*, respect
m; **reverent** respectueux
reverse [rɪ'vɜːrs] **1** *adj sequence* inverse **2** *n* (*opposite*)
contraire *m*; (*back*) verso *m*;
MOT *gear* marche *f* arrière **3**
v/i MOT faire marche arrière
review [rɪ'vjuː] **1** *n of book,
movie* critique *f*; *of troops* revue *f*; *of situation etc* bilan *m*
2 *v/t book, movie* faire la critique de; *troops* passer en revue; *situation etc* faire le bilan de; EDU réviser; **reviewer**
of book, movie critique *m*
revise [rɪ'vaɪz] *opinion* revenir sur; *text* réviser; **revision**

of text révision *f*

revival [rɪˈvaɪvl] *of custom,*
old style renouveau *m; of pa-*
tient rétablissement *m;* **re-**
vive 1 *v/t custom, old style*
faire renaître; *patient* ranimer **2** *v/i of business* reprendre

revoke [rɪˈvəʊk] *law* abroger;
license retirer

revolt [rɪˈvəʊlt] **1** *n* révolte *f* **2**
v/i se révolter; **revolting** répugnant; **revolution** révolu-
f; **revolutionary 1** *adj*
révolutionnaire **2** *n* révolutionnaire *m/f;* **revolutionize**
révolutionner

revolve [rɪˈvɒlv] tourner
(**around** autour de); **revolver**
revolver *m*

revulsion [rɪˈvʌlʃn] répu-
gnance *f*

reward [rɪˈwɔːrd] *n financial*
récompense *f; (benefit de-*
rived) gratification *f* **2** *v/t* financially récompenser; **re-**
warding *experience* grati-
fiant, valorisant

rewind [riːˈwaɪnd] *film, tape*
rembobiner

rewrite [riːˈraɪt] réécrire

rhetoric [ˈretərɪk] rhétorique *f*

rhyme [raɪm] **1** *n* rime *f* **2** *v/i*
rimer (**with** avec)

rhythm [ˈrɪðm] rythme *m*

rib [rɪb] ANAT côte *f*

ribbon [ˈrɪbən] ruban *m*

rice [raɪs] riz *m*

rich [rɪtʃ] **1** *adj person, food* ri-

che **2** *npl:* **the ~** les riches *mpl*

ricochet [ˈrɪkəʃeɪ] ricocher
(**off** sur)

rid [rɪd]: **get ~ of** se débarrasser de

ride [raɪd] **1** *n on horse* promenade *f* (à cheval); *excursion*
in vehicle tour *m; (journey)*
trajet *m;* **do you want a ~ in-**
to town? est-ce que tu veux
que je t'emmène en ville? **2**
v/t horse monter; *bike* se déplacer en; **can I ~ your bike?**
est-ce que je peux monter
sur ton vélo? **3** *v/i on horse*
monter à cheval; *on bike* rouler (à vélo); **rider** *on horse* ca-
valier(-ière) *m(f); on bike*
cycliste *m/f*

ridge [rɪdʒ] *(raised strip)* arête
f (saillante); *of mountain* crête *f; of roof* arête *f*

ridicule [ˈrɪdɪkjuːl] **1** *n* ridicule *m* **2** *v/t* ridiculiser; **ridicu-**
lous ridicule; **ridiculously**
ridiculement

riding [ˈraɪdɪŋ] *on horseback*
équitation *f*

rifle [ˈraɪfl] fusil *m,* carabine *f*

rift [rɪft] *in earth* fissure *f; in*
party etc scission *f*

rig [rɪg] **1** *n (oil ~)* tour *f* de forage; *at sea* plateforme *f* de
forage; *(truck)* semi-remorque *m* **2** *v/t elections* truquer

right [raɪt] **1** *adj bon; (not left)*
droit; **be ~** *of answer* être juste; *of person* avoir raison; *of*
clock être à l'heure; **it's not ~**
to ... ce n'est pas bien de ...;

put things ~ arranger les choses; **that's ~!** c'est ça!; **that's all ~** *(doesn't matter)* ce n'est pas grave; **when s.o. says thank you** je vous en prie; **it's all ~** *(is acceptable)* ça me va; **I'm all ~** *not hurt* je vais bien; **have enough** ça ira pour moi **2** *adv (directly)* directement, juste; *(correctly)* correctement, bien; *(not left)* à droite; **~ now** *(immediately)* tout de suite; *(at the moment)* en ce moment; **it's ~ here** c'est juste là **3** *n civil, legal* droit *m*; POL droite *f*; **be in the ~** avoir raison; **right-angle** angle *m* droit; **rightful** *owner etc* légitime; **right-handed** *person* droitier; **right-hand man** bras *m* droit; **right of way** *in traffic* priorité *f*; *across land* droit *m* de passage; **right wing** POL droite *f*; SP ailier *m* droit; **right-wing** POL de droite

rigid ['rɪdʒɪd] *also fig* rigide

rigor ['rɪgər] *of discipline* rigueur *f*; **rigorous** rigoureux; **rigorously** *check* rigoureusement

rigour *Br* → **rigor**

rile [raɪl] F agacer

rim [rɪm] *of wheel* jante *f*; *of cup* bord *m*; *of eyeglasses* monture *f*

ring[1] [rɪŋ] *n (circle)* cercle *m*; *on finger* anneau *m*; *in box-*ing ring *m*; *at circus* piste *f*

ring[2] [rɪŋ] **1** *n of bell* sonnerie *f*; *of voice* son *m* **2** *v/t bell* (faire) sonner; Br TELEC téléphoner à **3** *v/i of bell* sonner, retentir

'ringleader meneur(-euse) *m(f)*; **ring-pull** anneau *m* (d'ouverture)

rink [rɪŋk] patinoire *f*

rinse [rɪns] **1** *n for hair color* rinçage *m* **2** *v/t* rincer

riot ['raɪət] **1** *n* émeute *f* **2** *v/i* participer à une émeute; **start to ~** créer une émeute; **rioter** émeutier(-ière) *m(f)*; **riot police** police *f* anti-émeute

rip [rɪp] **1** *n in cloth etc* accroc *m* **2** *v/t cloth etc* déchirer

◆ **rip-off** F *customers* arnaquer F

ripe [raɪp] *fruit* mûr; **ripen** *of fruit* mûrir; **ripeness** *of fruit* maturité *f*

'rip-off F arnaque *f* F

ripple ['rɪpl] *on water* ride *f*

rise [raɪz] **1** *v/i from chair, bed, of sun* se lever; *of rocket, price, temperature* monter **2** *n in price, temperature* hausse *f*; *in water level* élévation *f*; Br: *in salary* augmentation *f*

risk [rɪsk] **1** *n* risque *m*; **take a ~** prendre un risque **2** *v/t* risquer; **risky** risqué

ritual ['rɪtʊəl] **1** *adj* rituel **2** *n* rituel *m*

rival ['raɪvl] **1** *n* rival(e) *m(f)* **2**

v/t (match) égaler; *(compete with)* rivaliser avec; **rivalry** rivalité *f*

river ['rɪvər] rivière *f*; *bigger* fleuve *m*; **riverbank** rive *f*; **riverbed** lit *m* de la rivière/ du fleuve; **riverside 1** *adj* en bord de rivière **2** *n* berge *f*, bord *m* de l'eau

riveting ['rɪvɪtɪŋ] fascinant

road [roud] route *f*; *in city* rue *f*; **roadblock** barrage *m* routier; **road-holding** *of vehicle* tenue *f* de route; **road map** carte *f* routière; **road safety** sécurité *f* routière; **roadsign** panneau *m* (de signalisation; **roadway** chaussée *f*; **roadworthy** en état de marche

roam [roum] errer

roar [rɔːr] **1** *n* rugissement *m*; *of traffic* grondement *m*; *of engine* vrombissement *m* **2** *v/i* rugir; *of traffic* gronder; *of engine* vrombir

roast [roust] **1** *n of beef etc* rôti *m* **2** *v/t* rôtir **3** *v/i of food* rôtir; **roast beef** rosbif *m*

rob [raːb] *person* voler, dévaliser; *bank* cambrioler, dévaliser; *robber* voleur(-euse) *m(f)*; **robbery** vol *m*

robe [roub] *of judge, priest* robe *f*; *(bath~)* peignoir *m*; *(dressing gown)* robe *f* de chambre

robot ['roubaːt] robot *m*

robust [rou'bʌst] robuste

rock [raːk] **1** *n* rocher *m*; MUS

rock *m* **2** *v/t baby* bercer; *cradle* balancer; *(surprise)* secouer **3** *v/i on chair, of boat* se balancer; **rock-bottom** *price* le plus bas possible; **rock climber** varappeur(-euse) *m(f)*; **rock climbing** varappe *f*

rocket ['raːkɪt] **1** *n* fusée *f* **2** *v/i of prices etc* monter en flèche

rocking chair ['raːkɪŋ] rocking-chair *m*; **rock 'n' roll** rock-and-roll *m inv*; **rocky** *beach* rocheux

rod [raːd] baguette *f*; *for fishing* canne *f* à pêche

rodent ['roudnt] rongeur *m*

rogue [roug] vaurien *m*

role [roul] rôle *m*; **role model** modèle *m*

roll [roul] **1** *n (bread ~)* petit pain *m*; *of film* pellicule *f*; *(list, register)* liste *f* **2** *v/i of ball, boat* rouler

◆ **roll over 1** *v/i* se retourner **2** *v/t person, object* tourner; *(renew)* renouveler; *(extend)* prolonger

'roll call appel *m*; **roller** *for hair* rouleau *m*; **roller blade®** roller *m* (en ligne); **roller coaster** montagnes *fpl* russes; **roller skate** patin *m* à roulettes

ROM [raːm] COMPUT (= **read only memory**) ROM *f*, mémoire *f* morte

Roman 'Catholic 1 *adj* REL catholique **2** *n* catholique *m/f*

romance ['roumæns] *(affair)*

idylle f; *novel, movie* histoire f d'amour; **romantic** romantique

root [ruːf] toit m; **roof-rack** MOT galerie f

rookie ['rʊkɪ] F bleu m F

room [ruːm] pièce f, salle f; (*bed~*) chambre f; (*space*) place f; **room clerk** réceptionniste m/f; **roommate** in *apartment* colocataire m/f; *in room* camarade m/f de chambre; **room service** service m en chambre; **room temperature** température f ambiante; **roomy** spacieux; *clothes* ample

root [ruːt] racine f

rope [roʊp] corde f

rosary ['roʊzərɪ] REL rosaire m, chapelet m

rose [roʊz] BOT rose f

roster ['rɑːstər] tableau m de service

rostrum ['rɑːstrəm] estrade f

rosy ['roʊzɪ] *also fig* rose

rot [rɑːt] **1** n pourriture f **2** v/i pourrir

rotate [roʊ'teɪt] **1** v/i tourner **2** v/t (*turn*) (faire) tourner; *crops* alterner; **rotation** rotation f

rotten ['rɑːtn] *also* F *weather, luck* pourri

rough [rʌf] **1** adj *surface* rugueux; *hands, skin* rêche; *voice* rude; (*violent*) brutal; *crossing, seas* agité; (*approximate*) approximatif; **~ draft** brouillon m **2** n in *golf* rough

m; **roughage** in *food* fibres fpl; **roughly** (*approximately*) environ; (*harshly*) brutalement

roulette [ruː'let] roulette f

round [raʊnd] **1** adj rond **2** n of *mailman, doctor, drinks* tournée f; of *competition* manche f, tour m; *in boxing* round m **3** v/t *corner* tourner **4** adv & prep → **around**

◆ **round up** *figure* arrondir; *suspects* ramasser

roundabout ['raʊndəbaʊt] **1** adj détourné, indirect **2** n Br: *on road* rond-point m; **round-the-world** autour du monde; **round trip** aller-retour m; **round-up** of *cattle* rassemblement m; of *suspects* rafle f; of *news* résumé m

rouse [raʊz] *from sleep* réveiller; *emotions* soulever; **rousing** exaltant

route [ruːt] itinéraire m

routine [ruː'tiːn] **1** adj de routine; *behavior* routinier **2** n routine f

row[1] [roʊ] n (*line*) rangée f; of *troops* rang m; **5 days in a ~** 5 jours de suite

row[2] [roʊ] v/i *in boat* ramer

rowboat ['roʊboʊt] bateau m à rames

rowdy ['raʊdɪ] tapageur, bruyant

royal ['rɔɪəl] royal; **royalty** (*membres* mpl de) la famille royale; *on book, recording*

droits *mpl* d'auteur
rub [rʌb] frotter
rubber ['rʌbər] **1** *n material* caoutchouc *m* **2** *adj* en caoutchouc; **rubber band** élastique *m*
rubble ['rʌbl] *from building* gravats *mpl*, décombres *mpl*
ruby ['ru:bɪ] *jewel* rubis *m*
rudder ['rʌdər] gouvernail *m*
ruddy ['rʌdɪ] *complexion* coloré
rude [ru:d] impoli; *language, gesture* grossier; **rudely** (*impolitely*) impoliment; **rudeness** impolitesse *f*
rudimentary [ru:dɪ'mentərɪ] rudimentaire; **rudiments** rudiments *mpl*
rueful ['ru:fl] contrit, résigné; **ruefully** avec regret; *smile* d'un air contrit
ruffian ['rʌfɪən] voyou *m*, brute *f*
ruffle ['rʌfl] **1** *n on dress* ruche *f* **2** *v/t hair* ébouriffer; *person* énerver
rug [rʌg] tapis *m*; *blanket* couverture *f*
rugby ['rʌgbɪ] rugby *m*
rugged ['rʌgɪd] *scenery, cliffs* escarpé; *face* aux traits rudes; *resistance* acharné
ruin ['ru:ɪn] **1** *n* ruine *f* **2** *v/t* ruiner; *party, plans* gâcher
rule [ru:l] **1** *n* règle *f*; *of monarch* règne *m*; **as a** ~ en règle générale **2** *v/t country* gouverner **3** *v/i of monarch* régner; **ruler** *for measuring* rè-

gle *f*; *of state* dirigeant(e) *m(f)*; **ruling 1** *n* décision *f* **2** *adj party* dirigeant, au pouvoir
rum [rʌm] *drink* rhum *m*
rumble ['rʌmbl] *of stomach* gargouiller; *of thunder* gronder
rumor, *Br* **rumour** ['ru:mər] **1** *n* bruit *m*, rumeur *f* **2** *v/t*: **it is ~ed that** ... le bruit court que ...
rump [rʌmp] *of animal* croupe *f*
rumple ['rʌmpl] *clothes, paper* froisser
rumpsteak rumsteck *m*
run [rʌn] **1** *n on foot* course *f*; *in pantyhose* échelle *f*; **go for a** ~ *for exercise* aller courir; **in the short/long** ~ à court/long terme **2** *v/i* courir; *of river, paint, makeup* couler; *of trains, buses* passer, circuler; *of play* tenir à l'affiche; *of engine, machine* marcher, tourner; *of software* fonctionner; *in election* se présenter; ~ **for President** être candidat à la présidence **3** *v/t race* courir; *business, hotel etc* diriger; *software* exécuter, faire tourner; *car* entretenir
◆ **run away** s'enfuir; *from home for a while* faire une fugue; *for good* s'enfuir de chez soi
◆ **run down 1** *v/t* (*knock down*) renverser; (*criticize*)

critiquer; *stocks* diminuer **2** *v/i of battery* se décharger
- **run off 1** *v/i* s'enfuir **2** *v/t* (*print off*) tirer
- **run out** *of contract* expirer; *of time* s'écouler; *of supplies* s'épuiser
- **run out of** ne plus avoir de
- **run over 1** *v/t* (*knock down*) renverser **2** *v/i of water etc* déborder
- **run up** *debts* accumuler

'runaway fugueur(-euse) *m(f)*; **run-down** *person* épuisé; *area* délabré

rung [rʌŋ] *of ladder* barreau *m*

runner ['rʌnər] *athlete* coureur(-euse) *m(f)*; **runner beans** haricots *mpl* d'Espagne; **runner-up** second(e) *m(f)*; **running 1** *n* SP course *f*; *of business* gestion *f* **2** *adj*: **for two days ~** pendant deux jours de suite; **running water** eau *f* courante; **runny substance** liquide; *nose* qui coule; **run-up** SP élan *m*; **in the ~ to** pendant la période

qui précède; **runway** AVIA piste *f*

rupture ['rʌptʃər] **1** *n also fig* rupture *f* **2** *v/i of pipe* éclater

rural ['rʊərəl] rural

ruse [ruːz] ruse *f*

rush [rʌʃ] **1** *n* ruée *f*; **do sth in a ~** faire qch à la hâte; **be in a ~** être pressé **2** *v/t person* presser; *meal* avaler (à toute vitesse) **3** *v/i* se presser; **rush hour** heures *fpl* de pointe

Russia ['rʌʃə] Russie *f*; **Russian** ['rʌʃən] **1** *adj* russe **2** *n* Russe *m/f*; *language* russe *m*

rust [rʌst] **1** *n* rouille *f* **2** *v/i* se rouiller; **rust-proof** anti-rouille *inv*; **rusty** *also fig* rouillé

rut [rʌt] *in road* ornière *f*; **be in a ~** *fig* être tombé dans la routine

ruthless ['ruːθlɪs] impitoyable, sans pitié; **ruthlessly** impitoyablement; **ruthlessness** dureté *f* (impitoyable)

rye [raɪ] seigle *m*; **rye bread** pain *m* de seigle

S

sabotage ['sæbətɑːʒ] **1** *n* sabotage *m* **2** *v/t* saboter; **saboteur** saboteur(-euse) *m(f)*

sachet ['sæʃeɪ] sachet *m*

sack [sæk] **1** *n bag* sac *m* **2** *v/t* F virer F

sacred ['seɪkrɪd] sacré

sacrifice ['sækrɪfaɪs] **1** *n* sacrifice *m* **2** *v/t also fig* sacrifier

sacrilege ['sækrɪlɪdʒ] REL, *fig* sacrilège *m*

sad [sæd] triste

saddle ['sædl] **1** *n* selle *f* **2** *v/t*

horse seller

sadism ['seɪdɪzm] sadisme *m*; **sadist** sadique *m/f*; **sadistic** sadique

sadly ['sædlɪ] tristement; (*regrettably*) malheureusement; **sadness** tristesse *f*

safe [seɪf] **1** *adj* (*not dangerous*) pas dangereux; *driver* prudent; (*not in danger*) en sécurité **2** *n* coffre-fort *m*; **safeguard 1** *n*: **as a ~ against** par mesure de protection contre **2** *v/t* protéger; **safely** *arrive, drive, assume* sans risque; **safety** sécurité *f*; *of investment, prediction* sûreté *f*; **safety pin** épingle *f* de nourrice

sag [sæg] *of ceiling* s'affaisser; *of rope* se détendre; *fig: of output* fléchir

saga ['sɑːɡə] saga *f*

sage [seɪdʒ] *herb* sauge *f*

sail [seɪl] **1** *n of boat* voile *f*; *trip* voyage *m* (en mer) **2** *v/i* faire de la voile; (*depart*) partir; **sailboard 1** *n* planche *f* à voile **2** *v/i* faire de la planche à voile; **sailboarding** planche *f* à voile; **sailboat** bateau *m* à voiles; **sailing** SP voile *f*; **sailor** marin *m*

saint [seɪnt] saint(e) *m(f)*

sake [seɪk]: **for my ~** pour moi

salad ['sæləd] salade *f*

salary ['sælərɪ] salaire *m*

sale [seɪl] vente *f*; *reduced prices* soldes *mpl*; **for ~** *sign* à vendre; **be on ~** être en

vente; *at reduced prices* être en solde; **sales** *department* vente *f*; **sales clerk** *in store* vendeur(-euse) *m(f)*; **sales figures** chiffre *m* d'affaires; **salesman** vendeur *m*; (*rep*) représentant *m*; **saleswoman** vendeuse *f*

salient ['seɪlɪənt] marquant

saliva [sə'laɪvə] salive *f*

salmon ['sæmən] saumon *m*

saloon [sə'luːn] (*bar*) bar *m* Br MOT berline *f*

salt [sɔːlt] sel *m*; **salty** salé

salute [sə'luːt] **1** *n* MIL salut *m* **2** *v/t* MIL saluer **3** *v/i* MIL faire un salut

salvage ['sælvɪdʒ] *from wreck* sauver

salvation [sæl'veɪʃn] *also fig* salut *m*

same [seɪm] **1** *adj* même **2** *pron*: **the ~** le/la même; *pl* **the ~** les mêmes; **Happy New Year – the ~ to you** Bonne année – à vous aussi; **all the ~** (*even so*) quand même **3** *adv*: **look/sound the ~** se ressembler, être pareil

sample ['sæmpl] *of work, cloth* échantillon *m*; *of blood* prélèvement *m*

sanction ['sæŋkʃn] **1** *n* (*approval*) approbation *f*; (*penalty*) sanction *f* **2** *v/t* (*approve*) approuver

sand [sænd] **1** *n* sable *m* **2** *v/t with sandpaper* poncer au papier de verre

sandal ['sændl] sandale *f*

'sandbag sac *m* de sable; **sand dune** dune *f*; **sander tool** ponçeuse *f*; **sandpaper 1** *n* papier *m* de verre **2** *v/t* poncer au papier de verre

sandwich ['sænwɪtʃ] sandwich *m*

sandy ['sændɪ] *beach* de sable; *soil* sablonneux; *feet, towel* plein de sable; *hair* blond roux

sane [seɪn] sain (d'esprit)

sanitarium [sænɪ'terɪəm] sanatorium *m*

sanitary ['sænɪterɪ] sanitaire; *(clean)* hygiénique; **sanitary napkin** serviette *f* hygiénique; **sanitation installations** *fpl* sanitaires; *(removal of waste)* système *m* sanitaire

sanity ['sænətɪ] santé *f* mentale

Santa Claus ['sæntəklɔːz] le Père Noël

sap [sæp] **1** *n* in tree sève *f* **2** *v/t s.o.'s energy* saper

sapphire ['sæfaɪr] saphir *m*

sarcasm ['sɑːrkæzm] sarcasme *m*; **sarcastic** sarcastique; **sarcastically** sarcastiquement

sardine [sɑːr'diːn] sardine *f*

sardonic [sɑːr'dɑːnɪk] sardonique

satellite ['sætəlaɪt] satellite *m*; **satellite dish** antenne *f* parabolique; **satellite TV** télévision *f* par satellite

satin ['sætɪn] satin *m*

satire ['sætaɪr] satire *f*; **satiri**cal satirique; **satirize** satiriser

satisfaction [sætɪs'fækʃn] satisfaction *f*; **satisfactory** satisfaisant; *(just good enough)* convenable; **satisfy** satisfaire; *conditions* remplir

Saturday ['sætərdeɪ] samedi *m*

sauce [sɔːs] sauce *f*; **saucepan** casserole *f*; **saucer** soucoupe *f*

Saudi Arabia [saʊdɪəˈreɪbɪə] Arabie *f* saoudite; **Saudi Arabian 1** *adj* saoudien **2** *n* Saoudien(ne) *m(f)*

sausage ['sɔːsɪdʒ] saucisse *f*; *dried* saucisson *m*

savage ['sævɪdʒ] **1** *adj* féroce **2** *n* sauvage *m/f*; **savagery** férocité *f*

save [seɪv] **1** *v/t (rescue)*, SP sauver; *(economize, put aside)* économiser; *(collect)* faire collection de; COMPUT sauvegarder **2** *v/i (put money aside)* faire des économies; SP arrêter le ballon **3** *n* SP arrêt *m*; **saver** *person* épargneur (-euse) *m(f)*; **savings** économies *fpl*; **savings account** compte *m* d'épargne; **savings and loan** caisse *f* d'épargne-logement; **savings bank** caisse *f* d'épargne

savior, *Br* **saviour** ['seɪvjər] REL sauveur *m*

savor ['seɪvər] savourer; **savory** *not sweet* salé

savour etc *Br* → **savor** etc

saw [sɔː] **1** *n tool* scie *f* **2** *v/t scier; sawdust* sciure *f*

saxophone ['sæksəfoʊn] saxophone *m*

say [seɪ] *v/t* dire; *that is to* ~ c'est-à-dire; **saying** dicton *m*

scab [skæb] *on wound* croûte *f*

scaffolding ['skæfəldɪŋ] échafaudage *m*

scald [skɔːld] ébouillanter

scale[1] [skeɪl] *n on fish* écaille *f*

scale[2] [skeɪl] **1** *n of project, map etc, on thermometer* échelle *f*; MUS gamme *f* **2** *v/t cliffs etc* escalader

scales [skeɪlz] *for weighing* balance *f*

scallop ['skæləp] *shellfish* coquille *f* Saint-Jacques

scalp [skælp] *cuir m* chevelu

scalpel ['skælpl] scalpel *m*

scam [skæm] F arnaque *m* F

scampi ['skæmpɪ] scampi *m*

scan [skæn] **1** *n* MED scanner *m*; *during pregnancy* échographie *f* **2** *v/t* horizon, page parcourir du regard; COMPUT scanner

♦ **scan in** COMPUT scanner

scandal ['skændl] scandale *m*; **scandalize** scandaliser; **scandalous** scandaleux

scanner ['skænər] MED, COMPUT scanner *m*

scanty ['skæntɪ] *dress* réduit au minimum

scapegoat ['skeɪpgoʊt] bouc

m émissaire

scar [skɑːr] **1** *n* cicatrice *f* **2** *v/t* marquer d'une cicatrice

scarce [skers] rare; **scarcely** ['skersli] à peine; ~ *anything* presque rien; **scarcity** manque *m*

scare [sker] **1** *v/t* faire peur à; *be* ~*d of* avoir peur de **2** *n* (*panic, alarm*) rumeurs *fpl* alarmantes; **scaremonger** alarmiste *m/f*

scarf [skɑːrf] *around neck* écharpe *f*; *over head* foulard *m*

scarlet ['skɑːrlət] écarlate

scary ['skerɪ] effrayant

scathing ['skeɪðɪŋ] cinglant

scatter ['skætər] **1** *v/t leaflets, seed* éparpiller **2** *v/i of people* se disperser; **scattered** *showers* intermittent; *villages* éparpillé

scavenge ['skævɪndʒ]: ~ *for sth* fouiller pour trouver qch; **scavenger** charognard *m*; *person* fouilleur(euse) *m(f)*

scenario [sɪ'nɑːrɪoʊ] scénario *m*

scene [siːn] scène *f*; *of accident, crime* lieu *m*; *make a* ~ faire une scène; *behind the* ~*s* dans les coulisses; **scenery** paysage *m*; THEA décor(s) *m(pl)*

scent [sent] odeur *f*; *Br* (*perfume*) parfum *m*

sceptic *etc Br* ► **skeptic** *etc*

schedule ['skedjuːl] **1** *n of*

events calendrier *m*; *for trains* horaire *m*; *of lessons, work* programme *m*; **be on ~ of work,** *workers* être dans les temps; *of train* être à l'heure; **be behind ~** être en retard **2** *v/t* (*put on ~*) prévoir; *scheduled flight* vol *m* régulier

scheme [skiːm] **1** *n* plan *m* **2** *v/i* (*plot*) comploter; **scheming** intrigant

schizophrenia [skɪtsəˈfriːnɪə] schizophrénie *f*; **schizophrenic 1** *adj* schizophrène **2** *n* schizophrène *m/f*

scholar [ˈskɑːlər] érudit(e) *m(f)*; **scholarly** savant, érudit; **scholarship** (*learning*) érudition *f*; *financial award* bourse *f*

school [skuːl] école *f*; (*university*) université *f*; **school bag** cartable *m*; **schoolchildren** écoliers *mpl*

science [ˈsaɪəns] science *f*; **scientific** scientifique; **scientist** scientifique *m/f*

scissors [ˈsɪzərz] ciseaux *mpl*

scoff[1] [skɑːf] *food* engloutir

scoff[2] [skɑːf] (*mock*) se moquer

scold [skoʊld] réprimander

scoop [skuːp] *for ice-cream* cuiller *f* à glace; *of ice cream* boule *f*; *story* scoop *m*

scooter [ˈskuːtər] *with motor* scooter *m*; *child's* trottinette *f*

scope [skoʊp] ampleur *f*;

(*freedom, opportunity*) possibilités *fpl*

scorch [skɔːrtʃ] brûler; **scorching** très chaud

score [skɔːr] **1** *n* sp score *m*; (*written music*) partition *f*; *of movie etc* musique *f* **2** *v/t* *goal, point* marquer; (*cut: line*) rayer **3** *v/i* sp marquer; (*keep the ~*) marquer les points; **scoreboard** tableau *m* des scores; **scorer** marqueur(-euse) *m(f)*

scorn [skɔːrn] **1** *n* mépris *m* **2** *v/t* idea mépriser; **scornful** méprisant; **scornfully** avec mépris

Scot [skɑːt] Écossais(e) *m(f)*; **Scotch whiskey** scotch *m*; **Scotch tape**® scotch *m*; **Scotland** Écosse *f*; **Scottish** écossais

scoundrel [ˈskaʊndrəl] gredin *m*

scour [ˈskaʊər] (*search*) fouiller

scowl [skaʊl] **1** *n* air *m* renfrogné **2** *v/i* se renfrogner

scramble [ˈskræmbl] **1** *n* (*rush*) course *f* folle **2** *v/t* message brouiller **3** *v/i:* **he ~d to his feet** il se releva d'un bond; **scrambled eggs** œufs *mpl* brouillés

scrap [skræp] **1** *n* *metal* ferraille *f*; (*fight*) bagarre *f*; *of food, paper* bout *m* **2** *v/t* idea, plan abandonner

scrape [skreɪp] **1** *n* on paint, skin éraflure *f* **2** *v/t paint-*

work, arm etc érafler

'scrap metal ferraille f

scrappy ['skræpi] work, essay décousu

scratch [skrætʃ] **1** n mark égratignure f; **start from ~** partir de zéro; **not up to ~** pas à la hauteur **2** v/t (mark: skin, paint) égratigner; of cat griffer; because of itch se gratter **3** v/i of cat griffer

scrawl [skrɔːl] **1** n gribouillis m **2** v/t gribouiller

scrawny ['skrɔːni] décharné

scream [skriːm] **1** n cri m **2** v/i pousser un cri

screech [skriːtʃ] **1** n of tires crissement m; (scream) cri m strident **2** v/i of tires crisser; (scream) pousser un cri strident

screen [skriːn] **1** n in room, hospital paravent m; in movie theater, of TV, computer écran m **2** v/t (protect, hide) cacher; movie projeter; for security reasons passer au crible; **screenplay** scénario m; **screen saver** COMPUT économiseur m d'écran; **screen test** for movie bout m d'essai

screw [skruː] **1** n vis m **2** v/t attach visser (**to** à); F (cheat) rouler F; V (have sex with) baiser V; **screwdriver** tournevis m; **screwed up** F psychologically paumé F; **screwy** F déjanté F

scribble ['skrɪbl] **1** n griffonnage m **2** v/t (write quickly)

griffonner **3** v/i gribouiller

script [skrɪpt] for movie scénario m; for play texte m; form of writing script m; Scripture: **the (Holy) ~s** les Saintes Écritures fpl; **scriptwriter** scénariste m/f

◆ **scroll down** COMPUT faire défiler vers le bas

◆ **scroll up** COMPUT faire défiler vers le haut

scrounge [skraundʒ] se faire offrir; **scrounger** profiteur(-euse) m(f)

scrub [skrʌb] floor laver à la brosse

scruples ['skruːplz] scrupules mpl; **scrupulous** morally, (thorough) scrupuleux; **scrupulously** (meticulously) scrupuleusement

scrutinize ['skruːtɪnaɪz] (examine closely) scruter; **scrutiny** examen m minutieux

scuba diving ['skuːbə] plongée f sous-marine autonome

scuffie ['skʌfl] bagarre f

sculptor ['skʌlptər] sculpteur(-trice) m(f); **sculpture** sculpture f

scum [skʌm] on liquid écume f; pej: people bande f d'ordures f

sea [siː] mer f; **seabird** oiseau m de mer; **seafood** fruits mpl de mer; **seagull** mouette f

seal¹ [siːl] n animal phoque m

seal² [siːl] **1** n on document

sceau m; TECH étanchéité f **2**
v/t container sceller

'sea level: **above/below** ~ au-
-dessus/au-dessous du niveau
de la mer

seam [siːm] on garment couture f; of ore veine f

'seaman marin m; seaport
port m maritime

search [sɜːrʧ] **1** n recherche f
(**for** de) **2** v/t chercher dans
◆ **search for** chercher

searching ['sɜːrʧɪŋ] look,
question pénétrant; search-
light projecteur m

'seashore plage f; seasick:
get ~ avoir le mal de mer;
seaside: **at the** ~ au bord
de la mer

season [siːzn] saison f; seasonal vegetables, employ-
ment saisonnier; seasoned
wood sec; traveler, cam-
paigner expérimenté; sea-
soning assaisonnement m;
season ticket carte f d'abonnement

seat [siːt] place f; chair siège
m; of pants fond m; **please
take a** ~ veuillez vous asseoir; seat belt ceinture f
de sécurité

'seaweed algues fpl

secluded [sɪˈkluːdɪd] retiré
second ['sekənd] **1** n of time
seconde f **2** adj deuxième **3**
adv come in deuxième **4** v/t
motion appuyer; secondary
secondaire; second floor
premier étage m, Br deuxiè-

me étage m; second-hand
d'occasion; secondly
deuxièmement; second-
-rate de second ordre

secrecy ['siːkrəsɪ] secret m;
secret **1** n secret m **2** adj secret

secretarial [sekrəˈterɪəl] job
de secrétariat; secretary secrétaire m/f; POL ministre
m/f; Secretary of State secrétaire m/f d'État

secretive ['siːkrətɪv] secret;
secretly en secret

sect [sekt] secte f

section ['sekʃn] section f

sector ['sektər] secteur m

secular ['sekjulər] séculier

secure [sɪˈkjur] **1** adj shelf etc
bien fixé; job, contract sûr **2**
v/t shelf etc fixer; s.o.'s help,
finances se procurer; securities market FIN marché m
des valeurs; security sécurité f; for investment garantie
f; security alert alerte f de
sécurité; security forces forces fpl de sécurité; security
guard garde m de sécurité;
security risk menace poten-
tielle à la sécurité de l'État
ou d'une organisation

sedan [sɪˈdæn] MOT berline f

sedate [sɪˈdeɪt] donner un
calmant à; sedative calmant
m

sedentary ['sedəntərɪ] job sédentaire

sediment ['sedɪmənt] sédi-
ment m

seduce [sɪ'djuːs] séduire; **seduction** séduction f; **seductive** *dress, offer* séduisant

see [siː] *with eyes,* (*understand*) voir; ~ *you!* F à plus! F ◆ **see off** *at airport etc* raccompagner; (*chase away*) chasser

seed [siːd] *single* graine f; *collective* graines fpl; *of fruit* pépin m; *in tennis* tête f de série; **seedy** miteux

seeing *'eye dog* chien m d'aveugle; **seeing** (*that*) étant donné que

seek [siːk] chercher

seem [siːm] sembler; **seemingly** apparemment

seesaw ['siːsɔː] bascule f

'see-through transparent

segment ['segmənt] segment m; *of orange* morceau m

segregate ['segrɪgeɪt] séparer; **segregation** ségrégation f; *of sexes* séparation f

seismology [saɪz'mɑːlədʒɪ] sismologie f

seize [siːz] *opportunity, arm, of police etc* saisir; *power* s'emparer de; **seizure** MED crise f; *of drugs etc* saisie f

seldom ['seldəm] rarement

select [sɪ'lekt] **1** *v/t* sélectionner **2** *adj group of people* choisi; *hotel etc* chic *inv*; **selection** sélection f; **selective** sélectif

self [self] moi m; **self-assurance** confiance f en soi; **self-assured** sûr de soi;

self-centered, *Br* **self-centred** égocentrique; **self-confidence** confiance en soi; **self-confident** sûr de soi; **self-conscious** intimidé; *about sth* gêné (**about** par); **self-consciousness** timidité f; *about sth* gêné f (**about** par rapport à); **self-control** contrôle m de soi; **self-defense,** *Br* **self-defence** autodéfense f; LAW légitime défense f; **self-employed** indépendant; **self-evident** évident; **self-expression** expression f; **self-government** autonomie f; **self-interest** intérêt m (personnel); **selfish** égoïste; **selfless** désintéressé; **self-made man** self-made man m; **self-pity** apitoiement m sur soi-même; **self-portrait** autoportrait m; **self-reliant** autonome; **self-respect** respect m de soi; **self-satisfied** *pej* suffisant; **self-service** libre-service; **self-service restaurant** self-service m; **self-taught** autodidacte

sell [sel] **1** *v/t* vendre **2** *v/i of products* se vendre; **sell-by date** date f limite de vente; **seller** vendeur(-euse) m(f); **selling** COM vente f; **selling point** COM point m fort

Sellotape® ['seləteɪp] *Br* scotch m

semester [sɪ'mestər] semestre m

semi ['semɪ] *truck* semi-remorque f; **semicircle** demi-cercle m; **semiconductor** ELEC semi-conducteur m; **semifinal** demi-finale f; **semifinalist** demi-finaliste m/f

seminar ['semɪnɑːr] séminaire m

semi'skilled worker spécialisé

senate ['senət] Sénat m; **senator** sénateur(-trice) m(f)

send [send] envoyer (**to** a)
♦ **send back** renvoyer
♦ **send for** doctor faire venir; help envoyer chercher

sender ['sendər] of letter expéditeur(-trice) m(f)

senile ['siːnaɪl] sénile; **senility** sénilité f

senior ['siːnjər] (older) plus âgé; in rank supérieur; **senior citizen** personne f âgée; **seniority** in job ancienneté f

sensation [sen'seɪʃn] sensation f; **sensational** sensationnel

sense [sens] **1** n sens m; (common ~) bon sens m; (feeling) sentiment m; **come to one's ~s** revenir à la raison; **it doesn't make ~** cela n'a pas de sens **2** v/t sentir; **senseless** (pointless) stupide

sensible ['sensəbl] sensé; clothes, shoes pratique; **sensibly** raisonnablement

sensitive ['sensətɪv] sensible; **sensitivity** sensibilité f

sensor ['sensər] détecteur m

sensual ['senʃʊəl] sensuel; **sensuality** sensualité f

sensuous ['senʃʊəs] voluptueux

sentence ['sentəns] **1** n GRAM phrase f; LAW peine f **2** v/t LAW condamner

sentiment ['sentɪmənt] (sentimentality) sentimentalité f; (opinion) sentiment m; **sentimental** sentimental; **sentimentality** sentimentalité f

sentry ['sentrɪ] sentinelle f

separate 1 ['sepərət] adj séparé **2** ['sepəreɪt] v/t séparer (**from** de) **3** v/i of couple se séparer; **separated** couple séparé; **separately** séparément; **separation** séparation f

September [sep'tembər] septembre m

septic ['septɪk] septique

sequel ['siːkwəl] suite f

sequence ['siːkwəns] ordre m

serene [sɪ'riːn] serein

sergeant ['sɑːrdʒənt] sergent m

serial ['sɪrɪəl] feuilleton m; **serialize** novel on TV adapter en feuilleton; **serial number** of product numéro m de série

series ['sɪriːz] série f

serious ['sɪrɪəs] person, company sérieux; illness, situation, damage grave; **seriously** injured gravement; under-

staffed sérieusement; **take s.o. ~** prendre qn au sérieux; **seriousness** *of person, situation, illness etc* gravité *f*

sermon ['sɜːmən] sermon *m*

servant ['sɜːrvənt] domestique *m/f*

serve [sɜːrv] **1** *n in tennis* service *m* **2** *v/t & v/i* servir; **server** *in tennis* serveur(-euse) *m(f)*; COMPUT serveur *m*; **service 1** *n also in tennis* service *m*; *for vehicle, machine* entretien *m*; **~s** services *mpl* **2** *v/t vehicle, machine* entretenir; **service charge** service *m*; **serviceman** MIL militaire *m*; **service station** station-service *f*; **serving of food** portion *f*

session ['seʃn] session *f*; *meeting, talk* discussion *f*

set [set] **1** *n* (*collection*) série *f*; (*group of people*) groupe *m*; MATH ensemble *m*; THEA (*scenery*) décor *m*; *for movie* plateau *m*; *in tennis* set *m* **2** *v/t* (*place*) poser; *movie, novel etc* situer; *date, time, limit* fixer; *alarm* mettre; *broken limb* remettre en place; *jewel* sertir; **~ the table** mettre la table **3** *v/i of sun* se coucher; *of glue* durcir **4** *adj ideas* arrêté; (*ready*) prêt

◆ **set off** *v/i on journey* partir **2** *v/t alarm etc* déclencher

◆ **set out** *v/i on journey* partir **2** *v/t ideas, goods* exposer

◆ **set up 1** *v/t company,* equipment, machine* monter; *market stall* installer; *meeting* arranger; F (*frame*) faire un coup à **2** *v/i in business* s'établir

setback revers *m*

settee [se'tiː] *Br* (*couch, sofa*) canapé *m*

setting ['setɪŋ] *of novel, play, house* cadre *m*

settle ['setl] **1** *v/i of bird* se poser; *of dust* se déposer; *of building* se tasser; *to live* s'installer **2** *v/t dispute, issue, debts* régler; *nerves, stomach* calmer; *that ~s it!* ça règle la question!

◆ **settle down** (*stop being noisy*) se calmer; (*stop wild living*) se ranger; *in an area* s'installer

◆ **settle for** (*accept*) accepter

settled ['setld] *weather* stable; **settlement** *of claim, debt, dispute,* (*payment*) règlement *m*; *of building* tassement *m*; **settler** *in new country* colon *m*

'set-up (*structure*) organisation *f*; (*relationship*) relation *f*; F (*frame-up*) coup *m* monté

seven ['sevn] sept; **seventeen** dix-sept; **seventeenth** dix-septième; **seventh** septième; **seventieth** soixante-dixième; **seventy** soixante-dix

sever ['sevər] sectionner; *relations* rompre

several ['sevrl] plusieurs

severe [sɪ'vɪr] *illness* grave; *penalty* lourd; *winter, weather* rigoureux; *teacher* sévère; **severely** *punish, speak* sévèrement; *injured* grièvement; *disrupted* fortement; **severity** *of illness* gravité f; *of penalty* lourdeur f; *of winter* rigueur f; *of teacher* sévérité f

sew [sou] coudre

sewage ['suːɪdʒ] eaux *fpl* d'égouts; **sewer** égout *m*

sewing ['souɪŋ] *skill* couture f; *(that being sewn)* ouvrage *m*

sex [seks] sexe *m*; **have ~ with** coucher avec; **sexist 1** *adj* sexiste **2** *n* sexiste *m/f*; **sexual** sexuel; **sexuality** sexualité f; **sexually** sexuellement; **sexy** sexy *inv*

shabbily ['ʃæbɪlɪ] *dressed* pauvrement; *treat* mesquinement; **shabby** *coat etc* usé; *treatment* mesquin

shack [ʃæk] cabane f

shade [ʃeɪd] **1** *n for lamp* abat-jour *m*; *of color* nuance f; *on window store m*; **in the ~** à l'ombre **2** *v/t from sun* protéger du soleil; *from light* protéger de la lumière

shadow ['ʃædou] ombre f

shady ['ʃeɪdɪ] *spot* ombragé; *character* louche

shaft [ʃæft] *of axle* arbre *m*; *of mine* puits *m*

shake [ʃeɪk] **1** *n*: **give sth a good ~** bien agiter qch **2**

v/t bottle agiter; *emotionally* bouleverser; **~ one's head** *in refusal* dire non de la tête; **~ hands with s.o.** serrer la main à qn **3** *v/i of hands, voice, building* trembler; **shaken** *emotionally* bouleversé; **shake-up** remaniement *m*; **shaky** *table etc* branlant; *after illness, shock* faible; *voice, hand* tremblant; *grasp of sth, grammar etc* incertain

shall [ʃæl] ◇ *future*: **I ~ do my best** je ferai de mon mieux ◇ *suggesting*: **~ we go now?** si nous y allions maintenant?

shallow ['ʃælou] *water* peu profond; *person* superficiel

shame [ʃeɪm] **1** *n* honte f; **what a ~!** quel dommage! **2** *v/t* faire honte à; **shameful** honteux; **shameless** effronté

shampoo [ʃæm'puː] shampo(o)ing *m*

shape [ʃeɪp] **1** *n* forme f **2** *v/t clay, character* façonner; *the future* influencer; **shapeless** *dress etc* informe; **shapely** *figure* bien fait

share [ʃer] **1** *n part* f; FIN action f **2** *v/t & v/i* partager; **shareholder** actionnaire *m/f*

shark [ʃɑːrk] requin *m*

sharp [ʃɑːrp] **1** *adj knife* tranchant; *mind, pain* vif; *taste* piquant **2** *adv* MUS trop haut; **at 3 o'clock ~** à 3 heures pile; **sharpen** *knife, skills* aiguiser

shatter ['ʃætər] **1** v/t glass, illusions briser **2** v/i of glass se briser; **shattered** ['ʃætərd] F (exhausted) crevé F; F (very upset) bouleversé; **shattering** news bouleversant

shave [ʃeɪv] **1** v/t raser **2** v/i se raser **3** n: **have a ~** se raser; **shaven** head rasé; **shaver** rasoir m électrique

shawl [ʃɔːl] châle m

she [ʃiː] elle; **there ~ is** la voilà

sheath [ʃiːθ] for knife étui m; contraceptive préservatif m

shed[1] [ʃed] v/t blood, tears verser; leaves perdre

shed[2] [ʃed] n abri m

sheep [ʃiːp] mouton m; **sheepdog** chien m de berger; **sheepish** penaud

sheer [ʃɪr] cur; cliffs abrupt

sheet [ʃiːt] drap m; of paper, metal, glass feuille f

shelf [ʃelf] étagère f; **shelves** set of shelves étagère(s) f(pl)

shell [ʃel] **1** n of mussel, egg coquille f; of tortoise carapace f; MIL obus m **2** v/t peas écosser; MIL bombarder; **shellfire** bombardements mpl; **shellfish** fruits mpl de mer

shelter ['ʃeltər] **1** n abri m **2** v/i s'abriter (**from** de) **3** v/t (protect) protéger; **sheltered** place protégé; **lead a ~ life** mener une vie protégée

shelve [ʃelv] fig mettre en suspens

shepherd ['ʃepərd] berger (-ère) m(f)

sheriff ['ʃerɪf] shérif m

shield [ʃiːld] **1** n MIL bouclier m; sports trophy plaque f; badge: of policeman plaque f **2** v/t (protect) protéger

shift [ʃɪft] **1** n (change) changement m; (move, switchover) passage m (**to** à); at work poste m; people équipe f **2** v/t (move) déplacer; production, employee transférer; stains etc faire partir **3** v/i (move) se déplacer; in attitude virer; **shifty** pej: person louche; eyes fuyant

shin [ʃɪn] tibia m

shine [ʃaɪn] **1** v/i briller; fig: of student être brillant (**at, in** en) **2** n on shoes etc brillant m; shiny brillant

ship [ʃɪp] **1** n bateau m, navire m **2** v/t (send) expédier **3** v/i of new product être lancé (sur le marché); **shipment** envoi m; **shipowner** armateur m; **shipping** (sea traffic) navigation f; (sending) expédition f; **shipwreck** naufrage m; **shipyard** chantier m naval

shirt [ʃɜːrt] chemise f

shit [ʃɪt] **1** n P merde f P **2** v/i P chier **3** int P merde P; **shitty** F dégueulasse F

shiver ['ʃɪvər] trembler

shock [ʃɑːk] **1** n choc m; ELEC décharge f; **be in ~** MED être en état de choc **2** v/t choquer

shock absorber MOT amortisseur *m*; **shocking** choquant; *F (very bad)* épouvantable

shoddy [ˈʃɑːdɪ] *goods* de mauvaise qualité; *behavior* mesquin

shoe [ʃuː] chaussure *f*, soulier *m*; **shoelace** lacet *m*; **shoemaker** cordonnier(-ière) *m(f)*; **shoe mender** cordonnier(-ière) *m(f)*; **shoestore** magasin *m* de chaussures

shoot [ʃuːt] **1** *n* BOT pousse *f* **2** *v/t tirer* sur; *and kill* tuer d'un coup de feu; *movie* tourner **3** *v/i* tirer

◆ **shoot down** *airplane* abattre; *fig: suggestion* descendre

◆ **shoot up** *of prices* monter en flèche; *of children, new buildings etc* pousser

shooting star [ˈʃuːtɪŋ] étoile *f* filante

shop [ʃɑːp] **1** *n* magasin *m* **2** *v/i* faire ses courses; **go ~ping** faire les courses; **shopkeeper** commerçant *m*,-ante *f*; **shoplifter** voleur(-euse) *m(f)* à l'étalage; **shoplifting** vol *m* à l'étalage; **shopping** *items* courses *fpl*; **go ~** faire des courses; **shopping bag** sac *m* à provisions; **shopping list** liste *f* de commissions; **shopping mall** centre *m* commercial

shore [ʃɔːr] rivage *m*; **on ~** *not at sea* à terre

short [ʃɔːrt] **1** *adj* court; *in*

height petit; **be ~ of** manquer de 2 *adv*: **cut ~** abréger; **go ~ of** se priver de; **in ~** bref; **shortage** manque *m*; **shortcoming** défaut *m*; **shortcut** raccourci *m*; **shorten** raccourcir; **shortfall** déficit *m*; **short-lived** de courte durée; **shortly** *(soon)* bientôt; **~ before/after that** peu avant/après; **shortness** *of visit* brièveté *f*; *in height* petite taille *f*; **shorts** short *m*; *underwear* caleçon *m*; **shortsighted** myope; *fig* peu perspicace; **short-sleeved** à manches courtes; **short-tempered** *by nature* d'un caractère emporté; *at a particular time* de mauvaise humeur; **short-term** à court terme

shot [ʃɑːt] *from gun* coup *m* de feu; *(photograph)* photo *f*; *(injection)* piqûre *f*; **shotgun** fusil *m* de chasse

should [ʃʊd]: **what ~ I do?** que dois-je faire?; **you ~n't do that** tu ne devrais pas faire ça; **you ~ have heard him** tu aurais dû l'entendre

shoulder [ˈʃoʊldər] épaule *f*

shout [ʃaʊt] **1** *n* cri *m* **2** *v/t & v/i* crier; **shouting** cris *mpl*

shove [ʃʌv] **1** *n*: **give s.o. a ~** pousser qn **2** *v/t & v/i* pousser

shovel [ˈʃʌvl] pelle *f*

show [ʃoʊ] **1** *n* THEA, TV spectacle *m*; *(display)* démonstration *f* **2** *v/t* montrer; *at exhibition* présenter; *movie* projeter 3 *v/i (be visible)* se voir; *of movie* passer

◆ **show in** faire entrer

◆ **show off 1** *v/t skills* faire étalage de **2** *v/i pej* crâner

◆ **show up 1** *v/t shortcomings etc* faire ressortir **2** *v/i F (arrive, turn up)* se pointer F; *(be visible)* se voir

'**show business** monde *m* du spectacle; **showcase** *also fig* vitrine *f*; **showdown** confrontation *f*

shower ['ʃaʊər] **1** *n of rain* averse *f*; *to wash* douche *f*; *party: petite fête avant un mariage ou un accouchement à laquelle tout le monde apporte un cadeau*; **take a ~** prendre une douche **2** *v/i* prendre une douche

'**show-off** *pej* prétentieux (-euse) *m(f)*; **showroom** salle *f* d'exposition; **showy** voyant

shred [ʃred] **1** *n of paper etc* lambeau *m*; *of meat etc* morceau *m* **2** *v/t documents* déchiqueter; *in cooking* râper; **shredder** *for documents* déchiqueteuse *f*

shrewd [ʃruːd] perspicace; **shrewdness** perspicacité *f*

shriek [ʃriːk] **1** *n* cri *m* aigu **2** *v/i* pousser un cri aigu

shrill [ʃrɪl] perçant

shrimp [ʃrɪmp] crevette *f*

shrine [ʃraɪn] lieu *m* saint

shrink¹ [ʃrɪŋk] *v/i of material* rétrécir; *of support* diminuer

shrink² [ʃrɪŋk] *n* F *(psychiatrist)* psy *m* F

shrivel ['ʃrɪvl] se flétrir

shrub [ʃrʌb] arbuste *m*; **shrubbery** massif *m* d'arbustes

shrug [ʃrʌg] **~ (one's shoulders)** hausser les épaules

shudder ['ʃʌdər] **1** *n of fear, disgust* frisson *m*; *of earth* vibration *f* **2** *v/i with fear, disgust* frissonner; *of earth* vibrer

shuffle ['ʃʌfl] *v/t cards* battre

shun [ʃʌn] fuir

shut [ʃʌt] **1** *v/t* fermer **2** *v/i of door, box* se fermer; *of store* fermer

◆ **shut down 1** *v/t business* fermer; *computer* éteindre **2** *v/i of business* fermer ses portes; *of computer* s'éteindre

◆ **shut up** F *(be quiet)* se taire; **shut up!** tais-toi!

shutter ['ʃʌtər] *on window* volet *m*; PHOT obturateur *m*

shuttle bus ['ʃʌtl] *at airport* navette *f*

shy [ʃaɪ] timide; **shyness** timidité *f*

sick [sɪk] malade; *sense of humor* noir; **be ~** *Br (vomit)* vomir; **sicken 1** *v/t (disgust)* écœurer; *(make ill)* rendre malade **2** *v/i:* **be ~ing for** couver; **sickening** écœurant; **sick leave** congé *m* de mala-

die; **sickness** maladie *f*;
(*vomiting*) vomissements
mpl

side [saɪd] côté *m*; SP équipe *f*;
take ~s (*favor one ~*) prendre parti; **~ by ~** côte à côte;
side effect effet *m* secondaire; **sidestep** éviter; *fig also*
contourner; **side street** rue
f transversale; **sidewalk** trottoir *m*; **sideways** de côté

siege [siːdʒ] siège *m*

sieve [sɪv] *for flour* tamis *m*

sift [sɪft] tamiser; *data* passer
en revue

sigh [saɪ] **1** *n* soupir *m* **2** *v/i*
soupirer

sight [saɪt] spectacle *m*; (*power of seeing*) vue *f*; **~s** *of city*
monuments *mpl*; **know by ~**
connaître de vue; **sightsee-
ing: go ~** faire du tourisme;
sightseer touriste *m/f*

sign [saɪn] **1** *n* signe *m*;
(*road~*) panneau *m*; *outside
shop* enseigne *f* **2** *v/t & v/i* signer

signal [ˈsɪɡnl] **1** *n* signal *m* **2**
v/i of driver mettre son clignotant

signatory [ˈsɪɡnətɔːrɪ] signa-
taire *m/f*

signature [ˈsɪɡnəʧər] signature *f*

significance [sɪɡˈnɪfɪkəns]
importance *f*; **significant
event, sum of money, im-
provement etc** important;
significantly *larger, more expensive* nettement

signify [ˈsɪɡnɪfaɪ] signifier

'sign language langage *m* des
signes; **signpost** poteau *m*
indicateur

silence [ˈsaɪləns] **1** *n* silence
m **2** *v/t* faire taire; **silent** silencieux

silhouette [sɪluːˈet] silhouette
f

silicon [ˈsɪlɪkən] silicium *m*

silk [sɪlk] **1** *adj shirt etc* en soie
2 *n* soie *f*; **silky** soyeux

silliness [ˈsɪlɪnɪs] stupidité *f*;
silly bête

silo [ˈsaɪloʊ] silo *m*

silver [ˈsɪlvər] **1** *adj ring* en argent; *hair* argenté **2** *n* argent
m; **silverware** argenterie *f*

similar [ˈsɪmɪlər] semblable
(**to** à); **similarity** ressemblance *f*; **similarly** de la même façon

simple [ˈsɪmpl] simple; **sim-
ple-minded** *pej* simple, sim-
plet; **simplicity** simplicité *f*;
simplify simplifier; **simplis-
tic** simpliste; **simply** (*absolutely*) absolument; (*in a simple way*) simplement

simultaneous [saɪməlˈteɪ-
nɪəs] simultané; **simulta-
neously** simultanément

sin [sɪn] **1** *n* péché *m* **2** *v/i* pécher

since [sɪns] **1** *prep & adv* depuis; **I've been here ~ last
week** je suis là depuis la semaine dernière **2** *conj in expressions of time* depuis que;
(*seeing that*) puisque

sincere [sɪn'sɪr] sincère; **sincerely** sincèrement; **Sincerely yours** Je vous prie d'agréer, Madame/Monsieur, l'expression de mes sentiments les meilleurs; **sincerity** sincérité f

sinful ['sɪnfʊl] *deeds* honteux; **~ person** pécheur m, pécheresse f

sing [sɪŋ] chanter

singe [sɪndʒ] brûler légèrement

singer ['sɪŋər] chanteur(-euse) m(f)

single ['sɪŋgl] **1** *adj* (*sole*) seul; (*not double*) simple; *bed* à une place; (*not married*) célibataire **2** *n* MUS single m; (*~ room*) chambre f à un lit; *person* personne f seule; **~s** *in tennis* simple m; **single-handed** tout seul; **single-minded** résolu; **single parent** mère/père qui élève ses enfants tout seul; **single parent family** famille f monoparentale; **single room** chambre f à un lit

singular ['sɪŋgjʊlər] GRAM **1** *adj* au singulier **2** *n* singulier m

sinister ['sɪnɪstər] sinistre

sink [sɪŋk] **1** *n* évier m **2** *v/i of ship, object* couler; *of sun* descendre; *of interest rates etc* baisser **3** *v/t ship* couler; *money* investir

sinner ['sɪnər] pécheur m, pécheresse f

sip [sɪp] **1** *n* petite gorgée f **2** *v/t* boire à petites gorgées

sir [sɜːr] monsieur m

siren ['saɪrən] sirène f

sirloin ['sɜːrlɔɪn] aloyau m

sister ['sɪstər] sœur f; **sister-in-law** belle-sœur f

sit [sɪt] (*down*) s'asseoir; **she was sitting** elle était assise

◆ **sit down** s'asseoir

sitcom ['sɪtkɑːm] sitcom m

site [saɪt] **1** *n* emplacement m; *of battle* site m **2** *v/t new offices etc* situer

sitting ['sɪtɪŋ] *of committee, court, for artist* séance f; *for meals* service m; **sitting room** salon m

situated ['sɪtʃueɪtɪd] situé; **situation** situation f; *of building etc* emplacement m

six [sɪks] six; **sixteen** seize; **sixteenth** seizième; **sixth** sixième; **sixtieth** soixantième; **sixty** soixante

size [saɪz] *of room, jacket* taille f; *of project* envergure f; *of loan* montant m; *of shoes* pointure f; **sizeable** *meal, house* assez grand; *order, amount* assez important

skate [skeɪt] **1** *n* patin m **2** *v/i* patiner; **skateboard** skateboard m; **skateboarding** skateboard m; **skater** patineur(-euse) m(f); **skating** patinage f; **skating rink** patinoire f

skeleton ['skelɪtn] squelette

m

skeptic ['skeptik] sceptique *m/f*; **skeptical** sceptique; **skepticism** scepticisme *m*

sketch [sketʃ] **1** *n* croquis *m*, THEA sketch *m* **2** *v/t* esquisser; **sketchy** *knowledge etc* sommaire

ski [ski:] **1** *n* ski *m* **2** *v/i* faire du ski

skid [skid] **1** *n* dérapage *m* **2** *v/i* déraper

skier ['ski:ər] skieur(-euse) *m(f)*; **skiing** ski *m*

skilful *etc Br* → **skillful**

skill [skil] technique *f*; **~s** compétences *fpl*; **skilled** habile; **skillful** habile; **skillfully** habilement

skim [skim] *surface* effleurer

skimpy ['skimpi] *account etc* sommaire; *dress* étriqué

skin [skin] **1** *n* peau *f* **2** *v/t animal* écorcher; *tomato* peler; **skin diving** plongée *f* sous-marine autonome; **skinny** maigre; **skin-tight** moulant

skip [skip] **1** *n* (*little jump*) saut *m* **2** *v/i* sautiller **3** *v/t* (*omit*) sauter; **skipper** capitaine *m/f*

skirt [skɜːrt] jupe *f*

skull [skʌl] crâne *m*

skunk [skʌŋk] mouffette *f*

sky [skai] ciel *m*; **skylight** lucarne *f*; **skyline** silhouette *f*; **skyscraper** gratte-ciel *m inv*

slab [slæb] *of stone, butter* plaque *f*; *of cake* grosse tranche *f*

slack [slæk] *rope* mal tendu; *work* négligé; *period* creux; **slacken** *rope* détendre; *pace* ralentir; **slacks** pantalon *m*

slam [slæm] claquer

slander ['slændər] **1** *n* calomnie *f* **2** *v/t* calomnier; **slanderous** calomnieux

slang [slæŋ] *also of a specific group* argot *m*

slant [slænt] **1** *v/i* pencher **2** *n* inclinaison *f*; *given to a story* perspective *f*; **slanting** *roof* en pente; *eyes* bridé

slap [slæp] (*blow*) claque *f* **2** *v/t* donner une claque à

slash [slæʃ] **1** *n* *cut* entaille *f*, *in punctuation* barre *f* oblique **2** *v/t* *painting, skin* entailler; *prices* réduire radicalement

slaughter ['slɔːtər] **1** *n of animals* abattage *m*; *of people, troops* massacre *m* **2** *v/t animals* abattre; *people, troops* massacrer; **slaughterhouse** abattoir *m*

slave [sleiv] esclave *m/f*

slay [slei] tuer; **slaying** (*murder*) meurtre *m*

sleaze [sli:z] POL corruption *f*; **sleazy** *bar, character* louche

sleep [sli:p] **1** *n* sommeil *m*; **go to ~** s'endormir **2** *v/i* dormir

◆ **sleep with** (*have sex with*) coucher avec

'sleeping bag sac *m* de couchage; **sleeping car** RAIL wagon-lit *m*; **sleeping pill** somnifère m; **sleepwalker** somnambule m/f; **sleepwalking** somnambulisme m; **sleepy** *person* qui a envie de dormir; *yawn, town* endormi; **I'm ~** j'ai sommeil

sleet [sliːt] neige f fondue

sleeve [sliːv] *of jacket etc* manche f; **sleeveless** sans manches

slender ['slendər] mince; *chance, margin* faible

slice [slaɪs] **1** n *of bread, pie* tranche f; *fig: of profits* part f **2** v/t *loaf etc* couper en tranches

slick [slɪk] **1** adj *performance* habile; *pej (cunning)* rusé **2** n *of oil* marée f noire

slide [slaɪd] **1** n *for kids* toboggan m; PHOT diapositive f **2** v/i *glisser*; *of exchange rate etc* baisser **3** v/t *item of furniture* faire glisser

slight [slaɪt] *person, figure* frêle; *(small)* léger; **no, not in the ~est** pas le moins du monde; **slightly** légèrement

slim [slɪm] *person* mince; *chance* faible

slime [slaɪm] *(mud)* vase f; *of slug etc* bave f; **slimy** *liquid etc* vaseux

sling [slɪŋ] **1** n *for arm* écharpe f **2** v/t F *(throw)* lancer

slip [slɪp] **1** n *(mistake)* erreur f **2** v/i *glisser*; *in quality, quantity* baisser

◆ **slip up** *(make a mistake)* faire une gaffe

slipped 'disc [slɪpt] hernie f discale

slipper ['slɪpər] chausson m

slippery ['slɪpərɪ] glissant

'slip-up *(mistake)* gaffe f

slit [slɪt] **1** n *(tear)* déchirure f; *(hole)*, *in skirt* fente f **2** v/t ouvrir, fendre

sliver ['slɪvər] petit morceau m; *of wood, glass* éclat m

slob [slɑːb] *pej* rustaud(e) m(f)

slog [slɑːg] *long walk* trajet m pénible; *hard work* corvée f

slogan ['sloʊgən] slogan m

slop [slɑːp] *(spill)* renverser

slope [sloʊp] **1** n inclinaison f; *of mountain* côté m **2** v/i être incliné

sloppy ['slɑːpɪ] F *work, in dress* négligé; *(too sentimental)* gnangnan F

slot [slɑːt] fente f; *in schedule* créneau m; **slot machine** *for vending* distributeur m *(automatique)*; *for gambling* machine f à sous

slovenly ['slʌvnlɪ] négligé

slow [sloʊ] lent; **be ~** *of clock* retarder

◆ **slow down 1** v/t ralentir **2** v/i ralentir; *in life* faire moins de choses

'slowdown *in production* ralentissement m; **slowly** lentement; **slowness** lenteur f

sluggish ['slʌgɪʃ] lent; *river* à cours lent

slum [slʌm] *area* quartier m

pauvre; *house* taudis *m*

slump [slʌmp] **1** *n in trade* effondrement *m* **2** *v/i of economy* s'effondrer; *of person* s'affaisser

slur [slɜːr] **1** *n on character* tache *f* **2** *v/t words* mal articuler

slush [slʌʃ] neige *f* fondue; *pej* (*sentimental stuff*) sensiblerie *f*; **slush fund** caisse *f* noire

slut [slʌt] *pej* pute *f* F

sly [slaɪ] (*furtive*) sournois; (*crafty*) rusé

small [smɔːl] petit

smart¹ [smɑːrt] *adj* élégant; (*intelligent*) intelligent; *pace* vif

smart² [smɑːrt] *v/i* (*hurt*) brûler

'smart card carte *f* à puce; **smartly** *dressed* avec élégance

smash [smæʃ] **1** *n noise* fracas *m*; (*car crash*) accident *m*; *in tennis* smash *m* **2** *v/t break* fracasser; (*hit hard*) frapper **3** *v/i break* se fracasser

smattering ['smætərɪŋ]: **have a ~ of** *Chinese* savoir un peu de chinois

smear [smɪr] **1** *n of ink etc* tache *f*; *Br* MED frottis *m*; *on character* diffamation *f* **2** *v/t character* entacher

smell [smel] **1** *n* odeur *f*; **sense of ~** odorat *m* **2** *v/t* sentir **3** *v/i unpleasantly* sentir mauvais; (*sniff*) renifler; **smelly** qui sent mauvais

smile [smaɪl] **1** *n* sourire *m* **2** *v/i* sourire

smirk [smɜːrk] petit sourire *m* narquois

smoke [smoʊk] **1** *n* fumée *f* **2** *v/t also food* fumer **3** *v/i of person* fumer; **smoker** fumeur(-euse) *m(f)*; **smoke-free** non-fumeur *inv*; **smoking**: **no ~** défense de fumer; **smoky** enfumé

smolder ['smoʊldər] *of fire* couver

smooth [smuːð] **1** *adj surface, skin, sea* lisse; *ride, flight, crossing* bon; *pej: person* mielleux **2** *v/t hair* lisser; **smoothly** *without any problems* sans problème

smother ['smʌðər] *person, flames* étouffer

smoulder *Br* → **smolder**

smudge [smʌdʒ] **1** *n* tache *f* **2** *v/t paint* faire des traces sur; *ink, mascara* étaler

smug [smʌg] suffisant

smuggle ['smʌgl] passer en contrebande; **smuggler** contrebandier(-ière) *m(f)*; **smuggling** contrebande *f*

smutty ['smʌtɪ] *joke* grossier

snack [snæk] en-cas *m*

snag [snæg] (*problem*) hic *m* F

snake [sneɪk] serpent *m*

snap [snæp] **1** *n sound* bruit *m* sec; PHOT instantané *m* **2** *v/t break* casser **3** *v/i break* se casser net **4** *adj decision, judgement* rapide, subit;

snappy *person, mood* cassant; *decision* prompt; **be a ~ dresser** s'habiller chic; **snapshot** photo *f*

snarl [snɑːrl] **1** *v/i of dog* grondement **2** *v/i of dog* gronder en montrant les dents

snatch [snætʃ] *(grab)* saisir; F *(steal)* voler; F *(kidnap)* enlever

snazzy ['snæzɪ] F *necktie etc* qui tape F

sneakers ['sniːkərz] tennis *mpl*

sneaky ['sniːkɪ] F *(underhanded)* sournois

sneer [snɪr] **1** *n* ricanement *m* **2** *v/i* ricaner

sneeze [sniːz] **1** *n* éternuement *m* **2** *v/i* éternuer

snicker ['snɪkər] pouffer de rire

sniff [snɪf] renifler

sniper ['snaɪpər] tireur *m* embusqué

snitch [snɪtʃ] **1** *n* *(telltale)* mouchard(e) *m(f)* F **2** *v/i (tell tales)* vendre la mèche

snivel ['snɪvl] pleurnicher

snob [snɑːb] snob *m/f*; **snobbery** snobisme *m*; **snobbish** snob *inv*

◆ **snoop around** [snuːp] fourrer le nez partout

snooty ['snuːtɪ] arrogant

snooze [snuːz] **1** *n* petit somme *m* **2** *v/i* roupiller F

snore [snɔːr] ronfler; **snoring** ronflement *m*

snorkel ['snɔːrkl] tuba *m*

snort [snɔːrt] *of bull, horse* s'ébrouer; *of person* grogner

snow [snoʊ] **1** *n* neige *f* **2** *v/i* neiger; **snowball** boule *f* de neige; **snowdrift** amoncellement *m* de neige; **snowman** bonhomme *m* de neige; **snowplow** chasse-neige *m inv*; **snowstorm** tempête *f* de neige; **snowy** *weather* neigeux; *roads, hills* enneigé

snub [snʌb] **1** *n* rebuffade *f* **2** *v/t* snober; **snub-nosed** au nez retroussé

snug [snʌg] bien au chaud; *(tight-fitting)* bien ajusté

so [soʊ] **1** *adv* si, tellement; **~ kind** tellement gentil; **not ~ much for me** pas autant pour moi; **~ much easier** tellement plus facile; **drink ~ much** tellement boire; **~ many people** tellement de gens; **I miss you ~** tu me manques tellement; **~ am/do I** moi aussi; **~ is/does she** elle aussi; **and ~ on** et ainsi de suite **2** *pron*: **I hope ~** je l'espère bien; **I think ~** je pense que oui; **~ or ~** une cinquantaine, à peu près cinquante **3** *conj (for that reason)* pour que; *(in order that)* pour que (+*subj*); **~ (that) I could come too** pour que je puisse moi aussi venir; **~ what?** F et alors?

soak [soʊk] *(steep)* faire tremper; *of water* tremper; **soaked** trempé soap [soup] *for washing* savon *m*; **soap (opera)** feuilleton *m*; **soapy** savonneux

soar [sɔːr] *of rocket, prices etc* monter en flèche

sob [sɑːb] **1** *n* sanglot *m* **2** *v/i* sangloter

sober ['soubər] en état de sobriété; *(serious)* sérieux

so-'called *(referred to as)* comme on le/la/les appelle; *(incorrectly referred to as)* soi-disant *inv*

soccer ['sɑːkər] football *m*

sociable ['souʃəbl] sociable

social ['souʃl] social; *(recreational)* mondain; **social democrat** social-démocrate *m/f*; **socialism** socialisme *m*; **socialist 1** *adj* socialiste **2** *n* socialiste *m/f*; **socialize** fréquenter des gens; **social worker** assistant sociale *m*, assistante sociale *f*

society [sə'saɪətɪ] société *f*

sociologist [sousɪ'ɑːlədʒɪst] sociologue *m/f*; **sociology** sociologie *f*

sock¹ [sɑːk] *n for wearing* chaussette *f*

sock² [sɑːk] *v/t (punch)* donner un coup de poing à

socket ['sɑːkɪt] ELEC *for light bulb* douille *f*; *Br (wall ~)* prise *f* de courant; *of eye* orbite *f*

soda ['soudə] *(~ water)* eau *f* gazeuse; *(soft drink)* soda *m*; *(ice-cream ~)* soda *m* à la crème glacée

sofa ['soufə] canapé *m*

soft [sɑːft] doux; *(lenient)* gentil; **soften** *position* assouplir; *impact, blow* adoucir; **softly** doucement; **software** logiciel *m*

soggy ['sɑːgɪ] *soil* détrempé; *pastry* pâteux

soil [sɔɪl] **1** *n (earth)* terre *f* **2** *v/t* salir

solar energy ['soulər] énergie *f* solaire

soldier ['souldʒər] soldat *m*

sole¹ [soul] *n of foot* plante *f*; *of shoe* semelle *f*

sole² [soul] *adj* seul; *responsibility* exclusif

solely ['soulɪ] exclusivement

solemn ['sɑːləm] solennel; **solemnity** solennité *f*; **solemnly** solennellement

solicit [sə'lɪsɪt] *of prostitute* racoler

solid ['sɑːlɪd] *(hard)* dur; *(without holes)* compact; *gold, silver etc* massif; **solidarity** solidarité *f*; **solidify** se solidifier; **solidly** *built* solidement; *in favor of* massivement

solitaire [sɑːlɪ'ter] *card game* réussite *f*

solitary ['sɑːlɪterɪ] *life, activity* solitaire; *(single)* isolé; **solitude** solitude *f*

solo ['soulou] **1** *adj* en solo **2** *n* MUS solo *m*; **soloist** soliste *m/f*

soluble ['sɑːljubl] *substance, problem* soluble; **solution** *also* **mixture** solution *f*

solve [sɑːlv] résoudre; **solvent** *financially* solvable

somber, *Br* **sombre** ['sɒmbər] sombre

some [sʌm] **1** *adj*: **~ cream/chocolate/cookies** de la crème/du chocolat/des biscuits; **people say that ...** certains disent que ... **2** *pron*: **~ of the money** une partie de l'argent; **~ of the group** certaines personnes du groupe, certains du groupe; **would you like ~?** est-ce que vous en voulez?; **give me ~** donnez-m'en **3** *adv* (*a bit*) un peu; **somebody** quelqu'un; **someday** un jour; **somehow** (*by one means or another*) d'une manière ou d'une autre; (*for some unknown reason*) sans savoir pourquoi; **someone** → **somebody**; **someplace** → **somewhere**

somersault ['sʌmərsɔːlt] **1** *n* roulade *f*; *by vehicle* tonneau *m* **2** *v/i of vehicle* faire un tonneau

'something quelque chose; **sometime** *one of these days*: **~ last year** dans le courant de l'année dernière; **sometimes** parfois; **somewhat** quelque peu; **somewhere 1** *adv* quelque part **2** *pron*: **let's go ~ quiet** allons dans un endroit calme; **~ to park** un endroit où se garer

son [sʌn] fils *m*

song [sɑːŋ] chanson *f*

'son-in-law beau-fils *m*; **son of a bitch** V fils *m* de pute V

soon [suːn] (*in a short while*) bientôt; (*quickly*) vite; (*early*) tôt; **how~?** dans combien de temps?; **as ~ as** dès que; **as ~ as possible** le plus tôt possible; **~er or later** tôt ou tard; **the ~er the better** le plus tôt sera le mieux

soothe [suːð] calmer

sophisticated [sə'fɪstɪkeɪtɪd] sophistiqué; **sophistication** sophistication *f*

sophomore ['sɑːfəmɔːr] étudiant(e) *m(f)* de deuxième année

soprano [sə'prɑːnoʊ] soprano *m/f*

sordid ['sɔːrdɪd] sordide

sore [sɔːr] **1** *adj* F (*angry*) fâché; (*painful*): **is it ~?** ça vous fait mal? **2** *n* plaie *f*

sorrow ['sɑːroʊ] chagrin *m*

sorry ['sɑːrɪ] *day* triste; *sight* misérable; (**I'm**) **~!** (*apologizing*) pardon!; **be ~** être désolé

sort [sɔːrt] **1** *n* sorte *f*; **~ of ...** F plutôt **2** *v/t also* COMPUT trier

SOS [esoʊ'es] S.O.S. *m*; *fig*: *plea for help* appel *m* à l'aide

so-so F comme ci comme ça F

soul [soʊl] *also fig* âme *f*

sound[1] [saʊnd] **1** *adj* (*sensible*) judicieux; *judgment* solide; (*healthy*) en bonne santé; *sleep* profond **2** *adv*: **be ~**

asleep être profondément endormi

sound² [saʊnd] **1** *n* son *m*; (*noise*) bruit *m* **2** *v/i*: *that ~s interesting* ça a l'air intéressant

soundly ['saʊndlɪ] *sleep* profondément; *beaten* à plates coutures; **soundproof** insonorisé; **soundtrack** bande *f* sonore

soup [suːp] soupe *f*

sour ['saʊər] *apple, milk* aigre; *comment* désobligeant

source [sɔːrs] *of river, information etc* source *f*

south [saʊθ] **1** *n* sud *m*; *the South of France* le Midi **2** *adj* sud *inv*; *wind* du sud **3** *adv travel* vers le sud; **South Africa** Afrique *f* du sud; **South African 1** *adj* sud-africain **2** *n* Sud-Africain *m*, Sud-Africaine *f*; **South America** Amérique *f* du sud; **South American 1** *adj* sud-américain **2** *n* Sud-Américain(e) *m(f)*; **southeast 1** *n* sud-est *m* **2** *adj* sud-est *inv* **3** *adv travel* vers le sud-est; **southeastern** sud-est *inv*; **southerly** *wind* du sud; *direction* vers le sud; **southern** du Sud; **southerner** habitant(e) *m(f)* du Sud; **southernmost** le plus au sud; **South Pole** pôle *m* Sud; **southward** vers le sud; **southwest 1** *n* sud-ouest *m* **2** *adj* sud-ouest *inv* **3** *adv vers*

le sud-ouest; **southwestern** sud-ouest *inv*

souvenir [suːvə'nɪr] souvenir *m*

sovereign ['sɑːvrɪn] *state* souverain

sow¹ [saʊ] *n* (*female pig*) truie *f*

sow² [soʊ] *v/t seeds* semer

space [speɪs] espace *m*; (*room*) place *f*; **space shuttle** navette *f* spatiale; **space station** station *f* spatiale; **spacious** spacieux

spade [speɪd] *for digging* bêche *f*; *~s in card game* pique *m*

spaghetti [spə'getɪ] spaghetti *mpl*

Spain [speɪn] Espagne *f*

spam (**mail**) [spæm] spam *m*

span [spæn] (*cover*) recouvrir; *of bridge* traverser

Spaniard ['spænjərd] Espagnol *m*, Espagnole *f*; **Spanish 1** *adj* espagnol **2** *n language* espagnol *m*; *the ~* les Espagnols

spanner ['spænər] *Br* clef *f*

spare [sper] **1** *v/t time* accorder; (*lend: money*) prêter; (*do without*) se passer de; *can you ~ the time?* est-ce que vous pouvez trouver un moment? **2** *adj* (*extra*) *cash* en trop; *pair of glasses, clothes* de rechange **3** *n* pièce *f* de rechange; **spare part** pièce *f* de rechange; **spare ribs** côtelette *f* de porc dans l'échine; **spare room** chambre f d'ami; **spare time** temps m libre; **spare wheel** roue f de secours; **sparing**: *be ~ with* économiser; **sparingly** en petite quantité

spark [spɑːk] étincelle f

sparkle ['spɑːkl] étinceler; **sparkling wine** vin m mousseux

'**spark plug** bougie f

sparse [spɑːrs] *vegetation* épars

spartan ['spɑːtn] *room* spartiate

spasmodic [spæz'mɑːdɪk] intermittent; *conversation* saccadé

spate [speɪt] *fig* série f, avalanche f

spatial ['speɪʃl] spatial

speak [spiːk] **1** v/i parler (**to, with** à); **~ing** TELEC lui-même, elle-même **2** v/t *foreign language* parler; **speaker** *at conference* intervenant(e) m(f); (*orator*) orateur(-trice) m(f); *of sound system* haut-parleur m; *French/Spanish* **~** francophone m/f / hispanophone m/f

special ['speʃl] spécial; *effort, day etc* exceptionnel; **specialist** spécialiste m/f; **specialize** se spécialiser (**in** en, dans); **specially** → **especially**; **specialty** spécialité f

species ['spiːʃiːz] espèce f

specific [spə'sɪfɪk] spécifique; **specifically** spécifique-ment; **specifications** *of machine etc* spécifications fpl; **specify** préciser

specimen ['spesɪmən] *of work* spécimen m; *of blood, urine* prélèvement m

spectacular [spek'tækjʊlər] spectaculaire

spectator [spek'teɪtər] spectateur(-trice) m(f)

spectrum ['spektrəm] *fig* éventail m

speculate ['spekjʊleɪt] *also* FIN spéculer; **speculation** spéculations fpl; FIN spéculation f; **speculator** FIN spéculateur(-trice) m(f)

speech [spiːtʃ] discours m; (*ability to speak*) parole f; (*way of speaking*) élocution f; **speechless** *with shock, surprise* sans voix

speed [spiːd] **1** n vitesse f **2** v/i (*go quickly*) se précipiter; *of vehicle* foncer; *drive too quickly* faire de la vitesse; **speedboat** vedette f; *with outboard motor* hors-bord m *inv*; **speed bump** dos d'âne m, ralentisseur m; **speed-dial button** bouton m de numérotation abrégée; **speedily** rapidement; **speeding** *when driving excess* m de vitesse; **speed limit** limitation f de vitesse; **speedometer** compteur m de vitesse; **speedy** rapide

spell[1] [spel] **1** v/t *word* écrire, épeler; *how do you ~ it?*

comment ça s'écrit? **2** v/i: **he can/can't ~** il a une bonne/ mauvaise orthographe

spell² n of time période f

spelling ['spelɪŋ] orthographe f

spend [spend] *money* dépenser; *time* passer; **spendthrift** *pej* dépensier(-ière) m(f)

sperm [spɜːm] spermatozoïde m; (*semen*) sperme m

sphere [sfɪr] *also fig* sphère f

spice [spaɪs] (*seasoning*) épice f; **spicy** *food* épicé

spider ['spaɪdər] araignée f; **spiderweb** toile f d'araignée

spike [spaɪk] pointe f; *on plant, animal* piquant m

spill [spɪl] **1** n/t renverser **2** v/i se répandre **3** n of oil déversement m accidentel

spin¹ [spɪn] **1** n (*turn*) tour m **2** v/t faire tourner **3** v/i of wheel tourner

spin² v/t *wool etc* filer; *web* tisser

spinach ['spɪnɪdʒ] épinards mpl

spinal ['spaɪnl] de vertèbres; **spinal column** colonne f vertébrale; **spinal cord** moelle f épinière; **spine** colonne f vertébrale; of book dos m; on plant, hedgehog épine f; **spineless** (*cowardly*) lâche

'spin-off retombée f

spiny ['spaɪnɪ] épineux

spiral ['spaɪrəl] **1** n spirale f **2** v/i rise quickly monter en spirale

spire ['spaɪr] of church flèche f

spirit ['spɪrɪt] esprit m; (*courage*) courage m; **spirited** (*energetic*) énergique; **spirits** (*alcohol*) spiritueux mpl; (*morale*) moral m; **be in good/poor ~** avoir/ne pas avoir le moral; **spiritual** spirituel

spit [spɪt] of person cracher

spite [spaɪt] malveillance f; **in ~** en dépit de; **spiteful** malveillant; **spitefully** avec malveillance

splash [splæʃ] **1** n noise plouf m; small amount of liquid goutte f; of color tache f **2** v/t person éclabousser; water, mud asperger **3** v/i of person patauger; **~ against sth** of waves s'écraser contre qch; **splashdown** amerrissage m

splendid ['splendɪd] magnifique; **splendor**, Br **splendour** splendeur f

splint [splɪnt] MED attelle f

splinter ['splɪntər] **1** n of wood, glass éclat m; in finger écharde f **2** v/i se briser

split [splɪt] **1** n damage fente f; (disagreement) division f; (of profits etc) partage m; (share) part f **2** v/t wood fendre; log fendre en deux; (cause disagreement in, divide) diviser **3** v/i of wood etc se fendre; (disagree) se diviser

♦ **split up** *of couple* se séparer

spoil [spɔɪl] *child* gâter; *surprise, party* gâcher; **spoilsport** F rabat-joie *m/f*; **spoilt** *child* gâté

spoke [spəʊk] *of wheel* rayon *m*

spokesperson
['spəʊkspɜːrsən] porte-parole *m/f*

sponge [spʌndʒ] éponge *f*; **sponger** F parasite *m/f*

sponsor ['spɒnsər] **1** *n for club membership* parrain *m*, marraine *f*; RAD, TV, SP sponsor *m/f* **2** *v/t for club membership* parrainer; RAD, TV, SP sponsoriser; **sponsorship** RAD, TV, SP sponsorisation *f*

spontaneous [spɑːnˈteɪnɪəs] spontané; **spontaneously** spontanément

spool [spuːl] bobine *f*

spoon [spuːn] cuillère *f*; **spoonful** cuillerée *f*

sporadic [spəˈrædɪk] intermittent

sport [spɔːrt] sport *m*; **sporting** *event* sportif; *(fair, generous)* chic *inv*; **sports car** voiture *f* de sport; **sportsman** sportif *m*; **sportswoman** sportive *f*; **sporty** *person* sportif

spot[1] [spɑːt] *n on skin* bouton *m*; *in pattern* pois *m*

spot[2] *n (place)* endroit *m*

spot[3] *v/t (notice, identify)* repérer

'spot check contrôle *m* au hasard; **spotless** impeccable; **spotlight** *beam* feu *m* de projecteur; *device* projecteur *m*; **spotty** *with pimples* boutonneux

spouse [spaʊs] *fml* époux *m*, épouse *f*

spout [spaʊt] **1** *n* bec *m* **2** *v/i of liquid* jaillir **3** *v/t* F débiter

sprain [spreɪn] **1** *n* foulure *f*; *serious* entorse *f* **2** *v/t ankle, wrist* se fouler; *seriously* se faire une entorse à

sprawl [sprɔːl] s'affaler; *of city* s'étendre; **sprawling** tentaculaire

spray [spreɪ] **1** *n of sea water* embruns *mpl*; *from fountain* gouttes *fpl* d'eau; *for hair* laque *f*; *container* atomiseur *m* **2** *v/t perfume, lacquer* vaporiser; *paint, weed-killer etc* pulvériser; **~ graffiti on sth** peindre des graffitis à la bombe sur qch; **spraygun** pulvérisateur *m*

spread [spred] **1** *n of disease, religion etc* propagation *f*; F *(big meal)* festin *m* **2** *v/t (lay), butter* étaler; *news, rumor, disease* répandre; *arms, legs* étendre **3** *v/i* se répandre; **spreadsheet** COMPUT feuille *f* de calcul; *program* tableur *m*

sprightly ['spraɪtlɪ] alerte

spring[1] [sprɪŋ] *n season* printemps *m*

spring² [sprɪŋ] n device ressort m

spring³ [sprɪŋ] **1** n (jump) bond m; (stream) source f **2** v/i bondir

'springboard tremplin m; **springtime** printemps m

sprinkle ['sprɪŋkl] saupoudrer; **sprinkler** for garden arroseur m; in ceiling extincteur m

sprint [sprɪnt] **1** n sprint m **2** v/i SP sprinter; fig piquer un sprint F; **sprinter** SP sprinteur(-euse) m(f)

spy [spaɪ] **1** n espion(ne) m(f) **2** v/i faire de l'espionnage **3** v/t (see) apercevoir

♦ **spy on** espionner

squabble ['skwɒbl] **1** n querelle f **2** v/i se quereller

squalid ['skwɒlɪd] sordide; **squalor** misère f

squander ['skwɒndər] gaspiller

square [skwer] **1** adj in shape carré; ~ **mile** mile carré **2** n shape, MATH carré m; in town place f; in board game case f

squash¹ [skwɒʃ] n vegetable courge f

squash² [skwɒʃ] n game squash m

squash³ [skwɒʃ] v/t (crush) écraser

squat [skwɒt] **1** adj in shape ramassé **2** v/i sit s'accroupir; illegally squatter

squeak [skwiːk] **1** n of mouse couinement m; of hinge grincement m **2** v/i of mouse couiner; of hinge grincer

squeal [skwiːl] **1** n cri m aigu; of brakes grincement m **2** v/i pousser des cris aigus; of brakes grincer

squeamish ['skwiːmɪʃ] trop sensible

squeeze [skwiːz] hand serrer; shoulder, (remove juice from) presser; fruit, parcel palper

squid [skwɪd] calmar m

squirm [skwɜːrm] se tortiller

St (= **saint**) St(e) (= saint(e)); (= **street**) rue

stab [stæb] poignarder

stability [stə'bɪlətɪ] stabilité f;

stabilize ['steɪbɪlaɪz] v/t stabiliser **2** v/i se stabiliser; **stable 1** adj stable **2** n for horses écurie f

stack [stæk] **1** n (pile) pile f **2** v/t empiler

stadium ['steɪdɪəm] stade m

staff [stæf] (employees) personnel m; (teachers) personnel m enseignant

stage¹ [steɪdʒ] n in project etc étape f

stage² [steɪdʒ] **1** n THEA scène f **2** v/t play mettre en scène; demonstration organiser

stagger ['stægər] **1** v/i tituber **2** v/t (amaze) ébahir; coffee breaks etc échelonner; **staggering** stupéfiant

stagnant ['stægnənt] water, economy stagnant; **stagnate** fig stagner

'stag party enterrement m de

vie de garçon

stain [steɪn] **1** n (dirty mark) tache f; for wood teinture f **2** v/t (dirty) tacher; wood teindre; **stained-glass window** vitrail m; **stainless steel** acier m inoxydable

stair [ster] marche f; **the ~s** l'escalier m; **staircase** escalier m

stake [steɪk] **1** n of wood pieu m; when gambling enjeu m; (investment) investissements mpl; **be at ~** être en jeu **2** v/t tree soutenir avec un pieu; money jouer; person financer

stale [steɪl] bread rassis; air empesté; fig: news plus très frais

stalk[1] [stɔːk] n of fruit, plant tige f

stalk[2] [stɔːk] v/t animal, person traquer

stall[1] [stɔːl] n at market étalage m; for cow, horse stalle f

stall[2] [stɔːl] **1** v/i of vehicle, engine caler; (play for time) chercher à gagner du temps **2** v/t engine caler; person faire attendre

stalls [stɔːlz] THEA orchestre m

stalwart ['stɔːlwərt] supporter fidèle

stamina ['stæmɪnə] endurance f

stammer ['stæmər] **1** n bégaiement m **2** v/i bégayer

stamp[1] [stæmp] n for letter timbre m; device, mark tampon m **2** v/t letter timbrer; passport tamponner

stamp[2] [stæmp] v/t: **~ one's foot** taper du pied

stance [stæns] position f

stand [stænd] **1** n at exhibition stand m; (witness ~) barre f des témoins; (support, base) support m; **take the ~** LAW venir à la barre **2** v/i (be situated) se trouver; as opposed to sit rester debout; (rise) se lever **3** v/t (tolerate) supporter; (put) mettre

◆ **stand by 1** v/i (not take action) rester là sans rien faire; (be ready) se tenir prêt **2** v/t person soutenir; decision s'en tenir à

◆ **stand down** (withdraw) se retirer

◆ **stand for** (tolerate) supporter; (represent) représenter

◆ **stand out** be visible ressortir

◆ **stand up 1** v/i se lever **2** v/t F poser un lapin à

◆ **stand up for** défendre

◆ **stand up to** (face) tenir tête à

standard ['stændərd] **1** adj procedure etc normal; **~ practice** pratique f courante **2** n (level) niveau m; moral critère m; TECH norme f; **standardize** normaliser; **standard of living** niveau m de vie

'standby fly en stand-by;

standing *in society* position *f* sociale; *(repute)* réputation *f*; **standoffish** distant; **standpoint** point *m* de vue; **standstill**: **be at a ~** être paralysé; **bring to a ~** paralyser

staple[1] ['steɪpl] *n foodstuff* aliment *m* de base

staple[2] ['steɪpl] **1** *n fastener* agrafe *f* **2** *v/t* agrafer

stapler ['steɪplər] agrafeuse *f*

star [stɑːr] **1** *n in sky* étoile *f*; *fig also* vedette *f* **2** *v/t of movie* avoir comme vedette(s); *starboard* de tribord

stare [ster]: **~ into space** regarder dans le vide; **it's rude to ~** ce n'est pas poli de fixer les gens

stark [stɑːrk] **1** *adj landscape, color* austère; *reminder, contrast etc* brutal **2** *adv*: **~ naked** complètement nu

starry ['stɑːrɪ] *night* étoilé; **Stars and Stripes** bannière *f* étoilée

start [stɑːrt] **1** *n* début *m* **2** *v/i* commencer; *of engine, car* démarrer; **~ing from tomorrow** à partir de demain **3** *v/t* commencer; *engine, car* mettre en marche; *business* monter; **starter** *of meal* entrée *f*; *of car* démarreur *m*

startle ['stɑːrtl] effrayer; **startling** surprenant

starvation [stɑːr'veɪʃn] inanition *f*; **starve** souffrir de la faim; **I'm starving** F je meurs de faim F

state[1] [steɪt] **1** *n (condition, country, part of country)* état *m*; **the States** les États-Unis *mpl* **2** *adj capital, police etc* d'état; *banquet, occasion etc* officiel

state[2] [steɪt] *v/t* déclarer; *name and address* décliner

'State Department Département *m* d'État (américain); **statement** *to police* déclaration *f*; *(announcement)* communiqué *m*; *(bank ~)* relevé *m* de compte; **state of emergency** état *m* d'urgence; **state-of-the-art** de pointe; **statesman** homme *m* d'État

static (electricity) ['stætɪk] électricité *f* statique

station ['steɪʃn] **1** *n* RAIL gare *f*; *of subway*, RAD station *f*; TV chaîne *f* **2** *v/t guard etc* placer; **stationary** immobile

stationery ['steɪʃənərɪ] papeterie *f*

'station wagon break *m*

statistical ['stə'tɪstɪkl] statistique; **statistically** statistiquement; **statistician** statisticien(ne) *m(f)*; **statistics** *science* statistique *f figures* statistiques *fpl*

statue ['stætʃuː] statue *f*; **Statue of Liberty** Statue *f* de la Liberté

status ['steɪtəs] statut *m*; *(prestige)* prestige *m*; **status symbol** signe *m* extérieur de richesse

statute ['stætʃuːt] loi *f*

staunch [stɔːntʃ] *supporter* fervent

stay [steɪ] **1** *n* séjour *m* **2** *v/i* rester; **~ in a hotel** descendre dans un hôtel; **~ right there!** tenez-vous là!

◆ **stay behind** rester; *in school* rester après la classe

◆ **stay up** (*not go to bed*) rester debout

steadily ['stedɪlɪ] *improve etc* de façon régulière; **steady 1** *adj hand* ferme; *voice* posé; (*regular*) régulier; (*continuous*) continu **2** *adv*: **be going ~ of couple** sortir ensemble **3** *v/t person* soutenir; *voice* raffermir

steak [steɪk] bifteck *m*

steal [stiːl] **1** *v/t* voler **2** *v/i* (*be a thief*) voler; **~ in/out** entrer/ sortir à pas feutrés

stealthy ['stelθɪ] furtif

steam [stiːm] **1** *n* vapeur *f* **2** *v/t food* cuire à la vapeur; **steamed up** F fou de rage; **steamer** *for cooking* cuiseur *m* à vapeur

steel [stiːl] **1** *adj* (*made of ~*) en acier **2** *n* acier *m*; **steel-worker** ouvrier(-ière) *m(f)* de l'industrie sidérurgique

steep¹ [stiːp] *adj hill etc* raide; F *prices* excessif

steep² [stiːp] *v/t* (*soak*) faire tremper

steer¹ [stɪr] *n animal* bœuf *m*

steer² [stɪr] *v/t* diriger

steering ['stɪrɪŋ] MOT direction *f*; **steering wheel** volant *m*

stem¹ [stem] *n of plant* tige *f*; *of glass* pied *m*; *of word* racine *f*

stem² [stem] *v/t* (*block*) enrayer

stench [stentʃ] odeur *f* nauséabonde

stencil ['stensɪl] **1** *n* pochoir *m*; *pattern* peinture *f* au pochoir **2** *v/t pattern* peindre au pochoir

step [step] **1** *n* (*pace*) pas *m*; (*stair*) marche *f*; (*measure*) mesure *f* **2** *v/i*: **~ forward/ back** faire un pas en avant/ en arrière

◆ **step down** *from post etc* se retirer

◆ **step up** (*increase*) augmenter

'**stepbrother** demi-frère *m*; **stepdaughter** belle-fille *f*; **stepfather** beau-père *m*; **stepladder** escabeau *m*; **stepmother** belle-mère *f*; **stepsister** demi-sœur *f*; **stepson** beau-fils *m*

stereo ['sterɪoʊ] (*sound system*) chaîne *f* stéréo; **stereotype** stéréotype *m*

sterile ['sterɪl] stérile; **sterilize** stériliser

sterling ['stɜːrlɪŋ] FIN sterling *m*

stern¹ [stɜːrn] *adj* sévère

stern² [stɜːrn] *n* NAUT arrière *m*

sternly ['stɜːrnlɪ] sévèrement

steroids ['sterɔɪdz] stéroïdes

mpl

stew [stu:] ragoût *m*

steward ['stu:ərd] *on plane, ship* steward *m; at demonstration, meeting* membre *m* du service d'ordre; **stewardess** *on plane, ship* hôtesse *f*

stick¹ [stɪk] *n* morceau *m* de bois; *of policeman* bâton *m; (walking ~)* canne *f*

stick² [stɪk] **1** *v/t with adhesive* coller (**to** à); F *(put)* mettre **2** *v/i* se coincer; *(adhere)* adhérer

◆ **stick by** F ne pas abandonner

◆ **stick to** *(adhere to)* coller à; F *(keep to)* s'en tenir à; F *(follow)* suivre

◆ **stick up for** F défendre

sticker ['stɪkər] autocollant *m;* **stick-in-the-mud** F encroûté(e) *m(f);* **sticky** gluant; *label* collant

stiff [stɪf] *brush, cardboard, mixture etc* dur; *muscle, body* raide; *in manner* guindé; *drink* bien tassé; *competition* acharné; *fine* sévère; **stiffness** *of muscles* raideur *f; in manner* aspect *m* guindé

stifle ['staɪfl] étouffer; **stifling** étouffant

stigma ['stɪgmə] honte *f*

still¹ [stɪl] **1** *adj* calme **2** *adv:* **keep ~!** reste tranquille!; **stand ~!** ne bouge pas!

still² [stɪl] *adv (yet)* encore, toujours; *(nevertheless)* quand même

'stillborn: be ~ être mort à sa naissance; **still life** nature *f* morte

stilted ['stɪltɪd] guindé

stimulant ['stɪmjulənt] stimulant *m;* **stimulate** stimuler; **stimulating** stimulant; **stimulation** stimulation *f;* **stimulus** *(incentive)* stimulation *f*

sting [stɪŋ] **1** *n from bee, jellyfish* piqûre *f* **2** *v/t & v/i* piquer; **stinging** *criticism* blessant

stink [stɪŋk] **1** *n (bad smell)* puanteur *f;* F *(fuss)* grabuge *m* F **2** *v/i (smell bad)* puer; *(be very bad)* être nul

stipulate ['stɪpjuleɪt] stipuler; **stipulation** condition *f; of will, contract* stipulation *f*

stir [stɜːr] **1** *v/t* remuer **2** *v/i of sleeping person* bouger; **stirring** *music, speech* émouvant

stitch [stɪtʃ] **1** *n* point *m; ~es* MED points *mpl* de suture **2** *v/t (sew)* coudre; **stitching** *(stitches)* couture *f*

stock [stɑːk] **1** *n (reserve)* réserves *fpl;* COM *of store* stock *m; animals* bétail *m;* FIN *actions fpl; for soup etc* bouillon *m;* **be in/out of ~** être en stock/épuisé **2** *v/t* COM avoir (en stock)

'stockbreeder éleveur *m;* **stockbroker** agent *m* de change; **stock exchange** bourse *f;* **stockholder** actionnaire *m/f;* **stockist** revendeur *m;* **stock market**

marché *m* boursier; **stock-
pile 1** *n of food, weapons*
stocks *mpl* de réserve **2** *v/t*
faire des stocks de

stocky ['stɒkɪ] trapu

stodgy ['stɒdʒɪ] *food* bourratif

stoical ['stəʊɪkl] stoïque; **sto-
icism** stoïcisme *m*

stomach ['stʌmək] **1** *n (insides)* estomac *m*; *(abdomen)*
ventre *m* **2** *v/t (tolerate)* supporter

stone [stəʊn] pierre *f*; *(pebble)* caillou *m*; **stoned** F *on
drugs* défoncé F

stool [stuːl] *seat* tabouret *m*

stoop¹ [stuːp] *v/i (bend down)*
se pencher

stoop² [stuːp] *n (porch)* perron *m*

stop [stɒp] **1** *n for train, bus*
arrêt *m* **2** *v/t* arrêter; *(prevent)* empêcher; *check* faire
opposition à; ~ **doing sth** arrêter de faire qch **3** *v/i* s'arrêter

◆ **stop over** faire escale

'stopgap bouche-trou *m*;
stoplight *(traffic light)* feu
m rouge; *(brake light)* stop
m; **stopover** étape *f*; **stopper** *for bottle* bouchon *m*;
stop sign stop *m*; **stop-
watch** chronomètre *m*

storage ['stɔːrɪdʒ] COM emma-
gasinage *m*; *in house* rangement *m*; **store 1** magasin
m; *(stock)* provision *f*;
(~house) entrepôt *m* **2** *v/t* en-

treposer; COMPUT stocker;
storefront devanture *f* de
magasin; **storekeeper**
commerçant(e) *m(f)*

storey *Br* → **story²**

storm [stɔːrm] *with rain, wind*
tempête *f*; *(thunder~)* orage
m; **stormy** orageux

story¹ ['stɔːrɪ] *(tale, account,
F: lie)* histoire *f*; *(newspaper
article)* article *m*

story² ['stɔːrɪ] *of building* étage
m

stout [staʊt] *person* corpulent, costaud

stove [stəʊv] *for cooking* cuisinière *f*; *for heating* poêle *m*

stow [stəʊ] ranger

◆ **stow away** s'embarquer
clandestinement

'stowaway passager clandestin *m*, passagère clandestine
f

straight [streɪt] **1** *adj line,
back, knees* droit; *hair* raide;
(honest, direct) franc; *(not
criminal)* honnête; *whiskey
etc* sec; *(tidy)* en ordre; *(con-
servative)* sérieux; *(not homosexual)* hétéro F **2** *adv*
(in a straight line) droit; *(directly, immediately)* directement; **go ~** F *of criminal* revenir dans le droit chemin; ~
ahead tout droit; ~ **away,** ~
off tout de suite; ~ **out** très
clairement; ~ **up** *without ice*
sans glace; **straighten** redresser; **straightforward**
(honest, direct) direct; *(sim-*

ple) simple

strain¹ [streɪn] **1** *n* on rope, engine tension *f*; *on heart* pression *f*; **suffer from ~** souffrir de tension nerveuse **2** *v/t* back se fouler; eyes s'abîmer; finances grever

strain² [streɪn] *v/t vegetables* faire égoutter; *oil, fat etc* filtrer

strained [streɪnd] *relations* tendu; **strainer** *for vegetables etc* passoire *f*

strait [streɪt] détroit *m*; **strait-laced** collet monté *inv*

strange [streɪndʒ] *(odd, curious)* étrange, bizarre; *(unknown, foreign)* inconnu; **strangely** *(oddly)* bizarrement; **~ enough, ...** c'est bizarre, mais ...; **stranger** étranger(-ère) *m* (*f*); **he's a complete ~** je ne le connais pas du tout; **I'm a ~ here myself** moi non plus je ne suis pas d'ici

strangle ['stræŋgl] étrangler

strap [stræp] *of purse, shoe* lanière *f*; *of brassiere, dress* bretelle *f*; *of watch* bracelet *m*; **strapless** sans bretelles

strategic [strə'tiːdʒɪk] stratégique; **strategy** stratégie *f*

straw [strɔː] *material, for drink* paille *f*; **strawberry** fraise *f*

stray [streɪ] **1** *adj animal, bullet* perdu **2** *n animal m* errant **3** *v/i of animal* vagabonder; *of child* s'égarer; *fig: of eyes,*

thoughts errer (**to** vers)

streak [striːk] **1** *n of dirt, paint* traînée *f*; *in hair* mèche *f*; *fig: of nastiness etc* pointe *f* **2** *v/i move quickly* filer

stream [striːm] ruisseau *m*; *fig: of people* flot *m*; **streamline** *fig* rationaliser; **streamlined** *car, plane* caréné; *organization* rationaliser

street [striːt] rue *f*; **streetcar** tramway *m*; **streetlight** réverbère *m*; **street people** sans-abri *mpl*; **street value** *of drugs* prix *m* à la revente; **strength** [streŋθ] force *f*; *(strong point)* point *m* fort; **strengthen 1** *v/t body* fortifier; *bridge, currency, bonds etc* consolider **2** *v/i* se consolider

strenuous ['strenjuəs] fatigant; **strenuously** *deny* vigoureusement

stress [stres] **1** *n (emphasis)* accent *m*; *(tension)* stress *m* **2** *v/t syllable* accentuer; *importance etc* souligner; **stressed out** F stressé F; **stressful** stressant

stretch [stretʃ] **1** *n of land, water* étendue *f*; *of road* partie *f* **2** *adj fabric* extensible **3** *v/t material* tendre; *small income* tirer le maximum de; *F rules* assouplir **4** *v/i to relax muscles, to reach sth* s'étirer; *(spread)* s'étendre; **stretcher** brancard *m*

strict [strɪkt] strict; **strictly**

strictement; *it is ~ forbidden* c'est strictement défendu

stride [straɪd] **1** *n* (grand) pas *m* **2** *v/i* marcher à grandes enjambées

strident ['straɪdnt] strident; *demands* véhément

strike [straɪk] **1** *n of workers* grève *f*; *in baseball* balle *f* manquée; *of oil* découverte *f*; *be on ~* être en grève **2** *v/i of workers* faire grève; (*attack: of wild animal*) attaquer; *of killer* frapper; *of disaster* frapper; *of clock* sonner **3** *v/t also fig* frapper; *match* allumer; *of oil* découvrir

♦ **strike out** *delete* rayer

strikebreaker ['straɪkbreɪkər] briseur(-euse) *m(f)* de grève; **striker** (*person on strike*) gréviste *m/f*; *in soccer* buteur *m*; **striking** (*marked, eye-catching*) frappant

string [strɪŋ] ficelle *f*; *of violin, tennis racket* corde *f*; **stringed instrument** instrument *m* à cordes

stringent ['strɪndʒnt] rigoureux

strip [strɪp] **1** *n* bande *f*; (*comic ~*) bande *f* dessinée **2** *v/t* (*remove*) enlever; (*undress*) déshabiller **3** *v/i* (*undress*) se déshabiller; *of stripper* faire du strip-tease; **strip club** boîte *f* de strip-tease

stripe [straɪp] rayure *f*; MIL galon *m*; **striped** rayé

stripper ['strɪpər] strip-teaseuse *f*; *male ~* strip-teaseur *m*; **striptease** strip-tease *m*

stroke [strouk] **1** *n* MED attaque *f*; *when painting* coup *m* de pinceau; *style of swimming* nage *f* **2** *v/t* caresser

stroll [stroul] **1** *n* balade *f* **2** *v/i* flâner; **stroller** *for baby* poussette *f*

strong [strɔːŋ] *fort*; *structure* solide; *candidate* sérieux; *support, supporter* vigoureux; **strongly** fortement; **strong-minded**: *be ~* avoir de la volonté; **strong point** point *m* fort; **strongroom** chambre *f* forte; **strong-willed** qui sait ce qu'il/elle veut

structural ['strʌktʃərl] *damage* de structure; *fault, problems* de construction; **structure 1** *n* (*something built*) construction *f*; *of novel, poem etc* structure *f* **2** *v/t* structurer

struggle ['strʌgl] **1** *n* lutte *f* **2** *v/i with a person* se battre; *~ to do sth* avoir du mal à faire qch

strut [strʌt] se pavaner

stub [stʌb] *of cigarette* mégot *m*; *of check, ticket* souche *f*

stubborn ['stʌbərn] *person, refusal etc* entêté; *defense* farouche

stubby ['stʌbɪ] boudiné

stuck [stʌk] F: *be ~ on s.o.* être fou de qn

student ['stu:dnt] *at high school* élève *m/f*; *at college, university* étudiant(e) *m(f)*

studio ['stu:diəʊ] studio *m*; *of artist* atelier *m*

studious ['stu:diəs] studieux; **study 1** *n room* bureau *m*; *(learning)* études *fpl*; *(investigation)* étude *f* **2** *v/t & v/i* étudier

stuff [stʌf] **1** *n (things)* trucs *mpl*; *substance, powder etc* truc *m*; *(belongings)* affaires *fpl* **2** *v/t turkey* farcir; **~ sth into sth** fourrer qch dans qch; **stuffing** *for turkey* farce *f*; *in chair, toy* rembourrage *m*; **stuffy** *room* mal aéré; *person* vieux jeu *inv*

stumble ['stʌmbl] trébucher; **stumbling block** pierre *f* d'achoppement

stump [stʌmp] **1** *n of tree* souche *f* **2** *v/t*: **I'm ~ed** je le colle F

stun [stʌn] étourdir; *animal* assommer; *fig (shock)* abasourdir; **stunning** *(amazing)* stupéfiant; *(very beautiful)* épatant

stunt [stʌnt] *for publicity* coup *m* de publicité; *in movie* cascade *f*; **stuntman** *in movie* cascadeur *m*

stupefy ['stu:pɪfaɪ] stupéfier

stupendous [stu:'pendəs] prodigieux

stupid ['stu:pɪd] stupide; **stupidity** stupidité *f*

sturdy ['stɜ:rdɪ] robuste

stutter ['stʌtər] bégayer

style [staɪl] *(method, manner)* style *m*; *(fashion)* mode *f*; *(fashionable elegance)* classe *f*; **stylish** qui a de la classe; **stylist** *hair ~* styliste *m/f*

subcommittee ['sʌbkəmɪtɪ] sous-comité *m*

subconscious [sʌb'kɑ:nʃəs] subconscient; **subconsciously** subconsciemment

subcontract [sʌbkən'trækt] sous-traiter; **subcontractor** sous-traitant *m*

subdivide [sʌbdɪ'vaɪd] sous-diviser

subdue [səb'du:] contenir

subheading ['sʌbhedɪŋ] sous-titre *m*

subhuman [sʌb'hju:mən] sous-humain

subject 1 ['sʌbdʒɪkt] *n of country,* GRAM, *(topic)* sujet *m*; *(branch of learning)* matière *f* **2** [sʌb'dʒɪkt] *adj*: **be ~ to** être sujet à **3** [səb'dʒɪkt] *v/t* soumettre (**to** à); **subjective** subjectif

sublet ['sʌblet] sous-louer

submachine gun [sʌbmə-'ʃi:ŋgən] mitraillette *f*

submarine ['sʌbməri:n] sous-marin *m*

submission [səb'mɪʃn] *(surrender)*, *to committee etc* soumission *f*; **submissive** soumis; **submit 1** *v/t plan* soumettre **2** *v/i* se soumettre

subordinate [sə'bɔ:rdɪnət] **1** *adj position* subalterne **2** *n* subordonné(e) *m(f)*

subpoena [sə'pi:nə] LAW **1** n assignation f **2** v/t person assigner à comparaître

◆ **subscribe to** [səb'skraɪb] magazine etc s'abonner à; theory souscrire à

subscriber [səb'skraɪbər] to magazine abonné(e) m(f); **subscription** abonnement m

subsequent ['sʌbsɪkwənt] ultérieur

subside [səb'saɪd] of waters baisser; of winds se calmer; of building s'affaisser; of fears s'apaiser

subsidiary [səb'sɪdɪrɪ] filiale f

subsidize ['sʌbsɪdaɪz] subventionner; **subsidy** subvention f

substance ['sʌbstəns] substance f

substandard [sʌb'stændərd] de qualité inférieure

substantial [səb'stænʃl] considérable; meal consistant; **substantially** (considerably) considérablement; (in essence) de manière générale

substantive [səb'stæntɪv] réel

substitute ['sʌbstɪtu:t] **1** n substitut m (for de); SP remplaçant(e) m(f) (for de) **2** v/t remplacer; **~ X for Y** remplacer Y par X; **substitution** remplacement m

subtitle ['sʌbtaɪtl] sous-titre m

subtle ['sʌtl] subtil

subtract [səb'trækt] soustraire

suburb ['sʌbɜːrb] banlieue f; **the ~s** la banlieue; **suburban** typique de la banlieue; attitudes etc de banliusards

subversive [səb'vɜːrsɪv] **1** adj subversif **2** n personne f subversive

subway ['sʌbweɪ] métro m

succeed [sək'si:d] **1** v/i réussir; to throne succéder à; **~ in doing sth** réussir à faire qch **2** v/t (come after) succéder à; **success** réussite f; **be a ~** avoir du succès; **successful** person qui a réussi; talks, operation réussi; **be ~ in doing sth** réussir à faire qch; **successfully** avec succès; **successive** successif; **on three ~ days** trois jours de suite; **successor** successeur m

succinct [sək'sɪŋkt] succinct

succumb [sə'kʌm] (give in) succomber

such [sʌtʃ] **1** adj: **~ a** (so much of a) un tel, une telle; **it was ~ a surprise** c'était une telle surprise; (of that kind): **~ as** tel/telle que; **there is no ~ word as ...** le mot ... n'existe pas **2** adv tellement; **an easy question** une question tellement facile

suck [sʌk] **1** v/t candy etc sucer **2** v/i P: **it ~s** c'est merdique P; **sucker** F person niais(e) m(f); F (lollipop) sucette f; **suction** succion f

sudden ['sʌdn] soudain; **suddenly** tout à coup, soudain

sue [suː] poursuivre en justice

suede [sweɪd] daim m

suffer ['sʌfər] 1 v/i souffrir 2 v/t experience subir; **suffering** souffrance f

sufficient [sə'fɪʃnt] suffisant; **not ~ funds** pas assez d'argent; **sufficiently** suffisamment

suffocate ['sʌfəkeɪt] 1 v/i s'étouffer 2 v/t étouffer; **suffocation** étouffement m

sugar ['ʃʊgər] 1 n sucre m 2 v/t sucrer

suggest [sə'dʒest] suggérer; **suggestion** suggestion f

suicide ['suːɪsaɪd] suicide m

suit [suːt] 1 n for man costume m; for woman tailleur m; in cards couleur f 2 v/t of clothes, color aller à; **suitable** approprié, convenable; **suitably** convenablement; **suitcase** valise f

suite [swiːt] of rooms suite f; furniture salon m trois pièces; MUS suite f

sulk [sʌlk] bouder; **sulky** bouderie

sullen ['sʌlən] maussade

sultry ['sʌltrɪ] climate lourd; sexually sulfureux

sum [sʌm] (total, amount) somme f; in arithmetic calcul m

◆ **sum up** 1 v/t (summarize) résumer; (assess) se faire

une idée de 2 v/i LAW résumer les débats

summarize ['sʌməraɪz] résumer; **summary** résumé m

summer ['sʌmər] été f

summit ['sʌmɪt] also POL sommet m

summon ['sʌmən] staff, meeting convoquer; **summons** LAW assignation f (à comparaître)

sun [sʌn] soleil m; **sunbathe** prendre un bain de soleil; **sunbed** lit m à ultraviolets; **sunblock** écran m solaire; **sunburn** coup m de soleil; **sunburnt: be ~** avoir des coups de soleil; **Sunday** dimanche m; **sunglasses** lunettes fpl de soleil; **sunny** day ensoleillé; disposition gai; **it's ~** il y a du soleil; **sunrise** lever m du soleil; **sunset** coucher m du soleil; **sunshade** handheld ombrelle f; over table parasol m; **sunshine** soleil m; **sunstroke** insolation f; **suntan** bronzage m; **get a ~** bronzer

super ['suːpər] 1 adj F super inv F 2 n (janitor) concierge m/f

superb [suˈpɜːrb] excellent

superficial [suːpərˈfɪʃl] superficiel

superfluous [suˈpɜːrfluəs] superflu

superintendent [suːpərɪnˈtendənt] of apartment block concierge m/f

superior [suː'pɪrɪər] **1** adj supérieur **2** n in organization supérieur m

superlative [suː'pɜːrlətɪv] **1** adj (superb) excellent **2** n GRAM superlatif m

supermarket supermarché m

'superpower POL superpuissance f

supersonic [suːpər'saːnɪk] supersonique

superstition [suːpər'stɪʃn] superstition f; **superstitious** superstitieux

supervise ['suːpərvaɪz] children activities etc surveiller; workers superviser; **supervisor** at work superviseur m

supper ['sʌpər] dîner m

supplement ['sʌplɪmənt] (extra payment) supplément m

supplier [sə'plaɪr] COM fournisseur(-euse) m(f); **supply 1** n of electricity, water etc alimentation f (of en); ~ **and demand** l'offre et la demande; **supplies** of food provisions fpl **2** v/t goods fournir

support [sə'pɔːrt] **1** n for structure support m; (backing) soutien m **2** v/t structure supporter; (financially entretenir; (back) soutenir; **supporter** of politician, football etc team supporteur(-trice) m(f); of theory partisan(e) m(f); **supportive** attitude de soutien; **be very ~ of s.o.** beaucoup soutenir qn

suppose [sə'pouz] (imagine)

supposer; **be ~d to do sth** (be meant to, said to) être censé faire qch; **supposing ... (et) si ...**; **supposedly** apparemment

suppress [sə'pres] réprimer; **suppression** répression f

supremacy [suː'preməsɪ] suprématie f; **supreme** suprême; **Supreme Court** Cour f suprême

surcharge ['sɜːrtʃɑːrdʒ] surcharge f

sure [ʃʊr] **1** adj sûr; **make ~ that ... s'assurer que ... 2** adv: ~ **enough** en effet; **it is hot today** F il fait vraiment chaud aujourd'hui; **~!** F mais oui, bien sûr!; **surety** for loan garant(e) m(f)

surf [sɜːrf] **1** n on sea écume f **2** v/t the Net surfer sur

surface ['sɜːrfɪs] **1** n surface f **2** v/i from water faire surface; (appear) refaire surface; **surface mail** courrier m par voie terrestre ou maritime

'surfboard planche f de surf; **surfer** surfeur(-euse) m(f); **surfing** surf m; **go ~** aller faire du surf

surge [sɜːrdʒ] in electric current surtension f; in demand etc poussée f

surgeon ['sɜːrdʒən] chirurgien m(f); **surgery** chirurgie f; **surgical** chirurgical; **surgically** remove par opération chirurgicale

surly ['sɜːrlɪ] revêche

surmount [sər'maunt] *difficulties* surmonter

surname ['sɜːrneɪm] nom *m* de famille

surpass [sər'pæs] dépasser

surplus ['sɜːrpləs] **1** *n* surplus *m* **2** *adj* en surplus

surprise [sər'praɪz] **1** *n* surprise *f* **2** *v/t* étonner; **be/look ~d** être/avoir l'air surpris; **surprising** étonnant; **surprisingly** étonnamment

surrender [sə'rendər] **1** *v/i* of army se rendre **2** *v/t* weapons etc rendre **3** *n* capitulation *f*; (handing in) reddition *f*

surrogate mother ['sʌrəgət] mère *f* porteuse

surround [sə'raund] **1** *v/t* entourer **2** *n* of picture etc bordure *f*; **surrounding** environnant; **surroundings** environs *mpl*; setting cadre *m*

survey ['sɜːrveɪ] *n* of modern literature etc étude *f*; Br of building inspection *f*; (poll) sondage *m* **2** [sər'veɪ] *v/t* (look at) contempler; Br building inspecter; **surveyor** Br expert *m*

survival [sər'vaɪvl] survie *f*; **survive** **1** *v/i* survivre **2** *v/t* accident, (outlive) survivre à; **survivor** survivant(e) *m(f)*

suspect 1 ['sʌspekt] *n* suspect(e) *m(f)* **2** [sə'spekt] *v/t* person soupçonner; (suppose) croire; **suspected** murderer soupçonné; cause, heart attack etc présumé

suspend [sə'spend] (hang), from office suspendre; **suspenders** for pants bretelles *fpl*; Br porte-jarretelles *m*

suspense [sə'spens] suspense *m*; **suspension** in vehicle, from duty suspension *f*

suspicion [sə'spɪʃn] soupçon *m*; **suspicious** (causing suspicion) suspect; (feeling suspicion) méfiant; **be ~ of s.o.** se méfier de qn; **suspiciously** behave de manière suspecte; ask avec méfiance

sustain [sə'steɪn] soutenir; **sustainable** durable

SUV [esjuː'viː] (= sports utility vehicle) véhicule *m* utilitaire sport

swab [swɑːb] tampon *m*

swallow[1] ['swɑːloʊ] *v/t* & *v/i* avaler

swallow[2] ['swɑːloʊ] *n* bird hirondelle *f*

swamp [swɑːmp] **1** *n* marécage *m* **2** *v/t*: **be ~ed with** être submergé de; **swampy** marécageux

swap [swɑːp] échanger (for contre)

swarm [swɔːrm] **1** *n* of bees essaim *m* **2** *v/i*: the town was ~ing with ... la ville grouillait de ...

swarthy ['swɔːrðɪ] basané

swat [swɑːt] insect écraser

sway [sweɪ] **1** *n* (influence, power) emprise *f* **2** *v/i* in wind se balancer; because drunk, ill tituber

swear [swer] **1** v/i (use swear-word) jurer; **~ at s.o.** injurier qn **2** v/t LAW, (promise) jurer
◆ **swear in** witnesses etc faire prêter serment à
'**swearword** juron m
sweat [swet] **1** n sueur f **2** v/i transpirer, suer; **sweat band** bandeau m en éponge; **sweater** pull m; **sweatshirt** sweat(-shirt) m; **sweaty** plein de sueur
sweep [swiːp] **1** v/t floor, leaves balayer **2** n (long curve) courbe f; **sweeping** statement hâtif; changes radical
sweet [swiːt] taste, tea sucré; F (kind) gentil; F (cute) mignon; **sweetcorn** maïs m; **sweeten** sucrer; **sweetheart** amoureux(-euse) m(f)
swell [swel] **1** v/i of wound, limb enfler **2** adj F (good) super F inv **3** n of the sea houle f; **swelling** MED enflure f
swerve [swɜːrv] of driver, car s'écarter brusquement
swift [swift] rapide
swim [swim] **1** v/i nager **2** n baignade f; **go for a ~** aller se baigner; **swimmer** nageur(-euse) m(f); **swimming** natation f; **swimming pool** piscine f; **swimsuit** maillot m de bain
swindle ['swindl] **1** n escroquerie f **2** v/t escroquer; **~ s.o. out of sth** escroquer qch à qn

swing [swiŋ] **1** n oscillation f; for child balançoire f; **~ to the Democrats** revirement m d'opinion en faveur des démocrates **2** v/t object in hand, hips balancer **3** v/i se balancer; (turn) tourner; of public opinion etc virer
Swiss [swis] **1** adj suisse **2** n person Suisse m/f; **the ~** les Suisses mpl
switch [swiʧ] **1** n for light bouton m; (change) changement m **2** v/t (change) changer de **3** v/i (change) passer
◆ **switch off** lights, engine, PC éteindre; engine arrêter
◆ **switch on** lights, engine, PC allumer; engine démarrer
Switzerland ['switsərlənd] Suisse f
swivel ['swivl] pivoter
swollen ['swəʊlən] stomach ballonné; ankles, face enflé
syllabus ['siləbəs] programme m
symbol ['simbəl] symbole m; **symbolic** symbolique; **symbolism** symbolisme m; **symbolist** symboliste m/f; **symbolize** symboliser
symmetrical [si'metrikl] symétrique; **symmetry** symétrie
sympathetic [simpə'θetik] (showing pity) compatissant; (understanding) compréhensif
◆ **sympathize with** ['simpə-

θaɪz] *person* compatir avec; *views* avoir des sympathies pour

sympathizer ['sɪmpəθaɪzər] POL sympathisant(e) *m(f)*; **sympathy** *(pity)* compassion *f*; *(understanding)* compréhension **for** de)

symphony ['sɪmfənɪ] symphonie *f*

symptom ['sɪmptəm] MED, *fig* symptôme *m*

synchronize ['sɪŋkrənaɪz] synchroniser

synonym ['sɪnənɪm] synonyme *m*; **synonymous** synonyme

synthesizer ['sɪnθəsaɪzər]

MUS synthétiseur *m*; **synthetic** synthétique

syphilis ['sɪfɪlɪs] syphilis *f*

Syria ['sɪrɪə] Syrie *f*; **Syrian 1** *adj* syrien **2** *n* Syrien(ne)

syringe [sɪ'rɪndʒ] seringue *f*

syrup ['sɪrəp] sirop *m*

system ['sɪstəm] système *m*; *(orderliness)* ordre *m*; *(computer)* ordinateur *m*; **systematic** systématique; **systematically** systématiquement

systems analyst COMPUT analyste-programmeur(-euse) *m(f)*

T

table ['teɪbl] table *f*; *of figures* tableau *m*; **tablecloth** nappe *f*; **table lamp** petite lampe *f*; **table of contents** table *f* des matières; **tablespoon** cuillère *f* à soupe

tablet ['tæblɪt] MED comprimé *m*

tabloid ['tæblɔɪd] *newspaper* journal *m* à sensation

taboo [tə'buː] tabou *inv* in *feminine*

tacit ['tæsɪt] tacite

tack [tæk] **1** *n nail* clou *m* **2** *v/t in sewing* bâtir **3** *v/i of yacht* louvoyer

tackle ['tækl] **1** *n (equipment)* attirail *m*; SP tacle *m*; *in rug-*

by plaquage *m* **2** *v/t* SP tacler; *in rugby* plaquer; *problem* s'attaquer à; *(confront)* confronter; *physically* s'opposer à

tacky ['tækɪ] *paint, glue* collant; F *(cheap, poor quality)* minable F

tact [tækt] tact *m*; **tactful** diplomate; **tactfully** avec tact

tactical ['tæktɪkl] tactique; **tactics** tactique *f*

tactless ['tæktlɪs] qui manque de tact, peu délicat

tag [tæg] *(label)* étiquette *f*

tail [teɪl] queue *f*; **tail light** feu *m* arrière

tailor ['teɪlər] tailleur *m*; **tai-**

lor-made *also fig* fait sur mesure

'tail pipe *of car* tuyau *m* d'échappement

take [teɪk] prendre; (*transport, accompany*) amener; *subject at school, photograph, photocopy, stroll* faire; *exam* passer; (*endure*) supporter; (*require: courage etc*) demander; **how long will it ~ you to ...?** combien de temps est-ce que tu vas mettre pour ...?

◆ **take after** ressembler à

◆ **take away** *object* enlever; *pain* faire disparaître; MATH soustraire (**from** de)

◆ **take back** *object* rapporter; *person to a place* ramener; **she wouldn't take him back** *husband* elle ne voulait pas qu'il revienne

◆ **take down** *from shelf* enlever; *scaffolding* démonter; *pants* baisser; (*write down*) noter

◆ **take in** (*take indoors*) rentrer; (*give accommodation to*) héberger; (*make narrower*) reprendre; (*deceive*) duper; (*include*) inclure

◆ **take off 1** *v/t clothes, hat* enlever; *10% etc* faire une réduction de; (*mimic*) imiter **2** *v/i of airplane* décoller; (*become popular*) réussir

◆ **take on** *job* accepter; *staff* embaucher

◆ **take out** *from bag, pocket* sortir (**from** de); *tooth, word from text* enlever; *money from bank* retirer; *to dinner, theater etc* emmener; *insurance policy* souscrire à

◆ **take over 1** *v/t company etc* reprendre **2** *v/i* POL arriver au pouvoir; *of new director* prendre ses fonctions; (*do sth in s.o.'s place*) prendre la relève

◆ **take up** *carpet etc* enlever; (*carry up*) monter; *dress etc* raccourcir; *judo, Spanish etc* se mettre à; *new job* commencer; *space, time* prendre; *offer* accepter

'takeoff *of airplane* décollage *m*; (*impersonation*) imitation *f*; **takeover** COM rachat *m*; **takeover bid** offre *f* publique d'achat, OPA *f*; **takings** recette *f*

tale [teɪl] histoire *f*

talent ['tælənt] talent *m*; **talented** doué; **talent scout** dénicheur(-euse) *m(f)* de talents

talk [tɔːk] **1** *v/t & v/i* parler; **~ business** parler affaires **2** *n* (*conversation*) conversation *f*; (*lecture*) exposé *m*; **~s** pourparlers *mpl*

◆ **talk back** répondre

talkative ['tɔːkətɪv] bavard; **talk show** talk-show *m*

tall [tɔːl] grand

tally ['tælɪ] **1** *n* compte *m* **2** *v/i* correspondre; *of stories* concorder

tame [teɪm] apprivoisé; *not wild* pas sauvage; *joke etc* fade

◆ **tamper with** [ˈtæmpər] toucher à

tampon [ˈtæmpɑːn] tampon *m*

tan [tæn] **1** *n from sun* bronzage; *color* marron *m* clair **2** *v/i in sun* bronzer **3** *v/t leather* tanner

tangent [ˈtændʒənt] MATH tangente *f*

tangible [ˈtændʒɪbl] tangible

tangle [ˈtæŋgl] enchevêtrement *m*

tango [ˈtæŋgou] tango *m*

tank [tæŋk] MOT, *for water* réservoir *m*; *for fish* aquarium *m*; MIL char *m*; *for skin diver* bonbonne *f* d'oxygène; **tanker** (*oil* ~) pétrolier *m*; *truck* camion-citerne *m*

tanned [tænd] bronzé

tantalizing [ˈtæntəlaɪzɪŋ] alléchant

tantrum [ˈtæntrəm] caprice *m*

tap [tæp] **1** *n Br (faucet)* robinet *m* **2** *v/t (knock)* taper; *phone* mettre sur écoute

tape [teɪp] **1** *n for recording* bande *f*; *recording* cassette *f*; *sticky* ruban *m* adhésif **2** *v/t conversation etc* enregistrer; *with sticky tape* scotcher; **tape deck** platine *f* cassettes; **tape drive** COMPUT lecteur *m* de bandes; **tape measure** mètre *m* ruban

taper [ˈteɪpər] *of stick* s'effiler; *of column, pant legs* se rétrécir

tape recorder magnétophone *m*; **tape recording** enregistrement *m*

tar [tɑːr] goudron *m*

tardy [ˈtɑːrdɪ] tardif

target [ˈtɑːrgɪt] **1** *n in shooting* cible *f*; *fig* objectif *m* **2** *v/t market* cibler

target audience public *m* cible; **target date** date *f* visée; **target market** marché *m* cible

tariff [ˈtærɪf] *(customs* ~) taxe *f*; *(prices)* tarif *m*

tarmac [ˈtɑːrmæk] *at airport* tarmac *m*

tarnish [ˈtɑːrnɪʃ] ternir

tarpaulin [tɑːrˈpɔːlɪn] bâche *f*

tart [tɑːrt] tarte *f*

task [tæsk] tâche *f*; **task force** MIL corps *m* expéditionnaire

taste [teɪst] **1** *n* goût *m* **2** *v/t* goûter; *(perceive taste of)* sentir; *try, fig* goûter à **3** *v/i: it ~s like ...* ça a (un) goût de ...; **tasteful** de bon goût; **tastefully** avec goût; **tasteless** *food* fade; *remark, décor* de mauvais goût; **tasting** *of wine* dégustation *f*; **tasty** délicieux

tattered [ˈtætərd] en lambeaux

tattoo [təˈtuː] tatouage *m*

taunt [tɔːnt] **1** *n* raillerie *f* **2** *v/t* se moquer de

taut [tɔːt] tendu

tax [tæks] **1** *n* on income impôt *m*; on goods, services taxe *f* **2** *v/t* income imposer; goods, services taxer; **taxable income** revenu *m* imposable; **taxation** act imposition *f*; (taxes) charges *fpl* fiscales; **tax bracket** fourchette *f* d'impôts; **tax-deductible** déductible des impôts; **tax evasion** fraude *f* fiscale; **tax-free** hors taxe; **tax haven** paradis *m* fiscal

taxi ['tæksɪ] taxi *m*; **taxi driver** chauffeur *m* de taxi

taxing ['tæksɪŋ] exténuant

'**taxi stand**, *Br* '**taxi rank** station *f* de taxis

'**taxpayer** contribuable *m/f*; **tax return** déclaration *f* d'impôts; **tax year** année *f* fiscale

TB [tiː'biː] (= **tuberculosis**) tuberculose *f*

tea [tiː] drink thé *m*; **teabag** sachet *m* de thé

teach [tiːtʃ] enseigner; person enseigner à; **teacher** professeur *m/f*; in elementary school instituteur(-trice) *m(f)*; **teaching** profession enseignement *m*

'**teacup** tasse *f* à thé

teak [tiːk] tek *m*

team [tiːm] équipe *f*; **team spirit** esprit *m* d'équipe; **teamster** camionneur(-euse) *m(f)*; **teamwork** travail *m* d'équipe

teapot ['tiːpɒt] théière *f*

tear[1] [ter] **1** *n* in cloth etc dé-

chirure *f* **2** *v/t* paper, cloth déchirer **3** *v/i* (run fast, drive fast): **she tore down the street** elle a descendu la rue en trombe

◆ **tear down** poster arracher; building démolir

◆ **tear out** page arracher

◆ **tear up** déchirer; contract etc annuler

tear[2] [tɪr] *n* in eye larme *f*; **be in ~s** être en larmes; **tearful** look plein de larmes; **tear gas** gaz *m* lacrymogène

tease [tiːz] taquiner

'**teaspoon** cuillère *f* à café

technical ['teknɪkl] technique; **technically** (strictly speaking) en théorie; **technician** technicien(ne) *m(f)*; **technique** technique *f*

technological [teknə'lɑːdʒɪkl] technologique; **technology** technologie *f*; **technophobia** plein de technophobie *f*

teddy bear ['tedɪber] ours *m* en peluche

tedious ['tiːdɪəs] ennuyeux

tee [tiː] in golf tee *m*

teenage ['tiːneɪdʒ] fashion pour adolescents; **teenager** adolescent(e) *m(f)*

teens [tiːnz] adolescence *f*

teeny ['tiːnɪ] F tout petit

teeth [tiːθ] *pl* → **tooth**

teethe [tiːð] faire ses dents

telecommunications [telɪkəmjuːnɪ'keɪʃnz] télécommunications *fpl*

telegraph pole ['telɪɡræfpool] *Br* poteau *m* télégraphique

telepathic [telɪˈpæθɪk] télépathique; **telepathy** télépathie *f*

telephone [ˈtelɪfoʊn] **1** *n* téléphone *m* **2** *v/t person* téléphoner à **3** *v/i* téléphoner; **telephone book** annuaire *m*; **telephone booth** cabine *f* téléphonique; **telephone call** appel *m* téléphonique; **telephone conversation** conversation *f* téléphonique; **telephone directory** annuaire *m*; **telephone number** numéro *m* de téléphone

telephoto lens [telɪˈfoʊtoʊlenz] téléobjectif *m*

telesales [ˈtelɪseɪlz] télévente *f*

telescope [ˈtelɪskoʊp] télescope *m*

televise [ˈtelɪvaɪz] téléviser

television [ˈtelɪvɪʒn] *also set* télévision *f*; **on ~** à la télévision; **television program**, *Br* **television programme** émission *f* télévisée; **television studio** studio *m* de télévision

tell [tel] **1** *v/t story* raconter; *lie* dire; **I can't ~ the difference** je n'arrive pas à faire la différence; **~ s.o. sth** dire qch à qn; **~ s.o. to do sth** dire à qn de faire qch **2** *v/i* (*have effect*) se faire sentir; **teller** *in bank* guichetier(-ière) *m(f)*; **telling off**: **get a ~** se faire remonter les bretelles; **telltale 1** *adj signs* révélateur **2** *n* rapporteur(-euse) *m(f)*

temp [temp] **1** *n* *employee* intérimaire *m/f* **2** *v/i* faire de l'intérim

temper [ˈtempər] (*bad ~*) mauvaise humeur *f*; **lose one's ~** se mettre en colère

temperament [ˈtemprəmənt] tempérament *m*; **temperamental** (*moody*) capricieux

temperate [ˈtempərət] tempéré

temperature [ˈtemprətʃər] température *f*

temple¹ [ˈtempl] REL temple *m*

temple² [ˈtempl] ANAT tempe *f*

tempo [ˈtempoʊ] MUS tempo *m*

temporarily [tempəˈrerɪlɪ] temporairement *f*; **temporary** temporaire

tempt [tempt] tenter; **temptation** tentation *f*; **tempting** tentant

ten [ten] dix

tenacious [tɪˈneɪʃəs] tenace; **tenacity** ténacité *f*

tenant [ˈtenənt] locataire *m/f*

tend¹ [tend] *v/t lawn* entretenir; *sheep* garder; *the sick* soigner

tend² [tend] *v/i*: **~ to do sth** avoir tendance à faire qch

tendency [ˈtendənsɪ] tendance *f*

tender¹ [ˈtendər] *adj* (*sore*) sensible; (*affectionate*), *steak* tendre

tender² ['tendər] *n* COM offre *f*

tenderness ['tendənɪs] *of kiss etc* tendresse *f*; *of steak* tendreté *f*

tendon ['tendən] tendon *m*

tennis ['tenɪs] tennis *m*; **tennis ball** balle *f* de tennis; **tennis court** court *m* de tennis; **tennis player** joueur(-euse) *m(f)* de tennis

tenor ['tenər] MUS ténor *m*

tense¹ [tens] *n* GRAM temps *m*

tense² [tens] *adj* tendu

tension ['tenʃn] tension *f*

tent [tent] tente *f*

tentative ['tentətɪv] *smile, steps* hésitant; *conclusion, offer* provisoire

tenth [tenθ] dixième

tepid ['tepɪd] *also fig* tiède

term [tɜːrm] *(period, word)* terme *m*; *Br* EDU trimestre *m*; *(condition)* condition *f*; **be on good/bad ~s with s.o.** être en bons/mauvais termes avec qn; **in the long/short ~** à long/court terme

terminal ['tɜːrmɪnl] **1** *n at airport* aérogare *m*; *for buses* terminus *m*; *for containers,* COMPUT terminal *m*; ELEC borne *f* **2** *adj illness* incurable; **terminally: ~ ill** in phase terminale; **terminate 1** *v/t* mettre fin à; *pregnancy* interrompre **2** *v/i* se terminer; **termination** *of contract* résiliation *f*; *in pregnancy* interrup-

tion *f* volontaire de grossesse

terminus ['tɜːrmɪnəs] terminus *m*

terrace ['terəs] terrasse *f*

terrain [te'reɪn] terrain *m*

terrible ['terəbl] horrible, affreux; **terribly** *(very)* très

terrific [tə'rɪfɪk] génial; **terrifically** *(very)* extrêmement, vachement *F*

terrify ['terɪfaɪ] terrifier; **terrifying** terrifiant

territorial [terə'tɔːrɪəl] territorial; **territory** territoire *m*; *fig* domaine *m*

terror ['terər] terreur *f*; **terrorism** terrorisme *m*; **terrorist** terroriste *m/f*; **terrorist attack** attentat *m* terroriste; **terrorize** terroriser

terse [tɜːrs] laconique

test [test] **1** *n scientific, technical* test *m*; *academic, for driving* examen *m* **2** *v/t* tester, mettre à l'épreuve; **test-drive** *car* essayer

testicle ['testɪkl] testicule *m*

testify ['testɪfaɪ] LAW témoigner

testimony ['testɪmənɪ] témoignage *m*

testy ['testɪ] irritable

tetanus ['tetənəs] tétanos *m*

text [tekst] **1** *n* texte *m*; *message* texto *m* **2** *v/t* envoyer un texto à; **textbook** manuel *m*; **text-message** texto *m*, SMS *m*

textile ['tekstaɪl] textile *m*

texture ['tekstʃər] texture *f*

than [ðæn] que; *with numbers* de; *faster ~ me* plus rapide que moi

thank [θæŋk] remercier; *~ you* merci; *no ~ you* (non) merci; **thankful** reconnaissant; **thankfully** (*luckily*) heureusement; **thankless** *task* ingrat; **thanks** remerciements *mpl*; *~!* merci!; *~ to* grâce à; **Thanksgiving** (Day) jour *m* de l'action de grâces, Thanksgiving *m*

that [ðæt] **1** *adj* ce, cette; *masculine before vowel* cet; *~ one* celui-là, celle-là **2** *pron* cela, ça; *give me ~* donne-moi ça; *~'s tea* c'est du thé; *what is ~?* qu'est-ce que c'est que ça?; *who is ~?* qui est-ce? **3** *rel pron* que; *the car ~ you see* la voiture que vous voyez **4** *adv* (*so*) aussi; *~ expensive* aussi cher **5** *conj* que; *I think ~ ...* je pense que ...

thaw [θɔ:] *of snow* fondre; *of frozen food* se décongeler

the [ðə] le, la; *pl* les; *to the station/theater* à la gare/au théâtre; *~ more I try* plus j'essaie

theater, *Br* **theatre** ['θɪətər] théâtre *m*; **theatrical** *also fig* théâtral

theft [θeft] vol *m*

their [ðer] leur; *pl* leurs; (*his or her*) son, sa; *pl* ses; **theirs** le leur, les leurs; *it's ~* c'est à eux/elles

them [ðem] *object* les; *indirect object* leur; *with prep* eux, elles; *I know ~* je les connais; *I gave ~ a dollar* je leur ai donné un dollar; *this is for ~* c'est pour eux/elles; *who? – ~* qui? – eux/elles

theme [θi:m] thème *m*; **theme park** parc *m* à thème

themselves [ðem'selvz] eux-mêmes, elles-mêmes; *reflexive* se; *after prep* eux, elles; *they gave ~ a holiday* ils se sont offerts des vacances

then (*at that time*) à l'époque; (*after that*) ensuite; *deducing* alors; *by ~* alors

theoretical [θɪə'retɪkl] théorique; **theoretically** en théorie; **theory** théorie *f*

therapeutic [θerə'pju:tɪk] thérapeutique; **therapist** thérapeute *m/f*; **therapy** thérapie *f*

there [ðer] là; *over ~/down ~* là-bas; *~ is/are ...* il y a ...; *is/are ~ ...?* est-ce qu'il y a...?, y a-t-il ...?; *~ is/are not ...* il n'y a pas ...; *~ you are* voilà; *~ and back* aller et retour; *~ he is!* le voilà!; *~, ~!* allons, allons; *we went ~ yesterday* nous y sommes allés hier; *thereabouts $500 or ~* environ 500 $; **therefore** donc

thermometer [θər'mɑ:mɪtər] thermomètre *m*

thermos flask ['θɜ:rməs-flæsk] thermos *m*

these [ðiːz] **1** *adj* ces **2** *pron* ceux-ci, celles-ci

thesis ['θiːsɪs] thèse *f*

they [ðeɪ] ils, elles; (*he or she*) il; **there ~ are** les voilà; **~ say that** ... on dit que ...

thick [θɪk] épais; F (*stupid*) lourd; **it's 3 cm ~** ça fait 3 cm d'épaisseur; **thicken** *sauce* épaissir; **thick-skinned** *fig* qui a la peau dure

thief [θiːf] voleur(-euse) *m(f)*

thigh [θaɪ] cuisse *f*

thin [θɪn] *material* léger, mince; *layer* mince; *person* maigre; *line* fin; *soup* liquide

thing [θɪŋ] chose *f*; **~s** (*belongings*) affaires *fpl*

think [θɪŋk] penser; **I ~ so** je pense que oui; **I don't ~ so** je ne pense pas; **I'll ~ about it** *offer* je vais y réfléchir
◆ **think over** réfléchir à
◆ **think through** bien examiner
◆ **think up** *plan* concevoir

'think tank comité *m* d'experts

thin-skinned ['θɪnskɪnd] *fig* susceptible

third [θɜːd] **1** *adj* troisième **2** *n* troisième *m/f*; **thirdly** troisièmement; **third-party** tiers *m*; **third-party insurance** *Br* assurance *f* au tiers; **Third World Tiers-Monde** *m*

thirst [θɜːst] soif *f*; **thirsty** assoiffé; **be ~** avoir soif

thirteen [θɜːˈtiːn] treize; **thir-**teenth treizième; **thirtieth** trentième; **thirty** trente

this [ðɪs] **1** *adj* ce, cette; *masculine before vowel* cet; **~ one** celui-ci, celle-ci **2** *pron* cela, ça; **~ is good** c'est bien; **~ is** ... c'est ...; *introducing s.o.* je vous présente ... **3** *adv*: **~ high** haut comme ça

thorn [θɔːrn] épine *f*; **thorny** *also fig* épineux

thorough ['θɜːrəʊ] *search, knowledge* approfondi; *person* méticuleux; **thoroughbred** *horse* pur-sang *m*; **thoroughly** complètement; *clean, search for, know* à fond

those [ðəʊz] **1** *adj* ces **2** *pron* ceux-là, celles-là

though [ðəʊ] **1** *conj* (*although*) bien que (+*subj*), quoique (+*subj*); **as ~** comme si **2** *adv* pourtant

thought [θɔːt] pensée *f*; **thoughtful** pensif; *book* profond; (*considerate*) attentionné; **thoughtless** inconsidéré

thousand ['θaʊznd] mille *m*; **~s of** des milliers *mpl* de; **thousandth 1** *adj* millième **2** *n* millième *m/f*

thrash [θræʃ] rouer de coups; *SP* battre à plates coutures
◆ **thrash out** *solution* parvenir à

thrashing volée *f* de coups; **get a ~** *SP* se faire battre à plates coutures

tick

thread [θred] **1** *n* fil *m*; *of screw* filetage *m* **2** *v/t needle, beads* enfiler; **threadbare** usé jusqu'à la corde

threat [θret] menace *f*; **threaten** menacer; **threatening** menaçant

three [θriː] trois; **three-quarters** les trois-quarts *mpl*

threshold ['θreʃhoʊld] *of house, new era* seuil *m*

thrifty ['θrıftı] économe

thrill [θrıl] **1** *n* frisson *m* **2** *v/t*: **be ~ed** être ravi; **thriller** thriller *m*; **thrilling** palpitant

thrive [θraıv] *of plants* bien pousser; *of business* prospérer

throat [θroʊt] gorge *f*; **throat lozenge** pastille *f* pour la gorge

throb [θrɑːb] **1** *n of heart* pulsation *f*; *of music* vibration *f* **2** *v/i of heart* battre fort; *of music* vibrer

throne [θroʊn] trône *m*

throttle ['θrɑːtl] **1** *n on motorbike, boat* papillon *m* des gaz **2** *v/t (strangle)* étrangler

through [θruː] **1** *prep* ◇ *(across)* à travers; **go ~ the city** traverser la ville ◇ *(during)* pendant; **all the night** toute la nuit; **Monday ~ Friday** du lundi au vendredi (inclus) ◇ *(by means of)* par: **wet ~** mouillé jusqu'aux os **3** *adj*: **be ~** *(have arrived: of news etc)* être parvenu; **we're**

~ of couple c'est fini entre nous; **be ~ with s.o./sth** en avoir fini avec qn/qch; **throughout 1** *prep* tout au long de, pendant tout(e) **2** *adv (in all parts)* partout

throw [θroʊ] **1** *v/t* jeter, lancer; *of horse* désarçonner; *(disconcert)* déconcerter; *party* organiser **2** *n* jet *m*; **it's your ~** c'est à toi de lancer

◆ **throw away** jeter

◆ **throw out** *old things* jeter; *from bar, home* jeter dehors, mettre à la porte; *from country* expulser; *plan* rejeter

◆ **throw up 1** *v/t ball* jeter en l'air **2** *v/i (vomit)* vomir

throw-away ['θroʊəweı] *(disposable)* jetable; *remark* en l'air; **throw-in** SP remise *f* en jeu

thru [θruː] → **through**

thrust [θrʌst] *(push hard)* enfoncer

thud [θʌd] bruit *m* sourd

thug [θʌg] brute *f*

thumb [θʌm] **1** *n* pouce *m* **2** *v/t*: **~ a ride** faire de l'auto-stop; **thumbtack** punaise *f*

thunder ['θʌndər] tonnerre *m*; **thunderous** *applause* tonitruant; **thunderstorm** orage *m*; **thunderstruck** abasourdi; **thundery** *weather* orageux

Thursday ['θɜːrzdeı] jeudi *m*

thus [ðʌs] ainsi

thwart [θwɔːrt] contrarier

tick [tık] **1** *n of clock* tic-tac *m*;

Br (*checkmark*) coche *f* **2** *v/i* faire tic-tac

ticket ['tɪkɪt] *for bus, museum* ticket *m; for train, airplane, theater, concert, lottery* billet *m; for speeding, illegal parking* P.V. *m;* **ticket machine** distributeur *m* de billets; **ticket office** billetterie *f*

ticking ['tɪkɪŋ] *noise* tic-tac *m*

tickle ['tɪkl] chatouiller

tidal wave ['taɪdlweɪv] raz-de-marée *m*

tide [taɪd] marée *f*

tidiness ['taɪdɪnɪs] ordre *m;*

tidy *person, habits* ordonné; *room, house, desk* en ordre

◆ **tidy up 1** *v/t room, shelves* ranger; **tidy o.s. up** remettre de l'ordre dans sa tenue **2** *v/i* ranger

tie [taɪ] **1** *n* (*necktie*) cravate *f;* SP (*even result*) match *m* à égalité; **he doesn't have any ~s** il n'a aucune attache **2** *v/t laces* nouer; *knot* faire; **hands** lier **3** *v/i* SP *of teams* faire match nul; *of runner* finir *ex æquo*

◆ **tie down** attacher; *fig* (*restrict*) restreindre

◆ **tie up** *hair* attacher; *person* ligoter; *boat* amarrer

tier [tɪr] *of hierarchy* niveau *m; of seats* gradin *m*

tight [taɪt] **1** *adj clothes, knot, screw* serré; *shoes* trop petit; (*properly shut*) bien fermé; *not leaving much time* juste; *security* strict; F (*drunk*)

bourré **2** *adv hold* fort; *shut* bien; *tighten control, security* renforcer; *screw* serrer; (*make tighter*) resserrer

tight-fisted radin; **tightly** *adv* → **tight** *adv;* **tightrope** corde *f* raide; **tights** *Br* collant *m*

tile [taɪl] *on floor, wall* carreau *m; on roof* tuile *f*

till¹ [tɪl] → **until**

till² [tɪl] (*cash register*) caisse *f*

tilt [tɪlt] pencher

timber ['tɪmbər] bois *m*

time [taɪm] **1** *n* temps *m;* (*occasion*) fois *f;* **have a good ~** bien s'amuser; **what's the ~?** quelle heure est-il?; **the first ~** la première fois; **all the ~** pendant tout ce temps; **at the same ~** *speak, reply etc,* (*however*) en même temps; **in ~** à temps; **on ~** à l'heure **2** *v/t* chronométrer; **time bomb** bombe *f* à retardement; **time difference** décalage *m* horaire; **time-lag** laps *m* de temps; **time limit** limite *f* dans le temps; **timely** opportun; **time out** SP temps *m* mort; **timer** *device* minuteur *m;* **timesaving** économie *f* de temps; **timescale** *of project* durée *f;* **time switch** minuterie *f;* **time zone** fuseau *m* horaire

timid ['tɪmɪd] timide

tin [tɪn] *metal* étain *m;* **tinfoil** papier *m* aluminium

tinge [tɪndʒ] soupçon *m*

tingle ['tɪŋgl] picoter

tinkle ['tɪŋkl] *of bell* tintement *m*

tinsel ['tɪnsl] guirlandes *fpl* de Noël

tint [tɪnt] **1** *n of color* teinte *f*; *for hair* couleur *f* **2** *v/t*: **~ one's hair** se faire une coloration; **tinted** *glasses* teinté; *paper* de couleur pastel

tiny ['taɪnɪ] minuscule

tip¹ [tɪp] *n (end)* bout *m*

tip² [tɪp] **1** *n* advice conseil *m*; *money* pourboire *m* **2** *v/t waiter etc* donner un pourboire à

◆ **tip off** informer

'tip-off renseignement *m*, tuyau *m* F

tipped [tɪpt] *cigarettes* à bout filtre

tippy-toe ['tɪpɪtoʊ]: **on ~** sur la pointe des pieds

tipsy ['tɪpsɪ] éméché

tire¹ ['taɪr] *n* pneu *m*

tire² ['taɪr] **1** *v/t* fatiguer **2** *v/i* se fatiguer

tired ['taɪrd] fatigué; **tiredness** fatigue *f*; **tireless** *efforts* infatigable; **tiresome** *(annoying)* fatigant; **tiring** fatigant

tissue ['tɪʃuː] ANAT tissu *m*; *handkerchief* mouchoir *m* en papier; **tissue paper** papier *m* de soie

title ['taɪtl] *of novel, person etc* titre *m*; LAW titre *m* de propriété (**to** de); **titleholder** SP tenant(e) *m(f)* du titre

to [tuː] **1** *prep* à; **~ Japan** au Japon; **~ Chicago** à Chicago; **~ my place** chez moi; **~ the north of** au nord de; **give sth ~** donner qch à qn **2** *with verbs*: **~ speak**, **~ shout** parler, crier; **learn ~ drive** apprendre à conduire; **too heavy ~ carry** trop lourd à porter **3** *adv*: **~ and fro** walk, pace de long en large

toast [toʊst] **1** *n for eating* pain *m* grillé; *when drinking* toast *m*; **propose a ~ to s.o.** porter un toast à qn **2** *v/t when drinking* porter un toast à

toaster grille-pain *m inv*

tobacco [tə'bækoʊ] tabac *m*

today [tə'deɪ] aujourd'hui

toddler ['tɑːdlər] jeune enfant *m*

to-do [tə'duː] F remue-ménage *m*

toe [toʊ] orteil *m*; *of sock, shoe* bout *m*; **toenail** ongle *m* de pied

together [tə'geðər] ensemble; *(at the same time)* en même temps

toilet ['tɔɪlɪt] toilettes *fpl*; **toilet paper** papier *m* hygiénique; **toiletries** articles *mpl* de toilette

token ['toʊkən] *sign* témoignage *m*; Br *(gift ~)* bon *m* d'achat; *instead of coin* jeton *m*

tolerable ['tɑːlərəbl] *pain etc* tolérable; *(quite good)* acceptable; **tolerance** tolérance *f*; **tolerant** tolérant *m*; **tolerate** tolérer

toll¹ [toul] *v/i* of bell sonner

toll² [toul] *n (deaths)* bilan *m*

toll³ [toul] *n* for bridge, road péage *m*

'toll booth poste *m* de péage; **toll-free** TELEC gratuit; **~ number** numéro *m* vert

tomato [tə'meɪtou] tomate *f*; **tomato ketchup** ketchup *m*

tomb [tu:m] tombe *f*; **tombstone** pierre *f* tombale

tomcat ['tɑ:mkæt] matou *m*

tomorrow [tə'mɔːrou] demain; *the day after ~* après-demain; *~ morning* demain matin

ton [tʌn] tonne *f* courte (=907 kg)

tone [toun] *of color, conversation* ton *m*; *of musical instrument* timbre *m*; *of neighborhood* classe *f*; *~ of voice* ton *m*; **toner** toner *m*

tongue [tʌŋ] langue *f*

tonic ['tɑ:nɪk] MED fortifiant *m*; **tonic (water)** Schweppes® *m*, tonic *m*

tonight [tə'naɪt] ce soir; *sleep* cette nuit

too [tu:] *(also)* aussi; *(excessively)* trop; *me ~* moi aussi; *~ much rice* trop de riz

tool [tu:l] outil *m*

tooth [tu:θ] dent *f*; **toothache** mal *m* de dents; **toothbrush** brosse *f* à dents; **toothpaste** dentifrice *m*; **toothpick** cure-dents *m*

top [tɑ:p] *n* also *clothing* haut *m*; *(lid: of bottle etc)* bouchon *m*; *of pen* capuchon *m*; *of the class, league* premier(-ère) *m(f)*; MOT: *gear* quatrième *f*/cinquième *f*; *on ~ of* sur; *be at the ~ of* en haut de; *be at the ~ of league* être premier du haut; *get to the ~ of company, mountain etc* arriver au sommet **2** *adj branches* du haut; *floor* dernier; *player etc* meilleur; *speed* maximum; *note* au plus élevé; *~ official* haut fonctionnaire *m*

topic ['tɑ:pɪk] sujet *m*; **topical** d'actualité

topless ['tɑ:plɪs] aux seins nus; **topmost** *branch* le plus haut; *floor* dernier; **topping** *on pizza* garniture *f*

topple ['tɑ:pl] **1** *v/i* s'écrouler **2** *v/t government* renverser

top 'secret top secret *inv*

topsy-turvy [tɑ:psɪ'tɜːrvɪ] sens dessus dessous

torment 1 ['tɔːrment] *n* tourment *m* **2** [tɔːr'ment] *v/t person, animal* harceler

tornado [tɔːr'neɪdou] tornade *f*

torpedo [tɔːr'pi:dou] **1** *n* torpille *f* **2** *v/t* also *fig* torpiller

torrent ['tɑːrənt] also *fig* torrent *m*

torture ['tɔːrtʃər] **1** *n* torture *f* **2** *v/t* torturer

toss [tɑːs] **1** *v/t ball* lancer;

rider désarçonner; *salad re-*
muer

total ['toutl] **1** *adj* total; *disaster* complet; *idiot* fini; **he's a ~ stranger** c'est un parfait inconnu **2** *n* total *m*; **totalitarian** totalitaire; **totally** totalement

totter ['tɑːtər] tituber

touch [tʌʃ] **1** *n sense* toucher *m*; **lose ~ with s.o.** perdre contact avec qn; **in ~** SP en touche **2** *v/t also emotionally* toucher; *exhibits etc* toucher à **3** *v/i of two things* se toucher

◆ **touch down** *of airplane* atterrir; SP faire un touché-en-but

'**touchdown** *of airplane* atterrissage *m*; SP touché-en-but; **touching** touchant; **touchline** SP ligne *f* de touche; **touch screen** écran *m* tactile; **touchy** personne susceptible

tough [tʌf] *person, material* résistant; *meat, question, exam, punishment* dur

tour [tʊr] **1** *n* visite *f*; *as part of package* circuit *m* (**of** dans); *of band etc* tournée *f* **2** *v/t area* visiter **3** *v/i of tourist* faire du tourisme; *of band* être en tournée; **tour guide** accompagnateur(-trice) *m(f)*; **tourism** tourisme; **tourist** touriste *m/f*; **tourist industry** industrie *f* touristique; **tourist information office** office *m*

de tourisme

tournament ['tʊrnəmənt] tournoi *m*

'**tour operator** tour-opérateur *m*, voyagiste *m*

tow [toʊ] remorquer

◆ **tow away** *car* emmener à la fourrière

toward [tɔːrd] vers; *with attitude, feelings etc* envers

towel ['taʊəl] serviette *f*

tower ['taʊər] tour *f*

town [taʊn] ville *f*; **town center**, *Br* **town centre** centre-ville *m*; **town council** conseil *m* municipal; **town hall** hôtel *m* de ville

toxic ['tɑːksɪk] toxique; **toxin** toxine *f*

toy [tɔɪ] jouet *m*

◆ **trace** [treɪs] **1** *n of substance* trace *f* **2** *v/t (find)* retrouver; *draw* tracer

track [træk] *path, (racecourse)* piste *f*; *motor racing* circuit *m*; *on record, CD* morceau *m*; RAIL voie *f* (ferrée); **~ 10** RAIL voie 10; **keep ~ of sth** suivre qch

◆ **track down** *person* retrouver; *criminal* dépister; *object* dénicher

tracksuit *Br* survêtement *m*

tractor ['træktər] tracteur *m*

trade [treɪd] **1** *n* commerce *m*; *(profession, craft)* métier *m* **2** *v/i (do business)* faire du commerce **3** *v/t (exchange)* échanger (**for** contre); **trade fair** foire *f* commerciale;

trademark marque *f* de commerce; **trade mission** mission *f* commerciale; **trader** commerçant(e) *m(f)*

tradition [trə'dɪʃn] tradition *f*; **traditional** traditionnel; **traditionally** traditionnellement

traffic ['træfɪk] circulation *f*; *at airport*, *in drugs* trafic *m*
◆ **traffic in** *drugs* faire du trafic de

'**traffic circle** rond-point *m*; **traffic cop** F agent *m* de la circulation; **traffic jam** embouteillage *m*; **traffic light** feux *mpl* de signalisation; **traffic sign** panneau *m* de signalisation

tragedy ['trædʒədɪ] tragédie *f*; **tragic** tragique

trail [treɪl] **1** *n* (*path*) sentier *m*; *of blood* traînée *f* **2** *v/t* (*follow*) suivre à la trace; (*tow*) remorquer **3** *v/i* (*lag behind*) traîner; **trailer** *pulled by vehicle* remorque *f*; (*mobile home*) caravane *f*; *of movie* bande-annonce *f*

train[1] [treɪn] *n* train *m*

train[2] [treɪn] **1** *v/t* entraîner; *dog* dresser; *employee* former **2** *v/i* *of team*, *athlete* s'entraîner; *of teacher etc* faire sa formation

trainee stagiaire *m/f*; **trainer** SP entraîneur(-euse) *m(f)*; *of dog* dresseur(-euse) *m(f)*; **~s** *Br*: *shoes* tennis *mpl*; **training** *of new staff* for-

mation *f*; SP entraînement *m*

'**train station** gare *f*

traitor ['treɪtər] traître *m*, traîtresse *f*

◆ **trample on** piétiner

trampoline ['træmpəliːn] trampoline *m*

tranquil ['træŋkwɪl] tranquille; **tranquility**, *Br* **tranquillity** tranquillité *f*; **tranquilizer**, *Br* **tranquillizer** tranquillisant *m*

transaction [træn'zækʃn] *of business* conduite *f*; *piece of business* transaction *f*

transatlantic [trænzət'læntɪk] transatlantique

transcript ['trænskrɪpt] transcription *f*

transfer 1 [træns'fɜːr] *v/t* transférer **2** [træns'fɜːr] *v/i* *when traveling* changer; *in job* être muté (*to* à) **3** ['trænsfɜːr] *n* transfert *m*; **transferable** *ticket* transférable; **transfer fee** *for sportsman* prix *m* de transfert

transform [træns'fɔːrm] transformer; **transformation** transformation *f*; **transformer** ELEC transformateur *m*

transfusion [træns'fjuːʒn] transfusion *f*

transit ['trænzɪt] **in ~** en transit; **transition** transition *f*; **transitional** de transition; **transit lounge** *at airport* salle *f* de transit; **transit pas-**

senger passager(-ère) *m(f)* en transit

translate [træns'leɪt] traduire; **translation** traduction *f*; **translator** traducteur(-trice) *m(f)*

transmission [trænz'mɪʃn] TV, AUT transmission *f*; transmit *news, program* diffuser; *disease* transmettre; transmitter RAD, TV émetteur *m*

transparency [træns'pærənsɪ] PHOT diapositive *f*; **transparent** transparent; (*obvious*) évident

transplant MED **1** ['trænsplænt] transplantation *n f*; *organ transplanted* transplant *m* **2** [træns'plænt] *v/t* transplanter

transport 1 ['trænspɔːrt] *n* transport *m* **2** [træn'spɔːrt] *v/t* transporter; **transportation** *of goods, people* transport *m*

transvestite [træns'vestaɪt] travesti *m*

trap [træp] **1** *n also fig* piège *m* **2** *v/t also fig* piéger; **trappings** *of power* signes extérieurs *mpl*

trash [træʃ] (*garbage*) ordures *fpl*; F *goods etc* camelote *f* F; *fig: person* vermine *f*; **trash can** poubelle *f*; **trashy** *goods* de pacotille; *novel* de bas étage

traumatic [trɔː'mætɪk] traumatisant; **traumatize** traumatiser

travel ['trævl] **1** *n* voyages *mpl* **2** *v/i* voyager **3** *v/t* miles parcourir; **travel agency** agence *f* de voyages; **travel agent** agent *m* de voyages; **traveler,** *Br* **traveller** voyageur(-euse) *m(f)*; **traveler's check,** *Br* **traveller's cheque** chèque-voyage *m*; **travel expenses** frais *mpl* de déplacement; **travel insurance** assurance-voyage *f*

trawler ['trɔːlər] chalutier *m*

tray [treɪ] *for food, photocopier* plateau *m*; *to go in oven* plaque *f*

treacherous ['tretʃərəs] traître; **treachery** traîtrise *f*

tread [tred] **1** *n* pas *m*; *of staircase* dessus *m* des marches; *of tire* bande *f* de roulement **2** *v/i* marcher

treason ['triːzn] trahison *f*

treasure ['treʒər] **1** *n* trésor *m* **2** *v/t gift etc* chérir; **treasurer** trésorier(-ière) *m(f)*; **Treasury Department** ministère *m* des Finances

treat [triːt] **1** *n* plaisir *m*; **it's my ~** (*I'm paying*) c'est moi qui paie **2** *v/t* traiter; **~ s.o. to sth** offrir qch à qn; **treatment** traitement *m*

treaty ['triːtɪ] traité *m*

treble ['trebl] **1** *adv*: **~ the price** le triple du prix **2** *v/i* tripler

tree [triː] arbre *m*

tremble ['trembl] trembler

tremendous [trɪ'mendəs]

(*very good*) formidable; (*enormous*) énorme; **tremendously** (*very*) extrêmement; (*a lot*) énormément

tremor ['tremər] *of earth* secousse *f* (sismique)

trench [trentʃ] tranchée *f*

trend [trend] tendance *f*; (*fashion*) mode *f*; **trendy** branché

trespass ['trespæs] entrer sans autorisation; **no ~ing** défense d'entrer; **trespasser** personne qui viole la propriété d'une autre

trial ['traɪəl] LAW procès *m*; *of equipment* essai *m*; **be on ~** LAW passer en justice

triangle ['traɪæŋgl] triangle *m*; **triangular** triangulaire

tribe [traɪb] tribu *f*

tribunal [traɪ'bju:nl] tribunal *m*

tributary ['trɪbjətərɪ] *of river* affluent *m*

trick [trɪk] **1** *n to deceive* tour *m*; (*knack*) truc *m* **2** *v/t* rouler; **trickery** tromperie *f*

trickle ['trɪkl] **1** *n* filet *m*; *fig* tout petit peu *m* **2** *v/i* couler goutte à goutte

tricky ['trɪkɪ] (*difficult*) délicat

trifling ['traɪflɪŋ] insignifiant

trigger ['trɪgər] *on gun* détente *f*

◆ **trigger off** déclencher

trim [trɪm] **1** *adj* (*neat*) bien entretenu; *figure* svelte **2** *v/t* *hair* couper un peu; *hedge* tailler; *costs* réduire; (*deco-*

rate: *dress*) garnir **3** *n* cut taille *f*

trinket ['trɪŋkɪt] babiole *f*

trip [trɪp] **1** *n* (*journey*) voyage *m*; (*outing*) excursion *f* **2** *v/i* (*stumble*) trébucher **3** *v/t* (*make fall*) faire un croche-pied à

◆ **trip up 1** *v/t* (*make fall*) faire un croche-pied à; (*cause to go wrong*) faire trébucher **2** *v/i* (*stumble*) trébucher; (*make a mistake*) faire une erreur

triple ['trɪpl] → **treble**

trite [traɪt] banal

triumph ['traɪʌmf] triomphe *m*

trivial ['trɪvɪəl] insignifiant; **triviality** banalité *f*

trolley ['trɒlɪ] (*streetcar*) tramway *m*

troops [tru:ps] troupes *fpl*

trophy ['trəʊfɪ] trophée *m*

tropic ['trɒpɪk] GEOG tropique *m*; **tropical** tropical; **tropics** tropiques *mpl*

trot [trɒt] trotter

trouble ['trʌbl] **1** *n* (*difficulties*) problèmes *mpl*; (*inconvenience*) dérangement *m*; (*disturbance*) affrontements *mpl*; **get into ~** s'attirer des ennuis **2** *v/t* (*worry*) inquiéter; (*bother*, *disturb*) déranger; *of back*, *liver etc* faire souffrir; **troublemaker** fauteur(-trice) *m(f)* de troubles; **troubleshooting** dépannage *m*; **troublesome** pénible

turn

trousers ['traʊzərz] *Br* pantalon *m*

trout [traʊt] truite *f*

truant ['truːənt]: **play ~** faire l'école buissonnière

truce [truːs] trêve *f*

truck [trʌk] camion *m*; **truck driver** camionneur(-euse) *m(f)*; **truck stop** routier *m*

trudge [trʌdʒ] **1** *v/i* se traîner **2** *n* marche *f* pénible

true [truː] vrai; *friend, American* véritable; **come ~** *of hopes, dream* se réaliser; **truly** vraiment; **Yours ~** je vous prie d'agréer mes sentiments distingués

trumpet ['trʌmpɪt] trompette *f*

trunk [trʌŋk] *of tree, body* tronc *m*; *of elephant* trompe *f*; *(large suitcase)* malle *f*; *of car* coffre *m*

trust [trʌst] **1** *n* confiance *f*; FIN fidéicommis *m* **2** *v/t* faire confiance à; **trusted** éprouvé; **trustee** fidéicommissaire *m/f*; **trustful, trusting** confiant; **trustworthy** fiable

truth [truːθ] vérité *f*; **truthful** honnête

try [traɪ] **1** *v/t & v/i* essayer; LAW juger; **~ to do sth** essayer de faire qch; **you must ~ harder** tu dois faire plus d'efforts **2** *n* rugby essai *m*; **trying** *(annoying)* éprouvant

T-shirt ['tiːʃɜːrt] tee-shirt *m*

tub [tʌb] *(bath)* baignoire *f* for liquid bac *m*; for yoghurt pot

m; **tubby** boulot

tube [tuːb] *(pipe)* tuyau *m*; *of toothpaste* tube *m*; **tubeless** *tire* sans chambre à air

Tuesday ['tuːzdeɪ] mardi *m*

tuft [tʌft] touffe *f*

tug [tʌɡ] **1** *n* NAUT remorqueur *m* **2** *v/t* tirer

tuition [tuːˈɪʃn] cours *mpl*

tumble ['tʌmbl] tomber; **tumbledown** qui tombe en ruines; **tumbler** for drink verre *m*; in circus acrobate *m/f*

tummy ['tʌmɪ] F ventre *m*; **tummy ache** mal *m* de ventre

tumor, *Br* **tumour** tumeur *f*

tumult ['tuːmʌlt] tumulte *m*; **tumultuous** tumultueux

tuna ['tuːnə] thon *m*

tune [tuːn] **1** *n* air *m* **2** *v/t* instrument accorder

◆ **tune up** *v/i of orchestra* s'accorder **2** *v/t engine* régler

tuneful ['tuːnfl] harmonieux; **tune-up** *of engine* règlement *m*

tunnel ['tʌnl] tunnel *m*

turbine ['tɜːrbaɪn] turbine *f*

turbulence ['tɜːrbjələns] in air travel turbulences *fpl*; **turbulent** agité

turf [tɜːrf] gazon *m*; piece motte *f* de gazon

turkey ['tɜːrkɪ] dinde *f*

turmoil ['tɜːrmɔɪl] confusion *f*

turn [tɜːrn] **1** *n (rotation)* tour *m*; in road virage *m*; in vaudeville numéro *m*; **take ~s doing sth** faire qch à tour

de rôle; **it's my~** c'est à moi **2**
v/t wheel tourner; **~ the cor-**
ner tourner au coin de la rue
3 *v/i of driver, car, wheel*
tourner; *of person* se retourner; **it has ~ed cold** le temps
s'est refroidi

◆ **turn around 1** *v/t object*
tourner; *company* remettre
sur pied; COM *order* traiter
2 *v/i* se retourner; *with a*
car faire demi-tour

◆ **turn away 1** *v/t (send away)*
renvoyer **2** *v/i (walk away)*
s'en aller; *(look away)* détourner le regard

◆ **turn back 1** *v/t edges, sheets*
replier **2** *v/i of walkers, in*
course of action faire demi-
tour

◆ **turn down** *offer* rejeter;
volume, heating baisser; *edge*
replier

◆ **turn off 1** *v/t TV, heater*
éteindre; *faucet* fermer; *en-*
gine arrêter **2** *v/i of car, driv-*
er tourner; *of machine*
s'éteindre

◆ **turn on 1** *v/t TV, heater* allumer; *faucet* ouvrir; *engine*
mettre en marche; F *sexually*
exciter **2** *v/i of machine* s'allumer

◆ **turn over 1** *v/i in bed* se retourner; *of vehicle* se renverser **2** *v/t (put upside down)*
renverser; *page* tourner; FIN
avoir un chiffre d'affaires de

◆ **turn up 1** *v/t collar* remonter; *volume* augmenter; *heat-*
ing monter **2** *v/i (arrive)* arriver, se pointer F

turning ['tɜːrnɪŋ] *in road* virage; **turning point** tournant
m; **turnout** *at game etc* nombre *m* de spectateurs; **turno-**
ver FIN chiffre *m* d'affaires;
turnpike autoroute *f*
payante; **turn signal** MOT clignotant *m*
turquoise ['tɜːrkwɔːz] turquoise
turtle ['tɜːrtl] tortue *f* de mer;
turtleneck sweater pull *m* à
col cheminée
tusk [tʌsk] défense *f*
tutor ['tuːtər] Br: *at university*
professeur *m/f*; **(private)** ~
professeur *m* particulier
tuxedo [tʌk'siːdou] smoking
m
TV [tiːˈviː] télé *f*; **on ~** à la télé;
TV dinner plateau-repas *m*;
TV guide guide *m* de télé;
TV program, Br **TV pro-**
gramme programme *m* télé
twang [twæŋ] **1** *n in voice* accent *m* nasillard **2** *v/t guitar*
string pincer
tweezers ['twiːzərz] pince *f* à
épiler
twelfth [twelfθ] douzième;
twelve douze
twentieth ['twentɪɪθ] vingtième; **twenty** vingt
twice [twaɪs] deux fois; **~ as**
much deux fois plus
twig [twɪg] brindille *f*
twilight ['twaɪlaɪt] crépuscule
m

twin [twɪn] jumeau *m*, jumelle *f*; **twin beds** lits *mpl* jumeaux

twinge [twɪndʒ] *of pain* élancement *m*

twinkle ['twɪŋkl] scintiller

'twin room chambre *f* à lits jumeaux

twirl [twɜːrl] **1** *v/t* faire tourbillonner; *mustache* tortiller **2** *n of cream etc* spirale *f*

twist [twɪst] **1** *v/t* tordre; **~ one's ankle** se tordre la cheville **2** *v/i of road* faire des méandres; *of river* faire des lacets **3** *n in rope* entortillement *m*; *in road* lacet *m*; *in plot* dénouement *m* inattendu; **twisty road** qui fait des lacets

twitch [twɪtʃ] *nervous* tic *m*

twitter ['twɪtər] *of birds* gazouiller

two [tuː] deux; **the ~ of them** les deux

tycoon [taɪ'kuːn] magnat *m*

type [taɪp] **1** *n (sort)* type *m* **2** *v/i (use a keyboard)* taper **3** *v/t with a typewriter* taper à la machine

typhoon [taɪ'fuːn] typhon *m*

typhus ['taɪfəs] typhus *m*

typical ['tɪpɪkl] typique; **that's ~ of you!** c'est bien de vous!; **typically** typiquement

typist ['taɪpɪst] dactylo *m/f*

tyrannical [tɪ'rænɪkl] tyrannique; **tyrannize** tyranniser; **tyranny** tyrannie *f*; **tyrant** tyran *m*

tyre *Br* → **tire¹**

U

ugly ['ʌglɪ] laid

UK [juː'keɪ] (= **United Kingdom**) R.-U. *m* (= Royaume-Uni)

ulcer ['ʌlsər] ulcère *m*

ultimate ['ʌltɪmət] *(best, definitive)* meilleur possible; *(final)* final; *(fundamental)* fondamental; **ultimately** *(in the end)* en fin de compte

ultimatum [ʌltɪ'meɪtəm] ultimatum *m*

ultrasound ['ʌltrəsaʊnd] MED ultrason *m*

ultraviolet [ʌltrə'vaɪələt] ul-

traviolet

umbrella [ʌm'brelə] parapluie *m*

umpire ['ʌmpaɪr] arbitre *m/f*

UN [juː'en] (= **United Nations**) O.N.U. *f* (= Organisation des Nations unies)

unable [ʌn'eɪbl]: **be ~ to do sth** not know how to ne pas savoir faire qch; not be in a position to ne pas pouvoir faire qch

unacceptable [ʌnək'septəbl] inacceptable

unaccountable [ʌnə-

'kauntəbl] inexplicable

un-American [ʌnə'merɪkən] (*not fitting*) antiaméricain

unanimous [ju:'nænɪməs] *verdict* unanime; **unanimously** à l'unanimité

unapproachable [ʌnə'prəʊtʃəbl] *person* d'un abord difficile

unarmed [ʌn'ɑ:rmd] *person* non armé

unassuming [ʌnə'su:mɪŋ] modeste

unattached [ʌnə'tætʃt] *without a partner* sans attaches

unattended [ʌnə'tendɪd] laissé sans surveillance

unauthorized [ʌn'ɔ:θəraɪzd] non autorisé

unavoidable [ʌnə'vɔɪdəbl] inévitable

unbalanced [ʌn'bælənst] *also* PSYCH déséquilibré

unbearable [ʌn'berəbl] insupportable

unbeatable [ʌn'bi:təbl] imbattable

unbeaten [ʌn'bi:tn] *team* invaincu

unbelievable [ʌnbɪ'li:vəbl] *also* F incroyable

unbias(s)ed [ʌn'baɪəst] impartial

unblock [ʌn'blɑ:k] *pipe* déboucher

unbreakable [ʌn'breɪkəbl] incassable

unbutton [ʌn'bʌtn] déboutonner

uncanny [ʌn'kænɪ] étrange, mystérieux

unceasing [ʌn'si:sɪŋ] incessant

uncertain [ʌn'sɜ:rtn] incertain; **uncertainty** *of the future* caractère *m* incertain; **there is still ~ about** des incertitudes demeurent quant à …

uncle [ʌŋkl] oncle *m*

uncomfortable [ʌn'kʌmftəbl] inconfortable

uncommon [ʌn'kɑ:mən] inhabituel

uncompromising [ʌn'kɑ:prəmaɪzɪŋ] intransigeant

unconditional [ʌnkən'dɪʃnl] sans conditions

unconscious [ʌn'kɑ:nʃəs] MED, PSYCH inconscient

uncontrollable [ʌnkən'trəʊləbl] incontrôlable

unconventional [ʌnkən'venʃnl] non conventionnel

uncooperative [ʌnkəʊ'ɑ:pərətɪv] peu coopératif

uncover [ʌn'kʌvər] découvrir

undamaged [ʌn'dæmɪdʒd] intact

undecided [ʌndɪ'saɪdɪd] *question* laissé en suspens; **be ~ about** être indécis à propos de

undeniable [ʌndɪ'naɪəbl] indéniable

under [ʌndər] sous; (*less than*) moins de; **it is ~ investigation** cela fait l'objet d'une enquête 'under**carriage** *train* m d'atterrissage

'under**cover** clandestin; ~ **agent** agent m secret

under'**cut** COM: ~ **the competition** vendre moins cher que la concurrence

under'**done** *meat* pas trop cuit; *pej* pas assez cuit

under'**estimate** sous-estimer

under'**fed** mal nourri

under'**go** subir

under'**graduate** *Br* étudiant(e) (de D.E.U.G. ou de licence)

'under**ground 1** *adj* souterrain; POL clandestin **2** *adv* *work* sous terre

under'**hand** (*devious*) sournois

under'**line** *text* souligner

under'**lying** sous-jacent

under'**mine** saper

under**neath** [ʌndər'niːθ] **1** *prep* sous **2** *adv* dessous

'under**pants** slip m

'under**pass** *for pedestrians* passage m souterrain

under**privileged** [ʌndər'prɪvɪlɪdʒd] défavorisé

under'**rate** sous-estimer

under**staffed** [ʌndər'stæft] en manque de personnel

under'**stand** comprendre; understandable compréhensible; understandably naturellement; understanding **1** *adj* *person* compréhensif **2** *n* compréhension *f*;

(*agreement*) accord m

under**take** *task* entreprendre; ~ **to do sth** (*agree to*) s'engager à faire qch; undertaking (*enterprise*) entreprise *f*; (*promise*) engagement m

under'**value** sous-estimer

'under**wear** sous-vêtements mpl

'under**world** *criminal* monde m du crime organisé

under'**write** FIN souscrire

undeserved [ʌndɪ'zɜːrvd] non mérité

undesirable [ʌndɪ'zaɪrəbl] indésirable

undisputed [ʌndɪ'spjuːtɪd] *champion* incontestable

undo [ʌn'duː] défaire

undoubtedly [ʌn'daʊtɪdlɪ] à n'en pas douter

undress [ʌn'dres] **1** *v/t* déshabiller; **get ~ed** se déshabiller **2** *v/i* se déshabiller

undue [ʌn'duː] excessif; unduly (*excessively*) excessivement

unearth [ʌn'ɜːrθ] *also fig* déterrer

uneasy [ʌn'iːzɪ] *relationship, peace* incertain vouloir signer cela

uneatable [ʌn'iːtəbl] immangeable

uneconomic [ʌniːkə'nɒmɪk] pas rentable

uneducated [ʌn'edʒəkeɪtɪd] sans instruction

unemployed [ʌnɪm'plɔɪd] **1** *adj* au chômage **2** *npl*: **the**

~ les chômeurs(-euses); **unemployment** chômage *m*

unequal [ʌnˈiːkwəl] inégal

unerring [ʌnˈɜːrɪŋ] *judgment,
instinct* infaillible

uneven [ʌnˈiːvn] *surface,
ground* irrégulier

uneventful [ʌnɪˈventfl] *day,
journey* sans événement

unexpected [ʌnɪkˈspektɪd]
inattendu; **unexpectedly**
inopinément

unfair [ʌnˈfer] injuste

unfaithful [ʌnˈfeɪθfl] *husband, wife* infidèle; **be ~ to
s.o.** tromper qn

unfamiliar [ʌnfəˈmɪljər] peu
familier

unfasten [ʌnˈfæsn] *belt* défaire

unfavorable [ʌnˈfeɪvərəbl]
défavorable

unfinished [ʌnˈfɪnɪʃt] inachevé

unfold [ʌnˈfoʊld] **1** *v/t letter*
déplier; *arms* ouvrir **2** *v/i of
story etc* se dérouler; *of view*
se déployer

unforeseen [ʌnfɔːrˈsiːn] imprévu

unforgettable [ʌnfərˈgetəbl]
inoubliable

unforgivable [ʌnfərˈgɪvəbl]
impardonnable

unfortunate [ʌnˈfɔːrtʃənət]
malheureux; **unfortunately**
malheureusement

unfounded [ʌnˈfaʊndɪd] non
fondé

unfriendly [ʌnˈfrendlɪ] *per-*

son, welcome, hotel froid

ungrateful [ʌnˈgreɪtfl] ingrat

unhappiness [ʌnˈhæpɪnɪs]
chagrin *m*; **unhappy**
malheureux; *customers etc*
mécontent (**with** de)

unharmed [ʌnˈhɑːrmd] indemne

unhealthy [ʌnˈhelθɪ] *person*
en mauvaise santé; *food, atmosphere* malsain; *economy*
qui se porte mal

unheard-of [ʌnˈhɜːrdəv]: **be ~**
ne s'être jamais vu

unhygienic [ʌnhaɪˈdʒiːnɪk]
insalubre

unification [juːnɪfɪˈkeɪʃn]
unification *f*

uniform [ˈjuːnɪfɔːrm] **1** *n* uniforme *m* **2** *adj* uniforme

unify [ˈjuːnɪfaɪ] unifier

unilateral [juːnɪˈlætərəl] unilatéral

unimaginable [ʌnɪˈmædʒɪ-
nəbl] inimaginable

unimaginative [ʌnɪˈmædʒɪ-
nətɪv] qui manque d'imagination

unimportant [ʌnɪmˈpɔːrtənt]
sans importance

uninhabitable [ʌnɪnˈhæbɪt-
əbl] inhabitable; **uninhabited** inhabité

unintentional [ʌnɪnˈtenʃnl]
non intentionnel; **uninten-
tionally** sans le vouloir

uninteresting [ʌnˈɪntrəstɪŋ]
inintéressant

uninterrupted [ʌnɪntəˈrʌpt-
ɪd] ininterrompu

union [' juːnjən] POL union *f*; (*labor* ~) syndicat *m*

unique [juː'niːk] unique

unit ['juːnɪt] unité *f*

unite [juː'naɪt] **1** *v/t* unir **2** *v/i* s'unir; **united** uni; *efforts* conjoint; **United Kingdom** Royaume-Uni *m*; **United Nations** Nations *fpl* Unies

United States (of A'merica) États-Unis *mpl* (d'Amérique)

unity ['juːnətɪ] unité *f*

universal [juːnɪ'vɜːrsl] universel; **universe** univers *m*

university [juːnɪ'vɜːrsətɪ] université *f*

unjust [ʌn'dʒʌst] injuste

unkind [ʌn'kaɪnd] méchant, désagréable

unknown [ʌn'noʊn] inconnu

unleaded [ʌn'ledɪd] *gas* sans plomb

unless [ən'les] à moins que (+*subj*)

unlikely [ʌn'laɪklɪ] improbable

unlimited [ʌn'lɪmɪtɪd] illimité

unload [ʌn'loʊd] décharger

unlock [ʌn'lɑːk] ouvrir

unluckily [ʌn'lʌkɪlɪ] malheureusement; **unlucky** *day* de malchance; *choice* malheureux; *person* malchanceux; *that was so* ~ *for you!* tu n'as vraiment pas eu de chance!

unmanned [ʌn'mænd] *spacecraft* sans équipage

unmarried [ʌn'mærɪd] non marié

unmistakable [ʌnmɪ'steɪkəbl] reconnaissable entre mille

unnatural [ʌn'nætʃrəl] contre-nature

unnecessary [ʌn'nesəserɪ] non nécessaire

unnerving [ʌn'nɜːrvɪŋ] déstabilisant

unobtainable [ʌnəb'teɪnəbl] *goods* qu'on ne peut se procurer; TELEC hors service

unobtrusive [ʌnəb'truːsɪv] discret

unoccupied [ʌn'ɑːkjʊpaɪd] (*empty*) vide; *position* vacant; *person* vacant

unofficial [ʌnə'fɪʃl] non officiel; **unofficially** non officiellement

unorthodox [ʌn'ɔːrθədɑːks] peu orthodoxe

unpack [ʌn'pæk] **1** *v/t case* défaire **2** *v/i* défaire sa valise

unpaid [ʌn'peɪd] *work* non rémunéré

unpleasant [ʌn'pleznt] désagréable

unplug [ʌn'plʌg] *TV, computer* débrancher

unpopular [ʌn'pɑːpjələr] impopulaire

unprecedented [ʌn'presɪdentɪd] sans précédent

unpredictable [ʌnprɪ'dɪktəbl] imprévisible

unpretentious [ʌnprɪ'tenʃəs] modeste

unproductive [ʌnprə'dʌktɪv]

meeting, discussion, land improductif

unprofessional [ʌnprə'feʃnl] non professionnel; *workmanship* peu professionnel

unprofitable [ʌn'prɒfɪtəbl] non profitable

unprovoked [ʌnprə'vʊkt] *attack* non provoqué

unqualified [ʌn'kwɒlɪfaɪd] non qualifié

unquestionably [ʌn'kwestʃnəblɪ] sans aucun doute; **unquestioning** *attitude* aveugle

unreadable [ʌn'riːdəbl] *book* illisible

unrealistic [ʌnrɪə'lɪstɪk] irréaliste

unreasonable [ʌn'riːznəbl] déraisonnable

unrelated [ʌnrɪ'leɪtɪd] sans relation (**to** avec)

unrelenting [ʌnrɪ'lentɪŋ] incessant

unreliable [ʌnrɪ'laɪəbl] pas fiable

unrest [ʌn'rest] agitation *f*

unrestrained [ʌnrɪ'streɪnd] *emotions* non contenu

unroll [ʌn'rəʊl] *carpet* dérouler

unruly [ʌn'ruːlɪ] indiscipliné

unsanitary [ʌn'sænɪterɪ] *conditions, drains* insalubre

unsatisfactory [ʌnsætɪs'fæktərɪ] insatisfaisant; (*unacceptable*) inacceptable

unscathed [ʌn'skeɪðd] (*not injured*) indemne; (*not dam-*

aged) intact

unscrew [ʌn'skruː] *sth screwed on* dévisser; *top* décapsuler

unscrupulous [ʌn'skruːpjələs] peu scrupuleux

unselfish [ʌn'selfɪʃ] désintéressé

unsettled [ʌn'setld] incertain; *lifestyle* instable; *bills* non réglé; *issue* non décidé

unshaven [ʌn'ʃeɪvn] mal rasé

unskilled [ʌn'skɪld] *worker* non qualifié

unsophisticated [ʌnsə'fɪstɪkeɪtɪd] peu sophistiqué

unstable [ʌn'steɪbl] instable

unsteady [ʌn'stedɪ] *on feet* chancelant; *ladder* branlant

unsuccessful [ʌnsək'sesfl] *attempt* infructueux; *writer* qui n'a pas de succès; *candidate, marriage* malheureux; **unsuccessfully** sans succès

unsuitable [ʌn'suːtəbl] inapproprié

unswerving [ʌn'swɜːrvɪŋ] *loyalty* inébranlable

unthinkable [ʌn'θɪŋkəbl] impensable

untidy [ʌn'taɪdɪ] en désordre

untie [ʌn'taɪ] *knot* défaire; *prisoner, hands* détacher

until [ən'tɪl] **1** *prep* jusqu'à; *from Monday ~ Friday* de lundi à vendredi; *not ~ Friday* pas avant vendredi **2** *conj* jusqu'à ce que; *can you wait ~ I'm ready?* est-ce que vous pouvez attendre que je sois prêt?

untiring [ʌnˈtaɪrɪŋ] *efforts* infatigable

untold [ʌnˈtoʊld] *riches, suffering* inouï; *story* inédit

untrue [ʌnˈtruː] faux

unused [ʌnˈjuːzd] *goods* non utilisé

unusual [ʌnˈjuːʒl] inhabituel; *(strange)* bizarre; **unusually** anormalement, exceptionnellement

unveil [ʌnˈveɪl] *statue etc* dévoiler

unwell [ʌnˈwel] malade

unwilling [ʌnˈwɪlɪŋ] **be ~ to do** refuser de faire; **unwillingly** à contre-cœur

unwind [ʌnˈwaɪnd] **1** *v/t tape* dérouler **2** *v/i of tape, story* se dérouler; *(relax)* se détendre

unwise [ʌnˈwaɪz] malavisé

unwrap [ʌnˈræp] déballer

unzip [ʌnˈzɪp] *dress etc* descendre la fermeture-éclair de; COMPUT décompresser

up [ʌp] **1** *adv*: **~ in the sky/on the roof** dans le ciel/sur le toit; **~ here** ici; **~ there** là-haut; **be ~** *(out of bed)* être debout; *of sun* être levé; *of temperature* avoir augmenté; *(have expired)* être expiré; **what's ~?** F qu'est-ce qu'il y a?; **~ to 1989** jusqu'à 1989; **he came ~ to me** il s'est approché de moi; **what are you ~ to these days?** qu'est-ce que tu fais en ce moment?; **be ~ to something (bad)** être sur un mauvais coup; **I don't feel ~ to it** je ne m'en sens pas le courage; **it's ~ to you** c'est toi qui décides; **it's ~ to them to solve it** c'est à eux de le résoudre **2** *prep*: **further ~ the mountain** un peu plus haut sur la montagne; **they ran ~ the street** ils ont remonté la rue en courant; **we traveled ~ to Paris** nous sommes montés à Paris **3** *n*: **~s and downs** hauts *mpl* et bas

'upbringing éducation *f*

up'date *file* mettre à jour

up'grade moderniser; *ticket* surclasser

upheaval [ʌpˈhiːvl] bouleversement *m*

up'hold *rights* maintenir

'upkeep maintien *m*

'upload COMPUT transférer

up'market *Br restaurant, hotel* chic; *product* haut de gamme

upon [əˈpɒn] → **on**

upper [ˈʌpər] supérieur

'upright 1 *adj citizen* droit **2** *adv sit* (bien) droit; **upright piano** piano *f* droit

'uprising soulèvement *m*

'uproar vacarme *m*; *fig* protestations *fpl*

up'set 1 *v/t* renverser; *emotionally* contrarier **2** *adj emotionally* contrarié, vexé; **upsetting** contrariant

upside 'down à l'envers; *car* renversé

up'stairs 1 adv en haut; ~ **from us** au-dessus de chez nous **2** adj room d'en haut

up'stream en remontant le courant

up'tight F (nervous) tendu; (inhibited) coincé

up-to-'date à jour

'upturn in economy reprise f

upward ['ʌpwəd]: **move sth** ~ élever qch; ~ **of 100** au-delà de 100

uranium [jʊ'reɪnɪəm] uranium m

urban ['ɜːrbən] urbain

urge [ɜːrdʒ] **1** n (forte) envie f **2** v/t: ~ **s.o. to do sth** encourager qn à faire qch; **urgency** urgence f; **urgent** urgent

urinate ['jʊrəneɪt] uriner; **urine** urine f

US [juː'es] (= **United States**) USA mpl

us [ʌs] nous

USA [juːes'eɪ] (= **United States of America**) USA mpl

usage ['juːdʒ] usage m

use 1 [juːz] v/t also pej: person utiliser **2** [juːs] n utilisation f; **it's no** ~ **waiting** ce n'est pas la peine d'attendre

◆ **use up** épuiser

used¹ [juːzd] car etc d'occasion

used² [juːst]: **be** ~ **to** être habitué à; **get** ~ **to** s'habituer à

used³ [juːst]: **I** ~ **to work there** je travaillais là-bas avant; **I** ~ **to know him well** je l'ai bien connu autrefois

useful ['juːsfʊl] utile; **usefulness** utilité f; **useless** inutile; F (no good) nul F; **user** of product utilisateur(-trice) m(f); **user-friendly** facile à utiliser; COMPUT convivial

usual ['juːʒl] habituel; **as** ~ comme d'habitude; **usually** d'habitude

utensil [juː'tensl] ustensile m

utilize ['juːtɪlaɪz] utiliser

utter ['ʌtər] **1** adj total **2** v/t sound prononcer; **utterly** totalement

V

vacant ['veɪkənt] building inoccupé; look vide, absent; Br: position vacant; **vacantly** stare d'un air absent; **vacate** room libérer

vacation [veɪ'keɪʃn] vacances fpl; **be on** ~ être en vacances

vaccinate ['væksɪneɪt] vacci-

ner; **vaccination** vaccination f; **vaccine** vaccin m

vacuum ['vækjʊəm] **1** n vide m **2** v/t floors passer l'aspirateur sur

vagrant ['veɪgrənt] vagabond m

vague [veɪg] vague; **vaguely**

vaguement

vain [veɪn] **1** *adj person* vaniteux; *hope* vain **2** *n:* **in ~** en vain

valiant ['væljənt] vaillant

valid ['vælɪd] valable; **validate** *with official stamp* valider; *theory* confirmer; **validity** validité *f;* *of argument* justesse *f;* *of claim* bien-fondé *m*

valley ['vælɪ] vallée *f*

valuable ['væljʊbl] **1** *adj* de valeur; *colleague, help, advice* précieux **2** *npl:* **~s** objets *mpl* de valeur; **valuation** estimation *f,* expertise *f;* **value 1** *n* valeur *f* **2** *v/t* tenir à, attacher un grand prix à

valve [vælv] soupape *f,* valve *f;* *in heart* valvule *f*

van [væn] *small* camionnette *f; large* fourgon *m*

vandal ['vændl] vandale *m;* **vandalism** vandalisme *m;* **vandalize** vandaliser

vanilla [və'nɪlə] **1** *n* vanille *f* **2** *adj* à la vanille

vanish ['vænɪʃ] disparaître; *of clouds, sadness* se dissiper

vanity ['vænɪtɪ] *of person* vanité *f*

vapor ['veɪpər] vapeur *f;* **vaporize** *of atomic bomb, explosion* pulvériser; **vapour** *Br* → **vapor**

variable ['ve'rɪəbl] **1** *adj* variable; *moods* changeant **2** *n* MATH, COMPUT variable *f;* **variant** variante *f;* **variation** va-

riation *f;* **varied** varié; **variety** variété *f;* **various** (*several*) divers, plusieurs; (*different*) divers, différent

varnish ['vɑːrnɪʃ] **1** *n* vernis *m* **2** *v/t* vernir

vary ['verɪ] varier; *it varies* ça dépend

vase [veɪz] vase *m*

vast [væst] vaste; *improvement* considérable; **vastly** *improve etc* considérablement; *different* complètement

Vatican ['vætɪkən]: *the ~* le Vatican

vault¹ [vɔːlt] *n in roof* voûte *f;* **~s** *of bank* salle *f* des coffres

vault² [vɔːlt] **1** *n sp* saut *m* **2** *v/t beam etc* sauter

VCR [viːsiːˈɑːr] (= *video cassette recorder*) magnétoscope *m*

veal [viːl] veau *m*

veer [vɪr] virer; *of wind* tourner

vegetable ['vedʒtəbl] légume *m;* **vegetarian 1** *n* végétarien(ne) *m(f)* **2** *adj* végétarien; **vegetation** végétation *f*

vehement ['viːəmənt] véhément

vehicle ['viːɪkl] véhicule *m*

veil [veɪl] voile *m*

vein [veɪn] ANAT veine *f*

velocity [vɪˈlɑːsətɪ] vélocité *f*

velvet ['velvɪt] velours *m*

vendetta [ven'detə] vendetta *f*

vending machine ['vendɪŋ]

distributeur *m* automatique;
vendor LAW vendeur(-euse)
m(f)

veneer [vəˈnɪr] placage *m*; *of
politeness* vernis *m*

venerable [ˈvenərəbl] vénérable; **veneration** vénération *f*

venereal disease [vəˈnɪrɪəl]
M.S.T. *f*, maladie *f* sexuellement transmissible

venetian blind [vəˈniːʃn] store *m* vénitien

venom [ˈvenəm] venin *m*

ventilate [ˈventɪleɪt] ventiler;
ventilation ventilation *f*;
ventilator ventilateur *m*;
MED respirateur *m*

venture [ˈventʃər] **1** *n* (*undertaking*) entreprise *f*; COM tentative *f* **2** *v/i* s'aventurer

venue [ˈvenjuː] *for meeting,
concert etc* lieu *m*; *hall also*
salle *f*

veranda [vəˈrændə] véranda *f*

verb [vɜːrb] verbe *m*; **verbal**
(*spoken*) oral, verbal; **verbally** oralement, verbalement

verdict [ˈvɜːrdɪkt] LAW verdict
m; (*opinion, judgment*) avis
m, jugement *m*

verge [vɜːrdʒ] *of road* accotement *m*, bas-côté *m*; **be on
the ~ of ...** être au bord de...

verification [verɪfɪˈkeɪʃn]
(*check*) vérification *f*; **verify**
(*check*) vérifier, contrôler;
(*confirm*) confirmer

vermin [ˈvɜːrmɪn] (*insects*)
vermine *f*, parasites *mpl*;
(*rats etc*) animaux *mpl* nuisi-
bles

vermouth [vərˈmuːθ] vermouth *m*

versatile [ˈvɜːrsətəl] *person*
plein de ressources, polyvalent; *piece of equipment* multiusages; **versatility** *of person* adaptabilité *f*, polyvalence *f*; *of piece of equipment*
souplesse *f*, *of song* couplet *m*

verse [vɜːrs] (*poetry*) vers
mpl, poésie *f*; *of poem* strophe *f*; *of song* couplet *m*

version [ˈvɜːrʃn] version *f*

versus [ˈvɜːrsəs] contre

vertical [ˈvɜːrtɪkl] vertical

vertigo [ˈvɜːrtɪɡoʊ] vertige *m*

very [ˈverɪ] **1** *adv* très; **was it
cold? – not ~** faisait-il froid?
– non, pas tellement; **the ~
best** le meilleur **2** *adj* même;
at that ~ moment à cet instant même, à ce moment
précis; **that's the ~ thing I
need** c'est exactement ce
dont j'ai besoin

vessel [ˈvesl] NAUT bateau *m*,
navire *m*

vest [vest] gilet *m* Br: *undershirt* maillot *m* (de corps)

vestige [ˈvestɪdʒ] vestige *m*;
fig once *f*

vet¹ [vet] *n* (*veterinarian*) vétérinaire *m/f*, véto *m/f* F

vet² [vet] *v/t applicants etc*
examiner

vet³ [vet] *n* MIL F ancien combattant *m*

veteran [ˈvetərən] **1** *n* vétéran
m **2** *adj* (*old*) antique; (*old*

557

and experienced) aguerri, chevronné

veterinarian [vetərə'neriən] vétérinaire *m/f*

veto ['viːtou] **1** *n* veto *m inv* **2** *v/t* opposer son veto à

via ['vaiə] par

viable ['vaiəbl] viable

vibrate [vai'breit] vibrer; **vibration** vibration *f*

vice¹ [vais] *n* vice *m*

vice² [vais] *Br* → **vise**

vice '**president** vice-président *m*

vice '**versa** [vais'vɜːrsə] vice versa

vicious ['viʃəs] vicieux; *dog* méchant; *person, temper* cruel; *attack* brutal; **viciously** brutalement

victim ['viktim] victime *f*; **victimize** persécuter

victorious [vik'tɔːriəs] victorieux; **victory** victoire *f*

video ['vidiou] **1** *n* vidéo *f*; *actual object* cassette *f* vidéo **2** *v/t* filmer; *tape off TV* enregistrer; **video camera** caméra *f* vidéo; **video cassette** cassette *f* vidéo; **video recorder** magnétoscope *m*; **videotape** bande *f* vidéo

vie [vai] rivaliser

Vietnam [vjet'næm] Vietnam *m*; **Vietnamese 1** *adj* vietnamien **2** *n* Vietnamien(ne) *m(f)*; *language* vietnamien *m*

view [vjuː] **1** *n* vue *f*; (*assessment, opinion*) opinion *f*, avis

m; **in** ~ **of** compte tenu de, étant donné **2** *v/t* considérer, envisager **3** *v/i* (*watch TV*) regarder la télévision; **viewer** *TV* téléspectateur(-trice) *m(f)*; **viewpoint** point *m* de vue

vigor ['vigər] vigueur *f*; **vigorous** vigoureux; **vigorously** vigoureusement; **vigour** *Br* → **vigor**

village ['vilidʒ] village *m*; **villager** villageois(e) *m(f)*

villain ['vilən] escroc *m*; *in drama* méchant *m*

vindicate ['vindikeit] (*prove correct*) confirmer, justifier; (*prove innocent*) innocenter

vindictive [vin'diktiv] vindicatif

vine [vain] vigne *f*

vinegar ['vinigər] vinaigre *m*

vineyard ['vinjərd] vignoble *m*

vintage ['vintidʒ] **1** *n of wine* millésime *m* **2** *adj* (*classic*) classique

violate ['vaiəleit] violer; **violation** violation *f*; (*traffic* ~) infraction *f* au code de la route

violence ['vaiələns] violence *f*; **violent** violent

violin [vaiə'lin] violon *m*; **violinist** violoniste *m/f*

VIP [viːaiˈpiː] (= **very important person**) V.I.P. *m*

viral ['vairəl] viral

virgin ['vɜːrdʒin] vierge *f*;

virgin

male puceau *m* F; **virginity** virginité *f*

virile ['vɪrəl] viril; **virility** virilité *f*

virtual ['vɜːrtʃʊəl] quasi-; **virtually** (*almost*) pratiquement, presque

virtue ['vɜːrtʃuː] vertu *f*; **virtuous** vertueux

virus ['vaɪrəs] virus *m*

visa ['viːzə] visa *m*

vise [vaɪz] étau *m*

visibility [vɪzə'bɪlətɪ] visibilité *f*; **visible** visible

vision ['vɪʒn] (*eyesight*) vue *f*; REL vision *f*

visit ['vɪzɪt] **1** *n* visite *f*; (*stay*) séjour *m* **2** *v/t* rendre visite à; *doctor, dentist* aller voir; *city, country* aller à/en; *castle, museum* visiter; *website* consulter; **visitor** (*guest*) invité *m*; (*tourist*) visiteur *m*

visor ['vaɪzər] visière *f*

visual ['vɪʒʊəl] visuel; **visualize** (*imagine*) (s')imaginer; (*foresee*) envisager, prévoir; **visually** visuellement

vital ['vaɪtl] (*essential*) vital, essentiel; **vitality** vitalité *f*; **vitally**: ~ *important* d'une importance capitale

vitamin ['vaɪtəmɪn] vitamine *f*; **vitamin pill** comprimé *m* de vitamines

vivacious [vɪ'veɪʃəs] plein de vivacité, vif; **vivacity** vivacité *f*

vivid ['vɪvɪd] vif; *description* vivant; **vividly** vivement; *re-member* clairement; *describe* de façon vivante

V-neck ['viːnek] col *m* en V

vocabulary [voʊ'kæbjʊlərɪ] vocabulaire *m*; (*list of words*) glossaire *m*

vocal ['voʊkl] vocal; **vocalist** MUS chanteur(-euse) *m(f)*

vocation [voʊ'keɪʃn] vocation *f*; **vocational** *guidance* professionnel

vodka ['vɑːdkə] vodka *f*

vogue [voʊg] vogue *f*; *be in ~* être en vogue

voice [vɔɪs] **1** *n* voix *f* **2** *v/t* *opinions* exprimer; **voice-mail** messagerie *f* vocale

volcano [vɑːl'keɪnoʊ] volcan *m*

volley ['vɑːlɪ] volée *f*

volt [voʊlt] volt *m*; **voltage** tension *f*

volume ['vɑːljəm] volume *m*

voluntarily [vɑːlən'terɪlɪ] de son plein gré, volontairement; **voluntary** volontaire; *work* bénévole; **volunteer 1** *n* volontaire *m/f*; (*unpaid worker*) bénévole *m/f* **2** *v/i* se porter volontaire

vomit ['vɑːmɪt] **1** *n* vomi *m*, vomissure *f* **2** *v/i* vomir

voracious [və'reɪʃəs] vorace; *reader* avide

vote [voʊt] **1** *n* vote *m* **2** *v/i* POL voter (*for* pour; *against* contre); **voter** POL électeur *m*; **voting** POL vote *m*

◆ **vouch for** [vaʊtʃ] *truth, person* se porter garant de

vow [vaʊ] **1** n vœu m, serment m **2** v/t: **~ to do** jurer de faire
vowel [vaʊl] voyelle f
voyage ['vɔɪɪdʒ] voyage m

vulgar ['vʌlgər] vulgaire
vulnerable ['vʌlnərəbl] vulnérable
vulture ['vʌltʃər] vautour m

W

waddle ['wɑːdl] se dandiner
wade [weɪd] patauger
wafer ['weɪfər] cookie gaufrette f; REL hostie f
waffle ['wɑːfl] to eat gaufre f
wag [wæg] remuer
wages [weɪdʒɪz] salaire m
waggle ['wægl] remuer
wail [weɪl] hurler
waist [weɪst] taille f
wait [weɪt] **1** n attente **2** v/i attendre
◆ **wait for** attendre
◆ **wait on** (serve) servir
◆ **wait up: don't wait up (for me)** ne m'attends pas pour aller te coucher
waiter ['weɪtər] serveur m; **~!** garçon!; **waiting list** liste f d'attente; **waiting room** salle f d'attente; **waitress** serveuse f
waive [weɪv] renoncer à
wake [weɪk] **1** v/i: **~ (up)** se réveiller **2** v/t person réveiller
walk [wɔːk] **1** n marche f; (path) allée f; **go for a ~** aller se promener **2** v/i marcher; as opposed to driving aller à pied; (hike) faire de la marche **3** v/t dog promener
◆ **walk out** of spouse prendre

la porte; from theater etc partir; (go on strike) se mettre en grève
walker ['wɔːkər] (hiker) randonneur(-euse) m(f); for baby trotte-bébé m; for old person déambulateur m; **walking** (hiking) randonnée f; **walkout** (strike) grève f; **walkover** (easy win) victoire f facile
wall [wɔːl] mur m
wallet ['wɑːlt] (billfold) portefeuille m
'wallpaper 1 n also COMPUT papier m peint **2** v/t tapisser; **wall-to-wall carpet** moquette f
waltz [wɔːlts] valse f
wan [wɑːn] face pâlot
wander ['wɑːndər] (roam) errer; (stray) s'égarer
wangle ['wæŋgl] F réussir à obtenir (par une combine)
want [wɑːnt] **1** n: **for ~ of** par manque de, faute de **2** v/t vouloir; (need) avoir besoin de; **~ to do sth** vouloir faire qch; **I ~ to stay here** je veux rester ici; **she ~s you to go back** elle veut que tu reviennes (subj) **3** v/i: **for nothing**

ne manquer de rien; **wanted by police** recherché

war [wɔːr] guerre *f*; *fig* lutte *f*

ward [wɔːrd] *Br: in hospital* salle *f*; *child* pupille *m/f*

◆ **ward off** éviter

warden ['wɔːrdn] *of prison* gardien (ne) *m(f)*; *Br: of hostel* directeur (-trice) *m (f)*

'**wardrobe** *for clothes* armoire *f*; *(clothes)* garde-robe *f*

warehouse ['werhaʊs] entrepôt *m*

'**warfare** guerre *f*; **warhead** ogive *f*

warily ['werɪlɪ] avec méfiance

warm [wɔːrm] chaud; *welcome, smile* chaleureux

◆ **warm up 1** *v/t* réchauffer **2** *v/i* se réchauffer; *of athlete etc* s'échauffer

warmly ['wɔːrmlɪ] chaudement; *welcome, smile* chaleureusement; **warmth** *also fig* chaleur *f*; **warm-up** SP échauffement *m*

warn [wɔːrn] prévenir; **warning** avertissement *m*

warp [wɔːrp] *of wood* gauchir; **warped** *fig* tordu

warrant ['wɔːrənt] **1** *n* mandat *m* **2** *v/t* justifier; **warranty** garantie *f*

warrior ['wɔːrɪər] guerrier (-ière) *m(f)*

wart [wɔːrt] verrue *f*

wary ['werɪ] méfiant; **be ~ of** se méfier de

wash [wɑːʃ] **1** *n*: **have a ~** se laver **2** *v/t clothes, dishes* laver **3** *v/i* se laver

◆ **wash up** *(wash one's hands and face)* se débarbouiller

washable ['wɑːʃəbl] lavable; **washbasin, washbowl** lavabo *m*; **washcloth** gant *m* de toilette; **washed out** *(tired)* usé; **washer** *for faucet etc* rondelle *f*; **washing** lessive *f*; **do the ~** faire la lessive; **washing machine** machine *f* à laver; **washroom** toilettes *fpl*

wasp [wɑːsp] guêpe *f*

waste [weɪst] **1** *n* gaspillage *m*; *from industrial process* déchets *mpl*; **it's a ~ of time/money** c'est une perte de temps/d'argent **2** *adj* non utilisé **3** *v/t* gaspiller; **waste basket** corbeille *f* à papier; **waste disposal (unit)** broyeur *m* d'ordures; **wasteful** gaspilleur; **wasteland** désert *m*; **wastpaper** papier(s) *m(pl)* (jetés) à la poubelle

watch [wɑːtʃ] **1** *n* timepiece montre *f*; **keep ~** monter la garde **2** *v/t* regarder; *(look after)* surveiller **3** *v/i* regarder; **watchful** vigilant

water ['wɔːtər] **1** *n* eau *f* **2** *v/t plant* arroser **3** *v/i*: **my mouth is ~ing** j'ai l'eau à la bouche; **watercolor**, *Br* **watercolour** aquarelle *f*; **watered down** *fig* atténué; **waterfall** chute *f* d'eau; **waterline** ligne *f* de flottaison; **waterlogged** dé-